SPURS

A COMPLETE RECORD

SPURS

A COMPLETE RECORD

BOB GOODWIN

The Breedon Books
Publishing Company
Derby

First published in Great Britain by
The Breedon Books Publishing Company Limited
44 Friar Gate, Derby DE1 1DA
1993

ISBN 1 873626 29 0

Printed and bound by Butler and Tanner Ltd, Frome and London.
Jacket printed by BDC Printing Services Ltd of Derby.

Contents

Photographic Credits

Photographs have been supplied by Action Images, Colorsport, EMPICS of Nottingham, Hulton-Deutsch Picture Library and Les Gold.

Introduction

WHEN I wrote the introduction to the second edition of *Spurs: A Complete Record* in May 1991, the very future of Tottenham Hotspur was in jeopardy. A club that had just won the FA Cup for a record eighth time faced the very real possibility of going out of existence after 109 years due to financial problems brought about by off-field activities.

A saviour was desperately needed and Spurs were fortunate to find one, not merely on their doorstep, but within the very portals of White Hart Lane.

Terry Venables, boyhood supporter, former player and then manager, worked harder than the proverbial Trojan to put together a rescue package. His determination and commitment earned him the respect not just of Spurs' supporters and football fans in general but the public at large. When he could have merely turned his back and walked away he was prepared to risk everything he had worked long and hard to achieve (and even more that he had yet to achieve) to save the club.

But he could not do it alone and it was only when millionaire businessman Alan Sugar threw his financial muscle behind Venables that a rescue could be completed.

The combination of two 'East End lads made good,' one in business, one in football, has been described as a 'Dream Ticket' and for the last two years the dream seemed to be coming true. Between them the club' finances were turned round, debts of £18 million or more becoming profits of £5 million and a team being built that looks destined to bring more honours to the club playing the type of football Spurs fans demand.

All the sadder, therefore, that Sugar and Venables should fall out and throw the club back into crisis.

At the time of writing, the future of Spurs is again clouded in doubt, Venables clinging to office courtesy of a High Court Judge, and I can but express the views of many Spurs fans in hoping that the problems are soon resolved. Terry Venables has done far too much for Spurs, and can yet do even more, to be tossed aside.

On a happier note I am again grateful to Anton Rippon and Breedon Books for publishing this third edition. My thanks also go to Carolyn Tingay, Mick Osborne, 'Ossie', Mark Hammond and Dave Whitton for all their help and encouragement. A special word must be reserved for Graham Betts who has been good enough to allow me access to documents that, I think, answer a question I know has puzzled many Spurs supporters — against whom did they play their first match. The answer is on page 365.

Bob Goodwin
London
May 1993

The Spurs Story

TOTTENHAM Hotspur! A unique name for a unique club. But why Hotspur? Why not Rovers or Albion, Wanderers or Athletic? Where does the name originate and why should a football club carry such an unusual and unlikely title?

In the early 1880s, the Tottenham district of North London bore little resemblance to the Tottenham of today. Much of the area was still marshland. But there were also many playing fields for the youth of the day to pursue sports like football, rugby and cricket.

One of the many small clubs was The Hotspur Cricket Club, which played on a field owned by Captain Delano, an uncle of two of the members. Its membership was derived from two local schools, Tottenham Grammar and St John's Middle Class, the latter being a Scottish Presbyterian Academy run by a man called Cameron.

Clearly the cricket club members must have enjoyed each other's company. The boys endeavoured to find a winter pastime which would keep the club together when the cricket season ended.

Football was an increasingly popular sport at the time. The Royal Engineers and the Old Etonians, FA Cup winners only a few years earlier, played in the locality, and many junior clubs had sprung up to try and emulate these early footballing heroes. The precise turn of events is unrecorded and therefore unclear but legend appears to indicate that at the behest of three individuals, Robert Buckle, Sam Casey and John Anderson, a meeting of The Hotspur Cricket Club was called, probably in August 1882, under a gas-lamp in Tottenham High Road, no more than 100 yards from the club's present White Hart Lane stadium.

That meeting resolved to form a football club and the name 'Hotspur' was adopted. No records survive but it is believed that the original members were Messrs Buckle, Casey and Anderson, together with T.Anderson, E.Beaven, L.R.Casey, F.Dexter, S.Leaman, J.H.Thompson, P.Thompson and E.Wall. They were soon joined by others including T.W.Bumberry, R.Howlett, C.Iverson, J.Tyrell, D.Davies, J.T.Fisher, Lovell and Jack Jull, a former pupil of St John's then at boarding school. Jull was a stalwart for years to come and was the first Spurs player to win representative honours when selected to play for Middlesex in 1889.

Although the exact date of that first meeting is unknown, the first subscriptions were due by 5 September 1882, a date now accepted as that of the club's formation.

Apart from subscriptions, the club's funds were supplemented by a grant from the cricket club, and the reason for Spurs adopting the name Hotspur is therefore simple. But this does not tell us how the name originated and to ascertain this it is necessary to go back to the reign of King Henry IV.

In 1399, Henry deposed his brother, King Richard II, whom he later had murdered at Pontefract Castle. Apart from the King, the most powerful man in the land was probably The Earl of Northumberland, head of the Percy family, whose power base was on the border with Scotland.

The Percy family remained loyal to Richard after his demise and continued to fight for the overthrow of Henry. Principal among the leaders of the rebel forces was Sir Henry Percy, the Earl's teenage son. Such were Henry's exploits on the field of battle that he was soon nicknamed 'Harry Hotspur'.

Hotspur met his end at the hands of the King's troops at the Battle of Shrewsbury in 1403, but his place in history was firmly established. He was immortalised by William Shakespeare in both *Richard II* and *Henry IV* and his fame spread throughout the world by the football club that adopted his name. Legend suggests that The Hotspur

Cricket Club was so-named because two founder-members, the Casey brothers, were studying 15th-century history and an elder brother put the name forward. And what an appropriate name. Much of the land in Tottenham was owned by the Percy family, many of the boys lived in houses in Northumberland Park, and all knew Percy House, the High Road home of the local YMCA.

From such origins came one of the world's greatest football clubs, one to stand alongside Real Madrid, Juventus, Manchester United and Santos. None of those boys, meeting under a flickering gas-lamp, could have imagined, even in their wildest dreams, that within 20 years their club would be the first professional side to bring the FA Cup to the South. Or that it would go on, in time, to become Football League Champions, achieve the glorious League and Cup 'double' and, finally, conquer Europe.

No matter what their aspirations, the boys soon set to work on the road to football glory. The club's inaugural funds were used to purchase timber for goal-posts (made and painted blue and white by the father of the Casey brothers), flags and tape for 'crossbars'. The first match-ball was donated by the same Casey brother who had suggested the name Hotspur for the cricket club.

Where to play presented no problem. Tottenham Marshes provided more than enough free accommodation for Hotspur and local clubs Park, Star and Radicals.

Results of matches played in the first season of 1882-3 have proved impossible to trace, except for an 8-1 defeat against local rivals, Latymer. This is not surprising, for nobody would have thought that over 100 years later, researchers would be interested in the Saturday afternoon activities of a group of schoolboys.

That first season had its problems. Apart from gangs of local bullies who frequented the Marshes and taunted the Hotspur members, the players also had to literally fight to keep their pitch. Other teams preferred to take by force the painstakingly prepared Hotspur surface rather than prepare their own.

Come the summer, the boys looked for adult help in running their club. They turned to John Ripsher, a pillar of the local community. He was warden of Tottenham YMCA and also took Bible classes at the Parish Church of All Hallows.

Ripsher suggested a club meeting and took the chair when one was called (in August 1883) by John Randall, an ex-Radicals player, working in Edmonton County Court. The venue was a basement kitchen at the YMCA and 21 young lads attended.

John Ripsher was elected president, a position he held throughout the club's formative years. John Randall was captain, Billy Harston vice-captain and the committee comprised T.W.Bumberry, W.G.Herbert, F.Dexter and W.Tyrell. Subscriptions were payable on or before 8 September 1883, matches were to be played at the Park Lane end of Tottenham Marshes and all members were requested to wear the club colours of navy-blue with a scarlet shield bearing the letter 'H'.

The 1883-4 season was highly successful. Results were good and the playing strength was enhanced by players from disbanded clubs. Hotspur were able to field a second team regularly.

The only sour note came when Hotspur were asked to leave the YMCA. A council member, investigating noise in the YMCA basement, had been struck by a soot-covered ball. Thereafter the club practised elsewhere.

John Ripsher came to the rescue and with Rev Wilson, the Vicar of Tottenham, a new home was found at 1 Dorset Villas, Northumberland Park. The only condition for use of these premises was that the Hotspur members had to attend church every Wednesday evening.

Season 1884-5 saw the continued growth of the club with more experienced recruits joining and the publication of the club's fixture list in the local newspaper. The club's name was changed to Tottenham Hotspur to prevent confusion with another club, called London Hotspur.

Tottenham Hotspur's players pictured in 1884-5, the first season that the word Tottenham was added to the Hotspur title. Back row (left to right): R.Amos, L.Brown, T.Wood, T.W.Bumberry, J.Anderson, J.Ripsher (president), H.D.Casey. Middle row: J.H.Thompson, W.C.Tyrell, F.Lovis, J.C.Jull (captain), H.Goshawk, W.Hillyer, S.Leaman (captain of the second team), F.Bayne, J.Randall. Front row: J.G.Randall, R.Buckle, G.F.Burt, G.Bush, P.Moss, W.Mason, W.Harston, F.Cottrell, H.Bull.

Ambition was now fired and at the end of the season, Spurs cancelled a match and the entire membership went to Kennington Oval to watch Blackburn Rovers defeat Queen's Park in the FA Cup Final.

Clearly impressed, Spurs changed their club colours to the Blackburn style of blue-and-white halves for the 1885-6 season. They also entered a cup competition for the first time. In the London Association Cup they defeated St Albans in front of 400 spectators before losing 8-0 to the Casuals.

There was another change in the club's headquarters. For two years, the members had dutifully attended church every Wednesday evening but when some members were caught playing cards in a church pew, they were asked to vacate Dorset Villas.

Again John Ripsher came to the club's rescue. Although a religious man himself, he clearly had faith in the young men under his wing and found them new quarters at the Red House in Tottenham High Road, a building which is now part of the club offices.

Further progress came in 1886-7, when the club competed in the London Association and East End Cups, and reached the semi-final of the latter competition, losing 1-0 to Caledonians at Tottenham.

Tracing details of matches played in the late 1880s is extremely difficult. Whilst cup-ties were reported in the local press, little attention was given to friendly matches which continued to account for the bulk of the club's fixtures.

One match that was reported was played on 19 November 1886 when, with Spurs leading 2-1, the first-ever meeting with Arsenal (then Royal Arsenal) was abandoned with 15 minutes left. It was too dark to continue.

Spurs' success and growing reputation led to a new problem — supporters. In about 1887, the committee felt it necessary to have ropes and stakes erected around the playing surface to prevent encroachment, and it was reported that at times 4,000 people were turning up on the Marshes to see Spurs play.

Would these supporters pay to see Spurs perform? Some doubted it. Others fervently believed that paying customers would come, and were happy to discourage the rowdier element who had proved so troublesome that complaints had been made to Spurs about their coarse comments.

The men behind the plan for Spurs to acquire a private ground were Bobby Buckle,

Frank Hatton, Jack Jull and Sam Casey. Due to their perseverance and efforts, a suitable site was found just off Northumberland Park and so a further step forward was taken.

The first match played at Northumberland Park was on 13 October 1888, when Spurs 'B' entertained Stratford St John's in a London Junior Cup match. The highlight of that season was the visit of Old Etonians in the London Senior Cup. As one might expect, Spurs were overwhelmed. They lost 8-2, although they were clinging on 3-2 at half-time.

The move to Northumberland Park seemed to be a success. A profit of nine shillings (45p) at the end of 1884-5 had increased to £6 at the end of 1888-9 and the club became members of the Football Association. The ground was used for a North-South match in the London Medal Competition.

For the next three seasons, Spurs' growth continued at a steady rate. Around this time Spurs came into contact with John Oliver, who was to guide the club through some of its most important years and most difficult decisions.

Oliver, president of Westminster Criterion, was clearly a pioneer of football at this time and in 1892, he promoted the formation of the Southern Alliance. Spurs were invited to be one of the ten founder-members and lost only three matches in this league in 1892-3, but from their point of view it was not a success and it was their only season in the competition

One oddity of the 1892-3 season was a decision to change the club colours to red shirts and blue shorts. The reason for this has never been explained but those colours were retained until Spurs joined the Southern League in 1896-7 when they were changed to chocolate and gold.

The legalisation of professional football in 1885 had helped to concentrate national success in the North and Midlands. The amateur clubs had little prospect of success in the FA Cup and pressure was brought upon the Football Association to institute a national cup competition open only to amateur clubs. That pressure resulted in the introduction of the FA Amateur Cup in season 1893-4 and Spurs were invited to compete in the inaugural competition.

After a bye in the first round, Spurs beat Vampires in the second. Although drawn to play Clapham Rovers in the third round, they went out of the Amateur Cup without playing a further match.

The reason has become known as 'The Payne's Boots Affair', one of the most important events in the club's history.

Throughout 1892-3, Fulham had on their books an outside-left by the name of Ernie Payne. He had not been selected to play for Fulham throughout that season and when Spurs asked him to fulfil a vacancy on 21 October 1893, he jumped at the chance.

Having been to Fulham on the morning of the match only to find that all his kit had 'disappeared' Payne arrived at Northumberland Park totally unprepared. Shirt, shorts and stockings were quickly provided but, despite trying on many pairs, no suitable boots could be found. Payne was therefore given ten shillings to buy a pair.

Fulham heard about this and immediately complained to the London Football Association, accusing Spurs of poaching and professionalism.

The charge of poaching was not sustained but to the amazement of the football world, the London FA found that Spurs had breached the rules by giving Payne the money to buy new boots, and their act should be considered an unfair inducement. Spurs were guilty of misconduct.

Payne returned the money to Spurs but was suspended for a week. The Tottenham club, after an unsuccessful appeal, were suspended for two weeks. The ground was closed for the same length of time, and Spurs were not allowed to play within six miles of Northumberland Park during the closure. They were unable to play the Amateur Cup match against Clapham Rovers and went out of the competition unbeaten.

Tottenham Hotspur in 1895, pictured with some of their supporters. Back row (left to right): The Briggs brothers. Standing: A.Petter, J.Campbell, J.Hurry, C.Williams, G.Baldock, C.Smith, T.Jull, S.Leaman, F.S.Walford, J.Allen, J.Jull (junior), H.Godfrey, R.Bullock, A.Norris, C.Monk, J.H.Thompson (junior), J.Jull (senior), F.Dexter. Seated: S.Casey, J.M.Baxter, H.Bull, J.Oliver, R.Buckle. On ground: W.Mason, A.Logan, W.Harston.

The consequences of the London FA's decision were quite astounding. Spurs received a tremendous amount of sympathetic publicity, attendances increased and the standard of opposition wanting to meet Spurs improved.

John Oliver must have seen the enormous potential of Tottenham Hotspur FC. When John Ripsher resigned as president in 1894, Oliver was elected to that office. Ripsher remained associated with the club as Patron, an honour richly deserved, for Spurs would not have survived without his help and staunch support in the early years.

With Oliver's financial support the club erected their first stand at Northumberland Park (although it blew down a few weeks later) and engaged their first professional trainer in Arthur Norris. Being the owner of a carpet-making factory, Oliver could offer employment to Spurs players and this helped them to attract the best.

The result of these developments was immediate. Spurs reached the third round of the Amateur Cup, before losing to the Old Carthusians, and the fourth qualifying round of the FA Cup.

Tottenham Hotspur was clearly a club going places. But progress was being shackled. The London FA had set itself against professionalism, yet Spurs saw it as the only way to compete with the top clubs in the land.

A meeting of the club was called for 16 December 1895. With the full support of the committee, Robert Buckle, a founding member, put the resolution that professionalism should be adopted. Much debate followed but the resolution was carried. Only one member voted against although several abstained.

One notable opponent of the proposal was club captain Stanley Briggs, who refused to attend the meeting. Strangely, Briggs was one of the few players to remain with the club after it turned professional although he continued to play as an amateur.

Spurs' increasing strength had been recognised by their exemption from the qualifying rounds of the Amateur Cup. They were drawn against Chesham in the first round. The change to professionalism meant that the game never took place.

The only competitive match played by Spurs as a professional club in 1895-6 was a first-round FA Cup-tie at Stoke where they lost 5-0. Friendly matches, many of them against other professional clubs, brought greater success.

Action from one of Spurs' last games at Northumberland Park. The visitors are Newton Heath (later Manchester United) who drew 1-1 in an FA Cup match there in January 1899. Spurs won the replay at Clayton, 5-3.

In June 1896, an application for membership of the Football League was rejected, Spurs finishing bottom of the poll with two votes. The following month they applied to join the Southern League. Such was the obvious strength of Spurs that they were elected straight into Division One.

The playing staff was strengthened and several newcomers were from Scotland. Welsh international J.L.Jones was signed and John Campbell was appointed trainer.

Spurs finished fourth in their first season in the Southern League, but the success on the field was not matched by events off it. Spectators were not coming through the gates in the numbers expected and the club was slipping into the red. Matters were not helped by the closure of the ground for two weeks. Spectators, incensed by the tactics of Luton Town, had encroached upon the pitch and assaulted three Luton players.

Spurs sought the help of Charles D. Roberts, a renowned local fund-raiser. He quickly saw that one or two fund-raising events would be of little help. The club had to be put on a firmer financial footing and those guiding the Spurs encouraged to invest in the future without fear of incurring personal liability.

He advised that the club should be wound-up, with assets and debts transferred to a new limited company, a step being taken by many other clubs at the time. It would mean the injection of urgently needed funds and allow the directors of the new company to operate the club as a truly commercial venture without running the risk of personal liability if it failed.

The suggestion was unanimously approved at a meeting on 2 March 1898. C.D.Roberts, J.Oliver, J.H.Thompson, R.Buckle and R.Bullock were elected as directors of the new Tottenham Hotspur Football and Athletic Company Limited, and 8,000 shares of £1 each were offered to the public. At about the same time, Frank Brettell was appointed as Spurs' first secretary-manager although he only held the position until the start of the following season.

The share issue did not go well. Only 1,558 were taken up in the first year. Spurs finished third in the Southern League in 1897-8 and seventh in 1898-9, but more spectators were attending. On 29 April 1899, 14,000 people crammed into Northumberland Park to witness a United League match against Woolwich Arsenal. To get a view of proceedings, some of them climbed on to the roof of the refreshment bar. The weight was too much and it collapsed. Nobody was seriously injured.

14

The warning signs were there though. Northumberland Park was simply not big enough. A new ground had to be found.

Prior to the start of the 1899-1900 season, John Oliver resigned as chairman and was replaced by Charles Roberts. W.Johnston was appointed trainer. Spurs also changed their colours, this time to white shirts and blue shorts as a tribute to Preston North End, the most successful team of the time. Strangely, Spurs were to meet Preston in the FA Cup for the next two seasons.

At about this time, Charles Roberts heard a rumour that a football club was moving to some vacant ground at the rear of the White Hart public house in Tottenham High Road. Charrington's Brewery had purchased Beckwith's Nursery, intending to build houses to provide custom for the White Hart, which they owned. It would make the perfect site for a football ground.

The landlord of the White Hart was all in favour of Spurs taking up residence there. He had run a pub near Millwall's ground and the demand from supporters for liquid refreshment had made it a lucrative business. Indeed, it has been reported that the landlord was so keen for Spurs to move to the site that it was he who had spread the rumours that a football club was interested in acquiring the land.

Charringtons were approached and they soon agreed to lease the land to Spurs, requiring only a guarantee that 1,000 spectators would attend for first-team games and 500 for reserve fixtures. Spurs knew that they could meet these targets easily and indeed, the first match at the ground, a friendly against Notts County on 4 September 1899, drew a crowd of 5,000.

Spurs now had two grounds but luck was with them. They were approached by the landlord of Northumberland Park, who did not know of the arrangements with Charringtons, and asked whether they were prepared to surrender their lease. They agreed to do so for a small consideration.

Spurs converted the stands at Northumberland Park for use at the new ground. The ground was never officially named, although suggestions such as Gilpin Park and Percy Park were put forward. It simply became known as White Hart Lane.

The move to a new ground had a stirring effect on Spurs. Under the guidance of

Tottenham Hotspur pictured in 1899-1900, their first season at White Hart Lane. Back row (left to right): J.L.Jones, H.Erentz, J.Melia, G.Clawley, A.Tait, D.Copeland. Middle row: W.Johnson (trainer), C.D.Roberts (chairman), R.Stormont, J.McNaught, T.Morris, E.Hughes, T.A.Deacock (director), C.Taylor (assistant trainer). Front row: T.Smith, T.Pratt, J.Cameron (secretary), J.Raby, L.Hyde, J.Kirwan.

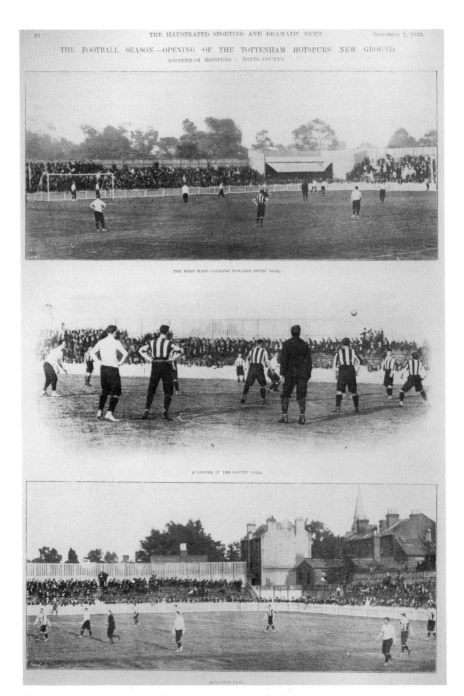

THE FOOTBALL SEASON—OPENING OF THE TOTTENHAM HOTSPURS' NEW GROUND.
TOTTENHAM HOTSPURS v. NOTTS COUNTY.

THE FIRST HALF—LOOKING TOWARDS SPURS' GOAL.

A CORNER AT THE COUNTY GOAL.

MIDFIELD PLAY.

Photographs taken at the opening of White Hart Lane in September 1899 when Notts County were the visitors for a friendly match which attracted 5,000 spectators to Spurs' new ground.

John Cameron, who had joined the club in the autumn of 1898 and was now player-manager, and trainer W.Briley, Spurs won the Southern League in 1899-1900, their first major competitive success.

Such success did not appear likely to continue in 1900-01. By Christmas, Spurs had picked up 12 out of 24 points and prospects of retaining the title looked slim. However, performances began to improve in the New Year, just in time for the first round of the FA Cup which was delayed until 11 February by the death of Queen Victoria.

Spurs were drawn against Preston North End who had beaten them at Deepdale the previous season. Hopes of revenge seemed dashed when Preston took the lead, against the run of play, after 28 minutes and then concentrated on defence. Preston goalkeeper McBridge appeared the match-winner until Spurs centre-forward Sandy Brown equalised with only eight minutes left, a goal described as a 'superhuman effort'.

In the replay, Brown scored three times as Spurs won the match 4-2. John Cameron scored the other goal.

The second round saw Spurs drawn at home again, this time against the FA Cup holders Bury, one of the strongest teams in the country at the time. Over 20,000 spectators were there to see Bury take a second-minute lead. Sandy Brown replied with two goals and Spurs held out for a 2-1 win.

The third round paired Spurs with Southern League rivals Reading at Elm Park. A ground record of 14,417 saw a 1-1 draw with John Kirwan getting Spurs' equaliser. It is said that every Cup-winning team has one moment of great fortune on their way to success and this match contained Spurs'.

Throughout the match they had been second best to a Reading team which could not compete with Spurs for artistry, but which had sufficient determination to bridge the gap in class. Reading's spoiling tactics, criticised in some quarters, had seen them on top for almost the whole game and pressing strongly for the winner with only minutes to go. Spurs goalkeeper Clawley was beaten by a shot from the left and the ball was just about to cross the line when Alexander Tait arrived to punch the ball away. A clear penalty thought 14,417 people. Two people did not. The referee's view had been obscured by Clawley and the linesman had not seen the incident either. Spurs escaped.

The replay took place the following Wednesday. Spurs were vastly superior and strolled to a 3-0 victory with Sandy Brown scoring twice and David Copeland getting the other.

The draw for the semi-final had already been made and Spurs were to meet West Bromwich Albion who were represented at the Reading replay. They suggested that

Spurs goalkeeper George Clawley (far left) claims an infringement as the ball goes harmlessly past his post during the FA Cup second round tie against holders Bury at White Hart Lane in 1901.

Sandy Brown (hidden) about to score Tottenham's third goal in the 1901 FA Cup Final replay against Sheffield United at Burnden Park.

the semi-final should take place at Villa Park and surprisingly, in view of the proximity of that venue to The Hawthorns, Spurs agreed.

What was not so easily agreed upon was the date of the match. Both clubs wanted to play on Saturday 6 April, but Spurs had a dispute with the Southern League, the first of several that were to see them leave that competition.

Spurs were due to fulfil a fixture at Bristol City, who would not cancel the match. The Southern League would not intervene or allow Spurs to field a reserve team in the fixture. (Spurs had done that in a Western League match at Bristol City on 27 March, keeping the first team fresh for the replay with Reading the next day.) The FA Cup semi-final was therefore arranged for 8 April. This was probably to both clubs' advantage as it was Easter Monday and must have helped the attendance.

A crowd of 46,000 turned up to watch Spurs turn in their best performance of the competition. No goals were scored in the first half but Spurs romped home in the second, scoring four without reply. Sandy Brown scored them all. Thousands of Spurs fans had travelled to Birmingham and they returned convinced that Spurs had nothing to fear from Sheffield United in the Cup Final at the Crystal Palace on 20 April.

Such was the interest in Spurs' bid for the Cup that 114,815 spectators turned up, a record for any match played in the country and the first time a crowd into six figures had been recorded.

According to contemporary reports, the match was excellent. United, with the sun and wind at their backs, had the best of the early play and scored the first goal after 12 minutes through Priest. They continued to have the better of the play but in the 25th minute, Spurs equalised, Brown heading in a free-kick from Kirwan. The wind must have been very influential for the reporters felt that United had to get at least one more goal before half-time if they were to have a realistic chance of winning the match.

The second half was only five minutes old when Brown put Spurs ahead from a pass by Cameron. A minute later, however, United were back on terms. Lipsham sent in a shot that Clawley fumbled, Bennett raced in to charge the goalkeeper and the ball went out of play. Clawley appealed for a goal-kick, Bennett for a corner. The linesman signalled a corner but the referee, Mr Kingscott, signalled a goal.

The Derby-based referee refused to consult his linesman, subsequently explaining that he thought the ball had crossed the line when Clawley fumbled Lipsham's shot. The match was the first ever filmed and pictures proved that the ball was never within a foot of the line.

Spurs were most aggrieved and much of the sparkle went out of their play. The Final finished a 2-2 draw.

The replay took place at Burnden Park, Bolton, the following Saturday. Why Bolton? Only the Football Association can answer that. Their original choice had been Goodison Park but Liverpool had a home game the same day. One of the Midlands grounds could have been used — Aston Villa were away from home that day — but Burnden Park was chosen. The journey for Spurs supporters was made worse by the fact that Bolton station was under reconstruction and the Lancashire and Yorkshire Railway Company refused to issue any cheap tickets. Just over 20,000 spectators saw a scrappy game spoilt by the weather.

Again Spurs conceded the first goal, Priest scoring in the 40th minute. On the balance of play Spurs had been the better team in the first half but the interval arrived with them a goal down. It took Spurs only ten second-half minutes to equalise through John Cameron. Shortly afterwards Tom Smith put Spurs ahead. Spurs now took command and a third goal, scored by Sandy Brown six or seven minutes from the end, was no more than they deserved.

Lord Kinnaird, president of the Football Association, presented the Cup to Spurs' captain J.L.Jones and Tottenham Hotspur became the first and only non-League club to win the FA Cup since the Football League's formation.

The Spurs team which won the FA Cup in 1901. Back row (left to right): C.Taylor (assistant secretary), H.Erentz, G.Clawley, A.Tait, W.Johnson (trainer). Middle row: J.Cameron, T.Morris, E.Hughes, T.L.Jones (captain), J.Kirwan. Front row: T.Smith, A.Brown, D.Copeland.

Whilst few Spurs supporters had travelled to Bolton, a large crowd had gathered at White Hart Lane to see the reserves fulfil a Southern League fixture against Gravesend United. When the result came through it started scenes of wondrous celebration. Those celebrations continued until the small hours of the next day when the Cup-winners returned to White Hart Lane to be greeted by over 40,000 supporters.

The next few seasons, through to 1907-08, were undistinguished. Whilst runners-up in the Southern League in 1901-02 and 1903-04, Spurs finished well behind the winners and could progress no further than the third round of the FA Cup.

The only noteworthy incident in the Cup came in the third round match against Aston Villa at White Hart Lane in 1903-04, and that for the wrong reasons. Such was the interest in the match that Spurs decided to put extra seating around the pitch perimeter. At half-time, with Spurs losing 1-0, the patrons occupying those seats invaded the pitch, to be followed by many other spectators. Despite all efforts they refused to leave and the referee had no alternative but to abandon the match. Spurs were fined £350 and ordered to replay the match at Villa Park. Quite unjustly they won the second game 1-0.

During this period, Spurs also made their first foreign tours. A lengthy trip to Vienna and Budapest, taking in seven games, was made in May 1905, and a shorter two-match trip to Ostend in 1907 saw Spurs play the local club and Southern League champions, Fulham.

Perhaps the major event of this time was the emergence of Vivian J. Woodward as Spurs' centre-forward. Woodward, who remained an amateur throughout his career, was highly respected on and off the field and was probably the outstanding footballer of his era. Captain of England and of the United Kingdom's Olympic-winning teams of 1908 and 1912, he was also a Spurs director before he transferred his allegiance to Chelsea in 1909.

One other matter that should be mentioned was the resignation of manager John Cameron during the 1906-07 season. At the start of that season, Cameron had passed

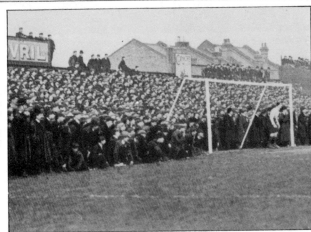

Photographs from the FA Cup match between Spurs and Aston Villa at White Hart Lane in February 1904 when the crowd invaded the pitch with Villa leading 1-0. The FA ordered the game to be replayed at Villa Park where Spurs won 1-0.

On 1 September 1906, football was played in temperatures in the 90s. This picture shows West Ham's visit to White Hart Lane for a Southern League match which the Hammers won 2-1.

his duties as secretary to the newly-appointed Arthur Turner, but he was unable to repeat the success of his earlier years, when player-manager, and in March 1907 he resigned.

He was replaced by Fred Kirkham, with Jack Nie being appointed trainer. Kirkham, however, left the club before the end of the next season, with Arthur Turner taking over responsibility for team affairs.

The 1907-08 season was Spurs' last in the Southern League which had become increasingly conservative in its attitude to professional clubs. The Southern League had rejected Chelsea and Clapton Orient, clubs which were welcomed by the Football League. And with Fulham leaving them, in 1907, the Southern League's traditional hold on the paying customer was under threat.

Spurs had tried hard to reverse this trend but without success. When director Morton Cadman returned from a meeting of the Southern League on 12 February 1908, he reported that his important resolution — just what it was has never been disclosed — put forward on behalf of Spurs, had not even found a seconder. Chairman Charles Roberts decided enough was enough. Spurs had to leave the Southern League and join the Football League. Apparently the rest of the board had been waiting for just such a decision and he was given their whole-hearted support.

Rumours immediately abounded and Spurs were forced to make an official announcement of their intentions as early as 17 February. Queen's Park Rangers, then on their way to the championship of the Southern League, and Bradford (Park Avenue) quickly followed suit with announcements that they too would leave the Southern League. Park Avenue had, in fact, applied to the Football League the previous year

The Southern League was incensed. A special meeting was called for 23 March and all three clubs were vehemently attacked by the other members. Millwall proposed that the action of the clubs in announcing their intentions to apply for membership of the Football League whilst still members of the Southern League was objectionable. Seconded by Northampton Town, the resolution was passed. Only Spurs and QPR voted against. Bradford abstained.

Identical voting saw a further resolution, again proposed by Millwall, calling for the three clubs to resign from the Southern League by 30 April. This was also passed but all three clubs stood firm, refusing to bow to the pressure. The Southern League called a further meeting, and a rule change gave the League power to expel the rebels.

22

Unofficially Spurs were told that if their application to the Football League failed they would be welcomed back to the Southern League, but only to the Second Division.

The general meeting of the Football League at which Spurs' application was to be decided was fixed for 27 May. The Southern League fixed their meeting for the same day and brought it forward half an hour so the two clashed exactly.

Despite Queen's Park Rangers' last-minute withdrawal of their application to the Football League, the first subject discussed at the Southern League meeting was the position of Spurs and Rangers. (Bradford had formally resigned.) A resolution that both clubs should be excluded from membership was passed, and Coventry City and Southend United were elected in their places.

Meanwhile, at the Football League meeting, things were not going well for Spurs. Having decided to leave the Southern League, they had immediately begun to canvass support for their membership of the Football League. Initial response was good and confidence was high. But the clubs forced to apply for re-election — Chesterfield, Grimsby Town and Lincoln City — would attract a strong loyalty vote. And Bradford City's promotion to the First Division had removed the major obstacle to the Park Avenue club's application.

Although the first ten votes counted were all for Spurs, the final voting was: Grimsby 32, Chesterfield 23, Bradford (PA) 20, Lincoln 18, Spurs 14 and Boston United one.

The future looked bleak for Spurs. Queen's Park Rangers had been re-elected to the Southern League but only on the financially crippling condition that almost all their matches were to be played in midweek. Spurs were determined not to compromise. It appeared that they would be limited to FA Cup and friendly matches.

The one ray of hope seemed to be in the possibility of the Football League forming a Third Division. An advertisement in *The Athletic News* invited applications but the matter went no further.

In mid-June, however, Stoke decided that Second Division crowds would not

Tottenham Hotspur in 1908-09, their first season of League football. Back row (left to right): T.A.Deacock (director), J.Walton, T.Morris, W.Minter, R.Hewitson, O.Burton, E.Coquet, M.F.Cadman (director), J.Nie (trainer). Front row: R.Steel, V.J.Woodward, D.Steele, H.Middlemiss, J.Darnell.

support the club and resigned from the Football League. Their decision was communicated to Spurs even before they told the League, a deal was done and Stoke gave Spurs their support.

A special meeting of the Football League was called for 29 June. Stoke had decided by then that their earlier decision had been too hasty but they were too late to withdraw their resignation. They went into the ballot with Spurs, Lincoln, Rotherham Town and Southport. To say the issue was close is an understatement.

In the first ballot the voting was: Spurs 17, Lincoln 17, Stoke six, Rotherham and Southport both nil. In the second, Spurs and Lincoln both received 20 votes. The matter went to the Management Committee — and Spurs squeezed home by five votes to three.

Spurs took over Stoke's fixtures and the first match brought FA Cup holders, Wolverhampton Wanderers, to White Hart Lane on 1 September 1908. Goals by Tom Morris and Vivian Woodward (2) gave Tottenham a 3-0 victory and a foretaste of things to come.

Having played 37 matches, West Bromwich Albion led the table by one point from Spurs and Bolton Wanderers. Each club had to play Derby County in their last match. West Brom lost, Spurs drew 1-1 and Bolton won. Spurs therefore won promotion on goal-average from Albion, but how close it was. If Spurs had drawn 2-2 instead of 1-1, West Bromwich would have gone up.

At the end of this most exciting of seasons, Spurs undertook their most adventurous tour so far. They travelled to South America for matches in Argentina and Uruguay. Spurs won all their matches against local opposition but lost two games against Everton.

One of the souvenirs Spurs acquired was a parrot. On the voyage home, a fancy-dress contest was held. Due to the efforts of Charles Roberts it was won by two Spurs players in the guise of Robinson Crusoe and Man Friday. The ship's parrot was used as one of their props and to mark the event, the parrot was presented to Roberts. The bird remained a Spurs mascot until 1919.

The 1909-10 season saw as exciting a conclusion to the League campaign as the previous one, but for different reasons. On the last day of the season, Spurs had to face Chelsea. If Bristol City lost they would join Bolton Wanderers in being relegated. If they won, then the losers of the Spurs-Chelsea match would go down. To be safe, Spurs had to win. Goals by Billy Minter and Percy Humphreys saw them home 2-1, and with Bristol City also victorious, it was Chelsea who were relegated.

Spurs continually battled against relegation for the next three seasons. It is not a period worthy of recall, save for one development.

At the end of the 1912-13 season, during which Peter McWilliam had been appointed Spurs manager, Woolwich Arsenal finished bottom of Division One.

Nine seasons in the top flight had been a struggle for the Plumstead club and there were now financial difficulties. Arsenal called on Henry Norris, then at Fulham, and he moved the club lock, stock and barrel.....to Highbury.

Hearing the news, Spurs and Clapton Orient complained bitterly to the Football League and the Football Association, for here was a club moving in on their territory. The protests were to no avail. There was then nothing in the rules of either body which gave them the power to dictate where a club should have its headquarters and the Arsenal move went through in time for the 1913-14 season.

End-of-season tours abroad were now becoming a regular feature of Spurs' programme, and in 1914 a tour to Europe was undertaken with games in Germany, Switzerland, Italy and Austria-Hungary. One game in Germany was a particularly unhappy affair for Tottenham who complained of violent opposition players, dishonest refereeing and unruly spectators. Goalkeeper 'Tiny' Joyce had his head split open by one umbrella-wielding fan and on the return to England, Charles Roberts

Top and bottom: Spurs in action against Newcastle United at White Hart Lane in November 1911. Newcastle, then First Division leaders, won 2-1 but eventually failed to win the Championship.

announced that Spurs would never again visit Germany while he remained chairman.

When war was declared later that year, the Government encouraged the football authorities to continue as normal. But the Armed Forces' appeal to patriotism was considerable and Spurs were very quickly affected by players joining the services. It would be easy to blame Spurs' disastrous performance on the praiseworthy response of their players to the call-to-arms, but that would be concealing the truth. Ever since promotion, Spurs had struggled to make an impact and relegation had been a constant threat. In 1914-15, they finished in last place.

Spurs, however, would have to wait four years before resuming their place in the Second Division. In the summer of 1915, the FA felt that soccer should be suspended altogether. The Government, however, felt that some form of football should remain, to boost morale as much as anything, but that travelling should be restricted.

Arsenal's Henry Norris, encouraged by the London FA, set out to form the London Combination, but there was opposition from the Football League, including the threat of expulsion for any club playing a wartime match not organised by the League. Eventually the Football Association intervened, and a compromise was reached

Spurs in 1913-14. Back row (left to right): Webster, Weir, Steel, King, Grimsdell, Nie (trainer), Cartwright. Front row: Walden, Fleming, Cantrell, Bliss, Oliver.

whereby clubs were allowed to organise their own competitions provided there was no interference with war work.

Instead, war work interfered with Spurs. In the summer of 1915, White Hart Lane was taken over for the manufacture of gas-masks. Manager Peter McWilliam, secretary Arthur Turner and assistant-secretary Coleman were directed to turn their efforts to assisting the war effort. Perhaps in a bid to overcome some of the bitterness caused by Arsenal's move, Highbury was made available for some of Spurs' home games. Clapton Orient's Homerton ground was used for the remainder but, although the London Combination continued throughout the war, Spurs' performances were only moderate.

There was no community in Britain that was not touched by the tragedy of World War One and Tottenham Hotspur were no exception with several of their players not returning from military service. They were: J.Fleming, J.Heddon, A.Hobday, J.Jarvie, E.Lightfoot, W.Lloyd, A.McGregor, F.Weir, A.Wilson, N.Wood and W.Tull. In addition, Tom Collins was so seriously injured that he was unable to resume his career.

In 1919, it was decided to resume normal League football and extend the First Division to 22 clubs. On previous occasions when the League had been extended, the top clubs in Division Two had been promoted as normal and the clubs that would normally have been relegated had retained their position in the top flight, with new members being added to the Second Division. Spurs therefore expected that they would remain in Division One, but that was not to be the case.

Derby County and Preston North End, who had finished first and second in

Division Two, were promoted as expected but the Management Committee called for nominations to replace Spurs and Chelsea. This was totally unexpected.

League President John McKenna of Liverpool said that there were special reasons why the fate of Chelsea should not be voted upon and they were re-elected unopposed.

Special reasons? In the last month of 1914-15, Manchester United had defeated Liverpool 2-0 and in the course of a long libel action it was established that some of the players (not the clubs) had 'fixed' the result. Had Manchester United not got those two points they would have finished below Chelsea, although they would have had to lose 8-0 to have finished below Spurs.

McKenna urged the meeting to vote for Arsenal to take Spurs' place. The basis of this was that Arsenal had been members of the Football League for longer than Spurs and loyalty should be rewarded.

It was true that Arsenal had been members of the League longer than Spurs, but Wolverhampton Wanderers, fourth in Division Two in 1914-15, were founder-members of the League in 1888. Birmingham had finished fifth and they had joined the League (as Small Heath) in 1892, one year before Arsenal.

Length of membership could not have been the real reason; nor could results in the last pre-war season. Arsenal had performed better than Spurs during the war years but not that much better. There must have been another reason. Could it have been McKenna's close friendship with Henry Norris? It remains a mystery.

The matter was put to the vote and the president's influence was clearly decisive. Arsenal were elected to Division One with 18 votes, despite having finished in sixth place in the last peacetime season. Spurs had eight, Barnsley five, Wolves four, Nottingham Forest three, Birmingham two and Hull City one. Arsenal have remained in the First Division ever since.

The decision astounded not only those associated with Spurs but the whole of football. Could it have been the reason why the parrot, bought back from Spurs' tour of South America in 1909, died the same day?

Spurs had to spend the 1919-20 season in Division Two and they determined to right what they saw as a grave injustice. The first seven matches were all won and they remained unbeaten at home. They lost only four games all season, scored 102 goals and totalled 70 points, easily a League record at the time. Spurs won the title six points clear of Huddersfield Town and a further eight points clear of third-placed Birmingham.

In 1920-21, Spurs finished sixth in the First Division, easily the club's highest position in the Football League up to that point, but the real success came in the FA Cup.

In the first round, Tottenham were drawn at home to Bristol Rovers and overwhelmed the visitors 6-2. In the second round, Bradford City were outclassed 4-0 in another home tie when Jimmy Seed hit a hat-trick. The third round took Spurs to Third Division Southend where they were not at their best and were perhaps flattered by the 4-1 scoreline.

As in 1901, fortune smiled on Tottenham. After half an hour, with the score 1-1, Southend were awarded a penalty for a foul by Bert Smith. Southend captain Fairclough placed the ball to take the kick but the referee decided it was not on the spot and re-positioned it. Fairclough went to adjust it to suit himself but the referee would not let him touch the ball. The Southend man shot wide.

For the fourth round, Spurs were drawn at home to Cup-holders, Aston Villa. Villa were the most attractive team around and the match drew the highest 'gate' of the round when a crowd of 56,991 set a record for White Hart Lane. The previous season Villa had beaten Spurs in the fourth round at White Hart Lane when a tragic own-goal by Tommy Clay had deprived Spurs after a splendid performance by the home side. The chance for revenge had come quickly.

Left: Jimmy Dimmock, who scored the winning goal in the 1921 FA Cup Final. Right: King George V presents Tottenham with the Cup. Below: Spurs with the trophy. Back row (left to right): W.Minter (trainer), T.Clay, B.Smith, F.Hunter, C.Walters, E.MacDonald. Front row: J.Banks, J.Seed, A.Grimsdell (captain), J.Cantrell, B.Bliss, J.Dimmock.

Spurs won what was later described as the 'greatest Cup-tie of the season' with a solitary goal scored by John Banks after a run and cross by outside-left Jimmy Dimmock. Try as Villa might, they were unable to draw level and it was Spurs who seemed more likely to score again.

The semi-final took place at Hillsborough on 19 March and Spurs' opponents were Preston North End. Birkenhead referee Mr Forshaw was the subject of much criticism for the number of questionable decisions he gave against Spurs, including disallowing two goals and refusing what appeared to be two blatant penalties. But nothing was going to stop Spurs' march to the Final and two second-half goals by Bert Bliss, both set up by Arthur Grimsdell, were nothing less than Spurs deserved. Preston made the score look more respectable with a late goal which was due to a wicked deflection off Tommy Clay's knees.

After a replay, Wolves beat Cardiff City in the other semi-final and Spurs met the Second Division side at Stamford Bridge on 23 April before a 72,805 crowd which included King George V and the future King George VI. Not since Spurs' victory in 1901 had a southern club won the Cup.

Spurs were easily the favourites but the weather was atrocious, the pitch was a quagmire due to non-stop rain, and Wolves' players raised themselves to give the match a more balanced look.

Centre-half Charlie Walters was the star for Spurs. He dominated the Wolves forwards and found time to prompt the attack from deep positions. He was not the most accomplished of footballers but the conditions were perfect for a player of his style and he probably gave his best performance for the club.

The only goal of the game was scored in the 54th minute by Jimmy Dimmock. Taking a pass from Bert Bliss he moved towards goal, only to lose the ball to Woodward. But Woodward was slow in clearing and Dimmock regained possession, advanced to within 15 yards of goal and beat the goalkeeper with an oblique shot which hardly left the ground and went in at the far post.

Two major successes in two years. Could Spurs make it three on the trot? They certainly tried, finishing second in the League to Liverpool in 1921-2, the highest position ever achieved by a London club, and reaching the semi-final of the FA Cup.

On 25 March 1922, when they again met Preston North End at Hillsborough in a semi-final, Tottenham were the better side in the first half but had only one goal to show for it at the interval, when Preston were reportedly given champagne. The second half saw roles reversed with Preston taking command and equalising early on. With the score at 1-1, Bert Bliss 'scored' for Spurs but the referee ruled that, before the ball crossed the line, he had blown the whistle for an injured Preston player to be treated. The goal was disallowed, Spurs were dejected and before they could regain their composure Preston netted the winner.

Tottenham's run of success had now come to an end and for the next few seasons the club was to finish no higher than 12th in the League, making no progress of note in the FA Cup. The highlight of this period was in October 1925 when the club was top of the table, but captain Arthur Grimsdell broke his leg and performances deteriorated rapidly. First place was also reached in 1927-8 but it did not last.

In February 1927, manager Peter McWilliam left to join Middlesbrough. Earning £850 a year at Tottenham, McWilliam was offered £1,500 by the Ayresome Park club. He wanted to stay at White Hart Lane and asked for an extra £150 from Spurs who refused. Billy Minter, who had joined the club as a player in 1907 and had been promoted to trainer after World War One, took McWilliam's place.

Throughout this period, the directors were constantly criticised for not buying players. They had adopted a rigid policy that the club would rely on producing its own talent — quite different to 30 or so years later when Spurs continually broke the transfer-fee record.

Top: High kicking in an FA Cup tie between Spurs and Bolton Wanderers in February 1925. Bottom: Arthur Grimsdell and Arsenal centre-forward Donald Cock tussle at Highbury in August 1925.

The policy of not buying players appeared to be vindicated when Spurs reached the sixth round of the FA Cup in 1928, but they were thrashed 6-1 by the great Huddersfield team of the era, managed by Herbert Chapman (a Spurs player in their Southern League days). Things then went from bad to worse. Whether new players would have made any difference is open to debate, but the sale of players certainly contributed to the demise. For seven seasons, Jimmy Seed had been one of the most important and influential members of the Spurs team. Towards the end of 1926-7 he had been injured and replaced by Eugene 'Taffy' O'Callaghan, a player of immense talent and even more promise. Unable to displace O'Callaghan, Seed had spent almost the whole of 1927-8 in the reserves. In March 1928, Sheffield Wednesday, looking doomed to relegation, sought his transfer. Terms were agreed and Seed moved to Yorkshire to become more than just a saviour.

By Easter, Wednesday were in with a chance of survival. The holiday fixtures paired Spurs and the Owls twice. Wednesday won 3-1 at White Hart Lane and 4-2 at Hillsborough with Seed scoring in each game. Wednesday finished with 39 points.

At the end of March, Spurs had been seventh with 35 points from 35 games. Only three more were picked up, Spurs finishing the season earlier than most and embarking on a tour of Holland. In their absence, results conspired against them and seven clubs finished with 39 points. Spurs were 21st and relegated. Thirty-eight is the record number of points obtained by a relegated club under the two-points-for-a-win system. And, as if to rub salt into the wound, Jimmy Seed went on to lead Sheffield Wednesday to the League Championship in 1928-9 and 1929-30.

Spurs finished tenth in Division Two in 1928-9 and were on their way to 12th position in 1929-30 when Billy Minter was moved to assistant secretary and Percy Smith brought from Bury as manager. Second Division football was not good enough for Spurs but it took until 1929 for the directors to decide that the transfer market

Arthur Grimsdell clears off the Spurs line in an FA Cup tie at Leicester in February 1928.

Acrobatics following a corner at White Hart Lane during the match against Bury in September 1929. Tottenham drew 2-2 with goals from Crompton and Osborne and finished the season in 12th place under new manager Percy Smith, the former Bury boss.

32

In March 1931, Spurs were battling with Everton and West Brom for promotion to the First Division. West Brom gained a valuable point in this match at White Hart Lane and went on to win promotion and the FA Cup that year.

would have to be entered. In March 1929, Ted Harper, who had played once for England, was signed from Sheffield Wednesday at considerable cost. In the 11 games left that season he scored 11 goals, and in 1929-30 netted 14 in 19 games.

Further signings were made for the start of the 1930-31 season and it appeared that the investment would pay off. In the middle of March, Spurs were battling with Everton and West Bromwich Albion for the two promotion places. On 21 March, Harper — who by then had scored 34 goals in 28 games — was injured. He played only two more games that season (not completing one of those), scoring two more goals to set a League scoring record for Spurs. Tottenham secured only four points in the six games he missed and finished third, three points behind second-placed West Bromwich.

The 1931-2 season saw a backward step — Spurs finished eighth. After seven games of 1932-3, the talk was of relegation. The next ten matches produced eight victories and two draws and of the last 35 matches, only three were lost. Stoke won the title, but Spurs were only one point behind and back in the First Division.

Basically the same team that had secured promotion appeared throughout the 1933-4 season and did so most satisfactorily. At Christmas, hopes were harboured that the title might be won, but Arsenal and Huddersfield were the outstanding teams of the era and in a class of their own. They finished first and second respectively with Spurs third.

The same players were available again the next season but results were dreadful. The injury list was always crowded, new recruits were unobtainable at the right price and the team plummeted to finish bottom of the table, at one stage going 16 League games without a win.

Percy Smith left in June 1935 amid allegations that the directors had frequently interfered with his team selections. Despite strong denials by the board, his replacement, Jack Tresadern, faced a difficult situation when he arrived from Crystal Palace.

Promotion was the aim again, but in the next three seasons Spurs were never really in with a chance. They finished sixth, tenth and fifth. The only redeeming factor of this spell was the moderate success obtained in the FA Cup.

33

Tottenham's amateur inside-forward A.H.Gibbons heads the ball past Barnsley goalkeeper Ellis to score Spurs' third goal at White Hart Lane in September 1937. The Londoners were still trapped in Division Two at the season's end and manager Jack Tresadern had resigned, his unpopular sales of George Hunt and Taffy O'Callaghan still rankling the fans.

In 1935-6, Tottenham reached the sixth round, disposing of Southend (after a 4-4 draw at home), Huddersfield at home and Bradford at home (after a draw at Park Avenue). In the quarter-final they met Sheffield United at Bramall Lane but lost 3-1.

In the third round of 1936-7, Spurs pulled off a minor miracle in winning 5-0 at Portsmouth, who were then going extremely well in Division One. Plymouth Argyle were defeated 1-0 at White Hart Lane in the fourth round and then Spurs travelled to Goodison Park. Five minutes from the end of a poor game, Everton were given a dubious penalty. Jack Hall saved the legendary Dixie Dean's spot kick and blocked his rebound effort. The ball was cleared upfield and Jimmy McCormick promptly put Spurs ahead. But there was still time for Everton to equalise and set up a replay which was to prove one of the most dramatic matches in Spurs' history.

With only six minutes remaining, Everton had a 3-1 lead. It could have been 4-1. Joe Mercer had taken a throw-in, play had proceeded and an Everton player had been fouled in the penalty area. The referee gave a penalty but then consulted his linesman. Mercer's throw-in had not been taken properly and play was called back for a throw-in to Spurs. Jack Morrison got a second goal for Tottenham and with four minutes left, Joe Meek grabbed the equaliser. With the last kick of the match, Morrison got the winner.

The sixth round brought Preston North End to White Hart Lane but the Cup run came to an end, Preston winning 3-1.

Spurs' progress to the sixth round in 1937-8 was not so dramatic. Blackburn Rovers, New Brighton and Chesterfield were defeated, and another home draw saw Sunderland stand between Spurs and a semi-final place.

A crowd of 75,038, Spurs record attendance, squeezed into White Hart Lane to witness a 1-0 victory for the Wearsiders. The match was not without incident and there

West Ham visit Spurs in October 1938. From left, Tottenham's Whatley, Hammers' Fenton and Spurs' goalkeeper Hooper.

were those partisan Tottenham fans who felt that if a linesman had been more up-with-play, Spurs would have won. With no goals scored, Spurs outside-left Colin Lyman beat the Sunderland goalkeeper with a fierce shot. As the ball was entering the net Jackie Gibbons rushed in and touched it with his hand. The referee gave the goal but, after Sunderland protests, consulted the linesman and then gave a free-kick instead. There seems no doubt that Gibbons was guilty of hand-ball, but those in a position to see were convinced the ball had crossed the line before he touched it.

Some measure of success in the Cup was very welcome but escape from the Second Division was the main objective and under Tresadern's guidance this seemed unlikely. His sales of George Hunt and Taffy O'Callaghan were never forgiven by the fans and towards the end of 1937-8, he resigned.

Peter McWilliam was called back to replace Tresadern but with only one full season before World War Two, he had little opportunity to impress. In 1938-9, Spurs finished eighth, but the foundations for future glory were being laid, particularly with the promotion of players from the nursery club at Northfleet.

Only three League matches had been played in 1939-40 when war was declared and all further competition suspended. As in World War One, the Government wanted football to continue, but severe restrictions were imposed upon travelling and the size of attendances. Clubs in the London area took part in an emergency competition which consisted of two groups of ten teams each.

On the outbreak of war, Peter McWilliam had returned north and Arthur Turner took on the responsibility for getting a team together. It was difficult job. Players had left the area, joined the forces or were simply unable to get to games. To get eleven players together at kick-off time was a success in itself.

Spurs managed only 11 points in 18 games and finished one from bottom. Most of the games were played in the first half of the season, so another competition was arranged for the second half of the campaign. This competition, known as Regional League South 'C', finished with Spurs as 'champions'.

Chelsea and Spurs meet in a wartime friendly match at Stamford Bridge in September 1939.

36

The restrictions on attendances and difficulty in raising teams did not make the running of football a profitable enterprise. Losses were inevitable but like most clubs Spurs felt that the losses would be greater if they were to close down altogether. When the Football League Management Committee suggested a total shutdown (in March 1940), Spurs were amongst those who disagreed. The Management Committee agreed to extend the season and introduce a Football League War Cup competition in which Spurs fell in the two-legged first round, to Crystal Palace. The 1940-41 season again featured a League War Cup, with Spurs losing over two legs to Arsenal. The League structure was altered and Spurs competed in the South Regional League (along with 33 other clubs). It was obvious that not all the clubs would be able to meet each other even once, let alone twice, and in a competition decided on goal-average, Spurs finished ninth. The structure of the League meant that there were insufficient matches to satisfy needs and, accordingly, the London clubs, with Football Association approval, set up the London War Cup on a league and then knock-out basis. Spurs lost in the semi-final to Brentford.

The overall structure of wartime football had not proved satisfactory and so in June 1941, the Management Committee suggested splitting the competing clubs into groups divided into two Leagues, North and South. Receiving their fixture lists, the London clubs were aghast at the amount of travelling they were expected to do. They felt they would not be able to fulfil their fixtures. After complaints the Management Committee amended them slightly but still the clubs found them unsatisfactory, feeling the amount of travelling was against the Government's wishes.

The London clubs decided to run their own league, relying on the decision of July 1915. The Football League warned the 'London League' clubs to toe the line. They refused and the Football League issued a notice stating that, by their actions, the rebels had ceased to be in membership. In other words, the 16 clubs were expelled. An appeal was lodged and in the meantime the clubs proceeded, with Football Association blessing, with the London War League and London War Cup competitions. Spurs finished fifth in the league but did not get past the league stage of the Cup.

The 'rebels' appeal against the Football League's decision was never formally decided. The Appeal Board indicated that the League and the rebel clubs should resolve the dispute between themselves. A settlement was reached. The rebels accepted that they had been in technical breach of League rules. They forfeited their £10 appeal fee as a fine and agreed to place their competitions under League control. In return they were accepted back as members of the League.

In seasons 1942-3, 1943-4 and 1944-5, the South League and Cup competitions were run on identical lines to the London War League and Cup of 1941-2 with the addition of two other clubs. In 1942-3, Spurs finished second to Arsenal in the League. In 1943-4 and 1944-5, they won the competition. Only in 1942-3 did Spurs get past the league stage of the Cup, again losing in the semi-final, this time to Charlton Athletic.

Throughout the war years, and even in 1945-6, football was regarded as much as an entertainment as a competition. Clubs were able to call on any available player to make up their teams and the use of guests was more the rule than the exception, particularly for clubs near military bases (such as Aldershot). However, no record would be complete without details of these seasons, during which many young players gained valuable experience.

World War Two allowed Spurs to repay Arsenal for the use of Highbury during the World War One. Highbury was requisitioned and Spurs made White Hart Lane available to their neighbours.

With the end of the war in 1945, the Football League suggested that football should go back to its pre-war set-up. The clubs agreed but then realised that transport was still difficult and players were to be discharged from the services slowly. They suggested that League competition should continue on a regional basis for at least one more year.

This affected only the First and Second Division clubs as the Third Division was already divided into North and South sections. In the Football League South, consisting of eight First and 14 Second Division clubs, Spurs finished ninth.

The wartime period brought many changes. Chairman Charles Roberts had died in 1943 and was replaced by Fred Bearman. Manager Peter McWilliam retired and was replaced by former Arsenal star Joe Hulme. Hulme was in charge for three seasons but failed to get Spurs out of the Second Division. In these seasons, Tottenham finished sixth, fifth and eighth, although an FA Cup semi-final was reached in 1948.

Bolton Wanderers, West Bromwich Albion, Southampton and Leicester City were disposed of in the early rounds, leaving Spurs to meet Blackpool at Villa Park. Len Duquemin scored in the 64th minute and Spurs got to within four minutes of their first visit to Wembley before Blackpool equalised through Mortensen. Two more goals for Mortensen in extra-time gave Blackpool a somewhat flattering 3-1 victory.

In May 1949, Hulme left to be replaced by Arthur Rowe, the Spurs centre-half and captain for most of the 1930s. In 1939, Rowe had taken up coaching, initially in Hungary, and he had spent four years as secretary-manager of Chelmsford City before rejoining Spurs. Although Rowe was given the credit for Spurs' subsequent success under his guidance, he was perhaps fortunate to find that the players he needed were already with the club, except for full-back Alf Ramsey. He can certainly be credited, however, with the introduction of what became known as 'Push and Run'.

The 1949-50 season started with 4-1 victories over Brentford and Plymouth Argyle before a 3-2 defeat by Blackburn Rovers. Spurs then went 23 League and Cup games without defeat, including two runs of seven successive victories. Promotion was secured on 1 April and the title a week later (with five games still to go). They finished nine points clear of Sheffield Wednesday and it could have been more had Spurs not eased up in the last five games.

Would the 'Push and Run' style prove effective in the First Division? Stoke City and Sunderland had been beaten in the FA Cup before Spurs went out at Everton, so the omens were good.

Spurs in 1949-50, the season they won the Second Division title. Back row (left to right): G.Ludford, A.Ramsey, W.Nicholson, E.Ditchburn, R.Burgess, C.Withers, S.McClellan. Front row: W.Walters, W.Rees, L.Duquemin, E.Baily, L.Medley, R.Clarke.

Back in Division One in 1950-51, Spurs won the League Championship. Back row (left to right): C.Poynton (trainer), A.Ramsey, L.Duquemin, P.Murphy, E.Ditchburn, H.Clarke, L.Bennett, C.Withers. Front row: W.Nicholson, W.Walters, A.Willis, R.Burgess, E.Baily, L.Medley.

After the first game of the 1950-51 season, they did not look so good. Blackpool had won 4-1 at White Hart Lane. But that was only a temporary hiccup and Spurs soon got the measure of First Division football and moved in with the Championship-chasing pack. The most impressive period of the season was in October and November when, during the course of an eight-match winning sequence, successive home matches saw Stoke defeated 6-1, Portsmouth, the League Champions of 1948-49 and 1949-50, 5-1 and Newcastle 7-0. Spurs were the sensation of the season with their new, fast-flowing brand of football watched by over 1.5 million fans at White Hart Lane. The League title was won in the penultimate game of the season and Spurs finished three points ahead of Manchester United. Only one team managed to get the full measure of Spurs. Despite finishing in 19th position, Huddersfield Town won both League matches and for good measure even put Spurs out of the FA Cup at the third-round stage.

But no matter. For the first time in their history, Spurs were Champions of The Football League.

In 1951-2, Tottenham lost in the fourth round of the FA Cup and finished second in the League to Manchester United. By any standard that was no poor performance. Perhaps the League could have been won again had it not been for the bad weather and heavy pitches during the winter months. This clearly did not help the Spurs style of play. At the end of the season the White Hart Lane pitch was ripped up and replaced.

Success led to many tour invitations. In the summer of 1952, Spurs accepted an offer to go to Canada. All ten games, including two against Manchester United, were won handsomely and included Spurs' highest scoring result in any first-team match — an 18-1 victory over the Saskatchewan FA in Saskatoon on 26 May. Sid McClellan scored nine goals in that game.

By 1952-3, the 'Push and Run' team was growing old and the style of play was being countered by their opponents. Tottenham finished an unremarkable tenth. But the 'Push and Run' team still had one target — Wembley — and they made the most determined effort to reach it. Tranmere Rovers were beaten in a replay at White Hart Lane in the third round, as were Preston North End in the fourth. Halifax were overcome on their ground in the fifth before Spurs managed to beat Birmingham City in a sixth-round second replay at Molineux.

Ted Ditchburn and Sheffield Wednesday's Shaw in a tangle at Hillsborough in the 1954-5 season. The Spurs goalkeeper managed to scramble the ball away for a corner.

As in 1948, the semi-final pitted Spurs against Blackpool and again the venue was Villa Park. A first-half goal by Perry was equalised by Len Duquemin early in the second half and the match looked to be heading for extra-time. It did not reach that stage. Only ten seconds from the end, Alf Ramsey underhit a back-pass, Jackie Mudie nipped in to score and there was time only for the ball to be placed on the centre-spot before the final whistle blew.

The 1953-4 and 1954-5 seasons saw the end of the 'Push and Run' side. It was hard on Arthur Rowe, who became very ill. His health was not helped by the team's performances. In both seasons, Spurs could manage only 16th place in the First Division, but the low point was the fifth-round FA Cup defeat at Third Division York City in 1955.

When Rowe officially retired at the end of 1954-5, his assistant, Jimmy Anderson, who had been at the club for almost 50 years, was appointed manager. Slowly but surely, the greatest team in Spurs' history was beginning to take shape.

By the end of 1955-6, Peter Baker, Danny Blanchflower, Terry Dyson, Ron Henry, Maurice Norman and Bobby Smith were, to varying degrees, establishing themselves. Tottenham could manage only 18th place in the First Division but again reached the semi-final of the FA Cup.

Boston United, Middlesbrough, Doncaster Rovers and West Ham United were all beaten. The semi-final again sent Spurs to Villa Park, to meet Manchester City. Spurs gave a poor performance and Manchester City deservedly won 1-0.

The next two seasons saw a definite improvement in League performances. Positions of second in 1956-7 and third in 1957-8 were largely due to the creative combination of Tommy Harmer and Danny Blanchflower and the goalscoring prowess of Bobby Smith. But Bournemouth became the second Third Division side in three years to beat Spurs in the FA Cup when they won 3-1 in 1957. And two seasons later, Norwich City made it three, while Spurs could only finish 18th in the League in 1958-9.

Jimmy Anderson resigned in October and on the 11th of that month Bill Nicholson was promoted from trainer to take his place. Everton were defeated 10-4 that day, a great result and, although results for the rest of the season were terribly disappointing, it was the start of great things to come. Cliff Jones was settling into the team, having been signed in February 1958, and by the end of the season Dave Mackay had arrived.

The start of the 1959-60 season was encouraging, 12 unbeaten games, but that included four draws in five home games. Spurs stayed in the hunt until successive defeats over Easter. The last two games were won. The last defeat was against Chelsea whose only goal was scored by the brilliant youngster, Jimmy Greaves, who had been persuaded to go to Chelsea instead of Spurs. If he had scored that winning goal for Spurs, the title would have been won, for champions Burnley were only two points ahead in the final table with an inferior goal-average. During the season Les Allen, Bill Brown and John White were signed. The team was now complete.

The winning of the Football League title and FA Cup 'double' made Spurs the greatest team in English football history. Let the facts of 1960-61 speak for themselves.

In the League, the first 11 games were all won — a record. The first defeat came in the 17th game — a record. Thirty-one were won — a record, only seven were lost, two of those in the last three games when the title had been won and the FA Cup Final was approaching. Sixteen away matches were won — a record. Sixty-six points were secured — equalling a record. Thirty-three away points were secured — a record. Fifty points came from only 29 games — a record. Only 17 players were used (three of them only once) — yet another record. Four players were ever-present, three missed only one game, one missed only two. The Championship was won by eight points from Sheffield Wednesday. A total of 2,054,306 spectators saw the games.

41

In 1951, it was a victory over Sheffield Wednesday that gave Spurs the title. In 1961, it was the defeat of Sheffield Wednesday on 17 April that gave them the first leg of the 'double'.

In the FA Cup, Charlton Athletic were beaten in the third round, Crewe Alexandra in the fourth and Aston Villa in the fifth. The only time Spurs looked in any difficulty was in the sixth round when Sunderland held them 1-1 at Roker Park before being thrashed 5-0 in the replay. The semi-final was perhaps the most worrying game. Not because the opponents were League Champions Burnley, but because the game was at Villa Park, scene of Spurs' semi-final defeats in 1948, 1953 and 1956. The bogey was laid to rest with a comfortable 3-0 win.

And so to Spurs first-ever appearance at Wembley. Leicester City provided the opposition. The match itself was something of a disappointment as a football spectacle. Leicester full-back Len Chalmers was injured in the 19th minute and a virtual passenger for the rest of the game. Yet it was not until 67 minutes had gone that Bobby Smith put Spurs ahead. When Terry Dyson added a second 10 minutes later, the 'double' was complete.

Spurs might have done it all again in 1961-2. The FA Cup was retained after Birmingham City, Plymouth Argyle, West Bromwich Albion and Aston Villa were beaten in the early rounds, followed by Manchester United in the semi-final at Hillsborough. At Wembley, they met Burnley, who had been fighting it out with Spurs and Ipswich Town for the League title. Although Burnley were slight favourites, an early goal by Jimmy Greaves put Spurs in charge and whilst Burnley did equalise, further goals by Bobby Smith and Danny Blanchflower, from a penalty, ensured that the Cup returned to White Hart Lane.

Terry Dyson's header skims the Leicester City crossbar at Wembley with Gordon Banks beaten.

Cliff Jones back-heads the ball which Leicester City full-back Richie Norman appears to be twirling on his fingers.

43

Top: Bobby Smith scores for Spurs against Burnley at Wembley in 1962; Bottom: Spurs appeal for a penalty which Danny Blanchflower put away to seal the game.

In the League, newly-promoted Ipswich, under the guidance of Alf Ramsey, proved a real shock. It was their first season in Division One and with Ramsey's revolutionary style of football they took the rest of the division by surprise. Ipswich were not a great team, evidenced by the fact that they were relegated two years later, but they took the title by three points from Burnley, with Spurs one point further behind. It was their away form that let Spurs down, only 20 points being picked up on travels, although had Spurs beaten Ipswich at home by 3-1 instead of losing by that score, the title would have been retained on goal average.

The real disappointment of 1961-2 was in the European Cup, the trophy Bill Nicholson had set his heart on winning. It was Spurs' first venture into European competition and their first game taught them a lesson. It was away to Górnik Zabrze, the champions of Poland. Within an hour, Spurs were 4-0 down. Two late goals gave them slight hope and they held on to it with relish in the second leg, winning 8-1. The lesson learnt, Feyenoord and Dukla Prague were beaten with much less difficulty and the semi-final set Spurs against the European Cup holders, Benfica.

Controversial decisions by referees have already figured large in Spurs' history. In the first-leg of the semi-final, Benfica won 3-1 in Portugal but Spurs had two goals disallowed by debatable offside decisions.

In the second leg, Spurs soon went a goal down. Then Greaves netted, only for it to be disallowed for offside. Again, film of the match has showed the decision questionable. Spurs did get two goals, though, and in the last 40 minutes put Benfica under unbelievable pressure. Three times the woodwork saved the Portuguese, however, and Spurs were out.

The loss of the title to Ipswich pained Tottenham. They felt they were much the better team and the FA Charity Shield of 1962 gave them an early opportunity to prove it. At Portman Road, Spurs won 5-1.

Spurs with the FA Cup which they retained. Back row (left to right): Baker, Norman, Brown, Henry, Mackay. Front row: Medwin, White, Blanchflower, Smith, Greaves, Jones.

Top: Spurs team pictured with the European Cup-winners' Cup. Right: Manager Bill Nicholson and skipper Danny Blanchflower show the trophy to Tottenham supporters.

The FA Cup was finally surrendered in January 1963 when Burnley won 3-0 at White Hart Lane in the third round. The League title went to Everton with Spurs six points behind. Due to the atrocious winter, only one League game was played between 26 December and 23 February, and the backlog of fixtures proved too much, although every club faced the same problems.

There was, however, one further trophy for the 'double' team to win before it split up. Having retained the FA Cup, Spurs were now in the European Cup-winners' Cup and they sailed through to the Final with comparative ease, beating Glasgow Rangers, Slovan Bratislava and OFK Belgrade on the way. The Final was in Rotterdam on 15 May, against Atletico Madrid.

The scoreline is deceptive, for Atletico made Spurs fight all the way, but three goals by Terry Dyson and two from Jimmy Greaves gave Tottenham a 5-1 victory. Spurs were the first British club to win a major European trophy.

The European Cup-winners' Cup was the last major trophy won by the 'double' side, which now began to break up. Fourth in the table in 1963-4 became sixth in 1964-5 and eighth in 1965-6, but all the time Nicholson was rebuilding, looking for that next great success.

It came in 1966-7, with the FA Cup. Millwall, Portsmouth, Bristol City and Birmingham City were defeated to put Spurs in the semi-final. The opposition was Nottingham Forest, on the way to pipping Tottenham to second place in the First Division on goal-average, and they were defeated 2-1 at Hillsborough. For the first time in modern history, the FA Cup Final had an all-London cast — Spurs against Chelsea.

The 2-1 scoreline hardly reflects the ease with which Spurs won. Goals by Jimmy Robertson in the first half and Frank Saul in the second were scant reward. The only time Chelsea looked like getting anywhere near the trophy was in the last five minutes after they had scored a consolation goal.

Including the FA Cup run, Spurs finished the season unbeaten in 24 games, and they finished third in the League.

Spurs celebrate their first goal of the 1967 FA Cup Final.

The promise of the 1967 team was not fulfilled. Inconsistency and poor away form were the biggest problems in the next four seasons. Though Tottenham finished third in 1970-71, they were 13 points behind 'double' winners Arsenal, who had emulated Spurs' feat of ten years earlier.

The early 1970s brought new trophies to White Hart Lane — two Football League Cups and the UEFA Cup.

Spurs had scorned the League Cup when it was first introduced but moving the Final to Wembley and then, from 1970-71, giving the winners a place in the UEFA Cup gave the competition new credibility.

In 1968-9, Spurs had reached the semi-final — losing to Arsenal over two legs — but in 1970-71 they improved on that. Home wins against Swansea City, Sheffield United, West Bromwich Albion and Coventry City, followed by a two-leg semi-final victory over Bristol City put them in the Final against Third Division Aston Villa.

The Football League Cup had proved lucky for Third Division clubs at Wembley — Queen's Park Rangers had won it there in 1967, and Swindon Town in 1969. Villa made Spurs work hard and it was only in the last 12 minutes that Martin Chivers scored the two goals that wrecked the Third Division's record.

Now Spurs embarked upon their first venture into the UEFA Cup. Keflavik were easily overcome in the first round (15-1 on aggregate) but FC Nantes proved much tougher in the next. One goal in the second leg at White Hart Lane decided the tie. Rapid Bucharest were beaten in the next round (5-0 on aggregate) followed by UT Arad (3-1 on aggregate) before AC Milan journeyed to London for the first leg of the semi-final.

Typical of all Italian teams, the Milanese based their game on defence, hoping to score on the break. They did just that after 25 minutes. From that moment on, the match was simply one long siege of the Milan goal. Only two chances fell to Spurs. Both on the edge of the penalty area and both taken by Steve Perryman. But that did not look sufficient for the second-leg in the San Siro Stadium.

The match proved to be Spurs' best performance of the season. Alan Mullery, having returned from a loan spell with Fulham, gave them a wonderful start by scoring after five minutes. The rest of the match was then a reverse of the first leg. Now it was Spurs under continual pressure, but they cracked only once to win 3-2 on aggregate.

In the UEFA Cup Final, Tottenham met Wolverhampton Wanderers. The first-leg was at Molineux where Chivers opened the scoring for Spurs, but within two minutes Wolves had equalised. Again it became a case of the defence having to hold out, hoping for breakaways to take the pressure off. One such breakaway did better than that. A clearance by Mullery was picked up by Chivers. From 40 yards he hit an unstoppable shot to give Spurs a 2-1 first-leg lead.

The second-leg was expected to be a formality and when Mullery scored for Tottenham, it looked likely to be just that. But Wolves equalised on the night and tried desperately to send the game into extra-time. They were by far the better team in the second half, but again the Spurs defence held firm.

Tottenham had now won two of the three European trophies, the first British team to do so.

The second leg of the Final had been Spurs' 26th Cup game of the season. In the FA Cup they got as far as the sixth round and in the Football League Cup as far as the semi-final before being beaten by Chelsea. Two matches had been played in winning the Anglo-Italian League Cup-winners' Cup from AC Torino. Whilst Cup performances had been consistently successful, League form had not reached the same level and Spurs could finish only sixth.

The 1972-3 season was very similar to the previous campaign. Tottenham's League form was inconsistent and they could finish no better than eighth. But again the Cup

Top: Alan Mullery and Gianni Rivera exchange pennants before Spurs' semi-final match against AC Milan in the San Siro Stadium. Bottom: Spurs pictured with the UEFA Cup in 1972. Back row (left to right): P.Beal, R.Evans, C.Knowles, P.Collins, P.Jennings, M.England, M.Chivers, A.Gilzean, T.Naylor. Front row: R.Coates, J.Kinnear, J.Pearce, M.Peters, S.Perryman, J.Pratt, R.Morgan, J.Neighbour.

Ralph Coates crowns himself King of Wembley after scoring the only goal of the 1973 Football League Cup Final for Spurs against Norwich.

competitions provided some relief. Ten matches were played in the UEFA Cup before Liverpool put Spurs out in the semi-final on the away-goals rule.

In the FA Cup, Spurs were leading Derby County 3-1 with only 12 minutes remaining in their fourth-round replay at White Hart Lane. Derby had always looked threatening, despite the score, and with the help of a Roger Davies hat-trick they won a thrilling tie, 5-3 in extra-time.

The Football League Cup provided Tottenham with their greatest success. The path to Wembley was hard, three games being needed to defeat Middlesbrough and two to dispose of Liverpool. Even after a 2-1 win in the first-leg of the semi-final at Wolverhampton, Spurs were never able to relax. Wolves forced extra-time in the second-leg before a Chivers goal put Tottenham through. The 1973 Football League Cup Final, between Spurs and Norwich City, will go down as one of the most tedious games ever staged at Wembley. Ralph Coates scored the only goal of match to ensure that Spurs maintained their record of never losing a major Cup Final.

That record fell in the following season's UEFA Cup Final when a 2-2 draw in the home leg against Feyenoord never looked sufficient. Spurs lost 2-0 in Holland and a proud sequence had ended.

The first four matches of 1974-5 produced four defeats and only one goal, and a disillusioned Bill Nicholson resigned. His replacement was Terry Neill, the former Arsenal defender and manager of Hull City and the Northern Ireland international team.

The arrival of a new manager bought an immediate, albeit temporary, improvement in results. After victories in Neill's first two games in charge, Spurs won only five of their next 27 matches, including a run of 14 games which produced only one victory. The end result was that Tottenham had to beat Leeds in the last match of the season if they were to avoid relegation.

A crowd of almost 50,000 roared them on to a 4-2 victory which was greeted with the sort of celebrations normally reserved for Cup Final success.

Terry Neill's reign at White Hart Lane lasted only one more season. It saw the club improve to finish ninth in the League and again reach the League Cup semi-final, only to lose to Newcastle United. At the end of the season, Spurs embarked on their longest-ever tour, visiting Canada, Fiji, New Zealand and Australia. Shortly after their return, Neill's resignation was accepted, leaving him free to move down the road to Arsenal.

His replacement was found from within the club. Keith Burkinshaw, who had joined Spurs as first-team coach after leaving Newcastle, was new to the job of managing a top club. His previous managerial experience had been restricted to brief spells at Workington and Scunthorpe United, but he was popular with the players at White Hart Lane and the Tottenham board obviously felt that he had the right qualities.

Unfortunately for Burkinshaw, the team under Neill had continued to deteriorate. In his first season there was little he could do to arrest the slide and Spurs finished 1976-7 bottom of the table. Almost three decades of great success had come to an end. For most clubs that would have meant the sack for the manager, but Tottenham had a tradition of loyalty to their managers in times of crisis and, indeed, Burkinshaw certainly deserved more time.

It was vital that a club of Spurs' pedigree returned to Division One at the first attempt — as had Manchester United two years earlier — and Burkinshaw's team achieved instant promotion in style.

Playing the kind of attacking football for which Tottenham Hotspur had long been renowned, they had to wait until the very last match of the season to clinch the point needed to go up with Bolton and Southampton. Brighton missed a First Division place on goal-difference.

Spurs' squad which won promotion was the same which had taken the club into the

Second Division in the first place and Burkinshaw needed to bring in new players. He began the injection of new blood with a double-signing which proved to be one of the most imaginative pieces of transfer dealing in the modern game.

In 1978, Argentina won the World Cup and one of their stars was the little midfield maestro Osvaldo Ardiles. Burkinshaw was tipped off that Ardiles and his fellow countryman, Ricardo Villa, were available for transfer and wanted to come to England. Burkinshaw wasted no time and football was soon buzzing at the prospect of the South Americans performing in the First Division.

The signing of Ardiles and Villa — exciting though it was — was not, of course, going to solve all Tottenham's problems overnight. Other new faces were needed, and the Argentinians themselves required time to adapt to a life-style and language half a world away from their home. They also had to come to terms with the very different world of British domestic football.

For Spurs, 1978-9 and 1979-80 were seasons of consolidation. In the first of these, Tottenham finished 11th in the table; in the second, 14th. It was not spectacular progress but a team capable of challenging for top honours was being built — and in 1980-81, success began to arrive.

Spurs' old problem of inconsistency meant that the season saw only a slight improvement in League results and a move up the table to tenth position, but in the FA Cup, the new-look team took Tottenham to Wembley again.

Queen's Park Rangers, Hull, Coventry and Exeter were beaten at White Hart Lane before a disputed late penalty at Hillsborough earned Wolves a semi-final replay at Highbury where Tottenham won easily, 3-0.

The Centenary FA Cup Final, between Spurs and Manchester City, was an exciting affair. City had been 're-born' under new manager John Bond, having seemed certainties for relegation earlier in the season. They took a 29th-minute lead at Wembley through Tommy Hutchison — and it was the same City player who deflected Glenn Hoddle's free-kick into his own net for Tottenham's equaliser with ten minutes left.

Ricky Villa swerves around Manchester City's defence to score one of the most spectacular goals seen at Wembley.

The replay, the first at Wembley, was one of the most exciting in FA Cup history. Villa gave Spurs the lead in the eighth minute, but three minutes later City were level through Steve Mackenzie's beautifully-struck goal. A Reeves penalty gave City the lead in the 50th minute, but Garth Crooks equalised ten minutes later. Six minutes after that Villa got the winner with one of the greatest goals ever seen at Wembley. How sweet those goals were for Villa, for in the first match he had walked to the dressing-room in tears having been substituted after an anonymous performance.

Spurs now embarked on a further period of success which, although not as great as the heady days of the early 1960s, stands comparison.

The 1981-2 season marked the club's Centenary and they went close to sweeping all the honours, despite losing their first two home League games.

They reached the semi-final of the European Cup-winners' Cup before losing to Barcelona, and were beaten in the League Cup Final (now re-named the Milk Cup) by Liverpool at Wembley after taking an 11th-minute lead through Steve Archibald. A magnificent defensive display was not enough and Liverpool got the equaliser they deserved and two more goals in extra-time to win 3-1.

Spurs had now lost their first major domestic Cup Final and their first match at Wembley, in each case after eight successes.

In the League, Tottenham always seemed in with a chance, but the old problem of inconsistency was still apparent and there was also a fixture backlog to overcome. A bad winter and success in Cup competitions meant that in the last two months of the season, Spurs had to play 19 games. Injuries and fatigue took their toll, performances tailed off and Spurs finished fourth.

The FA Cup provided the trophy Spurs so desperately wanted to mark their 100 years. Arsenal, Leeds United, Aston Villa and Chelsea fell in the early rounds and Second Division Leicester City were beaten in the Villa Park semi-final. Spurs faced Queen's Park Rangers in the Final without Ardiles and Villa. Ardiles had returned to Argentina for the Gold Cup after the semi-final and was not to return for nine months because of the Falklands conflict. Villa was left out of the Wembley game because of that conflict.

Queen's Park Rangers' Bob Hazell slides in to tackle Garth Crooks at Wembley.

Glenn Hoddle's penalty seals the 1982 FA Cup Final replay for Spurs.

Second Division Rangers provided stubborn opposition and 20 minutes extra-time had been played before Hoddle got the first goal. Five minutes later Rangers equalised.

For the second successive year, a replay was needed. It took place the following Thursday, again at Wembley where one goal decided the issue. It came from a sixth-minute Hoddle penalty which saw Spurs join Aston Villa as the only clubs to have won the FA Cup seven times.

The next season, 1982-3, was less successful. The FA Cup was surrendered at Everton in the fifth round and interest in the Cup-winners' Cup ended in the second round. Although Spurs finished fourth in the League, and thereby qualified for the next season's UEFA Cup, the biggest blow was in the Milk Cup when Second Division Burnley pulled off a sensational 4-1 win at White Hart Lane in the fifth round.

In 1983, Spurs took a unique step when a new company, Tottenham Hotspur plc, was formed. Shares in the new company were offered to the public through the Stock Market. Unlike the share offer of 1898, this was a great success with the issue being considerably over-subscribed.

Early exits from the FA and Milk Cups, and eighth place in the League, left only the UEFA Cup if Spurs were to salvage something from the 1983-4 season.

An easy first-round victory over Drogheda had been followed by much harder victories over Feyenoord, Bayern Munich, FK Austria and Hajduk Split to put Spurs in the Final against Anderlecht.

A Paul Miller goal earned them a 1-1 draw in Belgium and left them favourites to win the trophy at White Hart Lane. They did, but only in the most dramatic fashion. A surprise goal by Anderlecht after an hour's play was equalised six minutes from the end by Graham Roberts. With no further scoring in extra-time, the result hinged on a penalty shoot-out.

Anderlecht's first kick was saved and Spurs went into a 4-3 lead. Danny Thomas had only to put his kick away and the trophy was won, but his shot was saved. Then Spurs' goalkeeper Tony Parks, playing because of injury to regular goalkeeper Ray Clemence, pulled off a splendid save to give Spurs their third win in European Finals.

Top: Graham Roberts celebrates his goal against Anderlecht in the 1984 UEFA Cup Final. Bottom: Victorious Spurs team with the UEFA Cup.

During the course of the season, Keith Burkinshaw had become disenchanted with the new regime at Spurs and announced his decision to resign at the end of the season. He left on a high note, having been the second most successful manager in Spurs' history. Only the legendary Bill Nicholson stood ahead of him.

Burkinshaw's replacement was Peter Shreeve, promoted from assistant-manager, and he did well in his first season in charge. Although Spurs got no further than the fourth round of either the FA or Milk Cups, and lost in the second round of the UEFA Cup to the great Real Madrid, the best performance was in the League. Spurs battled with Everton and Liverpool for the title, their challenge evaporating only in the last few games due to the backlog of fixtures. They finished third and were undefeated in their last 16 away League games, but it was their home form which cost Spurs the title. Seven League games were lost at White Hart Lane, a run of five in six games late in the season proving the nail in the coffin of their ambitions.

The 1985-6 season again proved a disappointment. Early exits from the FA and Milk Cups were matched by a drop to tenth place in the League. In May 1986, Shreeve was replaced by David Pleat who had made his name as manager of Luton Town.

Pleat brought a reputation of providing entertaining football on limited resources. At Spurs, money was available and he set about restructuring the team, in particular the defence, although not at the expense of Spurs' great tradition of playing attacking football.

A five-man midfield was introduced and proved particularly effective for the lone striker, Clive Allen, who scored 49 competitive goals during the 1986-7 season to set a new goalscoring record for the club.

Exciting and effective as Spurs were, the season did not produce any tangible reward although they went desperately close to a trophy. They finished third in the League, reached the Littlewoods Cup semi-final before losing in a replay, and won through to their eighth FA Cup Final.

At Wembley, Tottenham Hotspur finally lost their 100 per cent record in FA Cup Finals when Coventry won one of the most entertaining Wembley games for years, in extra-time.

Steve Hodge (left) and Chris Waddle — two of the men brought in to try and bring the glory days back to White Hart Lane, along with the likes of Chris Fairclough, and more recently, Bobby Mimms and Paul Walsh.

Despite the shock of a Wembley defeat, Spurs fans looked forward optimistically to 1987-8 and, indeed, the season got off to a good start with a victory over Southampton on 12 September setting a club record of 14 successive home League wins. Liverpool, however, were soon romping away with the Championship, and Spurs did not have the consistency to mount a realistic challenge to the Merseysiders.

Soon events off the field took the club's name on to the front pages of the nation's newspapers. Manager David Pleat, amid lurid accusations about his private life, resigned in October and Terry Venables was quickly appointed to succeed him. Venables, though, was unable to take up his post until December and in the intervening period, Spurs' fortunes went rapidly downhill.

Assistant manager Trevor Hartley and coach Doug Livermore had taken charge for a short time, and team selection had even passed to a committee of senior players. The decline was not reversed, however, and Second Division promotion candidates, Aston Villa, knocked Spurs out of the Littlewoods Cup.

Venables' arrival was greeted with universal optimism but it was soon clear that a transitional period was about to dawn. Spurs won only six out of 23 League matches under the new manager and reached a low spot when they crashed to Third Division Port Vale in the FA Cup. Eventually, despite the £500,000 signing of Paul Walsh from Liverpool, they finished 13th and at one time could have been involved in the relegation play-offs. The one consolation was the experience gained by youngsters developed by the club, players like Brian Statham, Vinny Samways, Neil Ruddock and Paul Moran.

But the time gave Venables the opportunity to assess the playing staff available and in the summer of 1988 he plunged into the transfer market, spending a club record £1.7 million on the signing of Paul Stewart and, almost immediately, exceeding that with the purchase of Paul Gascoigne for £2 million.

Those signings showed that the board were prepared to back the new manager with hard cash and gave Spurs' supporters great hope, but those hopes were dealt a wicked blow even before a ball had been kicked in the 1988-9 season.

During the summer, work had commenced on the redevelopment of the East Stand but the building work had not gone as well as planned and the first match of the season, at home to Coventry City, had to be called off only a matter of hours before kick-off because of safety worries. The embarassment was bad enough, but the Football League then deducted two points which, although later reduced to a £10,000 fine, seemed to have an immediate demoralizing effect on the team.

Spurs' new manager, Terry Venables, returns to White Hart Lane.

A season of high hopes turned into a season of struggle with a third-round exit from the FA Cup at the hands of Bradford City perhaps being the lowest point. It was only in the last ten weeks that Spurs managed to put together the consistent results that enabled the club to finish the season in a respectable sixth place in the League.

If the team's performances were not impressive, at least the supporters found some consolation in the form of England winger Chris Waddle and when the signing of England's premier striker, Gary Lineker, was announced in June 1990, the thought of Gascoigne, Waddle and Lineker was enough to raise the pulse-rate of any football fan.

However, the dreams were again shattered before the new season kicked off. So impressive had Waddle performed that Europe's top clubs were soon sniffing around and when Olympique Marseille made a £4.25 million offer for his transfer, even Spurs could not refuse.

At the start of the season Spurs again struggled and it was some time before they learnt to compensate for Waddle's departure. Eventually, with Gascoigne taking over Waddle's linchpin role, Spurs managed to find some consistency and finished the season well to take third place in the First Division, although without ever challenging for the title. The FA Cup provided no consolation with another exit at the third-round stage.

However, it was now clear that Venables was beginning to get together a team capable of putting Spurs back at the top and after the success of England in the World Cup, early results in 1990-91 seemed to indicate that Spurs would at last offer a serious challenge to Liverpool and Arsenal for the top honours.

But now Spurs were to be rocked by the type of off-field problems that the club had never before encountered. It was revealed that Tottenham Hotspur FC was in serious financial difficulties. The bold move of making the club part of a Stock Exchange quoted public company and venturing into non-football activities rebounded badly. Financially, the football club did well, but on building and leisure wear substantial losses were suffered. Debts of up to £20 million were rumoured.

Amid speculation of take-overs, receivership, sale of players and even liquidation, manager Venables did well to keep the pressures such stories generated from the players. The lack of funds prevented Venables from strengthening the team and eventually the pressures began to be reflected in League results. With Venables himself fronting a consortium seeking to take over the club, the FA Cup took on enormous

Steve Sedgley and Manchester United's Brian McClair with Howells and Nayim looking on.

58

significance. It provided not only the one chance of winning honours for the season but also the financial lifeline that might keep Spurs afloat.

Victories over Blackpool, Oxford United, Portsmouth and Notts County took Tottenham through to a Wembley semi-final against their double-chasing neighbours, Arsenal. In an electric atmosphere, and inspired by Gascoigne, Spurs gave their best performance of the season to almost dominate the match and run out 3-1 winners.

The opposition in the Final was provided by Nottingham Forest and with two teams who play football the way it was meant to be played, a great game was expected. The spectacle was almost ruined after only 15 minutes when Paul Gascoigne, who had done so much to get Spurs through to Wembley, was carried off with serious knee ligament damage after a rash challenge on Gary Charles.

But if Gascoigne's departure deprived Spurs of the country's most talented player, it revealed the depth of team spirit that Venables had built.

Forest took the lead through Stuart Pearce's free-kick, awarded for Gascoigne's foul on Charles, but Spurs then had much the better of the game. A goal by Gary Lineker was disallowed for offside, wrongly as television was later to prove, and Lineker then had a penalty saved by Mark Crossley.

Ten minutes into the second half, Paul Stewart grabbed the equaliser after Nayim and Paul Allen had combined to set him free. And three minutes into extra-time, Spurs got the winner when Nayim's corner was flicked on by Stewart and headed into his own net by Des Walker.

No further goals were forthcoming and when Gary Mabbutt went up to collect the Cup, Spurs had again won a major trophy when the year ends in '1'. For the moment, all gloomy thoughts were banished as Spurs and their fans celebrated a day of Wembley glory.

But the overall future of Tottenham Hotspur remained uncertain. Gascoigne was in hospital, his multi-million pound move to Lazio in doubt; and manager Terry Venables went on holiday to Sardinia, still unable to clinch the take-over deal which clearly meant so much to him.

Paul Gascoigne (left) celebrates a goal against Luton Town and Gary Lineker (right) with the FA Cup after Tottenham's extra-time win over Nottingham Forest.

The season over, attention now focussed on the club's survival. Terry Venables worked long and hard to bring about a rescue, but it was only when he won the support of millionaire electronics magnate, Alan Sugar, that a deal was put together. Sugar became the largest shareholder of the parent PLC with Venables risking everything he had to become the second largest. But the takeover was only the start, for the financial problems still had to be resolved.

Venables was appointed chief executive with Peter Shreeve recalled as team manager, leaving Venables free to concentrate on the commercial side.

After a traumatic season it was perhaps expecting too much for Spurs to do much in 1991-2. With Gascoigne's Cup Final injury putting him out of action for the season and the announcement of Gary Lineker's imminent departure for Japan, the club did well to reach the Littlewoods Cup semi-finals, but a mid-season slump saw an early departure from the FA Cup. In the third round of the European Cup-winners' Cup, Spurs were unable to overcome a defence-minded Feyenoord and it was only a late-season run that took them away from the relegation zone to 15th place in the table.

Shreeve was not retained for the 1992-3 season, Venables returning to overall control of playing affairs, although day-to-day management was left in the hands of coaches Doug Livermore and Ray Clemence. The Venables-Sugar partnership had done an amazing job, in just one year reversing the club's financial decline to such an extent that £1.7 million could be invested in Darren Anderton and £2.2 million in Teddy Sheringham. To supplement big-money imports, Venables gave a chance to youngsters of the calibre of Andy Turner, Dean Austin, Nick Barmby, Kevin Watson and Danny Hill.

Teddy Sheringham (extreme right) scores for Tottenham against Norwich City at Carrow Road in the FA Cup fourth round in January 1993.

Sheringham, a £2.2 million signing from Nottingham Forest, in action at Ipswich.

Gary Mabbutt (left), proved an inspiration as Spurs' skipper. Neil Ruddock (right), played in 38 League games after his £750,000 return from Southampton.

A season for rebuilding, eighth place in the new FA Premier League was a creditable performance and the only real disappointment came in the FA Cup semi-final. For the second time in three years Spurs were drawn against Arsenal and interest was again so great that Wembley was the only realistic venue. The match was settled

Darren Anderton (left) cost Spurs £1.7 million after bursting on to the scene with Portsmouth. Nicky Barmby (right), an exciting first season in Tottenham's senior side.

by a second-half Tony Adams goal but if an early penalty decision had gone Spurs' way, the result could have been different.

A mixture of experienced stars, promising youngsters and an improving financial picture gave supporters justifiable cause for optimism, but that was all but destroyed on the eve of the FA Cup Final. Venables and Sugar had fallen out. Sugar contrived to sack Venables, who was only reinstated with the help of a temporary High Court injunction. Battle was again joined for the future of Tottenham Hotspur FC.

Spurs Managers

Frank Brettell
1898-1899

SPURS' first-ever manager, Frank Brettell, was appointed in February 1898, although he did not take up his duties until 14 March of that year, after watching his new team for the first time two days earlier.

Brettell's appointment as secretary-manager was prior to the club becoming a limited company. No doubt the pending flotation was in the directors' minds when they appointed the man who had been secretary-manager of Bolton Wanderers before joining Spurs.

Originally from Liverpool, Brettell had been one of the pioneers of Everton, having served on their committee in their first season of existence. He had also played for that club, at centre- or inside-forward, until injury, to which he was prone, had forced him to revert to half-back, sometimes even playing in goal.

When his playing career finished, he became a reporter on the *Liverpool Mercury*, although keeping in close touch with football through an association with Liverpool. In 1895, he joined Bolton.

Brettell's appointment was well received. He was well-liked in Lancashire and it was anticipated that he would do equally well in London. His popularity in the North dwindled when he persuaded players of the calibre of Cain, Erentz, McNaught, Melia, Smith, Atherton, Bradshaw, McKay, Hickson and Cameron to leave their clubs and move to Spurs.

Brettell remained at Spurs for less than a year, tendering his resignation on 8 February 1899 to take effect on 1 April. The reason for this was quite simple. He was offered substantially more money to take on the manager's job at Portsmouth.

John Cameron
1899-1907

FOLLOWING Frank Brettell's resignation, Spurs immediately advertised the position and received a huge number of applications. They appointed from within the club in giving the job to John Cameron.

Cameron had been one of Brettell's first signings, joining Spurs in May 1898 from Everton. Although in his early 20s, he had clearly impressed in his short time with the club and on 17 February 1899, he was appointed player-manager-secretary.

Born in Ayr, Cameron began his career with the local club before joining the mighty amateur side Queen's Park. Thereafter he had moved to Everton but continued to play as an amateur, a move which was not popular with his team-mates. He was eventually persuaded to join the professional ranks but soon afterwards moved to Spurs.

A goalscoring inside-forward, Cameron was immediately successful in his new role, helping Tottenham to the Southern League championship in 1899-1900, and victory in the 1901 FA Cup Final.

Perhaps not surprisingly, after such early success, Cameron was unable to maintain such high standards, although second place in the Southern League was achieved in 1901-02 and 1903-04. Gradually Cameron took a less active role on the pitch, preferring to concentrate on his managerial duties.

Although the team was not successful,

Cameron's popularity was such that no pressure was put upon him to tender his resignation and, indeed, Spurs even brought Arthur Turner from Rotherham in 1906 to take over the secretarial duties so that Cameron could give his full attention to team affairs.

Alas, this did nothing to improve results, a situation that Cameron was apparently unable to tolerate. It was a shock to supporters when Cameron resigned on 13 March 1907, giving 'differences with the directorate' as his reason.

Fred Kirkham
1907-1908

WITH Cameron's resignation, Spurs again advertised for a manager and again received many applications. This time the directors took much longer over announcing the new man — and when they finally reached a decision, it was a very strange one in the eyes of many outsiders.

The appointee was Fred Kirkham, a well-known referee from Preston. For 17 years, Kirkham had been working as a commercial traveller, and his only football involvement was as a referee. He had been in charge of the 1902 and 1906 FA Cup Finals and many internationals.

Having refereed Spurs' match with Watford on 13 April 1907, Kirkham was appointed manager on 18 April, although no official announcement was made until 22 April. He was given a five-year contract worth £350-per-annum.

For one of the country's top referees, he apparently had little respect for his colleagues. In November 1907, he was censured for making improper remarks to the referee in his dressing-room after Spurs' match with Brighton on 19 October.

Kirkham was not a success as a manager. He was unpopular with the players and fans alike and came in for a great deal of criticism from all quarters. It was no surprise when, after a settlement on the balance of his contract had been negotiated, Kirkham resigned on 20 July 1908.

The directors decided not to replace him. Engagement of players and team selection would be left to the directors, although these duties fell very much on the shoulders of Arthur Turner.

Peter McWilliam
1913-1927 & 1938-1939

BY December 1912, the Tottenham board concluded that if Spurs were going to make any real impact in the Football League, then a full-time manager had to be appointed. On 21 December, Peter McWilliam was named as that new manager.

Inverness-born McWilliam joined Newcastle United in 1903 and went on to play at half-back in their great teams of 1905-10, winning three Football League Championship medals and one FA Cup winners' medal.

A Scottish international, he suffered a serious knee injury in the match against Wales on 7 March 1911 and his playing career in League football came to an end. His decision to seek a manager's position was therefore understandable and he seemed eminently suitable. McWilliam took up his position with Spurs on 1 January 1913, and was to remain with the club for 14 years, becoming both the most popular and most successful manager Tottenham had had up to that point.

McWilliam was a quiet man, not given to lavishing much praise, but still extremely popular with the players. His football philosophy was very simple: he left the game to the players. He was not a man who spent time giving tactical talks. He simply surrounded himself with good players and left them to get on with it.

There is no better example of this than when

the offside law was changed for the 1925-6 season. McWilliam did not bother to have any tactical discussions with the players, leaving it to them to work out how the change in the law would affect play — and congratulating them when they came off the pitch after winning their first match under the new law. It was perhaps this style of management that earned him so much respect from the players.

After the traumas of World War One and relegation, McWilliam's teams won the Second Division title in 1919-20, the FA Cup in 1921, and took Spurs to their highest-ever First Division position of second in 1921-2.

The success was not maintained and McWilliam set out to build a new team to challenge for honours. But in late-1926 he was approached by Middlesbrough, then top of the Second Division, and offered £1,500 a year to take over as team manager.

At Spurs, McWilliam was on a salary of £850 a year but he wanted to stay at White Hart Lane. He asked the Spurs directors to give him a £150 rise but they refused. In December 1926, he handed in his notice although he did not leave until 26 February 1927.

Spurs were to regret their decision not to increase McWilliam's salary and it was rumoured over the next few years, with the club's fortunes fluctuating, that several attempts were made to persuade him to return.

However, McWilliam stayed with Middlesbrough until 1933 when he became Arsenal's chief scout, although he remained in the North-East and was rarely seen at Highbury.

Towards the end of 1937-8, Spurs' board decided that under Jack Tresadern's guidance it was unlikely that the club would get out of

the Second Division. New approaches were made to McWilliam and on 6 April 1938, Tresarden handed in his resignation. It was immediately announced that McWilliam would return as manager. He took up the post on 16 May 1938, but was to remain at White Hart Lane for little more than a year.

In that short time he realised that drastic changes had to be made and immediately began to promote juniors from the Northfleet nursery, with the long-term aim of producing a team that could get Spurs out of the Second Division and go on to challenge for top honours. World War Two put an end to McWilliam's plans. He returned to the North-East and by the time the war had ended he decided that he was too old for football management and retired.

Billy Minter
1927-1929

BORN in Woolwich, Billy Minter began his football career as an amateur with Norwich before returning to Woolwich to play for Arsenal. He moved to Reading before being transferred to Spurs in 1908, being almost ever-present in the team until normal football was suspended due to the outbreak of World War One. From inside-forward, he scored almost 100 League and Cup goals for the club.

His appearances were greatly reduced during the war, but he was back regularly in the 1919-20 Second Division championship team, retiring at the end of that season. In June 1920, Minter was appointed trainer and served under Peter McWilliam until 1927, when he was selected to replace him.

Officially appointed on 1 February 1927, he took up the position on 27 February, having spent the intervening period being eased into the job by the departing manager. Regretfully, Minter was not a success in his new role. He was a modest man, deeply concerned for the club, and he was the type of person who could never leave problems in the office. In his first full season in charge, Spurs were relegated.

Although he did everything possible, working as hard as any man could, he was unable to get them back into the First Division and eventually the burden took its toll. Anxiety brought on illness and on 20 November he resigned. He was not pushed into doing so, indeed he had the full support of the board, but felt that it was in Tottenham's best interests that he should move over. It was typical of the

man that his first thoughts were for the club not his own well-being.

He was appointed assistant-secretary and remained in that position until his death in May 1940.

Percy Smith
1929-1935

UPON Billy Minter's resignation, the successful applicant was Percy Smith, team manager of Bury.

Born in Leicester, Smith had moved to Preston when he was 18 years old. He played centre-forward for Preston North End for seven years, then joined Blackburn Rovers and stayed with them for six years, playing at half-back in their Championship sides of 1911-12 and 1913-14. He retired as a player in 1920 to become manager of Nelson and had been manager of Bury for three years before his move to Spurs.

As an outsider, Smith was remarkably successful in persuading the board to spend money on new players, and he was able to construct a team in the true traditions of his new club. They played attractive short-passing football with the emphasis on attack. Promotion was won in 1932-3 and third position in the First Division was reached the following season.

Why things should have gone so badly for Smith in 1934-5 is not clear. After a reasonable start, injuries piled up and from Christmas 1934 to April 1935 results were disastrous. The team plunged to the bottom of the table and in April 1935, Smith handed in his resignation claiming that his team selections had been interfered with by the board, an allegation that was strenuously denied.

His resignation was to take effect at the end of the season but in view of the atmosphere that his statements generated, he was encouraged to leave early, team affairs being temporarily in the hands of Walter Hardinge, the trainer.

Jack Tresadern
1935-1938

BORN in West Ham, Jack Tresadern started his career with the local club, appearing in the first Wembley Cup Final in 1923 and winning one England cap that year.

In October 1924, he was transferred to Burnley but stayed only a short time before moving to Northampton Town as player-manager. A broken leg in December 1926 brought his playing career to an end, but he remained as manager until 1930 when he moved to Crystal Palace in the same capacity. It was from Palace that he joined Spurs.

His application for the manager's position was accepted on 19 June 1935 and he took up the post on 1 July. He was not a success. Not only was he unable to produce the results on the field, but he was also unpopular with the supporters and club officials. He was not helped by continual rumours that the directors were trying to get Peter McWilliam to return. In March 1938, newspaper reports suggested that Tresadern would leave of his own accord before being asked to go.

The manager's job at Plymouth Argyle was vacant and, with his contract at Spurs due to expire on 20 June, Tresadern made a successful last-minute application. On 6 April, he handed in his resignation. It was accepted immediately, although no announcement was made until after the match on 9 April, when news of Peter McWilliam's return was made public.

Joe Hulme
1946-1949

PETER McWilliam's decision not to return to Spurs after the war again left Spurs looking for a replacement. The man selected was Joe Hulme, who had found fame with arch-rivals Arsenal.

Born in Staffordshire, but having lived in York from the age of nine, Hulme was an all-round athlete at school and had the option of playing either football or cricket professionally. He chose football and signed for York City in 1923.

After only six months with York, he moved to Blackburn Rovers, then joined Arsenal in 1925. During his time at Highbury he played cricket for Middlesex but it was at football that he excelled.

A goalscoring winger, Hulme was a part of the great Arsenal side of the 1930s, winning League Championship and FA Cup winners' medals together with England caps before moving to Huddersfield Town. His last game for Huddersfield was in the 1938 FA Cup Final against Preston North End.

He was appointed Spurs manager in January 1946, midway through the first full post-war season. His three-year reign was not a great success, the high point being the 1948 FA Cup semi-final against Blackpool, but he assembled almost all the players that were to bring Spurs their first League title.

In March 1949, Hulme returned to White Hart Lane after a short illness to receive a letter from the chairman inviting him to hand in his resignation if he was still unwell. He replied that he was perfectly fit and produced a letter from a doctor to confirm this. The chairman then gave him one month's notice.

Hulme was no doubt very unlucky. He had worked hard to build up Spurs after the war and was assembling a team that was showing signs of the great times to come, but obviously the directors were not prepared to wait any longer for the club to escape the clutches of the Second Division.

Arthur Rowe
1949-1955

BORN in Tottenham, Arthur Rowe was a Spurs man through and through. He first became associated with the club in 1921 as a schoolboy, and he worked his way through the junior ranks and the nursery clubs of Cheshunt and Northfleet to sign as a professional in 1929.

A centre-half, Rowe played throughout the 1930s and won an England cap against France in 1933-4. He was a 'footballing centre-half', not only performing defensive duties but looking to pass the ball to a colleague and set the attack going whenever possible. He also thought deeply about the game. A popular captain, his playing career came to an end in 1939 when he was released by Spurs after failing to recover fully from cartilage operations.

Rowe went to Budapest to take up a coaching position with the Hungarian government. The appointment was short-lived and with the outbreak of war he returned to Britain to serve in the army as a physical training instructor and took charge of the Army football team.

On his demob in 1945, Rowe became secretary-manager of Chelmsford City and was immediately successful. Chelmsford won the

Southern League Cup in his first season. In the short time he was with them he made them one of the top non-League teams in the country. His potential was spotted by Spurs and although the manager's position was advertised after Hulme's dismissal, Rowe was always favourite for the job. His appointment was announced in May 1949.

The only addition that Rowe made to the playing staff was that of Alf Ramsey from Southampton, a signing that Hulme had tried to make on the 1949 transfer deadline. The difference was in style — 'Push and Run'. 'Push' the ball to a colleague; 'Run' into an open space to take the return.

It was simple but so effective and in Rowe's first season in charge it won Spurs the Second Division title. That was followed in 1950-51 by the greatest success in Spurs' history to date — the League Championship.

The momentum was maintained in 1951-2 with second place in the First Division, and in 1953 the FA Cup semi-final was reached.

If one criticism can be levelled at Rowe it is that he was too loyal to the players who had won the Championship. But, against that, the young players were not coming through to replace the old guard and he had little option but to persevere with the established players while looking for the new talent so desperately needed.

Rowe was a man who felt passionately for Spurs and the decline of his great team, combined with some bad results, had a detrimental effect on his health. Having suffered a breakdown in 1954, followed by six months' complete rest, Rowe again fell ill in April 1955. His assistant Jimmy Anderson was made acting manager in June 1955 pending the expiration of Rowe's contract in January 1956, but in the July, Rowe resigned.

Jimmy Anderson
1955-1958

JIMMY Anderson joined Spurs as a groundstaff boy in 1908 and did a variety of jobs at White Hart Lane until being appointed manager in July 1955, on Rowe's resignation.

As Rowe's assistant he had already taken charge of team matters in the manager's absences and he knew the players well. However, he was probably already a little too old for the position when he was appointed. With Bill Nicholson

as coach, though, he provided the perfect stop-gap between Rowe and Nicholson, who was clearly being groomed for the manager's position.

Anderson knew that new blood was urgently needed and he soon set about trying to rebuild the team. The FA Cup semi-final was reached in 1956, but the team also struggled against relegation. As with his two predecessors, the pressure began to affect Anderson's health and in October 1958 he resigned.

Bill Nicholson
1958-1974

ALL great clubs can point to one man who has made them into the power they are today. In Spurs' case that man is Bill Nicholson.

Born in Scarborough, Nicholson joined Spurs as a groundstaff boy in 1936 and went to play for the nursery club at Northfleet. Having signed professional at the age of 18, he made his League debut in 1938 as a full-back and was about to establish himself in the team when World War Two intervened and he joined the Durham Light Infantry.

Most of his army service was spent in England, initially as an infantry training instructor and then as a PTI, and he was able to make only the occasional wartime guest appearance for Darlington and Newcastle United.

After the war he returned to Spurs and established himself as the first choice centre-half towards the end of the transitional 1945-6

season. He moved to right-half in 1947-8 and it was in this position that he won his only England cap, against Portugal at Goodison Park on 19 May 1951, scoring with his first touch after only 19 seconds.

He remained the regular Spurs right-half until 1954, a crucial member of the 1949-50 Second Division championship and 1950-51 League Championship team. In 1954, Nicholson suggested to Arthur Rowe that he was getting too old for first-team football and that it was time a replacement was found.

As a player Nicholson had taken a keen interest in coaching, passing his FA badge at the first attempt and taking charge of the Cambridge University team, and on retiring from playing he moved to the Spurs coaching staff. He became first-team coach in 1955 when Anderson replaced Rowe as manager.

Having helped England manager Walter Winterbottom with the England Under-23 team, Nicholson was the obvious choice as the next Tottenham manager. He was offered the job

on 8 October 1958, and the greatest period in Spurs' history started with a 10-4 victory over Everton three days later, the day of his appointment.

Under Nicholson, Spurs won the 'double' in 1960-61, the FA Cup again in 1962 and the European Cup-winners' Cup in 1963. He then rebuilt the team to win the FA Cup in 1967 and built a third team to win the Football League Cup in 1971, the UEFA Cup in 1972, the Football League Cup again in 1973 and to reach the UEFA Cup Final in 1974 before Spurs suffered their first defeat in a major Cup Final.

The teams that Nicholson built always played in the true Tottenham style, with great players allowed to show their skills, to attack and most of all to entertain.

In his 16 years as manager, Nicholson was a perfectionist. At the start of 1974-5 Spurs lost their first four matches and Nicholson decided it was time to go. On 29 August, he announced his resignation. The directors did not want him to leave, and even the players tried to persuade him to stay, but his mind was made up. He did agree to remain in charge until the club were able to find a replacement but this meant his last game was a 4-0 home defeat against Middlesbrough in the League Cup, an inglorious way to end the greatest era in the club's history.

For the rest of the season, Nicholson took a deserved rest from football, but he was back the following year when he agreed to help West Ham United in their preparations for European games. Much criticism was directed at Spurs for allowing Nicholson to completely sever his connections with the club. But it was not long before he was back at White Hart Lane. When Keith Burkinshaw was appointed manager in July 1976, the first 'signing' he made was to ask Nicholson to return as a consultant. Nicholson continued to serve the club in that capacity until May 1991 when he was appointed club president.

On 21 August 1983, Bill Nicholson's services to Spurs were rewarded with a testimonial against West Ham and in 1984 he was awarded the Professional Footballers' Association Merit Award.

Terry Neill
1974-1976

IT was a surprise when the Tottenham board decided to appoint a manager who had no previous connection with the club. It was even more surprising that he should be Terry Neill, a man who was, and always will be, associated with Arsenal.

Neill was appointed in September 1974. Born in Belfast, he joined Arsenal in December 1959 from Bangor and served as their captain and centre-half until moving to Hull City as player-manager in 1970. Neill was a Northern Ireland international, his country's player-manager and

held the then record of 59 Irish caps. It was always felt that his time as manager of Hull was preparation for his return to Highbury.

Neill stayed at Spurs for two years, handing in his resignation in June 1976 and almost immediately taking on the manager's job at Arsenal. Although he helped keep Spurs in the First Division in his first season in charge and saw them reach the Football League Cup semi-final in 1975-6, Neill was never universally accepted by the fans.

Keith Burkinshaw
1976-1984

KEITH Burkinshaw, a native of Higham (Yorkshire), had been rejected as a youth by Wolverhampton Wanderers and then played for Denaby United before being asked to join Liverpool. He jumped at the chance, giving up his job in the local pit, but, although he stayed at Anfield for seven years, he did not make the grade, playing only one Football League game.

Burkinshaw moved to Workington in 1957 and remained there until 1965, latterly as player-manager. He signed for Scunthorpe United solely as a player, although he also spent some of his three years at the Old Show Ground as caretaker-manager.

He was a coach at Newcastle United for seven

years until he was dismissed in 1975. In that summer he joined Spurs as first-team coach.

Extremely popular with the players, Burkinshaw had their full support when he decided to apply for the manager's job. Being relatively unknown, his prospects did not seem particularly favourable, but his appointment was announced in July 1976.

The task facing him was enormous. He was unable to arrest the slump and at the end of his first season Spurs were relegated. Burkinshaw rewarded the board's faith in him with promotion at the first attempt, but he knew that the players who had won back Tottenham's First Division place were not good enough to make an impact there. In the summer of 1978, he pulled off one of the greatest transfer deals of all time with the signing of Argentinian stars Osvaldo Ardiles and Ricardo Villa.

The team Burkinshaw fashioned won the FA Cup in 1981 and 1982, and followed this with the UEFA Cup in 1984, making him second only to Bill Nicholson as Spurs' most successful manager.

Burkinshaw became disillusioned after the boardroom takeover at White Hart Lane in 1983-4. He announced that he would resign when the season was over. His departure was on good terms and on 29 May, he was rewarded with a testimonial against an England XI before going to coach in the Middle East.

Peter Shreeve
1984-1986 & 1991-1992

BORN in Neath, South Wales, where his mother had been evacuated during the war, Peter Shreeve was brought up in Islington, North London.

He started his football career as a forward with Finchley before joining Reading, making his Football League debut in 1958-9. Injury caused his retirement from League football in 1966, although he was able to assist Southern League clubs Chelmsford City and Wimbledon before taking up coaching. From Charlton Athletic he moved to Spurs in 1974 as youth-team manager, being upgraded to reserve-team manager in 1977 and assistant-manager in 1980.

With Keith Burkinshaw's departure, Shreeve made the further step up to manager in June 1984, but was never given the opportunity to impress. During his two years in charge he tried to continue Burkinshaw's good work but immediate rewards were not forthcoming. Although sustained challenges were made on all trophies, injuries and backlogs of fixtures did not help and at the end of 1985-6, he left the club.

He joined Queen's Park Rangers as assistant manager and was expected to take over as manager on the departure of Jim Smith but after a short spell as caretaker manager was passed over in favour of Trevor Francis. He later moved to Watford where he worked under Steve Perryman until being recalled to White Hart Lane in June 1991 on Terry Venables' elevation to chief executive.

Given just a one year contract Shreeve had an almost impossible task trying to build upon the previous season's FA Cup success. Deprived of Paul Gascoigne's services and still handicapped by the lack of money that had almost seen the club's demise Spurs struggled. Shreeve worked hard to improve things but an approach that was sometimes over-cautious and a willingness to resort to long-ball tactics did little to endear him to Spurs' fans. At the end of his contract it was not renewed.

David Pleat
1986-1987

BORN in Nottingham, David Pleat started his career with Nottingham Forest before being transferred to Luton Town, then Shrewsbury Town, Exeter City and Peterborough United. He moved to Southern League Nuneaton Borough as player-manager and stayed with them for three years before returning to Luton Town as a coach.

In 1978, Pleat was promoted to manager and over the next eight years was mainly responsible for establishing Luton as a First Division club renowned for attractive, attacking play.

An innovative manager, receptive to new ideas, he joined Spurs in May 1986. In the following season he was responsible for the introduction of the style of play that had been so successful for Belgium in the 1986 World Cup — five men in midfield in support of a lone front runner.

Although this style clearly suited the players at White Hart Lane and proved highly entertaining, it was not quite good enough to provide any trophies. Spurs' third position in Division One, an FA Cup Final place and a semi-final spot in the Littlewoods Cup was ample proof of Pleat's influence, though.

Early in the 1987-8 season, however, he resigned after renewed newspapers reports concerning his private life. He was not out of football for long, however, and after turning down the chance of a job in Greece, Pleat accepted the manager's job at Second Division Leicester City. He lost his job when Leicester were nearly relegated to Division Three in 1991 and returned to Luton as manager.

Terry Venables
1987-1993

THE demise of David Pleat in October 1987 could have placed Spurs in an extremely difficult position. League club boards had agreed not to approach other managers during the season and there was no top-class manager available in the country. Tottenham were fortunate, then, that their former player, Terry Venables, had just resigned his job at Barcelona. At the time of Pleat's departure, Venables was on holiday in Florida. Spurs wasted no time in offering him the job and after sorting out his business and personal matters in Spain, he took over on 1 December 1987, although he was on the bench three days earlier for Spurs' game against Liverpool.

Signed by Spurs from Chelsea in May 1966, having won England honours at Schoolboy, Youth, Amateur, Under-23 and Full level, Venables was a skilful midfield player who showed remarkable vision both on and off the field. A victim of having to follow some of the

greatest names in Spurs' history, he did not have a particularly happy time in his three years as a player at White Hart Lane and it was only after his departure to Queen's Park Rangers in June 1969 that his true value was appreciated.

He enjoyed five years at Loftus Road before signing for Crystal Palace but his playing career was almost immediately brought to an end by injury and he then turned his attention to coaching. He spent two years working under Malcolm Allison before taking over the manager's role in June 1976 and built an exciting young team tipped as the 'Team of the Eighties' at Selhurst Park. Having led them from the Third to First Division he went back to Rangers as manager in October 1980 and, after taking them to the FA Cup Final against Spurs in 1982, led them to the Second Division title and established the West London club in the First Division before, in May 1984, accepting the offer to take over as manager of Barcelona on the departure of Argentina's 1978 World Cup winning manager, Cesar Luis Menotti.

In his first season, with ex-Spur Steve Archibald leading the attack, Barcelona won the Spanish League title. The following season they reached the European Cup Final before losing on penalties to Steau Bucharest, but although Barcelona finished second in 1986-7 it was their arch rivals, Real Madrid, who won the title and with a bad start to the following season Venables came under the type of pressure that only the Spanish or Italians can generate. Much to Spurs' good fortune he left Barcelona by mutual consent.

An innovative and progressive coach, tipped as a future England manager, he gave the established staff and youngsters the opportunity to impress before moving into the transfer market and signing experienced players — Terry Fenwick, Bobby Mimms and Paul Walsh — and leading Spurs to a respectable if not exciting mid-table position at the end of the season.

During the close season his plans for Spurs' future took shape as he backed his judgement of young talent by plunging into the transfer market to sign the exciting Paul Gascoigne and Paul Stewart for £2 million and £1.7 million respectively.

Slowly he began to build a team of flair and skill that looked capable of mounting a serious challenge for the League title but in the early part of 1990-91 his plans looked to be shattered by the financial difficulties that threatened the club's continued existence.

Venables was now faced not only with the problems associated with trying to bring success to a club like Spurs on the playing field, but he also had to cope with the pressures of persistent takeover rumours and the upheaval that automatically follows. Venables rose to the challenge, not only keeping the pressure off the team and leading them to FA Cup Final success, but with computer tycoon Alan Sugar putting together a rescue package that could at last fulfil Venables' long-held ambition of controlling a major football club from the top down.

With the success of the Sugar-Venables rescue Venables took on the role of chief executive and appointed Peter Shreeve as team manager for one season whilst he concentrated on turning round the club's financial position. That target almost achieved and Shreeve's contract not renewed Venables resumed control of team affairs in a continental style structure that saw Venables in overall command of playing affairs but with first-team coaches Doug Livermore and Ray Clemence in day-to-day control and responsible for team selection.

With the loss of Paul Gascoigne, Paul Stewart and Gary Lineker, Venables was forced to embark upon a rebuilding programme but with the promotion of promising youngsters and wise investment in the transfer market, by the end of 1992-93 he appeared to be well on course to build a title-challenging team.

However, all his hard work appeared to have been wasted when a rift with Alan Sugar saw Venables dismissed from all involvement with Spurs in May 1993 and only reinstated on a temporary basis after resorting to the Law Courts. Venables appeared to have a battle on his hands every bit as difficult as that which he had faced two years earlier.

Arthur Turner

ALTHOUGH never officially Spurs' manager, Arthur Turner fulfilled that position on several occasions and no history of the club could be complete without mentioning his contribution to their success.

Turner, one of the founders of Rotherham County, joined Spurs in 1906 as secretary in order to take some of the pressures off manager John Cameron. An accountant by profession and an expert in tax and rating law, Turner served Spurs for 43 years until his death in March 1949.

When the directors decided not to replace Fred Kirkham as manager in 1908, but to take control of team affairs themselves, the burdens fell on Turner, who was responsible for many of the club's most important players being signed.

Spurs Stars A-Z

Born of a Yugoslavian father at Newcastle-under-Lyme, Staffordshire, in 1951, Milija Aleksic was Spurs' goalkeeper in the 1981 FA Cup Final. He first came to national prominence when he helped Stafford Rangers win the FA Trophy in 1972, and his entry to the Football League (with Plymouth Argyle) came during the next season. While with Plymouth he went to Ipswich and Oxford on loan, then signed for Luton Town in December 1976. Two years later he was signed by Tottenham, the third 'keeper used by Spurs in the 1978-9 season, the others being Barry Daines and Mark Kendall. After an 18-month period of serious injuries and a spell on loan to Sheffield United, an injury to Daines gave him an opportunity late in the 1980-81 season. The first FA Cup tie Aleksic played that season was the semi-final, but his swift reflexes and courage helped Spurs to Wembley and through two exciting games against Manchester City. That summer, Ray

Clemence arrived at White Hart Lane. Aleksic stayed another season, including a spell on loan to Luton (November 1981).

MILIJA ALEKSIC

	LEAGUE		FA CUP		TOTAL	
	App	Gls	App	Gls	App	Gls
1978-79	5	0	1	0	6	0
1979-80	8	0	2	0	10	0
1980-81	10	0	4	0	14	0
1981-82	2	0	-	-	2	0
	25	0	7	0	32	0

When Clive Allen joined Spurs from Queen's Park Rangers in August 1984 he became the second member of the famous footballing family to play for Tottenham, following his father Les who had been a regular in the 'double' team of 1960-61. Clive's uncle Dennis played for Reading, his cousin Martin was a Queen's Park Rangers player, and another cousin, Paul, was transferred from West Ham to Spurs, and both Paul and Clive were in the team beaten by Coventry in the 1987 FA Cup Final. Clive Allen began his career at Loftus Road and established himself as a prolific scorer before moving to Arsenal in June 1980, for £1.25 million. Barely two months later, and having played only three friendly games for the Gunners, Allen was on the move again, this time transferring to Crystal Palace in exchange for full-back Kenny Sansom. After one season with Palace he returned to Rangers and from there signed for Tottenham. His first two seasons at Spurs were restricted by injury but in 1986-7, playing as the lone striker in David Pleat's new-look team, he responded magnificently with 49 goals in all first-class matches to beat Jimmy Greaves' long-standing record. That feat earned Allen 'player of the year' awards from both the Professional Footballers' Association and the Football Writers' Association. Allen made his full England debut against Brazil in June 1984. In March 1988 he signed for Bordeaux in the third £1 million move of his career but spent only one season in the French league before returning to England with Manchester City in another £1 million move. He maintained an excellent scoring rate at Maine Road but it was soon clear that his style of play was not appreciated by City manager Peter Reid and in December 1991 he moved to Chelsea. Three months

later he was surprisingly allowed to join his fifth London club, West Ham. His goals were not enough to save them from relegation but did help them to return at the first attempt.

CLIVE ALLEN

	LEAGUE		FA CUP		FL CUP		EUROPE		TOTAL	
	App	Gls	App	Gls	App	Gls	App	Gls	App	Gls
1984-85	12/1	7	-	-	3	1	3/1	2	18/2	10
1985-86	16/3	9	3/1	3	1	0	-	-	20/4	12
1986-87	38/1	33	6	4	8/1	12	-	-	52/2	49
1987-88	31/3	11	2	2	1	0	-	-	34/3	13
	97/8	60	11/1	9	13/1	13	3/1	2	124/11	84

Dagenham-born Les Allen had been an amateur on Spurs' books before joining Chelsea via Briggs Sports. In five years at Chelsea he played in 44 League games (11 goals) and was in the Reserves when Spurs manager Bill Nicholson negotiated his transfer in December 1959. Allen, signed in part-exchange for England international Johnny Brooks, and whilst he did not score on his debut, scored twice in his next game, hit five in an FA Cup game against Crewe a few weeks later and generally proved a prolific goalscorer, instinctive inside the penalty area. Hard-working and unselfish, Allen was ever-present in the League and FA Cup in the 'double' winning season of 1960-61. He scored 23 League goals that season and four in the Cup. He was capped for England Under-23s and represented the Football League, but the arrival of Jimmy Greaves left his place in jeopardy. He competed with Bobby Smith for the centre-forward spot before moving to Queen's Park Rangers in July 1965. With Third Division Rangers he won a League Cup winners' medal (1967) and helped their rise to the First Division, playing alongside Rodney Marsh and the Morgans. His son, Clive, came to Spurs after spells with Queen's Park Rangers (twice), Arsenal and Crystal Palace.

LES ALLEN

	LEAGUE		FA CUP		EUROPE		TOTAL	
	App	Gls	App	Gls	App	Gls	App	Gls
1959-60	15	7	4	8	-	-	19	15
1960-61	42	23	7	4	-	-	49	27
1961-62	23	9	3	1	2	0	28	10
1962-63	25	5	0	0	1	1	26	6
1963-64	8	1	1	0	-	-	9	1
1964-65	6	2	0	0	-	-	6	2
	119	47	15	13	3	1	137	61

Blond-haired Steve Archibald was born in Glasgow in 1956 and his first professional club was Clyde. He cost Aberdeen £25,000 in January 1978 and his 23 goals in 1979-80 helped the Dons to the Scottish Premier Division Championship. He was capped as a substitute while at Aberdeen and won 22 caps with Tottenham, who he joined for £800,000 in May 1980. The fee was a record for a transfer between Scottish and English clubs. Forming a striking partnership with Garth Crooks, Archibald more than justified the expense. He helped Spurs win the FA Cup twice (1981 and 1982) and the UEFA Cup (1984). He won a League (Milk) Cup runners-up medal in 1982 and scored Spurs' only goal in the Final. His skill on the ball, strong-running and effectiveness near goal made Archibald very popular with Spurs supporters, but in August 1984 he was transferred to Barcelona for £1,150,000. Barcelona won the Spanish League in his first season — their first such success for 11 years — and they reached the European Cup Final the following year. In 1987-8, Archibald, out of favour with the Spaniards, joined Blackburn Rovers on loan in an effort to provide the final impetus for their Second Division promotion campaign. At the end of the season he was released by the Spanish giants and joined Hibernian but in January 1990 bought out his contract so that he could return to Barcelona and play for the Second Division side, Espanol. In January 1991 he returned to Scotland joining St Mirren and later played for Ayr United.

STEVE ARCHIBALD

	LEAGUE		FA CUP		FL CUP		EUROPE		TOTAL	
	App	Gls	App	Gls	App	Gls	App	Gls	App	Gls
1980-81	40/1	20	9	3	6		2	-	55/1	25
1981-82	26/1	6	4/1	1	5		2	7	0	42/2	9
1982-83	31	11	1	0	4		2	4	2	40	15
1983-84	31/1	21	3	1	3		1	11	6	48/1	29
	128/3	58	17/1	5	18		7	22	8	185/4	78

Small and apparently frail, Argentinian Osvaldo Ardiles was the modern-day Walden and Harmer, darling of the Spurs fans, popular throughout football and possessor of a unique charm. Born at Cordoba in 1952, he played for Instituto de Cordoba before joining Huracán of Buenos Aires when he was 22. In 1978, he displayed his superb abilities in the World Cup Finals and after helping his country win the trophy, was signed by Keith Burkinshaw for £325,000. Cynics doubted whether he could sustain his standards through long English seasons but he combined silky skills with excellent defensive qualities, and once Spurs had adjusted to accommodate him, rewards followed. In 1981, Spurs won the FA Cup. By then his popularity was such that the marketing of the Spurs pop record *Ossie's Dream* revolved around Ardiles. The Falklands conflict caused him to miss the 1982 FA Cup Final and the first part of the next season when he was on loan to Paris Saint-Germain. He returned to Spurs in January 1983 but his appearances were limited by injuries, although he came on as a substitute in the second leg of the 1984 UEFA Cup Final. Honoured with a testimonial against Inter-Milan in May 1986, he was by then back to his best. He joined Blackburn on loan in 1987-8 but injuries prevented him from playing much of a role in their final push for promotion from the Second Division. Released on a free transfer by Spurs he joined Queen's Park Rangers but a broken leg limited his appearances. After only one season at Loftus Road he played briefly in the United States before accepting the job of manager of Swindon Town. He took Swindon up to Division One via the play-offs in 1990 but they were denied promotion because of 'financial irregularities' committed before Ardiles joined them. He built an exciting Swindon team but was always hampered by lack of money. However his managerial reputation was established and in March 1991 he took over at Newcastle, only to be cruelly dismissed less than a year later to make way for the return of Kevin Keegan. In May 1992 he took over as manager of West Brom, leading them to promotion at the first attempt.

OSSIE ARDILES

	LEAGUE		FACUP		FLCUP		EUROPE		TOTAL	
	App	Gls	App	Gls	App	Gls	App	Gls	App	Gls
1978-79	38	3	5	1	2	0	-	-	45	4
1979-80	40	3	6	2	1	0	-	-	47	5
1980-81	36	5	7	1	6	1	-	-	49	7
1981-82	26	2	5	0	8	1	6	1	45	4
1982-83	2	0	1	0	1	0	-	-	4	0
1983-84	8/1	0	1	0	-	-	2/1	1	11/2	1
1984-85	10/1	2	0	0	0	0	-	-	10/1	2
1985-86	20/3	1	2	0	3/1	0	-	-	25/4	1
1986-87	15/9	0	4	0	7	0	-	-	26/9	0
1987-88	26/2	0	1	0	3	1	-	-	30/3	1
	221/16	16	32	4	31/1	3	8/1	2	292/19	25

Through his 21-year association as a professional with Tottenham Hotspur, first as a player, later as assistant-manager to Bill Nicholson, Eddie Baily became an institution. He first played for Spurs as an amateur during World War Two, a chirpy Londoner born in Clapton. Having signed professional in 1946 he was to come to glory as a key link in the 'Push and Run' team. He was an inside-forward, known to many as 'The Cheeky Chappie' for one-touch creative skills which were well-suited to the Tottenham style of the time. But he could also hold the ball and dribble if necessary. He was capped for England nine times, scoring five goals in his first five internationals. In four games for England he was partnered by Spurs winger Les Medley, a true testament to a left-wing club pairing which helped Spurs to the League Championship with flowing movements and exciting interchanges. And Baily was also an off-the-field personality. Even the normally poker-faced Alf Ramsey was forced to comment on Baily's humour in his autobiography; the occasion was the England team flying over the Alps, the snowy peaks just below the bouncing fuselage of the aeroplane. "The terraces look a bit empty this afternoon," said Baily. 'It must be the weather'. The 'Cheeky Chappie' moved to Port Vale for £6,000 early in 1956, helped Nottingham Forest into Division One and ended his playing career with Leyton Orient. He returned to White Hart Lane in October 1963 and stayed 11 years as assistant-manager. He was later chief scout at West Ham.

EDDIE BAILY

	LEAGUE		FA CUP		TOTAL	
	App	Gls	App	Gls	App	Gls
1946-47	1	0	-	-	1	0
1947-48	22	5	5	0	27	5
1948-49	42	11	0	0	42	11
1949-50	40	8	3	1	43	9
1950-51	40	12	1	0	41	12
1951-52	30	4	2	1	32	5
1952-53	30	6	9	2	39	8
1953-54	33	5	6	1	39	6
1954-55	41	12	3	0	44	12
1955-56	18	1	0	0	18	1
	297	64	29	5	326	69

Peter Baker played right-back in the 1961 'double' team. He won an FA Cup winners' medal the following season and a European Cup-winners' medal in 1963. Hampstead-born, he first played for Spurs as an amateur while with Enfield. He signed professional in September 1952 and made his first-team debut that same season. For a time he was second-choice to Alf Ramsey and he took quite a while to establish himself. Eventually he formed an exceptionally reliable full-back partnership with Ron Henry, and of the 'double' winning team Baker and Henry were the only two who had not cost a substantial fee. Baker was a good positional player, a strong tackler and his passing was vital in turning defence into attack. His style of feeding short passes to the likes of Blanchflower, Henry or Norman was very much in keeping with the 'Push and Run' tradition. An England youth international, Baker

never quite achieved the stardom of his Spurs colleagues. After 13 seasons at White Hart Lane he left to join Durban City and eventually settled permanently in South Africa.

PETER BAKER

	LEAGUE		FA CUP		EUROPE		TOTAL	
	App	Gls	App	Gls	App	Gls	App	Gls
1952-53	1	0	0	0	-	-	1	0
1953-54	4	1	0	0	-	-	4	1
1954-55	8	0	0	0	-	-	8	0
1955-56	5	0	0	0	-	-	5	0
1956-57	38	0	3	0	-	-	41	0
1957-58	18	0	0	0	-	-	18	0
1958-59	36	0	4	0	-	-	40	0
1959-60	41	0	3	0	-	-	44	0
1960-61	41	1	7	0	-	-	48	1
1961-62	36	0	7	0	8	0	51	0
1962-63	33	0	1	0	6	0	40	0
1963-64	35	1	2	0	2	0	39	1
1964-65	3	0	0	0	-	-	3	0
	299	3	27	0	16	0	342	3

Jimmy Banks joined Spurs as an inside-forward from Willington Athletic in the summer of 1913. During the latter years of World War One, he was a high-scoring centre-forward but he had difficulty re-establishing himself when peacetime soccer resumed. He played about half the games in the 1919-20 Second Division championship season, but the signing of Jimmy Seed added further competition for forward places. Early in 1921, however, Fanny Walden was injured and Banks was reinstated at outside-right. He was a strong, resolute player who proved a direct winger, an ideal contrast to Dimmock's devastating dribbling. Banks took Spurs into the semi-final with a quick-thinking goal against Aston Villa in the fourth round, and he fully earned his FA Cup winners' medal in 1921. Yet he played only a few more games for Tottenham before his transfer to Norwich City in September 1923.

JIMMY BANKS

	LEAGUE		FA CUP		TOTAL	
	App	Gls	App	Gls	App	Gls
1913-14	12	0	-	-	12	0
1914-15	5	0	-	-	5	0
1919-20	18	2	4	1	22	3
1920-21	21	3	5	3	26	6
1921-22	11	1	0	0	11	1
1922-23	2	0	0	0	2	0
	69	6	9	4	78	10

Phil Beal joined Spurs as an amateur in May 1960 and turned professional early in 1962 when he was 17 years old. He made his Football League debut in the 1963-4 season. Although he could play full-back, it was as a central defender that Beal became a pillar of the Spurs team in the late-1960s and early-1970s. A close-marking defender, Beal played in both the 1971 and the 1973 League Cup Finals, alongside Peter Collins in the first and Mike England in the second. He was also in the 1972 UEFA Cup-winning side, and he appeared in a second UEFA Cup Final in 1974. He was awarded a testimonial against Bayern Munich but Beal reputedly lost money on the game because of the fee agreed with the German side. In the summer of 1975 he moved to Brighton & Hove Albion but he played only ten League games before moving on to American team Memphis Rogues and then Crewe Alexandra.

PHIL BEAL

	LEAGUE		FA CUP		FL CUP		EUROPE		TOTAL	
	App	Gls	App	Gls	App	Gls	App	Gls	App	Gls
1963-64	16	0	2	0	-		-	-	18	0
1964-65	8	0	0	0	-		-	-	8	0
1965-66	21	0	3	0	-		-	-	24	0
1966-67	26	0	1	0	1	0	-		28	0
1967-68	34/1	0	4	0	0	0	2	0	40/1	0
1968-69	39	1	4	0	6	0	-		49	1
1969-70	29/2	0	4	0	1	0	-		34/2	0
1970-71	32	0	4	0	7	0	-		43	0
1971-72	32	0	5	0	7	0	10	0	54	0
1972-73	24	0	2	0	3	0	6	0	35	0
1973-74	41	0	1	0	1	0	12	0	55	0
1974-75	28	0	0	0	1	0	-		29	0
	330/3	1	30	0	27	0	30	0	417/3	1

Tall, long-striding Les Bennett was the most unconventional and individualistic member of the great 'Push and Run' team. Top scorer in 1948-9 and 1951-2, Bennett had a clever turn and deceptive dribble, an inside-forward who was difficult to mark. Born at Wood Green in 1918, Bennett played for nursery-team Northfleet before signing professional for Spurs in May 1939, which was not the best of times to settle into a professional career. During World War Two he saw service in India, Egypt and Burma, and when the war was over he soon showed excellent form. But all this disruption meant Bennett was almost 29 when he made his debut in the Football League. One of three uncapped players in the 1950-51 Championship team, Bennett scored over 100 League goals for Spurs, one of only seven players to achieve this. He could also deputise as a wing-half. In December 1954 he signed for West Ham, and he had a spell as captain of the Hammers. Later he was player-manager of Clacton Town.

LES BENNETT

	LEAGUE		FA CUP		TOTAL	
	App	Gls	App	Gls	App	Gls
1946-47	38	16	2	1	40	17
1947-48	35	8	2	1	37	9
1948-49	43	19	1	0	44	19
1949-50	35	14	2	2	37	16
1950-51	25	7	1	0	26	7
1951-52	35	20	0	0	35	20
1952-53	30	14	8	5	38	19
1953-54	26	4	6	5	32	10
1954-55	6	2	0	0	6	2
	273	104	22	14	295	118

Possibly the greatest attacking wing-half of all-time, Danny Blanchflower captained Spurs to a string of soccer trophies — the League and FA Cup 'double' in 1961, the FA Cup again in 1962 and the European Cup-winners' Cup in 1963 — as well as playing 56 times for Northern Ireland, skippering them in the 1958 World Cup Finals. Blanchflower was born in 1926, in the Bloomfield area of Belfast, and arrived in English soccer when Barnsley signed him from Glentoran for £6,500 in 1949. Blanchflower soon showed his strong opinions by demanding more ball-work in training. A £15,000 transfer took him to Aston Villa in 1951 and three years later he moved to Tottenham for twice that amount. He was never a speedy player, nor particularly strong in the tackle, but he read the game superbly, distributed the ball effectively and was capable of making tactical decisions on the pitch. The latter could be controversial and he was temporarily stripped of the Spurs captaincy after his decision to change a player's position during the 1956 FA Cup semi-final. He was voted Footballer of the Year in 1958 and might have achieved greater glory that summer had his younger brother, Manchester United's Jackie Blanchflower, not had to miss the World Cup Finals with injuries received at Munich. Danny Blanchflower was again Footballer of the Year in 1961 but an injury in December 1962 contributed to his retirement 18 months later. He had a period as Chelsea manager (December 1978 to September 1979) and a spell in charge of the Northern Ireland team. Until recently he wrote a hard-hitting column in the *Sunday Express*.

DANNY BLANCHFLOWER

	LEAGUE		FA CUP		EUROPE		TOTAL	
	App	Gls	App	Gls	App	Gls	App	Gls
1954-55	22	0	3	0	-	-	25	0
1955-56	40	0	6	0	-	-	46	0
1956-57	39	1	3	1	-	-	42	2
1957-58	40	0	2	0	-	-	42	0
1958-59	36	1	1	0	-	-	37	1
1959-60	40	2	4	1	-	-	44	3
1960-61	42	6	7	0	-	-	49	6
1961-62	39	2	7	2	8	2	54	6
1962-63	24	3	0	0	4	0	28	3
1963-64	15	0	0	0	-	-	15	0
	337	15	33	4	12	2	382	21

In the season before World War One and the two seasons immediately after the conflict, Bert Bliss was Spurs' leading goalscorer. Playing inside-left, Bliss benefited from the strengths and skills of colleagues, particularly Arthur Grimsdell and Jimmy Dimmock, and capitalised on their moves with some ferocious shooting. In 1919-20, as an ever-present in Spurs' Second Division championship season, Bliss scored 31 goals. Born in Staffordshire in 1890, Bliss was signed from Willenhall Swifts in April 1912. He was only 5ft 6in and when he returned from the war with receding hair he looked little like a footballer, but his confidence and the power of his shooting encouraged tremendous accolades. Perhaps 'blistering' would be the most apt description of his shooting. Under the old offside law, Grimsdell, Bliss and Dimmock worked closely as a trio to break down defences. All three were selected to play for England against Scotland in 1921 (along with Bert Smith) and Bliss was at the peak of his career, scoring two goals in the semi-final against Preston and winning a Cup winners' medal against Wolves. In December 1922 he moved to Clapton Orient, and finished his career with Bournemouth & Boscombe Athletic.

BERT BLISS

	LEAGUE		FA CUP		TOTAL	
	App	Gls	App	Gls	App	Gls
1911-12	5	1	0	0	5	1
1912-13	19	5	0	0	19	5
1913-14	29	6	3	4	32	10
1914-15	33	21	2	1	35	22
1919-20	42	31	4	2	46	33
1920-21	36	17	6	4	42	21
1921-22	23	7	6	2	29	9
1922-23	8	3	0	0	8	3
	195	91	21	13	216	104

Garry Brooke may go down in history as the only player to appear as a substitute in three FA Cup Final matches. He came on for Ricky Villa when Spurs trailed to Manchester City in 1981, then was used as a substitute twice against Queen's Park Rangers the following year. Born in Bethnal Green, he joined Spurs as an apprentice in June 1977 and was upgraded to full-time professional in October 1978. He was 5ft 6in tall and built very strongly, and at Tottenham he developed into a midfield player with a powerful and accurate long-range shot. He scored two goals in his first full League game and his goal against Hull in 1981 helped Spurs on their path to Wembley. Brooke had spent the early part of that season (1980-81) with Swedish club Gais. The next season he was hampered by injuries, and generally he was unable to establish himself in the Spurs side. In May 1985 he left for Norwich City but was unable to establish himself at Carrow Road and moved to the Dutch club, Groningen, before returning to London with Wimbledon. Unable to adapt his style of play, he spent the end of the 1989-90 season on loan to Stoke City before joining Brentford on a free transfer in August 1990. In January 1991 he joined Colchester United on loan and then had a trial with Reading before signing for Wivenhoe Town where he linked up with former Spurs teammates John Lacy and Paul Price. He then went on to play for St Albans City, the newly reformed Romford and Worthing.

GARRY BROOKE

	LEAGUE		FA CUP		FL CUP		EUROPE		TOTAL	
	App	Gls	App	Gls	App	Gls	App	Gls	App	Gls
1980-81	10/8	3	2/5	1	0	0	-	-	12/13	4
1981-82	12/4	4	0/2	0	0	0	-	-	12/6	4
1982-83	19/4	7	1/1	0	3/1	1	4	1	27/6	9
1983-84	7/5	0	1	0	1	0	2/2	0	11/7	0
1984-85	1/3	1	0	0	0	0	0/3	0	1/6	1
	49/24	15	4/8	1	4/1	1	6/5	1	63/38	18

Alexander 'Sandy' Brown was with Spurs for only two seasons but his goalscoring impact was staggering. In 1901, when Spurs won the FA Cup, Brown scored in every round of the competition proper, and his total of 15 FA Cup goals that season is still a record. He scored two in the first game of the Final and another to seal a Tottenham win in the replay. Brown was one of five Scots in that victorious 1901 team. He was born in Glenbuck, a small village which produced other Scottish international players. He played with St Bernard's and Preston North End before moving to Portsmouth for their first season (1899-1900). Although Brown was one of a contingent of Scottish players helping to launch Pompey, one newspaper reporter felt compelled to inform his public that Brown was called 'Sandy' as a common adaptation of Alexander and it had nothing to do with his hair colouring. While with Spurs he was selected for the Ibrox-disaster Scotland-England game of 1902, and soon afterwards he returned to Portsmouth. In the close season of 1903 he moved to Middlesbrough, where he won his only official Scottish cap.

SANDY BROWN

	Southern		Western		FA CUP		TOTAL	
	App	Gls	App	Gls	App	Gls	App	Gls
1900-01	20	12	10	6	8	15	38	33
1901-02	26	18	12	9	3	0	41	27
	46	30	22	15	11	15	79	60

Bob Brown was a solid and dependable full-back who played 20 games when Tottenham Hotspur won the Second Division title in the first season after World War One. Brown had joined Spurs from Thorneycrofts in the summer of 1919 but despite playing his part in the club's promotion to the First Division, he could never hold a regular place and his cause was not helped by a number of injuries. His best season was certainly that title-winning campaign and thereafter he managed only a handful of appearances before leaving White Hart Lane in the summer of 1924.

| | LEAGUE | | FA CUP | | TOTAL | |
	App	Gls	App	Gls	App	Gls
1919-20	20	0	4	0	24	0
1920-21	2	0	0	0	2	0
1922-23	12	0	4	0	16	0
1923-24	3	0	0	0	3	0
	37	0	8	0	45	0

BOB BROWN

Goalkeeper Bill Brown was already a Scottish international when he was signed from Dundee for £16,500 in June 1959, and he went on to win 28 caps, which was a record for a Scottish goalkeeper at the time. Born in Arbroath in 1931, Brown played with Arbroath Cliffburn, Carnoustie Juveniles and Carnoustie Panmure before joining Dundee, who were fast becoming a top Scottish team. Brown was a Scottish schoolboy, Under-23 and 'B' international, and he established himself as number-one 'keeper in the full international team. He was tall, lean and athletic, and his powers of concentration and calmness rubbed off on fellow defenders, giving Spurs a defensive assurance during the high-quality years of the early 1960s. Brown missed only one game during the 'double' season of 1960-61 and he helped Spurs to the FA Cup in 1962 and the European Cup-winners' Cup in 1963. On the way to the Final of the latter competition he gave one brilliant performance in Bratislava, and generally his displays were consistent. Like his predecessors he could start attacks with accurate throws. By the mid-1960s a combination of injuries and the arrival of Pat Jennings restricted his appearances, although he played for Scotland as late as November 1965. His last game for Spurs was a friendly at Dundee in October 1966. That same month he moved to First Division Northampton Town, and later he had a spell with Toronto Falcons.

| | LEAGUE | | FA CUP | | EUROPE | | TOTAL | |
	App	Gls	App	Gls	App	Gls	App	Gls
1959-60	40	0	4	0	-	-	44	0
1960-61	41	0	7	0	-	-	48	0
1961-62	35	0	7	0	8	0	50	0
1962-63	40	0	1	0	7	0	48	0
1963-64	27	0	0	0	2	0	29	0
1964-65	19	0	4	0	-	-	23	0
1965-66	20	0	0	0	-	-	20	0
	222	0	23	0	17	0	262	0

BILL BROWN

In 16 years as a Spurs player Vic Buckingham never played in the First Division, an unusually frustrating record which may go some way to help explain why this stylish, debonair man later sought, and achieved, success as a coach and manager. Buckingham was born in Greenwich and nursed through the Northfleet team which introduced a number of Spurs professionals in the late 1930s. He had barely established himself as a first-team wing-half when World War Two took him into the Royal Air Force. Buckingham guested for Fulham during the war, played for Spurs when he could, and resumed as a full-back in post-war soccer, by which time Nicholson and Burgess were the Spurs wing-halves. In 1947-8 he was a Division Two ever-present. He became chief coach to Middlesex FA and then achieved a national reputation by coaching Pegasus to the Amateur Cup in 1951. He became manager of Bradford (June 1951 to Feb 1953), West Brom (Feb 1953 to May 1959), Ajax (Amsterdam), Sheffield Wednesday (May 1961 to January 1965) and Fulham (January 1965 to January 1968). Later he coached on the Continent.

VIC BUCKINGHAM

	LEAGUE		FA CUP		TOTAL	
	App	Gls	App	Gls	App	Gls
1935-36	16	0	2	0	18	0
1936-37	25	0	5	0	30	0
1937-38	29	0	6	0	35	0
1938-39	41	1	4	0	45	1
1939-40	3	0	0	0	3	0
1945-46	0	0	1	0	1	0
1946-47	27	0	2	0	29	0
1947-48	41	0	5	0	46	0
1948-49	26	0	1	0	27	0
	208	1	26	0	234	1

Welsh international Ron Burgess captained Spurs for eight seasons after the end of World War Two, leading his club to the Second Division championship and the League Championship in successive seasons. 'Push and Run' brought him four great years, for so much of Arthur Rowe's system revolved around this energetic attacking wing-half. Burgess was born in Cwm and played for Cwm Villa before Spurs. It was not the first time a player had taken the route from Rhondda to Tottenham; Burgess followed Spurs players like Billy Whatley, 'Taffy' O'Callaghan, Alf Day, Willie Evans and Jimmy Seed (and Harry Clarke was to come later). When he came to Spurs in May 1936, Burgess was a forward, and a year later he was about to be released when he played for the 'A' team at wing-half as a late deputy. Spurs changed their minds and kept him on — for another 17 years. He learned wing-half play under Jimmy Anderson's tutelage at Northfleet and joined the Spurs ground-staff. A natural right-footer, he gained a first-team place at right-half and made his debut for Wales just after the start of the war, in November 1939. After serving with the Royal Air Force and playing wartime soccer with Spurs and Notts County, Burgess settled into the left-half position. He had to wait almost ten years for his FA Cup debut, but in the post-war period honours came thick and fast. He was the first Welshman to play for the English Football League, he played for Great Britain against the Rest of Europe in 1947, and altogether he won 32 Welsh caps, many of them as captain. On the field his receding hairline belied his incredible stamina. He was like a marathon-runner, a human dynamo who was always in support, always running to take a push-pass from a colleague. He never lost his original urge to attack, and late in his career he even played for Spurs on the left wing. In August 1954, he moved to Swansea Town as player-manager and after four years (latterly as a manager) became coach (later manager) of Watford, where he signed Pat Jennings and transferred him to Spurs for a healthy profit.

RON BURGESS

	LEAGUE		FA CUP		TOTAL	
	App	Gls	App	Gls	App	Gls
1938-39	17	1	0	0	17	1
1939-40	3	0	-	-	3	0
1945-46	-	-	2	1	2	1
1946-47	40	5	2	0	42	4
1947-48	32	2	4	0	36	2
1948-49	41	3	1	0	42	3
1949-50	39	0	3	0	42	0
1950-51	35	2	1	0	36	2
1951-52	40	0	2	0	42	0
1952-53	30	2	7	0	37	2
1953-54	24	0	5	0	29	0
	301	15	27	1	328	16

The signing of John Cameron was a major catalyst in the rise of Tottenham Hotspur. He arrived in 1898 and within three years the club had won the Southern League championship (1899-1900) and the FA Cup (1901). Cameron, born in Ayr, first won fame with Queen's Park, winning one Scotland international cap. He had two years as an amateur at Everton, earning his money through a job with Cunard, before signing for Spurs. By then he had a reputation as a clever footballer and clever person, and he soon became secretary-manager of Spurs and secretary of the Players & Trainers' Union. Relying substantially on his Scottish contacts, he helped bring together the first Spurs team to reach national prominence. Cameron made his own contribution on the pitch. He was a scheming inside-forward, almost 6ft tall, who could distribute the ball well, and he could finish off moves. He was top-scorer in his first season at Spurs, and his goal in the 1901 FA Cup Final replay equalised the scores and set up Tottenham for a famous victory. After 1903, Cameron devoted his time solely to adminstrative duties, relinquishing his role of secretary to Arthur Turner in 1906. A year later he resigned as manager.

	Southern		United		Western		FA CUP		TOTAL	
	App	Gls	App	Gls	App	Gls	App	Gls	App	Gls
1898-99	25	12	19	7	0	0	9	5	53	24
1899-1900	30	13	0	0	0	0	1	0	31	13
1900-01	21	5	0	0	10	6	8	2	39	13
1901-02	25	11	0	0	11	7	3	0	39	18
1902-03	14	2	0	0	8	2	4	0	26	4
1903-04	3	0	0	0	4	1	0	0	7	1
	118	43	19	7	33	16	25	7	195	73

JOHN CAMERON

Jimmy Cantrell was an unusually subtle centre-forward in an era when the role was typically filled by the battering-ram, blood-and-thunder kind of player. He was later described by Jimmy Seed as playing something more akin to an inside-forward's game from the centre-forward position, for Cantrell was a dainty player, an artist who preferred to stroke the ball towards goal rather than blast his shots. In the Second Division championship team of 1919-20 and the FA Cup Final side of the following season, Cantrell's skills complemented the power of Seed and Bert Bliss. Cantrell came to Tottenham from Notts County in October 1912. Through most of his time he was to average a goal every other game. He was brave, had a good eye for goal and was able to bring others into the action. Never capped for England, he was frequently first reserve but did not get the break his talent perhaps deserved. In October 1923 he was transferred to Sutton United.

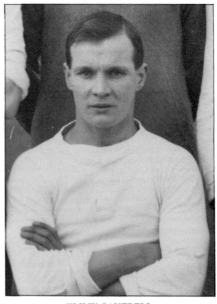

	LEAGUE		FA CUP		TOTAL	
	App	Gls	App	Gls	App	Gls
1912-13	25	12	3	2	28	14
1913-14	33	16	2	1	35	17
1914-15	26	14	1	1	27	15
1919-20	29	18	2	3	31	21
1920-21	23	7	6	2	29	9
1921-22	13	3	1	1	14	4
1922-23	10	4	0	0	10	4
	159	74	15	10	174	84

JIMMY CANTRELL

Tottenham's main striker during the early 1970s, when they won the League Cup twice and the UEFA Cup, Martin Chivers made an immense contribution to modern-day Spurs. A grammar-school boy, he scored goals alongside Ron Davies in Southampton's promotion team (1966-7) before joining Spurs in January 1968. The value of the transfer (£125,000) was a British record fee, although Frank Saul, valued at £45,000, moved in the opposite direction as part of the deal. Chivers was injured against Nottingham Forest the following September and spent a year nursing a serious injury to his left knee. His recovery was such that by February 1971 he was in the England team. Already the holder of a record number of Under-23 caps (17), he played 24 times, scoring 13 goals, for the full international team. Chivers could look clumsy and casual, but he was deceptive and extremely talented. He was a gentle giant, and people wondered how he would fare with more aggression in the Bobby Smith style. The goals came anyway, and his long throw-in was a creative weapon. In the 1971 League Cup Final his two goals beat Aston Villa, and the following year his superb goals at Molineux set up a UEFA Cup Final win. Chivers stayed with Spurs until the summer of 1976 when he moved to Servette of Switzerland. Later he had short spells with Norwich and Brighton.

MARTIN CHIVERS

	LEAGUE		FACUP		FLCUP		EUROPE		TOTAL	
	App	Gls	App	Gls	App	Gls	App	Gls	App	Gls
1967-68	18	7	5	3	-	-	-	-	23	10
1968-69	10	3	0	0	1	3	-	-	11	6
1969-70	27/4	11	1/2	0	1	0	-	-	29/6	11
1970-71	42	21	5	1	7	7	-	-	54	29
1971-72	39	25	5	2	7	7	11	8	62	42
1972-73	38	17	3	4	10	4	10	8	61	33
1973-74	39/1	17	1	0	1	0	11	6	52/1	23
1974-75	27/1	10	1	1	1	0	-	-	29/1	11
1975-76	28/4	7	1	0	5	2	-	-	34/4	9
	268/10	118	22/2	11	33	23	32	22	355/12	174

Henry Alfred Clarke, better known as Harry, was born at Woodfield Green in 1923. A 6ft 3in centre-half at Lovells Athletic, he was signed by Spurs in March 1949, thus making an unusually late entry into the Football League. He was a determined character and it was two-and-a-half years before he missed a League game. During that time the team won the Second Division title and the League Championship. After missing the start of the 1951-2 season through injury, Clarke came back to continue his impressive performances. He won an England 'B' cap and then played for the full international team in a 4-2 win at Hampden Park in 1954. He stayed registered as a Spurs player until 1959 although his latter days at the club were spent coaching the younger players. He went to Llanelli as player-manager in February 1959 and later managed Romford.

	LEAGUE		FA CUP		TOTAL	
	App	Gls	App	Gls	App	Gls
1948-49	10	0	0	0	10	0
1949-50	42	0	3	0	45	0
1950-51	42	0	1	0	43	0
1951-52	33	0	2	0	35	0
1952-53	31	0	6	0	37	0
1953-54	41	0	6	0	47	0
1954-55	36	0	3	0	39	0
1955-56	39	4	6	0	45	4
1956-57	21	0	0	0	21	0
	295	4	27	0	322	4

HARRY CLARKE

George Clawley made his name as Southampton's goalkeeper in the 1890s. He had one season with Stoke (1898-9) before John Cameron enticed him to play for Spurs in the summer of 1899. Clawley fractured his leg soon after his arrival at the newly-opened White Hart Lane and he missed most of the Southern League championship season, but was fit to play most games in 1900-01. He was particularly strong at dealing with corner-kicks and crosses (in an era when goalkeepers were offered little protection) and his form helped Spurs reach the 1901 FA Cup Final. In the Final he was involved in a controversial incident when Sheffield United were awarded a goal, Clawley dropped the ball but there was evidence to suggest that it did not go over the line. He stayed for two more seasons at Spurs before returning to Southampton in 1903. He won a Southern League championship medal with the Saints before retiring to become a publican. He died in July 1920, aged 44.

	Southern		Western		FA CUP		TOTAL	
	App	Gls	App	Gls	App	Gls	App	Gls
1899-1900	9	0	0	0	0	0	9	0
1900-01	25	0	9	0	8	0	42	0
1901-02	20	0	9	0	0	0	29	0
1902-03	29	0	13	0	4	0	46	0
	83	0	31	0	12	0	126	0

GEORGE CLAWLEY

A hard-tackling full-back, idolised by youngsters of the time, England international Tommy Clay was a Spurs regular for 12 years after his transfer from Leicester Fosse in January 1914. He was born in Leicester in 1892 and joined his local club in the close-season of 1911. Renowned for his positional play, he always looked to pass the ball constructively rather than just boot it upfield as many of his contemporaries seemed prepared to do. Clay played regularly for Spurs during World War One and was a reliable penalty-taker for the club. In 1919-20 he captained Tottenham to the Division Two championship but later handed over the captaincy to Grimsdell who thus stepped up to receive the FA Cup in 1921 after Clay had given a typically immaculate full-back display in the Final against Wolves. The fair-haired Clay won four England caps around that time, and in 1921 he even played one whole match in goal, when both Spurs goalkeepers were injured. Clay kept a clean sheet that day. He stayed with Spurs until the summer of 1929 when he moved to Northfleet to coach players at Spurs' nursery club. In 1931 he joined St Albans as a coach. Clay died in February 1949.

	LEAGUE		FA CUP		TOTAL	
	App	Gls	App	Gls	App	Gls
1913-14	15	0	0	0	15	0
1914-15	38	4	2	0	40	4
1919-20	27	2	3	0	30	2
1920-21	35	1	6	1	41	2
1921-22	37	8	6	0	43	8
1922-23	34	3	4	0	38	3
1923-24	40	1	1	0	41	1
1924-25	21	2	4	0	25	2
1925-26	34	2	3	0	37	2
1926-27	16	0	1	0	17	0
1927-28	16	0	3	0	19	0
1928-29	5	0	0	0	5	0
	318	23	33	1	351	24

TOMMY CLAY

Signed from Liverpool for £300,000 in August 1981, Ray Clemence had already won virtually every honour in the British game. Skegness-born Clemence played for Scunthorpe United until Liverpool spent £15,000 on his transfer. He became Liverpool's regular goalkeeper in the 1970-71 season and, incredibly, missed only six League games in his 11 seasons as first choice. During that time Liverpool won the League five times, the European Cup on three occasions, the UEFA Cup twice, the FA Cup once and the League Cup. Clemence also received two FA Cup runners-up medals and was on the losing side in the 1978 League Cup Final. In 1982, Liverpool won the League Cup for a second time, but by now Clemence was playing for opponents Spurs, doing his utmost to prevent his former colleagues from scoring at Wembley. Shortly afterwards, however, he won his first winners' medal for Tottenham — the FA Cup success against Queen's Park Rangers. Five years later Clemence was back at Wembley, keeping goal against Coventry City. With Spurs he had increased his England caps to 61, a number restricted by the simultaneous career of Peter Shilton. In September 1985, Clemence completed 1,000

first-class appearances and yet showed no sign of retiring. In 1987-8 his career was interrupted by injury which kept him out of the team whereupon he joined the Spurs coaching staff, working his way up to assistant first-team coach.

RAY CLEMENCE

	LEAGUE		FACUP		FLCUP		EUROPE		TOTAL	
	App	Gls	App	Gls	App	Gls	App	Gls	App	Gls
1981-82	38	0	7	0	8	0	8	0	61	0
1982-83	41	0	3	0	5	0	4	0	53	0
1983-84	26	0	1	0	3	0	7	0	37	0
1984-85	42	0	3	0	5	0	8	0	58	0
1985-86	42	0	5	0	6	0	-	-	53	0
1986-87	40	0	6	0	9	0	-	-	55	0
1987-88	11	0	0	0	2	0	-	-	13	0
	240	0	25	0	38	0	27	0	330	0

In May 1971, Bill Nicholson agreed a fee of £190,000 with Burnley for their England international right winger Ralph Coates. Burnley had been relegated and yet the strong running and skilfulness of the stocky Coates had made him a star. He had won eight England Under-23 caps, played for the Football League and his first two games as a Spurs player were for England, his third and fourth caps. Still in his mid-20s, Coates looked to have a spectacular future, but somehow he never quite fulfilled his promise. He played for Spurs in the 1972 UEFA Cup Final, scored the only goal of the 1973 League Cup Final (when he came on as a substitute) and his four UEFA Cup goals in 1973-4 helped Tottenham to the Final that season. Coates was an energetic player with Spurs, Bobby Charlton-like strands of fair hair covering a receding hair-line (and like Charlton he came from the north-east), but whether on the wing or in midfield, he never really recaptured his earlier England form. In the summer of 1978 he

joined an Australian club, St George's of Sydney, returning to England in October that year to play for Orient.

RALPH COATES

	LEAGUE		FACUP		FLCUP		EUROPE		TOTAL	
	App	Gls	App	Gls	App	Gls	App	Gls	App	Gls
1971-72	32	2	3/1	0	5	0	9	2	49/1	4
1972-73	29/3	3	3	0	4/3	1	7	3	43/6	7
1973-74	36	3	0	0	1	0	10	4	47	7
1974-75	26/4	1	2	0	1	0	-	-	29/4	1
1975-76	21/3	2	2	0	6	0	-	-	29/3	2
1976-77	28/3	3	1	0	2	0	-	-	31/3	3
1977-78	1/2	0	-	-	-	-	-	-	1/2	-
	173/15	14	11/1	0	19/3	1	26	9	229/19	24

Peter Collins was signed from Chelmsford City in January 1968. The fee was a mere £5,500, plus £4,000 when he made ten first-team appearances, a landmark he reached in the 1968-9 season. A big, yet very quick central defender, Collins came to the Football League late and left far too early, his career curtailed by injury when he was 26 years old. During most of his time at Spurs he was a deputy defender for Mike England or Phil Beal. England's injury gave him a long run in the 1970-71 season and Collins took the opportunity well, winning a League Cup winners' medal in the process. The next season, however, he was back in the Reserves. It was always going to be very competitive for him at Tottenham, with the experienced defenders plus the up-and-coming Terry Naylor, but the likelihood was that Collins would seal a first-team place. However, arthritis in his ankle was diagnosed and he was forced to retire from Football League soccer early. He was later player-manager of Folkestone and manager of Malden Town.

	LEAGUE		FA CUP		FL CUP		EUROPE		TOTAL	
	App	Gls	App	Gls	App	Gls	App	Gls	App	Gls
1968-69	22/3	0	4	0	3/1	1	-	-	29/4	1
1969-70	17/2	2	0	0	1	0	-	-	18/2	2
1970-71	26	0	4	0	1	0	-	-	31	0
1971-72	6/1	0	0/1	0	0/1	0	1/1	0	7/4	0
1972-73	7	2	-	-	-	-	-	-	7	2
	78/6	4	8/1	0	5/2	1	1/1	0	92/10	5

PETER COLLINS

David Copeland was a hard-working inside-left in the Southern League championship team (1899-1900) and the 1901 FA Cup winning team. Like John Cameron, the man who recruited him in 1899, Copeland came from Ayr. He had played for Ayr Parkhouse, Walsall and Bedminster, mainly as a winger or centre-forward. At Spurs it was a little time before Cameron moved him to inside-forward, where he achieved most of his success. With the arrival of Sandy Brown (in 1900) Spurs were able to field their famous all-Scottish inside-forward trio of Cameron, Brown and Copeland, and undoubtedly much of the credit for Brown's record-breaking scoring feats in the FA Cup was due to the other two. Also, Copeland had a marvellous understanding with his winger, John Kirwan. Copeland stayed with Spurs until May 1905, when he moved to Chelsea, continuing to forage unceasingly, although his goalscoring capabilities waned in the later years.

	Southern		Western		FA CUP		TOTAL	
	App	Gls	App	Gls	App	Gls	App	Gls
1899-1900	29	17	0	0	1	0	30	17
1900-01	9	5	5	3	8	1	22	9
1901-02	29	13	14	6	3	1	46	20
1902-03	28	8	11	2	3	1	42	11
1903-04	32	6	15	5	5	0	52	11
1904-05	19	2	15	5	0	0	34	7
	146	51	60	21	20	3	226	75

DAVID COPELAND

When Garth Crooks joined Spurs in July 1980, he was only just too old for the England Under-21 team, for whom he had played four times, but the pay-off for the £600,000 outlay was as swift as could have been expected from a much more experienced striker. Crooks scored in his first three games and formed a partnership with Steve Archibald which was to take Tottenham to two FA Cup Finals in two seasons. In fact, Crooks played 17 FA Cup games for Spurs before he was on the losing side. During that time he scored eight FA Cup goals, and many of them were crucial, like the two which killed off Wolves in the 1981 semi-final, the replay equaliser against Manchester City in the Final and the half-hit winner against Arsenal the following year. The strong-running left-footed Crooks also won a League Cup runners-up medal in 1982, but, inevitably, there came the usual hard times for a striker. He went on loan to Manchester United in 1983-4, only to be brought back when Spurs ran into injury problems. Crooks eventually signed for West Brom in July 1985, moving closer to the region where he was raised. He was born in Stoke and had played for Stoke City before joining Spurs. He helped Stoke into the First Division in 1978-9. In March 1987 he

moved back to London when he joined Charlton Athletic and despite continual injury problems played his part in keeping them in the First Division until injury finally led to his retirement in November 1990. A former chairman of the PFA there must be a place for him in the game's top level administration.

	LEAGUE		FACUP		FLCUP		EUROPE		TOTAL	
	App	Gls	App	Gls	App	Gls	App	Gls	App	Gls
1980-81	40	16	9	4	6	2	-	-	55	22
1981-82	27	13	7	3	7	0	5	2	46	18
1982-83	26	8	2	1	4	3	4	3	36	15
1983-84	6/4	1	0	0	0/1	0	1	1	7/5	2
1984-85	22	10	3	1	2	4	5/1	3	32/1	18
	121/4	48	21	9	19/1	9	15/1	9	176/6	75

GARTH CROOKS

Ally Dick, a Scottish Youth international, joined Tottenham Hotspur as an apprentice in July 1981 and was upgraded to the full-time professional ranks in May 1982, having made his Football League debut in February of that year, at home to Manchester City when he was substituted by Graham Roberts. Dick's appearances thereafter amounted to only a handful and in the summer of 1986 he moved to Ajax of Amsterdam. His one moment of glory with Tottenham, however, came in the second leg of the UEFA Cup Final in 1984 when he came on as substitute to replace Gary Mabbutt. Tottenham were a goal down against Anderlecht but Graham Roberts equalised, Spurs won the penalty shoot-out in dramatic fashion, and Dick had a UEFA Cup winners' medal to show for his modest career at White Hart Lane.

	LEAGUE		FACUP		FLCUP		EUROPE		TOTAL	
	App	Gls	App	Gls	App	Gls	App	Gls	App	Gls
1981-82	1	0	0	0	0	0	0	0	1	0
1982-83	2	0	2	0	0	0	0	0	4	0
1983-84	10/1	2	0	0	0	0	3/1	0	13/2	2
1984-85	2	0	0	0	0	0	0/2	0	2/2	0
1985-86	1	0	0	0	0	0	0	0	1	0
	16/1	2	2	0	0	0	3/3	0	21/4	2

ALISTAIR DICK

89

Jimmy Dimmock, Spurs left winger through the 1920s, was a man of mazy dribbles and touch-line trickery. He was clever with the ball to the point of being cheeky, over-individualistic or selfish, but his style made him a favourite of the fans and still brought plenty of tangible rewards. He was a member of the Second Division championship team in 1919-20, was capped by England, and then his goal won Spurs the FA Cup in 1921, a well-angled left-foot shot early in the second half of the game. All this success came before Dimmock's 21st birthday, for he was born in Edmonton late in 1900. He played a little as an amateur with Clapton Orient during World War One, and joined Spurs in May 1919 from Edmonton Ramblers. Clapton Orient were obviously interested in signing him too, but the verdict went to Spurs, the club based about a mile from where Dimmock was born. He proved a magnificent asset, a well-built winger who was elusive on the pitch. Early in his career it was surprising that he did not get more goals, but he righted this in the mid-1920s when he became a more prolific goalscorer. His form earned him two more England caps in 1926. He stayed with Spurs until August 1931, by which time he had put on weight, although losing none of his artistry on the ball. He next played for Thames, then Clapton Orient and Ashford.

	LEAGUE		FA CUP		TOTAL	
	App	Gls	App	Gls	App	Gls
1919-20	27	5	4	0	31	5
1920-21	41	9	6	1	47	10
1921-22	42	7	6	1	48	8
1922-23	42	6	5	1	47	7
1923-24	25	2	0	0	25	2
1924-25	29	5	4	2	33	7
1925-26	40	14	3	3	43	17
1926-27	41	19	1	1	42	20
1927-28	38	11	4	2	42	13
1928-29	30	12	1	0	31	12
1929-30	32	6	2	0	34	6
1930-31	13	4	2	1	15	5
	400	100	38	12	438	112

JIMMY DIMMOCK

The sight of Ted Ditchburn running on to the field — usually immediately behind his captain in accordance with a superstition — was one to leave Spurs fans feeling secure. His goalkeeping had both acrobatics and safety, and his consistency and freedom from injury can be gauged by his remarkable record of 247 consecutive League appearances. Before Jennings and Perryman, he held the club record of appearances, despite losing seven seasons to World War Two. He joined Spurs in 1939, Gillingham-born and Northfleet-nursed (in the football sense). Ted Ditchburn's father had been a professional boxer, although, perversely, the one part of the goalkeeper's game which received criticism was his punching. He was daring at the feet of forwards, brilliant at stopping ground-shots and with Alf Ramsey he pioneered the art of the short throw-out, thus temporarily playing an opposing winger out of the game and starting a Spurs attack. He was a one-club man who deserved more than his six England caps which were spread over eight years. He was kept out of the England team by Frank Swift and Bert Williams, and his cause was not helped by a surprise defeat in Sweden in one of his early games. He was ever-present in Tottenham's two championship seasons and was still playing in the First Division in his late-30s, when he finally suffered serious injuries. After 20 years with Spurs he moved to Romford in April 1959 and had a spell with them as manager.

	LEAGUE		FA CUP		TOTAL	
	App	Gls	App	Gls	App	Gls
1946-47	41	0	2	0	43	0
1947-48	41	0	5	0	46	0
1948-49	43	0	1	0	44	0
1949-50	42	0	3	0	45	0
1950-51	42	0	1	0	43	0
1951-52	42	0	2	0	44	0
1952-53	42	0	9	0	51	0
1953-54	39	0	6	0	45	0
1954-55	16	0	0	0	16	0
1955-56	14	0	0	0	14	0
1956-57	29	0	3	0	32	0
1957-58	26	0	2	0	28	0
1958-59	2	0	0	0	2	0
	419	0	34	0	453	0

TED DITCHBURN

Len Duquemin was Spurs' workmanlike centre-forward during the astoundingly successful seasons shortly after World War Two. He relied far more on perspiration than ball-playing inspiration but this made him ideally suited to Arthur Rowe's 'Push and Run' team. 'The Duke' scored many vital goals for Spurs, including the only goal of the game against Sheffield Wednesday which sealed the League Championship in the 1950-51 season. He also scored in two FA Cup semi-finals — against Blackpool in 1948 and 1953 — and was particularly unfortunate not to play in a Wembley Final. He was a 'player's player' who was good in the air and strong in support, but he lacked the skill of some of his contemporaries. Duquemin was unusual in being a Channel Islander in League football. Born in Guernsey in 1924, he lived there through the German occupation and came to Tottenham Hotspur from the Vauxbelet club. He became a professional in September 1946, after nine months as an amateur, and came into the team in 1947-8, finishing that season as Spurs' top

scorer. Chunky but mobile, Duquemin had a knack for goalscoring and helping his fellow roving forwards. The costly signing of Dave Dunmore in 1954 provided stiff competition but Duquemin stayed until the 1958-9 season, when he moved to Bedford Town.

LEN DUQUEMIN

	LEAGUE		FA CUP		TOTAL	
	App	Gls	App	Gls	App	Gls
1947-48	36	16	5	5	41	21
1948-49	38	15	0	0	38	15
1949-50	40	16	2	0	42	16
1950-51	33	14	1	0	34	14
1951-52	25	12	2	2	27	14
1952-53	38	18	9	6	47	24
1953-54	27	9	6	0	33	9
1954-55	19	8	2	1	21	9
1955-56	17	5	6	3	23	8
1956-57	2	1	0	0	2	1
	275	114	33	17	308	131

It is ironic that the first 20th-century League and FA Cup 'double' was virtually assured by a headed goal from the smallest man in British football at the time. Scorer of the second goal in the 1961 FA Cup Final against Leicester, Terry Dyson stood 5ft 3in, weighed less than 10st and was the son of a Yorkshire jockey. Born in Malton, Dyson joined Spurs in 1955, yet the 'double' winning season was his first campaign as Tottenham's number-one left winger. Even then he was not assured of a place, competing with the more expensive Terry Medwin, who cost Spurs £18,000 rather than a £10 signing-on fee. Not until Medwin was injured (in 1963) did Dyson have another season as a regular. Yet Dyson contributed some glorious moments to those days of the early 1960s. He scored a key European Cup goal against Feyenoord, a winner in

Belgrade in the first leg of the European Cup-winners' Cup semi-final and followed that with three goals (two from unlikely long-range positions) in the Final. He moved to Fulham in 1965 — as did Cliff Jones later — and after three years signed for Colchester United.

TERRY DYSON

	LEAGUE		FA CUP		EUROPE		TOTAL	
	App	Gls	App	Gls	App	Gls	App	Gls
1954-55	1	0	0	0	-	-	1	0
1955-56	3	0	0	0	-	-	3	0
1956-57	8	3	1	0	-	-	9	3
1957-58	12	2	2	0	-	-	14	2
1958-59	7	0	0	0	-	-	7	0
1959-60	6	0	0	0	-	-	6	0
1960-61	40	12	7	5	-	-	47	17
1961-62	23	6	0	0	4	4	27	10
1962-63	13	2	1	0	3	3	17	5
1963-64	39	11	2	1	2	1	43	13
1964-65	32	5	3	0	-	-	35	5
	184	41	16	6	9	8	209	55

Albert John Elkes, who was born at Wellington, Shropshire, on the last day of 1894, had a dream start to his career with Southampton, scoring two goals on his League debut in March 1922 after joining the Saints from Birmingham. Elkes, a tall, clever footballer, soon suffered a setback, however, when he broke his collar-bone in the very next game and spent the rest of the season on the sidelines. In the summer of 1923, Tottenham paid a reported £1,000 fee for his transfer and Elkes went on make exactly 200 League and Cup appearances for the club before moving to Middles-brough in the summer of 1929. Equally at home at inside-forward or centre-half, Elkes was close to an England cap and was named as reserve. He also toured Australia with an FA party in 1925. Jack Elkes ended his career with Watford. He died in January 1972, aged 78.

	LEAGUE		FA CUP		TOTAL	
	App	Gls	App	Gls	App	Gls
1923-24	37	11	1	0	38	11
1924-25	33	10	5	1	38	11
1925-26	32	11	3	0	35	11
1926-27	40	2	1	0	41	2
1927-28	22	5	0	0	22	5
1928-29	27	11	0	0	27	11
	191	50	10	1	201	51

JACK ELKES

Signed in the summer of 1966, after his first club, Blackburn Rovers, had been relegated, Mike England cost Spurs a record British fee for a defender but gave nine seasons' service as first-choice in the heart of the defence. England was a lean and strong player with tremendous 'stopper' qualities. He also had skill and at times turned out at centre-forward. There were plenty of personal rewards for the £95,000 signing. In his first season he won an FA Cup winners' medal, and there followed a UEFA Cup win in 1972 and another Final two years later, a League Cup success in 1973 — he missed the 1971 win through injury — and his inter-national appearances for Wales moved on to 44. Earlier he had played 11 times for the Welsh Under-23 side. Signed to replace the injured Maurice Norman, he was one of Bill Nicholson's last truly great signings. He retired, surprisingly suddenly, at the end of the 1974-5 season. England, who was born at Prestatyn, came back to play for Cardiff City, but later fame has come through his management of the Welsh national team until his dismissal in February 1988.

	LEAGUE		FACUP		FLCUP		EUROPE		TOTAL	
	App	Gls	App	Gls	App	Gls	App	Gls	App	Gls
1966-67	42	1	8	0	0	0	-	-	50	1
1967-68	31	3	5	0	0	0	2	0	38	3
1968-69	36	3	4	1	5	0	-	-	45	4
1969-70	36	1	4	0	1	0	-	-	41	1
1970-71	22	1	0	0	6	0	-	-	28	1
1971-72	38	2	5	0	7	0	11	1	61	3
1972-73	31	1	3	1	10	0	10	0	54	2
1973-74	33	0	1	0	1	0	12	2	47	2
1974-75	31	2	2	0	0	0	-	-	33	2
	300	14	32	2	30	0	35	3	397	19

MIKE ENGLAND

There were five Scotsmen in the 1901 FA Cup winning team and one of them was big Harry Erentz at right-back. Erentz was a hard-tackling full-back, fast and hard-working, and he provided a good balance with his full-back partner, the more constructive Sandy Tait. Erentz was signed from Newton Heath in May 1898 and had previously played for Dundee in his home town. He played a majority of games in Spurs' Southern League championship season (1899-1900) and was ever-present the season after the FA Cup win. He stayed with Spurs until the end of the 1903-04 season, when he joined Swindon Town. His brother, Fred Erentz, played over 300 games as a wing-half or full-back for Manchester United from their Newton Heath days. The two played in the same Newton Heath team in 1897-8.

	Southern		United		Western		FA CUP		TOTAL	
	App	Gls	App	Gls	App	Gls	App	Gls	App	Gls
1898-99	24	0	19	1	0	0	9	0	52	1
1899-1900	18	0	0	0	0	0	1	0	19	0
1900-01	20	0	0	0	12	0	8	0	40	0
1901-02	30	0	0	0	15	0	3	0	48	0
1902-03	24	0	0	0	10	0	0	0	34	0
1903-04	16	0	0	0	8	0	0	0	24	0
	132	0	19	1	45	0	21	0	217	1

HARRY ERENTZ

Welsh international winger Willie Evans was one of the stars of Tottenham's team of the early 1930s that was known as 'The Greyhounds' because of the incredible speed shown by the entire forward line. Evans, a regular goalscorer himself, was also responsible for creating many of the goals scored by George Hunt and Taffy O'Callaghan. He signed for Tottenham in May 1931, from Haywards Heath, and was soon playing regularly in Spurs' League team. In his second season he was an ever-present and missed few matches right up until injury ended his career. A head injury suffered whilst playing for Wales against England at Cardiff in February 1936 has often been regarded as the beginning of the end of Willie Evans' career, but in fact it was a knee injury sustained in a match at Villa Park in November of that year which led to his departure from White Hart Lane at the end of the season. In May 1937, Evans signed for Fulham but did not play in the Cottagers' League team and his career ended there.

	LEAGUE		FA CUP		TOTAL	
	App	Gls	App	Gls	App	Gls
1932-32	28	5	2	1	30	6
1932-33	42	28	2	1	44	29
1933-34	36	16	3	3	39	19
1934-35	32	12	4	2	36	14
1935-36	33	15	6	1	39	16
1936-37	7	2	0	0	7	2
	178	78	17	8	195	86

WILLIE EVANS

A big, strong central striker, more like a traditional British centre-forward, Mark Falco was signed as an apprentice in July 1977. Twelve months later he turned professional, and made his League debut at the end of the 1978-9 season. By then he was an England Youth international. Falco had a great start to the 1981-2 season but injury put him out in October and he found it difficult to re-establish himself in time for that season's FA Cup Final against Queen's Park Rangers. He did take part in the UEFA Cup success in 1984, however, and stayed another two seasons before moving to Watford in October 1986. Two more big-money moves followed in the next 16 months, first to Glasgow Rangers then to Queen's Park Rangers. In August 1991 he moved to Millwall but injury soon forced him to retire from the first class game and he spent a month at Worthing under his former teammate Gerry Armstrong before joining another old Tottenham star, Graham Roberts, at Enfield.

	LEAGUE		FA CUP		FL CUP		EUROPE		TOTAL	
	App	Gls	App	Gls	App	Gls	App	Gls	App	Gls
1978-79	1	1	0	0	0	0	-	-	1	1
1979-80	7/2	2	2	0	0/1	0	-	-	9/3	2
1980-81	3	1	0	0	0	0	-	-	3	1
1981-82	21	5	3	1	4	0	3/2	3	31/2	9
1982-83	11/5	5	0	0	1/1	0	0/1	0	12/7	5
1983-84	32/4	13	4	1	3	1	10/1	7	49/5	22
1984-85	42	22	3	1	5	2	8	4	58	29
1985-86	40	19	3	2	6	0	-	-	49	21
1986-87	5/1	0	0	0	0/1	0	-	-	5/2	0
	162/12	68	15	5	19/3	3	21/4	14	217/19	90

MARK FALCO

A winger with a seemingly endless appetite for hard work, Tony Galvin joined Spurs from Goole Town in January 1978 but was not able to command a regular first-team place until three years later, just in time for the 1981 FA Cup run. In fact, he had played only 28 League games when he impressed so much with his strong running on the left wing during both games with Manchester City that year. And he had spent most of 1980 out of action through injury. Born in Huddersfield, in 1956, he eventually won international honours with the Republic of Ireland. Brother of Chris Galvin, another League professional, he graduated from the University of Hull with a BA in Russian Studies. After the 1981 FA Cup Final success he became an automatic, if unsung, member of the Spurs team. He collected a second FA Cup winners' medal in 1982 and his star performances in the two legs of the 1984 UEFA Cup Final confirmed him as a man for big occasions. He also won a League Cup runners-up medal in 1982, altogether an impressive record for a £30,000 signing from the Northern Premier League. He moved to Sheffield Wednesday in August 1987 and two years later joined his former Spurs teammate Ossie Ardiles at Swindon Town where he was made assistant manager. He followed the little Argentine to Newcastle United, even finding time to play for Gateshead when his duties at St James' Park allowed, but was dismissed in February 1992 along with Ardiles.

	LEAGUE		FA CUP		FL CUP		EUROPE		TOTAL	
	App	Gls	App	Gls	App	Gls	App	Gls	App	Gls
1978-79	1	0	0	0	0	0	-	-	1	0
1979-80	7/3	4	0	0	0	0	-	-	7/3	4
1980-81	17	1	8/1	1	0	0	-	-	25/1	2
1981-82	32	3	7	0	8	0	8	1	55	4
1982-83	26	2	1	0	1	0	1	0	29	2
1983-84	30	1	3	0	3	1	9	4	45	6
1984-85	38	4	3	1	3	0	7	1	51	6
1985-86	23	4	0	0	3	1	-	-	26	5
1986-87	20/4	1	1	0	2/3	1	-	-	23/7	2
	194/7	20	23/1	2	20/3	3	25	6	262/11	31

TONY GALVIN

When Spurs signed Paul Gascoigne for £2 million from Newcastle United in July 1988, many questioned the wisdom of paying so much for a 21-year-old with barely three years' top-flight experience and a temperament some described as 'questionable'. But Gascoigne soon justified every penny of that record British fee. First associated with Newcastle as a schoolboy, he signed professional in May 1985, a month after making his First Division debut, and quickly established himself as the most exciting talent of his generation. A player who wants to enjoy football and wants the paying public to enjoy it too, his sense of humour sometimes got him into trouble but Venables knew that he could harness Gascoigne's talents without taking away any of the impishness that endeared him to the public. An Under-21 international when he arrived at Spurs, Gascoigne

made his full debut as a substitute against Denmark in September 1988 and was immediately hailed as the player around whom England should build its team for the 1990 World Cup. A richly talented midfield player always prepared to try the unorthodox, he can open up opposing defences with long, sweeping passes, or dribble his way through the most packed defences, and exhibits a remarkably cool finishing ability. Despite public pressure, he had great difficulty in persuading Bobby Robson that he was ready for the challenge of international football but in Italy he showed the world his talents, buckled down to the discipline needed at that level and was unquestionably the star of England's march to the semi-final. The tears he shed when he realized that a booking in the semi-final would mean him missing the Final if England got through endeared him to the nation. Voted BBC TV's Sports Personality of the Year on his return, he continued where he left off in the 1990-91 season, almost single-handedly pushing Spurs through to the FA Cup Final. His great day was ruined after only 15 minutes by a serious ligament injury, caused by a rash challenge on Gascoigne's part, and he was carried off, a world record £8.5 million move to Lazio now in jeopardy. A year long battle to regain fitness followed but in July 1992 he finally moved to the Eternal City and was soon back showing the form that makes him one of the most exciting talents in the modern game.

PAUL GASCOIGNE

	LEAGUE		FA CUP		FL CUP		TOTAL	
	App	Gls	App	Gls	App	Gls	App	Gls
1988-89	31/1	6	0	0	5	1	36/1	7
1989-90	34	6	0	0	4	1	38	7
1990-91	26	7	6	6	4/1	6	36/1	19
	91/1	19	6	6	13/1	8	110/2	33

A superb £72,500 signing from Dundee in December 1964, Alan Gilzean gave Spurs almost ten years' service, probing and prompting in attack. Originally an out-and-out centre-forward with Dundee — he had starred in their Scottish League Championship side and their European Cup run, and had scored over 100 Scottish League goals for the club — Gilzean adapted to form deadly striking partnerships with Jimmy Greaves, and,

later, with Martin Chivers. Capped 22 times for Scotland, Gilzean's great strength was his amazing heading ability, a combination of power and deft control. The sight of him holding off a defender as he jumped, then flicking the ball from his balding pate is one that Spurs fans of the era will cherish. He won winners' medals in the FA Cup (1967), the League Cup (1971 and 1973) and the UEFA Cup (1972). He continued into his mid-30s and narrowly failed to be the first player to score 100 League goals for one Scottish League club and a century for an English League club. He finished his career in South Africa and had a testimonial against Red Star Belgrade in November 1974.

	LEAGUE		FA CUP		FL CUP		EUROPE		TOTAL	
	App	Gls	App	Gls	App	Gls	App	Gls	App	Gls
1964-65	20	11	4	5	-	-	-	-	24	16
1965-66	40	12	3	3	-	-	-	-	43	15
1966-67	40	17	8	4	1	0	-	-	49	21
1967-68	32/2	8	5	0	0	0	4	2	41/2	10
1968-69	37	7	4	0	6	0	-	-	47	7
1969-70	34/2	10	4	0	0	0	-	-	38/2	10
1970-71	38	9	3	4	7	4	-	-	48	17
1971-72	38	11	5	4	4	0	11	6	58	21
1972-73	35	5	3	1	8/1	2	9	3	55/1	11
1973-74	21/4	3	1	0	1	0	3/1	2	26/5	5
	335/8	93	40	21	27/1	6	27/1	13	429/10	133

ALAN GILZEAN

Without doubt the greatest goalscorer in Spurs' history — and perhaps in the history of British football — Jimmy Greaves was signed for nearly £100,000 from AC Milan in December 1961. He celebrated with a hat-trick on his debut and that was a foretaste of what was to come. Greaves had made his Football League debut against Spurs, with Chelsea, on the first day of the 1957-8 season. He scored then, as he did on all his debut days. Only 5ft 8in, he had superb balance, unnerving anticipation in opponents' penalty areas and an incredibly cool assurance when chances arose. At Spurs he joined other ex-Chelsea forwards, Bobby Smith and Les Allen, and won an FA Cup winners' medal in his first season, scoring the opening goal at Wembley. He scored twice in the European Cup-winners' Cup Final and ended that season (1962-3) with Spurs' highest-scorer-in-a-season record. He went on to break Bobby Smith's career-aggregate record for Spurs and his spectacular goal in the 1967 FA Cup semi-final helped take Tottenham to another Cup success. However, a serious illness in 1965-6 meant he was unable to reach full fitness for the World Cup Finals that summer. In March 1970, he moved to West Ham as part of the deal that took Martin Peters to White Hart Lane but he retired — still only 31 years old — just over a year later, unable to recapture the form that had brought him 57 England caps (and 44 goals). He became the first modern-day Spurs player to receive a testimonial when Feyenoord visited White Hart Lane in October 1972. Typically, Greaves scored. Accustomed to feeding off Scottish centre-forwards (like Gilzean), Greaves later went into partnership with Ian St John in a television programme, having overcome a serious drink problem.

JIMMY GREAVES

	LEAGUE		FA CUP		FL CUP		EUROPE		TOTAL	
	App	Gls	App	Gls	App	Gls	App	Gls	App	Gls
1961-62	22	21	7	9	-	-	2	0	31	30
1962-63	41	37	1	0	-	-	6	5	48	42
1963-64	41	35	2	0	-	-	2	1	45	36
1964-65	41	29	4	6	-	-	-	-	45	35
1965-66	29	15	2	1	-	-	-	-	31	16
1966-67	38	25	8	6	1	0	-	-	47	31
1967-68	39	23	4	3	0	0	4	3	47	29
1968-69	42	27	4	4	6	5	-	-	52	36
1969-70	29	8	4	3	1	0	-	-	34	11
	322	220	36	32	8	5	14	9	380	266

Arthur Grimsdell was an aggressive, determined wing-half who always gave great support to his forwards. Although slightly built and light of foot, he was strong in defence and attack, one of the best-ever all-round wing-halves and possibly the most complete wing-half in the history of the game after Duncan Edwards of Manchester United. At half-back Grimsdell could be the best forward on the field, and he had a powerful long-range shot, as demonstrated by his two goals for England against Scotland in the 1919 Victory inter-national. At Spurs, covered by Seed or Bliss, it was customary for him to move forward strongly. He skippered the club in the years after World War One and was unfortunate in that his peacetime international

caps were restricted to six. He was even tried at centre-forward after Bliss left. Born in Watford, he was an England schoolboy international before signing for his home-town club. He joined Spurs in March 1912 and remained their regular left-half until he broke his leg at Leicester in 1926. He moved to Clapton Orient in 1929 as player-manager. Later he was a director of Watford.

ARTHUR GRIMSDELL

	LEAGUE		FA CUP		TOTAL	
	App	Gls	App	Gls	App	Gls
1911-12	2	0	0	0	2	0
1912-13	25	0	3	0	28	0
1913-14	37	1	3	0	40	1
1914-15	8	0	0	0	8	0
1919-20	37	14	4	1	41	15
1920-21	38	3	6	0	44	3
1921-22	35	3	6	0	41	3
1922-23	40	2	5	0	45	2
1923-24	27	1	1	0	28	1
1924-25	14	0	4	0	18	0
1925-26	13	0	0	0	13	0
1926-27	2	0	0	0	2	0
1927-28	35	2	4	0	39	2
1928-29	11	0	0	0	11	0
	324	26	36	1	360	27

Curly-haired inside-forward Willie Hall was signed from Notts County in December 1932 to take over from George Greenfield, who had broken a leg against Fulham. That season Spurs gained promotion to the First Division and were grateful for the creative skills of Hall, a clever ball-player who worked well with his winger. Born in Newark, Hall had been with Notts County for just two years and was not yet 21 when he signed for Spurs. Yet Notts County very sensibly inserted a clause whereby they would receive extra money (£500) if Hall was capped for England. In 1934 that happened, and Hall went on to win ten caps. He also scored nine times for his country, a remarkable record for someone who was not generally known as a goalscorer. In November 1938, Hall scored five in the international against Ireland. By then he was playing in the Second Division with Spurs, and it is no coincidence that Hall was injured in the season they were relegated. He also represented England against the Rest of Europe and played regularly for Spurs as late as 1943. But a serious leg disease forced his retirement and then caused him to have both legs amputated. In 1946, he was awarded a testimonial — Spurs against an FA XI — and it was particularly well supported. He had periods managing Clapton Orient and Chingford Town.

WILLIE HALL

	LEAGUE		FA CUP		TOTAL	
	App	Gls	App	Gls	App	Gls
1932-33	21	1	2	0	23	1
1933-34	42	3	3	0	45	3
1934-35	18	3	0	0	18	3
1935-36	32	6	5	0	37	6
1936-37	19	1	0	0	19	1
1937-38	29	4	6	0	35	4
1938-39	40	9	4	2	44	11
1939-40	3	0	-	-	3	0
	204	27	20	2	224	29

Ball-juggling Tommy Harmer, from the East End of London, was probably one of the most entertaining players to wear a Spurs shirt. Signed in August 1948, he made his name in Army football as an inside-foward. He was perhaps too individualistic for the 'Push and Run' era and his 12-year career with Spurs was erratic. Harmer was very slight of build, and various schemes were tried to help him put on weight in his early days, but on the pitch his confidence would take him into tight corners where he could rely on occasional backheels or other such pieces of wizardry. He was tried in most forward positions for Spurs, but not until 1956-7 was he a regular choice. As a forward who cost a mere signing-on fee, he was beginning to look a little out of place among Bill Nicholson's string of big signings when he was transferred in October 1960. Two years later he moved to Chelsea, played a few games in their promotion-winning team and even returned to White Hart Lane to help Chelsea win a First Division game against his old club. Harmer was unfortunate to miss out on major honours with Spurs, scoring well in 1956-7, when the team finished second to Manchester United, and scheming the club to third place on two other occasions. His only individual honour was an England 'B' cap.

TOMMY HARMER

	LEAGUE		FA CUP		TOTAL	
	App	Gls	App	Gls	App	Gls
1951-52	13	3	2	0	15	3
1952-53	17	4	0	0	17	4
1953-54	6	2	0	0	6	2
1954-55	5	0	0	0	5	0
1955-56	10	5	3	2	13	7
1956-57	42	17	3	1	45	18
1957-58	40	9	2	0	42	9
1958-59	35	4	3	0	38	4
1959-60	37	3	4	1	41	4
	205	47	17	4	222	51

Sunderland-born Mike Hazard signed as an apprentice in July 1976 and as a professional in February 1978. A highly talented midfield player, he was unfortunate to be at Spurs at the same time as Glenn Hoddle, who was liable to attract far more of the limelight. However, he was a key member of the squad and came into the side for the successful 1981-2 season, when Spurs finished fourth in the League, won the FA Cup and were runners-up in the League Cup. Two years later he played a major role in the UEFA Cup success, appearing in the Final after his excellent goal had helped Spurs conquer Hajduk Split in the semi-final. Hazard moved to Chelsea, in September 1985, in an effort to secure regular first-team football. Never truly able to command a regular first-team place at Stamford Bridge in January 1990 Hazard moved to Portsmouth and eight months later joined the ex-Spurs colony at Swindon Town.

MIKE HAZARD

	LEAGUE		FA CUP		FL CUP		EUROPE		TOTAL	
	App	Gls	App	Gls	App	Gls	App	Gls	App	Gls
1979-80	3	0	0	0	0	0	-	-	3	0
1980-81	2/2	0	0	0	0	0	-	-	2/2	0
1981-82	26/2	5	4/1	1	5/1	3	6	1	41/4	10
1982-83	15/3	1	2	1	3	0	3/1	0	23/4	2
1983-84	9/2	2	1/2	0	0/1	0	6	1	16/5	3
1984-85	15/8	4	0	0	3/1	2	7	1	25/9	7
1985-86	3/1	1	0	0	0	0	-	-	3/1	1
	73/18	13	7/3	2	11/3	5	22/1	3	113/25	23

In the late 1950s, Ron Henry waited five years for his chance as a regular first-team defender but his patience was rewarded with a place in one of the most successful club sides of all time. He was ever-present at left-back in the 'double' winning team of 1960-61 and a regular for the next four seasons. During that time he was capped for England once, in a heavy defeat in France. Shoreditch-born Henry played for Harpenden Town and Redbourne before signing for Spurs in January 1955. Three months later he made his First Division debut against Huddersfield Town. He played centre-half that day, but eventually it was an injury to left-back Mel Hopkins, who broke his nose in an international against Scotland, that brought him into the team to stay. He formed an excellent full-back partnership with Peter Baker and they were the only locally-born players (and the only ones who did not cost a big fee) in the great 1960-61 team. Henry, originally an outside-left, and a left-half in his early days at Spurs, was stockily built but very skilled. Tottenham Hotspur were his only League club and his career lasted more than 14 years, although he was troubled by cartilage injury in the later stages. Having won a League Championship medal, two FA Cup winners' medals and playing in the Cup-winners' Cup success, Henry later turned his attention to coaching Spurs' junior side.

RON HENRY

	LEAGUE		FA CUP		EUROPE		TOTAL	
	App	Gls	App	Gls	App	Gls	App	Gls
1954-55	1	0	0	0	-	-	1	0
1955-56	1	0	0	0	-	-	1	0
1956-57	1	0	0	0	-	-	1	0
1957-58	15	0	0	0	-	-	15	0
1958-59	8	0	0	0	-	-	8	0
1959-60	25	0	4	0	-	-	29	0
1960-61	42	0	7	0	-	-	49	0
1961-62	41	0	7	0	8	0	56	0
1962-63	42	0	1	0	7	0	50	0
1963-64	29	0	0	0	2	0	31	0
1964-65	41	1	4	0	-	-	45	1
1965-66	1	0	0	0	-	-	1	0
	247	1	23	0	17	0	287	1

One of the most gifted footballers of his generation, Glenn Hoddle signed professional for Spurs in April 1975 after overcoming a serious knee injury in his early teens. Born in Hayes in 1957, he won England Youth international honours and then played 12 times for the Under-21 team. His first full season in the Spurs first team was marred by relegation to the Second Division but he soon helped them back into the top flight. In the late 1970s, the football public was split in its admiration and criticism. On the positive side was his cunning from free-kicks and long-range shooting positions, plus his uncanny vision that led to perfect passes of 50 yards or more. On the debit side was a question-mark about his defensive qualities and doubts about his ability to work consistently over 90 minutes. But when he worked on the latter points he became an full England player, scoring on his debut in November 1979 and eventually becoming a regular. He won FA Cup winners' medals in 1981 (when his free-kick led to an equaliser) and 1982 (when he scored in both games), and he played in the losing team of 1987. In 1982 he was in Spurs' losing League Cup Final team, but injury kept him out of the 1984 UEFA Cup success. A six-footer, Hoddle has occasionally deputised in the Spurs goal during a game, while he also lent himself to popular music in 1987, recording a single with teammate Chris Waddle. In the 1987 close season he joined the French League club, AC Monaco where his talents were at last truly appreciated until persistent injury problems led to him being released from his contract in late 1990. He signed for Chelsea on a non-contract basis in an attempt to recover full fitness but without playing a game for them left in March 1991 to embark on what should prove a successful managerial career as successor to Ossie Ardiles at Swindon Town. In 1993 he took them to promotion.

GLENN HODDLE

| | LEAGUE | | FA CUP | | FL CUP | | EUROPE | | TOTAL | |
	App	Gls	App	Gls	App	Gls	App	Gls	App	Gls
1975-76	6/1	1	0	0	0	0	-	-	6/1	1
1976-77	39	4	1	0	2	1	-	-	42	5
1977-78	41	12	2	1	2	0	-	-	45	13
1978-79	34/1	7	5	1	2	1	-	-	41/1	9
1979-80	41	19	6	2	2	1	-	-	49	22
1980-81	38	12	9	2	6	1	-	-	53	15
1981-82	34	10	7	3	8	1	8	1	57	15
1982-83	22/2	1	0/1	0	3	0	0/1	0	25/4	1
1983-84	24	4	3	0	3	1	5/1	0	35/1	5
1984-85	26/2	8	3	0	3	0	4/2	0	36/4	8
1985-86	31	7	5	1	5	0	-	-	41	8
1986-87	35/1	3	6	1	8	4	-	-	49/1	8
	371/7	88	47/1	11	44	10	17/4	1	479/12	110

Mel Hopkins, a long-legged Welsh full-back from Astrad, had in many ways a very successful career, yet he was unfortunate to miss playing a part in team honours. He was capped once for the Welsh Under-23 team before playing 34 times for the full international side. However, an injury in an international against Scotland in 1959 caused him to lose his place in the Spurs first team. In the 'double' season of 1960-61 he was in the Reserves — the only season in 12 that he failed to make a First Division appearance. He joined the groundstaff at Spurs in 1951, just too late for the boom period under Arthur Rowe. He was left-back in the Championship-chasing teams of the late-1950s but ousted by Ron Henry just when the 'double' side had blended. Hopkins stayed with Spurs until October 1964, and he later played for Brighton & Hove Albion, Ballymena and Bradford.

MEL HOPKINS

| | LEAGUE | | FA CUP | | EUROPE | | TOTAL | |
	App	Gls	App	Gls	App	Gls	App	Gls
1952-53	2	0	0	0	-	-	2	0
1953-54	2	0	0	0	-	-	2	0
1954-55	32	0	3	0	-	-	35	0
1955-56	41	0	6	0	-	-	47	0
1956-57	35	0	3	0	-	-	38	0
1957-58	26	0	2	0	-	-	28	0
1958-59	34	0	4	0	-	-	38	0
1959-60	14	0	0	0	-	-	14	0
1960-61	0	0	0	0	0	0	0	0
1961-62	5	0	0	0	-	-	5	0
1962-63	9	0	0	0	1	-	10	0
1963-64	19	0	2	0	-	-	21	0
	219	0	20	0	1	0	240	0

Ruabon-born Ted Hughes was Spurs' centre-half in the 1901 FA Cup winning team. When he was signed from Everton in the close-season of 1899, Hughes was already a Welsh international although he made only eight League appearances for the Merseysiders. He added a further 12 caps to his international haul, making 14 in total, and in those days of relatively few international games, this meant Hughes was virtually a regular for eight years. At Tottenham, however, he was forced to wait for his chance. He replaced Spurs skipper James McNaught early in the 1901 FA Cup run and played well enough to retain his place. Hughes was a tireless worker with a great shot, always prepared to support his forwards. He remained with Spurs until early in the 1907-08 season.

	Southern		Western		FA CUP		TOTAL	
	App	Gls	App	Gls	App	Gls	App	Gls
1899-1900	3	0	0	0	-	-	3	0
1900-01	18	2	10	1	7	0	35	3
1901-02	24	2	12	1	3	2	39	5
1902-03	18	3	9	1	4	0	31	4
1903-04	24	0	8	0	5	0	37	0
1904-05	17	2	9	1	2	0	28	3
1905-06	22	0	5	0	4	0	31	0
1906-07	25	0	5	0	6	0	36	0
1907-08	1	0	4	0	0	0	5	0
	152	9	62	4	31	2	245	15

EDWARD HUGHES

Born in Forest Gate of a West Indian father, Chris Hughton signed for Spurs in June 1979 after completing his training as a lift engineer. A winger in his younger days, he was successfully converted to a full-back, capable of playing on either flank although naturally right-footed. Very quick on the turn, never resisting an opportunity to overlap, Hughton made his first-team debut in 1979 and settled into the left-back position. Qualifying to play for the Republic of Ireland through his mother he won his first cap against the United States in 1980 and has since made over 40 appearances for his country. With Spurs he played in the 1981 and 1982 FA Cup Finals and scored a couple of goals as Tottenham made their way to the UEFA Cup trophy in 1984. He won runners-up medals in the 1982 League Cup Final and 1987 FA Cup Final. His great service to Spurs was recognised with a free transfer in the summer of 1990 and although he was in demand with several clubs it was not until December that he decided to join West Ham permanently after a brief loan spell at Upton Park. In February 1992 he moved to Brentford but a knee injury forced him to retire in April 1993. His brother, Henry, was also a professional footballer.

	LEAGUE		FA CUP		FL CUP		EUROPE		TOTAL	
	App	Gls	App	Gls	App	Gls	App	Gls	App	Gls
1979-80	39	1	6	0	2	0	-	-	47	1
1980-81	34	1	6	1	6	0	-	-	46	2
1981-82	37	2	7	0	8	1	8	0	60	3
1982-83	38	3	3	0	4	0	3	1	48	4
1983-84	34	3	1	0	3	0	12	2	50	5
1984-85	29/2	1	2/1	0	4	1	6/1	1	41/4	3
1985-86	33	1	4	0	6	0	-	-	43	1
1986-87	9	0	2	0	0	0	-	-	11	0
1987-88	12/1	0	2	0	0/1	0	-	-	14/2	0
1988-89	20/1	0	0/1	0	0	0	0	0	20/2	0
1989-90	8	0	1	0	0/1	0	0	0	9/1	0
	293/4	12	34/2	1	33/2	2	29/1	4	389/9	19

CHRIS HUGHTON

100

George Hunt, Spurs' ball-playing centre-forward in the 1930s, held the club's aggregate goalscoring record until the advent of Bobby Smith. Although not so big and burly as Smith, he had all the stature of the later giant and probably more skill. Hunt's exciting solo runs made him a popular player and also brought him plenty of punishment from defenders. He was born in Barnsley, and his first professional club was Chesterfield. Spurs signed him from there in June 1930, and his goals helped Tottenham back into the First Division in the 1932-3 season. Around that time Hunt won three England caps, but after Jack Tresadern was appointed Spurs manager he was less a part of the Tottenham team. He was transferred to Arsenal in October 1937 and moved to Bolton Wanderers soon afterwards before finishing his career with Sheffield Wednesday. Hunt spent 20 years on the training staff of Bolton Wanderers after finishing as a player.

GEORGE HUNT

	LEAGUE		FA CUP		TOTAL	
	App	Gls	App	Gls	App	Gls
1930-31	9	5	0	0	9	5
1931-32	37	24	2	2	39	26
1932-33	41	33	2	3	43	36
1933-34	40	32	3	3	43	35
1934-35	30	10	3	3	33	13
1935-36	15	11	3	2	18	13
1936-37	13	10	0	0	13	10
	185	125	13	13	198	138

Pitched into the Spurs first team in February 1921, following an injury to regular goalkeeper Bill Jacques, Alex Hunter played so well that he won an FA Cup winners' medal less than two months later. It was a swift rise to fame, although the fall was almost as dramatic, Hunter losing his place to Jacques the next season. He was signed by Peter McWilliam from Queen's Park in May 1920, and altogether he was with Spurs for just two years before moving to Wigan Borough. Hunter was steady, courageous, and his temperament proved well-suited to the big occasion. He played in three FA Cup ties in 1921, conceding only one goal.

ALEX HUNTER

	LEAGUE		FA CUP		TOTAL	
	App	Gls	App	Gls	App	Gls
1920-21	11	0	3	0	14	0
1921-22	12	0	0	0	12	0
	23	0	3	0	26	0

In 1923, Tottenham Hotspur came within a whisker of being beaten by Midland League club Worksop Town. There were only four minutes of the match remaining when, with the score still at 0-0, Worksop's Rippon chipped the ball over goalkeeper Blake's head. The Spurs' 'keeper was completely beaten but the ball bounced off the crossbar and was scrambled clear. In the replay, also at White Hart Lane, Spurs won 9-0 but there was some consolation for tiny Worksop who took over £1,000 in 'gate' receipts from the two matches and were able to wipe off all their debts for that season.

Bill Jacques first found fame in the late 1900s in an excellent Gravesend & Northfleet team which included Charlie Buchan, later an England international. Jacques moved to Coventry and then signed for Spurs in the summer of 1914. He was first-choice goalkeeper for most of the next eight seasons. He played through World War One and missed only one League game in 1919-20, when Spurs won the Second Division championship. However, Jacques was desperately unlucky to miss the final part of the 1921 FA Cup success, injured in a game against West Brom late in February. Although he played as many FA Cup ties as Alex Hunter that season, it was the latter who took the medal.

	LEAGUE		FA CUP		TOTAL	
	App	Gls	App	Gls	App	Gls
1914-15	28	0	2	0	30	0
1919-20	42	0	4	0	46	0
1920-21	30	0	3	0	33	0
1921-22	22	0	6	0	28	0
1922-23	1	0	0	0	1	0
	123	0	15	0	138	0

BILL JACQUES

In his time Pat Jennings was one of the best — if not the best — goalkeeper in the world. Tall, strong and the possessor of huge hands, he retained his unflappable temperament through one of the longest-ever playing careers. Jennings first played for Newry Town in his native Northern Ireland. He joined Watford for £6,000 (May 1963) and Spurs for £27,000 just over a year later. After taking over from Bill Brown he went on to set the Spurs record for aggregate appearances (later overtaken by Steve Perryman). Jennings also established a world record for international appearances, winning 119 caps by the time he retired. He played in Spurs' 1967 FA Cup winning team, won Football League Cup winners' medals (1971 & 1973) and a UEFA Cup winners' medal (1972). He was elected Footballer of the Year (1972-3) and PFA Footballer of the Year (1975-6). In the Queen's 1976 Birthday Honours List he was awarded the MBE, and Spurs recognised his services with a testimonial against Arsenal in November 1976. He even managed a goal for Spurs — a mighty clearance in the 1967 FA Charity Shield game. Apart from his international honours, Jennings also played for the United Kingdom XI, the All-Ireland XI and The Three (against The Six) in a Common Market celebration game. When he finally suffered a serious injury — to his ankle in 1976-7 — Spurs were relegated and Jennings was released (far too soon). He spent eight seasons with Arsenal and added to his medals as an FA Cup winner (1979), as an FA Cup Finalist (1978 & 1980) and a European Cup-winners' Cup Finalist (1980). In May 1985, he was granted a second testimonial, this time against Spurs. He returned to White Hart Lane as goalkeeping cover in 1985-6, keeping fit enough to play for Northern Ireland in the 1986 World Cup Finals. Apart from friendlies, he made one further first-team appearance (in the Screen Sport Super Cup). Towards the end of the season he went to Everton on loan — to cover their FA Cup Final appearance — but officially finished his career as a Spurs player during the 1986 World Cup.

PAT JENNINGS MBE

	LEAGUE		FA CUP		FL CUP		EUROPE		TOTAL	
	App	Gls	App	Gls	App	Gls	App	Gls	App	Gls
1964-65	23	0	0	0	-	-	-	-	23	0
1965-66	22	0	3	0	-	-	-	-	25	0
1966-67	41	0	8	0	1	-	-	-	50	0
1967-68	42	0	5	0	0	0	4	0	51	0
1968-69	42	0	4	0	6	0	-	-	52	0
1969-70	42	0	4	0	1	0	-	-	47	0
1970-71	40	0	5	0	6	0	-	-	51	0
1971-72	41	0	5	0	7	0	12	0	65	0
1972-73	40	0	3	0	10	0	10	0	63	0
1973-74	36	0	1	0	0	0	10	0	47	0
1974-75	41	0	2	0	1	0	-	-	44	0
1975-76	40	0	2	0	6	0	-	-	48	0
1976-77	23	0	1	0	1	0	-	-	25	0
	473	0	43	0	39	0	36	0	591	0

Cliff Jones was only 5ft 7in but fast, tricky and braver than most wingers in the penalty area. He darted among the flurry of goalmouth bodies more like an old-fashioned centre-forward, often finishing moves with an excellent leap and firm header. Jones could play on either wing. He was on the right in the 'double' season and on the left in the successes soon afterwards. He was born into a football family; his father Ivor had been an inter-war Welsh international, his brother Bryn played for Swansea, Newport and Bournemouth, and his uncle Bryn had been transferred from Wolves to Arsenal for a British record fee just before World War Two. The £35,000 Spurs paid Swansea Town for Cliff Jones in February 1958 was also a record fee, for a winger. Jones had signed professional for Swansea in 1952 and was already a Welsh international when he joined Spurs. In his second international — against England in 1955 —he won the game with a headed goal, and he went on to make 59 appearances over a 15-year period. Soon after arriving at Spurs he fractured a leg in a pre-season training accident in 1958, but survived this early setback to more than justify his transfer fee. In June 1962, Juventus reputedly offered a six-figure sum for his services. Jones won three FA Cup winners' medals, the last as non-playing substitute in 1967, a League Championship medal and a European Cup-winners' Cup winners' medal. He left Spurs in October 1968 to join Fulham. Jones, who helped Wales to the 1958 World Cup quarter-finals, ended his career with King's Lynn and Wealdstone.

CLIFF JONES

	LEAGUE		FA CUP		FL CUP		EUROPE		TOTAL	
	App	Gls	App	Gls	App	Gls	App	Gls	App	Gls
1957-58	10	1	-	-	-	-	-	-	10	1
1958-59	22	5	4	2	-	-	-	-	26	7
1959-60	38	20	4	5	-	-	-	-	42	25
1960-61	29	15	6	4	-	-	-	-	35	19
1961-62	38	16	7	4	-	-	8	4	53	24
1962-63	37	20	1	0	-	-	6	2	44	22
1963-64	39	14	2	0	-	-	2	-	43	14
1964-65	39	13	4	0	-	-	-	-	43	13
1965-66	9	8	2	0	-	-	-	-	11	8
1966-67	20	6	4/1	0	0	0	0	-	24/1	6
1967-68	27/3	12	1/3	1	-	-	3	1	31/6	14
1968-69	6/1	5	0	0	2	1	-	-	8/1	6
	314/4	135	35/4	16	2	1	19	7	370/8	159

John (J.L.) Jones was the first Tottenham Hotspur captain to receive the FA Cup. He skippered the 1901 team from left-half. Although John Cameron was player-manager, Jones was captain on the field, a skilful Welsh international who often operated as a sixth forward. Before joining Spurs, in the summer 1897, Jack Jones had played for Bootle, Stoke, Grimsby Town and Sheffield United. He played in the majority of games during Spurs' 1899-1900 Southern League championship season and took over from McNaught as captain during the FA Cup-winning year. Suitably complemented by Tom Morris, Spurs' steady right-half, Jones proved an inspirational influence. He won 21 Welsh caps during his career, and 12 of these came while he was at Spurs. He was the brains of the team and one of the most skilful players of his day. Jones stayed with Spurs until May 1904, when he joined Watford.

	Southern		Western		United		FA CUP		TOTAL	
	App	Gls	App	Gls	App	Gls	App	Gls	App	Gls
1897-98	20	1	0	0	15	2	2	0	37	3
1898-99	16	0	0	0	11	0	10	1	37	1
1899-1900	20	1	0	0	0	0	0	0	20	1
1900-01	17	3	6	1	0	0	7	0	30	4
1901-02	25	1	11	0	0	0	3	0	39	1
1902-03	15	0	12	1	0	0	4	0	31	1
1903-04	19	1	8	1	0	0	5	0	32	2
	132	7	37	3	26	2	31	1	226	13

JACK JONES

Joe Kinnear was signed as an amateur in August 1963 and then as a professional 18 months later. His big chance came when Phil Beal broke an arm and Kinnear stepped into the right-back position in time to join the 1967 FA Cup winning team. Kinnear was the youngest player on the pitch for that Final and one of only two Spurs players who had not cost a big fee. Then a broken leg kept him out of action for 12 months. He returned to play in two League Cup winning teams (1971 and 1973) although another injury lost him his place to Ray Evans for a time in between. In 1973-4 he made a transfer request when he was left out of the team for much of the season. Kinnear was a quick, hard-tackling full-back who was very competent at overlapping. He won a UEFA Cup winners' medal in 1972, and earned 25 Republic of Ireland international caps, the last while at Brighton, whom he joined in August 1975. In March 1976, Spurs visited Brighton to play a testimonial match for him. He was still in football in 1987, teaming up with Dave Mackay as part of the Doncaster Rovers management staff. He took over as manager on Mackay's departure in March 1989 but left himself three months later. He then joined Wimbledon's coaching staff, rising to the post of manager in January 1992.

	LEAGUE		FACUP		FLCUP		EUROPE		TOTAL	
	App	Gls	App	Gls	App	Gls	App	Gls	App	Gls
1965-66	8	0	0	0	-	-	-	-	8	0
1966-67	19/1	0	7	0	1	0	-	-	27/1	0
1967-68	29/1	1	3	0	0	0	4	0	36/1	1
1968-69	24	0	1	0	6	0	-	-	31	0
1969-70	10	0	4	0	0	0	-	-	14	0
1970-71	35	0	5	0	7	0	-	-	47	0
1971-72	20/1	0	1	0	2	0	6	0	29/1	0
1972-73	24	1	1	0	4	0	6	0	35	1
1973-74	3/4	0	0	0	0	0	2	0	5/4	0
1974-75	17	0	2	0	0	0	-	-	19	0
1975-76	1	0	0	0	0	0	-	-	1	0
	190/7	2	24	0	20	0	18	0	252/7	2

JOE KINNEAR

John Kirwan was a very fast and exceptionally tricky left winger at the turn of the century. He would vary his tricks depending on the weaknesses of his opponents, and plenty of the credit for Sandy Brown's FA Cup scoring record in 1901 belonged to him. Kirwan was born in Wicklow, Ireland, and played for Southport before having a short spell with Everton in 1898. John Cameron partnered him for a time at Everton and obviously recognised the skills in the fair-haired winger, who won 17 caps for Ireland in his career and captained his country. Kirwan had been the subject of a dispute between Everton and Blackburn Rovers as to which club was entitled to his services, but at Tottenham he had the most stable period of his career. Signed in the summer of 1899, Kirwan stayed for six seasons, playing in the 1899-1900 Southern League championship and the 1901 FA Cup winning team. After the victory over Sheffield United, Kirwan was first to the match-ball and he kept it as a souvenir until he died. A total abstainer from drink and tobacco, he moved to Chelsea from Spurs, and later played for Clyde. He was good enough to be capped for Ireland as late as 1909.

	Southern		Western		FA CUP		TOTAL	
	App	Gls	App	Gls	App	Gls	App	Gls
1899-1900	29	13	0	0	1	0	30	13
1900-01	20	5	9	3	8	1	37	9
1901-02	28	9	14	9	3	1	45	19
1902-03	26	6	11	1	4	0	41	7
1903-04	28	4	12	2	5	0	45	6
1904-05	25	3	17	1	3	0	45	4
	156	40	63	16	24	2	243	58

JOHN KIRWAN

104

An extremely popular player, Cyril Knowles was a great attacking full-back, stylish and skilful. Born in Pontefract, his first professional club was Middlesbrough, for whom he signed in October 1962. He made his debut the following Easter and had made only 39 League appearances when he was signed by Spurs for £45,000 in May 1964. The brother of Peter Knowles, who gave up a professional career with Wolves to become a Jehovah's Witness, Cyril won six England Under-23 caps and four full caps in the late 1960s. A member of Spurs' FA Cup winning team in 1967, he also played in the 1971 and 1973 League Cup Final wins and the 1972 UEFA Cup success. He overcame the loss of his young son in a freak motorway accident and became a cult figure when the pop song *Nice One, Cyril* took off and the title became a national catchphrase.

From December 1973, Knowles was troubled by a serious knee injury. He added to his hero's reputation at the end of the 1974-5 season, when he scored against Leeds to help Spurs avoid relegation, but he broke down at the beginning of the next season. After a testimonial against Arsenal in October 1975, he retired the next year. Knowles stayed in football, coaching at Middlesbrough, and managing Darlington, Torquay United and Hartlepool United. A brain illness forced him to quit Hartlepool in June 1991 and he died two months later.

CYRIL KNOWLES

	LEAGUE		FA CUP		FL CUP		EUROPE		TOTAL	
	App	Gls	App	Gls	App	Gls	App	Gls	App	Gls
1964-65	38	0	4	0	-	-	-	-	42	0
1965-66	41	3	3	0	-	-	-	-	44	3
1966-67	42	1	8	0	1	0	-	-	51	1
1967-68	42	0	5	0	0	0	4	0	51	0
1968-69	36/1	2	4	0	5	0	-	-	45/1	2
1969-70	34	0	4	0	1	0	-	-	39	0
1970-71	38	0	5	0	6	0	-	-	49	0
1971-72	34	2	4	0	7	0	12	1	57	3
1972-73	35	0	3	1	10	0	10	0	58	1
1973-74	20	2	0	0	1	0	4	0	25	2
1974-75	31	5	2	0	0	0	-	-	33	5
1975-76	10	0	0	0	1/1	0	-	-	11/1	0
	401/1	15	42	1	32/1	0	30	1	505/2	17

Gary Lineker, signed by his home-town club, Leicester City, in December 1978, always looked to have the makings of a goalscorer but it was only on his transfer to Everton in June 1985 that he had the players around him to fully exploit his talent. He scored 40 goals in his season at Goodison, helping Everton finish runners-up to Liverpool in the League and FA Cup and winning him two Player of the Year awards. Although he had won seven full England caps at Leicester, his form at Everton elevated him to the position of England's number-one striker and in the 1986 World Cup he scored six goals to make him the competition's top scorer. Upon his return from Mexico, he moved to Terry Venables' Barcelona. Venables had been anxious to sign Lineker before the World Cup but Everton knew that a good performance would increase his value and Venables was forced to pay £2.5 million; Everton had paid Leicester only £800,000 barely a year earlier. He helped Barcelona finish runners-up in the League to Real Madrid in his first season and win the Spanish Cup in 1988. He had a poor European Championship in 1988 but it was later discovered that he had been suffering from hepatitis. When he recovered he found himself out of favour with Barcelona's new coach Johan Cruyff, although the fans were firmly behind him. He managed to end his Spanish career on a high note, setting up the goal that won the European Cup-winners' Cup in 1989. Venables had little difficulty in persuading Lineker to sign for Spurs in July 1989 at a bargain fee for a player still at the peak of his career. With Paul Gascoigne alongside him he scored 24 goals to head the First Division charts in his first season with Spurs. He continued in the same vein for both club and country, retiring from international football after the 1992 European Championships only one goal short of Bobby Charlton's record of 49. Announcing his departure from Spurs, he signed for Grampus Eight of Nagoya in November 1991, ready for the start of Japan's first professional football league in the summer of 1993. He was awarded the OBE in 1992.

GARY LINEKER

	LEAGUE		FA CUP		FL CUP		EUROPE		TOTAL	
	App	Gls	App	Gls	App	Gls	App	Gls	App	Gls
1989-90	38	24	1	0	6	2	-	-	45	26
1990-91	32	15	6	3	5	1	-	-	43	19
1991-92	35	28	2	0	5	5	8	2	50	35
	105	67	9	3	16	8	8	2	138	80

Bristol-born Gary Mabbutt has proved one of the most versatile players of the modern generation. He began his career as a striker but has played for England at full-back, central defender and midfield. At White Hart Lane he has been superbly consistent wherever he has been asked to play. Born in August 1961, the son of former Bristol Rovers player Ray Mabbutt, he signed apprentice for Rovers on his 16th birthday. He played for the England Youth and Under-21 teams before being transferred to Spurs for £105,000 in July 1982. Three months later he was in the full England team. Mabbutt was a member of the 1984 UEFA Cup winning team and played in the losing Spurs team in the 1987 FA Cup Final, when he became only the third player in history to score for both sides in an FA Cup Final. His achievements have been the more astounding because of his diabetic condition, and his stamina and athleticism have proved an inspiration to many other diabetics. In December 1987, he suffered a nasty head injury at Derby and had 16 stitches inserted into the wound. Happily, he was back in action within a couple of weeks. In May 1991, Mabbutt enjoyed the high point of his career, skippering Spurs to FA Cup glory.

	LEAGUE		FA CUP		FL CUP		OTHERS		TOTAL	
	App	Gls	App	Gls	App	Gls	App	Gls	App	Gls
1982-83	38	10	2/1	0	5	0	4	1	49/1	11
1983-84	21	2	2	0	2	0	7/2	2	32/2	4
1984-85	15/10	2	1/1	0	2/2	0	3/1	0	21/14	2
1985-86	29/3	3	5	0	5	1	-	-	39/3	4
1986-87	37	1	6	3	8	0	-	-	51	4
1987-88	37	2	2	0	3	0	-	-	42	2
1988-89	38	1	1	0	5	0	-	-	44	1
1989-90	36	0	1	0	7	1	-	-	44	1
1990-91	35	2	6	1	6	0	-	-	47	3
1991-92	40	2	2	0	6	0	8	1	56	3
1992-93	29	2	5	0	2	0	-	-	36	2
	355/13	27	33/2	4	51/2	2	22/3	4	461/20	37

GARY MABBUTT

Bob McDonald was a speedy, strong-tackling full-back who played in the FA Cup winning team of 1921. He was signed from Inverness Caledonians, where he played as an amateur, in August 1919, and he remained at Spurs until October 1927 when he moved to Clapton Orient. McDonald came to Spurs as a right-back but his way was initially barred by Tommy Clay's presence in the first team. McDonald played only once during the 1919-20 Second Division championship season, but early in the following season he came in for Bob Brown at left-back. He complemented Clay and won his FA Cup winners' medal in his first full season.

	LEAGUE		FA CUP		TOTAL	
	App	Gls	App	Gls	App	Gls
1919-20	1	0	0	0	1	0
1920-21	36	0	6	0	42	0
1921-22	40	0	6	0	46	0
1922-23	17	0	0	0	17	0
1923-24	3	0	0	0	3	0
1924-25	12	0	4	0	16	0
	109	0	16	0	125	0

BOB McDONALD

106

Edinburgh-born Dave Mackay, a Scottish schoolboy international, joined Spurs from Hearts in March 1959. The fee of £30,000 equalled the British record for a wing-half, set by Spurs when signing Blanchflower. A barrel-chested, craggy-faced warhorse, who never knew when he was beaten, Mackay is another contender for the mantle of greatest Spurs player of all time. He was only 5ft 8in and had no great pace, but a mere clap of his hands could inspire those around him, his long throw-in provoked much excitement and his great strength lay in his tackling. Much has been written about the Mackay tackle. Bryon Butler wrote that 'it could have earned him a good living felling trees, demolishing walls or breaking up tanks', and another writer likened it to a clap of thunder. A member of the 1960-61 'double' side and the 1962 FA Cup winning team, Mackay missed the 1963 European Cup-winners' Cup Final with a stomach injury. When Spurs attempted to retain their European trophy he broke a leg in the eighth minute of the game against Manchester United at Old Trafford. He broke the same leg in his comeback game, against Shrewsbury in the Football Combination, and only his tremendous fight brought him back to fitness. In 1967 he captained Spurs to an FA Cup Final victory. Capped 22 times for Scotland, he left for Derby County in July 1968, now a central defender. He led the Rams back into the First Division and was joint Footballer of the Year. It was yet another honour to add to his impressive stock, which included the major Scottish badges and representative honours for both the Scottish League and English League. He played until 1971 and then took up managerial responsibilities with Swindon Town, Nottingham Forest, Derby County (who won the League Championship under his charge) and Walsall. He spent nine years coaching in Kuwait before returning to manage Doncaster Rovers in 1987. He only stayed with Doncaster until March 1989 when he disagreed with the board over the sale of promising young players and resigned. He was soon back in management taking over at Birmingham City the following month but resigning in January 1991 with Birmingham struggling in the Third Division.

DAVE MACKAY

| | LEAGUE | | FA CUP | | EUROPE | | TOTAL | |
	App	Gls	App	Gls	App	Gls	App	Gls
1958-59	4	0	0	0	-	-	4	0
1959-60	38	11	3	0	-	-	41	11
1960-61	37	4	7	2	-	-	44	6
1961-62	26	8	7	0	7	2	40	10
1962-63	37	6	1	0	6	2	44	8
1963-64	17	3	0	0	2	1	19	4
1964-65	0	0	0	0	0	0	0	0
1965-66	41	6	2	2	-	-	43	8
1966-67	39	3	8	0	-	-	47	3
1967-68	29	1	5	0	2	0	36	1
	268	42	33	4	17	5	318	51

Tony Marchi was a solid, reliable defender who never received the credit he deserved during two lengthy spells with Spurs. Although his father was Italian, Marchi was London-born and he joined his local club as a professional in June 1950. In 1954, he settled into the left-half position and was an ever-present for two consecutive seasons in the mid-1950s. When he was transferred to Italian club, Lanerossi, for £40,000 in 1957, Marchi was Spurs' captain. The nephew of George Dorling, who played with Tottenham either side of World War Two, Marchi won England honours at schoolboy, Youth and 'B' levels but never graduated to the full international team. When Spurs re-signed him, from Juventus in July 1959, again for a big fee, Marchi became one of the finest — and probably the most costly — reserves in football. He played a few games during the famous 'double' season and made valuable contributions for a further four seasons. He captained Spurs in the 1963 European Cup-winners' Cup semi-final, yet only received his chance in the Final because of an injury to Dave Mackay. It was his only honour with Spurs. Marchi left the club in 1965.

| | LEAGUE | | FA CUP | | EUROPE | | TOTAL | |
	App	Gls	App	Gls	App	Gls	App	Gls
1949-50	2	0	0	0	0	0	2	0
1952-53	5	0	0	0	0	0	5	0
1953-54	8	1	0	0	0	0	8	1
1954-55	32	0	3	0	0	0	35	0
1955-56	42	1	6	0	0	0	48	1
1956-57	42	0	3	0	0	0	45	0
1959-60	14	1	1	0	0	0	15	1
1960-61	6	0	0	0	0	0	6	0
1961-62	21	0	0	0	5	0	26	0
1962-63	22	3	0	0	5	0	27	3
1963-64	21	0	1	0	2	0	24	1
1964-65	17	0	2	0	0	0	19	0
	232	7	16	0	12	0	260	7

TONY MARCHI

Such was the fluency and versatility of 'Push and Run' soccer that left-winger Les Medley was top goalscorer when Spurs won the Second Division championship in 1949-50 and he reached double figures when they won the League Championship the following season. He was a mobile winger who could appear in an inside-forward position and was always on the look-out for the game's action. His partnership with Eddie Baily dovetailed beautifully, while the left-wing triangle of Burgess, Baily and Medley was one to rival that of Grimsdell, Bliss and Dimmock in the 1920s. But Medley partnered other players in the 'Push and Run' era. When Alf Ramsey ran up to take a distant free-kick, Medley would often lounge on the edge of the penalty area group, then dart towards goal, timing his run and jump in accordance with the flight Ramsey had put on the ball. It is said that the move brought Spurs eight goals one season. Signed as an amateur in the summer of 1935, Medley was groomed at Northfleet before signing professional with Spurs in February 1939. He left Tottenham for Canada in 1946, as his wife was homesick, but returned in January 1948. He was a schoolboy international and Football League representative, played six times for England (four with Baily) and was never on the losing side. He retired in 1953 and emigrated to Canada.

LES MEDLEY

	LEAGUE		FA CUP		TOTAL	
	App	Gls	App	Gls	App	Gls
1945-46	-	-	1	0	1	0
1946-47	10	4	0	0	10	4
1947-48	2	0	1	0	3	0
1948-49	6	3	0	0	6	3
1949-50	42	18	3	1	45	19
1950-51	35	11	1	0	36	11
1951-52	34	8	2	0	36	8
1952-53	21	1	6	0	27	1
	150	45	14	1	164	46

A Welsh international signed from Swansea Town for £18,000 in May 1956, Terry Medwin could play on either wing and even at centre-forward if the need arose. He was reasonably tall, good in the air and a two-footed player who gave fine service with his excellent crosses from the wing. Born in Swansea, he grew up close to the Swansea Town ground, winning Welsh schoolboy international caps. He played 148 League games for Swansea, scoring 59 times, before his move to Spurs on the last day of the 1955-6 season. Capped by Wales when still only 21 years old, he won 29 caps altogether, all but the first three while with Spurs. Medwin had an excellent first season at White Hart Lane and Spurs finished second in Division One. Terry Dyson offered stiff competition for a wing place and Medwin was unfortunate not to be a regular in the 1960-61 'double' winning season, although he played 15 League and FA Cup games that season as deputy for either Jones or Dyson. In April 1959, he scored four goals against Leicester from the centre-forward position. Medwin gained some reward when he played in the 1962 FA Cup-winning team, but a broken leg on the 1963 tour of South Africa forced him into an early retirement.

TERRY MEDWIN

	LEAGUE		FA CUP		EUROPE		TOTAL	
	App	Gls	App	Gls	App	Gls	App	Gls
1956-57	37	14	2	2	-	-	39	16
1957-58	39	14	2	1	-	-	41	15
1958-59	35	14	1	0	-	-	36	14
1959-60	26	4	0	0	-	-	26	4
1960-61	14	5	1	0	-	-	15	5
1961-62	20	5	7	4	3	0	30	9
1962-63	26	9	0	0	2	0	28	9
	197	65	13	7	5	0	215	72

Born in Stepney, Paul Miller joined Spurs as an apprentice in April 1976 and was upgraded to full-time professional in May 1977. He spent a season with Skeid in the Norwegian League, then established himself as a Spurs regular. Although not an especially constructive player, Miller became effective as a central defender. He helped Spurs win successive FA Cup competitions, alongside Graham Roberts (in 1981) and Paul Price (in 1982). He also won a Milk Cup runners-up medal in 1982. In the first leg of the 1984 UEFA Cup Final, Miller headed in Hazard's corner to become the 11th Spurs player to score in the competition that season. The dramatic penalty shoot-out at White Hart Lane sealed Miller's third major trophy medal in three years, but he lost his first-team place in 1986 with the arrival of Richard Gough. Miller was transferred to Charlton Athletic in February 1987 later playing for Watford, Bournemouth and Brentford.

	LEAGUE		FACUP		FLCUP		EUROPE		TOTAL	
	App	Gls	App	Gls	App	Gls	App	Gls	App	Gls
1978-79	7	0	0	0	0	0	-	-	7	0
1979-80	27	2	6	0	2	0	-	-	35	2
1980-81	24/1	2	9	1	1	0	-	-	34/1	3
1981-82	35	0	6/1	0	8	0	7	1	56/1	1
1982-83	23	1	0	0	2	0	2	0	27	1
1983-84	20/1	0	3	0	0	0	6	1	29/1	1
1984-85	39	0	3	0	5	0	8	0	55	0
1985-86	29	2	3	0	2	0	-	-	34	2
1986-87	2	0	0	0	2/1	0	-	-	4/1	0
	206/2	7	30/1	1	22/1	0	23	2	281/4	10

PAUL MILLER

Grantham-born Tom Morris had the distinction of being the most southerly-born player in Tottenham's 1901 FA Cup winning team. He made his reputation as a dependable wing-half with Grantham Town and Gainsborough Trinity. Spurs signed him in 1899 and won the Southern League championship the following season. His robust, workmanlike play at right-half was a perfect foil to the more subtle skills of Jack Jones. Morris was the only member of the 1901 team to play in Spurs' first Football League game (in 1908) and he stayed with the club for 13 seasons, earning two benefits. Morris twice played in North-South England international trials but never won a full international cap.

	LEAGUE		Southern		Western		FA CUP		TOTAL	
	App	Gls	App	Gls	App	Gls	App	Gls	App	Gls
1899-1900	-	-	24	4	0	0	1	0	25	4
1900-01	-	-	19	3	12	4	8	0	39	7
1901-02	-	-	25	3	13	4	0	0	38	7
1902-03	-	-	25	3	10	0	4	0	39	3
1903-04	-	-	22	2	9	0	3	0	34	2
1904-05	-	-	28	3	16	2	4	0	48	5
1905-06	-	-	32	2	10	0	4	0	46	2
1906-07	-	-	33	1	4	0	7	0	44	1
1907-08	-	-	31	0	6	1	1	0	38	1
1908-09	24	1	-	-	-	-	3	1	27	2
1909-10	26	1	-	-	-	-	4	0	30	1
1910-11	11	0	-	-	-	-	0	0	11	0
1911-12	2	0	-	-	-	-	0	0	2	0
	63	2	239	21	80	11	39	1	421	35

TOM MORRIS

A midfield player signed from Fulham for £72,500 in March 1964, Alan Mullery had the unenviable task of succeeding Danny Blanchflower with a different style. Eventually he won over the fans and proved an inspirational captain after the departure of Mackay. Born in Notting Hill, Mullery signed professional for Fulham in December 1958 and helped his club to promotion to the First Division in his first season. He won three England Under-23 caps and went on to attain 35 full England caps, scoring against West Germany in the 1970 World Cup Finals. With Spurs, Mullery won an FA Cup winners' medal in 1967, and captained the team to successes in the League Cup (1971) and UEFA Cup (1972), scoring against Wolves in the Final of the latter competition after a pelvic-joint injury had kept him out for six months earlier in the season. He returned to Fulham for £65,000 in the 1972 close-season and in 1975 he won an FA Cup runners-up medal, was elected Footballer of the Year and awarded the MBE. In his first managerial job he helped Brighton into the First Division, and later he managed Charlton, Crystal Palace, Queen's Park Rangers and Brighton again.

ALAN MULLERY MBE

| | LEAGUE | | FACUP | | FLCUP | | EUROPE | | TOTAL | |
	App	Gls	App	Gls	App	Gls	App	Gls	App	Gls
1963-64	9	1	0	0	-	-	-	-	9	1
1964-65	42	2	4	0	-	-	-	-	46	2
1965-66	40	1	3	0	-	-	-	-	43	1
1966-67	39	5	8	0	1	0	-	-	48	5
1967-68	41	2	5	0	0	0	3	0	49	2
1968-69	41	1	4	0	6	0	-	-	51	1
1969-70	42	4	4	0	1	0	-	-	47	4
1970-71	41	6	5	1	7	0	-	-	53	7
1971-72	18	3	0	0	3	0	7	4	28	7
	313	25	33	1	18	0	10	4	374	30

A wholehearted defender, Islington-born Terry Naylor joined Spurs in July 1969 and stayed for more than 11 years. In the early 1970s, he generally played as a reserve central defender, coming in for Phil Beal, Peter Collins or Mike England, but Cyril Knowles' knee injury, in December 1973, brought him a chance at full-back. Naylor was in the team for both legs of the 1974 UEFA Cup Final. In 1975-6, following the departure of Kinnear and Evans, Naylor showed his versatility still further by playing in the number-two shirt in a reconstructed back-four consisting of Naylor, Young, Osgood and McAllister. Although Spurs were relegated in 1976-7, Naylor stayed to help the club to promotion the following season, always giving the impression that he would run until he dropped for the sake of Tottenham Hotspur. With Spurs back in Division One, Naylor was now in his 30s, and he moved to Charlton Athletic in November 1980.

TERRY NAYLOR

| | LEAGUE | | FACUP | | FLCUP | | EUROPE | | TOTAL | |
	App	Gls	App	Gls	App	Gls	App	Gls	App	Gls
1969-70	3	0	-	-	-	-	-	-	3	0
1970-71	3/1	0	2	0	0	0	-	-	5/1	0
1971-72	12	0	1	0	1	1	2/2	0	16/2	1
1972-73	14/2	0	1	0	7/1	0	3/3	0	25/6	0
1973-74	27/1	0	0	0	1	0	8/1	0	36/2	0
1974-75	37/1	0	2	0	1	0	-	-	40/1	0
1975-76	36	0	2	0	7	0	-	-	45	0
1976-77	40	0	1	0	2	0	-	-	43	0
1977-78	37	0	2	0	2	0	-	-	41	0
1978-79	22	0	5/1	0	2	0	-	-	29/1	0
1979-80	6/1	0	1	0	0	0	-	-	7/1	0
	237/6	0	17/1	0	23/1	1	13/6	0	290/14	1

110

A home-produced player, born in Chingford in 1950, Jimmy Neighbour signed professional forms for Spurs in November 1968 after being an apprentice with the club. As a winger he had to compete with Jimmy Pearce and Roger Morgan at first, but Neighbour's chance came in 1970-71 and he won a League Cup winners' medal after only a few first-team games. In the mid-1970s he became a regular choice under Terry Neill, then another change of managership, the appointment of Keith Burkinshaw, quickly brought the sale of Neighbour to Norwich for £75,000 in September 1976. On the same day Peter Taylor was signed from Crystal Palace for a much greater fee. It was that season that Spurs were relegated. After three years at Norwich he moved to West Ham. Although he did not play in the Hammers' FA Cup Final team in 1980, he was in their losing League Cup Final squad and helped them reach Wembley. Generally, Neighbour was a provider rather than a goalscorer, a strong-running and tricky winger.

	LEAGUE		FA CUP		FL CUP		EUROPE		TOTAL	
	App	Gls	App	Gls	App	Gls	App	Gls	App	Gls
1970-71	12/5	0	5	1	2/1	-	-	-	19/6	1
1971-72	12/2	1	2	0	2/1	0	3/1	0	19/4	1
1972-73	6/1	1	0	0	0/1	0	0/1	0	6/3	1
1973-74	11/3	0	1	0	0	0	3/1	1	15/4	1
1974-75	21/4	3	0/1	0	1	0	-	-	22/5	3
1975-76	35	3	2	0	7	0	-	-	44	3
1976-77	7	0	0	0	2	1	-	-	9	1
	104/15	8	10/1	1	14/3	1	6/3	1	134/22	11

JIMMY NEIGHBOUR

Bill Nicholson was not a spectacular player with breathtaking skills, but 'Push and Run' did not require two spectacular wing-halves. Instead, Nicholson was an unsettling opponent, a biting tackler who played simple passes and who never gave up when Spurs had lost the ball. He did not have the polish of a Ramsey or a Burgess, but he was a competent professional, deserving of the Second Division championship and League Championship honours he won in Arthur Rowe's great team. Born in Scarborough in January 1919, he joined Spurs as an amateur in 1936, was groomed at Northfleet for a couple of years and then signed professional in August 1938. He made his League debut at left-back early in the 1938-9 season and throughout his career also proved capable of deputising in his original position of centre-half. But it was as a wing-half, for eight seasons after World War Two, that Nicholson achieved fame. He played for England once, against Portugal in 1951, when he showed his typical long-range shooting powers by scoring with his first kick. He missed another cap through injury. Nicholson became club coach in 1954, assistant-manager in August 1957 and finally manager in October 1958.

	LEAGUE		FA CUP		TOTAL	
	App	Gls	App	Gls	App	Gls
1938-39	8	0	0	0	8	0
1939-40	3	0	-	-	3	0
1946-47	39	0	2	0	41	0
1947-48	38	0	5	0	43	0
1948-49	42	2	1	0	43	2
1949-50	39	2	3	0	42	2
1950-51	41	1	1	0	42	1
1951-52	37	1	2	0	39	1
1952-53	31	0	7	0	38	0
1953-54	30	0	6	0	36	0
1954-55	10	0	0	0	10	0
	318	6	27	0	345	6

BILL NICHOLSON

111

Norfolk-born Maurice Norman joined Spurs from Norwich City for £18,000 in November 1955. At first he played for Spurs as a full-back, but he made his name as a solid, uncompromising centre-half in the 'double' team. A giant player, whose hairstyle made him appear even taller than 6ft 1in, he was beautifully built and awesomely efficient. His long legs could lunge into unexpected tackles, he was a commanding figure in the air and an early exponent of joining his forwards for an attacking corner-kick. Norman was born in Mulbarton and was on the groundstaff at Norwich before Jimmy Anderson engineered a deal which saw Johnny Gavin go from Spurs to Carrow Road. Norman won three England Under-23 caps, then had a long wait for full international honours, often being a reserve to the England team. His chance came in the 1962 World Cup Finals and he went on to win 23 caps. Aside from his 1960-61 club honours, he won an FA Cup winners' medal the next season and was in the 1963 European Cup-winners' Cup winning team. He suffered a broken left leg during a friendly with a Hungarian XI in November 1965 and was forced to retire two years later without playing again.

MAURICE NORMAN

	LEAGUE		FA CUP		EUROPE		TOTAL	
	App	Gls	App	Gls	App	Gls	App	Gls
1955-56	27	1	6	1	-	-	33	2
1956-57	16	0	0	0	-	-	16	0
1957-58	33	1	2	0	-	-	35	1
1958-59	35	3	4	0	-	-	39	3
1959-60	39	1	4	0	-	-	43	1
1960-61	41	4	7	0	-	-	48	4
1961-62	40	0	7	0	8	0	55	0
1962-63	38	1	1	0	7	1	46	2
1963-64	42	3	2	0	2	0	46	3
1964-65	30	1	4	1	-	-	34	2
1965-66	16	1	0	0	-	-	16	1
	357	16	37	2	17	1	411	19

'Taffy' O'Callaghan was a star of Tottenham's forward line throughout the late 1920s and early 1930s. He was a clever player who packed a good shot in either foot and he scored plenty of goals for the club. O'Callaghan was born in Ebbw Vale in October 1906 and signed for Tottenham in 1924. At first he was loaned to Barnet and Northfleet but after gaining a League place he soon became a favourite with the White Hart Lane crowd who appreciated his dash and flair. He replaced the injured Jimmy Seed and did so well that Seed was unable to regain his place and eventually left the club for Sheffield Wednesday. O'Callaghan, meanwhile, went from strength to strength. He won 11 Welsh caps and scored twice when Wales beat Scotland 5-2 in October 1932. He spent ten years at Spurs before joining Leicester City in March 1935 and won a Second Division championship medal with the Midlands club in 1936-7. When Jack Peart, the former Ebbw Vale player-coach, was appointed Fulham manager he remembered the player from his days in Wales and O'Callaghan signed for the Cottagers in October 1937. He played for them until 1945-6, then worked on the training staff until his death in July 1956.

EUGENE 'TAFFY' O'CALLAGHAN

	LEAGUE		FA CUP		TOTAL	
	App	Gls	App	Gls	App	Gls
1926-27	13	5	0	0	13	5
1927-28	42	19	4	5	46	24
1928-29	36	9	1	0	37	9
1929-30	10	4	0	0	10	4
1930-31	37	9	1	0	38	9
1931-32	34	17	2	0	36	17
1932-33	32	14	2	1	34	15
1933-34	32	11	0	0	32	11
1934-35	16	4	1	0	17	4
	252	92	11	6	263	98

The son of an Army colonel, Frank Osborne was born in Wynberg, South Africa, and came to England in 1911, joining amateur club Bromley in 1919. His talent as a goalscorer was soon spotted and in 1921 he signed for Fulham, making 70 League and Cup appearances and winning two England caps in two-and-a-half seasons at Craven Cottage. In January 1924, Tottenham paid a large fee for his signature and over the next seven seasons he made over 200 senior appearances, scoring over 80 goals. He would probably have scored more had he played regularly at centre-forward — his first England cap had come in that position and his second at outside-right — but his slight build was considered more suitable to the wing. There is no doubt, however, that when he was given the centre-forward berth, he had an excellent scoring record. To emphasise his versatility, Osborne won two more caps as a Spurs player, again at centre-forward and on the wing, and it was as leader of the attack that he scored a hat-trick against Belgium in May 1926. He moved to Southampton in June 1931, his career now drawing to a close, but soon returned to London and subsequently became manager of Fulham and then a director of that club.

FRANK OSBORNE.

	LEAGUE		FA CUP		TOTAL	
	App	Gls	App	Gls	App	Gls
1923-24	12	1	-	-	12	1
1924-25	23	0	3	0	26	0
1925-26	39	25	1	2	40	27
1926-27	34	9	0	0	34	9
1927-28	31	18	3	1	34	19
1928-29	33	16	1	0	34	16
1929-30	32	9	2	1	34	10
1930-31	6	0	0	0	6	0
	210	78	10	4	220	82

FRANK OSBORNE

A little after 10.30pm on a May evening in 1984, one moment in Tony Parks' life sealed another glorious night in Spurs' history. Under the White Hart Lane floodlights, an Anderlecht player dressed in mauve strode up to take yet another penalty in the shoot-out. Parks dived to his right, clawed the ball away and immediately erupted into the celebrations of youth. It was his second save in that shoot-out and it brought the 1984 UEFA Cup to Spurs. Parks was only 21 then, and second choice to Ray Clemence, his standing for most of his time with the club which he joined as a professional in September 1980. Before he played the first leg of that UEFA Cup Final, he had appeared in only 18 League games. Like Aleksic before him, he was around at a time of glory. In 1987-8, when Clemence was again sidelined through injury, Parks' career was resurrected with a prolonged spell of First Division football. However Terry Venables' arrival in December 1988 Parks was unable to perform to the standard required and, with the signing Bobby Mimms, was allowed to leave in July 1988 when he joined former Spurs skipper Steve Perryman at Brentford. Parks later played for Queen's Park Rangers, Fulham, Southend United, West Ham United and Falkirk.

	LEAGUE		FACUP		FLCUP		EUROPE		TOTAL	
	App	Gls	App	Gls	App	Gls	App	Gls	App	Gls
1981-82	2	0	0	0	0	0	-	-	2	0
1982-83	1	0	0	0	0	0	0/1	0	1/1	0
1983-84	16	0	3	0	0	0	5	0	24	0
1986-87	2	0	0	0	0	0	-	-	2	0
1987-88	16	0	2	0	1	0	-	-	19	0
	37	0	5	0	1	0	5/1	0	48/1	0

TONY PARKS

Signed as a professional in May 1965, Jimmy Pearce could play in midfield or in any attacking position, although it was as a more orthodox winger that he had his best spells with Spurs. He was very skilful but perhaps not consistent enough to make a first-team place his own. Tottenham-born, in 1947, an England schoolboy international and an apprentice at Spurs, he had the unenviable task of following transfer-trail wingers like Cliff Jones, Terry Medwin and Jimmy Robertson. He was unfortunate to be omitted from the 1971 League Cup Final team and named substitute — he did not appear — especially after he had scored in the semi-final, but there was some compensation in gaining a League Cup winners' medal two years later. In general, he was in and out of the team, often used as a substitute (in 33 League games alone). However, in 1973, he was forced to yield to a serious injury, a rare bone complaint, although still only 26 years old. He retired from League football, took a year off, then played for Walthamstow Avenue.

Steve Perryman first came to prominence with Ealing Schoolboys, playing for England at that level. Signed as an apprentice in July 1967, he turned professional in January 1969 and when he played in the 1970 FA Youth Cup winning team he was already a first-team player. After making his League debut in September 1969, Perryman hardly missed a game until he left to join Oxford United in March 1986. He played in over 1,000 first-team games for Spurs — the only player to do so. Originally a midfield player, he dropped into the back-four in 1977 and later played as a full-back. He won more Spurs honours than any other player — League Cup winner (1971 & 1973), UEFA Cup winner (1972), captain of two winning FA Cup Final teams (1981 & 1982) and captain of the 1984 UEFA Cup winners, although he had to miss the second leg through suspension. He had won a UEFA Cup runners-up medal 10 years earlier. His only England cap was as a substitute against Iceland in June 1982, although he was in Ron Greenwood's 40-player pool for the World Cup Finals that summer. That season he was also voted Footballer of the Year. He was awarded a testimonial in April 1979 (against West Ham United), and he received the MBE in the Queen's 1986 Birthday Honours List. Steve Perryman will be remembered as the great professional, a superb club man who attained the club's record appearances. In fact, his last game, in a friendly at Brentford, came as late as May 1986, two months after he had joined Oxford. Perryman was later appointed Brentford's player-manager. In August 1990 he suprisingly resigned from Brentford but three months later took over as manager of Watford on the dismissal of his former Spurs teammate Colin Lee.

JIMMY PEARCE

	LEAGUE		FACUP		FLCUP		EUROPE		TOTAL	
	App	Gls	App	Gls	App	Gls	App	Gls	App	Gls
1968-69	24/3	3	2	0	5	2	-	-	31/3	5
1969-70	26/6	7	2/2	2	1	0	-	-	29/8	9
1970-71	23/10	2	0	0	3/3	2	-	-	26/13	4
1971-72	9/6	5	0/1	0	3/2	2	0/5	1	12/14	8
1972-73	27/8	4	0/3	1	9/1	1	8/2	3	44/14	9
	109/33	21	4/6	3	21/6	7	8/7	4	142/52	35

	LEAGUE		FACUP		FLCUP		EUROPE		TOTAL	
	App	Gls	App	Gls	App	Gls	App	Gls	App	Gls
1969-70	24	1	4	0	0	0	-	-	28	1
1970-71	42	3	5	0	6	1	-	-	53	4
1971-72	39	1	5	0	6	1	12	3	62	5
1972-73	41	2	3	0	10	1	10	0	64	3
1973-74	39	1	1	0	1	0	12	0	53	1
1974-75	42	6	2	0	1	0	-	-	45	6
1975-76	40	6	2	1	6	0	-	-	48	7
1976-77	42	1	1	0	2	0	-	-	45	1
1977-78	42	1	2	0	2	0	-	-	46	1
1978-79	42	1	7	1	2	0	-	-	51	2
1979-80	40	1	6	0	2	0	-	-	48	1
1980-81	42	2	9	0	6	0	-	-	57	2
1981-82	42	1	7	0	8	0	8	0	65	1
1982-83	32/1	1	3	0	2	0	2/1	0	39/2	1
1983-84	41	1	4	0	3	0	11	0	59	1
1984-85	42	1	3	0	5	0	8	0	58	1
1985-86	22/1	1	5	0	4	0	-	-	31/1	1
	654/2	31	69	2	66	3	63/1	3	852/3	39

114

STEVE PERRYMAN MBE

The signing of Martin Peters followed in the Spurs tradition of signings like Cliff Jones, Jimmy Greaves and Martin Chivers — a British record payment for a player's transfer. In March 1970, Peters was valued at £200,000, and the deal included Jimmy Greaves' transfer to West Ham. Peters was still only 26 years old but very experienced on the international stage. He had been capped for England at schoolboy, Youth, Under-23 and full level, and his role in England's 1966 World Cup victory was already legendary. He took a time to settle at Spurs but in five years with the club, he won two League Cup winners' medal, taking his international-cap haul to 67 in the process. A midfield player, with the knack of scoring goals from blind-side runs, Peters was Spurs' captain after the departure of Alan Mullery. His next club was Norwich City, who had full value for their £50,000 outlay with five seasons of top-class play, mainly in the First Division. Peters finished his career as player-manager of Sheffield United.

MARTIN PETERS

	LEAGUE		FA CUP		FL CUP		EUROPE		TOTAL	
	App	Gls	App	Gls	App	Gls	App	Gls	App	Gls
1969-70	7	2	0	0	0	0	-	-	7	2
1970-71	42	9	5	2	7	4	-	-	54	15
1971-72	35	10	5	2	7	3	12	2	59	17
1972-73	41	15	3	1	8	5	8	3	60	24
1973-74	35	6	1	0	1	0	12	8	49	14
1974-75	29	4	2	0	0	0	-	-	31	4
	189	46	16	5	23	12	32	13	260	76

115

Hackney-born John Pratt, a non-stop midfield player, signed as a professional for Spurs in November 1965 and made his debut in March 1969. An injury to Alan Mullery gave him an extended run in 1971-2 and, alongside midfield colleagues Perryman and Peters, he prompted attacks neatly. He won a UEFA Cup winners' medal that season. The following year he helped Spurs reach Wembley but, after 20 minutes of the League Cup Final against Norwich, he was forced to leave the field injured. It proved to be his only Wembley appearance. In 1974, he won a UEFA Cup runners-up medal and he was ever-present in the Second Division promotion team (1977-8). He was granted a testimonial in May 1978, against Arsenal. He moved to Portland Timbers in May 1980 but returned to Spurs in January 1983 as youth-team manager. Pratt continued to play in an occasional friendly and had spells as reserve-team manager and assistant to Peter Shreeve before he left the club again in May 1986.

JOHN PRATT

	LEAGUE		FA CUP		FL CUP		EUROPE		TOTAL	
	App	Gls	App	Gls	App	Gls	App	Gls	App	Gls
1968-69	8/1	0	0	0	0	0	-	-	8/1	0
1969-70	12	1	0	0	0/1	0	-	-	12/1	1
1970-71	4/2	0	2	0	1	0	-	-	7/2	0
1971-72	15/8	1	2	1	4	0	5/1	0	26/9	2
1972-73	37/1	5	3	1	10	2	7	1	57/1	9
1973-74	35	4	1	0	0/1	0	12	0	48/1	4
1974-75	27/2	1	2	0	1	0	-	-	30/2	1
1975-76	41	10	2	0	7	3	-	-	50	13
1976-77	30/4	4	1	0	0/2	0	-	-	31/6	4
1977-78	42	7	2	0	2	1	-	-	46	8
1978-79	37/1	4	7	0	0	0	-	-	44/1	4
1979-80	19/5	2	1/5	0	2	1	-	-	22/10	3
	307/24	39	23/5	2	27/4	7	24/1	1	381/34	49

A £250,000 signing from Luton Town in June 1981, Welsh international Paul Price found his early days at Spurs thwarted by injury setbacks. He waited a long time to impress himself on the Tottenham public but started a successful run in January 1982, starting 18 League games that season plus what seemed like as many in the various Cups. He won an FA Cup winners' medal against Queen's Park Rangers and a Milk Cup runners-up medal against Liverpool. But that was the pinnacle of his time at Spurs, and in the summer of 1984 he joined Minnesota Strikers on trial. On his return to the UK he played for Swansea City, Saltash United, Peterborough United, Chelmsford City and Wivenhoe before joining his home-town team St Albans City. Earlier in his career he had spent 10 years with Luton Town, and Spurs provided the opposition for his testimonial there in October 1981. Capped for Wales at Under-21 level, he went on to earn 11 full international caps.

PAUL PRICE

	LEAGUE		FA CUP		FL CUP		EUROPE		TOTAL	
	App	Gls	App	Gls	App	Gls	App	Gls	App	Gls
1981-82	18/3	0	5	0	3	0	4	0	30/3	0
1982-83	16	0	1	0	3	0	4	0	24	0
1983-84	1/1	0	0	0	1	0	2	0	4/1	0
	35/4	0	6	0	7	0	10	0	58/4	0

Alf Ramsey, Spurs' unflamboyant and unflappable right-back between May 1949 and May 1955, was a grocer's boy from Dagenham. Educated at Becontree High School, he was invited to join Southampton as a professional in 1944 after he had played against them for an Army team. When he moved to Spurs the deal was worth £21,000 — Welsh international Ernie Jones moved in the opposite direction — and Ramsey was the only one of the famous 'Push and Run' team to cost a large fee, a stark contrast to the expensive Spurs 'double' team. He was the final piece in the jigsaw which brought the Second Division championship and League title to White Hart Lane. Nicknamed 'The General', he rarely wasted a pass, developed a fine understanding with goalkeeper Ted Ditchburn, was studiously accurate from free-kicks and penalties, and even scored a fine individual goal against Grimsby in the Second Division championship season. It was a bold move for a Second Division side to pay a record fee (for a full-back) for a 29-year-old player but Ramsey proved almost irreplaceable. He took over as captain when Burgess left and captained England in Billy Wright's absence. He won 32 caps, including 29 in succession, and three times scored penalty goals for his country. He later managed Ipswich Town (League Champions in 1961-2), and his high-workrate, wingerless England team won the 1966 World Cup. In January 1967 he was knighted, and he later managed Birmingham City.

SIR ALF RAMSEY

	LEAGUE		FA CUP		TOTAL	
	App	Gls	App	Gls	App	Gls
1949-50	41	4	3	0	44	4
1950-51	40	4	1	0	41	4
1951-52	38	5	2	0	40	5
1952-53	37	6	9	0	46	6
1953-54	37	2	6	0	43	2
1954-55	33	3	3	0	36	3
	226	24	24	0	250	24

Charlie Rance, an ex-Clapton amateur player, gave Tottenham Hotspur great service between 1911 and 1921. He was an immaculate centre-half, hard-working and determined, and his displays in the early 1910s contributed much to Spurs' ability to retain their First Division status. During World War One, Rance made more appearances for Spurs than any other player and he remained first-choice centre-half for the 1919-20 Second Division championship season. In the next season, he lost his place to Charlie Walters just before Spurs set off on their run to the FA Cup Final. Rance was transferred to Derby County in March 1921, and moved back to London to join Queen's Park Rangers in September 1922.

CHARLIE RANCE

	LEAGUE		FA CUP		TOTAL	
	App	Gls	App	Gls	App	Gls
1910-11	11	0	0	0	11	0
1911-12	18	0	1	0	19	0
1912-13	33	1	3	1	36	2
1913-14	0	0	0	0	0	0
1914-15	3	0	0	0	3	0
1919-20	26	0	3	0	29	0
1920-21	14	0	0	0	14	0
	105	1	7	1	112	2

A hard midfielder or central defender, Graham Roberts joined Spurs in May 1980 from Weymouth. The fee of £35,000 was the most ever paid for a non-League player. Roberts had signed schoolboy forms with Southampton, his home-town club, then moved on to have spells as an amateur with Bournemouth and Portsmouth, where he broke an ankle. From Dorchester he went to Weymouth, where he was part-time, working as a shipyard fitter's mate until Spurs signed him full-time. A year later he was playing in the centenary FA Cup Final, spitting out two broken teeth before helping Spurs win the trophy after a replay. The next season he earned a second FA Cup winners' medal; his long attacking run early in the 1982 replay brought the penalty from which Glenn Hoddle scored the winning goal. In 1984, Roberts, captaining Spurs in the second leg of the UEFA Cup Final against Anderlecht, poked in a goal 12 minutes from time to equalise the scores. It was a true fairy-tale rise for he was still only 25 years old. In December 1986, soon after David Pleat's arrival as manager, Roberts was transferred to Glasgow Rangers. He soon became a favourite of the Ibrox supporters but, after a row with manager Graeme Souness, was transferred to Chelsea in May 1988. He helped them to promotion to the First Division in 1989 but then rowed with chairman Ken Bates and in November 1990 was transferred to West Bromwich Albion. Released by West Brom at the end of the 1991-2 season he returned to north London joining Spurs' non-League neighbours Enfield.

GRAHAM ROBERTS

	LEAGUE		FACUP		FLCUP		EUROPE		TOTAL	
	App	Gls	App	Gls	App	Gls	App	Gls	App	Gls
1980-81	21/3	0	9	1	0/1	0	-	-	30/4	1
1981-82	35/2	6	6	0	5	0	6/1	1	52/3	7
1982-83	20/4	2	2	0	2	0	-	-	24/4	2
1983-84	35	6	4	1	3	0	12	4	54	11
1984-85	40	7	3	0	4	1	7	1	54	9
1985-86	32	1	3	0	6	2	-	-	41	3
1986-87	17	1	0	0	4	2	-	-	21	3
	200/9	23	27	2	24/1	5	25/1	6	276/11	36

Signed for Spurs from St Mirren in March 1964, Jimmy Robertson was a fast, flying winger who had previously played for Cowdenbeath. Born in Glasgow in 1944, he was still young when signed and was undoubtedly a fine prospect. He played for Scotland against Wales soon after he came south — this was his only full cap —and he won four Under-23 caps. He was a perfect supplier for Greaves and Gilzean, and a popular star in the 1966-7 team, which reached Wembley and finished third in Division One. At Wembley, against Chelsea, Robertson's long-range shot registered the first goal of the game and Spurs went on to win the FA Cup. He could play on either wing, though was more often seen on the right. In October 1968, he moved to Arsenal in a deal which brought David Jenkins the other way and which was perhaps not one of Bill Nicholson's best. Robertson still had a lot of football left in him and he made four more moves — to Ipswich (March 1970), Stoke (June 1972), Walsall (September 1977) and Crewe (September 1978).

	LEAGUE		FACUP		FLCUP		EUROPE		TOTAL	
	App	Gls	App	Gls	App	Gls	App	Gls	App	Gls
1963-64	3	1	-	-	-	-	-	-	3	1
1964-65	36	7	4	1	-	-	-	-	40	8
1965-66	33	6	3	0	-	-	-	-	36	6
1966-67	40	5	8	1	1	0	-	-	49	6
1967-68	33/1	5	3	1	0	0	4	3	40/1	9
1968-69	8/3	1	0	0	1	0	-	-	9/3	1
	153/4	25	18	3	2	0	4	3	177/4	31

JIMMY ROBERTSON

Although most famous for his success as manager of the 'Push and Run' team of the early 1950s, it was as a centre-half throughout the 1930s that Arthur Rowe's deep affection for Tottenham Hotspur was developed. Born in 1906, only a stone's throw from White Hart Lane, Rowe seemed destined to make his name with the club. He enjoyed great success as a schoolboy footballer and in local junior soccer with Cheshunt before moving to Northfleet, Tottenham's nursery club in Kent. In May 1929, Spurs signed him as a professional and following his League debut in October 1931 he quickly established himself as first-choice centre-half. Rowe was almost an ever-present during the next two seasons as Spurs climbed out of Division Two and reached third place in Division One. Unlike many of his contemporaries, Rowe was not a purely 'stopper' centre-half. Indeed, he always sought to be constructive and some of his theories as a player were put to good effect when he became a manager. The highlight of Rowe's playing career came in December 1933 when he was selected to play for England against France at White Hart Lane. After that, injury severely restricted his appearances. His absences began to prove costly and at the end of the

1933-4 season, Tottenham were relegated. They were unable to regain their First Division place until Arthur Rowe returned to the club as manager.

	LEAGUE		FA CUP		TOTAL	
	App	Gls	App	Gls	App	Gls
1931-32	29	0	2	0	31	0
1932-33	41	0	0	0	41	0
1933-34	42	0	3	0	45	0
1934-35	18	0	0	0	18	0
1935-36	28	0	6	0	34	0
1936-37	15	0	5	0	20	0
1937-38	9	0	3	0	12	0
	182	0	19	0	201	0

ARTHUR ROWE

Born Canvey Island, Frank Saul joined the Spurs groundstaff from school and signed professional in August 1960. When 15 he played in the Football Combination and he became an England Youth international. During the 'double' season, as a teenage centre-forward deputy for Bobby Smith, he made as many League appearances as Tony Marchi (six) and was never on the losing side. Yet chances were limited during his stay at Spurs of over seven years, even though he could play on either wing. He appeared in early European games, was a star of the 1967 FA Cup run, but never played as much as two-thirds of any League campaign. His biggest moment of glory came in 1967 when his instinctive turn and shot hit the target for Spurs' second goal against Chelsea at Wembley. He had also scored in the semi-final against Nottingham Forest. This was his only honour with Tottenham. He moved to Southampton in January 1968 as part of the deal which

brought Martin Chivers to Spurs. He also had spells with Queen's Park Rangers and Millwall.

	LEAGUE		FACUP		FLCUP		EUROPE		TOTAL	
	App	Gls	App	Gls	App	Gls	App	Gls	App	Gls
1960-61	6	3	0	0	-	-	-	-	6	3
1961-62	8	3	0	0	-	-	2	2	10	5
1962-63	10	4	0	0	-	-	2	0	12	4
1963-64	2	0	0	0	-	-	-	-	2	0
1964-65	23	11	0	0	-	-	-	-	23	11
1965-66	26	8	3	3	-	-	-	-	29	11
1966-67	20/2	4	4	3	1	0	-	-	25/2	7
1967-68	17/2	4	0	0	-	-	1	0	18/2	4
	112/4	37	7	6	1	0	5	2	125/4	45

FRANK SAUL

Jimmy Seed was a brainy player, an inside-forward with excellent vision and a good shot. His career was a romantic rags-to-riches story, every setback acting as a catalyst to greater achievement. A Durham boy, born at Blackwell in 1895, he joined Sunderland just before World War One. On returning from military duty he found himself released by Sunderland, ostensibly on the scrapheap at 24 and still recovering from a slight gas attack during active service. He was signed by Mid-Rhondda and, like Jock Stein 30 years later, was to have his playing career resurrected and later achieve great managerial glory after a spell with a Welsh club. Spurs signed Seed in February 1920 and he won an FA Cup winners' medal the next season, scoring three goals in one tie against Bradford City. He was a fine tactician, capped five times for England in the early 1920s, and dropped into an even deeper link role after the change in offside law in 1925. Seed was an automatic choice until 1927, when an injury allowed Taffy O'Callaghan to take his place. His transfer to Sheffield Wednesday in August 1927 was probably the worst deal in Spurs' history. Spurs went down to the Second Division and Seed captained Wednesday to two League titles. His first administrative job was as secretary-manager to Clapton

	LEAGUE		FA CUP		TOTAL	
	App	Gls	App	Gls	App	Gls
1919-20	5	2	0	0	5	2
1920-21	36	12	6	5	42	17
1921-22	36	10	6	3	42	13
1922-23	36	9	5	2	41	11
1923-24	21	2	0	0	21	2
1924-25	41	17	5	2	46	19
1925-26	31	6	2	0	33	6
1926-27	23	7	1	0	24	7
	229	65	25	12	254	77

Orient, then in 23 years as Charlton Athletic manager he brought them from Third to First Division and into two FA Cup Finals, one victorious. He also had spells in charge of Bristol City and Millwall.

JIMMY SEED

Prior to World War One, Bert Smith had played as a forward for Metrogas and Huddersfield Town. During the war he played in the same services' team as Bert Bliss, whose recommendation led to Smith's transfer to Spurs in August 1919. They converted him to wing-half where he won two England caps and an FA Cup winners' medal. In 1921, he was one of four Spurs players — the others were Grimsdell, Bliss and Dimmock — who played for England against Scotland. Often overshadowed by the more illustrious left-half, Arthur Grimsdell, Smith was an unsung hero of the 1919-20 Second Division championship team and sides through the 1920s. He was a strong defensive player, a hard-working man who complemented the skills of others. He remained with Spurs until May 1930 when he became coach of the young players at the Northfleet nursery club. He also coached in Switzerland and worked with non-League clubs. Born in Higham, Kent, his first clubs had been Vanbrugh Park and Crawford United.

	LEAGUE		FA CUP		TOTAL	
	App	Gls	App	Gls	App	Gls
1919-20	40	2	4	0	44	2
1920-21	36	3	6	1	42	4
1921-22	25	0	6	0	31	0
1922-23	32	2	5	0	37	2
1923-24	41	1	1	0	42	1
1924-25	37	1	2	0	39	1
1925-26	38	0	3	0	41	0
1926-27	24	0	1	0	25	0
1927-28	8	0	0	0	8	0
1928-29	10	0	0	0	10	0
	291	9	28	1	319	10

BERT SMITH

Bobby Smith was probably the last of England's shoulder-charging, battering-ram centre-forwards, a big, bustling, round-faced, round-bodied player who was intimidating to centre-halves and a goalkeeper's nightmare. He broke Spurs' career-aggregate goal-scoring record, scored 36 League goals in one season (1957-8), top-scored in the 'double' season, scored in two FA Cup Finals, scored eight times in his first five England games, and yet there were still many who said he could not play. The son of a Yorkshire miner, Smith was born in Lingdale and first played for Redcar United. He joined the Chelsea groundstaff and made his first-team debut when only 17, helping Chelsea to avoid relegation. After six years at Chelsea he came to Spurs for £18,000 in December 1955. He played in all the trophy-winning teams of the early 1960s and his goals were often crucial — two in the 1961 semi-final against Burnley, the leading goal against Leicester at Wembley, putting Spurs ahead again in the 1962 FA Cup Final. The latter, scored with socks rolled down, followed a subtle turn which belied his physical bulk, and, indeed, there were many other moments of class, like his chipped goal against Spain, one of 13 he scored for England in 15 internationals. After 1962 his career

became more chequered; he lost his place to Les Allen in 1962-3 for a time, and was sacked by his next club, Brighton, over newspaper articles. Brighton had paid £5,000 for him in May 1964 and they were Fourth Division champions in Smith's only season with them. Having put on weight, Smith finished his career with Hastings United.

BOBBY SMITH

	LEAGUE		FA CUP		EUROPE		TOTAL	
	App	Gls	App	Gls	App	Gls	App	Gls
1955-56	21	10	6	3	-	-	27	13
1956-57	33	18	3	1	-	-	36	19
1957-58	38	36	2	2	-	-	40	38
1958-59	36	32	4	3	-	-	40	35
1959-60	40	25	4	5	-	-	44	30
1960-61	36	28	7	5	-	-	43	33
1961-62	26	6	4	3	6	6	36	15
1962-63	15	8	1	0	6	4	22	12
1963-64	26	13	1	0	2	0	29	13
	271	176	32	22	14	10	317	208

Signed from Preston North End in the summer of 1898, Tom Smith was an extremely speedy winger who hugged the touch-line and sent over accurate centres to create goals for John Cameron, David Copeland and, in particular, Sandy Brown. For four seasons he was rarely absent from the outside-right spot, and didn't miss a Southern League game in 1898-9. He was a regular in the 1899-1900 Southern League title team and then helped Spurs win the FA Cup for the first time. In the 1901 FA Cup Final replay, Tom Smith put Spurs 2-1 ahead and on the way to the trophy. He officially retired at the end of the 1901-02 season but subsequently turned out again for Preston North End.

TOM SMITH

	Southern		Western		United		FA CUP		TOTAL	
	App	Gls	App	Gls	App	Gls	App	Gls	App	Gls
1898-99	26	10	-	-	18	2	10	1	54	13
1899-1900	28	7	-	-	-	-	1	0	29	7
1900-01	17	4	6	2	-	-	8	1	31	7
1901-02	23	4	12	2	-	-	1	0	36	6
	94	25	18	4	18	2	20	2	150	33

Gary Stevens was signed by Spurs as a central defender in the summer of 1983 after his displays in that year's FA Cup Final had attracted national attention. Playing for Brighton he had defended brilliantly in the first game before scoring a late equaliser which took the game to extra-time and almost produced a surprise outcome against Manchester United, who won the replay comfortably. Spurs paid £300,000 for Stevens' services but he was unable to establish himself as a central defender at White Hart Lane. However, as a midfield player he proved highly successful, even winning himself a place in the England team. First capped against Finland as a substitute in October 1984 he became England's 'super-sub' of the 1980s. Stevens, who played for Spurs in the 1984 UEFA Cup-winners team, had his career disrupted by injuries and when he returned to the Tottenham team, it was as a fullback. Born in 1962, he joined Brighton as an apprentice and made his League debut in September 1982. In March 1990 Stevens left White Hart Lane to join Portsmouth after spending two months on loan at Fratton Park proving his fitness. Unfortunately injuries continued to blight his career and in February 1992 he retired to concentrate on a new career as a match summariser for radio.

GARY STEVENS

	LEAGUE		FA CUP		FL CUP		EUROPE		TOTAL	
	App	Gls	App	Gls	App	Gls	App	Gls	App	Gls
1983-84	37/3	4	4	0	3	0	9	1	53/3	5
1984-85	28	0	3	0	5	0	6	2	42	2
1985-86	28/1	2	5	0	5	0	-	-	38/1	2
1986-87	20	0	1/4	0	2/1	0	-	-	23/5	0
1987-88	18	0	0	0	2	0			20	0
1988-89	5	0	0	0	2	0	-	-	7	0
1989-90	4/3	0	0	0	0/1	0	-	-	4/4	0
	140/7	6	13/4	0	19/2	0	15	3	187/13	9

Paul Stewart started his career with Blackpool, joining them as a 17-year-old professional in October 1981, but it was not until he moved to Manchester City in March 1987, for £200,000, that he began to make a real impact. Although unable to save City from relegation in his first season, 24 goals in 40 League appearances the following season saw him force his way into the England Under-21 side. With the departure of Clive Allen and Nico Claesen at the end of the season, Spurs were obviously short of striking power and in June 1988, Terry Venables moved to sign the bustling centre-forward for what was, at the time, a record Spurs fee of £1.7 million. Suspended for the first few games of the season, Stewart was keen to do well in the team Venables was building but had the misfortune to miss a last-minute penalty on his League debut against Manchester United in October 1988. That seemed to set the pattern for his first season as he struggled to justify the fee. Not helped by having to adapt to the more intricate pattern of Spurs' play in a team trying to develop its own style, it was only towards the end of the season that he began to show his true ability. The arrival of Gary Lineker the following season meant that Stewart had to play a more supporting role. It took time for him to adjust and it was only midway through 1990-91 that he began to win over the fans, who at last began to appreciate his non-stop work and overall value. The real turning point came in December 1990, when Spurs had two men sent-off against Luton and Stewart was forced to fall back. So well did he perform that he remained in midfield, where his stamina and determination, allied to the extra time and space he was allowed, revealed a range of skills that had been submerged in the more frenetic area of the opposition penalty box. However, he was still able to get forward and showed the true calibre of his marksmanship with Spurs' first goal in the 1991 FA Cup victory. With personal pressures he was keen to return North and in July 1992 Spurs found Liverpool's £2.3 million offer too good to refuse.

PAUL STEWART

	LEAGUE		FA CUP		FL CUP		TOTAL	
	App	Gls	App	Gls	App	Gls	App	Gls
1988-89	19/1	12	1	0	4	1	24/1	13
1989-90	24/4	8	1	0	6	1	31/4	9
1990-91	35	3	5	2	6	4	46	9
	78/5	23	7	2	16	6	101/5	31

Generally regarded as the best left-back in the country, and a Scottish international trialist, Alexander Tait made his name with Motherwell and Preston North End before joining Spurs in the summer of 1899. He was only 26 years old then, young enough to give eight seasons of sterling service to Tottenham, captaining the team in the latter days. He was a regular member of the Southern League championship team of 1899-1900 and his play was heavily influential in Spurs' FA Cup success of 1901. Like his 1901 colleague Sandy Brown, Tait came from Glenbuck in Ayrshire. He had excellent positional sense, a determined professionalism and a football brain. He was not especially fast but his tackling ability carried him through, so much that he was nicknamed 'Terrible Tait'. He stayed with Spurs until May 1908 when he moved to Leyton.

SANDY TAIT

	Southern		Western		FA CUP		TOTAL	
	App	Gls	App	Gls	App	Gls	App	Gls
1899-1900	32	0	-	-	1	0	33	0
1900-01	22	0	13	0	8	0	43	0
1901-02	26	0	12	0	3	0	41	0
1902-03	25	1	12	0	4	0	41	1
1903-04	25	0	13	0	5	0	43	0
1904-05	25	1	11	2	4	0	40	3
1905-06	27	1	9	0	4	0	40	1
1906-07	24	0	3	0	7	0	34	0
1907-08	1	0	6	0	0	0	7	0
	207	3	79	2	36	0	322	5

A very popular and friendly player, Danny Thomas was signed from Coventry City in June 1983. Born at Worksop in 1961, Thomas made his League debut for Coventry in September 1979. His first five appearances were as a substitute, but he soon succeeded Mick Coop as Coventry's right-back and earned a place in the England Under-21 team. Altogether he won seven Under-21 caps — the last two after his £250,000 move to Spurs — and while with Coventry he was capped twice for the full-international side. A top-class full-back, who could play on either flank, Thomas showed the ability to push forward and add weight to the attack. He was a member of Spurs' UEFA Cup-winning team in 1984 but a serious injury, sustained in 1987, brought his career to an end and in January 1988, Thomas announced his retirement after fighting a losing battle to regain fitness. He set out to qualify as a physiotherapist and in May 1992 returned to football in that capacity with Ossie Ardiles' West Bromwich Albion.

DANNY THOMAS

	LEAGUE		FA CUP		FL CUP		EUROPE		TOTAL	
	App	Gls	App	Gls	App	Gls	App	Gls	App	Gls
1983-84	26/1	0	0	0	1	0	7/1	0	34/2	0
1984-85	14/2	0	0	0	1	0	1/3	0	16/5	0
1985-86	27	1	1	0	2/1	0	-	-	30/1	1
1986-87	13/4	0	3	0	7/1	0	-	-	23/5	0
	80/7	1	4	0	11/2	0	8/4	0	103/13	1

The first player to appear for England at all levels (schoolboy, amateur, Youth, Under-23 and full), Terry Venables joined Tottenham from Chelsea in May 1966 and played against his old club in Spurs' 1967 FA Cup winning team. Born in Dagenham, he became a professional with Chelsea in 1960 and was part of a young team which won promotion to Division One in 1962-3. He was a League Cup winner with Chelsea (1965) and valued at £80,000 in the deal which brought him to Spurs. He was an England international — two caps while with Chelsea were his only appearances — but it was hard to follow the likes of Blanchflower and White. He was not one of Bill Nicholson's greatest signings, but the £70,000 Tottenham received from Queen's Park Rangers in June 1969 was the most Spurs received for a player for almost a decade. Venables moved to Crystal Palace in September 1974 and later achieved managerial fame during a four-year spell in charge of Palace, taking them from the Third Division to the First. He took over as manager of Queen's Park Rangers in October 1980, and then moved to Barcelona, who he steered to the Spanish League Championship and into a European Cup Final. After parting company with Barcelona he returned to Spurs as manager, as cheerful and positive as ever.

TERRY VENABLES

	LEAGUE		FA CUP		FL CUP		EUROPE		TOTAL	
	App	Gls	App	Gls	App	Gls	App	Gls	App	Gls
1965-66	1	0	-	-	-	-	-	-	1	0
1966-67	41	3	8	2	1	0	-	-	50	5
1967-68	35/1	2	3/1	0	-	-	4	1	42/2	3
1968-69	37	0	4	0	5	1	-	-	46	1
	114/1	5	15/1	2	6	1	4	1	139/2	9

A deceptively skilful player for such a big man, Ricardo Villa was 'the other half' of Keith Burkinshaw's deal with Argentinian clubs in July 1978. He came with Ossie Ardiles and cost £375,000 from Racing Club of Buenos Aires. Previously with Quilmes and Tucuman, he had made two appearances as substitute during the 1978 World Cup Finals, when Argentina won the trophy. At Spurs, Villa proved more unpredictable than Ardiles, often used as a substitute in his early days, but the powerful midfielder-cum-striker became a folk-hero with his display in the 1981 FA Cup Final. Having scored a spectacular goal against Wolves in the semi-final replay, Villa was ineffective at Wembley and looked down-and-out when he was substituted midway through the second half. In the replay he scored twice, including the winner; his long, weaving run was followed by a strong right-foot shot and then an even longer, weaving run — around Wembley in delirious South American ecstacy. He came on as substitute during the 1982 Milk Cup Final but missed the FA Cup Final that year. His performances had suffered from crowd abuse during the Falklands conflict. Villa, who suffered from a series of injuries when he first came to Spurs, never found his true position with the club, but certainly found his moment of glory. He left in June 1983 to join Fort Lauderdale Strikers.

RICKY VILLA

	LEAGUE		FA CUP		FL CUP		EUROPE		TOTAL	
	App	Gls	App	Gls	App	Gls	App	Gls	App	Gls
1978-79	26/6	3	5	0	2	1	-	-	33/6	4
1979-80	22	3	6	0	0	0	-	-	28	3
1980-81	28/1	2	5	3	6	1	-	-	39/1	6
1981-82	26/1	8	2	0	3/1	0	4/1	1	35/3	9
1982-83	21/1	2	3	0	4	1	4	0	32/1	3
	123/9	18	21	3	15/1	3	8/1	1	167/11	25

Although associated with both Newcastle United and Coventry City as a schoolboy, Chris Waddle spent two years with Tow Law Town before signing for Newcastle in July 1980. He soon made up for lost time, making his Football League debut in October 1980, and under the guidance of Arthur Cox rapidly became a regular, benefiting enormously from the arrival of Kevin Keegan in August 1982. Playing alongside Keegan and Peter Beardsley, he helped Newcastle win promotion to Division One in 1984 and won his first full cap in March 1985. Spurs signed him in July 1985 for £590,000 and after scoring on his League debut, against Watford in August 1985, he soon struck up a fine understanding with Glenn Hoddle, a partnership that worked off the field as well with a hit record *Diamond Lights*. A member of Spurs' 1987 FA Cup Final team, he appeared regularly for England, although doubts were expressed as to whether an international team could accommodate two players of similiar style as Waddle and John Barnes and they were frequently in competition for a place. With the departure of Hoddle, Waddle took over as the focal point of Spurs' team and thrived on the responsibility. A tall, willowy player with a strange 'hunched shoulders' style of running, he was equally effective as an out-and-out winger, central striker or midfielder but was at his best when given the freedom to roam. It was playing in such a loose role that he had his best season for Spurs in 1988-9. At the end of that season, Spurs received an offer of £4.25 million from Marseille. It was hard to turn down such a bid, even for a club of Spurs' standing, but the final decision was left to Waddle, who decided to accept the challenge

to play in the French League, where Hoddle had been so successful. In the less frenetic atmosphere of Continental football, he was given the opportunity to show the full range of his talents and helped Marseille retain the French League title in 1990. A member of England's successful World Cup team that year, he was one of the most influential players in Marseille's march to the European Cup Final in 1991. Released by Marseille in July 1992 he joined Sheffield Wednesday.

CHRIS WADDLE

	LEAGUE		FA CUP		FL CUP		TOTAL	
	App	Gls	App	Gls	App	Gls	App	Gls
1985-86	39	11	5	2	6	1	50	14
1986-87	39	6	6	2	9	3	54	11
1987-88	21/1	2	2	1	1	0	24/1	3
1988-89	38	14	1	0	5	0	44	14
	137/1	33	14	5	21	4	172/1	42

Frederick 'Fanny' Walden once described his own measurements as '8st 9lbs and 5ft 2⅛in — 5ft 2in after a hair-cut'. He was one of the smallest players of all-time, too small to be shoulder-charged and too elusive to be tackled. He was a right-winger with a variety of tricks, very popular with the public, and the joke was that he could run through the legs of big full-backs. His first Football League club was Northampton Town, for whom he was signed by manager Herbert Chapman from Wellingborough Town, Walden's home-town club. That was in 1909, and four years later he moved to Tottenham for £1,700. He played in the 1919-20 Second Division championship team and was unfortunate to miss the later part of the 1921 FA Cup run through a cartilage injury. He reached the semi-final with Spurs in 1922, and returned to Northampton for his last playing season (1926-7). Walden's two England caps were eight years apart, and but for the intervention of World War One there might have been far more. He was also a Northamptonshire county cricket player, an excellent batsman and cover-point fielder. Later he was a first-class cricket umpire.

	LEAGUE		FA CUP		TOTAL	
	App	Gls	App	Gls	App	Gls
1912-13	1	0	0	0	1	0
1913-14	30	5	3	2	33	7
1914-15	38	1	2	1	40	2
1919-20	31	4	4	0	35	4
1920-21	22	5	1	1	23	6
1921-22	28	2	6	0	34	2
1922-23	30	3	5	0	35	3
1923-24	34	1	1	0	35	1
	214	21	22	4	236	25

FANNY WALDEN

Charlie Walters played one game as a guest for Spurs during World War One and was signed from Oxford City in 1920. He came in for Charlie Rance during the FA Cup-winning season and was part of the team which beat Wolves in the Final. He was a star of that match, his defensive work responsible for some crucial clearances late in the game. He was a speedy centre-half with good powers of recovery, destructive rather than constructive, perhaps unfortunate to be playing in an era when more constructive qualities were required of centre-halves. He was Spurs' centre-half for another couple of seasons, and he was with the club until October 1926, when he moved to Fulham. Walters ended his career with Mansfield Town and died in Bath in 1971, aged 74.

	LEAGUE		FA CUP		TOTAL	
	App	Gls	App	Gls	App	Gls
1919-20	1	0	0	0	1	0
1920-21	25	0	6	0	31	0
1921-22	33	0	5	0	38	0
1922-23	29	0	0	0	29	0
1923-24	15	0	0	0	15	0
1924-25	2	0	0	0	2	0
1925-26	1	0	0	0	1	0
	106	0	11	0	117	0

CHARLIE WALTERS

Sonny Walters was one of only three uncapped players in Arthur Rowe's great 'Push and Run' team, although he did play for the England 'B' team. Born in Edmonton in 1924, he played for Walthamstow Avenue before joining Spurs towards the end of World War Two. He was a goalscoring winger, yet an ideal link in the 'Push and Run' system, working well with Alf Ramsey and Bill Nicholson, pushing the ball quickly rather than indulging in individual wing sorties. He won a Second Division championship medal in 1949-50 and a League Championship medal the next season. He left the club in July 1957 and played for Aldershot for a couple of seasons.

	LEAGUE		FA CUP		TOTAL	
	App	Gls	App	Gls	App	Gls
1946-47	1	1	2	0	3	1
1947-48	1	0	0	0	1	0
1948-49	13	1	0	0	13	1
1949-50	35	14	3	2	38	16
1950-51	40	15	1	0	41	15
1951-52	37	10	2	0	39	10
1952-53	26	8	8	1	34	9
1953-54	37	14	6	2	43	16
1954-55	7	2	1	0	8	2
1955-56	14	1	0	0	14	1
	211	66	23	5	234	71

SONNY WALTERS

Ghosting into space on the left, acting as a decoy runner or ready to be picked out by a Blanchflower pass, John White was a difficult inside-forward to play against. They called him 'The Ghost' at White Hart Lane and he was a vital cog in the 'double' team but, tragically, White died in his mid-20s, struck by lightning while sheltering from the rain on Crews Hill golf course at Enfield on 21 July 1964. White was a Scottish international, capped 22 times for his country. Born in Musselburgh, Midlothian, he played for Alloa Athletic before Falkirk manager Reg Smith paid £3,300 for his services in September 1958. A year later Falkirk received £20,000 and White was on his way to London. He was not easily accepted by Spurs fans. His style was delicate and subtle, and local-hero Tommy Harmer was a similarly lightweight inside-forward. White played on the wing for a while, then became more of a goalscoring inside-forward than he had previously. He was an invaluable member of the 'double', 1962 FA Cup-winning and 1963 European Cup-winners' Cup-winning teams.

	LEAGUE		FA CUP		EUROPE		TOTAL	
	App	Gls	App	Gls	App	Gls	App	Gls
1959-60	28	5	4	0	-	-	32	5
1960-61	42	13	7	0	-	-	49	13
1961-62	36	8	7	1	8	1	51	10
1962-63	37	8	1	0	7	5	45	13
1963-64	40	6	0	0	2	0	42	6
	183	40	19	1	17	6	219	47

JOHN WHITE

Born in Denaby, Yorkshire, Arthur Willis played for Finchley before joining Spurs as an amateur in 1938. He signed professional in January 1944 and was a Spurs regular during the last seasons of wartime football, when he worked in a local engineering works. For much of the 1940s he was kept in the Reserves, first by the full-back pairing of Buckingham and Tickeridge, and later by Ramsey and Withers. But an injury to Withers, early in the 1950-51 season, gave him a chance for a prolonged spell at left-back (although he could play on either flank). He proved quick and sharp, and a good footballing full-back too; his reward was a League Championship medal in 1951 and an England cap against France — Alf Ramsey was his full-back partner — later that same year. However, he still had to compete for his place in the Spurs team with Charlie Withers still around. Willis stayed with Spurs until September 1954, when he left to join Ron Burgess at Swansea Town. Later he was on the training staff at Swansea.

	LEAGUE		FA CUP		TOTAL	
	App	Gls	App	Gls	App	Gls
1945-46	-	-	2	0	2	0
1946-47	37	0	2	0	39	0
1947-48	3	0	0	0	3	0
1948-49	11	0	0	0	11	0
1949-50	2	0	0	0	2	0
1950-51	39	0	1	0	40	0
1951-52	17	0	0	0	17	0
1952-53	27	1	5	0	32	1
1953-54	9	0	6	0	15	0
	145	1	16	0	161	1

ARTHUR WILLIS

127

Full-back Charlie Withers was Spurs' first-choice at left-back during the 1949-50 Second Division title season, but he lost his place to Arthur Willis the following season. He played with Tottenham Juniors and Finchley before signing professional with Spurs in October 1947. His career then closely paralleled that of Willis. Edmonton-born, Withers combined a never-say-die attitude and hard-tackling skills with a cool football brain, and he was a good servant to the 'Push and Run' system, which demanded more from full-backs than previous tactics. Withers re-established himself in 1951-2, having unfortunately lost his place during the Championship season, and was in and out until his retirement during the 1955-6 season. He earned an England 'B' cap and even played on the left wing for Spurs, scoring two goals in an FA Cup tie.

CHARLIE WITHERS

	LEAGUE		FA CUP		TOTAL	
	App	Gls	App	Gls	App	Gls
1947-48	1	0	0	0	1	0
1948-49	12	0	0	0	12	0
1949-50	40	0	3	0	43	0
1950-51	4	0	0	0	4	0
1951-52	29	0	2	0	31	0
1952-53	15	0	6	2	21	2
1953-54	31	0	0	0	31	0
1954-55	11	0	0	0	11	0
1955-56	10	0	0	0	10	0
	153	0	11	2	164	2

Vivian Woodward was one of the outstanding footballers of his generation, despite remaining an amateur throughout his lengthy career. Born at Kennington in June 1879, and an architect by profession, he began his career with Southern League Chelmsford City and was soon in demand as the bigger clubs eyed his abilities. In 1901 he accepted an invitation to join Spurs, although his business commitments restricted his appearances in his first two seasons with the club. When he was able to turn out regularly, his talent blossomed. Tall, slim and elegant, Woodward had an almost uncanny control of the ball and he could evade the hefty challenges of defenders of the day. At that time, most centre-forwards were big and bustling, and Woodward's cultured style lifted him above many of his contemporaries. The international selectors soon recognised his special talents and Woodward made 23 full England appearances (scoring 29 goals) and won a remarkable 67 caps for the England and United Kingdom amateur sides, captaining the UK teams which won Olympic titles in 1908 and 1912. Woodward scored Spurs' first Football League goal and was leading scorer in the promotion-winning team. He had the unique distinction of being a Tottenham director at the same time but just when Spurs were looking forward to their first season in Division One, Woodward shocked them by resigning as both player and director. He surprised Spurs even further in 1909-10 when he returned to the game as a Chelsea player. He remained with them until World War One and served as a director at Stamford Bridge between 1922 and 1930.

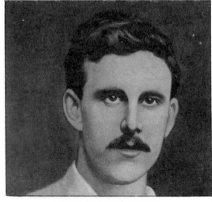

VIVIAN J. WOODWARD

	LEAGUE		Southern		Western		FA CUP		TOTAL	
	App	Gls	App	Gls	App	Gls	App	Gls	App	Gls
1900-01	-	-	2	2	1	1	0	0	3	3
1901-02	-	-	2	0	1	2	0	0	3	2
1902-03	-	-	12	4	3	0	4	3	19	7
1903-04	-	-	17	10	5	2	5	1	27	13
1904-05	-	-	20	7	3	0	4	0	27	7
1905-06	-	-	12	5	1	2	3	1	16	8
1906-07	-	-	20	7	0	0	3	0	23	7
1907-08	-	-	20	10	1	0	1	0	22	10
1908-09	27	18	-	-	-	-	4	0	31	18
	27	18	105	45	15	7	24	5	171	75

128

Spurs 3   West Herts 2

A CROWD of some 2,000 people gathered at Northumberland Park to see Spurs' first-ever match in the FA Cup, against the forerunners of Watford.

At the beginning of this first-qualifying-round game, West Herts showed the better play. They put Spurs' defence under pressure and got the ball into goal early on from a free-kick, only to have the score disallowed as the free-kick was indirect and nobody had touched the ball on the way.

Play went from end to end. Ernie Payne was conspicuous for his tricky ball control but he missed with a good chance from less than 12 yards. And Cubberley put in some good shots without reward.

West Herts had two chances to open the scoring, one shot being well saved by Monk and another flying over. Then Eccles got the ball out to Payne whose cross was headed in by Hunter and Spurs were one up.

From then until half-time, Spurs were totally in command but the visiting goalkeeper, King, kept them at bay, making fine saves from Eccles. Payne, Cubberley and Goodall, until Goodall eventually notched a second goal.

Up to the interval, West Herts were barely able to get the ball out of their half, such was Spurs' dominance, but King was performing miracles for his team and half-time arrived with Spurs still only 2-0 ahead.

The story of the second half was totally different. Within five minutes of the restart, Wright pulled one back for West Herts from a corner and then Hobbs headed an equaliser.

West Herts, if anything, now had the better of the play although Hunter almost regained the lead for Spurs. Eventually a winner came. Goodall took a pass from Cubberley and slipped it past King as the 'keeper came out to meet him.

Spurs were now pinned back in defence and their forwards were only seen in rare break-outs although Goodall should have scored on one occasion and Eccles claimed one shot had gone in but the referee ruled it had gone over the bar, a common dispute in the days when there were no nets.

Although West Herts kept up the pressure until the final whistle, Spurs held out and their debut in the FA Cup proved successful.

Spurs: Monk; Jull, Welham, Shepherd, Briggs, Julian, Cubberley, Goodall, Hunter, Eccles, Payne.
West Herts: King; Lidderdale, Paul, Penney, Robbins, Green, Wright, Hobbs, Anderson, Taylor, Strout.
Referee: Mr Bisiter   *Attendance: 2,000*

Match to Remember 2   4 September 1899

Spurs 4   Notts County 1

FOR Spurs' first-ever match at White Hart Lane they invited Notts County, the oldest and one of the most famous clubs in the country. On a warm day, a crowd of some 5,000 turned out to more than satisfy Spurs' new landlords, Charringtons, who had been guaranteed a minimum of 1,000 spectators at each first-team game.

Football League clubs had for some time looked on matches against Southern League teams as little more than exhibitions, a chance to show the South the skills that had concentrated football success in the hands of the more powerful professional clubs of the North and Midlands. But they were now coming to realise that the Southern clubs were improving rapidly. This match was to prove the point.

Spurs had already developed the close-passing style for which they have always been known and they pitted this against the more direct long-ball style favoured by County.

The ceremonial kick-off having been performed by Spurs chairman Charles Roberts, the opening play was very even with both goals being threatened and either team could have taken the lead. As it was, County got the first goal, a shot by McCairns being deflected in by Tait. They could soon have had a second, Clawley having to make a good save from Fletcher.

Spurs managed to get even before half-time. Smith's cross eluded everybody, Kirwan returned the ball and Pratt managed to force it home.

The second half opened with Spurs well on top. Cameron got through but pushed the ball too far and allowed Suter to take it off his toe, and Copeland hit the post. Then Suter made a good save from Pratt but was only able to push the ball into the path of Copeland, who put Spurs ahead.

After 15 minutes of the second half the match turned Spurs' way. Kirwan went up for a high ball with Suter but caught the 'keeper with his foot. Suter had to be taken off and Bull took his place.

Although Bull put up a great show in goal, his absence from midfield disturbed County's play and left Spurs well on top.

Copeland added a third goal from a Cameron pass and then completed his hat-trick from a Kirwan centre. Cameron also got the ball in the net twice but both efforts were disallowed for offside.

Spurs: Clawley; Erentz, Tait, Jones, McNaught, Morris, Smith, Pratt, Copeland, Cameron, Kirwan.
Notts County: Suter; Lewis, Montgomery, Ball, Bull, Lowe, Hadley, MacConachie, McCairns, Fletcher, Chalmers.
Referee: C.D.Crisp   *Attendance: 5,000*

Match to Remember 3   1 September 1908

Spurs 3   Wolverhampton Wanderers 0

SPURS' first-ever Football League match could not have been against more attractive opposition. The visitors were FA Cup holders Wolves and, not surprisingly, they were expected to win easily. But that was not to be — Spurs made a great League debut and the final scoreline was no exaggeration of their superiority.

For Spurs, Hewitson, McFarlane and Bob Steel were making their debuts, although Walter Bull was unable to appear as there was a problem with the Football League over his transfer from Notts County. The presence of Vivian Woodward, who usually did not play football until the cricket season had ended, perhaps indicates the importance of the occasion.

Although the weather was poor, with a blustery wind and grey clouds threatening to reproduce the downpours of earlier in the day, and the fact that the match was played on a Thursday, a crowd of 20,000 turned up.

Dan Steel won the toss and Spurs soon gave their supporters something to celebrate. After only six minutes Lunn, the Wolves 'keeper, carried the ball outside the penalty area; Walton took the free-kick and fired in a terrific shot which the 'keeper did well to block but the ball fell to Woodward who simply turned it into the net for Spurs' first Football League goal.

Within minutes Woodward had almost scored a second. McFarlane took a pass from Bob Steel and fired in a shot that Lunn had to go full-length to save. He could not hold the ball and it came out to Woodward, who put it just wide.

Midway through the first half Wolves made their only serious assault on the Spurs goal. Radford netted but was offside.

Just before half-time Spurs thought they had a second. Close work in front of the Wolves goal left McFarlane in a good position. His shot was pushed out by Lunn, Walton fired it back in and Middlemiss netted but was ruled offside. A minute later the same thing happened to Woodward.

From the restart Spurs again took up the attack and a left-wing cross was met by Woodward to put Spurs two ahead. Wolves now realised the extent of their task and began to put Spurs under considerable pressure, but their finishing was woefully off-form.

At the other end, Middlemiss almost scored and then after a wonderful dribble in which he beat three men, Woodward was just off-target with his shot. This inspired Spurs to a third goal and after Lunn had made a good save to deny Woodward his hat-trick, Tom Morris cracked home a tremendous shot from 30 yards. Later, Middlemiss hit the bar.

Spurs: Hewitson; Coquet, Burton, Morris, D.Steel, Darnell, Walton, Woodward, McFarlane, R.Steel, Middlemiss.
Wolves: Lunn; Jones, Collins, Hunt, Wooldridge, Bishop, Harrison, Shelton, Hedley, Radford, Pedley.
Referee: Mr Howcroft. *Attendance: 20,000*

Match to Remember 4   19 September 1925

Spurs 5   Huddersfield Town 5

A LARGE crowd assembled at White Hart Lane to witness this visit of Huddersfield, who had won the League title under the guidance of Herbert Chapman for the last two seasons and were on their way to a hat-trick.

Despite, or perhaps because of, the rain and slippery conditions, and the fact that the players were still getting used to the new offside law, they saw an incredible ten-goal bonanza.

The teams had totally contrasting styles. Huddersfield used a direct go-ahead approach; Spurs their more refined short-passing game. On this day they were equally effective.

The match had a flying start, Jackson putting Huddersfield ahead from a corner after four minutes. Three minutes later Osborne centred for Elkes to head a Spurs' equaliser. But by the 13th minute the visitors were back in the lead when a long run by Brown opened Spurs' defence for Jackson to make it 2-1.

Until this point Spurs had been the better team, but Skinner was injured and Huddersfield took control. Come half-time they were well on top but there had been no further scoring. That was to change dramatically in the second half.

Spurs changed their tactics, getting the ball out to Dimmock more and using their wingers to get behind the Huddersfield defence. With 51 minutes gone Dimmock curled the ball into the net from an almost impossibly acute angle on the left and only nine minutes later, having worked himself into a good position, Lindsay was fouled by Wordsworth. Clay took the penalty but it was saved by Taylor. However, the referee decided Taylor had moved before the kick was taken and ordered it to be retaken. Clay made no mistake with the second chance.

Only two minutes after this, Huddersfield were back on level terms. Jackson converting Cook's pass. But parity prevailed for only three minutes. First Osborne scored with a curling cross-shot and then, almost from the restart, Osborne crossed to Elkes, whose header put Spurs 5-3 ahead.

Spurs now seemed to have the match sewn-up but minutes later, Wadsworth committed a bad foul on Spurs master-craftsman Jimmy Seed, who was carried off unconscious.

Almost immediately a scramble in Spurs' goalmouth led to Jackson reducing the arrears. Spurs were in trouble. With only ten men, and three of those — Skinner, Lindsay and Forster — carrying injuries, they were under continuous bombardment. They held out until four mintutes from the end when Brown headed in from Jackson's cross to produce a final score of 5-5.

Spurs: Hinton; Clay, Forster, Skinner, B.Smith, Grimsdell, Osborne, Seed, Lindsay, Elkes, Dimmock.
Huddersfield: Taylor; Barkas, Wadsworth, Steele, Wilson, Watson, Jackson, Cook, Brown, Stephenson, Williams.
Referee: W.P.Harper *Attendance: 21,667*

Spurs 5   West Ham United 3

A CROWD of over 36,000 gathered at White Hart Lane to witness this London derby. They were thrilled by a superb exhibition of forward play from Spurs in an exciting game which had five goals in the first 25 minutes.

The goalscoring started as early as the fourth minute when Horler and Bailie left a long pass to each other. Bailie got his hands to the ball but O'Callaghan nipped in to push the ball away and put Spurs one up.

Three minutes later Elkes totally baffled the West Ham defence with a back-heel to Dimmock, whose centre was met with a full-blooded header from Handley. Spurs were now 2-0 ahead, but the West Ham were soon fighting back. Almost straight from the kick-off, Barrett fired in a speculative 35-yarder which put the Hammers back in the game.

In the 14th minute, O'Callaghan's shot was blocked by a defender. The ball spun to Handley and his centre was headed in by Elkes. But eight minutes later, Brittan dropped a centre by Yews and Ruffell nipped in to make it 3-2.

In the next 20 minutes or so, the goalscoring calmed down although Spurs were still by far the better team. With half-time only a minute away, poor ball-control by Hebden let O'Callaghan in to score again and give Spurs a 4-2 half-time lead.

With the second half barely 10 minutes old, West Ham got themselves back in the game. Gibbons chased a long ball down the middle. Forster left it to Brittan, but Gibbins got there first and lobbed the ball over the goalkeeper. Forster managed to get back to clear from the line, but West Ham appealed for a penalty. The referee consulted his linesman and gave a corner. Yews' flag-kick was headed home by Earlie.

West Ham now sensed that they could get a point, but Spurs held out and had the better chances. Only two minutes remained when Elkes chipped the ball in to Osborne and Spurs had won 5-3.

The match had been one long exhibition of sustained attacking football, both sides thinking that they could outscore their opponents. For Spurs, Dimmock, Elkes and Osborne were superb whilst O'Callaghan's performance prevented Seed from regaining his place.

Spurs: Brittan; Forster, Richardson, Lowdell, Skitt, Lindsay, Handley, O'Callaghan, Osborne, Elkes, Dimmock.
West Ham United: Bailie; Hebden, Horler, Collins, Barrett, Cox, Yews, Earle, Gibbins, Moore, Ruffell.
Referee: A.J.Caseley   *Attendance: 36,600*

Everton 2   Spurs 5

WHEN Spurs travelled to Goodison Park for this Division One match, Everton were top of the table and on their way to the League title. Spurs, on the other hand, were in a mid-table position and were on their way back to the Second Division. Some 25,000 people were at Goodison for what was expected to be an easy Everton victory.

How wrong they were. With Dixie Dean well controlled by Skitt, and Jimmy Dimmock tormenting Cresswell, Spurs turned on a splendid performance and thoroughly deserved their sensational victory. Taffy O'Callaghan just pipped Dimmock for the man-of-the-match title by virtue of his four goals.

'Taffy' O'Callaghan's four goals gave Spurs a memorable end to the season.

Spurs never allowed Everton to get into their stride. They took the lead in the 20th minute when Dimmock netted following a through-ball from Handley and went two ahead ten minutes later when O'Callaghan intercepted a Cresswell back-pass to Taylor, rounded the 'keeper and slipped the ball home.

Everton's fortunes lifted five minutes into the second half when Dean headed down a cross for Troup to pull one back, but Spurs immediately made it 3-1; O'Callaghan rounded Cresswell and beat Taylor with a perfectly placed drive. Ten minutes later, O'Callaghan got his third after a fine pass from Armstrong.

Troup managed his second for Everton, although he looked offside, but with two minutes left Dimmock robbed Cresswell, fed O'Callaghan and from the halfway line O'Callaghan went through to finish the scoring.

For Spurs it was the most memorable performance in an otherwise disappointing season.

Everton: Taylor; Cresswell, O'Donnell, Brown, Hart, Virr, Critchley, Irvine, Dean, Weldon, Troup.
Spurs: Spiers; Clay, Richardson, Lowdell, Skitt, Lindsay, Handley, O'Callaghan, Armstrong, Elkes, Dimmock.
Referee: W.Thomas   *Attendance: 25,000*

Match to Remember 7   6 January 1934

Aston Villa 1   Spurs 5

A BRILLIANT display by the Spurs forward line, coupled with a good solid defensive performance, gave Spurs their best away win of the season at Villa Park.

After only ten minutes Morton made a brave save at Hunt's feet but when the ball went up in the air, McCormick was the first to react, putting Spurs ahead. Immediately Colquhoun went off to have stitches put in a bad head wound but he returned just in time to see Meads hit home a 25-yard volley to put Spurs further ahead.

In the 23rd minute Hunt scored Spurs third with a glorious drive and 12 minutes later, Tottenham got their fourth when a Howe shot hit the bar and was adjudged to have crossed the line.

Comfortably ahead, Spurs eased up in the second half, protecting the injured Colquhoun, but they still managed a fifth goal when McCormick, having had a shot cleared off the line by Gibson only minutes earlier, beat Kingdon and both Villa full-backs before dribbling around Morton.

Ten minutes from the end Villa were reduced to ten men. Their centre-forward, 'Pongo' Waring, who had already been warned twice by the referee for bad fouls, charged into both Rowe and Nicholls. Although not a bad offence in itself, the referee decided something had to be done and ordered Waring off.

The 30,000 crowd who had been totally frustrated by Spurs' masterful performance, vented their anger by hurling apples, oranges and beer bottles on to the pitch. As if to calm them down, Astley scored a consolation goal for Villa five minutes from the end.

Aston Villa: Morton; Blair, Mort, Gibson, Kingdon, Wood, Mandley, Dix, Waring, Astley, Houghton.
Spurs: Nicholls; Channell, Whatley, Colquhoun, Rowe, Meads, McCormick, Howe, Hunt, G.W.Hall, W.Evans.
Referee: P.Snape *Attendance: 30,000*

A goalkeeper's nightmare? Spurs forwards pepper the goal during training in 1934.

Match to Remember 8   8 December 1934

Spurs 3   Stoke City 2

STOKE came to White Hart Lane as one of the top three teams in the country, having won five of their nine away games, whereas Spurs had injury problems and were forced to field what was little more than a reserve forward line. Matters were made worse when centre-half Arthur Rowe went off injured and then Taffy O'Callaghan had to go to outside-right because of a back injury.

The match had started well for Spurs with Hunt putting them ahead in the seventh minute, despite Stoke appeals for offside, but Channell then made a bad mistake which allowed Davies to score for the visitors.

The match was fairly evenly balanced, but early in the second half Rowe was forced to leave the field and two minutes later Matthews put Stoke ahead. Spurs still seemed in with a chance but after 70 minutes, O'Callaghan was injured and could do little more than limp along on the wing.

Spurs now showed real character. With only 18 minutes remaining, the nine fit men played an inspired game. Wave after wave of attacks staggered Stoke's defence and O'Callaghan managed to get an equaliser with his left foot. But Spurs were not satisfied and playing with a determination rarely seen they continued to hunt for the winning goal. It came in the 87th minute.

A brilliant individual run by Hunt resulted in a corner, taken by O'Callaghan. Bellamy rose highest in the area and nodded past Lewis to secure a fine victory.

Spurs: Nicholls; Channell, Whatley, T.Evans, Rowe, Meads, Howe, O'Callaghan, Hunt, Greenfield, Bellamy.
Stoke City: Lewis; McGrory, Spencer, Buller, Turner, Sellars, Matthews, Liddle, Sale, Davies, Johnson.

Attendance: 31,854

Match to Remember 9   28 March 1936

Spurs 8   Southampton 0

AFTER seeing his team go four games without winning and thereby effectively drop out of the promotion race, Spurs manager Jack Tresadern, in his first full season, decided that changes had to be made. Grice and Meek had come in for their first games the week before; and Ward made his second appearance. A 1-1 draw at Swansea had been an improvement but now the infusion of new blood had to maintain it. They did so with a vengeance, adding a variety to Spurs' play that had been sadly lacking of late.

After six minutes, good interpassing by Duncan, Meek and Hunt gave Willie Evans, who had wandered into the centre-forward position, the chance to give Tottenham the start they needed.

Seven minutes later, Sargent's corner was not cleared and Meek volleyed in from the edge of the box. Three minutes after that, Grice and Willie Evans interchanged to give Hunt an easy chance to put Spurs three up.

Tottenham were now totally in command. Only the heroic Scriven kept the score down, but even he erred. Four minutes from half-time he fumbled a shot from Hunt that squirmed past him for number four. On the stroke of half-time, Grice made a strong run and switched the ball inside to Meek, who gave Spurs a 5-0 interval lead.

Spurs eased up in the second half. Their sixth goal came in the 59th minute when Scriven failed to hold Hunt's drive and Meek had a simple job to tap in. Number-seven came in the 65th minute, when Bradford felled Hunt in the penalty area, and the Tottenham player picked himself up to score from the penalty. Spurs finished the scoring in the 78th minute when Willie Evans headed in Sargent's cross.

Spurs had been on top throughout the game and the Southampton forwards had not troubled Nicholls' goal once, although it must be said that all the luck went Spurs' way. On other occasions they had played better and lost, but on this day everything went right, and George Hunt was in particularly splendid form.

Spurs: Nicholls; Ward, Buckingham, Howe, Rowe, Grice, Sargent, Meek, Hunt, Duncan, W.Evans.
Southampton: Scriven; Adams, Sillett, King, Bradford, Woodhouse, Neal, Tully, Gurry, Holt, Fishlock.
Referee: J.M.Wiltshire   *Attendance: 29,732*

Spurs 4   Everton 3

THERE were nearly 47,000 people at White Hart Lane to see this FA Cup fifth-round replay and they hoped that the level of drama of the first match — when Spurs scored with only five minutes left and Everton equalised in the last minute — would be repeated. In fact it was surpassed.

Conditions for the match were poor. The pitch, flooded in the morning, had been cleared by groundstaff but was still very greasy. No doubt this contributed to the match's dramatic start and finish.

Everton bought in 17-year-old Tommy Lawton for the game and he justified his inclusion in only the second minute, when he crashed home a cross from Geldard. In the 20th minute Everton went further ahead when Dean scored from another cross from Geldard, who was giving Whatley a torrid time.

Everton's 2-0 lead was hardly a true reflection of the play, for Spurs had shown great approach work and remarkable skill on the tricky pitch.Morrison managed to pull one goal back in the 27th minute from a Miller pass and from then until half-time, Spurs could not force another breakthrough despite being well on top.

The second half started dramatically. Hall twice had to save at the feet of Everton forwards. Then, from a throw-in by Mercer, the ball was worked to Dean. He was fouled in the penalty area and the referee pointed to the spot until he noticed that a linesman was signalling that Mercer's throw-in had been wrongly taken.

Morrison then headed what appeared to be a good goal but the referee decided that Sagar had been pushed. Almost immediately, Dean got Everton's third and the tie seemed over. Two minutes later, in the 65th minute, Meek found Morrison with a through-ball and while Everton appealed for offside, Morrison went on to find the net.

For the next 20 minutes Everton were content to hold on to their lead and Spurs were unable to pierce a solid defence. Tottenham looked to be going out of the FA Cup. But with five minutes left, Morrison collected from a throw-in, drew the defence to him and then found the perfect pass to give Meek the opportunity to grab the equaliser.

The tie was not over yet. With two minutes left, Miller went like a greyhound down the wing and his cross was met perfectly by Morrison's head. Against all the odds Spurs had won.

Spurs: Hall; J.Ward, Whatley, Buckingham, Rowe, Grice, McCormick, Meek, Morrison, Duncan, Miller.
Everton: Sagar; Cook, Jones, Britton, Gee, Mercer, Geldard, Cunliffe, Dean, Lawton, Gillick.
Referee: H.N.Mee   *Attendance: 46,972*

Spurs' 1937 win over Everton was not the first time that they had scored a famous victory over the Merseysiders. Three years earlier, FA Cup holders Everton had been knocked out in the third round at White Hart Lane. Here, George Hunt scores Tottenham's first goal past Ted Sagar.

136

Spurs 7 Newcastle United 0

HAVING gained promotion with Arthur Rowe's 'Push and Run' football, the true test of Spurs new-look approach came with the visit of Division One leaders Newcastle. A crowd of 70,000 amassed to see if Spurs' good start to the season could continue. Many thousands more were turned away. At kick-off time everybody wanted to know if 'Push and Run' had a future in the top-flight. By four o'clock they knew the answer.

After only five minutes the perfect example of 'Push and Run' was seen. Duquemin collected the ball in midfield, beat his marker and passed to Baily. Baily laid it forward to Medley, who had cut inside, and raced down the wing to collect Medley's return pass. He centred immediately and Bennett was there to head home.

On 24 minutes Baily took the ball off Harvey, rounded him and put Spurs two up. Medley then scored twice to send Spurs in for the half-time break, 4-0 ahead.

If there had been any doubts about the power of 'Push and Run', then they had now been dispelled and in the second half, any lingering reservations were well and truly buried. In the 54th minute Walters made it 5-0 with a long-range shot before McMichael, the Newcastle full back, collided with him and had to be carried off. Newcastle played the last 15 minutes with ten men.

Three minutes after McMichael's departure, Medley completed his hat-trick and in the dying minutes Cowell, under pressure from Duquemin, handled; Ramsey scored the seventh from the penalty spot.

Spurs' win was greeted with astonishment. Newcastle were not a bad side, indeed their defence was considered invincible, but even without the injured Burgess, Spurs were able to rip through that defence almost at will, with Baily and Medley outstanding.

Spurs: Ditchburn; Ramsey, Willis, Nicholson, Clarke, Brittan, Walters, Bennett, Duquemin, Baily, Medley.
Newcastle United: Fairbrother; Cowell, McMichael, Harvey, Brennan, Crowe, Walker, Taylor, Milburn, Robledo, Mitchell.
Referee: H.E.Evans   *Attendance: 70,026*

Action from Spurs' 7-0 win over Newcastle United. Left: Bennett heads home the opening goal. Right: Fairbrother makes a daring dive to deny Duquemin.

Bobby Smith (centre) scores his third and Spurs' seventh after good work by Danny Blanchflower.

Match to Remember 12   11 October 1958

Spurs 10   Everton 4

ON the morning of this match it had been officially announced that Bill Nicholson was Spurs' new manager. In the afternoon he watched the last team picked by his predecessor, Jimmy Anderson, run up Spurs' record League score.

That team included a genius of an inside-forward in little Tommy Harmer, a brilliant ball player and a favourite with the crowd. Harmer was never able to command a first-team place, being unable to harness his unquestionable talent to the team effort. In this match, however, after a spell in the reserves, he showed his amazing ability for creating goals. Harmer was undoubtedly man of the match.

The goals started as early as the third minute, when Stokes scored, and continued unabated throughout the match. After 11 minutes Hickson tricked his way past Ryden and passed to Jimmy Harris, who had a simple job of beating Hollowbread. Four mintues later Smith nodded home from Harmer's pass and 14 minutes after that, Danny Blanchflower set up Robb to dance round a defender and put Spurs 3-1 up.

In the next minute Smith glided home Medwin's cross and just another minute later, Stokes converted another Medwin cross. On the stroke of half-time Medwin notched number six, his shot going in off a post.

Seven minutes into the second half, Jimmy Harris pulled another back for Everton, but Blanchflower soon set up Smith for Spurs' seventh.

With the injured Ryden having to move to the left wing, the next 20 minutes were quiet from a goalscoring point of view, but that was just the calm before a storm of five goals in the last ten minutes.

On the 80-minute mark, Harmer hit home a first-time drive from 15 yards. Harris immediately got his third, but on 85 minutes Stokes' corner was converted by Smith. Collins made it 9-4 in the 86th minute and two minutes from the end the hobbling Ryden rounded off the scoring with Spurs' tenth.

Spurs: Hollowbread; Baker, Hopkins, Blanchflower, Ryden, Iley, Medwin, Harmer, Smith, Stokes, Robb.
Everton: Dunlop; Sanders, Bramwell, King, Jones, B.Harris, Fielding, J.Harris, Hickson, Collins, O'Hara.
Referee: G.W.Pullin   *Attendance: 37,794*

Spurs 13   Crewe Alexandra 2

ON the previous Saturday, Spurs, then top of the table, were held to a humiliating 2-2 draw at Gresty Road by little Crewe. Some reporters considered that they were lucky to get away with a draw.

At White Hart Lane, however, Spurs expected to go into the fifth round of the FA Cup and a local Tottenham butcher painted his verdict in the window of his shop: Spurs 7 Crewe 0. What a pessimist, he turned out to be, for Spurs ran up their record score in a first-class match.

Right from the kick-off it was obvious that Spurs were going to put Crewe in their place. In the third minute, a corner by White was hit home, off a post, by Smith. Seven minutes later the Crewe right-half, Jones, slipped and Allen was through to make it 2-0. Only a minute later Smith scored number three when he turned sharply on an Allen pass. Crewe then pulled one back when a 25-yard drive from Coleman dropped over Brown's head, but Spurs were soon adding to their total.

On 21 minutes, Jones pulled the ball back from the bye-line for Harmer to crack home a gem of a drive. On 29 minutes, Allen netted number-five with a diving header from Jones' centre. On 30 minutes, Millar made a mistake and Smith completed his hat-trick. On 36 minutes, Allen centred for Smith to make it 7-1. On 39 minutes, a lovely Harmer dribble set up Jones from close range and in the last four minutes of the half, Allen scored two more, the first after a fine run and cross by White. The half-time score was an unbelievable 10-1.

Within five minutes of the restart, a White pass enabled Jones to score the 11th goal, and now Spurs eased up. A further 23 minutes passed before a Jones drive was parried by Evans for Allen to touch home the rebound.

All credit to Crewe, for they did not give up and a minute later Llewellyn burst through to get their second. The last goal of an incredible match came in the 79th minute with Jones scoring from the penalty spot after he had been fouled.

It had been one of Spurs' most dazzling and ruthless exhibitions ever. But it must be said that Crewe contributed to the entertainment. Outclassed they may have been but they always tried to play good open football and never resorted to dubious tactics.

Spurs: Brown; Hills, Henry, Blanchflower, Norman, Mackay, White, Harmer, R.Smith, Allen, C.Jones.
Crewe Alexandra: Evans; Millar, Campbell, D.Jones, Willmott, Warhurst, Coleman, Riley, Llewellyn, Keery, M.Jones.
Referee: L.H.Harris   *Attendance: 64,365*

Match to Remember 14   20 September 1961

Spurs 8   Górnik Zabrze 1

SPURS' very first venture into a European competition had an uneasy start. The 'double' winners had been beaten by the Polish champions, 4-2 in the first leg of this preliminary round tie, and were only saved by two goals in the last 20 minutes.

Everybody thought they would be disgraced and out of the competition at the first hurdle. But nearly 57,000 people turned up to witness the first of many famous European nights at White Hart Lane.

With the match only 30 seconds old, Spurs rocked Górnik, Allen stabbing a shot against the bar. Nine minutes later, Spurs got their first goal, a penalty by Blanchflower, and only ten minutes later, Blanchflower cut open the right flank of the Górnik defence to give Dyson time and space to lob the ball across for Jones to put Spurs level on aggregate.

On the 24-minute mark, a long throw-in by Mackay was cleared to Jones on the edge of the box. He scored with a left-foot drive; and only nine minutes later, it was Jones again, turning in a cross from the by-line by Allen.

Before half-time, Smith sewed the match up for Spurs with a header and repeated the feat in the 72nd minute with another splendid effort.

Spurs did not ease up. Their pride had been dented by the first-leg defeat and they wanted Europe to realise that they meant business. Dyson and Blanchflower combined before Blanchflower's return pass put Dyson in for a seventh and in the last minute White made it eight.

Spurs: Brown; Baker, Henry, Blanchflower, Norman, Mackay, Jones, White, Smith, Allen, Dyson.
Górnik Zabrze: Kostka; Franosz, Oslizlo, Olszowka, Gawlik, Ollejnik, Florenski, Wilczek, Jankowski, Pohl, Lentner.
Referee: L. Van Nuffell   *Attendance: 56,737*

Match to Remember 15   29 September 1962

Spurs 9   Nottingham Forest 2

WHEN Nottingham Forest arrived at White Hart Lane they had conceded only 11 goals in ten games. When they left they had goalkeeper Grummitt to thank that the figure had not doubled; it was only due to Grummitt's superb performance that Spurs did not reach double figures.

Yet after five minutes, nobody could have imagined how the result would turn out, for Hockey capitalised on a mistake by Henry and put Forest ahead. Inside ten minutes, however, the tables had been completely turned. Within 60 seconds of Hockey's goal, Greaves took a pass from Medwin to equalise; five minutes later, a similar move gave Greaves a second. Four minutes after that, Blanchflower put Jones through to make it 3-1.

In the 28th minute, White scored from Medwin's pass, then Allen supplied passes for goals by Medwin and Greaves. Tottenham had scored six by half-time.

Spurs were playing slick interchanging football at its best. Their fast approach work was destroying Forest's offside trap and disproving the theory that the Spurs team was growing old.

In the 51st minute, Jones was fouled in the box and Allen rammed home the penalty. This was followed, two minutes later, by Jones netting after Henry had created the opening.

The Forest attack now tried to make up for the shortcomings of their defence, forcing Brown to make three splendid saves before Greaves scored Spurs' last goal from a Mackay pass in the 72nd minute.

Spurs were still not finished, however, and in the last quarter of an hour, Grummitt was forced to make great saves to prevent first Greaves and then Henry making it ten. But Forest had the last word, Vowden netted from a Hockey cross four minutes from the final whistle.

Spurs: Brown; Baker, Henry, Blanchflower, Norman, Mackay, Medwin, White, Allen, Greaves, Jones.
Nottingham Forest: Grummitt; Wilson, Gray, Palmer, McKinlay, Winfield, Hockey, Adamson, Quigley, Vowden, Le Flem.
Referee: K. E. Walker   *Attendance: 48,336*

Spurs 5   Aston Villa 5

THIS was one of the highest scoring and most exciting games seen at White Hart Lane in recent years but was not one of Spurs' better performances. Coasting to victory, 5-1 ahead, they were stung by a Villa fightback inspired by Tony Hateley.

In the first 15 minutes, with Greaves in scintillating form and getting back to his best after a long illness, Spurs were untouchable. In the second minute Gilzean turned in a Mackay shot after a Greaves corner; and ten minutes later, Possee and Clayton combined to send Greaves through. His first effort was blocked by Withers but Greaves was first to the rebound to put Spurs two up. Only two minutes after that, Saul headed Spurs' third but it was only a further two minutes before Hateley provided a sample of what was to come. After Baker had got round Mullery, playing out of position at full-back, Hateley headed in the cross.

Five minutes before half-time, Laurie Brown shot home through a crowded penalty area and five minutes the other side of half-time, a diving header by Robertson gave Spurs what should have been a winning 5-1 lead.

It was now that Hateley started to give Laurie Brown the runaround. In the space of four minutes, two goals from Hateley and one from Deakin put a completely different complexion on the game.

Eleven minutes from the end, Hateley again got his head to the ball to equalise; and in the 87th minute, Deakin was clean through. He rounded Jennings but faced with an easy shot into an empty net, hesitated. By the time he managed to tap the ball goalwards, Mullery had recovered sufficiently to clear off the line.

Spurs: Jennings; Mullery, Knowles, Clayton, L.Brown, Mackay, Robertson, Greaves, Saul, Gilzean, Possee.

Aston Villa: Withers; Wright, Aitken, Pountney, Sleeuwenhoek, Tindall, McEwain, Hamilton, Hateley, Deakin, Baker.

Referee: P.R.Walters   *Attendance: 28,290*

Spurs 4   Leeds United 2

THIS was a match Spurs had to win to stay in Division One. It was the last game of the season and anything less than two points would mean relegation. Moreover, the opposition could not have been tougher. Although only ninth in the First Division, Leeds were through to the European Cup Final.

Martin Chivers had not started a first-team match for two months and it appeared that his great career at Spurs was over, but he was recalled to add his experience and it was the seasoned players, together with a crowd of almost 50,000, who saw Spurs safely home.

The match started well for Tottenham. In only the fifth minute, the magical Alfie Conn was fouled on the edge of the box and Cyril Knowles slammed home the free-kick to give Spurs the start they wanted.

The first half was one continual bombardment of the Leeds goal, with Knowles, playing one of his best games, sending over a continual stream of crosses. Yet the crucial second goal would not come although Pat Jennings was practically redundant except for two saves from Jordan.

The second half was five minutes old when Spurs got the goal they so desperately needed. A free-kick saw the ball go from Knowles to Perryman. Conn's shot was half saved but Chviers was on hand to net the rebound.

The result was made safe in the 63rd minute when Knowles netted a penalty after Perryman had been brought down by Cherry, although Jordan scored after a 30-yard Lorimer shot had come back off a post.

Conn rounded things off in the 75th minute when he took a pass from Chivers, beat three men and scored from an impossible angle. The celebrations of the Spurs fans were as great as if the FA Cup had just been won and a second Leeds goal by Lorimer in the 81st minute went almost unnoticed.

It did not matter. Spurs were still in the First Division and that was the only consideration. They had won with a style and bravado that had been missing through the earlier months of the season.

The stars were Knowles, who had scored twice and had a hand in another; Conn, who had continually kept the Leeds defence at full stretch with his scintillating runs; and Osgood, who had played on despite a bad head wound and continual pain from an ankle injury. But they were all heroes and the Spurs fans were still on the pitch celebrating half an hour after the final whistle.

Spurs: Jennings; Kinnear, Knowles, Beal, Osgood, Naylor, Conn, Perryman, Chivers, Jones, Pratt.
Leeds United: Stewart; Reaney, Cherry, Bremner, Madeley, Hunter, Lorimer, F.Gray, Jordan, Yorath, E.Gray.
Referee: K.H.Burns *Attendance: 49,886*

Match to Remember 18   26 October 1977

Spurs 9   Bristol Rovers 0

AT the end of the 1977-8 season, Spurs regained First Division status on goal-difference and this match provided the goals that proved so crucial.

Only 48 hours earlier, Spurs had paid Torquay United £60,000 for a little-known striker called Colin Lee. By the end of the afternoon the whole country was to know the name of this young man who, rejected by Bristol City, had spent half his short career as a full-back.

The first 20 minutes gave little indication of the mayhem to come but in the 21st minute, an immaculate cross by Hoddle was headed down by Moores for Lee to sweep it home. Four minutes later, Lee leapt high at the far post to get his second from Pratt's corner; and one minute from half-time, Taylor headed home another cross from Hoddle.

Moores scored number-four from Taylor's cross in the 56th minute but it was in the last 15 minutes that the game really began to explode.

First Pratt headed on a Taylor corner for Lee to grab his third; then Hoddle's cross was dummied for Moores to get his second. Eight minutes from the end, Lee turned provider and crossed for Moores to hit his third; and four minutes later Lee, on the floor, reacted swiftly to turn in the ball after Taylor's shot had been blocked.

With just two minutes left, the immaculate Hoddle collected Moores' pass over the defence to score a goal he richly deserved and give Tottenham their record Football League winning margin.

Spurs: Daines; Naylor, Holmes, Hoddle, McAllister, Perryman, Pratt, McNab, Moores, Lee, Taylor.
Bristol Rovers: Jones; Bater, T.Taylor, Day, S.Taylor, Prince(Hendrie), Williams, Aitken, Gould, Staniforth, Evans.
Referee: H.R.Robinson *Attendance: 26,311*

Leeds United's Joe Jordan seems in control for the European Cup Finalists but it was Spurs who triumphed to stay in Division One.

Spurs 6   Wolverhampton Wanderers 1

ON the day Spurs new West Stand was officially opened, the opposition was provided by Wolves, the same club who had met Tottenham in their first-ever Football League game 74 years earlier.

Again Wolves were to return to the Midlands beaten, but this time they were well and truly trampled by a Spurs team inspired by Glenn Hoddle. The big Argentinian, Ricky Villa, was the chief executioner.

It all started in the ninth minute when Wolves centre-half Gallagher fouled Mark Falco and the referee had no option but to give the penalty which Hoddle put away.

On the half-hour, Villa scored his first goal with a vicious swerving shot; and ten minutes later he netted with a powerful header from Tony Galvin's cross. On the stroke of half-time, Hibbitt made the score a little more respectable when he cracked home a short free-kick from Atkinson, but within three minutes of the restart, Villa collected his third when he picked up a loose ball and rifled his shot home.

After a further three minutes, Garth Crooks scored with a superb near-post header and the scoring was concluded in the final minutes when Falco turned home a Steve Perryman cross.

Spurs: Clemence; Hughton, Miller, Price, Villa, Perryman, Ardiles, Falco, Galvin, Hoddle, Crooks(Hazard).
Wolverhampton Wanderers: Bradshaw; Palmer, Humphrey, Atkinson, Gallagher, Berry, Hibbitt, Eves, Gray, Richards, Brazier(Clarke).
Referee: T.Spencer   *Attendance: 29,990*

Spurs 5   West Ham United 0

WITH Arsenal awaiting the winners in the semi-final, Spurs and West Ham had drawn 1-1 at Upton Park five days earlier, and Tottenham were now favourites to go through to a North London derby with their greatest rivals. West Ham were badly hit by injuries but no team could have lived with Spurs on this night, and in particular with the predatory Clive Allen in his record-breaking season.

Spurs made a flying start when Ossie Ardiles found Nico Claesen with a delicately chipped pass. Claesen took the ball on his chest before coolly flicking it past Parkes with his marker, Parris, floundering in his wake. Only six minutes had gone.

For the next 65 minutes those in attendance were treated to an exhibition of top-class English football mixed with the delicate foreign skills of Claesen and Ardiles. Spurs were well on top throughout practically all this period with Chris Waddle taking on defenders, and Paul Allen providing non-stop running in midfield to complement the marvellous skills of Glenn Hoddle at his best. Although there were brief glimpses of West Ham's cultured football, and Ray Clemence made a brilliant save from a McAvennie header, Spurs were running riot and it was only a matter of time before they got their second.

It came in the 71st minutes when, with the West Ham defence backing off and expecting a pass, Hoddle sent a lovely shot into the net from 20 yards, taking the entire defence and a good portion of the crowd by surprise. West Ham now had to throw caution to

144

Nico Claesen is congratulated by Clive Allen after scoring the first goal.

the wind if their interest in the competition was going to stay and that provided the perfect stage for Clive Allen to finish them off.

In the 80th minute, Claesen collected a clearance from Clemence, sped down the right wing and put over the perfect low cross. Allen arrived just before Parkes and got his toe to the ball. It ballooned up into the air beyond Parkes and dropped over the line. Six minutes later Paul Allen had twisted his way into the box when he was brought down by Alvin Martin and cousin Clive drilled the penalty home.

In the last minute, Paul Allen scampered down the left and sent a cross to the far post. Clive Allen was there to put away the easiest chance of the night.

In what was a season of great success for Spurs under the guidance of the newly-installed David Pleat, this was a performance *par excellence*.

Spurs: Clemence; D.Thomas, M.Thomas, Ardiles, Gough, Mabbutt, C.Allen, P.Allen, Waddle, Hoddle, Claesen.
West Ham United: Parkes; Bonds, Parris(Hilton), Gale, Martin, Devonshire, Ward, McAvennie, Orr, Cottee, Robson.
Referee: V.G.Callow   *Attendance: 41,995*

Match to Remember 21   14 April 1991

Spurs 3   Arsenal 1

WITH so many supporters wanting to witness this match and no other suitable venue available, the FA decided that these two great rivals should meet at Wembley in the first FA Cup semi-final to be staged there.

Even with an all-seater capacity of 80,000, the famous old stadium could have been sold out five times over for a match which was of crucial importance to both clubs, although for totally different reasons.

Arsenal went into the match odds-on favourites. Five points ahead of Liverpool in the race for the First Division title (and that after having two points deducted for a brawl at Old Trafford early in the season), they had lost only twice in 42 matches and were looking more than capable of repeating their double feat of 20 years earlier.

Spurs, on the other hand, had been going through a terrible time. Beset by financial problems throughout the season, the chance of an FA Cup Final provided not only the last hope of a major trophy but also the financial lifeline that might just avoid the need to sell England's World Cup hero Paul Gascoigne and avert perhaps even the threat of liquidation.

But Spurs' problems were not only off the field. After the sixth-round win over Notts County, Gascoigne had gone into hospital for a double hernia operation and had played only 60 minutes football in five weeks. His midfield partner, David Howells, had been absent for 11 weeks and had returned to first-team action only five days earlier. It was hardly the perfect build-up to such a vital match for Spurs and the inclusion of both Gascoigne and Howells was seen as a major gamble by manager Terry Venables.

After only five minutes Spurs were ahead. Paul Stewart, operating in a five-man midfield that left only Gary Lineker up front, was needlessly fouled by Anders Limpar more than 30 yards from goal. Gascoigne took the kick and hit the ball into the top left-hand corner of Seaman's goal with tremendous power.

A dream start for Spurs and five minutes later the dream began to look like becoming reality. Gascoigne and Paul Allen played an exquisite exchange of passes down the right-hand flank. Howells just missed Allen's perfect cross but when the ball bounced off the chest of Alan Smith, who had gone back into defence to cover Gary Mabbutt, Lineker pounced to poke the ball over the line.

For the next 20 minutes, Spurs' short-passing midfield movements had Arsenal chasing shadows and the speed with which the midfield men got up to support Lineker tore gaping holes in the best defence in the country. Gascoigne showed his full repertoire of tricks, Vinny Samways' neat flicks, deft lay-offs and continual support of colleagues always gave the man in possession plenty of options, and in the centre of the pitch Stewart was always there to pick up the pieces. Out on the wings Howells and Allen gave the Arsenal full-

Paul Gascoigne hammers home a superb goal from a free-kick to give Spurs a sensational start to the semi-final.

146

Five minutes later, Gary Lineker stabs home the ball from close range to put Spurs 2-0 ahead.

backs, Dixon and Winterburn, no peace and deprived the Gunners of their most potent attacking ploy.

Spurs deserved a third goal but it would not come and on the stroke of half-time Arsenal pulled one back. At last Dixon managed to get forward and fire a cross into the penalty box. Erik Thorstvedt started to come but then retreated to his line and was unable to get down as Smith beat Mabbutt in the air.

With Gascoigne and Howells sure to tire on Wembley's energy-sapping turf, Spurs knew that they were bound to come under severe pressure. But if the first half belonged to Spurs' forwards, the second was to belong to the defence. Steve Sedgley and Mabbutt worked tirelessly to keep Smith and Kevin Campbell under control. Pat Van den Hauwe showed the calm experience expected of such a seasoned professional and blotted out the threat of Anders Limpar so that the Swede was replaced by Perry Groves. On the opposite flank, young Justin Edinburgh had such a superb game that it was hard to believe that barely 12 months earlier he had been playing in the Fourth Division for Southend United. Behind them, Thorstvedt was immaculate, commanding his penalty area and thriving on the high balls Arsenal hurled at him.

The exhausted Gascoigne was withdrawn after 60 minutes, to be replaced by Nayim, but by then had done more than enough to justify his rapid return from surgery.

For 30 minutes, Spurs fought off Arsenal's increasingly desperate efforts to equalise and then broke away to clinch their place in the Final.

Mabbutt won the ball in the centre circle and slipped it between two Arsenal men to set Lineker on a run for goal. Samways raced ahead and drew Steve Bould, leaving Lineker with only Tony Adams to beat. Seaman seemed to get both hands to Lineker's shot but the ball slipped through them and into the far side of the goal.

It was all over but Arsenal were not a team to give up and Campbell hit the bar with Paul Merson putting the rebound inches wide.

Man of the match Samways was replaced by Paul Walsh and with Arsenal throwing everything forward, Spurs had several chances to increase the margin but were unable to take them. It mattered not, for when the whistle went Spurs had booked another day out at Wembley.

Spurs: Thorstvedt; Edinburgh, Van den Hauwe, Sedgley, Howells, Mabbutt, Stewart, Gascoigne(Nayim), Samways(Walsh), Lineker, Allen.
Arsenal: Seaman; Dixon, Winterburn, Thomas, Bould, Adams, Campbell, Davis, Smith, Merson, Limpar(Groves). Sub not used: O'Leary.
Referee: R.Lewis   *Attendance: 77,893*

Spurs League Records

	P	W	D	L	F	A	Pts	Pos
SOUTHERN ALLIANCE								
Division One								
1892-93	12	7	2	3	29	21	16	3rd
	12	7	2	3	29	21	16	

	P	W	D	L	F	A	Pts	Pos
SOUTHERN LEAGUE								
Division One								
1896-97	20	9	4	7	43	29	22	4th
1897-98	22	12	4	6	52	31	28	3rd
1898-99	24	10	4	10	40	36	24	3rd
1899-00	28	20	4	4	67	26	44	1st
1900-01	28	16	4	8	55	33	36	5th
1901-02	30	18	6	6	61	22	42	2nd
1902-03	30	14	7	9	47	31	35	4th
1903-04	34	16	11	7	54	37	43	2nd
1904-05	34	15	8	11	53	34	38	5th
1905-06	34	16	7	11	46	29	39	5th
1906-07	38	17	9	12	63	45	43	6th
1907-08	38	17	7	14	59	48	41	7th
	360	180	75	105	640	401	435	

	P	W	D	L	F	A	Pts	Pos
UNITED LEAGUE								
Division One								
1896-97	14	1	4	9	25	34	6	8th
1897-98	16	8	5	3	40	27	21	2nd
1898-99	20	11	2	7	36	25	24	3rd
	50	20	11	19	101	86	51	

	P	W	D	L	F	A	Pts	Pos
THAMES & MEDWAY LEAGUE								
Division One								
1898-99	16	10	0	6	43	28	20	4th
	16	10	0	6	43	28	20	

	P	W	D	L	F	A	Pts	Pos
SOUTHERN DISTRICT COMBINATION								
Division One								
1899-00	16	10	3	3	41	18	23	2nd
	16	10	3	3	41	18	23	

	P	W	D	L	F	A	Pts	Pos
WESTERN LEAGUE								
Division One								
1900-01	16	8	5	3	37	19	21	3rd
1901-02	16	11	3	2	42	17	25	2nd
1902-03	16	6	7	3	20	14	19	4th
1903-04	16	11	3	2	32	12	25	1st
1904-05	20	5	6	9	20	28	16	8th
1905-06	20	7	7	6	28	17	21	4th

	P	W	D	L	F	A	Pts	Pos
1906-07	10	3	3	4	13	15	9	4th
1907-08	12	7	0	5	26	15	14	2nd
	126	58	34	34	218	137	150	

	P	W	D	L	F	A	Pts	Pos
LONDON LEAGUE								
Division One								
1901-02	8	3	3	2	15	13	9	2nd
1902-03	10	7	1	2	19	4	15	1st
1903-04	12	7	1	4	23	14	15	2nd
	30	17	5	8	57	31	39	

	P	W	D	L	F	A	Pts	Pos
LONDON FOOTBALL COMBINATION								
Division One								
1915-16	22	8	8	6	38	35	24	6th
Division Two								
1915-16	14	8	3	3	32	22	19	2nd
Division One								
1916-17	40	24	5	11	112	64	53	4th
1917-18	36	22	2	12	86	56	46	4th
1918-19	36	13	8	15	52	72	34	8th
	148	75	26	47	320	249	176	

	P	W	D	L	F	A	Pts	Pos
FOOTBALL LEAGUE SOUTH								
Division One								
1940-41	23	9	5	9	53	41	23	10th
1941-42	30	15	8	7	61	41	38	5th
1942-43	28	16	6	6	68	28	38	2nd
1943-44	30	19	8	3	71	36	46	1st
1944-45	30	23	6	1	81	30	52	1st
1945-46	42	22	3	17	78	81	47	9th
	183	104	36	43	412	257	244	

	P	W	D	L	F	A	Pts	Pos
FOOTBALL LEAGUE								
Division Two								
1908-09	38	20	11	7	67	32	51	2nd
Division One								
1909-10	38	11	10	17	53	69	32	15th
1910-11	38	13	6	19	52	63	32	15th
1911-12	38	14	9	15	53	53	37	12th
1912-13	38	12	6	20	45	72	30	17th
1913-14	38	12	10	16	50	62	34	17th
1914-15	38	8	12	18	57	90	28	20th
Division Two								
1919-20	42	32	6	4	102	32	70	1st
Division One								
1920-21	42	19	9	14	70	48	47	6th

	P	W	D	L	F	A	Pts	Pos
1921-22	42	21	9	12	65	39	51	2nd
1922-23	42	17	7	18	50	50	41	12th
1923-24	42	12	14	16	50	56	38	15th
1924-25	42	15	12	15	52	43	42	12th
1925-26	42	15	9	18	66	79	39	15th
1926-27	42	16	9	17	76	78	41	13th
1927-28	42	15	8	19	74	86	38	21st
Division Two								
1928-29	42	17	9	16	75	81	43	10th
1929-30	42	15	9	18	59	61	39	12th
1930-31	42	22	7	13	88	55	51	3rd
1931-32	42	16	11	15	87	78	43	8th
1932-33	42	20	15	7	96	51	55	2nd
Division One								
1933-34	42	21	7	14	79	56	49	3rd
1934-35	42	10	10	22	54	93	30	22nd
Division Two								
1935-36	42	18	13	11	91	55	49	5th
1936-37	42	17	9	16	88	66	43	10th
1937-38	42	19	17		76	54	44	5th
1938-39	42	19	9	14	67	62	47	8th
1939-40	3	1	2	0	6	5	4	7th
1946-47	42	17	14	11	65	53	48	6th
1947-48	42	15	14	13	56	43	44	8th
1948-49	42	17	16	9	72	44	50	5th
1949-50	42	27	7	8	81	35	61	1st
Division One								
1950-51	42	25	10	7	82	44	60	1st
1951-52	42	22	9	11	76	51	53	2nd
1952-53	42	15	11	16	78	69	41	10th
1953-54	42	16	5	21	65	76	37	16th
1954-55	42	16	8	18	72	73	40	16th
1955-56	42	15	7	20	61	71	37	18th
1956-57	42	22	12	8	104	56	56	2nd
1957-58	42	21	9	12	93	77	51	3rd
1958-59	42	13	10	19	85	95	36	18th
1959-60	42	21	11	10	86	50	53	3rd
1960-61	42	31	4	7	115	55	66	1st
1961-62	42	21	10	11	88	69	52	3rd

	P	W	D	L	F	A	Pts	Pos
1962-63	42	23	9	10	111	62	55	2nd
1963-64	42	22	7	13	97	81	51	4th
1964-65	42	19	7	16	87	71	45	6th
1965-66	42	16	12	14	75	66	44	8th
1966-67	42	24	8	10	71	48	56	3rd
1967-68	42	19	9	14	70	59	47	7th
1968-69	42	14	17	11	61	51	45	6th
1969-70	42	17	9	16	54	55	43	11th
1970-71	42	19	14	9	54	33	52	3rd
1971-72	42	19	13	10	63	42	51	6th
1972-73	42	16	13	13	58	48	45	8th
1973-74	42	14	14	14	45	50	42	11th
1974-75	42	13	8	21	52	63	34	19th
1975-76	42	14	15	13	63	63	43	9th
1976-77	42	12	9	21	48	72	33	22nd
Division Two								
1977-78	42	20	16	6	83	49	56	3rd
Division One								
1978-79	42	13	15	14	48	61	41	11th
1979-80	42	15	10	17	52	62	40	14th
1980-81	42	14	15	13	70	68	43	10th
1981-82	42	20	11	11	67	48	71	4th
1982-83	42	20	9	13	65	50	69	4th
1983-84	42	17	10	15	64	65	61	8th
1984-85	42	23	8	11	78	51	77	3rd
1985-86	42	19	8	15	74	52	65	10th
1986-87	42	21	8	13	68	43	71	3rd
1987-88	40	12	11	17	38	48	47	13th
1988-89	38	15	12	11	60	46	57	6th
1989-90	38	19	6	13	60	47	63	3rd
1990-91	38	11	16	11	51	50	49	11th
1991-92	42	15	7	20	58	63	52	15th
	3027	1276	737	1014	5072	4297	3361	

FA Premier League

	P	W	D	L	F	A	Pts	Pos
1992-93	42	16	11	15	60	66	59	8th
	42	16	11	15	60	66	59	

1896-97

Manager: None

1	Sep	5	(a)	Sheppey U	D 3-3	Crump, Milliken, Clements	2,000
2		12	(a)	Wolverton	L 0-1		1,000
3	Oct	3	(a)	Gravesend	W 3-1	Newbigging, Clements, Payne	1,600
4		10	(h)	Chatham	L 2-3	Milliken, Payne	3,000
5		17	(h)	Gravesend	W 4-0	McElhaney, Milliken 2, Clements	3,000
6		24	(a)	R Ordnance*	W 2-1	Almond, Payne	500
7		31	(a)	Chatham	W 2-1	McElhaney, Milliken	5,000
8	Nov	7	(h)	Sheppey U	W 3-2	McElhaney, Clements, Payne	3,000
9		14	(h)	Swindon T	W 3-1	Devlin, Milliken, Newbigging	2,000
10		28	(h)	Millwall A	L 1-3	Fleming	6,000
11	Dec	5	(a)	Reading	L 1-2	Payne	3,500
12		25	(a)	Millwall A	W 4-0	McElhaney, Clements 2, Payne	6,000
13	Jan	9	(a)	Swindon T	L 0-1		2,000
14	Feb	13	(h)	Northfleet	W 5-0	Robertson, Clements 3, Stirling (og)	3,000
15		20	(a)	New Brompton	L 1-2	Clements	2,000
16	Mar	6	(a)	Northfleet	L 0-2		2,000
17		20	(h)	Reading	D 4-4	Almond, McElhaney, Wilson, Clements	4,000
18		27	(h)	New Brompton	W 2-0	Wilson, Clements	2,000
19		29	(a)	Soton St Mary's	D 1-1	Clements	3,000
20	Apr	1	(h)	Wolverton	W 2-0	McElhaney, Crump	2,000
21		8	(h)	Soton St Mary's	D 2-2	Wilson, Clements	3,000

FINAL LEAGUE POSITION: 4th in Southern League, Division One.
*Result not included in final league table due to Royal Ordnance's resignation.

Appearances
Goals

United League

22	Sep	19	(a)	Millwall A	L 5-6	Crump 2, Newbigging 2, Clements	6,000
23	Nov	2	(a)	Rushden	L 0-2		
24		9	(a)	W Arsenal	L 1-2	McElhaney	
25	Jan	30	(a)	Wellingborough	D 2-2	Burrrows (pen), Clements	1,200
26	Feb	25	(h)	W Arsenal	D 2-2	Devlin, Clements	2,000
27		27	(h)	Loughborough	L 1-2	Payne	4,000
28	Mar	4	(h)	Rushden	W 5-1	Briggs, Newbigging, Milliken, Allen, Crump	
29		13	(h)	Luton T	L 1-2	Devlin	7,000
30		15	(a)	Kettering T†	D 1-1	Milliken	200
31	Apr	3	(h)	Millwall A	L 1-3	Milliken	5,000
32		10	(a)	Luton T	L 1-2	Newbigging	2,500
33		13	(a)	Kettering T	L 2-5	Wilson, Draper (og)	
34		17	(h)	Kettering T	D 1-1	Clements	
35		19	(h)	Wellingborough	D 1-1	Lanham	
36		24	(a)	Loughborough	L 2-3	Clements, Hobson	

FINAL LEAGUE POSITION: 8th in United League, Division One.
†Abandoned after 25 minutes — a Kettering Town player broke his leg.

Appearances
Goals

FA Cup

1Q	Dec	12	(h)	Old St Stephen's	W 4-0	Newbigging, Clements 2, Payne	
2Q	Jan	6	(h)	Maidenhead	W 6-0	Crump 2, McElhaney, Newbigging 2, Payne	2,000
3Q		16	(a)	Luton T	L 0-3		5,000

Appearances
Goals

Wellingborough Charity Cup

P	Nov	19	(h)	Gravesend	W 3-2	Almond, Fleming 2	1,000
1	Dec	16	(a)	Wolverton	W 2-0	McElhaney, Lanham	
SF	Apr	5	(n§)	Rushden*	W 2-1	McElhaney (pen), Clements	1,000
F		29	(a)	Wellingborough	L 0-2		

§ Played at Wellingborough. * After extra-time.

Appearances
Goals

Football appearance and scorer grid (positions 1–11 by player and match). Empty cells indicate the player did not play in that match.

Allen	Almond	Ambler	Briggs	Brown	Burrows	Clements	Collins	Crump	Devlin	Fleming	Hatfield	Hobson	Hunter	Jull J	Jull TE	Lanham	Latham	Mair	Markham E	McElhaney	Milliken	Montgomery	Newbigging	Payne	Regan	Robertson	Shepherd	Stokeley	Wilson	Cook	
		1			2	10	4	6	5											7	8	3	9	11							1
	5	1			2	10		6	4									7			8	3	9	11							2
		1	5		2	10		6	4											7	8	3	9	11							3
		1	5		2	10		6	4											7	8	3	9	11							4
	5	1			2	10		6	4											7	8	3	9	11							5
	5	1			2	10		6	4											7	8	3	9	11							6
	5	1			2	10	4	6	8											7	9	3		11							7
	5	1	4		2	10		6	8											7	9	3		11							8
	5	1			2	10		6	4											7	8	3	9	11							9
	5	1			2	10		6	4	9										7	8	3		11							10
	5	1			2	10			4	11							6			7	8	3	9								11
	5	1			2	10		6	4											7	8	3	9	11							12
8		1			2	10		6	4									5		7		3	9	11							13
	5	1			2	10		6	4											7	8	3		11	9						14
	5	1			2	10		6	4								8			7	9	3		11							15
9	5	1			2	10		6	4												8	3	7	11							16
	5	1			2	10		6	4											7	8	3		11			9				17
	5	1	6			10		11	4										2	7		3		8			9				18
5		1	6			10		11	4										2	7	8	3					9				19
	5		6			10		11	4		1								2	7	8	3					9				20
2	5	1				10		6	4											7	8	3		11			9				21
4	16	20	6		17	21	2	20	21	2	1						2	2	3	19	19	21	10	19	1		5				
	2					14		2	1	1										6	6		2	6	1		3				

I own-goal

Allen	Almond	Ambler	Briggs	Brown	Burrows	Clements	Collins	Crump	Devlin	Fleming	Hatfield	Hobson	Hunter	Jull J	Jull TE	Lanham	Latham	Mair	Markham E	McElhaney	Milliken	Montgomery	Newbigging	Payne	Regan	Robertson	Shepherd	Stokeley	Wilson	Cook	
		1	5		2	10		6	4											7	8	3	9	11							22
		1	5		2	10	6		4											7	8	3	9	11							23
	5	1			2	10	4	6	8											7	11	3	9								24
5		1			2	10		6	4									9		7	8	3		11							25
	5	1			2	10		6	4											7	8	3	9	11							26
	5	1			2	10		6	4									3		7	8		9	11							27
9		1	6		2	10		11	5												8	3	7			4					28
9	5	1			2	10		6	4											7	8	3		11							29
5		1				10		11	4										6	2	7	8	3	9							30
	5	1	6		2	10			4											7	8	3		11			9				31
2		1	5			10		6	4										3	7		8		11			9				32
2			5			10		11	4		1								6	3	7	8					9				33
5					2	10		6				7		8	1	4					3	9	11								34
5		1			3	8		6					11	10	4					2	9	7									35
5						10		7				11	8		2						3	9			4	1					36
9	5	12	6		11	15	2	13	12	1	1	1	2	1	3	1	7	2		11	11	12	11	10	1	1	1	3			
1			1		1	5		3	2				1				1			1	3	4	1				1				

I own-goal

Allen	Almond	Ambler	Briggs	Brown	Burrows	Clements	Collins	Crump	Devlin	Fleming	Hatfield	Hobson	Hunter	Jull J	Jull TE	Lanham	Latham	Mair	Markham E	McElhaney	Milliken	Montgomery	Newbigging	Payne	Regan	Robertson	Shepherd	Stokeley	Wilson	Cook	
	5	1	6		2	10			4											7	8	3	9	11							1Q
	5	1			2	10	4	6												7	8	3	9	11							2Q
	5	1			2	10	4	6												7	8	3	9	11							3Q
	3	3	1		3	3	2	3												3	3	3	3	3							
						2		2												1		3	2								

Allen	Almond	Ambler	Briggs	Brown	Burrows	Clements	Collins	Crump	Devlin	Fleming	Hatfield	Hobson	Hunter	Jull J	Jull TE	Lanham	Latham	Mair	Markham E	McElhaney	Milliken	Montgomery	Newbigging	Payne	Regan	Robertson	Shepherd	Stokeley	Wilson	Cook	
	5	1			2	10		6	4	9										7	8	3		11							P
		5						11	4		1						8		6	7	10	3	9					2			1
2		1	5		11			6	4											7	8	3	10				9				SF
4		1	5	7		10		11									8			2	3	9			6						F
2	1	3	3	1	1	3		4	3	1	1					1		1	1	3	4	4	3	1	1		1	1			
	1					1				1						1			2												

151

1897-98

Manager: Frank Brettell from March

1	Sep	4	(a)	Sheppey U	D	1-1	Joyce	2,000
2		18	(h)	Southampton	W	2-0	Davidson 2	6,000
3		25	(h)	Millwall A	W	7-0	Tannahill, Davidson, Meade 3, Joyce, Black	10,000
4	Oct	2	(a)	New Brompton	L	0-1		4,000
5		9	(h)	Gravesend U	W	2-0	Hartley 2	2,000
6		23	(a)	Southampton	L	1-4	Tannahill	8,000
7	Nov	6	(a)	Reading	D	3-3	Tannahill, Joyce, Black	4,000
8		13	(h)	Bristol C	D	2-2	Burrows, Black	9,000
9		27	(a)	Bristol C	L	1-3	Joyce	4,000
10	Dec	18	(a)	Wolverton	W	2-1	Joyce, Stormont	1,500
11	Jan	15	(h)	Northfleet	W	4-0	Hartley, Joyce 3	2,000
12		22	(h)	Wolverton	W	7-1	Davidson 2, Joyce 4, Hartley	2,000
13		29	(a)	Chatham	L	2-4	Black, Joyce	2,500
14	Feb	5	(a)	Swindon T	L	0-3		4,000
15		19	(a)	Northfleet	W	3-1	Joyce 2, Black	2,000
16		26	(h†)	Reading	D	1-1	Jones	5,500
17	Mar	5	(a)	Gravesend U	W	2-1	Hartley 2	3,000
18		19	(h)	Sheppey U	W	4-0	Joyce 4	2,800
19	Apr	2	(h)	New Brompton	W	3-1	Joyce, Black 2	4,000
20		9	(h)	Chatham	W	2-1	Hartley, Black	3,000
21		11	(h)	Swindon T	W	2-0	Meade, Stormont	5,000
22		16	(a)	Millwall A	L	1-3	Meade	3,000

FINAL LEAGUE POSITION: 3rd in Southern League, Division One.
†Home match played at Millwall

Appearances
Goals

United League

23	Sep	16	(h)	Kettering T	D	1-1	Clements	2,000
24		29	(a)	Loughborough	W	2-1	Tannahill, Stormont	
25	Oct	11	(a)	Luton T	L	0-5		
26		16	(a)	Millwall A	W	1-0	Jones	8,000
27	Dec	4	(h)	Wellingborough	W	5-0	Tannahill, Joyce, Stormont 2, Black	1,000
28		25	(a)	W Arsenal	W	3-2	Joyce 2, Stormont	
29	Jan	1	(a)	Rushden	L	2-5	Hartley 2	
30		8	(h)	Rushden	W	3-1	Hartley 3	4,000
31		10	(a)	Kettering T	L	2-4	Joyce 2 (1 pen)	
32		19	(a)	Southampton	D	2-2	Tannahill, Joyce (pen)	3,000
33	Feb	2	(h)	Luton T	D	2-2	Stormont, Joyce	
34	Mar	12	(h)	Millwall A	W	3-2	Jones (pen), Davidson, Black	
35		24	(h)	Loughborough	W	5-0	Joyce 2, Stormont, Black 2	300
36		28	(h)	Southampton	W	7-0	Hartley, Joyce 4, Stormont, Black	
37	Apr	8	(h)	W Arsenal	D	0-0		15,000
38		23	(a)	Wellingborough	D	2-2	Stormont, Black	

FINAL LEAGUE POSITION: 2nd in United League, Division One.

Appearances
Goals

FA Cup

1Q	Oct	30	(h*)	2nd Cold'm Gds	W	7-0	Hall, Crump, Meade 2, Joyce, Stormont, Black	4,000
2Q	Nov	20	(h)	Luton T	L	3-4	Joyce 2, Black	12,000

*Drawn away but played at home by mutual consent

Appearances
Goals

Batting-order chart (each row a match; numbers indicate batting position).

Matches 1–22

	Ambler	Black	Briggs	Burrows	Clements	Crump	Cullen	Davidson	Downie	Hall	Hargreaves	Hartley	Jones	Joyce	Knowles	Madden	Meade	Montgomery	Payne	Stormont	Tannahill	
	11					1	10		6				5	9	2		8	3		4	7	1
	11		2	6		1	8		4				5	9	3					10	7	2
	11		2			1	8		4				5	10			9	3		6	7	3
	11		2			1	9		4				5	10	3		8			6	7	4
	11		2			1	8		4	9			5	10	3					6	7	5
	11		2			1	8		4	10			5	9	3					6	7	6
	11	5				1			4				6	9	2		8	3		10	7	7
	11		2	6		1			4				5	9	3		8			10	7	8
1	11		2	6			8		4				5	9	3					10	7	9
	11		2	6		1	8		4			7	5	9	3					10		10
						1	8		4			7	5	9	2	10	3			6	11	11
				11		1	8		4			10	5	9	2		3			6	7	12
	7			11		1	8		4			10	5	9	2		3			6		13
	11			6		1	8		4			7	5		2		9	3		10		14
	11			6		1	8	5	4			7		9	2		3			10		15
	11			6		1	8		4			7	5	9	2		3			10		16
	11			6		1	8		4			7	5	9	2		3			10		17
	11			6		1		5	4			7		9	2		8	3		10		18
	11					1	8	6	4			7	5	9	2		3			10		19
	11		2			1	8	6	4			7	5			9	3			10		20
	11					1		6	4			7	5	9	2		8	3		10		21
	7		3			1			4	6		11	5	9	2		10			8		22
1	20	1	10	11		21	17	7	21			15	20	19	19	2	10	15		22	11	
	8	1				5							7	1	20		5			2	3	

Matches 23–38

	Ambler	Black	Briggs	Burrows	Clements	Crump	Cullen	Davidson	Downie	Hall	Hargreaves	Hartley	Jones	Joyce	Knowles	Madden	Meade	Montgomery	Payne	Stormont	Tannahill	
	11		2	10		1	8		4				5	9	3					6	7	23
	11		2	6		1	8		4				5	9	3					10	7	24
	11		2			1	8		4	7	9		5	10			3			6		25
	11		2	6		1	8		4				5	9	3					10	7	26
1	11		2	6			8		4				5	9	3					10	7	27
	11		2	6		1	8		4			7	5	9	3					10		28
	11		2	6		1	8		4			7	5	9	3					10		29
	11					1	8		4			7	5	9	2	10	3			6		30
	11					1	8		4			7	5	9	2	10	3			6		31
				11		1	8		4			10	5	9	2		3			6	7	32
	11			6		1	8		4			7	5	9	2		3			10		33
	11		2	6		1	8		4			7	5	9	3					10		34
	11					1		6	4			7	5	9	2	8	3			10		35
	11			6		1		5	4			7		9	2	8	3			10		36
	11		2	6		1	8		4			7	5	9	3					10		37
	11		2	6		1		3	4			8	5	9					7	10		38
1	15	10	1	11		15	13	3	16	1		12	15	16	14	4	7	1		16	5	
	6	1				1							6	2	13					8	3	

Q matches

	Ambler	Black	Briggs	Burrows	Clements	Crump	Cullen	Davidson	Downie	Hall	Hargreaves	Hartley	Jones	Joyce	Knowles	Madden	Meade	Montgomery	Payne	Stormont	Tannahill	
	11		2	6		1			4				5	9			8	3		10	7	1Q
	11		2	6		1			4				5	9	3					10	7	2Q
	2		2	2		2			2				1	2	2	1	1	1		2	2	
	2		1			1								3			2			1		

1898-99

Southern League   Manager: Frank Brettell until February then John Cameron

1	Sep	10	(h)	Bedminster	D 1-1	Cameron	5,000
2		17	(h)	Sheppey U	W 3-2	Cameron 3	4,500
3		24	(h)	Warmley*	W 7-1	Smith 3, McKay, Joyce 3	4,000
4	Oct	8	(h)	Chatham	W 2-0	Smith, Cameron	10,000
5		22	(a)	Millwall A	L 2-4	Smith 2	14,000
6	Nov	5	(h)	Reading	W 3-0	McKay, Cameron, Bradshaw	12,000
7		26	(a)	R Artillery	W 3-2	Joyce 2, Smith	1,300
8	Dec	3	(a)	Bristol C	L 1-2	Joyce	6,000
9		17	(a)	Sheppey U	L 2-3	McKay, Penney (og)	900
10		24	(a)	Warmley*	W 5-1	Smith, Hartley, Joyce, Cameron, Bradshaw	2,000
11		26	(a)	Southampton	D 1-1	Smith	16,000
12		31	(a)	Swindon T	L 3-4	Cameron 3	6,000
13	Jan	7	(h)	R Artillery	W 1-0	McKay	3,500
14		14	(a)	Gravesend U	L 2-4	Joyce 2	3,500
15		21	(a)	Brighton U	W 1-0	Bradshaw	2,000
16	Feb	14	(a)	Reading	L 0-2		3,000
17		18	(h)	Bristol C	W 3-2	McKay, Hartley, Broadshaw	6,000
18	Mar	13	(a)	New Brompton	D 1-1	Joyce	3,000
19		18	(h)	New Brompton	W 3-0	Smith, Rule 2	3,000
20		25	(h)	Brighton U	L 1-3	Joyce	2,500
21		31	(h)	Southampton	L 0-1		8,500
22	Apr	1	(h)	Gravesend U	W 3-0	Joyce, Leach 2	4,000
23		3	(h)	Swindon T	D 1-1	Cameron	4,500
24		8	(a)	Chatham	L 0-1		3,000
25		15	(a)	Bedminster	L 0-1		1,500
26		22	(h)	Millwall A	W 3-1	Joyce, Cameron, Bradshaw	7,000

FINAL LEAGUE POSITION: 3rd in Southern League, Division One.   Appearances
*Results not included in final League table due to Warmley's resignation.   Goals

United League

27	Sep	5	(h)	Luton T	W 1-0	McKay	5,000
28		19	(a)	Luton T	W 4-3	Cameron, Joyce 2, McKay	
29	Oct	5	(a)	Brighton U	W 2-1	Cameron, Joyce	
30		10	(h)	Southampton	W 4-0	Smith, McKay, Cameron, Bradshaw	7,000
31		15	(a)	Bristol C	W 1-0	Cameron	
32	Nov	9	(a)	Reading	L 0-1		
33		12	(h)	Bristol C	W 2-1	McKay, Cameron	
34	Dec	5	(h)	Kettering T	W 3-0	Joyce 2, Bradshaw	
35	Jan	23	(h)	Reading	D 1-1	Bradshaw	
36	Feb	15	(a)	Southampton	L 1-2	Joyce	
37		20	(a)	Rushden	L 1-2	McKay	
38		27	(a)	Kettering T	W 1-0	McNaught	
39	Mar	4	(a)	Millwall A	L 1-2	Erentz	10,000
40		11	(a)	W Arsenal	L 1-2	Meade	6,000
41		27	(h)	Rushden	D 0-0		
42	Apr	4	(h)	Brighton U	W 3-0	Cameron (pen), Leach, Caldwell (og)	
43		17	(a)	Wellingborough	L 1-3	Joyce	
44		24	(h)	Wellingborough	W 5-2	Cain, Atherton, Hartley 3	800
45		26	(h)	Millwall A	L 1-3	Cameron	2,500
46		29	(h)	W Arsenal	W 3-2	Smith, Joyce, Ord (og)	5,000

FINAL LEAGUE POSITION: 3rd in United League, Division One.   Appearances
                                                                                      Goals

154

Ambler	Atherton	Bradshaw	Cain	Cameron	Cullen	Downie	Erentz	Hall	Hartley	Hickson	Hudson	Jones	Joyce	Kerry	Leach	Markham	McKay	McNaught	Meade	Melia	Payne	Rule	Smith	Stormont	Waller	
		11	3	10	1		2					4	9				8	5					7	6		1
		11	3	10	1		2					6	9				8	5					7	4		2
		11	3	10	1		2					4	9				8	5					7	6		3
			3	10	1		2					4	9				8	5			11		7	6		4
		11	3	10	1		2					4	9				8	5					7	6		5
		11	3	10	1		2					4	9				8	5					7	6		6
		11	3	10	1		2					4	9				8	5					7	6		7
		11	3	10	1		2					4	9				8	5					7	6		8
		11	3		1		4					5	10				8		9	2			7	6		9
		11	3	10	1		2	8				4	9					5					7	6		10
		11	3	10	1		2	8				4	9					5					7	6		11
		11	3	10	1	5						4	9				8			2			7	6		12
		11	3	10	1	5						4					8		9	2			7	6		13
		11		10	1		2	4					9				8	5		3			7	6		14
		11	3	10				4	5				9				8			2			7	6	1	15
1		11	3	10				5				4	9					2	8				7	6		16
		11	3	10	1							4	9				8	5		2			7	6		17
		11	3	10	1		2					4	9					5	8				7	6		18
	8	11	3	10	1	4												5		2		9	7	6		19
		11	3	8	1	4							10					5		2		9	7	6		20
		11	3	8		4							10					5		2		9	7	6	1	21
			2	10	1	6	4						9		11		8	5		3			7			22
		9	2	10	1	6	4								11		8	5		3			7			23
		9	3	10	1	4	2								11		8	5					7	6		24
	8	11		10	1	4	3						9				6	5		2			7			25
		11	3	10		4							9				8	5		2			7	6	1	26
1	2	24	24	25	22	4	24	3	3			16	21		4		18	21	5	13	1	3	26	23	3	
			5	12			2					13	2				5			2			2	10		

1 own-goal

Ambler	Atherton	Bradshaw	Cain	Cameron	Cullen	Downie	Erentz	Hall	Hartley	Hickson	Hudson	Jones	Joyce	Kerry	Leach	Markham	McKay	McNaught	Meade	Melia	Payne	Rule	Smith	Stormont	Waller	
1		11	3	10								4	9				8	5		2			7	6		27
			2	10	1	3	6	7				4	9				11	5					8			28
		11	3	10	1		2					4	9				8	5					7	6		29
		11	3	10	1		2					4	9				8	5					7	6		30
		11	2	10	1		3					4	9				8	5					7	6		31
		11	3	10	1		2					4	9				8	5					7	6		32
		11	3	10	1		2					4	9				8	5					7	6		33
		11	3	10	1		2	4				5	9				8						7	6		34
		11	3	10	1	6		4	5				9			2	8						7			35
		11	3	10	1		2	8				4	9		6				5				7			36
		11		10	1			4	7			5	9			3	8		2					6		37
		11	3	10	1			4				5	9				8			2			7	6		38
		11	3	10	1			4					9				8	5		2			7	6		39
		11	3	10	1		2					4						5	8			9	7	6		40
1		11	3	10	5			4					9				8		2				7	6		41
	8	9	3	10	1	4	2								11			5					7	6		42
	10	11	3		1	4	2						9					5	8				7	6		43
	9	11	3	10	1	5		4									8			2			7	6		44
		11	3	10		6		4					9				8	5		2			7		1	45
		11	3	10	1			4					9				8	5		2			7	6		46
2	3	19	19	19	17	6	19	3	5			11	17		2	2	14	14	2	9		1	18	17	1	
	1	3	1	7			1	3				8	1				5	1	1				2			

2 own-goals

155

1898-99 (continued)

47	Sep	3	(h)	Thames Iron	W	3-0	McKay, Cameron, Bradshaw	4,000
48		27	(a)	Sheppey U	W	3-2	Joyce, Cameron, McKay	
49	Oct	3	(h)	Gravesend U	W	3-1	Joyce 2, Cameron	2,500
50		17	(h)	New Brompton†	W	2-1	Smith, McKay	6,000
51		26	(a)	Dartford	W	3-2	Bradshaw, Cameron, McKay	
52	Nov	2	(a)	R Engineers	W	6-2	McKay 5, McNaught	100
53	Jan	2	(a)	Chatham	L	0-5		
54		9	(h)	Chatham	L	0-4		
55		16	(h)	Sheppey U	W	3-0	Hartley, Cameron, Bradshaw	1,500
56	Feb	6	(h)	Grays U	W	2-1	Atherton, Leach	
57	Mar	8	(a)	Gravesend U	W	3-0	Atherton, Cameron, Bradshaw	2,000
58		16	(a)	Thames Iron	L	1-2	Joyce	
59		20	(h)	R Engineers	L	1-2	Hartley	
60		22	(a)	Grays U	L	0-1		
61	Apr	10	(a)	New Brompton	L	4-5	Smith, Atherton, Cameron, Leach	
62		13	(h)	Dartford	W	9-0	Joyce 5, Cameron 2, Leach 2	

FINAL LEAGUE POSITION: 3rd in Thames & Medway League
†Also William Joyce's benefit match

Appearances
Goals

FA Cup

1Q	Oct	29	(h)	Wolverton	W	4-0	McKay, Joyce, Cameron, Bradshaw	3,000
2Q	Nov	19	(a)	Clapton	D	1-1	Bradshaw	7,000
R		23		Clapton	W	2-1	Cameron 2	2,500
3Q	Dec	10	(h)	Luton T	D	1-1	Joyce	12,000
R		14	(a)	Luton T	D	1-1	Joyce	4,000
2R		19	(n‡)	Luton T	W	2-0	Cameron, Bradshaw	8,000
1	Jan	28	(h)	Newton Heath	D	1-1	Joyce	13,721
R	Feb	1	(a)	Newton Heath	W	5-3	Jones, McNaught, Smith, Hartley, Joyce	6,000
2		11	(h)	Sunderland	W	2-1	Cameron, Bradshaw	12,371
3		25	(a)	Stoke	L	1-4	Bradshaw	25,000

‡Played at Tufnell Park

Appearances
Goals

156

Batting order grid (player columns left to right; rightmost column = innings/match reference):

Ambler	Atherton	Bradshaw	Cain	Cameron	Cullen	Downie	Erentz	Hall	Hartley	Hickson	Hudson	Jones	Joyce	Kerry	Leach	Markham	McKay	McNaught	Meade	Melia	Payne	Rule	Smith	Stormont	Waller	
	11	3	10				1						4	9			8	5		2			7	6		47
	11	2	10	1	3								4	9			8	5					7	6		48
	11	3	10	1	2								4	9			8	5					7	6		49
	11	3	10	1	2								4	9			8	5					7	6		50
	11	3	10	1									4	9			8	5		2			7	6		51
	11	3	10	1									4	9			8	5		2			7	6		52
	11							1		3		9	4	5		10	8			2			7	6		53
	11	3	10	1				4				9		5			8			2			7	6		54
1	5	9		8		6	3	4	7	10						11				2						55
1	8			5			4	7	10	9					6	11	3			2						56
8	11	3	10	1	2								4	9				5					7	6		57
8	11	3	10	1	2								5	9				4					7	6		58
8	11	3	10	1				4	6	7	9							5		2						59
8	9	3	10	1	4				7							11		5		2				6		60
8	9	3	10	1	4											11		5		2			7	6		61
8		3	10	1	4				7			9				11	2	5						6		62
2	8	14	13	14	13	5	9	4	7	3	1	10	10	1	6	2	8	12		10			11	13		
3	4		9				2						9				4	9	1				2			

Ambler	Atherton	Bradshaw	Cain	Cameron	Cullen	Downie	Erentz	Hall	Hartley	Hickson	Hudson	Jones	Joyce	Kerry	Leach	Markham	McKay	McNaught	Meade	Melia	Payne	Rule	Smith	Stormont	Waller	
	11	3	10	1									4	9			8	5		2			7	6		1Q
	11	3	10	1	2								4	9			8	5					7	6		2Q
	11	3	10	1	2								4	9			8	5					7	6		R
	11	3	10	1	4								5	9			8			2			7	6		3Q
	11	3		1	4								5	10			8	9	2				7	6		R
	11	3	10	1	2								4	9			8	5					7	6		2R
	11	3	10	1	2								4	9			8	5					7	6		1
		3	10	1	2			9					4	11			8	5					7	6		R
	11	3	10	1	2			8					4	9				5					7	6		2
	11	3	10	1	2								4	9				5					7	6		3
	9	10	9	10	9	2							10	10			9	8	1	3			10	10		
	5		5		1								1	5			1	1					1			

1899-1900

Southern League

Manager: John Cameron

1	Sep	2	(a)	Millwall A	W 3-1 Copeland, Kirwan 2	12,000
2		9	(h)	Queen's Park R	W 1-0 Smith	11,000
3		16	(a)	Chatham	W 3-2 Morris, Pratt, Kirwan	4,000
4		23	(h)	Reading	W 2-1 Smith 2	9,000
5	Oct	2	(h)	Gravesend U	W 4-0 Pratt, Copeland 2, Cameron	18,000
6		7	(h)	Brighton U†	W 6-1 Jones, Copeland 2, Kirwan 3	6,000
7		14	(a)	Bedminster	L 1-2 Copeland	3,000
8		21	(h)	Bristol R*	W 1-0 Pratt	4,000
9	Nov	4	(h)	Thames Iron	W 7-0 Morris 2, Pratt 3, Copeland, Kirwan	7,000
10	Dec	2	(a)	Swindon T	W 2-0 Pratt, Cameron	3,000
11		9	(h)	Bristol C	D 2-2 Copeland, Kirwan	5,000
12		16	(a)	Cowes†	W 6-1 Smith 2, Pratt, Copeland 3	500
13		25	(h)	Portsmouth	W 3-0 Pratt, Copeland, Kirwan	14,000
14		26	(a)	Southampton	L 1-3 Cameron	9,000
15		30	(h)	Millwall A	W 2-1 Cameron, Pratt	10,000
16	Jan	6	(a)	Queen's Park R	D 0-0	8,000
17		13	(h)	Chatham	W 2-1 Smith, Pratt (pen)	4,500
18		20	(a)	Reading	W 1-0 Cameron	2,000
19	Feb	3	(a)	Sheppey U	W 4-1 Cameron, Pratt 3	2,000
20		10	(a)	Brighton U†	W 3-0 Pratt 3 (1 pen)	1,800
21		17	(h)	Bedminster	W 5-2 Pratt 3, Kirwan 2	7,000
22		24	(a)	Bristol R	D 2-2 Copeland, Hyde	3,000
23	Mar	3	(a)	Portsmouth	L 0-1	7,000
24		10	(a)	Thames Iron	D 0-0	9,000
25		19	(h)	Bristol R	W 5-1 Morris, Cameron 2, Stormont, Kirwan	3,000
26		24	(h)	New Brompton	W 1-0 Pratt	5,000
27		31	(a)	Gravesend U	W 6-2 Cameron 2, Pratt 2, Copeland 2	2,000
28	Apr	7	(h)	Swindon T	W 3-0 Smith, Pratt, Copeland	7,000
29		13	(h)	Southampton	W 2-0 Cameron 2	15,000
30		14	(a)	Bristol C	L 0-3	4,000
31		16	(h)	Sheppey U	W 3-0 Hyde, Pratt, Kirwan	4,500
32		28	(a)	New Brompton	W 2-1 Cameron, Copeland	3,000

FINAL LEAGUE POSITION: 1st in Southern League, in Division One. *Abandoned after 55 minutes — fog.
†Results not included in League table due to Cowes and Brighton United's resignation

Appearances
Goals

Southern District Combination

33	Sep	18	(h)	Portsmouth	W 2-0 Cameron, Kirwan	4,000
34	Oct	9	(a)	Reading	L 1-2 Morris	
35		16	(h)	Millwall A	L 1-2 Cameron	6,000
36		23	(a)	Queen's Park R	W 3-1 Cameron 3	
37		30	(h)	Reading	W 3-0 Smith, Cameron, Copeland	3,000
38	Nov	6	(h)	Chatham	W 8-0 Morris (pen), Smith, Cameron, Pratt 3, Copeland, Kirwan	
39		15	(a)	Bristol C	D 3-3 Smith, Copeland, Kirwan	
40		20	(h)	Queen's Park R	W 3-1 Copeland, Kirwan 2	2,000
41	Dec	4	(a)	Chatham	W 1-0 Copeland	
42	Jan	8	(h)	Southampton	W 3-2 Cameron, Pratt, Durber (og)	
43		17	(a)	Portsmouth	D 2-2 Smith, Pratt	4,000
44	Mar	12	(h)	Bristol C	W 2-0 Cameron, Kirwan	3,000
45	Apr	17	(h)	W Arsenal	W 4-2 Smith, Pratt 2, Kirwan	4,000
46		24	(a)	W Arsenal‡	L 1-2 Pratt	500
47		26	(a)	Millwall A	D 0-0	
48		30	(a)	Southampton	W 4-1 Hyde, Roberts, Cameron, Leigh (og)	1,000

FINAL LEAGUE POSITION: 2nd in Southern District Combination, Division One.
‡Abandoned after 75 minutes — bad language — result stood.

Appearances
Goals

FA Cup

1	Jan	27	(a)	Preston NE	L 0-1	15,000

Appearances
Goals

158

Ambler	Cameron	Clawley	Copeland	Crump	Erentz	Haddow	Hughes	Hyde	Jones	Kirwan	McNaught	Melia	Morris	Pratt	Raby	Roberts	Rule	Smith	Stormont	Tait	Waller	
10	1	9	2					4	11	5			8			7	6	3				1
10	1	9	2					6	11	5		4	8			7		3				2
10	1	9	2					6	11	5		4	8			7		3				3
10	1	9	2					6	11	5		4	8			7		3				4
10	1	9	2					6	11	5		4	8			7		3				5
10	1	9	2		6			4	11	5			8			7		3				6
10	1	9	2					5	11			4	8			7	6	3				7
10	1	9						4	11		2	5	8			7	6	3				8
10		9						4	11		2	5	8			7	6	3	1			9
8		10		1				4	11		2	5	9			7	6	3				10
8		10		1				4	11		2	5	9			7	6	3				11
8		10	2	1	4				11	5			9			7	6	3				12
8		10	2	1				4	11	5			9			7	6	3				13
8		10	2	1				4	11	5			9			7	6	3				14
8		10	2	1		6	11	4		5			9			7		3				15
8		10	2	1				4	11	5			9			7	6	3				16
		10	2	1					11	5		4	9		8	7	6	3				17
8		10	2	1			11			5		4	9			7	6	3				18
8		10	2	1					11	5		4	9			7	6	3				19
8		10		1					11	5	2	4	9			7	6	3				20
		10		1					11	5	2	4	9		8	7	6	3				21
8		10		1			11	4		5	2		9			7	6	3				22
8		10		1					11	5	2	4	9	7			6	3				23
8				1			11			5	2	4	9	7	10		6	3				24
8				1	7	6	11	5		2		4	9		10			3				25
8			2	1		6	11			5		4	9			7		3		10		26
8		10		1					11	5	2	4	9			7	6	3				27
8		10		1					11	5	2	4	9			7	6	3				28
8		10		1					11	5	2	4	9			7	6	3				29
8		10		1					11	5	2	4	9			7	6	3				30
8		10	2	1		7		4	11	5			9				6	3				31
8	1	10	2			6			11	5		4	9			7		3				32
30	9	29	18	22	3	6		20	29	26	14	24	30	2	4	28	25	32	1			
13		17						2	1	13		4	25			7		1				

Ambler	Cameron	Clawley	Copeland	Crump	Erentz	Haddow	Hughes	Hyde	Jones	Kirwan	McNaught	Melia	Morris	Pratt	Raby	Roberts	Rule	Smith	Stormont	Tait	Waller	
10	1	9	2					6	11	5		4	8			7		3				33
9	1		2			6	11	4		5			8	10		7		3				34
10	1	9	2					5	11			4	8			7	6	3				35
10	1	9						4	11		2	5	8			7	6	3				36
1		10						4	11		2	5	8			7	6	3				37
1	10	9	2					4	11		2	5	8			7	6	3				38
8		9		1				4	11		2	5	10			7	6	3				39
8		10		1				4	11		2	5	9			7	6	3				40
8		10		1					11	4	2	5			9	7	6	3				41
8		10	2	1			11	4	7	5			9				6	3				42
8		10	2	1					11	5		4	9			7	6	3				43
9				1	7	6	11	5	2	4				8				3		10		44
8		10	2	1				4	11	5			9			7	6	3				45
8	1	10	2					4	11	5			9			7	6	3				46
1		6	2	3	11			5		4						10	9	8		7		47
8	1	10	2		11													9		7		48
2	15	7	13	1	10	7	2	5	12	13	8	6	12	12	3	2	2	14	12	14		
10		5		1				7		2			8		1			5				

2 own-goals

Ambler	Cameron	Clawley	Copeland	Crump	Erentz	Haddow	Hughes	Hyde	Jones	Kirwan	McNaught	Melia	Morris	Pratt	Raby	Roberts	Rule	Smith	Stormont	Tait	Waller	
8		10	2	1					11	5		4	9			7	6	3				1
1		1	1	1					1	1		1	1			1	1	1				

1900-01

Southern League   Manager: John Cameron

1	Sep	1	(h)	Millwall A	L 0-3		5,000
2		15	(h)	Chatham*	W 5-0	Smith, Cameron, Brown 3	3,000
3		22	(a)	Bristol C	D 1-1	Stormont	9,000
4		29	(h)	Swindon T	W 2-0	Smith, Stormont	7,000
5	Oct	6	(a)	Watford	L 1-2	Brown	7,000
6		20	(a)	Queen's Park R	L 1-2	Brown	5,000
7		27	(h)	West Ham U	D 0-0		5,000
8	Nov	10	(a)	New Brompton	W 2-1	Cameron, Brown	3,000
9		24	(a)	Reading	L 1-3	Morris	5,000
10	Dec	1	(h)	Kettering T	W 1-0	Morris	4,000
11		15	(a)	Millwall A	W 2-1	Cameron, Brown	8,000
12		25	(h)	Portsmouth	W 4-1	Smith, Brown, J.L.Jones, Kirwan	12,000
13		26	(a)	Southampton	L 1-3	Cameron	10,000
14	Jan	12	(a)	Swindon T	D 1-1	Brown	2,500
15		19	(h)	Watford	W 7-0	Smith, Brown, J.L.Jones 2, Kirwan 2, Nidd (og)	5,000
16		26	(h)	Bristol R	W 4-0	Morris (pen), Cameron, Copeland 2	6,000
17	Feb	16	(a)	West Ham U	W 4-1	Brown, Stormont 2, Hyde	5,000
18	Mar	2	(h)	New Brompton	W 2-1	Brown, Copeland	4,500
19		9	(a)	Bristol R	L 0-1		5,000
20		16	(h)	Reading	W 1-0	Hughes	5,000
21		30	(h)	Queen's Park R	W 4-1	Copeland 2, Kirwan, Hyde	4,000
22	Apr	3	(a)	Gravesend U	L 1-2	Stormont	5,000
23		5	(h)	Southampton	W 1-0	Hughes	12,000
24		6	(h)	Bristol C	W 1-0	Burton	5,000
25		24	(a)	Portsmouth	L 0-4		3,000
26		25	(h)	Luton T	W 3-2	Melia, Moffatt 2	4,000
27		27	(h)	Gravesend U	W 5-0	Burton, Fortnum, Woodward 2, Hyde	5,000
28		29	(a)	Luton T	W 4-2	Hawley 2, Moffatt, Kirwan	4,000
29		30	(a)	Kettering T	D 1-1	Jones AE	4,000

FINAL LEAGUE POSITION: 5th in Southern League, in Division One.   Appearances
*Result not included in League table due to Chatham's resignation.   Goals

Western League

30	Nov	17	(h)	Portsmouth	W 8-1	McNaught 2, A.E.Jones, Morris, Brown 2, Cameron, Kirwan	5,000
31		26	(h)	Bristol C	W 4-1	A.E.Jones 2, Morris, Kirwan	3,000
32	Dec	5	(a)	Swindon T	W 1-0	Cameron	4,000
33		8	(a)	Millwall A	D 1-1	Kirwan	
34		10	(h)	Bristol R	W 6-0	Morris 2 (2 pens), Smith, Brown 3 (1 pen)	
35		22	(h)	Southampton	W 2-0	McNaught, Cameron	5,000
36	Feb	18	(h)	Reading	W 3-2	Stormont, Smith, Copeland	2,000
37		27	(h)	Swindon T	W 5-0	Hughes, Cameron 2, Copeland 2	1,000
38	Mar	6	(a)	Reading	D 1-1	J.L.Jones	1,000
39		11	(a)	Southampton	D 1-1	Brown	
40		18	(a)	Queen's Park R	D 1-1	Stormont	1,000
41		27	(a)	Bristol C	L 1-4	A.E.Jones	
42	Apr	13	(h)	Millwall A	W 1-0	Cameron	
43		15	(h)	Queen's Park R	D 2-2	A.E.Jones, Woodward	
44		17	(a)	Portsmouth	L 0-1		
45		22	(a)	Bristol R	L 0-4		

FINAL LEAGUE POSITION: 3rd in Western League, Division One.   Appearances
                                                                              Goals

FA Cup

1	Feb	9	(h)	Preston NE	D 1-1	Brown	15,223
R		13	(a)	Preston NE	W 4-2	Brown 3, Cameron	6,000
2		23	(h)	Bury	W 2-1	Brown 2	20,250
3	Mar	23	(a)	Reading	D 1-1	Kirwan	14,417
R		28	(h)	Reading	W 3-0	Brown 2, Copeland	11,600
SF	Apr	8	(n§)	West Brom A	W 4-0	Brown 4	46,000
F		20	(n†)	Sheffield U	D 2-2	Brown 2	114,815
R		27	(n‡)	Sheffield U	W 3-1	Smith, Brown, Cameron	20,470

§ Played at Villa Park, Birmingham. † Played at the Crystal Palace. ‡ Played at Burnden Park, Bolton.   Appearances
                                                                                                          Goals

160

Appearances and goals grid (columns are players; right-hand column is the match number).

Section 1 (League)

Anson	Berry	Brown	Buckingham	Burton	Cameron	Clawley	Copeland	Erentz	Finch	Fortnum	Haddow	Hawley	Hudson	Hughes	Hyde	Jones AE	Jones JL	Kirwan	Leigh	McNaught	Melia	Moffatt	Moles	Morris	Pangbourne	Sands	Smith	Stevens	Stevenson	Stormont	Tait	Woodward	No.
					9	8	1											11		5	2			4	10		7			6	3		1
					9	8	1	4								5	6	11			2						7			10	3		2
					9	8	1	4						3			6	11		5	2						7			10			3
					9	8	1	4									6	11		5	2						7			10	3		4
					9	8	1										6	11		5	2			4			7			10	3		5
					9	10	1	2								4		11		5	8						7			6	3		6
					9	8	1	2						6		4		11		5							7			10	3		7
					9	8	1	2								4		11	7	10				5						6	3		8
					9	10	1	2								4	7	11		5	8									6	3		9
						10	1	2								4	7	11		5	9						8			6	3		10
					9	7	1	2								4	10	11		5	8									6	3		11
					9		1	2								4	10	11		5	8						7			6	3		12
					9	7	1	2								4	10	11		5	8									6	3		13
					9	8	1	10		2							6	11		4				5			7				3		14
					9	8	1	2						3			10	11		5				4			7			6			15
						8	1	9		2							10	11		5				4			7			6	3		16
					9	8	1	2								5		11		6				4			7			10	3		17
					9	8	1	10		2								11		5				4			7			6	3		18
					9	8	1	10		2						5		11						4			7			6	3		19
					9	8	1	10		3						5	6	11						4			7				2		20
					9	8	1			2						5	10	11	7					4						6	3		21
3	7	6	4								1						11	8		5	2	9								10			22
					9	8	1	10		2						5	6	11						4			7				3		23
4		8		1										3				11	7	5	2	10								6		9	24
4		6					8	1	10									11		5	2	9					7			3			25
	6	4					1	8				7						11		5	2	9								3	10		26
	6	4				8	1											11	7	5	2									3	10	9	27
	6						1	10				8				5		11			2	9		4			7				3		28
9	6						1	10				8				2	7	11		5				4							3		29
3	1	20	6	4	21	25	9	20		2	4	3	1			18	9	8	17	20	20	11	6	3	19	2	17		3	23	22	2	
	12		2	5		5		1			2					2	3	1	3	5		1	3		3		4			5	2		

1 own-goal

Section 2

Anson	Berry	Brown	Buckingham	Burton	Cameron	Clawley	Copeland	Erentz	Finch	Fortnum	Haddow	Hawley	Hudson	Hughes	Hyde	Jones AE	Jones JL	Kirwan	Leigh	McNaught	Melia	Moffatt	Moles	Morris	Pangbourne	Sands	Smith	Stevens	Stevenson	Stormont	Tait	Woodward	No.
					9	10	1	2								4	7	11		5	8									6	3		30
					9	10	1	2								4	7	11		5	8									6	3		31
					9		1	2								4	7	11	10	5	8									6	3		32
					9	7	1	2								4	10	11		5	8									6	3		33
					9		1									4	10	11		5	2					8	7			6	3		34
					9	7	1	2								4	10	11		5	8									6	3		35
					9	8		10	1	2								11		5				4			7			6	3		36
					9	10			1	2						5		11			8			4			7			6	3		37
					9	8		10	1	2						5		11						4			7			6	3		38
					9		1	10		2						5		11			8			4			7			6	3		39
					9	8	1	10		3						7	6	11						4			5				2		40
3		6												8		1	7	11		5	2	4								10		9	41
					9	10	1	2								6	8	11		5				4			7				3		42
	6	4					2						1					11	8	7	5	10								3		9	43
4							1										7			2	5						8			3			44
	7	4					1	10										11	8	5	2	9								3	6		45
1	1	10	2	3	10	9	5	12	1	7		2	10	6		10	7	9	1	10	4	2	2	12		1	6	2		13	13	1	
	6			6		3		1		5		1	3	3				4			2		2			1							

Section 3 (Cup)

Anson	Berry	Brown	Buckingham	Burton	Cameron	Clawley	Copeland	Erentz	Finch	Fortnum	Haddow	Hawley	Hudson	Hughes	Hyde	Jones AE	Jones JL	Kirwan	Leigh	McNaught	Melia	Moffatt	Moles	Morris	Pangbourne	Sands	Smith	Stevens	Stevenson	Stormont	Tait	Woodward	No.
					9	8	1	10		2								11		5				4			7			6	3		1
					9	8	1	10		2						5	6	11						4			7				3		R
					9	8	1	10		2						5	6	11						4			7				3		2
					9	8	1	10		2						5	6	11						4			7				3		3
					9	8	1	10		2						5	6	11						4			7				3		R
					9	8	1	10		2						5	6	11						4			7				3		SF
					9	8	1	10		2						5	6	11						4			7				3		F
					9	8	1	10		2						5	6	11						4			7				3		R
					8	8	8	8		8						7	7	8		1				8			8			1	8		
					15			2		1								1															

1901-02

Southern League

Manager: John Cameron

#		Date		Opponent	Result	Scorers	Att
1	Sep	7	(h)	Millwall A	W 2-0	Cameron, Brown	27,000
2		14	(h)	Queen's Park R	W 2-0	Cameron, Copeland	9,000
3		21	(a)	Reading	D 1-1	Morris (pen)	8,000
4	Oct	5	(a)	Bristol R	W 2-1	Smith, Brown	7,000
5		12	(h)	New Brompton	W 3-1	Brown, Kirwan 2	7,324
6		19	(a)	Northampton T	L 1-3	Smith	5,000
7		26	(h)	Watford	W 8-1	Cameron 2, Brown 3, Copeland 2, Kirwan	7,500
8	Nov	2	(a)	West Ham U	W 1-0	J.L.Jones	14,000
9		9	(a)	Wellingborough	W 1-0	Brown	4,500
10		23	(a)	Swindon T	W 3-1	Morris, Cameron 2	3,000
11	Dec	7	(a)	Kettering T	W 2-0	Cameron, Kirwan	1,200
12		21	(a)	Millwall A	D 1-1	Kirwan	4,000
13		25	(h)	Portsmouth	L 1-2	Cameron	14,000
14		26	(a)	Southampton	L 0-1		11,000
15		28	(a)	Queen's Park R	W 3-0	Brown 3	13,000
16	Jan	4	(h)	Reading	W 4-2	Hughes, Cameron, Copeland, Kirwan	8,500
17		18	(h)	Bristol R	W 1-0	Cameron	6,000
18	Feb	1	(h)	Northampton T	W 1-0	Kirwan	3,000
19		8	(a)	Watford	W 3-0	Brown 2, Copeland	2,500
20		15	(h)	West Ham U	L 1-2	Copeland	9,000
21		22	(h)	Wellingborough	W 3-0	Brown, Copeland 2	6,000
22	Mar	8	(h)	Swindon T	W 7-1	Cameron, Brown 3, Copeland 2, Kirwan	4,000
23		15	(a)	Brentford	L 1-2	Smith	11,000
24		22	(h)	Kettering T	W 4-0	Smith, Copeland 3	3,000
25		28	(h)	Southampton	D 2-2	Hughes, Kirwan	21,300
26		31	(a)	Luton T	D 0-0		3,000
27		31	(a)	Portsmouth	L 0-1		13,400
28	Apr	5	(a)	New Brompton	D 0-0		5,000
29		12	(h)	Luton T	D 0-0		6,000
30		26	(h)	Brentford	W 3-0	Morris (pen), Brown 2	3,000

FINAL LEAGUE POSITION: 2nd in Southern League, Division One.

Appearances

Goals

Western League

#		Date		Opponent	Result	Scorers	Att
31	Sep	9	(h)	Reading	W 4-0	Morris (pen), Cameron, Brown 2	4,000
32		28	(h)	Southampton	W 5-0	Hughes, Cameron, Copeland 2, Kirwan	
33		30	(a)	Queen's Park R	W 3-1	Morris, Copeland, Kirwan	4,000
34	Oct	7	(h)	Millwall A	W 3-1	Brown 2, Kirwan	
35		14	(h)	West Ham U	W 2-1	Cameron, Copeland	7,000
36		21	(h)	Bristol R	W 4-1	Brown, Cameron, Kirwan 2	
37	Nov	11	(h)	Swindon T	W 6-0	Morris, Woodward 2, Copeland, Kirwan 2	
38		16	(a)	Portsmouth	L 1-3	Brown	16,000
39		18	(a)	Bristol R	W 4-0	Morris, Smith, Brown, Kirwan	600
40	Dec	9	(h)	Queen's Park R	W 3-2	Brown, Smith, Kirwan	2,500
41	Jan	11	(a)	Southampton	L 1-5	Cameron	6,000
42		15	(a)	Reading	D 1-1	Gilhooley	
43	Feb	17	(a)	Millwall A	W 3-1	Barlow, Cameron 2	2,000
44	Mar	10	(a)	West Ham U	D 1-1	Brown	3,000
45		17	(h)	Portsmouth	D 0-0		4,000
46	Apr	9	(a)	Swindon T	W 1-0	Copeland	

FINAL LEAGUE POSITION: 2nd in Western League, Division One.

Appearances

Goals

162

Appearances grid (player columns = shirt/position number played in each match).

Barlow	Brown	Burton J	Cameron	Clawley	Copeland	Erentz	Fitchie	Gilhooley	Griffiths	Haig-Brown	Hughes	Hyde	Jones JL	Kirwan	McNaught	Moles	Montgomery	Morris	Smith	Soulsby	Stevenson	Tait	Woodward	#
	9		8	1	10	2							6	11	5			4		7		3		1
	9		8	1	10	2	7				3		6	11	5			4						2
		4	9	1	10	2		8			3		6	11	5					7				3
	9	6		1	10	2		8			5			11				4		7		3		4
	9			1	10	2		8			5		6	11				4		7		3		5
			9	1	10	2		8			5		6	11				4		7		3		6
	9		8	1	10	2							6	11	5			4		7		3		7
	9		8	1	10	2					5		6	11				4		7		3		8
8	9			1	10	2					5		6	11				4		7		3		9
	9		8	1	10	2							6	11	5			4		7		3		10
	9		8	1	10	2					5		6	11				4		7		3		11
			8		10	2	7		1		5		6	11				4				3	9	12
	9		8		10	2			1		5		6	11				4		7		3		13
	9		8		10	2			1		5		6	11				4		7		3		14
	9		10			2		8	1		4		6	11	5					7		3		15
	9		8		10	2			1		5		6	11				4		7		3		16
	9		8		10	2	7		1		5		6	11				4				3		17
	9		8		10	2	7		1		4		6	11	5							3		18
	9		8		10	2	7		1		6			11	5			4				3		19
	9		8		10	2			1		4	7	6	11	5							3		20
	9	6		1	10	2								11	5			4		7		3	8	21
	9		8	1	10	2	7				6			11	5			4				3		22
	9		8	1	10	2					4		6	11	5					7		3		23
	9		8	1	10	2							6	11	5			4		7		3		24
	9		8	1	10	2					5		6	11				4		7		3		25
	9		8	1	10	2					5		6	11				4		7		3		26
	9		8	1	10	2							6	11	5			4		7		3		27
10			8		9	2					3		6	11	5	1		4		7				28
	9			1	10	2		8			4		6	11	5					7		3		29
	9		8	1	10	2							6	11	5			4		7		3		30
2	26	3	25	20	29	30	1	10	9	2	24	2	25	28	16	1	25	23	1	26	2			
	18		11		13								2	1	9					3	4			

Barlow	Brown	Burton J	Cameron	Clawley	Copeland	Erentz	Fitchie	Gilhooley	Griffiths	Haig-Brown	Hughes	Hyde	Jones JL	Kirwan	McNaught	Moles	Montgomery	Morris	Smith	Soulsby	Stevenson	Tait	Woodward	#
	9		8		10	2	7		1				6	11	5			4				3		31
		6	9	1	10	2		8			5			11				4		7		3		32
		6	9	1	10	2		8			5			11				4		7		3		33
	9	6			10	2		8	1		5			11				4		7		3		34
	9		8	1	10	2	7				5		6	11				4				3		35
8	9	6	10			2			1		5			11				4		7		3		36
8					10				1		6			11	5			4		7	2	3	9	37
	9		8	1	10	2					5		6	11				4		7		3		38
8	9			1	10	2					5		6	11				4		7		3		39
	9			1	10	2		8			5		6	11				4		7		3		40
	9		10			2		8	1		3		6	11	5			4		7				41
	9	4			10	2		8	1				6	11	5					7		3		42
8		3	9		10	2	7		1		4		6	11	5									43
	9		8	1	10	2							6	11	5			4		7		3		44
7	9		8	1	10	2					4		6	11	5							3		45
	9		8	1	10	2					4		6	11	5					7		3		46
5	12	6	11	9	14	15		9	7		12	2	11	14	8			13		12	3	12	1	
1	9	7	6		1	1					9							4		2		2		

1901-02 (continued)

London League

47	Sep	16	(a)	W Arsenal	W 2-0	Gilhooley, Brown	4,000
48	Nov	4	(h)	W Arsenal	W 5-0	Barlow, Brown 3, Copeland	4,000
49	Dec	16	(a)	West Ham U	L 1-3	Gilhooley	2,000
50	Jan	6	(a)	Millwall A	D 1-1	Smith	
51	Feb	10	(h)	Queen's Park R	L 1-5	Brown	1,500
52	Mar	24	(h)	Millwall A	D 1-1	Cameron	
53	Apr	14	(a)	Queen's Park A	W 2-1	Hughes, Cameron	
54		21	(h)	West Ham U	D 2-2	Brown 2	2,000

FINAL LEAGUE POSITION: 2nd in London League, Premier Division.

Appearances
Goals

FA Cup

1	Jan	25	(h)	Southampton	D 1-1	Copeland	25,000
R		29	(a)	Southampton	D 2-2	Hughes 2	12,036
2R	Feb	3	(n*)	Southampton	L 1-2	Kirwan	10,000

*Played at Elm Park, Reading.

Appearances
Goals

Southern Charity Cup

SF	Apr	23	(a)	W Arsenal‡	D 0-0		3,000
R		29	(h)	W Arsenal	W 2-1	Coles (og), Copeland	2,000

‡West Bromwich Albion failed to appear for quarter-final, Spurs awarded a walkover.

Appearances
Goals

Dewar Shield

	Mar	1	(h)	Corinthians	W 5-2	Cameron 3, Brown, Kirwan

Appearances
Goals

Barlow	Brown	Burton J	Cameron	Clawley	Copeland	Erentz	Fitchie	Gilhooley	Griffiths	Haig-Brown	Hughes	Hyde	Jones JL	Kirwan	McNaught	Moles	Montgomery	Morris	Smith	Soulsby	Stevenson	Tait	Woodward	
	9			1	10	2		8			3		6	11			5	4	7					47
8	9			1	10	2					5		6	11				4	7		3			48
			9	1	10	2		8			3		6	11	5			4		7				49
	9				10			8	1		2		6	11	5			4	7		3			50
8	9	6			10	2		7	1					11	5			4			3			51
10		9	1								4	11	6		5			8	7		2	3		52
	9	8		1	10	2					4		6	11	5				7		3			53
	9			1	10	2		8			5		6	11				4	7		3			54
3	6	1	3	6	7	6		5	2		7	1	7	7	5	1		7	6	1	3	4		
1	7	2	1								2							1						

Barlow	Brown	Burton J	Cameron	Clawley	Copeland	Erentz	Fitchie	Gilhooley	Griffiths	Haig-Brown	Hughes	Hyde	Jones JL	Kirwan	McNaught	Moles	Montgomery	Morris	Smith	Soulsby	Stevenson	Tait	Woodward	
	9				10	2			1		4		6	11	5				7		3			1
	9				10	2	7		1		4		6	11	5						3			R
	9				10	2	7		1		4		6	11	5						3			2R
	3				3	3	2		3		3		3	3	3				1		3			
	1										2				1									

Barlow	Brown	Burton J	Cameron	Clawley	Copeland	Erentz	Fitchie	Gilhooley	Griffiths	Haig-Brown	Hughes	Hyde	Jones JL	Kirwan	McNaught	Moles	Montgomery	Morris	Smith	Soulsby	Stevenson	Tait	Woodward	
8			9	1	10	2							6	11	5			4	7		3			SF
	9	8		1	10	2							6	11	5			4	7		3			R
1	1	1	1	2	2	2							2	2	2			2	2		2			
					1																			

1 own-goal

Barlow	Brown	Burton J	Cameron	Clawley	Copeland	Erentz	Fitchie	Gilhooley	Griffiths	Haig-Brown	Hughes	Hyde	Jones JL	Kirwan	McNaught	Moles	Montgomery	Morris	Smith	Soulsby	Stevenson	Tait	Woodward	
	9	8		1	10	2					4		6	11	5				7		3			
	1	1	1	1	1						1		1	1				1	7		1			
	1	3											1											

1902-03

Southern League

Manager: John Cameron

1	Sep	6	(h)	Queen's Park R	D	0-0		13,000
2		20	(h)	Wellingborough	W	6-1	Morris, J.Jones, Cameron, Copeland, Kirwan, Dartnell (og)	8,000
3		27	(a)	Bristol R	L	2-3	J.Jones 2	12,000
4	Oct	4	(h)	Northampton T	W	2-0	Morris (pen), Copeland	7,000
5		11	(a)	Watford	W	2-1	Houston 2	4,000
6		18	(h)	Brentford	W	3-1	J.Burton, Morris, J.Jones	5,000
7		25	(a)	Millwall A	L	0-2		8,000
8	Nov	1	(h)	West Ham U	D	1-1	Copeland	9,000
9		22	(h)	Swindon T	W	2-0	Gilhooley, Kirwan	5,500
10	Dec	6	(h)	Luton T	D	1-1	Gilhooley	4,500
11		20	(a)	Queen's Park R	W	4-0	Hughes, Woodward 2, Kirwan	7,000
12		25	(h)	Portsmouth	D	2-2	Dryburgh, Warner	23,000
13		26	(a)	Southampton	W	1-0	Kirwan	12,000
14	Jan	3	(a)	Wellingborough	W	2-0	Warner, Kirwan	3,000
15		5	(h)	New Brompton	W	3-1	Tait (pen), Warner, Copeland	3,000
16		10	(h)	Bristol R	W	3-0	Warner 2, Woodward	11,000
17		17	(a)	Northampton T	L	1-3	Woodward	4,000
18		24	(h)	Watford	D	1-1	Kirwan	6,000
19		31	(a)	Brentford	D	1-1	Copeland	4,000
20	Feb	14	(a)	West Ham U	L	0-1		10,000
21	Mar	14	(h)	Kettering T	W	4-0	Hughes 2 (1 pen), Dryburgh, Warner	7,000
22		21	(a)	Luton T	L	0-3		6,000
23		28	(h)	Reading	W	2-0	Warner, Copeland	4,000
24	Apr	4	(a)	Reading	D	0-0		5,000
25		10	(h)	Southampton	W	2-1	Warner, Copeland	20,000
26		11	(a)	New Brompton	L	0-3		4,000
27		13	(a)	Portsmouth	L	0-2		12,000
28		14	(h)	Millwall A	W	2-0	Cameron, Copeland	8,000
29		22	(a)	Swindon T	L	0-2		3,000
30		25	(a)	Kettering T	L	0-1		2,000

FINAL LEAGUE POSITION: 4th in Southern League, Division One.

Appearances
Goals

Western League

31	Sep	13	(a)	Southampton	D	1-1	Houston	7,000
32		15	(h)	Millwall A	W	4-3	Hughes, J.L.Jones, Cameron, Barlow	5,000
33		22	(a)	Queen's Park R	W	2-0	J.Jones, Kirwan	5,000
34		29	(h)	Reading	W	2-1	Cameron, Copeland	
35	Oct	13	(h)	Bristol R	L	0-1		6,500
36		29	(a)	Reading	L	0-3		
37	Nov	3	(h)	Queen's Park R	W	3-0	J.Jones, Barlow 2	
38		8	(h)	Portsmouth	D	0-0		11,000
39		29	(a)	Portsmouth	D	2-2	Barlow 2	9,000
40	Dec	27	(h)	Southampton	D	0-0		20,000
41	Jan	28	(a)	Millwall A	D	1-1	Copeland	
42	Feb	16	(h)	West Ham U	W	1-0	Rainbird	4,000
43		23	(a)	Bristol R	L	0-2		
44	Mar	9	(a)	Brentford	D	0-0		
45		19	(a)	West Ham U	D	0-0		
46		26	(h)	Brentford	W	4-0	Gilhooley, Houston 2, Fredericks	1,000

FINAL LEAGUE POSITION: 4th in Western League, Division One.

Appearances
Goals

Football appearances/line-up grid. Column headers (left to right):

Barlow, Brown, Bugg, Burton J, Burton O, Cameron, Chalmers, Clawley, Copeland, Dryburgh, Erentz, Fredericks, Gilhooley, Haig-Brown, Houston, Hughes, Jones J, Jones JL, Kirwan, Moles, Morris, Quinn, Rainbird, Steven, Stevenson, Tait, Warner, Watson, Williams, Woodward

Barlow	Brown	Bugg	Burton J	Burton O	Cameron	Chalmers	Clawley	Copeland	Dryburgh	Erentz	Fredericks	Gilhooley	Haig-Brown	Houston	Hughes	Jones J	Jones JL	Kirwan	Moles	Morris	Quinn	Rainbird	Steven	Stevenson	Tait	Warner	Watson	Williams	Woodward	#
							1	10		2				9	5	8	6	11		4					3	7				1
						8	1	10		2				9	5	7	6	11		4					3					2
						8	1	10		2				9	5	7	6	11		4					3					3
					4	8	1	10		2				9		7	6	11		5					3					4
					4		1	10		2	7			9	5	8	6	11		.					3					5
					4		1	10		2	7			9		8	6	11		5							3			6
						8	1	10		3				9	5	7	6	11		4					2					7
9	6					8	1	10		2				5	7	4		11							3					8
9	4					8	1	10		2	7						6	11		5							3			9
8	4						1	10		2	7				5		6	11									3	9		10
	4						1	10			7				5		6	11							3	8	2	9		11
	4						1	10	7								6	11		5					3	8	2	9		12
	4						1	10	7								6	11		5					3	8	2	9		13
	4	6					1	10	7	2								11		5					3	8		9		14
9	4	6					1	10	7	2								11		5					3	8				15
	4	6					1	10	7	2								11		5					3	8		9		16
	4	6		11			1	10	7	2										5					3	8		9		17
	4	6						10	7	2				9	5					11					3	8	1			18
	4					8	1	10		2							6	11		5					3	7		9		19
	4			9	11	1			7			10	8				6			5					3		2			20
						1	10	7	2					5				11		4					3	8	6	9		21
	6		10	11	1		7	2						5				4							8	3		9		22
	4			11	1	10	7	2						6				5							3	8		9		23
	5					1	10	7	2					9				11		4					3	8	6			24
	6					1	10	7						5				11		4					3	8	2	9		25
	6	9				1	10	7						4				11		5					3	8	2			26
	6	9				1	10	7	2					4				11		5					3	8				27
		9				1	10		2			7		4				11		5					3	8	6			28
	3	9				1	10		2			7		4				11		5						8	6			29
	6	9				1	10	7	2		8			4				11		5					3					30
4	14	15		14	4	29	28	16	24	1	7	2	9	18	8	15	26		25					25	19	14	1	12		
	1	2			8	2			2		2	3	4		6			3						1	8		4		

I own-goal

Barlow	Brown	Bugg	Burton J	Burton O	Cameron	Chalmers	Clawley	Copeland	Dryburgh	Erentz	Fredericks	Gilhooley	Haig-Brown	Houston	Hughes	Jones J	Jones JL	Kirwan	Moles	Morris	Quinn	Rainbird	Steven	Stevenson	Tait	Warner	Watson	Williams	Woodward	#
						7	1	10		2				9	5	8	6	11		4					3					31
9			4			8		10		2				5			6	11								7	3	1		32
	4						1	10		2	7			9		8	6	11		5					3					33
	6				8	1	10		2					9	5	7		11		4					3					34
					10	1			2	7				5	8	6	11		4						3			9		35
	4				8	1	10							9			6	11		5			2		3	7				36
9	4		5		8	1	10		2							7	6	11							3					37
					8	1	10		2					5	7	6	11		4					3			9			38
9	4				8	1	10		2	7				5			6	11							3					39
	4			11	1	10	7							6				5						3	8	2	9			40
9	4				1	10	7	2						6				11		5					3	8				41
	5	2	6		11				7			10						4			8	9		3			1			42
	4					1				8	9				6	11		5	10	7		2	3						43
	4			11	1		7						9			6		5	10			2	3	8					44
	6				7	1	8	11	3				9	5		4						2		10					45
	4		6		11			10	8	9	5									2	3	7		1					46
4	7	1	7	2	8	5	13	11	5	10	1	6	8	9	6	12	11	1	10	3	2		6	12	7	3	3	3		
5					2		2			1	1	3	1	2	1	1		1												

1902-03 (continued)

London League

47	Oct	6	(a)	Brentford	W	5-1	Morris (pen), J.Jones 3, Copeland	500
48		20	(a)	West Ham U	D	0-0		4,000
49	Nov	17	(a)	W Arsenal	L	1-2	Morris (pen)	
50	Dec	1	(h)	W Arsenal	W	1-0	Warner	
51		15	(h)	West Ham U	W	4-0	Tait (pen), Hughes (pen), Barlow, Kirwan	3,000
52	Jan	!2	(h)	Brentford	W	1-0	Warner	
53	Mar	2	(a)	Millwall A	W	3-0	J.Burton, Houston 2	
54		16	(a)	Queen's Park R	L	0-1		
55		23	(h)	Millwall A	W	1-0	Chalmers	1,500
56		30	(h)	Queen's Park R	W	3-0	Hughes (pen), Copeland, Chalmers	2,500

FINAL LEAGUE POSITION: 1st in London League, Premier Division.

Appearances
Goals

FA Cup

1	Feb	7	(h)	West Brom A	D	0-0		25,641
R		11	(a)	West Brom A	W	2-0	Dryburgh (pen), Woodward	35,000
2		21	(h)	Bristol C	W	1-0	Woodward	18,750
3	Mar	7	(h)	Aston Villa	L	2-3	Woodward, Copeland	24,500

Appearances
Goals

Southern Charity Cup 1901-02

F	Sep	8	(n*)	West Ham U	W	2-1	Houston, Kirwan	6,000

*Played at Upton Park.

Appearances
Goals

Southern Charity Cup 1902-03

1	Nov	24	(h)	Reading	D	1-1	Kirwan	3,000
R	Jan	14	(a)	Reading	L	2-3	Houston, Quinn	

Appearances
Goals

Block 1

Barlow	Brown	Bugg	Burton J	Burton O	Cameron	Chalmers	Clawley	Copeland	Dryburgh	Erentz	Fredericks	Gilhooley	Haig-Brown	Houston	Hughes	Jones J	Jones JL	Kirwan	Moles	Morris	Quinn	Rainbird	Steven	Stevenson	Tait	Warner	Watson	Williams	Woodward	No.
	4					1	10			2		7		9		8	6	11		5					3					47
	4				8	1	10			2				9		7	6	11		5					3					48
9					8	1	10			2		7		5			6	11		4					3					49
	4				9		10			2		7		5			6	11								8	3	1		50
9	4						10							5			6	11						7		8	2	1		51
		4	6			1	10	7		2				9				11		5					3	8				52
		4			8	1		7		2				9			6	11		5	10				3					53
		6				1	10	7						9	5			11		4	10				3	8	2			54
		6	9	11		1		7		2					5					4	10					8	3			55
		4		11			10	7		2			8	9	6					5					3		1			56
2	4	3	3	5	2	7	8	5		8		4		6	6	2	6	8		8	2	1			7	5	5	3		
1	1		2		2									2	2	3		1		2					1	2				

Block 2

Barlow	Brown	Bugg	Burton J	Burton O	Cameron	Chalmers	Clawley	Copeland	Dryburgh	Erentz	Fredericks	Gilhooley	Haig-Brown	Houston	Hughes	Jones J	Jones JL	Kirwan	Moles	Morris	Quinn	Rainbird	Steven	Stevenson	Tait	Warner	Watson	Williams	Woodward	No.
					8	1	10	7						5			6	11		4					3		2	9		I
					10	1		7					8	5			6	11		4					3		2	9		R
					8	1	10	7						5			6	11		4					3		2	9		2
					8	1	10	7						5			6	11		4					3		2	9		3
					4	4	3	4					1	4			4	4		4					4		4	4		
							1	1																				3		

Block 3

Barlow	Brown	Bugg	Burton J	Burton O	Cameron	Chalmers	Clawley	Copeland	Dryburgh	Erentz	Fredericks	Gilhooley	Haig-Brown	Houston	Hughes	Jones J	Jones JL	Kirwan	Moles	Morris	Quinn	Rainbird	Steven	Stevenson	Tait	Warner	Watson	Williams	Woodward	No.
						1	10			2		7		9	5	8	6	11		4					3					F
						1	1			1		1		1	1	1	1	1		1					1					
														1			1													

Block 4

Barlow	Brown	Bugg	Burton J	Burton O	Cameron	Chalmers	Clawley	Copeland	Dryburgh	Erentz	Fredericks	Gilhooley	Haig-Brown	Houston	Hughes	Jones J	Jones JL	Kirwan	Moles	Morris	Quinn	Rainbird	Steven	Stevenson	Tait	Warner	Watson	Williams	Woodward	No.
	4				8	1	10			2				5		7	6	11							3	9				I
		6		11									8	9					4		10	7	5	2	3	1				R
1		1		1	1	1	1			1			1	1	1	1	1	1		1	1	1	1	2	1	1				
							1							1				1												

1903-04

Southern League

Managers: John Cameron

1	Sep	5	(a)	Fulham	D 0-0	10,000
2		12	(h)	Millwall	L 0-1	16,000
3		14	(a)	Brentford	D 0-0	4,000
4		19	(a)	Queen's Park R	L 0-2	6,000
5		26	(h)	Plymouth A	L 0-2	8,000
6	Oct	3	(a)	Reading	D 2-2 J.Jones, J.L.Jones	6,000
7		10	(h)	Wellingborough	W 1-0 J.Jones	9,000
8		17	(a)	Bristol R	L 0-1	8,000
9		24	(h)	Brighton & HA	D 2-2 Woodward, Chalmers	8,000
10	Nov	7	(h)	Northampton T	W 2-1 Morris (pen), J.Jones	8,000
11		21	(h)	West Ham U	W 2-1 J.Jones, Kirwan	8,000
12	Dec	5	(a)	Luton T	L 2-3 J.Jones (pen), Copeland	6,000
13		19	(a)	Kettering T	D 3-3 Woodward 2, Copeland	2,000
14		25	(h)	Portsmouth	D 1-1 J.Jones (pen)	20,000
15		26	(a)	Southampton	L 0-1	12,000
16	Jan	2	(h)	Fulham	W 1-0 Warner	10,000
17		9	(a)	Millwall	W 1-0 Woodward	1,000
18		16	(h)	Queen's Park R	D 2-2 J.Jones 2	10,000
19		23	(a)	Plymouth A	W 3-1 Brearley 2, Copeland	10,000
20		30	(h)	Reading	W 7-4 Warner, J.Jones, Woodward 3, Copeland 2	8,000
21	Feb	13	(h)	Bristol R	W 5-1 Warner, J.Jones (pen), Woodward 2, Kirwan	10,000
22		22	(h)	Swindon T	W 1-0 Walton	7,000
23	Mar	12	(h)	Brentford	D 1-1 J.Jones	5,000
24		19	(a)	West Ham U	W 2-0 Walton 2	8,000
25		26	(a)	Swindon T	D 0-0	3,000
26	Apr	1	(h)	Southampton	W 2-1 J.Jones, Woodward	21,300
27		2	(h)	Luton T	D 1-1 Turner	10,000
28		4	(a)	Portsmouth	L 0-1	11,000
29		5	(h)	New Brompton	W 1-0 Morris	6,000
30		9	(a)	New Brompton	W 1-0 Kirwan	10,000
31		13	(a)	Brighton & HA	W 2-1 Warner, Kirwan	8,000
32		16	(h)	Kettering T	W 5-1 Turner 4, Brearley	4,000
33		25	(a)	Northampton T	W 1-0 Copeland	3,000
34		30	(a)	Wellingborough	D 3-3 J.Jones 3	3,000

FINAL LEAGUE POSITION: 2nd in Southern League, Division One.

Appearances
Goals

Western League

35	Sep	7	(h)	Reading	W 3-1 Brearley 3	6,000
36	Oct	5	(h)	Queen's Park R*	W 3-0 O.Burton, J.Jones, J.L.Jones	
37		14	(a)	Reading	W 2-0 Cameron, Kirwan	
38		31	(a)	Portsmouth	W 3-0 Woodward 2, Copeland	
39	Nov	2	(h)	Brentford	D 1-1 Copeland	
40		9	(a)	Queen's Park R	L 0-2	
41		30	(h)	Bristol R	W 2-1 J.Jones, Badger	
42	Dec	14	(h)	West Ham U	W 4-1 J.Jones 3, Copeland	
43		28	(h)	Southampton	W 1-0 Kirwan	13,000
44	Feb	27	(h)	Portsmouth	D 1-1 Walton	12,000
45		29	(h)	Plymouth A	W 5-1 Walton 2, Gilhooley, Berry, Chalmers (pen)	
46	Mar	28	(a)	Brentford	W 2-1 J.Jones, Copeland	
47	Apr	18	(a)	West Ham U	W 1-0 J.Jones	
48		20	(a)	Plymouth A	D 0-0	
49		23	(a)	Southampton	L 0-1	
50		27	(a)	Bristol R	W 4-2 Warner 2, Copeland, Walton	

FINAL LEAGUE POSITION: 1st in Western League, Division One.
*Also Erentz benefit match.

Appearances
Goals

170

Archer	Badger	Berry	Brearley	Brown	Burton J	Burton O	Cameron	Chalmers	Copeland	Erentz	Gilhooley	Hughes	Jones J	Jones JL	Kirwan	Leach-Lewis	Mapley	McConachie	McNaught	Mearns	Milton	Morris	Pilch	Quinn	Smith	Stevenson	Tait	Turner	Vaughan	Walton	Warner	Watson	Williams	Woodward	
			9						10	2		4	8	6	11							5					3			7			1		1
			9						10	2		4		6	11				5								3			7	8		1		2
			9						10	2	8	4		6	11			7	5													3	1		3
			9		4		8		10	2				6	11			7	5													3	1		4
			8						10	2		4		6	11				5								3				7		1	9	5
			9			6			10	2		4	8	5	11			7									3						1		6
						6			10	2		4	8	5	11			7									3						1	9	7
						6			10			4	8	5	11			7									3					2	1	9	8
						6		11	10				8	5				7				4					3					2	1	9	9
						5			10			2	8	6	11					1		4					3			7				9	10
						6			10			2	8		11				5			4					3				7		1	9	11
						6			10			2	8		11				5			4					3				7		1	9	12
						6			10			2	8		11				5			4					3				7		1	9	13
					6				10			2	8		11				5			4					3				7		1	9	14
			9						10				8	6	11				5			4					3				7	2	1		15
					6				10			5	8		11							4					3				7	2	1	9	16
						6			10			5	8		11							4					3				7	2	1	9	17
						6			10			5	8		11							4					3				7	2	1	9	18
			9						10	2		5	8	6	11							4									7	3	1		19
									10	2			8	6	11				5			4									7	3	1	9	20
									10			5	8	6	11							4					3				7	2	1	9	21
			9	4		6		11		2							3		5	1				10				7		8					22
		9	5	4		6		11	10				8														3			7		2	1		23
			4						10			5	8	6	11												3			7		2	1	9	24
			4				9	11	10			5		6			3													7	8	2	1		25
									10	2		5	8	6	11							4					3			7			1	9	26
						6			10				8		11	5						4					3	7				2	1	9	27
		9				6			10				8		11	5			4								3	7				2	1		28
		9					10								11		3		5		6	4								7	8	2	1		29
			9						10	2			8	6	11				5			4					3				7		1		30
			9			6			10	2		5			11		3			1		4						7			8				31
			9			6			10	2		5			11		3			1		4						7			8				32
			9			6		11	10	2		5								1		4					3	7			8				33
			9					11	10	2		5	8	6								4					3			7			1		34
		3	17	2	3	17	3	6	32	16	1	24	24	19	28	2	5	6	14	5	1	22		1			25	6		10	19	17	29	17	
			3					1	6				15	1	4							2						5		3	4			10	

Archer	Badger	Berry	Brearley	Brown	Burton J	Burton O	Cameron	Chalmers	Copeland	Erentz	Gilhooley	Hughes	Jones J	Jones JL	Kirwan	Leach-Lewis	Mapley	McConachie	McNaught	Mearns	Milton	Morris	Pilch	Quinn	Smith	Stevenson	Tait	Turner	Vaughan	Walton	Warner	Watson	Williams	Woodward	
			9						10	2		4	8	6	11				5								3			7			1		35
				4		6			10	2			8	5	11			7		1							3							9	36
			9			6	8		10			4		5	11			7									3					2	1		37
						6		11	10				8	5								4				2	3			7			1	9	38
				4		6	8	11	10									7		1		5					3			9		2			39
						6	9		10	2			8	5	11							4					3			7			1		40
	9					6			10			2	8	5	11							4					3				7		1		41
	9					6			10			2	8		11				5			4					3				7		1		42
					6				10			5	8		11					1		4					3				7	2		9	43
				4					10			5		6	11												3			8	7	2	1	9	44
	5	10	4			6		11		2	9						3			1								7		8					45
				4		6			10	2		5	9		11												3	7			8		1		46
			9						10	2			8		11		3		5		6	4								7			1		47
	9		4						10			5	8		11						6						3			7		2	1		48
	5					6			10	2					11							4					3	7			8		1	9	49
							10	7	9	3				4					5			6								11	8	2	1		50
	5	1	5	4	1	10	4	4	15	8	1	8	10	8	12		2	3	4	4	2	9					1	13	3	9	7	6	12	5	
	1	1	3			1	1	1	5		1		7	1	2															4	2			2	

1903-04 (continued)

London League

51	Sep	1	(h)	W Arsenal	L	0-1	
52		21	(h)	Fulham	W	2-1 Cameron, Kirwan	3,000
53	Nov	14	(a)	W Arsenal	D	1-1 Kirwan	
54		16	(a)	Brentford	W	2-0 J.Jones, Kirwan	
55		23	(h)	Millwall	L	2-3 Warner, Badger	
56	Jan	11	(h)	Brentford	W	2-1 Walton, Brearley	
57		18	(h)	West Ham U	W	2-0 J.Jones, Brearley	
58	Feb	15	(a)	Queen's Park R	W	3-0 Walton 3	
59	Mar	7	(h)	Queen's Park R	L	1-3 Brown	2,500
60		14	(a)	Millwall	L	2-3 Turner, Chalmers	
61		21	(a)	West Ham U	W	1-0 Warner	
62	Apr	11	(a)	Fulham	W	5-1 Berry 2, Cameron, Badger, Copeland	

FINAL LEAGUE POSITION: 2nd in London League, Premier Division.

Appearances
Goals

South Eastern League*

63	Oct	19	(h)	New Brompton	W	4-2 O.Burton, J.Jones 2, McConachie	
64	Nov	28	(h)	Brighton & HA	W	7-0 J.Jones 2, Woodward 3, Copeland 2	

*Usually competed in by reserve team but on these occasions first team appeared.

Appearances
Goals

FA Cup

1	Feb	6	(a)	Everton	W	2-1 Woodward, Balmer (og)	25,000
2		20	(h)	Aston Villa†	L	0-1	32,000
R		25	(a)	Aston Villa	W	1-0 J.Jones	30,000
3	Mar	5	(h)	Sheffield W	D	1-1 J.Jones	15,500
R		10	(a)	Sheffield W	L	0-2	32,000

†Abandoned after 20 minutes — crowd overflow.

Appearances
Goals

Southern Charity Cup

1	Sep	28	(a)	Millwall	L	1-3 Brearley	

Appearances
Goals

Archer	Badger	Berry	Brearley	Brown	Burton J	Burton O	Cameron	Chalmers	Copeland	Erentz	Gilhooley	Hughes	Jones J	Jones JL	Kirwan	Leach-Lewis	Mapley	McConachie	McNaught	Mearns	Milton	Morris	Pilch	Quinn	Smith	Stevenson	Tait	Turner	Vaughan	Walton	Warner	Watson	Williams	Woodward	
		9							10	2		4	8	6	11						5						3	7				1			51
		9		6	4	8			10	2	7			5	11												3		1						52
				6					10	2			8		11						5		4				3	7				1	9		53
3				6					10		9	2	8		11						5		4					7				1			54
	9								10	2				5			1				4	6			3		11	8	7						55
3	9		4	6					10						11						5	1					8	7	2						56
3	9		4				11		10			8	6								5							7	2			1			57
3	9		4	6						11					2						5	1		10			7	8							58
3	5	10	4	6						11					2	9						1					7	8							59
	5		4	6						11	9	2	10		8										3			7				1			60
			4				10	6	9	11		2									5						3	7	8			1			61
	9	7	4	6	8				10	2					11						5							3		1					62
5	4	2	7	5	2	9	3	5	9	7	4	3	5	4	6	2					7	4		3	2	1	4	4	1	6	5	4	8	1	
2	2	2	1	2	1	1							2	3								1						4		2					

Archer	Badger	Berry	Brearley	Brown	Burton J	Burton O	Cameron	Chalmers	Copeland	Erentz	Gilhooley	Hughes	Jones J	Jones JL	Kirwan	Leach-Lewis	Mapley	McConachie	McNaught	Mearns	Milton	Morris	Pilch	Quinn	Smith	Stevenson	Tait	Turner	Vaughan	Walton	Warner	Watson	Williams	Woodward	
		9		6					10			4	8	5	11		7									2	3					1			63
				6					10	2			8		11						5		4				3	7				1	9		64
		1		2					2			2	2	1	2		1				1		1			1	2	1				2	1		
				1									2		4												1						3		

Archer	Badger	Berry	Brearley	Brown	Burton J	Burton O	Cameron	Chalmers	Copeland	Erentz	Gilhooley	Hughes	Jones J	Jones JL	Kirwan	Leach-Lewis	Mapley	McConachie	McNaught	Mearns	Milton	Morris	Pilch	Quinn	Smith	Stevenson	Tait	Turner	Vaughan	Walton	Warner	Watson	Williams	Woodward	
									10			5	8	6	11						4						3	7	2	1	9				1
									10			5	8	6	11						4						3	7	2	1	9				2
									10			5	8	6	11						4						3	7	2	1	9				R
			4						10			5	8	6	11												3	7	2	1	9				3
			4						10			5	8	6	11												3	7	2	1	9				R
			2						5			5	5	5	5						3						5	5	5	5	5				
													2																		1				

1 own-goal

Archer	Badger	Berry	Brearley	Brown	Burton J	Burton O	Cameron	Chalmers	Copeland	Erentz	Gilhooley	Hughes	Jones J	Jones JL	Kirwan	Leach-Lewis	Mapley	McConachie	McNaught	Mearns	Milton	Morris	Pilch	Quinn	Smith	Stevenson	Tait	Turner	Vaughan	Walton	Warner	Watson	Williams	Woodward	
		9		6					10			4	8	5	11											2	3	7				1			1
		1		1					1			1	1	1	1											1	1	1				1			
			1																																

1904-05

Manager: John Cameron

1	Sep	3	(h)	Fulham	L	0-1		17,000
2		10	(a)	Watford	W	1-0	Walton	7,000
3		17	(h)	Plymouth A*	W	2-0	Stansfield, Woodward	25,000
4		24	(a)	West Ham U	D	0-0		13,000
5	Oct	1	(h)	Reading	L	1-3	Copeland	13,000
6		8	(a)	Bristol R	L	1-3	Hughes	11,000
7		15	(h)	Northampton T	L	0-1		12,000
8		29	(h)	Brentford	D	1-1	Stansfield	9,800
9	Nov	5	(a)	Queen's Park R	W	2-1	Morris, Brearley	12,000
10		12	(h)	Millwall	W	1-0	Warner	2,000
11		19	(a)	Brighton & HA	D	1-1	Bull	9,000
12		26	(a)	Luton T	L	0-1		8,000
13	Dec	3	(h)	Swindon T	W	6-3	Morris (pen), Walton 2, Glen, O'Hagan 2	10,000
14		10	(a)	New Brompton	D	1-1	Woodward	6,000
15		17	(h)	Wellingborough	W	8-0	Morris (pen), Brearley, Walton 2, Woodward, Glen 3	5,000
16		26	(a)	Southampton	D	1-1	Kirwan	14,000
17		27	(h)	Portsmouth	D	1-1	Woodward	28,000
18		31	(a)	Fulham	L	0-1		9,000
19	Jan	7	(h)	Watford	W	2-0	Tait (pen), Woodward	8,000
20		21	(h)	West Ham U†	W	1-0	Kirwan	14,000
21		28	(a)	Reading	L	2-3	Brearley, Glen	1,000
22	Feb	11	(a)	Northampton T	W	3-0	Hughes, O'Hagan 2	8,000
23		25	(a)	Brentford	D	0-0		6,000
24	Mar	4	(h)	Queen's Park R	W	5-1	Stansfield 2, Woodward, Glen 2	7,000
25		11	(a)	Millwall	W	2-0	Woodward, Glen	5,000
26		18	(h)	Brighton & HA	D	1-1	Chapman	7,000
27		25	(h)	Luton T	W	1-0	O'Hagan	7,000
28	Apr	1	(a)	Swindon T	L	1-2	Stansfield	7,000
29		5	(a)	Plymouth A	L	1-2	Walton	8,000
30		8	(h)	New Brompton	W	2-0	Copeland, Glen	6,000
31		15	(a)	Wellingborough	W	1-0	Glen	3,000
32		21	(h)	Southampton	L	1-2	Kirwan	27,000
33		24	(a)	Portsmouth	L	2-3	Bull, Chapman	10,000
34		29	(h)	Bristol R	W	1-0	George	10,000

FINAL LEAGUE POSITION: 5th in Southern League, Division One.
*Also Hughes and Morris benefit match. †Also Copeland and Kirwan benefit match.

Appearances
Goals

Batting order chart. Columns are players (names printed vertically); the final column is the match number. The two bottom rows are the column totals.

Berry	Brearley	Bull	Burton J	Cameron	Chapman	Copeland	Eggett	Freeborough	Gallacher	George	Glen	Hughes	Kirwan	McCurdy	McNaught	Milton	Morgan	Morris	Murray	O'Hagan	Pilch	Stansfield	Swann	Tait	Walton	Warner	Watson	Williams	Woodward	#
	6					10				8	5	11					4				9		3	7	2	1				1
	6					10				9	5	11					4						3	7	8	2	1			2
	6					10					5	11					4				8		3	7	2	1		9		3
	6					10					5	11					4				8		3	7	2	1		9		4
	6					10					5	11					4				8		3	7	2	1		9		5
		6				10				8	5	11					4				7		3		2	1		9		6
8	6										5	11		2			4		10		7		3					9		7
	6					10	1				5						4		11		7		3		8	2		9		8
9	6	5				10	1					11					4					8	3	7	2					9
9	6	5				10	1					11					4					8	3	7	2					10
9	6	5				10	1					11					4						3	7	2		8			11
9	6	5					1					11					4		10				3	7	2		8			12
	6	5					1				9	11	2				4		10				3	7			8			13
	6	5	3				1	4			9	11	2						10					7			8			14
	6		3				1				9	11	2	5			4		10					7			8			15
9	6	5					1					11	2				4		10				3	7			8			16
						10	1				5	11	2				4						3	7	8	6		9		17
	6	5				10	1					11	2				4				7		3		8			9		18
	6	5					1				9	11					4		10		7		3			2	8			19
	6	5				10	1				9	4	11	2							7		3				8			20
	6	5					1				9	11	2				4		10		7		3				8			21
8		5					1				9	6					4		11		10		7	3		2				22
9		5	3				1				10	6	2				4		11		8		7							23
7		5					1				10	6					4		11		8		3			2		9		24
		5				8	1				10	6					4		11		7		3			2		9		25
		5				9	1				10	6					4		11		8		3	7		2				26
7		5				8	1					11			6		4		10		9		3			2				27
		5			8	10	1				9	6					4		11		7		3			2				28
		5				8	1				10	6					4		11				3	7		2		9		29
		5	3			8	1				10	6					4		11					7		2		9		30
		5	3			8	1			6	10	11					4				9			7		2				31
		5					1				6	11					4		10		9		3	7	8	2				32
		5	3		8	10	1				4	11	2		6						9		7							33
		5	3			8	1				4	11	2		6				10		9		7							34
9	19	26	7		5	19	27	1		4	18	17	25	12	7		28	9	12		22	2	25	19	9	25	7	20		
3	2				2	2		1		10	2	3					3		5		5		1	6	1			7		

175

1904-05 (continued)

Western League

35	Sep	7	(a)	Reading	W	1-0 Warner	
36		19	(h)	Queen's Park R	W	4-1 Morris (pen), Glen, Copeland 2	7,000
37		26	(h)	Bristol R	W	1-0 Morris (pen)	6,000
38	Oct	3	(a)	Millwall	L	2-3 Copeland, Kirwan	
39		19	(a)	Plymouth A	L	0-5	9,000
40		22	(a)	Portsmouth	L	0-1	15,000
41		24	(h)	West Ham U	L	0-1	
42	Nov	7	(h)	Reading	D	2-2 Berry 2	
43		14	(a)	Fulham	D	0-0	
44		21	(h)	Plymouth A	W	2-0 Brearley, Berry	
45	Dec	24	(h)	Southampton§	W	2-1 Tait (pen), O'Hagan	
46	Jan	2	(h)	Fulham	L	0-5	
47	Feb	27	(h)	Millwall	W	4-1 Hughes, Swann, Stansfield, Glen	
48	Mar	6	(a)	Bristol R	L	1-2 Copeland	
49		20	(a)	Queen's Park R	D	1-1 Copeland	
50		27	(a)	West Ham U	D	1-1 Walton	
51		29	(h)	Southampton	D	1-1 Tait (pen)	3,000
52	Apr	3	(a)	Brentford	L	0-2	
53		11	(h)	Brentford	D	0-0	
54		17	(h)	Portsmouth	L	0-1	
55		22	(a)	Southampton	L	0-1	

FINAL LEAGUE POSITION: 8th in Western League, Division One.
§Abandoned after 45 minutes — rain.

Appearances
Goals

FA Cup

1	Feb	4	(a)	Middlesbrough	D	1-1 Glen	25,000
R		9	(h)	Middlesbrough	W	1-0 O'Hagan	18,000
2		18	(h)	Newcastle U	D	1-1 Walton	19,013
R		22	(a)	Newcastle U	L	0-4	26,755

Appearances
Goals

Southern Charity Cup

1	Oct	10	(a)	W Arsenal	W	3-1 Brearley, Woodward 2
SF	Jan	9	(h)	West Ham U	W	10-0 Tait (pen), Brearley 2, Woodward 5, O'Hagan 2
F	Apr	27	(n§)	Reading	D	0-0

§Played at Craven Cottage, Fulham.

Appearances
Goals

Appearance/line-up grid (shirt numbers per match; bottom rows are totals).

Berry	Brearley	Bull	Burton J	Cameron	Chapman	Copeland	Eggett	Freeborough	Gallacher	George	Glen	Hughes	Kirwan	McCurdy	McNaught	Milton	Morgan	Morris	Murray	O'Hagan	Pilch	Stansfield	Swann	Tait	Walton	Warner	Watson	Williams	Woodward	
	6					10						5	11					4			9		3	7	8	2	1			35
8		6				10					9	5	11	2				4					3	7			1			36
	6					10					9	5	11					4		8			3	7		2	1			37
					6	10					9	5	11					4		8	7		3			2	1			38
9	4	6				10					8	5	11	2						7			3				1			39
	6					10	1					11	2	5				4		7					8	3		9		40
	6					9	1					11	2	5				4		10	7				8	3				41
9	6					10	1					5	11					4					8	3		7	2			42
9		6				10	1		5				11					4					8	3		7	2			43
9	6					10	1	5				11	2					4					3	7			8			44
	6	5				1					9	11	2					4		10			3	7			8			45
	6	5				10	1					11		4						9	7		3		8	2				46
	6		3			1	2				10	5			4				11		9	8			7					47
9		5	4			8	1	2									6	7		10				11		3				48
7		5		9	10	1	6							4				11		8		3			2					49
7		6				8	1				10		11	2	5		4						9			3				50
	5					8	1				6	11				4			10		9		3	7		2				51
9						1	5	7				11	2	6					10	4	8					3				52
	5	3				1				10			6			4	11		9	8		7			2					53
		3		8		1	6				10	11	2	5			4			9		7								54
		3				1				4	11	2	5			6		10		9		7	8							55
8	11	8	8		2	15	16	6	1	1	9	9	17	10	8	1	1	16	4	7	1	15	4	11	11	8	15	5	3	—
3	1				5						2	1	1					2		1			1	1	2	1	1			—

Berry	Brearley	Bull	Burton J	Cameron	Chapman	Copeland	Eggett	Freeborough	Gallacher	George	Glen	Hughes	Kirwan	McCurdy	McNaught	Milton	Morgan	Morris	Murray	O'Hagan	Pilch	Stansfield	Swann	Tait	Walton	Warner	Watson	Williams	Woodward	
	6	5				1					9		11					4		10			3	7		2		8		I
	6	5				1					9		11					4		10			3	7		2		8		R
10	6					1					9	5						4	11				3	7		2		8		2
	6	5				1					9	2	11					4		10	7		3					8		R
1	4	3				4					4	2	3					4	1	3	1		4	3		3		4		—
						1												1					1							—

Berry	Brearley	Bull	Burton J	Cameron	Chapman	Copeland	Eggett	Freeborough	Gallacher	George	Glen	Hughes	Kirwan	McCurdy	McNaught	Milton	Morgan	Morris	Murray	O'Hagan	Pilch	Stansfield	Swann	Tait	Walton	Warner	Watson	Williams	Woodward	
8	6					10						5	11	2				4			7		3			1		9		I
	6	5				1				4	9		11	2				4		10	7		3					8		SF
9		5	3	8		1						6						4	11	10				7		2				F
1	2	3	1	1		1	2			1	1	2	2	2				2	1	2	2		2	1		1	1	2		—
	3																			2			1				7			—

1905-06

Southern League   Manager: John Cameron

1	Sep	2	(a)	Reading	D	1-1	Kyle	12,000
2		9	(h)	Watford	W	1-0	Kyle	8,000
3		16	(a)	Brighton & HA	L	0-2		9,000
4		23	(h)	West Ham U	W	2-0	Chapman 2	14,000
5		30	(a)	Fulham	D	0-0		25,000
6	Oct	7	(h)	Queen's Park R	W	2-1	Chapman, Kyle	13,000
7		14	(a)	Bristol R	W	2-0	Tait (pen), Chapman	10,000
8		21	(h)	New Brompton *	W	6-0	Walton 2, Chapman 2, Kyle, Glen	15,000
9	Nov	4	(h)	Swindon T	W	2-1	Morris, Kyle	10,000
10		11	(a)	Millwall	L	1-2	Kyle	10,000
11		18	(h)	Luton T	W	1-0	Woodward	22,000
12		25	(h)	Northampton T	W	2-0	Bull, Carrick	13,000
13	Dec	2	(a)	Brentford	W	3-0	Walton, Chapman 2	10,000
14		16	(a)	Plymouth A	L	1-2	Morris (pen)	10,000
15		25	(h)	Portsmouth	W	3-1	Chapman, Kyle, Carrick	33,000
16		26	(a)	Southampton	L	0-1		12,000
17		30	(h)	Reading	W	1-0	Glen (pen)	12,000
18	Jan	6	(a)	Watford	D	0-0		5,000
19		20	(h)	Brighton & HA	W	3-1	Bull, Walton, Woodward	10,000
20		27	(a)	West Ham U	W	1-0	Kyle	18,000
21	Feb	10	(a)	Queen's Park R	D	0-0		10,000
22		12	(h)	Fulham	L	0-1		18,000
23		17	(h)	Bristol R	D	2-2	Walton, Carrick	4,000
24	Mar	5	(a)	New Brompton	L	0-1		6,000
25		10	(a)	Swindon T	L	0-2		3,000
26		17	(h)	Millwall	W	3-1	Shackleton, Brearley, Carrick	12,000
27		24	(a)	Luton T	L	0-2		10,000
28		31	(a)	Northampton T	D	0-0		6,000
29	Apr	7	(a)	Brentford	W	4-1	Berry, Chapman, Leach 2	8,000
30		13	(h)	Southampton	D	1-1	Chapman	22,000
31		14	(a)	Norwich C	L	1-4	Woodward	12,000
32		16	(a)	Portsmouth	L	0-1		12,000
33		17	(h)	Norwich C	W	3-0	Stansfield, Woodward 2	15,000
34		21	(h)	Plymouth A	L	0-1		8,000

FINAL LEAGUE POSITION: 5th in Southern League, Division One.   Appearances
* Also Tait's benefit match   Goals

178

Berry	Blake	Brearley	Bull	Burton O	Carrick	Chaplin	Chapman	Darnell	Eggett	Freeborough	Gaudson	George	Glen	Hickling	Hughes	Kyle	Leach	McMillan	McNaught	Milnes	Milton	Morris	Murray	O'Hagan	Page	Shackleton	Stansfield	Tait	Walton	Watson	Whitbourne	Whyman	Woodward	No.
	6	5				8		1							9							4	11	10				3	7	2				1
	6	5				8		1							9							4	11	10			7	3		2				2
9	6	5				8		1														4	11	10				3	7	2				3
		5				8	6	1							9							4	11	10			7	3		2				4
		5				8	6	1							9							4	11	10				3	7	2				5
		5				8	6	1							9							4	11	10				3	7	2				6
		5				8	6	1				10			9							4	11					3	7	2				7
		5				8	6	1				10			9							4	11					3	7	2				8
		5				8	6	1				10			9							4	11					3	7	2				9
		5				8	6	1				10			9							4	11					3	7	2				10
		5						1				10		6	8							4	11					3	7	2		9		11
		5		11		8		1						6	9							4						3	7	2		10		12
		5		11		8		1						6	10							4						3	7	2		9		13
	6		3	11		8		1						5	10							4							7	2		9		14
		5	3	11		8		1						6	10							4							7	2		9		15
		5	3	11		8		1				10		6	9							4							7	2				16
		5	3	11				1				8		6	10							4							7	2		9		17
		5	3	11		8		1						6	10							4							7	2		9		18
	6	5		11		8		1							10							4						3	7	2		9		19
	4	5		11		8		1				10		6	9													3	7	2				20
		5		11		8		1				10		6	9							4						3	7	2				21
		5		11		8		1				10		6	9							4						3	7	2				22
	6			11		8		1				10		5	9							4						3	7	2				23
7		5		11		8		1				10		6	9							4						3		2				24
	10	5		11				1			4			6	9							8					7	3		2				25
	10	5		11		8		1						6	9							4					7	3		2				26
7	10	5				8		1						6	9							4						3		2	11			27
	10	5				8		1						6								4					7	3		2	11	9		28
7	10					8	6	1						5	9							4						3		2	11			29
	10	5				8	6	1														4					7	3		2	11	9		30
	8	5	3				6	1							10							4	11						7	2		9		31
9	8		2				4	1	5					6							10						7	3			11			32
	8	5						1						6								4		10			7	3	2		11	9		33
9		5	3			8		1						6	10							4					7		2		11			34
6	16	30	6	15	2	28	10	34	1		1	14		22	25	2						32	12	7	1	3	7	27	21	33	7	12		
1	1	2		4		11	2					2			8	2						2					1	1	1	5		5		

1905-06 (continued)

Western League

35	Sep	4	(h)	Reading	W	5-1	Chapman 3, Kyle, Berry	
36		11	(a)	Queen's Park R	D	1-1	Kyle	3,000
37		25	(h)	Bristol R	L	0-1		4,000
38	Oct	2	(h)	Plymouth A	L	0-2		6,000
39		11	(a)	Reading	D	0-0		
40		16	(h)	Fulham	W	1-0	Kyle	6,000
41		23	(h)	Millwall	W	5-0	Berry 4, Blake	6,000
42		28	(a)	Portsmouth	D	0-0		
43	Nov	6	(a)	West Ham U	L	1-4	Berry	
44		13	(h)	Brentford	L	2-3	Freeborough, Stansfield	
45		20	(a)	Fulham	W	3-0	Stansfield, Kyle 2	
46	Dec	23	(h)	Southampton	W	5-0	Walton 2 (1 pen), Glen, Woodward 2	
47	Jan	29	(h)	Queen's Park R	L	1-2	O'Hagan	
48	Feb	19	(a)	Millwall	D	1-1	Brearley	
49		26	(a)	Brentford	W	1-0	Leach	
50	Mar	3	(h)	Portsmouth	D	1-1	Kyle	6,000
51		19	(a)	Bristol R	D	0-0		
52		21	(a)	Plymouth A	D	0-0		
53		26	(h)	West Ham U	W	1-0	Whyman	1,000
54	Apr	25	(a)	Southampton	L	0-1		

FINAL LEAGUE POSITION: 4th in Western League, Division One.

Appearances
Goals

FA Cup

1	Jan	13	(h)	Burnley	W	2-0	Woodward, Kyle	20,000
2	Feb	3	(h)	Reading	W	3-2	Bull, Walton, Kyle	26,000
3		24	(h)	Birmingham	D	1-1	Kyle	28,000
R		28	(a)	Birmingham	L	0-2*		34,000

*After extra-time

Appearances
Goals

Southern Charity Cup

1	Nov	8	(h)	Queen's Park R	W	2-0	Kyle, Glen	
SF	Apr	9	(h)	W Arsenal	D	0-0		8,000
R		28	(a)	W Arsenal	L	0-5		8,000

Appearances
Goals

Table 1

Berry	Blake	Brearley	Bull	Burton O	Carrick	Chaplin	Chapman	Darnell	Eggett	Freeborough	Gaudson	George	Glen	Hickling	Hughes	Kyle	Leach	McMillan	McNaught	Milnes	Milton	Morris	Murray	O'Hagan	Page	Shackleton	Stansfield	Tait	Walton	Watson	Whitbourne	Whyman	Woodward	
10		6	5				8		1							9						4	11					3	7	2				35
			5				8	6	1							9						4	11	10				3	7	2				36
			5		11			6	1					10		9						4					8	3	7	2				37
		6			2		8		1							9			5			4	11	10				3	7					38
		3					8	6	1	5				9				4					11	10					7	2				39
	11		5		2		8	6	1							4	9	10										3	7					40
9	11							6	1					10	5							4					8	3	7	2				41
			5				8	6	1					10		9						4	11					3	7	2				42
9	11		3						1	6	7	4			5										10		8			2				43
9		6			11		2						4		5										10		8	3	7		1			44
		6			2				1					10	5	9						4	11				8		7	3				45
	4	5	3	11				6	1					8	10														7	2		9		46
					2			6	1			4				9			5	3			11	10		7	8							47
9	10		3		2			6				4							5				11			7	8				1			48
			3		2			6				4				9	8	5					11	10		7					1			49
		6			2		8		1							9			5	3		4	11	10		7								50
	10		11		2		8	6		5		4				9										7		3			1			51
7	10		6		3		8			5						9						4								2	1	11		52
			5					6						10	3	9						4	7				8			2	1	11		53
																																		*54
6	3	8	7	7	4	10	9	12	13	6	1	4	7	1	5	10	5	1	5	2	1	10	11	8		6	7	9	11	11	6	2	1	
6	1	1					3					1				1						6	1				1	2	2		1	2		

*Team untraced

Table 2

Berry	Blake	Brearley	Bull	Burton O	Carrick	Chaplin	Chapman	Darnell	Eggett	Freeborough	Gaudson	George	Glen	Hickling	Hughes	Kyle	Leach	McMillan	McNaught	Milnes	Milton	Morris	Murray	O'Hagan	Page	Shackleton	Stansfield	Tait	Walton	Watson	Whitbourne	Whyman	Woodward	
			5		11				1					8	6	10						4						3	7	2	9			1
			5		11		8		1					10	6	9						4						3	7	2				2
			5		11				1					10	6	9						4						3	7	2		8		3
			5		11				1					10	6	9						4						3	7	2		8		R
			4		4		1		4					4	4	4						4						4	4	4	3			
									1							3						1								1				

Table 3

Berry	Blake	Brearley	Bull	Burton O	Carrick	Chaplin	Chapman	Darnell	Eggett	Freeborough	Gaudson	George	Glen	Hickling	Hughes	Kyle	Leach	McMillan	McNaught	Milnes	Milton	Morris	Murray	O'Hagan	Page	Shackleton	Stansfield	Tait	Walton	Watson	Whitbourne	Whyman	Woodward	
			5		2		8	6	1					10		9						4	11					3	7					1
7			5		2		8		1					10	6							4	11					3			9			SF
	10				3		9			1	5				6							4					7			2	11	8		R
1	1	2			3		3	1	3	1				2		2	1					3	2			1	2	1	1		1	2		
														1								1												

1906-07

Southern League   Manager: John Cameron until March then Fred Kirkham

1	Sep	1	(h)	West Ham U	L 1-2 Dow	16,000
2		5	(a)	Watford	D 1-1 Hewitt	4,000
3		8	(a)	Bristol R	W 3-2 Bull, Eames, Dow	10,000
4		15	(a)	Swindon T	D 0-0	6,000
5		22	(h)	Norwich C	D 2-2 Walton, Hewitt	16,000
6		24	(h)	Fulham	W 5-1 Walton, Hewitt, Reid 2, Dow	13,000
7		29	(a)	Luton T	W 2-0 Bull, Hewitt	10,000
8	Oct	6	(h)	Crystal P	W 3-0 Walton, Reid 2	20,000
9		13	(a)	Brentford	D 2-2 Reid 2 (1 pen)	8,000
10		27	(a)	Leyton	D 1-1 Woodward	15,000
11		29	(a)	Fulham	L 1-2 Stansfield	20,000
12	Nov	3	(h)	Portsmouth	D 1-1 Reid	20,000
13		10	(a)	New Brompton	W 1-0 Woodward	6,000
14		17	(h)	Plymouth A	W 4-2 Hewitt 2, Reid 2	20,000
15		24	(a)	Brighton & HA	L 0-2	8,000
16	Dec	1	(h)	Reading	W 2-0 Hewitt, Reid	10,000
17		15	(h)	Northampton T	W 6-0 Walton 2, Hewitt 2 (1 pen), Eames, Reid	7,000
18		22	(a)	Queen's Park R	L 1-3 Morris	15,000
19		25	(h)	Millwall	W 3-1 Hewitt, Chapman, Reid	20,000
20		26	(a)	Southampton	L 1-2 Reid	8,000
21		29	(a)	West Ham U	L 2-4 Woodward, Reid	13,000
22	Jan	5	(h)	Bristol R	W 4-0 Chapman, Woodward 2, Pickett	12,000
23		19	(h)	Swindon T	W 3-0 Hewitt, Whyman, Walton	7,000
24		26	(a)	Norwich C	L 0-5	5,000
25	Feb	9	(a)	Crystal P	W 1-0 Pickett	8,000
26		16	(h)	Brentford	W 2-1 Chapman, Pickett	15,000
27	Mar	2	(h)	Leyton	D 0-0	14,000
28		9	(a)	Portsmouth	L 1-3 Woodward	12,000
29		16	(h)	New Brompton	W 2-0 Walton, Reid	6,000
30		23	(a)	Plymouth A	D 0-0	5,000
31		25	(h)	Luton T	L 1-2 Stansfield	9,000
32		29	(h)	Southampton	W 2-0 Woodward, Reid	20,000
33		30	(h)	Brighton & HA	W 3-0 Walton, Walker, Pickett	12,000
34	Apr	1	(a)	Millwall	L 0-2	12,000
35		6	(a)	Reading	L 0-2	8,000
36		13	(h)	Watford	D 0-0	9,000
37		20	(a)	Northampton T	L 0-2	8,000
38		27	(h)	Queen's Park R	W 2-0 Reid 2 (1 pen)	7,000

FINAL LEAGUE POSITION: 6th in Division One, Southern League.   Appearances
Goals

182

Player appearances / line-up grid (shirt numbers by match):

Badenoch	Berry	Brearley	Bull	Burton	Chaplin	Chapman	Darnell	Dow	Eames	Eggett	Hewitt	Hughes	Jones	McDairmid	Morris	Page	Payne	Pickett	Reid	Reilly	Stansfield	Steel D	Tait	Walker	Walton	Watson C	Watson J	Whitbourne	Whyman	Wilkinson	Woodward	No.
			5									11	9	1	8		6	4		3			10	7								1
7	9		5	2	3									1	8		6	4					10					11				2
			5	2	3							11	9	1	8		6	4					10	7								3
			5	2	3							11	9	1	8		6	4					10	7								4
			5	2	3							11		1	8		6	4					10	7					9			5
			5		2	6						11		1	8			4		3			10	7					9			6
			5		2	6						11		1	8			4		3			10	7					9			7
			5		2	6						11		1	8			4		3			10	7					9			8
			5		2	6						11		1	8			4		3			10	7					9			9
			5		2	6						11		1	8			4		3			10	7					9			10
		11	5		2						6	4			8			10	1	3				7					9			11
		11	5		2						6	4			8			10	1			3		7					9			12
		11	5		2						6	4			8			10	1			3		7					9			13
		11	5		2						6	4			8			10	1			3		7					9			14
		11	5		2						6	4			8			10	1			3		7					9			15
		11	5		2						6	4			8			10	1			3		7					9			16
		11	5		2			9			6	4			8			10	1			3		7								17
		11	5		2						6	4			8			10	1			3		7					9			18
		11	5		2			9			6	4			8			10	1			3		7								19
		11	5		2			9			6	4			8			10	1			3		7								20
			5		2						6	4			8			10	1			3		7				11	9			21
		11	5		2						6	4			8			10	1			3		7					9			22
		11	5		2			9			6				8		10		1			3		7	4			11				23
		11	5		3			9			6	4			8		10		1					7		2						24
		11	5	3	2	6		9				4			8		7	5	1			10										25
		11	5		2	6		9				4			8		10		1			3		7								26
		11	5	3	2						6	4			8		10							7		1			9			27
		11	5	3	2						6	4			8		10							7		1			9			28
		11	5		2						6	4			8		10					3		7		1			9			29
		11	5		2			9			6	4			8		10			8		3		7		1						30
		11	5		2			9			6	4			8		10			8				7		1	3					31
		11	5		2						6	4			8		10			8		3		7		1			9			32
		11	5		2			9			6	4			8		10			8		3		7		1						33
		11	5	3				9			6	4			8		7					8	10			1		2				34
		11	5		2			9			6	4			8		10			8		3		7		1						35
		11	5		2						6	4			8		10			8		3		7		1			9			36
		11	5		2						6				8		9	10			8	4	3	7		1						37
		11	5		2			9			6	4			8		10					3		7		1						38
1	1	18	28	4	34	10	2	9	7	5	30	25	8	7	33		15	26	19	11	6	24	10	34	12	14	3	2	20			
			2		3	3		2				11			1		4	18	2			1		8		1			7			

Western League

							Appearances
39	Sep	3	(h)	Plymouth A	D	0-0	4,000
40		10	(h)	Southampton	L	2-3 Jones, Brearley	5,000
41	Oct	3	(a)	Southampton	L	0-2	
42		8	(a)	West Ham U	L	0-5	4,000
43		20	(h)	Millwall	W	1-0 Stevenson (og)	
44	Nov	7	(a)	Portsmouth	L	0-1	4,000
45		26	(h)	Portsmouth	W	4-2 Brearley, Hewitt (pen), Walton 2	8,000
46	Dec	12	(a)	Plymouth A	D	2-2 Reid, Orrell (og)	
47	Apr	8	(h)	West Ham U	W	4-0 Chapman, Whyman 3	
48		22	(a)	Millwall	D	0-0	

FINAL LEAGUE POSITION: 4th in Division One, Western League.

Appearances
Goals

FA Cup

							Appearances
1	Jan	12	(h)	Hull C	D	0-0	27,033
R		17	(a)	Hull C	D	0-0*	18,000
2R		21	(h†)	Hull C	W	1-0 Chapman	20,000
2	Feb	2	(a)	Blackburn R	D	1-1 Walton	24,963
R		7	(a)	Blackburn R	D	1-1‡ Reid	29,900
2R		11	(n§)	Blackburn R	W	2-1 Walton, Reid	18,000
3		23	(a)	Notts C	L	0-4	25,000

*Abandoned after ten minutes of extra-time — bad light — result stood.
†Played at home by mutual consent. ‡After extra-time. §Played at Villa Park, Birmingham.

Appearances
Goals

Southern Charity Cup

1	Oct	22	(h)	West Ham U	W	2-0 Stansfield, Reid	8,000
SF	Mar	4	(h)	Queen's Park R	W	4-0 Jones, Hewitt, Reid, Brearley	6,000
F	Apr	29	(h)	Southampton	W	2-0 Hewitt, Reid	10,000

Appearances
Goals

	Badenoch	Berry	Brearley	Bull	Burton	Chaplin	Chapman	Darnell	Dow	Eames	Eggett	Hewitt	Hughes	Jones	McDairmid	Morris	Page	Payne	Pickett	Reid	Reilly	Stansfield	Steel D	Tait	Walker	Walton	Watson C	Watson J	Whitbourne	Whyman	Wilkinson	Woodward	
		5			3	8		11	9	1			4	6			10									7		2						39
		5		2				11	9	1	8		4	6			10							3		7								40
	9	5			3			11				8	6		4					1					10	7		2						41
	7		6						9			8	5							10	1	11	4			3	2							42
		6			2	8		11					5							4	9			10	1			7	3					43
		11	5			2						8	6							4				10	1	9		7	3					44
		11	5						9			8					6				10			1	4	3		7	2					45
		11	5						9			8	6					4			10	1				3		7	2					46
		11		3	2	9	4					8			6									5				7		1	10			47
		11	5	3	2	9	6					8								10					4			7		1				48
1	1	10	4	3	6	4	2	5	4	2	8	5	2	4	4	1	1	2	5	6	2	4	3	1	9	1	7	2	1				
		2				1				1		1							1							2				3			

2 own-goals

	Badenoch	Berry	Brearley	Bull	Burton	Chaplin	Chapman	Darnell	Dow	Eames	Eggett	Hewitt	Hughes	Jones	McDairmid	Morris	Page	Payne	Pickett	Reid	Reilly	Stansfield	Steel D	Tait	Walker	Walton	Watson C	Watson J	Whitbourne	Whyman	Wilkinson	Woodward	
		11	5									8	6							4			10	1		3		7	2		9			1
		11	5									8	6							4			10	1		3		7	2		9			R
			5			9						8	6							4			10	1	11	3		7	2					2R
			5			9						8	6							4			10	1	11	3		7	2					2
			5			9						8	6							4			10	1	11	3		7	2					R
			5			9						8	6							4			10	1	11	3		7	2					2R
			5			8							6							4			10	1	11	3		7	2		9			3
		2	7			6	1					5	6							7			7	5	7	7		7	7		3			
						1														2						2							

	Badenoch	Berry	Brearley	Bull	Burton	Chaplin	Chapman	Darnell	Dow	Eames	Eggett	Hewitt	Hughes	Jones	McDairmid	Morris	Page	Payne	Pickett	Reid	Reilly	Stansfield	Steel D	Tait	Walker	Walton	Watson C	Watson J	Whitbourne	Whyman	Wilkinson	Woodward	
			2			11						5	6	4						10	1	8		3		7				9			1
		11			2	9						8	6	5		4				10				3		7		1					SF
			5		2							8	6		4					10		11		3		7		1		9			F
	1	1	3	1		1						2	3	1	1	3				3	1	2		3		3		2	1	1			
		1											2	1						3		1											

185

1907-08

Southern League

Manager: Fred Kirkham

1	Sep	2	(a)	Queen's Park R	D 3-3 Walton, Pass, McNair	6,000
2		7	(a)	West Ham U	D 1-1 McNair	10,000
3		14	(h)	Queen's Park R	W 3-2 Bull, Darnell, Pass	20,000
4		21	(h)	New Brompton	W 2-1 McNair 2	16,000
5		28	(a)	Swindon T	L 0-1	5,000
6	Oct	5	(h)	Crystal P	L 1-2 Stansfield	18,000
7		12	(a)	Luton T	L 1-3 McNair	7,000
8		19	(h)	Brighton & HA	D 1-1 Morris (og)	12,000
9		26	(a)	Portsmouth	W 2-1 Seeburg 2	10,000
10	Nov	2	(h)	Bradford	D 0-0	20,000
11		9	(a)	Millwall	W 2-1 Woodward 2	8,000
12		16	(h)	Brentford	W 1-0 Reid	12,000
13		23	(a)	Bristol R	D 0-0	8,000
14		30	(h)	Leyton	W 1-0 Woodward	12,000
15	Dec	7	(a)	Reading	L 1-3 Middlemiss	5,000
16		14	(h)	Watford	W 5-0 Steel, Woodward 2, Middlemiss, Hitch (og)	9,000
17		21	(a)	Norwich C	L 1-2 Middlemiss	5,000
18		25	(h)	Northampton T	W 2-0 Woodward 2	25,000
19		26	(a)	Southampton	D 1-1 Walker	18,000
20		28	(a)	Northampton T	L 1-2 Pass	9,000
21	Jan	4	(h)	West Ham U	W 3-2 Pass, Payne, Pickett	13,000
22		18	(a)	New Brompton	W 2-1 Woodward, Bull	5,000
23		20	(h)	Plymouth A	L 0-1	10,000
24		25	(h)	Swindon T	W 1-0 Reid	10,000
25	Feb	8	(h)	Luton T	L 1-2 Walker	11,000
26		12	(a)	Crystal P	W 2-0 Pass, Pickett	8,000
27		15	(a)	Brighton & HA	L 0-2	3,000
28		29	(a)	Bradford	W 2-1 Seeburg, Middlemiss	7,000
29	Mar	7	(h)	Millwall	L 1-2 Minter	20,000
30		14	(a)	Brentford	L 0-3	6,000
31		21	(h)	Bristol R	L 1-2 Woodward	11,000
32		28	(a)	Leyton	W 5-2 Woodruff 2, Woodward, Seeburg, Bidmead (og)	12,000
33	Apr	4	(h)	Reading	W 2-0 Minter 2	8,000
34		6	(h)	Portsmouth	L 2-3 Middlemiss, Phillips (og)	6,000
35		11	(a)	Watford	D 2-2 Woodruff, Minter	5,000
36		17	(h)	Southampton	W 3-0 Seeburg, Payne, Middlemiss	22,000
37		18	(h)	Norwich C	W 3-0 Payne, Middlemiss 2	10,000
38		20	(a)	Plymouth A	L 0-1	8,000

FINAL LEAGUE POSITION: 7th in Division One, Southern League.

Appearances
Goals

Western League

39	Sep	9	(h)	Bristol R	W 10-0 Morris, Walton, Pass 4, McNair, Reid 3	500
40		16	(a)	Bristol R	L 1-2 Walton	
41		23	(a)	Millwall	L 0-2	
42	Oct	2	(a)	Reading	W 2-1 Whyman, Seeburg	
43		7	(h)	West Ham U*	W 2-1 Bull, Pickett	5,000
44		14	(h)	Reading	L 0-2	
45		23	(a)	Crystal P	L 0-2	
46	Nov	4	(a)	West Ham U	W 3-1 Steel, Reid 2	
47		25	(h)	Millwall	L 0-3	3,000
48	Dec	2	(h)	Crystal P	W 1-0 Middlemiss	2,000
49		9	(a)	Luton T	W 5-1 Walton, Pass 2, McNair, Payne	1,500
50		16	(h)	Luton T	W 2-0 Seeburg, Payne	1,500

FINAL LEAGUE POSITION: 2nd in Section 'B', Western League.
*Also Watson benefit match.

Appearances
Goals

FA Cup

1	Jan	11	(a)	Everton	L 0-1	21,000

Appearances
Goals

Southern Charity Cup

1	Sep	30	(h)	Millwall	D 1-1 Walton	7,000
R	Nov	19	(a)	Millwall	L 1-2 Whyman	700

Appearances
Goals

186

Football season appearance and goal grid. Player columns (left to right): Brewster, Bull, Burton, Chaplin, Coquet, Cousins, Darnell, Dixon, Gipps, Gray, Hughes, Lee, Manning, Massey, McNair, Middlemiss, Minter, Morris, Pass, Payne, Pickett, Reid, Seeburg, Stansfield, Steel D, Tait, Walker, Walton, Watson, Whitbourne, Whyman, Woodruff, Woodward.

Brewster	Bull	Burton	Chaplin	Coquet	Cousins	Darnell	Dixon	Gipps	Gray	Hughes	Lee	Manning	Massey	McNair	Middlemiss	Minter	Morris	Pass	Payne	Pickett	Reid	Seeburg	Stansfield	Steel D	Tait	Walker	Walton	Watson	Whitbourne	Whyman	Woodruff	Woodward	#
	5	2		3						6		9				4	8			10						7		1	11				1
	5	2	6	3								9				4	8			10						7		1	11				2
	5	2	6	3								9				4	8					10				7		1	11				3
	5	2	6	3							1	9				4	8	11		10						7							4
	5	3	2	6							1	9				4	8	11	10							7							5
	5	3		6							1	10				4	8						11			7	2					9	6
	5	3	2	6							1	10				4	8						11			7						9	7
		3	2	6							1	9				4				10			11	5		7					8	9	8
	5	3	2					6			1					4	8					10	11			7						9	9
	5	3	2					6			1					4	8					10	11			7						9	10
		3						6			1					4				10			5		8	7	2		11			9	11
		3	2					6			1	11				4				10			5		8	7						9	12
		3	2					6			1	11				4				10			5		8	7						9	13
		3	2					6			1	11				4				10			5		8	7						9	14
		3	2					6			1	11				4			8				5		10	7		9					15
							10	6			1	11				4						5	3	8	7	2						9	16
		3	2				10	6			1	9	11			4						5		8	7								17
		3	2			6					1	11			4	10						5		8	7							9	18
		3	2			6					1	11	4	8	10							5		7							9	19
		3	2					6			1		4	8	10	11						5		7							9	20
		3	2					6			1		4	8	10	11						5		7							9	21
	10	3	2					6			1	7	11			4						5		8							9	22
7	10	3	2					6			1	9	11			4						5		8								23
	5	3	2					6			1	7	11	4	8		10	9														24
	5	3	2					6			1	7	11	4		10						8						9				25
	5	3	2			6					1	7	11		8	10	9	4														26
	5	3	2			6					1	7	11		8	10	9	4														27
	5	3	2			6					1		11	7	10		8	4								9						28
	5	3		2		6					1		11	8	7	10			4										9			29
	5	3		2	6						1		11	8	7	10			4							9						30
		3	2			6						11	10	4				7	5							1	9	8				31
		3	2			6					1	11	4		10	9	5											7	8			32
		3		2		6					1	11	8	4	10	9	5										7				33
	5	3	2			6					1	11	8		10	9	4								1	7						34
		2	3		6						1	11	10	4		9	5										7	8				35
		3	2			6					1	11	8	4	10	9	5										7					36
	5	3	2			6					1	11	8	4	10	9	7															37
	5			2		6	3				1	11	8	10	9	7	4															38
1	21	31	30	6		2	22	5		15	1	33		15	25	9	31	18	7	13	10	15	8	26	1	14	18	3	5	8	5	20	
	2			1						5	8	4		5	3	2	2	5	1	1		2	1			3	10						

4 own-goals

Brewster	Bull	Burton	Chaplin	Coquet	Cousins	Darnell	Dixon	Gipps	Gray	Hughes	Lee	Manning	Massey	McNair	Middlemiss	Minter	Morris	Pass	Payne	Pickett	Reid	Seeburg	Stansfield	Steel D	Tait	Walker	Walton	Watson	Whitbourne	Whyman	Woodruff	Woodward	#
	5	2		6								9				4	8			10				3		7		1	11				39
	5				3		6	4				9					8			10						7	2	1	11				40
		5	2	6	3					1		4	8	10		9									7			11				41
		2			3		6			1	4		8						10	11	5				7		9						42
	5			6	3					1	9					10	8	11	4						7	2						43
		3					11	1	6	9		4					8	5				7	2			10							44
				6						1		4	8	11	10		5	3	7			2		9									45
		2		4			6			1	9		8		10		11	5	3	7													46
			10		2		6	5		1		11	4			9		3	8	7													47
		2		5	4		6	1		7	11	8			10		3									9							48
	3			5	2		6			1	9	4	8	10			7									11							49
	5			6						1	4	11	8	10		7			3				2	9									50
	4	3	5	1		7	6	1	5	4	1	10	3	8	2	6	9	3	2	3	8	3	5	6	2	9	5	2	8	1			
	1									2	1		1	6	2	1	5	2		1			1		3		1						

Brewster	Bull	Burton	Chaplin	Coquet	Cousins	Darnell	Dixon	Gipps	Gray	Hughes	Lee	Manning	Massey	McNair	Middlemiss	Minter	Morris	Pass	Payne	Pickett	Reid	Seeburg	Stansfield	Steel D	Tait	Walker	Walton	Watson	Whitbourne	Whyman	Woodruff	Woodward	#
	10	3	2					6			1		11			4	8					5		7							9		1
	1	1	1					1			1		1			1	1					1		1							1		

Brewster	Bull	Burton	Chaplin	Coquet	Cousins	Darnell	Dixon	Gipps	Gray	Hughes	Lee	Manning	Massey	McNair	Middlemiss	Minter	Morris	Pass	Payne	Pickett	Reid	Seeburg	Stansfield	Steel D	Tait	Walker	Walton	Watson	Whitbourne	Whyman	Woodruff	Woodward	#
		3	2					6			1		9			4	8					10	11	5		7							1
		3	2					6			1		9			4			10			5		8	7		11						R
		2	2					2			2		2			2	1		1			1	2	1	2		1						
																	1						1										

187

1908-09

Manager: Directors

					Result	Scorers	Attendance
1	Sep	1	(h)	Wolves	W 3-0	Morris, Woodward 2	20,000
2		5	(a)	Leeds C	L 0-1		20,000
3		12	(h)	Barnsley	W 4-0	Walton, Woodward, Middlemiss 2	20,000
4		19	(h)	Bolton W	W 2-1	Minter, Middlemiss	25,000
5		26	(a)	Hull C	L 0-1		12,000
6	Oct	3	(h)	Derby C	D 0-0		25,000
7		10	(a)	Blackpool	D 1-1	R.Steel	6,000
8		17	(h)	Chesterfield	W 4-0	Walton, Minter 2, R.Steel	14,000
9		24	(a)	Glossop NE	D 1-1	Minter	3,000
10		31	(h)	Stockport C	D 0-0		16,000
11	Nov	7	(a)	West Brom A	L 0-3		20,000
12		14	(h)	Birmingham	W 4-0	Woodward 2, Middlesmiss 2	25,000
13		21	(a)	Gainsborough T	W 2-0	R.Steel, Middlemiss	6,000
14		28	(h)	Grimsby T	W 2-0	Woodward 2	14,000
15	Dec	5	(a)	Fulham	W 3-2	Minter 2, R.Steel	35,000
16		12	(h)	Burnley	W 4-2	Minter, Woodward 2, R.Steel	10,000
17		19	(a)	Bradford	W 2-0	Minter, Woodward	5,000
18		25	(a)	Oldham A	L 0-1		24,000
19		26	(h)	Oldham A	W 3-0	Minter, Woodward, Middlemiss	40,000
20		28	(a)	Wolves	L 0-1		9,000
21	Jan	2	(h)	Leeds C	W 3-0	Minter 2, Middlemiss	16,000
22		9	(a)	Barnsley	D 1-1	Minter	7,000
23		23	(a)	Bolton W	W 1-0	R.Steel	24,000
24		30	(h)	Hull C	D 0-0		21,000
25	Feb	13	(h)	Blackpool	W 4-1	Minter, R.Steel, Middlemiss 2	15,000
26		27	(h)	Glossop NE	D 3-3	McFarlane, R.Steel 2	12,000
27	Mar	6	(a)	Stockport C	W 3-1	Minter, R.Steel, Middlemiss	5,000
28		8	(a)	Chesterfield	W 3-1	Woodward, Middlemiss 2	5,000
29		13	(h)	West Brom A	L 1-3	Woodruff	35,000
30		20	(h)	Birmingham	D 3-3	D.Steel, Woodward, R.Steel	8,000
31		27	(h)	Gainsborough T	D 1-1	Woodward	15,000
32	Apr	3	(a)	Grimsby T	W 2-1	Minter, McFarlane	5,000
33		9	(h)	Clapton O	L 0-1		33,000
34		10	(h)	Fulham	W 1-0	Woodward	22,000
35		12	(a)	Clapton O	D 0-0		20,000
36		17	(a)	Burnley	W 2-1	Woodward 2	8,000
37		24	(a)	Bradford	W 3-0	Curtis, Minter, Woodward	20,000
38		28	(a)	Derby C	D 1-1	R.Steel	9,000

FINAL LEAGUE POSITION: 2nd in Division Two

Appearances

Goals

FA Cup

1	Jan	16	(a)	Manchester C	W 4-3	Morris (pen), Minter 2, R.Steel	20,000
2	Feb	6	(h)	Fulham	W 1-0	R.Steel	33,008
3		20	(h)	Burnley	D 0-0		21,838
R		24	(a)	Burnley	L 1-3	Coquet (pen)	30,000

Appearances

Goals

London FA Charity Cup

1	Oct	5	(h)	Queen's Park R	W 1-0	Minter	7,000
2	Nov	30	(a)	West Ham U	W 2-0	Walton, D.Steel	3,000
SF	Mar	22	(n*)	Millwall	L 0-2		5,000

*Played at Upton Park

Appearances

Goals

London Professional Football Charity Fund

	Nov	2	(h)	Clapton O	D 1-1	Minter	6,000

Appearances

Goals

Squad appearance grid. Columns are players (left→right): Bentley, Boreham, Brough, Bull, Burton, Coquet, Curtis, Darnell, Hewitson, Leslie, Massey, McFarlane, Middlemiss, Minter, Morris, Morton, Seeburg, Steel D, Steel R, Walton, Wilkes, Woodruff, Woodward. The far-right column is the match number.

Bentley	Boreham	Brough	Bull	Burton	Coquet	Curtis	Darnell	Hewitson	Leslie	Massey	McFarlane	Middlemiss	Minter	Morris	Morton	Seeburg	Steel D	Steel R	Walton	Wilkes	Woodruff	Woodward	#
			3	2		6	1			9	11		4			5	10	7			8		1
			3	2		6	1			9	11	8	4			5	10	7			8		2
			3	2		6	1				11	9	4			5	10	7			8		3
			3	2		6	1			9	11	8	4			5	10	7					4
			3	2		6	1				11	9	4		8	5	10	7					5
			3	2		6	1				11	9	4			5	10	7			8		6
			3	2			1	6		9	11	8	4			5	10	7					7
			3	2		6	1			9	11	8	4			5	10	7					8
			3	2		6	1			9	11	8	4			5	10	7					9
			3	2		6	1			9	11		4			5	10	7			8		10
			3	2		6	1			7	11	9	4			5	10				8		11
			3	2		6	1				11	8	4			5	10		7	9			12
			3	2		6	1			9	11	8	4			5	10		7				13
			3	2		6	1				11		4	9		5	10	7			8		14
			3	2		6	1				11	8	4			5	10	7			9		15
			3	2		6	1				11	8	4			5	10	7			9		16
			3	2		6	1				11	8	4			5	10	7			9		17
			3	2		6	1				11	8	4	9		5	10	7					18
			3	2		6	1				11	8	4			5	10	7			9		19
	4		3	2		6	1				11	8				5	10	7			9		20
			3	2		6	1				11	8	4			5	10	7			9		21
			3	2		6	1				11	8	4			5	10	7			9		22
			3	2		6	1				11	8	4			5	10	7			9		23
			3	2		6	1				11	8	4			5	10	7			9		24
			3	2		6	1			9	11	8	4			5	10	7					25
			3	2		6	1	4		9	11	8				5	10		7				26
		4	3	2		6	1				11	8				5	10		7	9			27
		4	3	2		6	1				11	8				5	10		7	9			28
		4	3	2		6	1				11	8				5	10		7	9			29
		4	3	2		6	1				11	8				5	10		7	9			30
1		4	3			6			8	10	11					5		2	7	9			31
1		4	3	2		6				9	11	8				5	10	7			9		32
1		4	3	2		6					11	8				5	10	7			9		33
1		4		2		6				7	11	8				5	10		3		9		34
1		4		2		6				7	11	8				5	10		3		9		35
1		4		2		6				7	11	8				5	10		3		9		36
1		4		2	7	6					11	8				5	10		3		9		37
1		4		2	7	6					11	8				5	10		3		9		38
8	1	12	33	37	2	37	30	2	1	16	38	34	24	2	1	38	37	24	6	8	27		
							1					2	13	16	1		1	12	2		1	18		

Bentley	Boreham	Brough	Bull	Burton	Coquet	Curtis	Darnell	Hewitson	Leslie	Massey	McFarlane	Middlemiss	Minter	Morris	Morton	Seeburg	Steel D	Steel R	Walton	Wilkes	Woodruff	Woodward	#
			3	2		6	1				11	8	4			5	10	7			9		1
			3	2		6	1				11	8	4			5	10	7			9		2
			3	2		6	1				11	8	4			5	10	7			9		3
	4		3	2		6	1				11	8				5	10	7			9		R
	1		4	4		4	4				4	4	3			4	4	4			4		
							1					2	1					2						

Bentley	Boreham	Brough	Bull	Burton	Coquet	Curtis	Darnell	Hewitson	Leslie	Massey	McFarlane	Middlemiss	Minter	Morris	Morton	Seeburg	Steel D	Steel R	Walton	Wilkes	Woodruff	Woodward	#
5			2	3		6	1				11	9	4		8	5		7			10		1
	4		3	2		6	1				11	8		9		5	10	7					2
1		4	3	2		6			8	10	11			9		5			7				SF
1	1	1	2	3	2	3	2	1	1	3	2	1	2	1	2	1	2	1		1	1		
												1					1	1						

Bentley	Boreham	Brough	Bull	Burton	Coquet	Curtis	Darnell	Hewitson	Leslie	Massey	McFarlane	Middlemiss	Minter	Morris	Morton	Seeburg	Steel D	Steel R	Walton	Wilkes	Woodruff	Woodward	#
			3	2		6	1			7	11	8	4			5	10				9		
			1	1		1	1			1	1	1	1			1	1				1		
												1												

1909-10

Manager: Directors

1	Sep	1	(a) Sunderland	L	1-3	Morris	10,000
2		4	(a) Everton	L	2-4	Minter, Middlemiss	20,000
3		11	(h) Manchester U	D	2-2	R.Steel 2 (2 pens)	32,275
4		18	(a) Bradford C	L	1-5	Tull	25,000
5		25	(h) Sheffield W	W	3-0	D.Steel, Curtis, Minter	24,000
6	Oct	2	(a) Bristol C	D	0-0		20,000
7		9	(h) Bury	W	1-0	Middlemiss	30,000
8		16	(h) Middlesbrough	L	1-3	Middlemiss	23,000
9		23	(a) Preston NE§	D	0-0		4,000
10		30	(h) Notts C	L	1-3	Minter	23,000
11	Nov	6	(a) Newcastle U	L	0-1		26,000
12		13	(h) Liverpool	W	1-0	Middlemiss	22,000
13		20	(a) Aston Villa	L	2-3	Minter, R.Steel	25,000
14		22	(a) Preston NE	L	1-4	R.Steel	
15		27	(h) Sheffield U	W	2-1	Minter, R.Steel (pen)	26,000
16	Dec	4	(a) W Arsenal	L	0-1		18,000
17		11	(h) Bolton W	D	1-1	Minter	20,000
18		18	(a) Chelsea	L	1-2	Minter	50,000
19		25	(h) Nottingham F	D	2-2	Humphreys 2	30,000
20		27	(a) Nottingham F	D	2-2	R.Steel, Middlemiss	22,300
21	Jan	1	(a) Blackburn R	L	0-2		15,000
22		8	(h) Everton	W	3-0	R.Steel, Middlemiss 2	24,000
23		22	(a) Manchester U	L	0-5		8,000
24		29	(h) Bradford C	D	0-0		22,000
25	Feb	12	(h) Bristol C	W	3-2	Minter, Humphreys, Middlemiss	25,000
26		26	(a) Middlesbrough	L	3-4	Minter 2, Steel R	5,000
27	Mar	5	(h) Preston NE	W	2-1	Minter, Humphreys	25,000
28		12	(a) Notts C	L	0-3		15,000
29		14	(a) Sheffield W	D	1-1	D.Steel	3,000
30		19	(h) Newcastle U	L	0-4		25,000
31		25	(h) Sunderland	W	5-1	Curtis, Humphreys 2, R.Steel, Middlemiss	35,000
32		26	(a) Liverpool	L	0-2		15,000
33		28	(h) Blackburn R	W	4-0	Minter 3, Humphreys	23,000
34	Apr	2	(h) Aston Villa	D	1-1	Humphreys	34,000
35		9	(a) Sheffield U	D	1-1	Humphreys	10,000
36		16	(h) W Arsenal	D	1-1	Curtis	39,800
37		20	(a) Bury	L	1-3	Humphreys	4,000
38		23	(a) Bolton W	W	2-0	Humphreys 2	3,000
39		30	(h) Chelsea	W	2-1	Minter, Humphreys	35,000

FINAL LEAGUE POSITION: 15th in Division One
§Abandoned after 50 minutes — rain.

Appearances
Goals

FA Cup

1	Jan	15	(a) Plymouth A	D	1-1	Humphreys	10,200
R		19	(h) Plymouth A	W	7-1	Minter, Humphreys 3, R.Steel, Middlemiss 2	17,000
2	Feb	5	(a) Chelsea	W	1-0	Humphreys	31,766
3		19	(a) Swindon T	L	2-3	Minter, R.Steel	11,818

Appearances
Goals

London FA Charity Cup

1	Sep	20	(a) Nunhead	W	9-0	Minter 2, R.Steel 4 (1 pen), Middlemiss 3	3,000
2	Oct	11	(h) Croydon C	W	7-1	Minter 2, I.Brown, Middlemiss 4	
SF	Nov	8	(n*) Queen's Park R	D	0-0		12,000
R		15	(n†) Queen's Park R	W	4-1	Curtis, I.Brown 2, R.Steel (pen)	10,000
F	Dec	6	(n*) Fulham	L	1-4	Minter	17,000

*Played at Stamford Bridge. †Played at Craven Cottage.

Appearances
Goals

London Professional Football Charity Fund

	Nov	1	(h) W Arsenal	W	3-0	Curtis 2, R.Steel	5,000

Appearances
Goals

190

Player appearance / batting-order grid (numbers indicate batting position per match; right-hand column is the match number).

Bentley	Boreham	Brown D	Brown I	Burton	Coquet	Curtis	Darnell	Drabble	Elkin	Gipps	Harris	Humphreys	Joyce	Kennedy	Kerry	Leslie	Lunn	Lyle	McFarlane	Middlemiss	Minter	Morris	Newman	Steel A	Steel D	Steel R	Tull	Wilkes	Woodruff	#
1					2	7	6													11	8	4			5	10	9	3		1
1					2	7	6													11	9	4			5	10	8	3		2
1					2	7	6													11	9	4			5	10	8	3		3
1					2	7	6													11	9	4			5	10	8	3		4
1					2	7	6										8	4		11	9				5	10		3		5
1			3		2	7	6											4	11	9				5	10		8		6
1			3		2	7	6											4	11	9				5	10		8		7
1			3		2	7	6											4	11	8				5	10		9		8
4	9		3		2	7	6	1												11	8				5	10				9
4	9		3		2	7	6	1												11	8				5	10				10
6	1		9			7						3								11	8	4			5	10		2		11
	1		9			7	6					3								11	8	4			5	10		2		12
	1		9			7	6					3								11	8	4			5	10		2		13
	1		9			7	6					3								11	8	4			5	10		2		14
4			9			7	6					3	1							11	8				5	10		2		15
4			9			7	6					3	1							11	8				5	10		2		16
4							6	3			2	9	1							11	8				5	10		7		17
4			3			9	6				2		1							11	8				5	10		7		18
4			3			7	6				2	9	1							11	8				5	10				19
6			3			7					2	9	1							11	8	4			5	10				20
6			3			7					2	9	1							11	8	4			5	10				21
6			3			7					2	9	1							11	8	4			5	10				22
			3			7	6				2	9	1						4	11	8				5	10				23
6	9		3			7					2		1							11	8			4	5	10				24
			3			7	6					9	1			2				11	8	4			5	10				25
6			3			7						9	1			2				11	8	4			5	10				26
6						7						9	1			2				11	8	4			5	10		3		27
6						7						9	1			2				11	8	4			5	10		3		28
						7	6					9	1			2				11	8	4			5	10		3		29
						7	6					9	1			2				11	8	4			5	10		3		30
6					2	7						9	1	5						11	8	4				10		3		31
6	9		3			7							1	5						11	8	4				10		2		32
6					2	7						9	1							11	8	4			5	10		3		33
6			3			7						9	1			2				11	8	4			5	10				34
			3			7	6					9	1							11	8	4			5	10		2		35
6					2	7						9	1							11	8	4			5	10		3		36
					2	7	6					9	1							11	8	4			5	10		3		37
					2	7	6					9	1								8	4	11		5	10		3		38
					2	7	6					9	1	11							8	4			5	10		3		39
20	12	1	9	5	28	38	26	2	8		7	20	23	2	1	7	2	1	5	37	39	26	1	1	37	39	7	23	2	
		3										13								9	15	1			2	9	1			

Bentley	Boreham	Brown D	Brown I	Burton	Coquet	Curtis	Darnell	Drabble	Elkin	Gipps	Harris	Humphreys	Joyce	Kennedy	Kerry	Leslie	Lunn	Lyle	McFarlane	Middlemiss	Minter	Morris	Newman	Steel A	Steel D	Steel R	Tull	Wilkes	Woodruff	#
6			3			7					2	9	1							11	8	4			5	10				1
6			3			7					2	9	1							11	8	4			5	10				R
			3			7	6					9	1			2				11	8	4			5	10				2
			3			7	6					9	1			2				11	8	4			5	10				3
2			4			4	2				2	4	4			2				4	4	4			4	4				
			5									2	2							2	2				2					

Bentley	Boreham	Brown D	Brown I	Burton	Coquet	Curtis	Darnell	Drabble	Elkin	Gipps	Harris	Humphreys	Joyce	Kennedy	Kerry	Leslie	Lunn	Lyle	McFarlane	Middlemiss	Minter	Morris	Newman	Steel A	Steel D	Steel R	Tull	Wilkes	Woodruff	#
1		3			2	7				6									4	11	9				5	10	8			1
1	9				2	7	6					3				4				11	8				5	10				2
6	1	9										3								11	8	4			5	10		2	7	SF
1	9					7	6					3				2				11	8	4			5	10				R
4	1					8	6					3								11	9	5				10		2	7	F
2	5	3	1	2	4	3				1	4				2				5	5	3			4	4	2	2	2	
	3				1							7	5								5									

Bentley	Boreham	Brown D	Brown I	Burton	Coquet	Curtis	Darnell	Drabble	Elkin	Gipps	Harris	Humphreys	Joyce	Kennedy	Kerry	Leslie	Lunn	Lyle	McFarlane	Middlemiss	Minter	Morris	Newman	Steel A	Steel D	Steel R	Tull	Wilkes	Woodruff	#
					8	1		6	3											11	9	4			5	10		2	7	
					1	1		1	1											1	1	1			1	1		1	1	
					2																1									

191

1910-11

Manager: Directors

1	Sep	1	(a)	Everton	L 0-2	22,000
2		3	(h)	Sheffield W	W 3-1 Darnell, R.Steel, Middlemiss	29,200
3		10	(a)	Bristol C	W 2-0 Humphreys, Middlemiss	20,000
4		17	(h)	Newcastle U	L 1-2 Minter	36,000
5		24	(a)	Oldham A	L 0-2	14,000
6	Oct	1	(a)	Middlesbrough	L 0-2	20,000
7		8	(h)	Preston NE	D 1-1 Minter	24,000
8		15	(a)	Notts C	L 0-1	14,000
9		22	(h)	Manchester U	D 2-2 Minter, Humphreys	28,000
10		29	(a)	Liverpool	W 2-1 Minter, Humphreys	12,000
11	Nov	5	(h)	Bury	W 5-0 Curtis, Minter, Humphreys 2, Middlemiss	20,000
12		12	(a)	Sheffield U	L 0-3	10,000
13		19	(h)	Aston Villa	L 1-2 Humphreys	28,000
14		26	(a)	Sunderland	L 0-4	12,000
15	Dec	3	(h)	W Arsenal	W 3-1 Darnell, Minter, Humphreys	16,000
16		10	(a)	Bradford C	L 0-3	10,000
17		17	(h)	Blackburn R	D 2-2 R.McTavish 2	16,000
18		24	(a)	Nottingham F	W 2-1 Minter, R.McTavish	10,000
19		26	(h)	Nottingham F	L 1-4 Minter	35,000
20		27	(h)	Manchester C	D 1-1 Tull	28,000
21		31	(a)	Sheffield W	L 1-2 Minter	25,000
22	Jan	3	(a)	Manchester C	L 1-2 Kennedy	10,000
23		7	(h)	Bristol C	W 3-2 Minter 3	18,000
24		21	(a)	Newcastle U	D 1-1 Minter	22,000
25		28	(h)	Oldham A*	D 1-1 Crompton	14,000
26	Feb	11	(a)	Preston NE	L 0-2	10,000
27		13	(h)	Middlesbrough	W 6-2 Minter, Humphreys, R.Steel 3, Forman	8,000
28		18	(h)	Notts C	W 3-0 Minter, Humphreys, R.Steel	26,000
29		25	(a)	Aston Villa	L 0-4	17,000
30	Mar	4	(h)	Liverpool	W 1-0 Minter	25,000
31		11	(a)	Bury	L 1-2 R.Steel	10,000
32		15	(a)	Manchester U	L 2-3 Birnie, Humphreys	13,000
33		18	(h)	Sheffield U	W 2-1 Humphreys, R.Steel	18,000
34		27	(h)	Oldham A	W 2-0 Minter, R.Steel	
35	Apr	1	(h)	Sunderland	D 1-1 Minter	26,000
36		8	(a)	W Arsenal	L 0-2	24,853
37		15	(h)	Bradford C	W 2-0 Minter, R.Steel	30,000
38		17	(h)	Everton	L 0-1	20,000
39		22	(a)	Blackburn R	L 0-3	14,000

FINAL LEAGUE POSITION: 15th in Division One
*Abandoned after 45 minutes — fog.

Appearances
Goals

FA Cup

1	Jan	14	(h)	Millwall	W 2-1 Minter, Carmichael (og)	21,464
2	Feb	4	(a)	Blackburn R	D 0-0	25,000
R		9	(h)	Blackburn R	L 0-2	26,946

Appearances
Goals

London FA Charity Cup

1	Sep	19	(h)	Clapton O	W 1-0 Rance	8,500
2	Oct	10	(h)	Chelsea	W 3-0 Minter, Brown, R.Steel	8,900
SF	Nov	7	(n§)	Millwall	D 2-2 Minter, R.Steel	5,000
R		21	(n†)	Millwall	W 2-0 Minter, Middlesmiss	7,827
F	Dec	5	(n‡)	Fulham	W 2-1 Minter, Middlesmiss	10,000

§Played at Leyton. †Played at Homerton. ‡Played at Stamford Bridge.

Appearances
Goals

London Professional Football Charity Fund

Oct	3	(a)	Chelsea	W 3-0 Minter, Brown 2	9,000

Appearances
Goals

192

Appearance / line-up grid (shirt numbers by player and match).

Bentley	Birnie	Brown	Bulling	Collins	Coquet	Crompton	Curtis	Darnell	Elkin	Forman	Gosnell	Humphreys	Joyce	Kennedy	Leslie	Lunn	McTavish J	McTavish R	Middlemiss	Minter	Morris	Newman	Rance	Steel D	Steel R	Tull	Wilkes	
							7	6	2		9					1			11	8	4			5	10		3	1
							7	6	2		9					1			11	8	4			5	10		3	2
							7	6	2		9					1			11	8	4			5	10		3	3
	9						7	6	2							1			11	8	4			5	10		3	4
	9						7	6	2							1			11	8	4			5	10		3	5
4				3			7	6	2	11		9				1				8				5	10			6
				3			7	6	2			9				1			11	8	4			5	10			7
				3			7	6	2			9				1			11	8	4			5	10			8
				3			7	6	2			9				1			11	8	4			5	10			9
			2	3			7	6				9				1			11	8	4			5	10			10
				3			7	6	2			9				1			11	8	4			5	10			11
				3			7	6	2			9				1			11	8	4			5	10			12
4				3			7	6	2			9				1			11	8				5	10			13
4			3		2		7	6				9				1			11	8				5	10			14
4			3		2		7	6				9				1		10	11	8				5				15
4	9		3		2		7	6								1		10	11	8				5				16
4			3		2		7	6								1		10	11	8			9	5				17
				3			7	6	2	11						1		10		8	4			5		9		18
				3			7	6	2	11	9					1		10		8	4			5				19
				3			7	6	2							1			11	8	4			5	10	9		20
	9			3			7	6	2							1			11	8	4			5	10			21
	9			3			7	6	2							1		10	11	8	4			5				22
	9			2			7	6	11							1		10		8	4			5			3	23
4	9			2			7	6								1		10		8			11	5			3	24
4	9		3	2			7	6								1		10		8			11	5				25
	9		3	2	7			6								1		10	11	8	4			5				26
4					2			6		11		9		7		1				8				5	10		3	27
4					2			6		11		9		7		1				8				5	10		3	28
4					2			6		11		9		7		1				8				5	10		3	29
4					2			6				9		7		1				8			11	5	10		3	30
4					2			6				9		7		1				8			11	5	10		3	31
4	5				2			6				9		7		1				8			11		10		3	32
4					2		7	6				9				1				8			11	5	10		3	33
4					2		7	6				9				1				8			11	5	10		3	34
4					2		7	6				9				1				8			11	5	10		3	35
4					2		7	6								1				8			11	5	10	9	3	36
4					2		7	6				9				1				8			11	5	10		3	37
4					2		7	6	3			9				1			11	8				5	10			38
					2			6				9		7		1		10	11	8				5			3	39
17	4	4	2	26	13	6	31	39	18	2	5	24	4	7	1	35	9	10	30	39	11	2	11	27	30	3	19	
1				1	1	2		1				11		1					3	3	19				9	1		

Bentley	Birnie	Brown	Bulling	Collins	Coquet	Crompton	Curtis	Darnell	Elkin	Forman	Gosnell	Humphreys	Joyce	Kennedy	Leslie	Lunn	McTavish J	McTavish R	Middlemiss	Minter	Morris	Newman	Rance	Steel D	Steel R	Tull	Wilkes	
4					2		9	7	6			11				1		10		8				5			3	1
4					2		9	7	6							1		10		8			11	5			3	2
4					2			7	6	11	9					1				8				5	10		3	R
3				3		2	3	3		2	1					3		1	1	3			2	3			3	
																				1								

1 own-goal

Bentley	Birnie	Brown	Bulling	Collins	Coquet	Crompton	Curtis	Darnell	Elkin	Forman	Gosnell	Humphreys	Joyce	Kennedy	Leslie	Lunn	McTavish J	McTavish R	Middlemiss	Minter	Morris	Newman	Rance	Steel D	Steel R	Tull	Wilkes	
6	4	9	3				7		2	11		1				10				8				5				1
	9			3			7	6	2			9	5		1				11	8				4	10			2
				3			7	6	2			9	5		1				11	8				4	10			SF
4			3				7	6	2			9	1						11	8				5	10			R
4				2			7	6	3			9			1		10	11	8				5				F
3	1	2	2		3		5	4	5		1	3	3	1		2		2	4	5	1		1	4	3			
	1															2			4		1			2				

Bentley	Birnie	Brown	Bulling	Collins	Coquet	Crompton	Curtis	Darnell	Elkin	Forman	Gosnell	Humphreys	Joyce	Kennedy	Leslie	Lunn	McTavish J	McTavish R	Middlemiss	Minter	Morris	Newman	Rance	Steel D	Steel R	Tull	Wilkes	
	9			3			7	6	2	11		1		5		10				8	4							
	1			1	1	1	1	1	1			1	1	1		1				1	1	1						
	2																			1								

193

1911-12

Manager: Directors

#	Month	Date		Opponent	Result	Scorers	Attendance
1	Sep	2	(a)	Everton	D 2-2	J.McTavish, Young	25,000
2		4	(h)	Sheffield W	W 3-1	Minter, Young 2	20,000
3		9	(h)	West Brom A	W 1-0	Minter	31,000
4		16	(a)	Sunderland	D 1-1	R.Steel	16,000
5		23	(h)	Blackburn R	L 0-2		37,820
6		30	(a)	Sheffield W	L 0-4		15,000
7	Oct	7	(h)	Bury	W 2-1	Minter 2	18,000
8		14	(a)	Middlesbrough	L 0-2		15,000
9		21	(h)	Notts C	D 2-2	Minter, Middlemiss	25,000
10		28	(h)	Preston NE	W 6-2	Newman 3, Minter, Middlemiss 2	20,000
11	Nov	4	(a)	Manchester U	W 2-1	Minter, Middlemiss	26,000
12		11	(h)	Liverpool	W 2-0	Minter, Middlemiss	23,000
13		18	(a)	Aston Villa	D 2-2	R.Steel 2	30,000
14		25	(h)	Newcastle U	L 1-2	Newman	37,541
15	Dec	2	(a)	Sheffield U	W 2-1	R.Steel, Middlemiss	
16		9	(h)	Oldham A	W 4-0	J.McTavish, Minter, R.Steel, Middlemiss	20,000
17		16	(a)	Bolton W	L 0-1		20,000
18		23	(h)	Bradford C	L 2-3	R.Steel 2	30,000
19		25	(h)	W Arsenal	W 5-0	Darnell, J.McTavish, Minter 2, Middlemiss	47,109
20		26	(a)	W Arsenal	L 1-3	Minter	22,000
21		30	(h)	Everton	L 0-1		24,500
22	Jan	6	(a)	West Brom A*	D 0-0		4,000
23		20	(h)	Sunderland	D 0-0		17,000
24		27	(a)	Blackburn R	D 0-0		14,000
25	Feb	10	(a)	Bury	L 1-2	Elliott	6,000
26		17	(h)	Middlesbrough	W 2-1	Minter, R.Steel	22,000
27		24	(a)	Notts C	D 2-2	Minter 2	10,000
28	Mar	2	(a)	Preston NE	W 1-0	Minter	5,000
29		13	(a)	West Brom A	L 0-2		12,000
30		16	(a)	Liverpool	W 2-1	Newman, Mason	15,000
31		23	(h)	Aston Villa	W 2-1	Middlemiss 2	19,000
32		30	(a)	Newcastle U	L 0-2		21,000
33	Apr	5	(a)	Manchester C	L 1-2	Newman	39,800
34		6	(h)	Sheffield U	D 1-1	Middlemiss (pen)	26,000
35		8	(h)	Manchester C	L 0-2		20,000
36		9	(h)	Manchester U	D 1-1	Bliss	14,000
37		13	(a)	Oldham A	L 1-2	Elliott	6,000
38		20	(h)	Bolton W	W 1-0	Minter	18,000
39		27	(a)	Bradford C	L 0-3		8,000

FINAL LEAGUE POSITION: 12th in Division One   Appearances
*Abandoned after 57 minutes — fog.   Goals

FA Cup

#	Month	Date		Opponent	Result	Scorers	Attendance
1	Jan	13	(a)	West Brom A	L 0-3		22,000

Appearances
Goals

London FA Charity Cup

#	Month	Date		Opponent	Result	Scorers	Attendance
1	Sep	18	(a)	Brentford	L 1-4	McTavish	3,000

Appearances
Goals

London Professional Football Charity Fund

Month	Date		Opponent	Result	Scorers	Attendance
Oct	23	(h)	Fulham	W 3-0	Minter, R.Steel, Middlemiss	3,981

Appearances
Goals

Daily Telegraph Titanic Fund

Month	Date		Opponent	Result	Scorers	Attendance
Apr	29	(n†)	W Arsenal	L 0-3		5,000

†Played at Park Royal Ground.   Appearances
Goals

Bentley	Bliss	Bowering	Brittan	Collins	Crompton	Curtis	Darnell	Elliott	Forman	Grimsdell	Humphreys	Joyce	Kennedy	Lightfoot	Lunn	Mason	McTavish J	McTavish R	Middlemiss	Minter	Morris	Newman	Rance	Steel D	Steel R	Tattersall	Webster	Wilkes	Young	#
		2		6	11									1		7				8				5	4	10	3	9		1
		2		6	11									1		7				8				5	4	10	3	9		2
		2		6	11									1		7				8				5	4	10	3	9		3
		2		6	11	9								1		7				8				5	4	10	3			4
		2		6	11									1		7				8				5	4	10	3	9		5
		2		6	11									1		7				8				5	4	10	3	9		6
		2	9	6										1		7			11	8				5	4	10	3			7
		2	9	6									5	1		7			11	8					4	10	3			8
	3	2	9	6										1		7			11	8				5	4	10				9
	3	2		6									5	1		7			11	9		8			4	10				10
		2		6									5	1		7			11	9	3	8			4	10				11
	3	2		6									5	1		7			11	9		8			4	10				12
	3	2		6									5	1		7			11	8		9			4	10				13
	3	2		6									5	1		7			11	9		8			4	10				14
	3	2		6									5	1		7			11	9		8			4	10				15
	3	2		6									5	1		7			11	9		8			4	10				16
	3	2		6									5	1		7			11	9		8			4	10				17
	3	2		4										1		7			11	9		8		5	6	10				18
		2		6										1		7			11	9		8		5	4	10	3			19
		2		6										1		7			11	9		8		5	4	10	3			20
		3		6										1		7			11	9		8		5	4	10	2			21
	3	2		6										1		7			11	9		8		5	4	10				22
		2	7	6	9								5	1					11	8					4	10	3			23
	6	3	2	7	9								5	1		8			11						4	10				24
	6	3	2	7	9								5	1					11	8					4	10				25
	4	3	2	7									6	1		8			11	9				5		10				26
	4	3	2	7									6	1		8			11	9				5		10				27
		3	2	7	4								6	1		8			11	9				5		10				28
	4	3	2	7	6								5	1		8			11	9						10				29
		3	2	4									6	1	10	7			11	9		8		5						30
		3	2	4									6	1		7			11	9		8		5		10				31
		3	2	4									6	1		7			11	9		8		5		10				32
		3	2	4									6	1		7			11	9		8		5		10				33
	6	3		4										1	10	7			11	9		8		5		2				34
	10	3		4	9									1	6	7			11	2		8		5						35
5	10	3		7	4								6	1		8			11	9						2				36
	10	6	3	7	4	9							5	1		8			11							2				37
	10	3	2	4	5								6	1					11	9		8				7				38
	10	3	2	4	5								6	1		8			11	9						7				39
1	5	7	27	34	3	9	35	5	6	2	1	4	4	21	35	7	31		33	36	2	20	18	29	32	2	6	9	5	
1				1	2									1	3		11	17		6			8				3				

Bentley	Bliss	Bowering	Brittan	Collins	Crompton	Curtis	Darnell	Elliott	Forman	Grimsdell	Humphreys	Joyce	Kennedy	Lightfoot	Lunn	Mason	McTavish J	McTavish R	Middlemiss	Minter	Morris	Newman	Rance	Steel D	Steel R	Tattersall	Webster	Wilkes	Young	#
		3	2	6										1		7			11	8				9	5	4	10			1
		1	1	1										1		1			1	1				1	1	1	1			

Bentley	Bliss	Bowering	Brittan	Collins	Crompton	Curtis	Darnell	Elliott	Forman	Grimsdell	Humphreys	Joyce	Kennedy	Lightfoot	Lunn	Mason	McTavish J	McTavish R	Middlemiss	Minter	Morris	Newman	Rance	Steel D	Steel R	Tattersall	Webster	Wilkes	Young	#
4		2		6	11							9	1	5		7	10			8							3			1
1		1		1	1							1	1	1		1	1			1							1			
															1															

Bentley	Bliss	Bowering	Brittan	Collins	Crompton	Curtis	Darnell	Elliott	Forman	Grimsdell	Humphreys	Joyce	Kennedy	Lightfoot	Lunn	Mason	McTavish J	McTavish R	Middlemiss	Minter	Morris	Newman	Rance	Steel D	Steel R	Tattersall	Webster	Wilkes	Young	#
		3	2	6									5	1		7			11	9		8			4	10				
		1	1	1									1	1		1			1	1		1			1	1				
																			1	1					1					

Bentley	Bliss	Bowering	Brittan	Collins	Crompton	Curtis	Darnell	Elliott	Forman	Grimsdell	Humphreys	Joyce	Kennedy	Lightfoot	Lunn	Mason	McTavish J	McTavish R	Middlemiss	Minter	Morris	Newman	Rance	Steel D	Steel R	Tattersall	Webster	Wilkes	Young	#
8		3		7	6								4	1					11	9				5	10	2				
1		1		1	1								1	1					1	1				1	1	1				

1912-13

Manager:Directors/Peter McWilliam

1	Sep	2	(h)	Everton	L	0-2		22,000
2		7	(h)	Sheffield W	L	2-4	Tattersall, Middlemiss	28,000
3		14	(a)	Blackburn R	L	1-6	Minter	25,000
4		21	(h)	Derby C	L	1-2	Collins (pen)	25,000
5		28	(a)	Sunderland	D	2-2	Bliss, Middlemiss	8,000
6	Oct	5	(a)	Middlesbrough	D	1-1	Minter	18,000
7		12	(h)	Notts C*	L	1-3	Rance	7,000
8		19	(a)	Manchester U	L	0-2		12,000
9		26	(h)	Aston Villa	D	3-3	Cantrell 2, Middlemiss	18,000
10	Nov	2	(a)	Liverpool	L	1-4	Minter	15,000
11		4	(h)	Notts C	L	0-3		11,000
12		9	(h)	Bolton W	L	0-1		23,000
13		16	(a)	Sheffield U	L	0-4		12,000
14		23	(h)	Newcastle U	W	1-0	Cantrell	26,000
15		30	(a)	Oldham A	L	1-4	Middlemiss	12,000
16	Dec	7	(h)	Chelsea	W	1-0	Tattersall	36,771
17		14	(a)	W Arsenal	W	3-0	Cantrell 2, Steel	13,000
18		21	(h)	Bradford C	W	2-1	Cantrell, Middlemiss	20,000
19		25	(a)	Manchester C	D	2-2	Cantrell, Middlemiss	30,000
20		26	(h)	Manchester C	W	4-0	Minter, Cantrell 3	20,000
21		28	(a)	Sheffield W	L	1-2	Tattersall	15,000
22	Jan	1	(a)	Everton	W	2-1	Minter 2	30,000
23		4	(h)	Blackburn R	L	0-1		33,000
24		18	(a)	Derby C	L	0-5		10,000
25		25	(h)	Sunderland	L	1-2	Minter	31,000
26	Feb	8	(h)	Middlesbrough	W	5-3	Minter 2, Elliott 2, Middlemiss	24,000
27		15	(a)	Notts C	W	1-0	Bliss	12,000
28		22	(h)	Sheffield U	W	1-0	Weir	25,000
29	Mar	1	(a)	Aston Villa	L	0-1		27,000
30		8	(h)	Liverpool	W	1-0	Middlemiss	20,000
31		15	(a)	Bolton W	L	0-2		25,000
32		21	(h)	West Brom A	W	3-1	Cantrell, Bliss 2	34,000
33		24	(a)	West Brom A	L	1-4	Middlemiss	20,000
34		29	(a)	Newcastle U	L	0-3		20,000
35		31	(h)	Manchester U	D	1-1	Minter	12,762
36	Apr	5	(h)	Oldham A	W	1-0	Bliss	20,000
37		12	(a)	Chelsea	L	0-1		50,500
38		19	(h)	W Arsenal	D	1-1	Minter	20,000
39		26	(a)	Bradford C	L	1-3	Cantrell	10,000

FINAL LEAGUE POSITION: 17th in Division One   Appearances
*Abandoned after 80 minutes — fog.   Goals

FA Cup

1	Jan	11	(h)	Blackpool	D	1-1	Rance	18,677
R		16	(h†)	Blackpool	W	6-1	Tattersall 2, Cantrell 2, Steel, Middlemiss	16,926
2	Feb	1	(a)	Reading	L	0-1		17,794

†Replay rights sold by Blackpool.   Appearances
     Goals

London FA Charity Cup

1	Sep	23	(h)	Bromley	W	3-0	Minter 3	2,000
2	Oct	21	(h)	Crystal P‡	W	2-0	Minter, Cantrell	4,449
R		28	(h)	Crystal P	D	3-3	Minter 2, Middlemiss	4,300
2R	Nov	11	(a)	Crystal P	L	1-4	Middlemiss	2,000

‡ Replay ordered as Cantrell unregistered in original match.   Appearances
     Goals

London Professional Football Charity Fund

	Oct	14	(a)	Fulham	L	0-1	

Appearances
Goals

Bliss	Brittan	Cantrell	Collins	Curtis	Darnell	Elliott	Grimsdell	Jones	Joyce	Lightfoot	Lunn	Middlemiss	Minter	Morris	Newman	Rance	Steel R	Tate	Tattersall	Upton	Walden	Webster	Weir	Williams	Young	#
10	3		2		4		5			6	1	11	8					7					9			1
	3		2					4		6	1	11	8		5	10		7					9			2
	3		2					4		6	1	11	8		5	10		7					9			3
	3		2				10			6	1	11	8		5			7				4	9			4
10			2					9		6	11	11	8		5			7			3	4				5
10			2					9		6	1	11	8		5			7			3	4				6
10	2							9		6	1	11	8		5			7			3	4				7
	2	9					5			6	1	11	8	7			10				3	4				8
		9	2							6	1	11	8		5	10		7			3	4				9
		9	2		4						1	11	8		5	10		7			3	6				10
			2				5			6	1	11	8	9			10	7			3	4				11
		9	2	6			5				1	11	8			10		7			3	4				12
		9	2	6		4					1	11	8			10		7			3	5				13
		9	2							6	1	11	8		5	10		7			3	4				14
		9	2	6			5				1	11	8			10		7			3	4				15
		9	2						1	6		11	8		5	10		7			3	4				16
		9	2						1	6		11	8		5	10		7			3	4				17
		9	2		4						1	11	8		5	10		7			3	6				18
		9	2		4						1	11	8		5	10		7			3	6				19
		9	2							6	1	11	8		5	10		7			3	4				20
		9	2							6	1	11	8		5	10		7			3	4				21
10	9	2			4					6	1	11	8		5			7			3					22
10	9	2								6	1	11	8		5			7			3	4				23
		9	2							6	1	11	8		5	10		7			3	4				24
		9	2							6	1	11	8		5	10		7			3	4				25
10	2			9	6						1	11	8		5			7			3	4				26
10	2			9	6						1	11	8		5			7			3	4				27
10	2			9	6						1	11	8		5			7			3	4				28
10	2			9	6						1	11	8		5			7			3	4				29
10	2			9	6						1	11	8		5			7			3	4				30
10	2			9	6						1	11			8	5		7			3	4				31
10	2	9								6	1	11	8		5			7			3	4				32
10	2	9								6	1	11	8		5			7			3	4				33
10	2	9								6	1	11	8		5			7			3	4				34
		9	2	7						6	1	11	8		5	10					3	4				35
10	9	2	7							6	1	11	8		5						3	4				36
10	9	2	7							6	1	11	8		5						3	4				37
10		9	2							6		11	8		5				1	7	3	4				38
10		9	2	7						6		11	8		5				1		3	4				39
19	15	25	28	4	4	6	25	8	20	16	17	39	38	3	33	19	2	31	2	1	35	35	4			
5	12	1		2								9	11			1	1	3			1					

Bliss	Brittan	Cantrell	Collins	Curtis	Darnell	Elliott	Grimsdell	Jones	Joyce	Lightfoot	Lunn	Middlemiss	Minter	Morris	Newman	Rance	Steel R	Tate	Tattersall	Upton	Walden	Webster	Weir	Williams	Young	#
		9	2							6	1	11	8		5	10		7			3	4				1
		9	2							6	1	11	8		5	10		7			3	4				R
	2	9								6	1	11	8		5	10		7			3	4				2
1	3	2			3		2		1	3	3	3	3		3	3	3	3			3	3				
	2									1					1	1		2								

Bliss	Brittan	Cantrell	Collins	Curtis	Darnell	Elliott	Grimsdell	Jones	Joyce	Lightfoot	Lunn	Middlemiss	Minter	Morris	Newman	Rance	Steel R	Tate	Tattersall	Upton	Walden	Webster	Weir	Williams	Young	#
	3		2				10			6	1	11	8		5			7				4	9			1
	2	9					5			6	1		8			10		7	11		3	4				2
	2				6		5				1	11	8	4		10		7			3		9			R
	2				6		4				1	11	8		5	10		7			3		9			2R
4	1	1	2	2	2	2	4	3	4	1	2	3	3	2	3	2	1	2								
	1											2	6													

Bliss	Brittan	Cantrell	Collins	Curtis	Darnell	Elliott	Grimsdell	Jones	Joyce	Lightfoot	Lunn	Middlemiss	Minter	Morris	Newman	Rance	Steel R	Tate	Tattersall	Upton	Walden	Webster	Weir	Williams	Young	#
		2						9		6	1	11	8		5	10		7			3	4				
		1						1		1	1	1	1		1	1		1			1	1				

197

1913-14

Manager: Peter McWilliam

1	Sep	1	(a)	Sheffield U	W 4-1	Walden, Minter, Bauchop 2	16,000
2		6	(a)	Chelsea	W 3-1	Grimsdell, Cantrell 2	65,000
3		8	(h)	Sheffield U	W 2-1	Cantrell 2	26,000
4		13	(h)	Derby C	D 1-1	Cantrell	40,000
5		20	(a)	Oldham A	L 0-3		18,000
6		27	(h)	Manchester C	W 3-1	Minter 2, Cantrell	30,513
7	Oct	4	(a)	Manchester U	L 1-3	Middlemiss	39,000
8		11	(h)	Bradford C	D 0-0		30,000
9		18	(a)	Burnley	L 1-3	Cantrell	22,000
10		25	(h)	Blackburn R	D 3-3	Minter, Cantrell, Middlemiss	46,128
11	Nov	1	(a)	Preston NE	W 2-1	Bauchop, Bliss	14,000
12		8	(h)	Sunderland	L 1-4	Cantrell	36,000
13		15	(a)	Newcastle U	L 0-2		23,000
14		22	(h)	Everton	W 4-1	Bauchop, Bliss 2, Middlemiss	22,000
15		29	(a)	Liverpool	L 1-2	Cantrell	21,000
16	Dec	6	(h)	West Brom A	W 3-0	Bauchop 2, Middlemiss	24,000
17		13	(a)	Aston Villa	D 3-3	Walden, Cantrell, Bliss	30,000
18		20	(h)	Sheffield W	D 1-1	Walden	22,000
19		26	(h)	Middlesbrough	L 0-1		37,055
20		27	(h)	Chelsea	L 1-2	Fleming	29,355
21	Jan	1	(a)	Bolton W	L 0-3		30,000
22		3	(a)	Derby C	L 0-4		10,000
23		17	(h)	Oldham A	W 3-1	Lightfoot, Sparrow 2	25,000
24		24	(a)	Manchester C	L 1-2	Sparrow	30,000
25	Feb	7	(h)	Manchester U	W 2-1	Minter, Cantrell	28,000
26		14	(a)	Bradford C	L 1-2	Cantrell	18,000
27		23	(h)	Burnley	W 2-0	Walden (pen), Bliss	15,000
28		28	(a)	Blackburn R	D 1-1	Walden	25,000
29	Mar	7	(h)	Preston NE	W 1-0	Cantrell	25,000
30		14	(a)	Sunderland	L 0-2		10,000
31		21	(h)	Newcastle U	D 0-0		20,000
32		28	(a)	Everton	D 1-1	Sparrow	15,000
33	Apr	4	(h)	Liverpool	D 0-0		19,800
34		10	(h)	Bolton W	W 3-0	Joyce, Cantrell, Bliss	39,020
35		11	(a)	West Brom A	D 1-1	Cantrell	15,000
36		13	(a)	Middlesbrough	L 0-6		22,000
37		18	(h)	Aston Villa	L 0-2		22,000
38		25	(a)	Sheffield W	L 0-2		12,000

FINAL LEAGUE POSITION: 17th in Division One

Appearances
Goals

FA Cup

1	Jan	10	(a)	Leicester F	D 5-5	Walden, Minter, Cantrell, Bliss 2	9,454
R		15	(h)	Leicester F	W 2-0	Walden, Bliss	20,252
2		31	(a)	Manchester C	L 1-2	Bliss	36,256

Appearances
Goals

London FA Charity Cup

1	Sep	22	(h)	Metrogas	W 11-2	Walden, Minter 2, Cantrell 3, Bauchop 4, Middlemiss	2,500
2	Oct	14	(a)	Fulham	W 2-0	Middlemiss 2	6,500
SF	Nov	10	(n*)	W Arsenal	W 2-1	Fleming, Cantrell	7,800
F	Dec	8	(n†)	Crystal P	L 1-2	Walden	14,000

*Played at Stamford Bridge. †Played at Arsenal Stadium, Highbury.

Appearances
Goals

London Professional Football Charity Fund

	Oct	27	(h)	Crystal P	L 1-2	Middlemiss	5,895

Appearances
Goals

Banks	Bauchop	Bliss	Bowler	Brittan	Cantrell	Cartwright	Clay	Collins	Crowl	Darnell	Elliott	Fleming	Gemmell	Grimsdell	Heggarty	Hobday	Joyce	King	Lightfoot	Middlemiss	Minter	Newman	Oliver	Sparrow	Steel R	Tate	Tattersall	Walden	Webster	Weir	
10		9				2						6						1		11	8		5			7	3	4			1
10		9				2						6						1		11	8		5			7	3	4			2
10		9				2						6						1		11	8		5			7	3	4			3
10		9				2						6						1		11	8		5			7	3	4			4
10		9				2						6						1		11	8		5			7	3	4			5
10		9				2						6						1		11	8		5			7	3	4			6
	10	9				2						6						1		11	8		5			7	3	4			7
	10	9				2						6						1		11	8		5			7	3	4			8
	10	9				2			7			6						1		11	8		5				3	4			9
	10	9				2						6						1		11	8		5			7	3	4			10
9	10					2						6						1		11	8		5			7	3	4			11
	10	9				2						6						1		11	8		5			7	3	4			12
	10	9			3						8	6						1		11			5		7		2	4			13
9	10				3						8	6						1		11			5		7		2	4			14
11	10	9			3						8	6						1					5		7		2	4			15
8	10	9			3							6						1		11			5		7		2	4			16
	10	9			3						8	6						1				11	5		7		2	4			17
	10	9			3						8	6						1				11	5		7		2	4			18
	10	9			3						8	6						1		11			5		7		2	4			19
	10	9				2					8	6						1		11			5			7	3	4			20
	10	9			3	2						6						1		11	8		5			7		4			21
	10	9			3	2						6						1		11	8		5			7		4			22
						2						6						1	4	11	8	10	9	5		7	3				23
	10					2						6						1	4	11		8	9	5		7	3				24
10		9			3	2						6						1		11	8		5			7		4			25
10		9			3	2						6						1		11	8		5			7		4			26
	10	9			3	2						6						1		11	8		5			7		4			27
8	10	9	4			2						6						1		11			5			7	3				28
8	10	9	4			2						6						1		11			5			7	3				29
8	10	9				2						6						1		11			5			7	3	4			30
8	10	9				2						6						1		11			5			7	3	4			31
8	10					2						6						1		11		9	5			7	3	4			32
8	10	9	4			2						6						1		11			5			7	3				33
8	10	9				2						6						1		11			5			7	3	4			34
8	10	9				2		5				6						1			11					7	3	4			35
	10	9				2						6								11	8		5		1	7	3	4			36
8	10	9				2						6						1		11			5			7	3	4			37
8	10	9				2				11		6						1					5			7	3	4			38
12	10	29	3	33	13	15	15	1	1	1	8	37			17	19	2	34	16	5	2	3	37	2	7	30	33	33			—
6	6	16								1	1	1			1	4	5					4				5					—

Banks	Bauchop	Bliss	Bowler	Brittan	Cantrell	Cartwright	Clay	Collins	Crowl	Darnell	Elliott	Fleming	Gemmell	Grimsdell	Heggarty	Hobday	Joyce	King	Lightfoot	Middlemiss	Minter	Newman	Oliver	Sparrow	Steel R	Tate	Tattersall	Walden	Webster	Weir	
	10	9			3	2						6						1	4	11	8		5			7					1
	10				3	2					9	6						1	4	11	8		5			7					R
	10	9				2						6						1	4	11		8	5			7	3				2
	3				2	2	3				1	3						2	1	3	3	2	1			3	3	1			—
	4				1							1											1			2					—

Banks	Bauchop	Bliss	Bowler	Brittan	Cantrell	Cartwright	Clay	Collins	Crowl	Darnell	Elliott	Fleming	Gemmell	Grimsdell	Heggarty	Hobday	Joyce	King	Lightfoot	Middlemiss	Minter	Newman	Oliver	Sparrow	Steel R	Tate	Tattersall	Walden	Webster	Weir	
10		9				2						6						1		11	8		5			7	3	4			1
	10	2	9									6						1		11	8		5			7	3	4			2
	10	9									8	6	11	2				1					5		7		3	4			SF
8	10	9	3								11	6						1					5			7	2	4			F
2	3		1	4	1		1			2	4	1	1	4				2	2				4			1	3	4	4		—
4		4									1												3	2							—

Banks	Bauchop	Bliss	Bowler	Brittan	Cantrell	Cartwright	Clay	Collins	Crowl	Darnell	Elliott	Fleming	Gemmell	Grimsdell	Heggarty	Hobday	Joyce	King	Lightfoot	Middlemiss	Minter	Newman	Oliver	Sparrow	Steel R	Tate	Tattersall	Walden	Webster	Weir	
10			4	2	9	3						6						1		11	8		5			7					
1		1	1	1	1							1						1		1	1		1			1					—

1914-15

Manager: Peter McWilliam

1	Sep	2	(h)	Everton	L	1-3	Cantrell	9,000
2		5	(h)	Chelsea	D	1-1	Cantrell	26,000
3		12	(a)	Bradford C	D	2-2	Bliss 2	10,000
4		19	(h)	Burnley	L	1-3	Bliss	25,000
5		26	(a)	Manchester C	L	1-2	Sparrow	13,000
6		28	(h)	West Brom A	W	2-0	Clay (pen), Fleming	8,500
7	Oct	3	(a)	Newcastle U	L	0-4		12,000
8		10	(h)	Middlesbrough	D	3-3	Lightfoot, Walden, Cantrell	15,000
9		17	(a)	Sheffield U	D	1-1	Bliss	20,000
10		24	(h)	Aston Villa	L	0-2		25,000
11		31	(a)	Liverpool	L	2-7	Clay (pen), Bliss	12,000
12	Nov	7	(h)	Bradford	W	3-0	Cantrell, Bliss 2	14,000
13		14	(a)	Oldham A	L	1-4	Bliss	10,000
14		21	(h)	Manchester U	W	2-0	Clay (pen), Cantrell	11,000
15		28	(a)	Bolton W	L	2-4	Clay (pen), Cantrell	8,000
16	Dec	5	(h)	Blackburn R	L	0-4		14,000
17		12	(a)	Notts C	W	2-1	Cantrell, Bliss	8,000
18		19	(h)	Sunderland	L	0-6		5,000
19		25	(a)	Sheffield W	L	2-3	Minter, Bliss	26,000
20		26	(h)	Sheffield W	W	6-1	Steel, Sparrow, Bliss 4	8,000
21	Jan	1	(a)	Everton	D	1-1	Bliss	17,000
22		2	(a)	Chelsea	D	1-1	Middlemiss	31,000
23		16	(h)	Bradford C	D	0-0		12,000
24		23	(a)	Burnley	L	1-3	Cantrell	4,000
25	Feb	13	(a)	Middlesbrough	L	5-7	Cantrell 4, Bliss	8,000
26		20	(h)	Notts C	W	2-0	Weir, Iremonger (og)	12,000
27		27	(a)	Aston Villa	L	1-3	Bliss	16,000
28	Mar	10	(h)	Liverpool	D	1-1	Minter	12,000
29		13	(a)	Bradford	L	1-5	Minter	9,000
30		15	(h)	Manchester C	D	2-2	Minter, Sparrow	6,000
31		20	(h)	Oldham A	W	1-0	Middlemiss	14,000
32		27	(a)	Manchester U	D	1-1	Minter	7,000
33	Apr	2	(h)	Newcastle U	D	0-0		18,000
34		3	(h)	Bolton W	W	4-2	Cantrell, Bliss 3	11,000
35		6	(a)	West Brom A	L	2-3	Steel, Cantrell	6,000
36		10	(a)	Blackburn R	L	1-4	Bliss	10,000
37		17	(h)	Sheffield U	D	1-1	Fleming	7,500
38		24	(a)	Sunderland	L	0-5		10,000

FINAL LEAGUE POSITION: 20th in Division One

Appearances
Goals

FA Cup

1	Jan	9	(h)	Sunderland	W	2-1	Walden, Bliss	17,000
2		30	(a)	Norwich C	L	2-3	Cantrell, Lansdale (og)	9,758

Appearances
Goals

London FA Charity Cup

1	Sep	21	(a)	Nunhead	W	2-1	Bliss, Cantrell
2	Oct	19	(a)	Crystal P	L	1-3	Walden

Appearances
Goals

London Professional Football Charity Fund

	Oct	28	(a)	Crystal P	D	2-2	Minter, Sparrow

Appearances
Goals

War Relief Fund

	Aug	22	(h)	Arsenal	L	1-5	Minter	13,500

Appearances
Goals

Banks	Bliss	Cantrell	Clay	Collins	Crowl	Darnell	Eadon	Fleming	Grimsdell	Jacques	Joyce	Lightfoot	Lowe	Middlemiss	Minter	Pearson	Rance	Rutherford	Sparrow	Steel R	Tattersall	Walden	Webster	Weir	Woodger	
	10	9	2						6	1				11	8					5		7	3	4		1
8	10	9	2					4	6	1				11						5		7	3			2
8	10		2					4	6	1				11		3			9	5		7				3
8	10	9	2					4	6	1				11		3				5		7				4
8	10		2						6	1				11					9	5		7	3	4		5
	10		2				8			1		6		11					9	5		7	3	4		6
	10		2				8			1		6		11					9	5		7	3	4		7
	10	9	2			4	8			1		6		11						5		7	3			8
	10	9	2			4	8			1		6		11						5		7	3			9
	10	9	2							1		6		11	8					5		7	3	4		10
	10	9	2	3				4		1		6			8					5	11	7				11
	10	9	2	3				4		1		6			8					5	11	7				12
	10	9	2	3						1		6			8					5	11	7	4			13
	10	9	2	3						1		6			8					5	11	7	4			14
	10	9	2	3						1		6			8					5	11	7	4			15
	10	9	2	3				4		1		6		11	8					5		7				16
	10	9	2	3						1		6		11	8					5		7		4		17
	10	9	2	3					6	1				11	8					5		7		4		18
	10	9	2	3						1		6		11	8					5		7		4		19
	10		2							1		6		11	8	3			9	5		7		4		20
8	10		2							1		6		11		3			9	5		7		4		21
	10		2							1		6		11	8	3			9	5		7		4		22
	10		2							1		6		11	8	3			9	5		7		4		23
	10	9	2							1		6		11	8	3				5		7		4		24
	10	9	2							1		6	8	11		3				5		7		4		25
	10	9	2							1		6	8	11		3				5		7		4		26
	10	9	2							1		6		11	8					5		7	3	4		27
	10		2	3					6	1	9			11	8					5		7		4		28
	10		2	3					6	1				11	8				9	5		7		4		29
	10		2	3				6		1				11	8				9	5		7		4		30
	10		2					6		1				11	8	3			9	5		7		4		31
	10		2					6		1				11	8	3			9	5		7		4		32
	10		2					6		1				11	8	3			9	5		7		4		33
	10	9	2					6		1				11	8	3				5		7		4		34
	10	9	2					6		1				11	8	3				5		7		4		35
8	10		2					6		1				11		3			9	5		7		4		36
			2							1	10	6		11	8	3			9	5		7		4		37
	10		2						9	1		6		11	8	3				5		7		4		38
5	33	26	38	12		11	5	11	8	28	5	23	2	33	26	17	3		15	36	5	38	9	29		
	21	14	4					2	1		2	5		3	2				2			1		1		

1 own-goal

Banks	Bliss	Cantrell	Clay	Collins	Crowl	Darnell	Eadon	Fleming	Grimsdell	Jacques	Joyce	Lightfoot	Lowe	Middlemiss	Minter	Pearson	Rance	Rutherford	Sparrow	Steel R	Tattersall	Walden	Webster	Weir	Woodger	
	10		2							1		6		11	8	3			9	5		7		4		1
	10	9	2							1		6		11	8	3				5		7		4		2
	2	1	2							2		2		2	2	2			1	2		2		2		
	1	1								1																

1 own-goal

Banks	Bliss	Cantrell	Clay	Collins	Crowl	Darnell	Eadon	Fleming	Grimsdell	Jacques	Joyce	Lightfoot	Lowe	Middlemiss	Minter	Pearson	Rance	Rutherford	Sparrow	Steel R	Tattersall	Walden	Webster	Weir	Woodger	
8	10		2					4	6	1				11					9	5		7	3			1
	9		2			6				1		10		11		5			8			7	3	4		2
1	2	1	1			1		1	1	2		1	2	2	1	1			2	2	1	2	2	1		
1	1									1																

Banks	Bliss	Cantrell	Clay	Collins	Crowl	Darnell	Eadon	Fleming	Grimsdell	Jacques	Joyce	Lightfoot	Lowe	Middlemiss	Minter	Pearson	Rance	Rutherford	Sparrow	Steel R	Tattersall	Walden	Webster	Weir	Woodger	
	10	11	2	3						1		6			8				5	9		4	7			
	1	1	1	1						1		1			1				1	1		1	1			

Banks	Bliss	Cantrell	Clay	Collins	Crowl	Darnell	Eadon	Fleming	Grimsdell	Jacques	Joyce	Lightfoot	Lowe	Middlemiss	Minter	Pearson	Rance	Rutherford	Sparrow	Steel R	Tattersall	Walden	Webster	Weir	Woodger	
	9		2	11				4	6	1				8						5		7	3	10		
	1		1	1				1	1	1				1						1		1	1	1		

201

1915-16

Manager: Peter McWilliam

1	Sep	4	(a)	Arsenal	L 0-2		14,879
2		11	(h)	Brentford	D 1-1	Glen	5,150
3		18	(a)	West Ham U	D 1-1	Rance	8,000
4		25	(h)	Chelsea	L 1-3	Bliss	8,683
5	Oct	2	(h)	Crystal P	L 2-4	Banks 2	1,800
6		9	(a)	Queen's Park R	W 4-0	Bassett 2, Minter, Thomas	3,000
7		16	(h)	Fulham	W 3-1	Banks, Bliss 2	4,200
8		23	(a)	Clapton O	D 0-0		9,000
9		30	(h)	Watford	W 3-0	Bassett, Steel, Bliss	3,000
10	Nov	6	(a)	Millwall	L 2-3	Morris, Bliss	8,000
11		13	(h)	Arsenal	D 3-3	Travers, Bliss, Steel	7,000
12		20	(a)	Brentford	D 1-1	Bliss	3,000
13		27	(h)	West Ham U	W 3-0	Morris, Bliss 2	4,000
14	Dec	4	(a)	Chelsea	L 1-8	Rance	8,000
15		11	(a)	Crystal P	L 2-4	Steel, Bliss	300
16		18	(h)	Queen's Park R	W 2-1	Knighton 2	2,000
17		25	(h)	Croydon C	W 3-0	Clay (pen), Lloyd 2	4,000
18		27	(a)	Croydon C	D 0-0		
19	Jan	1	(a)	Fulham	W 2-0	Bassett, Lloyd	5,000
20		8	(h)	Clapton O	D 1-1	Bassett	5,000
21		15	(a)	Watford	W 1-0	Lloyd	2,000
22		22	(h)	Millwall	D 2-2	Morris, Bassett	8,000

FINAL LEAGUE POSITION: 6th in London Combination, 1st Competition

Appearances
Goals

23	Feb	5	(a)	West Ham U	L 0-2		8,000
24		12	(h)	Croydon C	W 2-0	Bassett, Bliss	3,000
25		19	(a)	Fulham	L 1-3	Steel	3,000
26		26	(h)	Luton T	W 7-4	Clay (pen), Rance, Bassett, Banks, Bliss 3	3,000
27	Mar	4	(a)	Arsenal	W 3-0	Barton, Banks, Bliss	6,000
28		11	(h)	Queen's Park R	D 0-0		3,000
29		18	(a)	Croydon C	D 3-3	Clay (pen), Rance, Steel	1,500
30		25	(h)	Fulham	W 4-0	Lloyd 2, Bliss, Steel	6,000
31	Apr	1	(a)	Luton T	W 2-1	Banks, Bliss	3,000
32		8	(h)	Arsenal	W 3-2	Clay (pen), Bassett, Bliss	7,000
33		15	(a)	Queen's Park R	W 3-1	Banks 2, Hopkins	4,000
34		21	(h)	Crystal P	W 3-1	Bliss 3	10,000
35		22	(a)	Crystal P	L 0-4		10,000
36		29	(h)	West Ham U	D 1-1	Bliss	7,000

FINAL LEAGUE POSITION: 2nd in London Combination, 2nd Competition

Appearances
Goals

Banks	Barton	Bassett	Bliss	Chaplin	Clay	Darnell	Doyle	Elliott	Fricker	Glen	Hopkins	Jacques	Joyce	Knighton	Lloyd	Minter	Morris	Page	Ralston	Rance	Steel R	Thomas	Travers	Watkins	Weir	Wilson	#
9	6		10	3	2	4		7					1			8	11		5								1
10	6				2	4	3		9				1			8	7	11	5								2
8	6			3	2		4						1				7	11	5		10	9					3
8	6		10	3	2		4						1				7		5		11	9					4
9		8		3	2		4						1				7	11	5	6	10						5
10		8	6		2								1		9		7		5	3	11		4				6
8	3		10		2	6		4					1				7		5	9	11						7
	3	8	10			6	4						1				7	2	5	9	11						8
	3	8	10		2	6	4						1				7		5	9	11						9
	3	8	10		2	6	4						1				7		5	9	11						10
	6	8	10		2	4							1				7	3	5	11		9					11
	6	8	10		2		4						1				7	3	5	9	11						12
	6		10		2		4						1	8			7	3	5	9					11		13
	3	8	10		2	6	4						1				7		5	9					11		14
	3	8	10			4		2					1		9		7		5	6					11		15
	6	8	10		2		4						1		9		7		5	3					11		16
	6	8	10		2		4						1		9		7	3	5						11		17
	6	8	10		2		4						1				7	3	5	9					11		18
	6	8	10		2		4						1		9		7	3	5	11							19
	6	8	10		2	4							1		9		7	3	5	11							20
		8			2	4							1	10	9		7	3	5	6					11		21
		8	10		2	4							1		9		7	3	5	6					11		22
7	18	15	19	4	19	12		17	1	1		6	16	4	5	3	22	3	10	22	17	9	3		1	8	
3		6	10		1			1					1			2	4	1	3		2	3	1	1			

Banks	Barton	Bassett	Bliss	Chaplin	Clay	Darnell	Doyle	Elliott	Fricker	Glen	Hopkins	Jacques	Joyce	Knighton	Lloyd	Minter	Morris	Page	Ralston	Rance	Steel R	Thomas	Travers	Watkins	Weir	Wilson	#
	6	8	10		2			4					1		9		7	3	5		11						23
9	6	8	10			4	2						1				7	3	5		11						24
9		8	10		2	6	3	4									7		5		11			1			25
9		8	10		2	6	4						1				7		5	3					11		26
9	6	8	10		2		4						1				7		5	3					11		27
9	6	8	10		2		4						1				7	3	5		11						28
9	6	7	10		2		4						1		8			3	5		11						29
9	6		10		2		4						1		8		7	3	5		11						30
9	6	8	10		2		4						1				7	3	5		11						31
9	6	8	10		2		4				11		1				7		5	3							32
9		8	10		2	6		4			11		1				7		5	3							33
	6	8	10		2		4						1		9		7	3	5		11						34
	6	8	10		2	11		4					1		9		7		5	3							35
	6	8	10		2		4				11		1		9		7		5	3							36
10	11	13	14		13	5	1	14			3	12	1		7		13	7	14	13			1		1	2	
5	1	3	12		3			1					1			2			2	3							

203

1916-17

Manager: Peter McWilliam

#	Month	Date		Opponent	Result	Scorers	Att.
1	Sep	2	(h)	Chelsea	L 0-2		4,000
2		9	(a)	Arsenal	D 1-1	Bassett	6,000
3		16	(n*)	Luton T	L 2-3	Morris, Travers	6,000
4		23	(a)	Reading	W 4-2	Barton, Bassett, Potter, Bliss	10,000
5		28	(n*)	West Ham U	L 1-2	Bliss	3,000
6		30	(n†)	Millwall	L 1-4	Bliss	6,000
7	Oct	7	(a)	Watford	W 2-0	Bassett, Banks	2,000
8		14	(n†)	Clapton O	W 4-2	Bassett, Banks 2, Bliss	4,000
9		21	(a)	Fulham	L 1-2	Banks	4,000
10		28	(n†)	Queen's Park R	L 4-5	Walden 3, Grimes	4,000
11	Nov	4	(a)	West Ham U	L 1-5	Thwaites	8,000
12		11	(a)	Southampton	L 0-1		5,000
13		18	(n*)	Crystal P	W 3-1	Banks 2, Bliss	1,300
14		25	(a)	Chelsea	W 4-2	Clay (pen), Banks 2, Bliss	10,000
15	Dec	2	(n*)	Arsenal	W 4-1	Bassett, Banks 3	11,000
16		9	(a)	Luton T	W 3-1	Walden, Banks 2	5,000
17		16	(n*)	Portsmouth§	W 1-0	Banks	2,000
18		23	(a)	Millwall	D 3-3	Walden, Bassett, Bliss	3,000
19		25	(a)	Brentford	W 5-1	Elliott, Bassett, Hannaford, Bliss 2	3,000
20		26	(n†)	Brentford	W 5-2	Elliott, Bassett 3, Crowl	3,000
21		30	(n*)	Watford	W 3-0	Barton, Bassett, Darnell	6,000
22	Jan	6	(a)	Clapton O	W 2-1	Bassett, Barton	3,000
23		13	(n†)	Fulham	W 1-0	Barton	4,000
24		20	(a)	Queen's Park R	D 1-1	Bassett	3,000
25		27	(n†)	West Ham U	D 0-0		7,000
26	Feb	3	(n*)	Southampton	W 3-1	Potter, Banks, Bliss	5,000
27		10	(a)	Crystal P	W 1-0	Banks	2,000
28		17	(a)	Portsmouth	W 4-2	Bliss 4	5,000
29		24	(n*)	Crystal P	W 4-1	Bassett 2, Potter, Hawkins	5,000
30	Mar	3	(n†)	Luton T	W 3-2	Clay 2 (2 pens), Bassett	5,000
31		10	(a)	Southampton	W 4-2	Bassett 2, Banks, Hawkins	4,000
32		17	(n*)	Clapton O	W 5-2	Walden, Bassett 4	3,000
33		24	(a)	West Ham U	L 0-3		12,000
34		31	(n*)	Portsmouth	W 10-0	Elliott, Bassett, Banks 5, Thwaites 2, Hulme (og)	2,000
35	Apr	6	(n†)	Arsenal	D 0-0		5,000
36		7	(a)	Crystal P	W 3-0	Banks 3	5,000
37		9	(a)	Arsenal	L 2-3	Rance, Banks	12,000
38		10	(n*)	Portsmouth	W 2-1	Walden, Middlemiss	2,000
39		14	(a)	Luton T	L 4-5	Lloyd, Bliss 2, Barton	3,000
40		21	(n†)	Southampton	W 4-0	Bassett 2, Banks, Potter	2,000
41		28	(a)	Clapton O	W 8-0	Bassett, Banks 3, Bliss 4	4,000

FINAL LEAGUE POSITION: 4th in London Combination
§Abandoned after 15 minutes — fog. *Home game played at Highbury.
†Home game played at Homerton.

Appearances
Goals

Appearance and goalscoring grid (shirt numbers worn in each match; final two rows are total appearances and goals).

Banks	Barton	Bassett	Bearman	Bliss	Caldwell	Clay	Clayton	Croft T	Croft W	Crossley	Crowl	Darnell	Elliott	Grimes	Hannaford	Hawkins	Hood	Hunt	Jacques	Lloyd	McGlanachlan	McVey	Middlemiss	Morris	Potter	Powell	Ralston	Rance	Slade	Smith	Thwaites	Travers	Walden	Watkins	Weir	Williamson	
	6	7		10	11	2							4						1		8						3	5				9					1
	6	8		10		2							5						1	11						7	3				4	9					2
	6	8		10							11		4						1	2						7	3	5				9					3
	6	8		10		2					11		5						1	4				7	9		3										4
	6	8		10		2	2				11		5						1	9		4		7			3										5
	6			10		2					11		5						1	9				7			3					4			8		6
8	6	7		10		2					11		5						1	9						7	3					4					7
9	6	8		10		2					11		4						1					7			3	5									8
9	6	8				2					11		5	7					1								3		10			4					9
4	6	8		10		2			3		11		5			9			1														7				10
9	6			10		2							4						1	11							3	5			8		7				11
10	6	8				2					11		5						1	4				9			3						7				12
9	6	8		10		2					11		4						1							3	5						7				13
9	3	8		10		2					11	6	5						1	4													7				14
9	6	8		10		2							4						1							3	5	11					7				15
9	6	8		10		2						4	5						1					11		3							7				16
9	6	8				2					11		5				4		1	10						3							7				17
	3	8		10							11	6	4						1	9						2	5						7				18
	3	7		10							11	6	5			8			1	9						2						4					19
	6	8		10		2					11	4	5						1	9						3							7				20
9	6	8		10		2					11		5						1							3							7	4			21
9	10	8				2							6			11			1	4						3	5						7				22
9	10	8				2							6			11			1	4						3	5						7				23
9	6	8				2							5			11			1	4				10		3							7			1	24
9	6	8				2						4				11			1					10		3	5						7				25
9	6			10		2					11	4							1						8	3	5						7				26
9	6			10		2					11								1	8						3	5	4					7				27
		8		10		2		4	9		6								1						11	3	5						7				28
9	6	8				2										11			1	4					10	3	5						7				29
9	6	8				2										11			1	4					10	3	5						7				30
9	6	8				2						4				11			1	10						3	5						7				31
9	6	8				2						4				11			1						10	3	5						7				32
9	3	8										4				11			1	6					10	2	5						7				33
9	6	8				2						4	5			11			1	7						3					10						34
9	6	8		10		2						4				11			1							3	5						7				35
9	3	8		10								6	4			11			1	2							5						7				36
9	3	8		10								6	4						1				11			2	5						7				37
9		8		10									4		2	11										3	5						7		6	1	38
	10	8		9		2						6	5			11			1	4						3						7				39
9	6	8		10		2							4						1				11			3	5					7				40
9	6	8		10		2							4						1				11			3	5					7				41
30	39	37	1	27	1	30	1	2	3	1	13	14	37	3	1	9	4	1	39	24	1	2	2	5	13	1	38	23	1	1	9	3	30	1	3	1	
30	5	26		20		3					1	1	3	1	1	1	2			1		1	1	1	4		1				3	1	7				

1 own-goal

205

1917-18

Manager: Peter McWilliam

1	Sep	1	(a) Crystal P	W 4-2	Rance, Bassett, Minter 2	2,000
2		8	(n*) Chelsea	L 0-4		12,000
3		15	(a) Brentford	L 2-5	Banks, Nuttall	3,000
4		22	(n*) Arsenal	L 1-2	Potter	10,000
5		29	(a) West Ham U	L 0-1		8,000
6	Oct	6	(n*) Fulham	W 1-0	Banks (pen)	6,000
7		13	(a) Queen's Park R	W 3-2	Nuttall, Barnard 2	2,000
8		20	(n†) Clapton O	W 2-1	A.Lindsay 2	3,000
9		27	(n*) Crystal P	W 1-0	Banks	5,000
10	Nov	3	(a) Chelsea	D 0-0		8,000
11		10	(n*) Brentford	W 6-1	Walden 2, Banks, Nuttall, Lawrence, Hawkins	4,000
12		17	(n§) Arsenal	W 1-0	Nuttall	10,000
13		24	(n*) West Ham U	W 2-0	Banks 2	7,000
14	Dec	1	(a) Fulham	L 3-4	Banks 2, Coomber	7,000
15		8	(n†) Queen's Park R	L 0.1		4,000
16		15	(a) Clapton O	W 4-2	Banks 2, Nuttall, Spencer	4,000
17		22	(a) Crystal P	W 3-2	Nuttall 2, Coomber	2,000
18		25	(a) Millwall	W 6-0	Nuttall 2, Banks 3, Middlemiss	
19		26	(n†) Millwall	L 0-1		
20		29	(n*) Chelsea	W 2-0	Banks, Peake	8,000
21	Jan	5	(a) Brentford	W 3-2	Banks, Hawkins 2	2,000
22		12	(n*) Arsenal	W 4-1	Walden, Banks, Peake, Chipperfield (og)	9,000
23		19	(a) West Ham U	D 2-2	Banks 2	3,000
24		26	(n*) Fulham	L 0-1		15,000
25	Feb	2	(a) Queen's Park R	W 7-2	Rance, Walden, Nuttall, Peake 3, Hawkins	3,000
26		9	(n†) Millwall	W 4-2	Rance, Walden, Banks 2	7,000
27		16	(n*) Crystal P	W 8-0	Elliott, Banks 2 (1 pen), Peake, Potter 2, Hawkins 2	7,000
28		23	(a) Chelsea	L 0-3		20,000
29	Mar	2	(n*) Brentford	W 3-0	Banks, Minter, Hawkins	4,000
30		9	(a) Arsenal	L 1-4	Minter	15,000
31		16	(n*) West Ham U	L 0-5		10,000
32		23	(a) Fulham	W 3-0	Walden, Potter, Jack	3,000
33		29	(a) Clapton O	W 3-2	Walden, Jack Middlemiss	7,000
34		30	(n†) Queen's Park R	L 1-2	Goldthorpe	5,000
35	Apr	1	(n†) Clapton O	W 5-2	Goldthorpe 2, Jack 2, Middlemiss	3,000
36		6	(a) Millwall	W 1-0	Goldthorpe	2,000

FINAL LEAGUE POSITION: 4th in London Combination. *Home game played at Higbury. †Home game played at Homerton. §Away game played at Homerton.

Appearances
Goals

London Combination Subsidiary

37	Apr	13	(a) Chelsea	D 1-1	Peake	5,000
38		20	(n*) Chelsea	L 0-1		5,000
39		27	(a) Fulham	L 0-3		5,000
40	May	4	(n‡) Fulham	L 2-3	Thomas, Goldthorpe	2,000

*Home game played at Highbury. ‡Home game played at Upton Park.

Appearances
Goals

Ayres	Baldwin	Banks	Barnard	Barton	Bassett	Beaton	Bird	Bliss	Brown	Clay	Coomber	Cresswell	Crowl	Darnell	Elliott	Fleming	Goldthorpe	Hawkins	Hill	Hoffman	Jack	Jacques	Lawrence	Lindsay A	Lindsay D	Middlemiss	Minter	Nuttall	Peake	Potter	Ralston	Rance	Saunders	Thomas	Thwaites	Tomkins	Walden	Match
		10			8							4		6	2							1						9			3	5				11	7	1
		9			8					2			11	6	4							1									3	5				10	7	2
		9			8					2				6	4			11				1							10		3	5					7	3
		8								2				6	4			11				1			10			9			3	5					7	4
		8								2				6	4			11				1			10			9			3	5					7	5
		4			8					2				6				11				1			10			9			3	5					7	6
	10	4								2				6				11				1		8				9			3	5					7	7
		9								2				6	4			11				1		10	8						3	5					7	8
		8												6	2			11				1		10				9			3	5		4			7	9
		8								2				6	4			11				1		10							3	5					7	10
		8								2				6	4			11				1		10				9			3	5					7	11
		8								2				6	4			11				1						9			3	5					7	12
		8								2	10				4			11				1						9			3	5				6	7	13
		8								2	10			6	4			11		1								9			3	5					7	14
		8								2					4			11				1		10				9			3	5				6	7	15
		8								2	10				4							1						9			3	5				6	7	16
		8								2	10				4			11				1						9			3	5				6	7	17
		8		6						2					4		5	11				1						9	10		3						7	18
		8		6						2					4			11				1						9	10		3	5					7	19
		8								2					4			7				1					11	9	10		3	5				6		20
		8							11	2				6	4			9				1									3	5	10				7	21
		8								2				6	3			11				1						9	10			5		4			7	22
		8		6						2					4			11				1						9			3	5						23
		8									10			6	2			11				1						9			3	5		4			7	24
		8										4		6	2			11				1						9	10		3	5					7	25
		8												6	2			11				1						9	10		3	5		4			7	26
		8						7		2					4			11				1						9	10		3	5				6		27
		8								2					4			11				1						9	10		3	5				6	7	28
		8								2				6	4				10		11	1						9			3	5					7	29
		8		6						2								11				1						9	10		3	5		4			7	30
1		8						7		2				6	4		3	9	11										10			5						31
										2					4		9	11					1						10	8	3	5				6	7	32
11										2				6	4		3	9					1						10	8		5					7	33
11										2				6	4		8	3	9				1						10			5					7	34
		6								2					4		8	3			11		1					9	10			5					7	35
		9								2				6	3		8	11				1							10			5		4				36
3	1	30	1	4	6	1	1	2	2	17	13	11	1	16	34	1	4	33	1	1	6	29	5	5	5	6	3	18	11	6	30	35	1	4	1	12	31	
		23								2	1			2	1		4	7			4				1	2			3	4	10	6	4		3			7	

1 own-goal

Ayres	Baldwin	Banks	Barnard	Barton	Bassett	Beaton	Bird	Bliss	Brown	Clay	Coomber	Cresswell	Crowl	Darnell	Elliott	Fleming	Goldthorpe	Hawkins	Hill	Hoffman	Jack	Jacques	Lawrence	Lindsay A	Lindsay D	Middlemiss	Minter	Nuttall	Peake	Potter	Ralston	Rance	Saunders	Thomas	Thwaites	Tomkins	Walden	Match
		9								2				6	4		8	11				1							10		3	5					7	37
				2										6		7	8	11				1							10		3	5	4	9				38
		8								2	9			6				11											10		3	5		4			7	39
		9								2				6			8	11				1							10		3	5					7	40
		3		1						3	1			3	2	1	3	4			1	3							4		4	4	1	3			3	
		1															1												1									

W.Halle played number 10 in Match 23; Lightfoot played number 9 in Match 10 and number 10 in Match 12; Lloyd played number 7 in Match 23; Robinson played number 4 in Match 40; Spencer played number 11 in Match 16 and scored one goal; Wren played number 1 in Match 39.

1918-19

Manager: Peter McWilliam

1	Sep	7	(a) Fulham	D	2-2	Barnard, Thomas	8,000
2		14	(n†)Brentford	D	1-1	Thomas	3,000
3		21	(a) West Ham U	W	1-0	Thomas	8,000
4		28	(n†)Clapton O	W	2-0	Hadyn-Price 2	5,000
5	Oct	5	(n*)Chelsea	W	2-1	Goldthorpe, Thomas	12,000
6		12	(a) Arsenal	L	0-3		19,900
7		19	(n*)Crystal P	W	2-0	Rance, A.Lindsay	10,000
8		26	(a) Millwall	W	2-0	Hadyn-Price, Barnard	7,000
9	Nov	2	(n†)Fulham	W	1-0	Simons	5,000
10		9	(a) Brentford	L	1-7	Banks	6,000
11		16	(n†)West Ham U	L	1-4	Rance	6,000
12		23	(a) Clapton O	W	3-0	A.Lindsay 2, Simons	6,000
13		30	(a) Chelsea	L	1-3	Peake	14,000
14	Dec	7	(n*)Arsenal	W	1-0	McCalmont	12,000
15		14	(a) Crystal P	L	3-6	A.Lindsay, Goldthorpe 2	2,000
16		21	(n†)Millwall	L	0-3		8,000
17		25	(a) Queen's Park R	D	1-1	Rance	8,000
18		26	(n†)Queen's Park R	D	0-0		6,000
19		28	(a) Fulham	L	1-3	Banks	8,000
20	Jan	4	(n†)Brentford	D	1-1	R.Smith	12,000
21		11	(a) West Ham U	L	0-2		13,000
22		18	(n†)Clapton O	L	2-4	Jack 2	7,000
23		25	(n*)Chelsea	D	1-1	Goldthorpe	25,000
24	Feb	1	(a) Arsenal	W	3-2	Bennett, Minter, Jack	16,000
25		8	(n*)Crystal P	W	4-2	Minter 3, Banks	14,500
26		15	(a) Queen's Park R	L	1-7	Cain	10,000
27		22	(n†)Fulham	L	0-2		10,000
28	Mar	1	(a) Brentford	L	1-4	Walden	12,000
29		8	(n†)West Ham U	L	0-1		17,190
30		15	(a) Clapton O	W	2-1	Minter, Banks	16,000
31		22	(a) Chelsea	W	2-1	Minter, Banks	25,000
32		29	(n*)Arsenal	L	0-1		33,000
33	Apr	5	(a) Crystal P	D	2-2	Minter, Elliott	10,000
34		12	(n*)Queen's Park R	L	2-3	Minter, Bliss	20,000
35		18	(n†)Millwall	D	2-2	Minter, Middlemiss	18,000
36		21	(a) Millwall	W	4-2	Williams, Bliss, Middlemiss 2	18,000

FINAL LEAGUE POSITION: 8th in London Combination   Appearances
*Home game played at Highbury. †Home game played at Homerton.   Goals

Victory Cup

1	Mar	23	(n*)West Ham U	W	3-1	Minter 2, Banks	9,000
SF	Apr	19	(n§)Fulham	L	0-2		45,000

*Home game played at Highbury. §Played at Stamford Bridge.   Appearances
     Goals

National War Fund

	May	10	(h) Fulham	D	2-2	Grimsdell 2	5,000

     Appearances
     Goals

The table below records squad numbers worn by each player in each match. Column alignment in this very dense grid is approximate.

Banks	Barnard	Barton	Beaton	Bennett	Bliss	Cantrell	Chester	Clay	Darnell	Dockray	Elliott	Freeman	Goldthorpe	Grimsdell	Haydn-Price	Harbridge	Hawkins	Jack	Jacques	Lindsay A	Lindsay D	McIver	Middlemiss	Minter	Peake	Potter	Ralston	Rance	Simons	Smith P	Smith B	Thomas	Tomkins	Walden	Williams	Worrall	Match
8									4	7	3						11			10	1				2			5				9	6				1
	4								6	11	2						7			8	1				3			5				9					2
	4								6	11	2	10					7			8	1				3			5				9					3
	4								6	11	2	9		10			7			8	1							5	3								4
8					6				2		11	9					7				1						3	5				10	4				5
8									6	11							7	2		10	1						3	5					4				6
10	4								2			9					7		11	8	1							5	3		6						7
9	10								2	6							7		11	8	1							5					4				8
9	4								6								7		11	8	1						3			10	2			5			9
8	4								6		9							2			1						3	5	10				4				10
					6						9	8		11							1						3	5			2		4				11
	6								4	11	3	9					7			8	1							5	10						2		12
		3							6		2	7							11	10	1			8				5									13
7									2	11	4	8									1			10				5			6					3	14
									2	6	4	9				7	11				1		8	10				5								3	15
8	6								2		9					7			11		1			10				5					4			3	16
7	3								6		2							11	10		1							5				8					17
7	2								6		4							11	10		1		9				5				8				3	18
7	6								2		9							11	10		1						5				8	4			3	19
7		10							2	6								11		1		8					5				8		9		3	20
7		10							2	6								11		1		8	9				5					4			3	21
7		10							2	6	4							9	11		1		8				5								3	22
8			9						2				10		6		7		11		1						3	5					4				23
10		7							2	6	9							11			1			8				5					4			3	24
10		7							2						6		11				1		8	9				5					4			3	25
8		7							2	6	9				3		11				1							5					4				26
9	10								2									6	11	8	1							5					4	7			27
8	10								2									6	9		1						3	5					4	7			28
	3							7	2									6	11		1		8					5				9	4				29
10	3		8						2	11								6			1			9				5					4	7			30
10	3			9					2									6		11	1			8				5					4	7			31
10	3	7							2	11		9						6			1			8				5					4				32
10	3								2	7	11	9		5							1			8							6						33
7	3							10	2									6		11	1		8					5					4	9			34
10	7								2	6	3									11	1		8					5					4	9			35
		10							2					5					11		1		8				3			4		6	7	9			36
26	6	14	6	4	2	2	2	24	21	11	17	2	10	9	9	2	21	13	17	17	16	3	4	9	4	2	11	33	3	4	6	7	23	5	3	11	
5	2		1	2				1			4	3				3	3		4		3	9	1		3	2		1	4		1	1					

Additional competition appearances:

Banks	Barnard	Barton	Beaton	Bennett	Bliss	Cantrell	Chester	Clay	Darnell	Dockray	Elliott	Freeman	Goldthorpe	Grimsdell	Haydn-Price	Harbridge	Hawkins	Jack	Jacques	Lindsay A	Lindsay D	McIver	Middlemiss	Minter	Peake	Potter	Ralston	Rance	Simons	Smith P	Smith B	Thomas	Tomkins	Walden	Williams	Worrall	Match
10	3		9						2		4						6				1		11	8				5					7				1
		10							2								5				1		11	8			3			4		6	7	9			SF
1	1		1	1				2		1		2				2			2	2			1	1			1		1	2	1						
1																					2																

Banks	Barnard	Barton	Beaton	Bennett	Bliss	Cantrell	Chester	Clay	Darnell	Dockray	Elliott	Freeman	Goldthorpe	Grimsdell	Haydn-Price	Harbridge	Hawkins	Jack	Jacques	Lindsay A	Lindsay D	McIver	Middlemiss	Minter	Peake	Potter	Ralston	Rance	Simons	Smith P	Smith B	Thomas	Tomkins	Walden	Williams	Worrall
		10							3			6												8			5						4				
		1							1			1												1			1									
											2																									

In the London Combination Bee played number 9 in Match 17; Blake played number 9 in Match 6; Bowler played number 4 in Match 17; Brawn played number 7 in Match 10; Bully played number 10 in Match 11; Cain played number 10 in Match 26 and scored once; Couchman played number 11 in Match 28; Duncan played number 7 in Match 11; Frazer played number 4 in Match 33; Gee played number 3 in Match 8; Hoffman played number 11 in Match 10; Jennings played number 10 in Match 2; Lloyd played number 9 in Match 13; McCalmont played number 9 in Match 14 and scored once; Parsons played number 4 in Match 20; Patterson played number 3 in Match 27; Walters played number 10 in Match 29. In the National War Fund game Bay played number 9, Dimmock number 11, Forshaw number 2, Furr number 7 and Hatfield number 1.

1919-20

Manager: Peter McWilliam

#	Month	Date	H/A	Opponent	Result	Scorers	Attendance
1	Aug	30	(a)	Coventry C	W 5-0	Grimsdell, Bliss 2, Chipperfield 2	15,000
2	Sep	1	(h)	Leicester C	W 4-0	Clay (pen), Cantrell 2, Bliss	21,060
3		6	(h)	Coventry C	W 4-1	Grimsdell, Cantrell, Bliss, Chipperfield	30,610
4		11	(a)	Leicester C	W 4-2	Clay (pen), Minter, Cantrell, Bliss	20,000
5		13	(h)	South Shields	W 2-0	Cantrell, Bliss	33,172
6		20	(a)	South Shields	W 3-0	Wilson 3	20,000
7		27	(h)	Lincoln C	W 6-1	Grimsdell, Minter, Wilson, Bliss 2, Chipperfield	35,000
8	Oct	4	(a)	Lincoln C	D 1-1	Goodman	7,000
9		11	(h)	Clapton O	W 2-1	Minter, Bliss	44,268
10		18	(a)	Clapton O	W 4-0	Minter, Bliss 3	32,644
11		27	(a)	Port Vale	W 1-0	Cantrell	17,000
12	Nov	1	(h)	Port Vale	W 2-0	Smith, Bliss	28,603
13		8	(a)	Bury	L 1-2	Wilson	12,000
14		15	(h)	Bury	W 2-1	Bliss, Chipperfield	32,000
15		22	(a)	Nottingham F	D 1-1	Chipperfield	18,000
16		29	(h)	Nottingham F	W 5-2	Walden, Cantrell, Bliss 2, Dimmock	28,000
17	Dec	6	(a)	Fulham	W 4-1	Grimsdell, Minter, Cantrell, Bliss	30,000
18		13	(h)	Fulham	W 4-0	Walden, Minter 2, Bliss	38,000
19		20	(a)	Barnsley	L 0-3		12,000
20		25	(h)	Hull C	W 4-0	Grimsdell (pen), Cantrell, Bliss 2	40,008
21		26	(a)	Hull C	W 3-1	Cantrell, Dimmock, Bell (og)	28,000
22		27	(h)	Barnsley	W 4-0	Grimsdell, Banks, Cantrell, Bliss	43,071
23	Jan	3	(a)	Stockport C	W 2-1	Bliss, Dimmock	15,000
24		17	(h)	Stockport C	W 2-0	Walden, Bliss	38,000
25		24	(a)	Huddersfield T	D 1-1	Bliss	27,000
26	Feb	7	(a)	Blackpool	W 1-0	Walden	10,000
27		14	(h)	Blackpool	D 2-2	Banks, Wilson	40,000
28		16	(h)	Huddersfield T	W 2-0	Grimsdell, Wilson	35,000
29		25	(a)	Bristol C	W 2-1	Bliss 2	12,000
30		28	(h)	Bristol C	W 2-0	Grimsdell, Cantrell	38,000
31	Mar	13	(a)	West Ham U	L 1-2	Grimsdell (pen)	25,691
32		20	(h)	Rotherham C	W 2-0	Smith, Cantrell	28,000
33		22	(h)	West Ham U	W 2-0	Cantrell, Dimmock	26,000
34		27	(a)	Rotherham C	D 1-1	Grimsdell (pen)	18,000
35	Apr	2	(h)	Wolves	W 4-2	Cantrell, Bliss 3	38,000
36		3	(h)	Stoke	W 2-0	Grimsdell, Dimmock	36,000
37		5	(a)	Wolves	W 3-1	Grimsdell 2, Cantrell	25,000
38		10	(a)	Stoke	W 3-1	Seed, Cantrell 2	12,000
39		17	(h)	Grimsby T	W 3-1	Grimsdell, Bliss 2	32,000
40		24	(a)	Grimsby T	L 0-2		10,000
41		26	(h)	Birmingham	D 0-0		30,000
42	May	1	(a)	Birmingham	W 1-0	Seed	39,000

FINAL LEAGUE POSITION: 1st in Division Two

Appearances
Goals

FA Cup

#	Month	Date	H/A	Opponent	Result	Scorers	Attendance
1	Jan	10	(a)	Bristol R	W 4-1	Cantrell 3, Bliss	17,000
2		31	(h)	West Stanley	W 4-0	Banks, Wilson 2, Bliss	35,527
3	Feb	21	(h)	West Ham U	W 3-0	Grimsdell, Wilson 2	47,642
4	Mar	6	(h)	Aston Villa	L 0-1		52,179

Appearances
Goals

FA Charity Shield

	Month	Date	H/A	Opponent	Result	Scorers	Attendance
	May	15	(h)	West Brom A	L 0-2		3,600

Appearances
Goals

London FA Charity Cup

#	Month	Date	H/A	Opponent	Result	Scorers	Attendance
1	Sep	22	(h)	Millwall	W 6-0	Banks 2, Wilson 4	7,904
2	Oct	6	(a)	Crystal P	L 2-3	Clay 2 (2 pens)	4,000

Appearances
Goals

London Professional Football Charity Fund

	Month	Date	H/A	Opponent	Result	Scorers	Attendance
	Sep	29	(a)	Arsenal	W 1-0	Minter	10,000

Appearances
Goals

Archibald	Banks	Bliss	Brown	Cantrell	Castle	Chipperfield	Clay	Dimmock	Elliott	French	Goodman	Grimsdell	Jacques	Lindsay A	Lorimer	Lowe	McDonald	Middlemiss	Minter	Pearson	Rance	Sage	Seed	Skinner	Smith	Walden	Walters	Wilson	No.
		10		9		11	2					6	1	8						5	3				4	7			1
		10		9		11	2					6	1	8						5	3				4	7			2
		10		9		11	2					6	1	8						5	3				4	7			3
		10		9		11	2					6	1						8	3	5				4	7			4
		10		9		11	2					6	1		7				8	3	5				4				5
		10				11	2					6	1		7				8	3	5				4			9	6
		10			2	11						6	1		7				8	3	5				4			9	7
	8	10			2	11			6		9		1		7					5	3				4				8
		10					2	11				6	1						8	3	5				4	7		9	9
		10					2	11			9	6	1						8	3	5				4	7			10
		10		9			2	11				6	1						8	3	5				4	7			11
		10		9			2	11				6	1						8	3	5				4	7			12
		10					2	11				6	1						8	3	5				4	7		9	13
		10		9			2	11				6	1						8	3	5				4	7			14
		10		9			2	11				6	1						8	3	5				4	7			15
		10		9			2	11				6	1						8	3	5				4	7			16
		10		9			2	11				6	1						8	3	5				4	7			17
		10		9			2	11				6	1						8	3	5				4	7			18
		10					2	11				6	1						8	3	5				4	7		9	19
		10		9			2	11				6	1						8	3	5				4	7			20
		10		9			2	11				6	1						8	3	5				4	7			21
	8	10	3	9			2	11				6	1								5				4	7			22
	8	10	3	9			2	11				6	1								5				4	7			23
	8	10	3				2	11				6	1								5				4	7		9	24
	8	10	3				2	11				6	1								5				4	7		9	25
	8	10	3				2	11				6	1								5				4	7		9	26
	8	10	3				2	11				6	1								5				4	7		9	27
	8	10					2	11			3	6	1								5				4	7		9	28
	8	10	3				2	11					1								5	6			4	7		9	29
4	8	10	3	9			2	11				6	1											5	7			30
4	8	10	3	9			2	11				5	1				7								6				31
6	8	10	3	9			2	11					1				4							5	7			32
4	8	10	3	9			2	11				6	1											5	7			33
4	8	10	3	9			2	11				6	1			7								5				34
4	8	10	3	9			2	11				6	1											5	7			35
4	8	10	3	9			2	11				6	1											5	7			36
4		10	3	9			2	11				6	1			7							8	5				37
4		10	3	9	7		2	11			6		1										8				5		38
4		10	3	9	7		2	11				6	1										8	5				39
4		10	3				2	11				6	1			7							8	5			9	40
4	8	10	3	9			2	11				6	1											5	7			41
4	7	10	3	9				11				6	1					2						5	8			42
13	18	42	20	29	2	15	27	27	1		16	37	42	3	4	1	1	4	20	21	26	1	5	3	40	31	1	12	
	2	31		18		6	2	5			1	14								7		2				2	4		7	

1 own-goal

Archibald	Banks	Bliss	Brown	Cantrell	Castle	Chipperfield	Clay	Dimmock	Elliott	French	Goodman	Grimsdell	Jacques	Lindsay A	Lorimer	Lowe	McDonald	Middlemiss	Minter	Pearson	Rance	Sage	Seed	Skinner	Smith	Walden	Walters	Wilson	No.
	8	10	3	9				11				6	1								5				4	7			1
	8	10	3				2	11				6	1							5					4	7		9	2
	8	10	3				2	11				6	1							5					4	7		9	3
4	8	10	3	9			2	11				6	1											5	7			4
1	4	4	4	2			3	4				1	4	4						3				4	4	2			
	1	2		3				1																		4			

Archibald	Banks	Bliss	Brown	Cantrell	Castle	Chipperfield	Clay	Dimmock	Elliott	French	Goodman	Grimsdell	Jacques	Lindsay A	Lorimer	Lowe	McDonald	Middlemiss	Minter	Pearson	Rance	Sage	Seed	Skinner	Smith	Walden	Walters	Wilson	No.
4	7	10	3	9			2	11				6	1										8		5				
1	1	1	1	1			1	1				1	1										1		1				

Archibald	Banks	Bliss	Brown	Cantrell	Castle	Chipperfield	Clay	Dimmock	Elliott	French	Goodman	Grimsdell	Jacques	Lindsay A	Lorimer	Lowe	McDonald	Middlemiss	Minter	Pearson	Rance	Sage	Seed	Skinner	Smith	Walden	Walters	Wilson	No.
	8	10					11					3	6	1		7	2			5				4		9			1
6	8		3				2	10	1	9				7			11			5	4				1	2		1	2
1	2	1	1				1	1	1	1	2	1	1	2		1	1			1	1			1	2		1		
	2						2																	4					

Archibald	Banks	Bliss	Brown	Cantrell	Castle	Chipperfield	Clay	Dimmock	Elliott	French	Goodman	Grimsdell	Jacques	Lindsay A	Lorimer	Lowe	McDonald	Middlemiss	Minter	Pearson	Rance	Sage	Seed	Skinner	Smith	Walden	Walters	Wilson	No.
9		10					11				2	6	1	7						8	3	5				4			
1		1					1				1	1	1	1						1	1	1				1			

1920-21

Manager: Peter McWilliam

1	Aug	28	(h)	Blackburn R	L	1-2	Bliss	47,345
2		30	(a)	Derby C	D	2-2	Clay (pen), Bliss	18,628
3	Sep	4	(a)	Blackburn R	D	1-1	Seed	40,000
4		6	(h)	Derby C	W	2-0	Seed, Bliss	26,142
5		11	(a)	Aston Villa	L	2-4	Walden, Dimmock	55,000
6		18	(h)	Aston Villa	L	1-2	Bliss	42,000
7		25	(a)	Manchester U	W	1-0	Grimsdell	52,000
8	Oct	2	(h)	Manchester U	W	4-1	Walden 2, Seed 2	34,600
9		9	(h)	Chelsea*	W	5-0	Wilson, Bliss 3, Dimmock	47,000
10		16	(a)	Chelsea	W	4-0	Wilson 2, Bliss, Dimmock	76,000
11		23	(h)	Burnley	L	1-2	Banks	39,661
12		30	(a)	Burnley	L	0-2		40,000
13	Nov	6	(h)	Oldham A	W	5-1	Grimsdell 2, Seed 2, Bliss	27,824
14		13	(a)	Oldham A	W	5-2	Seed 2, Wilson 2, Bliss	15,000
15		20	(h)	Preston NE	L	1-2	Walden	33,338
16		27	(a)	Preston NE	L	1-4	Smith	20,000
17	Dec	4	(h)	Sheffield U	W	4-1	Walden, Wilson 2, Dimmock	23,500
18		11	(a)	Sheffield U	D	1-1	Dimmock	25,000
19		18	(h)	Bolton W	W	5-2	Seed, Cantrell, Bliss 2, Dimmock	33,000
20		25	(a)	Newcastle U	D	1-1	Cantrell	30,000
21		27	(h)	Newcastle U	W	2-0	Bliss, Dimmock	54,500
22	Jan	1	(a)	Bolton W	L	0-1		45,000
23		15	(h)	Arsenal	W	2-1	Cantrell, Bliss	39,221
24		22	(a)	Arsenal	L	2-3	Smith, Cantrell	60,600
25	Feb	3	(h)	Bradford	W	2-0	Cantrell, Bliss	20,000
26		5	(a)	Bradford	D	1-1	Dimmock	18,000
27		12	(h)	Manchester C	W	2-0	Cantrell, Dimmock	32,000
28		23	(a)	West Brom A	L	1-3	Seed	16,000
29		26	(h)	West Brom A	W	1-0	Bliss	38,000
30	Mar	9	(a)	Manchester C	L	0-2		30,000
31		12	(h)	Everton	W	2-0	Archibald, Seed	30,000
32		25	(a)	Liverpool	D	1-1	Bliss	40,000
33		26	(a)	Sunderland	W	1-0	Seed	35,000
34		28	(h)	Liverpool	W	1-0	Smith	35,000
35	Apr	2	(h)	Sunderland	D	0-0		35,000
36		9	(a)	Bradford C	L	0-1		15,000
37		16	(h)	Bradford C	W	2-0	Wilson 2	30,000
38		25	(a)	Huddersfield T	L	0-2		28,000
39		27	(a)	Everton	D	0-0		23,000
40		30	(h)	Huddersfield T	W	1-0	Banks	35,000
41	May	2	(a)	Middlesbrough	L	0-1		10,000
42		7	(h)	Middlesbrough	D	2-2	Banks, Cantrell	25,000

FINAL LEAGUE POSITION: 6th in Division One   Appearances

*Also Bliss, Cantrell and Dimmock benefit match.   Goals

FA Cup

1	Jan	8	(h)	Bristol R	W	6-2	Clay (pen), Smith, Walden, Seed, Cantrell, Bliss	35,175
2		29	(h)	Bradford C	W	4-0	Banks, Seed 3	39,048
3	Feb	19	(a)	Southend U	W	4-1	Banks, Seed, Cantrell, Bliss	11,600
4	Mar	5	(h)	Aston Villa	W	1-0	Banks	51,991
SF		19	(n†)	Preston NE	W	2-1	Bliss 2	44,668
F	Apr	23	(n‡)	Wolves	W	1-0	Dimmock	72,805

†Played at Hillsborough, Sheffield. ‡Played at Stamford Bridge, London.   Appearances

       Goals

FA Charity Shield

	May	16	(h)	Burnley	W	2-0	Cantrell, Bliss	18,000

       Appearances

       Goals

London FA Charity Cup

1	Oct	11	(a)	Barking	W	4-1	Wilson 2, Bliss, Dimmock	7,000
2	Nov	1	(h)	Arsenal	W	3-1	Grimsdell, Walden, Banks	14,500
SF	Apr	11	(n§)	Clapton O	L	1-2	Castle	16,033

§Played at Arsenal Stadium, Highbury, London.   Appearances

       Goals

London Professional Footballers Charity Fund

	Oct	25	(h)	Arsenal	W	2-0	Wilson 2	17,436

       Appearances

       Goals

Archibald	Banks	Bliss	Brown	Cantrell	Castle	Chipperfield	Clay	Dimmock	Findlay	Forster	Grimsdell	Hunter	Jacques	Lindsay A	Lorimer	Lowe	McDonald	Pearson	Rance	Ross	Seed	Skinner	Smith	Thompson	Walden	Walters	Wilson	
		10	3	9			2	11		6		1						8	4			7	5					1
		10		9			2	11		6		1			3			8	4			7	5					2
		10		9	7		2	11		6		1			3			8	4				5					3
	7	10					2	11		6		1			3		5	8	4					9				4
		10		9				11		6		1		2	3		5	8	4			7						5
		10		9				11		6		1		2	3		5	8	4			7						6
		10					2	11		6		1			3		5	8	4			7		9				7
		10					2	11		6		1		5	3			8	4			7		9				8
8		10					2	11		6		1			3		5		4			7		9				9
8		10					2	11		6		1			3		5		4			7		9				10
8		10					2	11				1			3		5	6	4			7		9				11
		10					2	11		6		1			3		5	8	4			7		9				12
		10					2	11		6		1			3		5	8	4			7		9				13
4		10					2	11		6		1			3		5	8				7		9				14
		10					2	11		6		1			3		5	8	4			7		9				15
		10					2	11		6		1			3		5	8	4			7		9				16
		10					2	11		6		1			3		5	8	4			7		9				17
		10					2	11		6		1			3		5	8	4			7		9				18
		10		9			2	11		6		1			3			8	4			7	5					19
		10		9			2	11		6		1			3			8	4			7	5					20
		10		9			2	11		6		1			3			8	4			7	5					21
		10		9			2	11		6		1			3			8	4			7	5					22
		10		9			2	11		6		1			3			8	4			7	5					23
		10		9			2	11		6		1			3			8	4			7	5					24
	7	10		9			2	11		6		1			3			8	4				5					25
	7	10		9			2	11		6		1			3			8	4				5					26
	7	10		9			2	11		6		1			3			8	4				5					27
4	7						2	11				1	10		6		3	8					5	9				28
	7	10		9			2	11	2	6		1			3			8	4				5					29
	7						2	11		6		1	10		3			8	4				5	9				30
4	7	10						11	2	6		1			3			8					5	9				31
4	7	10					2	11				1			8		6	3					5					32
	7						1	11	2	6					3			8	4		10		5	9				33
	7	10		9			2	11		6		1			3			8	4				5					34
	7	10		9			2	11		6		1			3			8	4				5					35
	7		9				2				1				6		3	8	4		10		5	11				36
	7	10					2	11		6		1		8			3		4				5	9				37
			7					11	2	6		1			5		3	8			4	10		9				38
4		10		9	7		2	11	3	6		1						8					5					39
	7	10		9			2	11		6		1			3			8	4				5					40
	7	10	3	9				11	2	6		1						8	4				5					41
5	7	10		9				11	2	6		1			3			8	4				5					42
6	21	36	2	23	3		35	41	7	38	11	30	5	5	36	5	14	36	2	36	3	22	25	20				
1	3	17		7			1	9		3					12		3			5				9				

Archibald	Banks	Bliss	Brown	Cantrell	Castle	Chipperfield	Clay	Dimmock	Findlay	Forster	Grimsdell	Hunter	Jacques	Lindsay A	Lorimer	Lowe	McDonald	Pearson	Rance	Ross	Seed	Skinner	Smith	Thompson	Walden	Walters	Wilson	
		10		9			2	11		6		1			3			8	4			7	5					1
	7	10		9			2	11		6		1			3			8	4				5					2
	7	10		9			2	11		6		1			3			8	4				5					3
	7	10		9			2	11		6	1				3			8	4				5					4
	7	10		9			2	11		6	1				3			8	4				5					SF
	7	10		9			2	11		6	1				3			8	4				5					F
	5	6		6			6	6		6	3	3			6			6	6			1	6					
	3	4		2			1	1										5	1				1					

Archibald	Banks	Bliss	Brown	Cantrell	Castle	Chipperfield	Clay	Dimmock	Findlay	Forster	Grimsdell	Hunter	Jacques	Lindsay A	Lorimer	Lowe	McDonald	Pearson	Rance	Ross	Seed	Skinner	Smith	Thompson	Walden	Walters	Wilson	
	7	10		9			2	11		6		1			3			8	4				5					1
	1	1		1			1	1		1	1				1			1	1				1					
		1		1																								

Archibald	Banks	Bliss	Brown	Cantrell	Castle	Chipperfield	Clay	Dimmock	Findlay	Forster	Grimsdell	Hunter	Jacques	Lindsay A	Lorimer	Lowe	McDonald	Pearson	Rance	Ross	Seed	Skinner	Smith	Thompson	Walden	Walters	Wilson	
8		10					2	11		6		1		7		3	5		4					9				1
10							2	11		6		1			3	5	8	4			7		9					2
	3			7	11			2			1	8		5			4	6		10			9					SF
2	1	1		1	1		2	2		1	2	3	1	1	1	2	2	1	1	1	1	2	1	1	3			
																									1	2		

Archibald	Banks	Bliss	Brown	Cantrell	Castle	Chipperfield	Clay	Dimmock	Findlay	Forster	Grimsdell	Hunter	Jacques	Lindsay A	Lorimer	Lowe	McDonald	Pearson	Rance	Ross	Seed	Skinner	Smith	Thompson	Walden	Walters	Wilson	
8							2	11	10	6		1			3	5		4					7	9				1
1							1	1	1	1		1			1	1		1					1	1				
																								2				

1921-22

Manager: Peter McWilliam

1	Aug	27	(a)	Cardiff C	W 1-0 Banks	50,000
2		29	(h)	Bolton W	L 1-2 Thompson	31,771
3	Sep	3	(h)	Cardiff C	W 4-1 Clay (pen), Thompson 2, Dimmock	35,000
4		5	(a)	Bolton W	L 0-1	40,000
5		10	(h)	Middlesbrough	L 2-4 Clay (pen), Bliss	34,882
6		17	(a)	Middlesbrough	D 0-0	20,000
7		24	(h)	Aston Villa	W 3-1 Clay (pen), Seed, Bliss	47,017
8	Oct	1	(a)	Aston Villa	L 1-2 Dimmock	40,000
9		8	(h)	Manchester U	D 2-2 Wilson 2	36,113
10		15	(a)	Manchester U	L 1-2 Dimmock	40,000
11		22	(h)	Liverpool	L 0-1	31,593
12		29	(a)	Liverpool	D 1-1 Dimmock	25,000
13	Nov	5	(h)	Newcastle U	W 4-0 Grimsdell, Seed 3	34,448
14		12	(a)	Newcastle U	W 2-0 Seed, Lindsay	20,000
15		19	(h)	Burnley	D 1-1 Seed	45,000
16		26	(a)	Burnley	L 0-1	25,000
17	Dec	3	(h)	Sheffield U	W 2-1 Clay (pen), Skinner	27,321
18		10	(a)	Sheffield U	L 0-1	27,000
19		17	(h)	Chelsea	D 0-0	44,035
20		24	(a)	Chelsea	W 2-1 Bliss 2	54,000
21		26	(h)	Bradford C	W 1-0 Clay (pen)	34,483
22		27	(a)	Bradford C	W 4-0 Seed, Wilson 2, Thompson	25,000
23		31	(h)	Preston NE	W 5-0 Seed, Wilson 2, Thompson, Dimmock	28,097
24	Jan	14	(a)	Preston NE	W 2-1 Walden, Cantrell	20,000
25		21	(a)	West Brom A	L 0-3	20,000
26		30	(h)	West Brom A	W 2-0 Clay (pen), Wilson	30,000
27	Feb	4	(a)	Manchester C	D 3-3 Wilson, Bliss 2	20,000
28		11	(h)	Manchester C	W 3-1 Grimsdell, Bliss, Dimmock	43,000
29		25	(h)	Everton	W 2-0 Wilson, Dimmock	34,871
30	Mar	11	(h)	Sunderland	W 1-0 Thompson	41,003
31		15	(a)	Everton	D 0-0	30,000
32		18	(h)	Huddersfield T	W 1-0 Skinner	36,187
33		27	(a)	Huddersfield T	D 1-1 Lindsay	16,000
34	Apr	1	(a)	Birmingham	W 3-0 Clay (pen), Seed, Roulsen (og)	34,000
35		5	(a)	Sunderland	L 0-2	37,000
36		8	(h)	Birmingham	W 2-1 Lindsay, Jones (og)	19,638
37		14	(h)	Oldham A	W 3-1 Clay (pen), Cantrell 2	34,881
38		15	(h)	Arsenal	W 2-0 Grimsdell, Seed	40,394
39		17	(a)	Oldham A	L 0-1	31,343
40		22	(a)	Arsenal	L 0-1	42,000
41		29	(h)	Blackburn R	W 2-1 Walden, Wilson	24,559
42	May	6	(a)	Blackburn R	D 1-1 Wilson	25,000

FINAL LEAGUE POSITION: 2nd in Division One

Appearances
Goals

FA Cup

1	Jan	7	(a)	Brentford	W 2-0 Seed, Cantrell	12,964
2		28	(h)	Watford	W 1-0 Bliss	47,660
3	Feb	18	(h)	Manchester C	W 2-1 Wilson, Bliss	53,810
4	Mar	4	(a)	Cardiff C	D 1-1 Seed	55,000
R		9	(h)	Cardiff C	W 2-1 Wilson, Dimmock	53,626
SF		25	(n*)	Preston NE	L 1-2 Seed	50,095

*Played at Hillsborough, Sheffield.

Appearances
Goals

London FA Charity Cup

1	Oct	17	(h)	London Cals	W 5-0 Walden 2, Seed, Whitton, Handley	5,000
2		31	(h)	Brentford	D 1-1 Grimsdell	6,600
R	Nov	7	(a)	Brentford	W 3-2 Wilson, Thompson, Dimmock	12,000
SF		14	(n†)	Arsenal	D 0-0*	11,000
R		21	(n‡)	Arsenal	L 1-2§ Clay (pen)	9,028

† Played at Stamford Bridge, London. ‡ Played at Homerton, London.
* Abandoned after 5 minutes of extra-time. § After extra-time.

Appearances
Goals

London Professional Football Charity Fund

	Sep	12	(a)	West Ham U	L 0-1	11,000

Appearances
Goals

Appearances and goals grid (shirt numbers shown per match; bottom rows give total appearances and goals).

Archibald	Banks	Blake	Bliss	Cantrell	Clay	Dimmock	Forster	French	Grimsdell	Handley	Hunter	Jacques	Lindsay	Lorimer	Lowe	McDonald	Pearson	Seed	Skinner	Smith	Thompson	Walden	Walters	Whitton	Wilson	#
	7	10	9		2	11			6			1				3		8	4			5				1
	7		9		2	11			6			1			8	3			4		10	5				2
	7		9		2	11			6			1			8	3			4		10	5				3
	7		9		2	11			6			1			8	3			4		10	5				4
4	7	10	9		2	11			6			1				3		8				5				5
4					2	11			6			1				3		8			10	7	5		9	6
4	7	10			2	11			6			1				3		8					5		9	7
4		10			2	11			6			1				3		8				7	5		9	8
4		10			2	11			6			1				3		8				7	5		9	9
					2	11			6			1				3		8	4		10	7	5		9	10
	9					11	2		6			1				3		8	4		10	7	5			11
					2	11			6			1	9	7		3		8	4		10		5			12
		10			2	11			6			1	9			3		8	4			7	5			13
		10			2	11			6			1	9			3		8	4			7	5			14
		10			2	11			6			1	9			3		8	4			7	5			15
		10			2	11			6			1	9		5	3		8	4			7				16
		10			2	11			6			1	9		5	3		8	4			7				17
		10			2	11			6			1	9		5	3		8	4			7				18
		10	9		2	11			6			1					3	8	4			7	5			19
		10	9		2	11			6			1				3		8	4			7	5			20
		10	9		2	11			6			1			5	3		8	4			7				21
	7					11	2		6			1			5	3		8	4		10				9	22
	7				2	11			6			1			5	3		8	4		10				9	23
		10	9		2	11			6			1			5	3		8	4			7				24
	7	10	9		2	11			6			1			5	3		8	4							25
		10			2	11			6			1				3		8	4			7	5		9	26
		10			2	11			6			1				3		8	4			7	5		9	27
		10			2	11			6			1				3		8	4			7	5		9	28
		10			2	11			6			1				3		8	4			7	5		9	29
					2	11						1				3		8	4	6	10	7	5		9	30
	7					11			6	10		1	8		5	3	2		4						9	31
		10			2	11			6			1			8	3			4			7	5		9	32
		10			2	11						1	7		6	3		8	4				5		9	33
					2	11						1			6	3		8	4		10	7	5		9	34
			1			11	2		6							3		8	4		10	7	5		9	35
			1			11	2		6						8	3			4		10	7	5		9	36
			1	9	2	11			6							3		8	4		10		5			37
			1	9	2	11			6							3		8	4		10	7	5			38
			1	10	2	11										3		8	4	6		7	5		9	39
			1	9	2	11			6							3		8	4		10	7	5			40
			1		2	11										3		8	4	6	10		5		9	41
			1		2	11						7				3		8	4	6	10		5			42
5	**11**	**8**	**23**	**13**	**37**	**42**	**4**		**35**	**1**	**12**	**22**	**16**	**1**	**12**	**40**	**3**	**36**	**16**	**25**	**18**	**28**	**33**		**21**	
1			7	3		8			7				3		3			10			2	6	2		11	

2 own-goals

Archibald	Banks	Blake	Bliss	Cantrell	Clay	Dimmock	Forster	French	Grimsdell	Handley	Hunter	Jacques	Lindsay	Lorimer	Lowe	McDonald	Pearson	Seed	Skinner	Smith	Thompson	Walden	Walters	Whitton	Wilson	#
		10	9		2	11			6			1			5	3		8	4			7				1
		10			2	11			6			1				3		8	4			7	5		9	2
		10			2	11			6			1				3		8	4			7	5		9	3
		10			2	11			6			1				3		8	4			7	5		9	4
		10			2	11			6			1				3		8	4			7	5		9	R
		10			2	11			6			1				3		8	4			7	5		9	SF
		6	1		6	6			6			6			1	6		6	6			6	5		5	
		2	1		1													3							2	

Archibald	Banks	Blake	Bliss	Cantrell	Clay	Dimmock	Forster	French	Grimsdell	Handley	Hunter	Jacques	Lindsay	Lorimer	Lowe	McDonald	Pearson	Seed	Skinner	Smith	Thompson	Walden	Walters	Whitton	Wilson	#
					2	11			6	10		1				3		8	4			7	5	9		1
					2	11			6			1	9	7		3		8	4		10		5			2
					2	11						1		7	6	3		8	4		10		5	9		R
	7	10			2	11			6	1			9			3		8	4				5			SF
4	7	10			2	11			6			1	9			3		6	8				5			R
1	2	2			4	5		1	1	3		2	2	3	2	5		4	5		3	1	5	1	1	
					1	1				1		1				1			1		1	2		1	1	

Archibald	Banks	Blake	Bliss	Cantrell	Clay	Dimmock	Forster	French	Grimsdell	Handley	Hunter	Jacques	Lindsay	Lorimer	Lowe	McDonald	Pearson	Seed	Skinner	Smith	Thompson	Walden	Walters	Whitton	Wilson	#
4	7				2	11	3		6			1						8			10		5		9	
1	1				1	1	1		1			1						1			1		1		1	

1922-23

Manager: Peter McWilliam

1	Aug	26	(h)	Cardiff C	D	1-1	Cantrell	43,168
2	Sep	2	(a)	Cardiff C	W	3-2	Smith, Seed, Bliss	50,000
3		4	(h)	Everton	W	2-0	Seed, Bliss	24,262
4		9	(h)	Burnley	L	1-3	Cantrell	39,434
5		16	(a)	Burnley	W	1-0	Bliss	20,000
6		23	(h)	Arsenal	L	1-2	Lindsay	40,582
7		30	(a)	Arsenal	W	2-0	Dimmock 2	55,000
8	Oct	7	(a)	Aston Villa	L	0-2		50,000
9		14	(h)	Aston Villa	L	1-2	Seed	43,252
10		21	(h)	West Brom A	W	3-1	Skinner, Walden, Brooks	26,188
11		28	(a)	West Brom A	L	1-5	Seed	23,000
12	Nov	4	(h)	Liverpool	L	2-4	Clay (pen), Grimsdell	35,068
13		11	(a)	Liverpool	D	0-0		29,000
14		18	(h)	Newcastle U	L	0-1		30,300
15		25	(a)	Newcastle U	D	1-1	Lindsay	25,000
16	Dec	2	(h)	Nottingham F	W	2-1	Seed, Dimmock	25,252
17		9	(a)	Nottingham F	W	1-0	Seed	15,000
18		16	(a)	Chelsea	D	0-0		50,000
19		23	(h)	Chelsea	W	3-1	Smith, Seed 2	33,068
20		25	(h)	Sheffield U	W	2-1	Cantrell, Handley	45,000
21		26	(a)	Sheffield U	L	0-2		42,000
22		30	(a)	Middlesbrough	L	0-2		8,000
23	Jan	1	(a)	Everton	L	1-3	Lindsay	20,000
24		6	(h)	Middlesbrough	W	2-0	Walden, Handley	35,000
25		20	(a)	Oldham A	W	3-0	Grimsdell, Lindsay, Dimmock	9,000
26		27	(h)	Oldham A	W	3-0	Clay 2 (2 pens), Lindsay	24,843
27	Feb	10	(a)	Blackburn R	L	0-1		6,000
28		14	(h)	Blackburn R	W	2-0	Lindsay 2	10,000
29		17	(h)	Bolton W	L	0-1		30,000
30	Mar	3	(h)	Manchester C	W	3-1	Walden, Seed, Handley	27,963
31		14	(a)	Manchester C	L	0-3		25,000
32		17	(a)	Stoke	D	0-0		30,000
33		24	(h)	Stoke	W	3-1	Lindsay, Handley, Dimmock	20,000
34		30	(h)	Preston NE	D	1-1	Handley	30,865
35		31	(a)	Sunderland	L	0-2		18,000
36	Apr	2	(a)	Preston NE	L	0-2		22,000
37		7	(h)	Sunderland	L	0-1		23,571
38		11	(a)	Bolton W	W	2-0	Cantrell, Dimmock	15,000
39		14	(a)	Birmingham	L	1-2	Lindsay	15,000
40		21	(h)	Birmingham	W	2-0	Lindsay 2	16,335
41		28	(a)	Huddersfield T	L	0-1		15,000
42	May	5	(h)	Huddersfield T	D	0-0		17,000

FINAL LEAGUE POSITION: 12th in Division One

Appearances

Goals

FA Cup

1	Jan	13	(h*)	Worksop T	D	0-0		23,928
R		15	(h)	Worksop T	W	9-0	Seed, Lindsay 4, Handley 3, Dimmock	23,122
2	Feb	3	(h)	Manchester U	W	4-0	Lindsay, Handley 3	38,333
3		24	(a)	Cardiff C	W	3-2	Seed, Lindsay, Handley	54,000
4	Mar	10	(h)	Derby C	L	0-1		50,349

*Played at home by mutual consent

Appearances

Goals

London FA Charity Cup

1	Oct	23	(a)	Arsenal	L	2-3	Handley 2	12,000

Appearances

Goals

London Professional Football Charity Fund

	Oct	2	(h)	West Ham U	W	2-1	Clay (pen), Wilson	7,000

Appearances

Goals

Batting order chart (cell values are batting positions; rightmost column is the match/row number).

Banks	Barnett	Blake	Bliss	Brooks	Brown	Cantrell	Clay	Dimmock	Forster	Grimsdell	Handley	Hartley	Jacques	Lindsay	Lowe	Maddison	McDonald	Pearson	Ross	Seed	Sharp	Skinner	Smith	Thompson	Walden	Walters	Wilson	#
		1		9		2		11		6							3			8			4	10	7	5		1
		1	10	9		2		11		6							3			8			4		7	5		2
		1	10			2		11		6				9			3			8			4		7	5		3
			10	9		2		11		6			1				3			8			4		7	5		4
		1	10	9		2		11		6							3			8			4		7	5		5
		1	10			2		11		6				9			3			8			4		7	5		6
		1	11			2		10		6							3			8			4		7	5	9	7
		1	11			2		10		6							3			8			4		7	5	9	8
		1	11	9		2		10		6							3			8			4		7	5		9
		1	10	11		2		9							8	6		3						4		7	5		10
		1	10	11			2	9		6							3			8			4		7	5		11
		1	10	11			2	9		6							3			8			4		7	5		12
		1	7				2	11	9	10							3			8		6	4			5		13
		1					2	11	9	10							3			8		6	4		7	5		14
		1					2	11	6	10				9			3			8			4		7	5		15
		1					2	11	6	10				9			3			8			4		7	5		16
		1					2	11	6	10				9			3			8			4		7	5		17
		1					2	11	3	6	10			9						8			4		7	5		18
		1					2	11	3	6	10			9						8			4		7	5		19
		1		9			2	11	3	6	10									8			4		7	5		20
7		1					2	11	3		10			9						8		6	4			5		21
		1					2	11	3	6	10			9	5					8			4		7			22
		1					2	11	3	6	10			9	5					8			4		7			23
		1					2	11		6	10			9	5		3			8			4		7			24
		1			3		2	11		6	10			9	5					8			4		7			25
		1					2	11	3	6	10			9	5					8			4		7			26
		1			3		2	11		6	10			9	5					8			4		7			27
		1			3		2	11			10			9	5					8		6	4		7			28
		1			3		2	11			10			9	5					8		6	4		7			29
		1			3		2	11		6	10			9	5					8			4		7			30
		1			3			11		6	10			9	5				2	8			4		7			31
		1			3			11		6	10			9	5				2	8			4		7			32
		1			3			11		6	10			9	5				2	8			4		7			33
		1			3			11		6	10			9	5				2	8			4		7			34
		1			3			11		6				9					2	8		10	4		7	5		35
9		1			3			11		6									2	8		10	4		7	5		36
		1		9	3		2	11		6	10									8			4		7	5		37
	7			9			2	11	3	6	10					1				8			4			5		38
	7			9			2	11	3	6	10					1				8			4			5		39
				9			2	11	3	6	10					1				8			4		7	5		40
							2	11	3	6	10			9		1				8			4		7	5		41
							2	11	3	6	10			9		1				8			4		7	5		42
2	2	36	8	7	12	10	34	42	12	40	30	1	1	34	14	5	17	1	6	36	2	15	32	2	30	29	2	
	3	1			4	3	6			2	5				11					9		1	2		3			

Banks	Barnett	Blake	Bliss	Brooks	Brown	Cantrell	Clay	Dimmock	Forster	Grimsdell	Handley	Hartley	Jacques	Lindsay	Lowe	Maddison	McDonald	Pearson	Ross	Seed	Sharp	Skinner	Smith	Thompson	Walden	Walters	Wilson	#
		1					2	11		6	10			9	5		3			8			4		7			1
		1			3		2	11		6	10			9	5					8			4		7			R
		1			3		2	11		6	10			9	5					8			4		7			2
		1			3		2	11			10			9	5					8		6	4		7			3
		1			3		2	11		6	10			9	5					8			4		7			4
		5			4		4	5		5	5			5	5		1			5		1	5		5			
					1					7				6						2								

Banks	Barnett	Blake	Bliss	Brooks	Brown	Cantrell	Clay	Dimmock	Forster	Grimsdell	Handley	Hartley	Jacques	Lindsay	Lowe	Maddison	McDonald	Pearson	Ross	Seed	Sharp	Skinner	Smith	Thompson	Walden	Walters	Wilson	#
		1					2	9		6	11			7	5		3			8			4		10			1
		1					1	1		1	1			1	1		1			1			1		1			
								2																				

Banks	Barnett	Blake	Bliss	Brooks	Brown	Cantrell	Clay	Dimmock	Forster	Grimsdell	Handley	Hartley	Jacques	Lindsay	Lowe	Maddison	McDonald	Pearson	Ross	Seed	Sharp	Skinner	Smith	Thompson	Walden	Walters	Wilson	#
		1	11				2	10		6				7			3			8			4			5	9	1
		1	1				1	1		1				1			1			1			1			1	1	
								1																			1	

217

1923-24

Manager: Peter McWilliam

1	Aug	25	(h)	Preston NE	W 2-0	Lindsay, Handley	33,405
2		27	(a)	Chelsea	W 1-0	Lindsay	40,000
3	Sep	1	(a)	Preston NE	D 2-2	Handley, Dimmock	16,000
4		3	(h)	Chelsea	L 0-1		31,996
5		8	(h)	Middlesbrough	W 2-1	Lindsay 2	32,772
6		15	(a)	Middlesbrough	W 1-0	Lindsay	25,000
7		22	(h)	Bolton W	D 0-0		35,012
8		29	(a)	Bolton W	L 1-3	Lindsay	25,000
9	Oct	6	(a)	Notts C	D 0-0		19,000
10		13	(h)	Notts C	L 1-3	Elkes	28,503
11		20	(a)	Sunderland	L 0-1		20,000
12		27	(h)	Sunderland	D 1-1	Lindsay	24,840
13	Nov	3	(a)	Nottingham F	D 0-0		18,000
14		10	(h)	Nottingham F	W 3-0	Lindsay, Elkes, Handley	23,831
15		17	(a)	Arsenal	D 1-1	Seed	50,000
16		24	(h)	Arsenal	W 3-0	Lindsay 2, Elkes	31,624
17	Dec	1	(h)	West Brom A	D 0-0		23,048
18		8	(a)	West Brom A	L 1-4	Seed	23,000
19		15	(h)	Blackburn R	W 2-1	Lindsay, Elkes	19,471
20		22	(a)	Blackburn R	W 1-0	Lindsay	15,000
21		25	(h)	Huddersfield T	W 1-0	Lindsay	44,274
22		26	(a)	Huddersfield T	L 1-2	Handley	29,000
23		29	(h)	Birmingham	D 1-1	Lindsay	24,414
24	Jan	1	(a)	Manchester C	L 0-1		24,000
25		5	(a)	Birmingham	L 2-3	Thompson, Elkes	25,000
26		19	(h)	Newcastle U	W 2-0	Poynton, Elkes	25,649
27		26	(a)	Newcastle U	D 2-2	Clay (pen), Osborne	27,000
28	Feb	9	(a)	West Ham U	D 0-0		30,000
29		16	(h)	Cardiff C	D 1-1	Smith	32,478
30	Mar	1	(h)	Sheffield U	L 1-2	Dimmock	25,925
31		8	(a)	Sheffield U	L 2-6	Lindsay, Elkes	25,000
32		15	(a)	Aston Villa	D 0-0		30,000
33		22	(h)	Aston Villa	L 2-3	Lindsay, Elkes	28,771
34		29	(a)	Liverpool	L 0-1		22,000
35	Apr	5	(h)	Liverpool	D 1-1	Grimsdell	22,470
36		7	(a)	Cardiff C	L 1-2	Lindsay	25,000
37		12	(h)	Everton	L 2-5	Walden, Lindsay	14,606
38		19	(a)	Everton	L 2-4	Lindsay, Raitt (og)	20,000
39		21	(h)	Manchester C	W 4-1	Elkes, Lindsay, Hargreaves 2	11,739
40		22	(h)	West Ham U	L 0-1		18,153
41		26	(a)	Burnley	D 2-2	Elkes, Hargreaves	50,000
42	May	3	(h)	Burnley	W 1-0	Elkes	20,000

FINAL LEAGUE POSITION: 15th in Division One

Appearances
Goals

FA Cup

1	Jan	12	(a)	Crystal P	L 0-2		17,000

Appearances
Goals

London FA Charity Cup

1	Oct	22	(a)	Crystal P	D 1-1	Clay (pen)	3,000
R		29	(h)	Crystal P	W 2-1	Sharp, Brooks	7,316
2	Nov	5	(a)	Clapton O	L 0-2		7,000

Appearances
Goals

London Professional Football Charity Fund

	Oct	8	(h)	Clapton O	L 1-3	Dimmock (pen)	6,742

Appearances
Goals

218

This page presents football season appearance-and-goals grids (player line-up numbers by match). Column headers (read vertically) are the player surnames.

Main table — player shirt numbers by match:

Barnett	Blake	Brooks	Brown	Clay	Dimmock	Duffus	Elkes	Forster	Grimsdell	Handley	Hargreaves	Jennings	Knott	Lindsay	Lowe	Maddison	McDonald	Osborne	Poynton	Ross	Sage	Seed	Sharp	Skinner	Smith	Thompson	Walden	Walters	White	#
				2	11			3	6	10				9		1						8	4				7	5		1
				2	11			3	6	10				9		1						8	4				7	5		2
				2	11			3		10				9	6	1						8	4				7	5		3
				2	11			3	6					9		1						8	4	10			7	5		4
				2	11		10	3	6					9		1						8	4				7	5		5
				2	11		10	3	6					9		1						8	4				7	5		6
				2	11		10	3	6					9		1						8	4				7	5		7
				2	11		10	3	6	8				9		1							4				7	5		8
				2	11		10	3	6					9		1						8	4				7	5		9
				2	11		10	3	6							1				9		8	4				7	5		10
	11			2			10	3	6					9		1						8	4				7	5		11
	11			2			10	3	6					9	5	1						8	4	7						12
	11			2			10		3					9	5	1						8	4				7		6	13
				2			10	3	6		11			9	5	1						8	4				7			14
				2			10	3	6		11			9	5	1						8	4				7			15
				2			10	3	6		11			9	5	1						8	4				7			16
				2			10	3	6		11			9	5	1						8	4				7			17
				2			19	3	6		11			9	5	1						8	4				7			18
				2			10	3	6		11			9	5	1						8	4				7			19
				2			10	3	6		11			9	5	1						8	4				7			20
				2			10	3	6		11			9	5	1						8	4				7			21
				2			10	3	6		11			9	5	1							4	8			7			22
				2			10	3			11			9	5	1			6			8	4				7			23
				2	11		10	3		7				9	5	1			6				4	8						24
					11		10	3	6	7				9	5	1				2			4	8						25
				2			10	3			11			9	5	1	8	6					4				7			26
				2			10	3			11			9	5	1	8	6					4				7			27
							10	3			11	9				1	2	8	4								7	5	6	28
				2			10	3			11	9				1	8	6					4				7	5		29
7	1			2	11			3		10				9			8	6					4					5		30
7	1			2	11		10	3				9					8	6					4					5		31
				2	11		10	3						8		1	9	6		5			4	7						32
				2	11		10	3	6					9		1	8			5			4				7			33
				2	11		10		6					9		1	8	3		5			4				7			34
				2	11		10	3	6					9		1	8			5			4				7			35
				2	11		10	3	6					9		1	8			5			4				7			36
				2	11		10	3	6					9	5	1	8						4				7			37
	1		3	2	11		10							9	5		8					6	4				7			38
	1		3	2	11		8					10		9	5							6	4				7			39
	1		3	2	11		8					10		9	5								4				7	6		40
	1			2	11		8					10		9	5			3					4				7	6		41
	1			2	11		8				7	10		9				3				5	4						6	42
2	7	3	3	40	25		37	35	27	22	7			39	22	35	3	12	10	1	7	21	41	7			34	15	5	(tot)
		1	2	11			1	4	3					20			1	1			2		1	1	1		1	1		(gls)

1 own-goal

Sub-table (appearances / goals):

Barnett	Blake	Brooks	Brown	Clay	Dimmock	Duffus	Elkes	Forster	Grimsdell	Handley	Hargreaves	Jennings	Knott	Lindsay	Lowe	Maddison	McDonald	Osborne	Poynton	Ross	Sage	Seed	Sharp	Skinner	Smith	Thompson	Walden	Walters	White	#
				2			10	3	6		11			9	5	1							4	8			7			1
				1			1	1	1		1			1	1	1							1	1			1			

Sub-table (cup ties):

Barnett	Blake	Brooks	Brown	Clay	Dimmock	Duffus	Elkes	Forster	Grimsdell	Handley	Hargreaves	Jennings	Knott	Lindsay	Lowe	Maddison	McDonald	Osborne	Poynton	Ross	Sage	Seed	Sharp	Skinner	Smith	Thompson	Walden	Walters	White	#
	11			2			10	3	6	7						1				9	8		4					5		1
	11			2		9		3	6					8	5	1							4	7	10					R
	11			2					6			9		5		1	3				8		4		10			7		2
	3			3		1	1	2	3	1		1		1	2	3	1			1	2	2	3	1	1	1		1		
	1			1												1														

Sub-table (charity / other):

Barnett	Blake	Brooks	Brown	Clay	Dimmock	Duffus	Elkes	Forster	Grimsdell	Handley	Hargreaves	Jennings	Knott	Lindsay	Lowe	Maddison	McDonald	Osborne	Poynton	Ross	Sage	Seed	Sharp	Skinner	Smith	Thompson	Walden	Walters	White	#
					11		9	3	6	10						1				2		8	4				7	5		1
					1		1	1	1	1						1				1		1	1				1	1		
					1																									

1924-25

Manager: Peter McWilliam

1	Aug	30	(h)	Bolton W	W 3-0 Clay (pen), Lindsay, Hargreaves	42,000
2	Sep	3	(a)	Birmingham	W 2-0 Seed, Dimmock	20,000
3		6	(a)	Notts C	D 0-0	20,000
4		8	(a)	West Brom A	L 0-2	17,000
5		13	(h)	Everton	D 0-0	35,039
6		20	(a)	Sunderland	L 1-4 Lindsay	30,000
7		22	(h)	West Brom A	L 0-1	16,281
8		27	(h)	Cardiff C	D 1-1 Elkes	38,324
9	Oct	4	(a)	Preston NE	W 3-0 Seed 2, Dimmock	20,000
10		11	(h)	Burnley	D 1-1 Handley	23,508
11		18	(a)	Leeds U	L 0-1	25,000
12		25	(a)	Arsenal	L 0-1	51,000
13	Nov	1	(h)	Aston Villa	L 1-3 Handley	19,054
14		8	(a)	Huddersfield T	W 2-1 Thompson, Seed	18,000
15		10	(h)	Manchester C	D 1-1 Smith	10,781
16		15	(h)	Blackburn R	W 5-0 Seed 2, Elkes 3	30,000
17		22	(a)	West Ham U	D 1-1 Elkes	30,000
18		29	(h)	Sheffield U	W 4-1 Seed, Hargreaves, Elkes, Handley	24,483
19	Dec	6	(a)	Newcastle U	D 1-1 Elkes	28,000
20		13	(h)	Liverpool	D 1-1 Hargreaves	25,604
21		20	(a)	Nottingham F	L 0-1	15,000
22		25	(h)	Bury	D 1-1 Elkes (pen)	35,716
23		27	(a)	Bolton W	L 0-3	18,000
24	Jan	1	(a)	Bury	L 2-5 Seed 2	18,000
25		3	(h)	Notts C	D 1-1 Elkes	23,933
26		17	(a)	Everton	L 0-1	30,000
27		24	(h)	Sunderland	W 1-0 Seed	26,696
28	Feb	7	(h)	Preston NE	W 2-0 Seed, Lane	35,000
29		14	(a)	Burnley	W 4-1 Clay (pen), Thompson, Seed, Lane	18,000
30		28	(h)	Arsenal	W 2-0 Elkes, Dimmock	29,457
31	Mar	7	(a)	Aston Villa	W 1-0 Lane	25,000
32		9	(h)	Leeds U	W 2-1 Seed, Lane	8,000
33		14	(h)	Huddersfield T	L 1-2 Lane	35,000
34		18	(a)	Cardiff C	W 2-0 Seed 2	31,126
35		21	(a)	Blackburn R	D 1-1 Thompson	15,000
36		28	(h)	West Ham U	D 1-1 Seed	29,321
37	Apr	4	(a)	Sheffield U	L 0-2	20,000
38		10	(h)	Birmingham	L 0-1	30,411
39		11	(h)	Newcastle U	W 3-0 Lane, Dimmock 2	23,144
40		18	(a)	Liverpool	L 0-1	12,000
41		25	(a)	Nottingham F	L 1-0 Seed	20,000
42	May	2	(a)	Manchester C	L 0-1	10,000

FINAL LEAGUE POSITION: 12th in Division One

Appearances
Goals

FA Cup

1	Jan	10	(h)	Northampton T	W 3-0 Seed, Lindsay, Elkes	32,718
2		31	(h)	Bolton W	D 1-1 Seed	52,635
R	Feb	4	(a)	Bolton W	W 1-0 Lane	51,774
3		21	(h)	Blackburn R	D 2-2 Lane, Dimmock	54,521
R		26	(a)	Blackburn R	L 1-3 Dimmock	48,000

Appearances
Goals

London FA Charity Cup

1	Oct	27	(h)	Fulham	W 5-1 Osborne, Hargreaves, Elkes 3	3,559
2	Nov	17	(h)	Kingstonians	W 5-0 Skitt, Osborne, Seed, Hargreaves, Elkes	
SF		24	(n*)	Clapton O	L 1-2 Hargreaves	

*Played at Arsenal Stadium, Highbury, London

Appearances
Goals

London Professional Football Charity Fund

Nov	3	(a)	Clapton O†	L 1-2 Hargreaves (pen)	2,300

†Abandoned after 20 minutes of extra-time — bad light — result stood.

Appearances
Goals

Clay	Dimmock	Elkes	Forster	Grimsdell	Handley	Hargreaves	Hinton	Lane	Lindsay	Lowe	McDonald	Osborne	Poynton	Sage	Seed	Sharp	Skinner	Skitt	Smith	Thompson	Walters	White	
2	11	5			10		1	9				7	3		8				4		6		1
2	11	5			10		1	9				7	3		8				4		6		2
2	11	5			10		1	9			3	7			8		6		4				3
2	11	5			10		1	9			3	7			8		6		4				4
2	11	5			10		1	9				7	3		8		6		4				5
2	11	5			10		1	9				7	3		8		6		4				6
2	11	5					1	9				7	3		8	10	6		4				7
2	11	10	6				1	9	5		3	7			8				4				8
2	11	10					1	9	5			7	3		8		6		4				9
2	11			10			1	9	5			7	3		8		6		4				10
	11	10	2				1	9	5			7	3		8				4			6	11
	11	10	2				1	9	5			7	3		8				4			6	12
		10	2		11	9	1					7	3		8		6	5	4				13
		10	2		11	9	1						3		8		6	4	7	5			14
		10	2		11	9	1						3		8		6	4	7	5			15
		10			11	9	1			2		7	3		8		6	5	4				16
		10	2		11	9	1					7	3		8		6	5	4				17
		10	2		11	9	1				3	7			8		6	5	4				18
		10	2		11	9	1				3	7			8		6	5	4				19
		10	2		11	9	1				3	7			8		6	5	4				20
2		10	3		11		1	9				7			8		6	5	4				21
		10	2		11		1	9				7	3		8		6	5	4				22
	11	10	2				1	9				7	3		8		6	5	4				23
	11	10	2				1	9				7	3		8		6	5	4				24
		10	2				1	9				7	3		8		6	5	4	11			25
		10	2				1	9				7	3		8		6	5	4	11			26
		10	2		7		1	9					3		8		6	5	4	11			27
2	11	10					1	9			3				8		5		4	7		6	28
2	11	10	6				1	9			3				8		4	5		7			29
	11	10	2				1	9			3				8		6	5	4	7			30
2	11	10	6				1	9			3				8		5		4	7			31
	11	10	2	6			1	9	5		3				8				4	7			32
	11		2	6	10		1	9			3				8		5		4	7			33
2	11		6		10		1	9			3				8		4	5		7			34
2	11	10	6				1	9			3				8		4	5		7			35
2	11	10	6				1	9			3				8		4	5		7			36
2	11		3		10		1	9							8		6	5	4	7			37
2	11		3		10		1	9							8		6	5	4	7			38
	11		2	3	10		1	9							8		6	5	4	7			39
2	11		3		10		1	9							8		6	5	4	7			40
2	11		3		10		1	9							8		6	5	4	7			41
	11		2	3	10		1	9							8		6	5	4	7			42
21	29	33	21	14	14	20	42	17	18	6	12	23	24	1	41	1	34	27	37	20	2	5	
2	5	10			3	3		6	2				17					1	3				

Clay	Dimmock	Elkes	Forster	Grimsdell	Handley	Hargreaves	Hinton	Lane	Lindsay	Lowe	McDonald	Osborne	Poynton	Sage	Seed	Sharp	Skinner	Skitt	Smith	Thompson	Walters	White	
		10	2				1	9				7	3		8		6	5	4	11			1
2	11	10	6				1	9			3	7			8		4	5					2
2	11	10	6				1	9			3				8		5		4	7			R
2	11	10	6				1	9			3				8		4	5		7			3
2	11	10	6				1	9			3				8		4	5		7			R
4	4	5	1		4		5	4	1		4	2	1		5		4	5	2	4			
	2	1					2	1							2								

Clay	Dimmock	Elkes	Forster	Grimsdell	Handley	Hargreaves	Hinton	Lane	Lindsay	Lowe	McDonald	Osborne	Poynton	Sage	Seed	Sharp	Skinner	Skitt	Smith	Thompson	Walters	White	
		10	2		11	9	1					7	3		8		6	5	4				1
		10			11	9	1			2		7	3		8		6	5	4				2
			2		11	10	1	9				7	3				6	5	4	8			SF
	2	2			3	3	3	1		1	3	3	2		3		3	3	1				
	4				3						2		1		1								

Clay	Dimmock	Elkes	Forster	Grimsdell	Handley	Hargreaves	Hinton	Lane	Lindsay	Lowe	McDonald	Osborne	Poynton	Sage	Seed	Sharp	Skinner	Skitt	Smith	Thompson	Walters	White	
		10	2		11	9	1		5				3		8		6		4	7			1
	1	1			1	1	1				1		1		1		1		1	1			
					1																		

221

1925-26

Manager: Peter McWilliam

#	Month	Date		Opponent	Result		Scorers	Attendance
1	Aug	29	(a)	Arsenal	W	1-0	Dimmock	53,183
2		31	(a)	Sheffield U	W	3-2	Osborne 2, Hargreaves	18,743
3	Sep	5	(h)	Manchester C	W	1-0	Seed	35,594
4		7	(h)	Sheffield U	W	3-2	Seed 2, Dimmock	21,978
5		12	(a)	Everton	D	1-1	Dimmock	37,506
6		14	(h)	Cardiff C	L	1-2	Elkes	26,716
7		19	(h)	Huddersfield T	D	5-5	Clay (pen), Osborne, Elkes 2, Dimmock	20,880
8		21	(a)	Cardiff C	W	1-0	Dimmock	20,698
9		26	(a)	Sunderland	L	0-3		30,700
10	Oct	3	(h)	Blackburn R	W	4-2	Thompson, Osborne 2, Dimmock	35,645
11		10	(a)	Bury	L	0-3		19,759
12		17	(a)	Manchester U	D	0-0		26,496
13		24	(h)	Liverpool	W	3-1	Osborne 3	29,952
14		31	(a)	Leicester C	L	3-5	Osborne 3	28,076
15	Nov	7	(h)	West Ham U	W	4-2	Osborne 3, Elkes	35,259
16		14	(a)	Newcastle U	L	1-3	Seed	23,391
17		21	(h)	Bolton W	L	2-3	Osborne, Elkes	26,792
18		28	(a)	Notts C	L	2-4	Elkes, Dimmock	12,191
19	Dec	5	(h)	Aston Villa	D	2-2	Osborne, Elkes	28,821
20		12	(a)	Burnley	W	2-1	Osborne, Dimmock	18,592
21		19	(h)	Leeds U	W	3-2	Thompson, Osborne, Elkes	19,200
22		25	(a)	Birmingham	L	1-3	Clay (pen)	29,586
23		26	(h)	Birmingham	W	2-1	Seed, Osborne	44,429
24	Jan	2	(h)	Arsenal	D	1-1	Thompson	43,221
25		16	(a)	Manchester C	D	0-0		25,244
26		23	(h)	Everton	D	1-1	Thompson	22,805
27	Feb	6	(h)	Sunderland	L	0-2		31,434
28		13	(a)	Blackburn R	L	2-4	Osborne, Dimmock	21,584
29		20	(h)	Bury	W	4-2	Lindsay 2, Osborne 2	33,023
30		27	(h)	Manchester U	L	0-1		25,466
31	Mar	3	(a)	Huddersfield T	L	1-2	Elkes	13,005
32		6	(a)	Liverpool	D	0-0		26,355
33		13	(h)	Leicester C	L	1-3	Osborne	23,911
34		20	(a)	West Ham U	L	1-3	Osborne	29,423
35		25	(h)	Newcastle U	W	1-0	Dimmock	11,774
36	Apr	2	(h)	West Brom A	W	3-2	Seed, Dimmock 2	27,914
37		3	(a)	Bolton W	D	1-1	Osborne	21,364
38		5	(a)	West Brom A	L	0-1		15,365
39		10	(h)	Notts C	W	4-0	Roe, Elkes, Dimmock 2	17,892
40		17	(a)	Aston Villa	L	0-3		11,774
41		24	(h)	Burnley	L	0-2		21,211
42	May	1	(a)	Leeds U	L	1-4	Elkes	16,158

FINAL LEAGUE POSITION: 15th in Division One

Appearances
Goals

FA Cup

#	Month	Date		Opponent	Result		Scorers	Attendance
1	Jan	9	(h)	West Ham U	W	5-0	Osborne 2, Dimmock 3	49,800
2		30	(h)	Manchester U	D	2-2	Thompson, Lindsay	43,653
R	Feb	3	(a)	Manchester U	L	0-2		46,929

Appearances
Goals

London FA Charity Cup

#	Month	Date		Opponent	Result		Scorers	Attendance
1	Sep	15	(h)	Brentford	L	1-2	Handley	1,980

Appearances
Goals

London Professional Football Charity Fund

	Month	Date		Opponent	Result		Scorers	Attendance
	Nov	16	(h)	Queen's Park R	W	1-0	Thompson	1,396

Appearances
Goals

222

Bann	Brittan	Clay	Dimmock	Elkes	Forster	Grimsdell	Handley	Hargreaves	Hinton	Kaine	Knott	Lane	Lindsay	Lowe	Osborne	Poynton	Roe	Sage	Seed	Skinner	Skitt	Smith B	Smith J	Thompson	Walters	White	
		2	11		3	6	10		1				9						8	4	5			7			1
		2	11		3	6		10	1				9		7				8	4	5						2
		2	11	10	3	6			1				9		7				8		5	4					3
		2	11	10	3	6			1				9		7				8		4				5		4
		2	11	10	3	6			1				9	5	7				8			4					5
		2	11	10	3	6			1				9	5	7				8			4					6
		2	11	10	3	6			1				9		7				8	4		5					7
		2	11	10	3	6			1			9			7			5				4		8			8
		2	11	10	3	6			1			9			7				8	4	5						9
		2	11	10	3	6			1						9					4	5	8		7			10
		2	11	10	3					1					9			5	8	6		4		7			11
		2	11	10	3	6				1					9			5	8			4		7			12
		2	11	10	3	6			1						9				8		5	4		7			13
		2	11	10	3	6									9				8		5	4	1	7			14
		2	11	10	3											9			8	6	5	4	1	7			15
		2	11	10	3										9				8	6	5	4	1	7			16
		2	11	10	3										9				8	6	5	4	1	7			17
		2	11	10	3					1					9				8	6	5	4		7			18
		2	11	10	3					1					9				8	6	5	4		7			19
		2	11	10	3					1					9				8	6	5	4		7			20
		2	11	10	3					1					9				8	6	5	4		7			21
		2	11		3					1			10		9			4	8		5	6		7			22
		2			3			10		1			11		9				8	6	5	4		7			23
		2	11	10	3					1			8		9					6	5	4		7			24
		2	11	10	3					1			8		9						5	4		7		6	25
		2	11	10	3					1			9						8		5	4		7		6	26
		2	11		3			10	1				8		9						5	4		7		6	27
		2	11		3			10	1				8		9						5	4		7		6	28
		2	11		3			10	1				8		9						5	4		7		6	29
		2	11		3			19	1				8		9						5	4		7		6	30
		2		10	3			11							9				8		5	4	1	7		6	31
		2	11	10	3										9				8		5	4	1	7		6	32
		2	11	10	3										9				8		5	4	1	7		6	33
	1	2	11	10	3							8			9						5	4		7		6	34
2	1		11	10	3								6		9				8		5	4		7			35
2	1		11	10	3								6		9				8		5	4		7			36
2	1		11		3								6		9		8		10		5	4		7			37
2	1		11	10	3								6		9				8		5	4		7			38
2	1		11	10	3								6		9		8				5	4		7			39
2	1		11		3								6		9		8		10		5	4		7			40
2	1		11	10	3								6		9				8		5	4		7			41
2	1		11	8	3		10					9	6								5	4		7			42
8	9	34	40	32	42	13	2	7	15	11		4	24	2	39		3	4	31	15	36	38	7	35	1	10	
		2	14	11				1					2		25		1		6			3		4			

Bann	Brittan	Clay	Dimmock	Elkes	Forster	Grimsdell	Handley	Hargreaves	Hinton	Kaine	Knott	Lane	Lindsay	Lowe	Osborne	Poynton	Roe	Sage	Seed	Skinner	Skitt	Smith B	Smith J	Thompson	Walters	White	
		2	11	10	3					1			8		9					6	5	4		7			1
		2	11	10	3				1				9						8		5	4		7		6	2
		2	11	10	3				1				9						8		5	4		7		6	R
		3	3	3	3				2	1			3		1				2	1	3	3		3		2	
			3										1		2									1			

Bann	Brittan	Clay	Dimmock	Elkes	Forster	Grimsdell	Handley	Hargreaves	Hinton	Kaine	Knott	Lane	Lindsay	Lowe	Osborne	Poynton	Roe	Sage	Seed	Skinner	Skitt	Smith B	Smith J	Thompson	Walters	White	
2			11		3		10		1		8	9				5						4		7		6	1
1			1		1		1		1		1	1				1						1		1		1	
							1																				

Bann	Brittan	Clay	Dimmock	Elkes	Forster	Grimsdell	Handley	Hargreaves	Hinton	Kaine	Knott	Lane	Lindsay	Lowe	Osborne	Poynton	Roe	Sage	Seed	Skinner	Skitt	Smith B	Smith J	Thompson	Walters	White
		2	11	10	3										9				8	6	5	4	1	7		
		1	1	1	1										1				1	1	1	1	1	1		
																								1		

1926-27

Manager: Peter McWilliam until February then Billy Minter

1	Aug	28	(h)	Everton	W 2-1	Blair, Osborne	28,324
2		30	(h)	Sheffield W	W 7-3	Elkes 2, Thompson, Blair, Osborne, Seed, Dimmock	19,726
3	Sep	4	(a)	Blackburn R	L 0-1		21,964
4		6	(h)	Leicester C	D 2-2	Dimmock 2	19,461
5		11	(h)	Huddersfield T	D 3-3	Thompson, Blair 2	29,516
6		13	(a)	Leicester C	D 2-2	Lane, Dimmock	24,928
7		18	(a)	Sunderland	L 2-3	Blair 2	17,459
8		25	(h)	West Brom A	W 3-0	Blair, Osborne, Seed	31,236
9	Oct	2	(a)	Bury	D 0-0		16,581
10		9	(h)	Birmingham	W 6-1	Blair 2, Roe 2, Seed, Dimmock	29,392
11		16	(h)	Sheffield U	W 3-1	Osborne 2, Seed	29,656
12		23	(a)	Derby C	L 1-4	Handley	20,325
13		30	(h)	Bolton W	W 1-0	Handley	29,999
14	Nov	6	(a)	Aston Villa	W 3-2	Seed 2, Dimmock	19,496
15		13	(h)	Cardiff C	W 4-1	Osborne 2, Handley, Dimmock	15,350
16		20	(a)	Burnley	L 0-5		17,957
17		27	(h)	Newcastle U	L 1-3	Dimmock	33,325
18	Dec	4	(a)	Leeds U	D 1-1	Dimmock	24,470
19		11	(h)	Liverpool	L 1-2	Blair	26,640
20		18	(a)	Arsenal	W 4-2	Seed, Osborne 2, Handley	49,429
21		25	(h)	Manchester U	D 1-1	Dimmock	37,287
22		27	(a)	Manchester U	L 1-2	Handley	50,665
23		28	(a)	Sheffield W	L 1-3	Dimmock	35,529
24	Jan	15	(a)	Everton	W 2-1	Blair, Dimmock	35,986
25		22	(h)	Blackburn R	D 1-1	Handley	14,323
26		29	(a)	Huddersfield T	L 0-2		15,147
27	Feb	5	(h)	Sunderland	L 0-2		32,506
28		12	(a)	West Brom A	L 0-5		15,388
29		19	(h)	Bury	W 1-0	Dimmock (pen)	19,759
30		26	(a)	Birmingham	L 0-1		21,145
31	Mar	5	(a)	Sheffield U	D 3-3	O'Callaghan 2, Sanders	21,732
32		12	(h)	Derby C	W 3-2	O'Callaghan, Roe, Dimmock	26,556
33		19	(a)	Bolton W	D 2-2	Sanders, Dimmock	17,762
34		26	(h)	Aston Villa	L 0-1		30,614
35	Apr	2	(a)	Cardiff C	W 2-1	O'Callaghan, Handley	13,384
36		9	(h)	Burnley	W 4-1	O'Callaghan, Sanders 2, Dimmock	15,481
37		15	(h)	West Ham U	L 1-3	Handley	42,010
38		16	(a)	Newcastle U	L 2-3	Sanders, Dimmock	32,151
39		18	(a)	West Ham U	W 2-1	Handley, Dimmock	21,354
40		23	(h)	Leeds U	W 4-1	Sanders 2, Handley, Dimmock (pen)	17,745
41		30	(a)	Liverpool	L 0-1		15,756
42	May	7	(h)	Arsenal	L 0-4		29,555

FINAL LEAGUE POSITION: 13th in Division One

Appearances

Goals

FA Cup

3	Jan	8	(a)	West Ham U	L 2-3	Handley, Dimmock	44,417

Appearances

Goals

London FA Charity Cup

1	Sep	27	(a)	Millwall	L 2-5	Lane, Seed	2,837

Appearances

Goals

London Professional Football Charity Fund

	Nov	8	(a)	Clapton O	W 3-1	Thompson, Roe, Dimmock	864

Appearances

Goals

Appearance grid (numbers indicate shirt number worn in each match; right-hand column is the match number).

Bann	Barnett	Bellamy	Blair	Brittan	Clay	Dimmock	Elkes	Forster	Grimsdell	Handley	Lane	Lindsay	Lowe	Nicholls	O'Callaghan	Osborne	Poynton	Richardson	Roe	Sanders	Seed	Skitt	Smith B	Smith J	Thompson	#
		8			11	5	2				6				9	3				10		4	1	7		1
		8			11	5	2				6				9	3				10		4	1	7		2
		8			11	5	2				6				9	3				10		4	1	7		3
		8			11	5	2		10						9	3				6		4	1	7		4
		8			11	5	2				6				9	3				10		4	1	7		5
		8			11	5	2				6				9	3				10		4	1	7		6
		8			11	5	2				6				9	3				10		4	1	7		7
		8			11	5	2				6				9	3				10		4	1	7		8
		8			11	5	3				6				9	2				10		4	1	7		9
		8		2	11	5					6					3			9	10		4	1	7		10
		8		2	11	5					6				9	3				10		4	1	7		11
				2	11	5			10		6				9	3				8		4	1	7		12
				2	11	5			8		6				9	3				10		4	1	7		13
		8		2	11	5					6				9	3				10		4	1	7		14
				2	11	5			10		6				9	3				8		4	1	7		15
		8		2	11	5					6				9	3				10		4	1	7		16
		8		2	11	5	3								9					10	6	4	1	7		17
		8		2	11	5	3								9					10	6	4	1	7		18
		8		2	11	5	3				6				9					10		4	1	7		19
				2	11	5	3		10		6				9					8		4	1	7		20
				2	11	5	3		10		6				9					8		4	1	7		21
				2	11	5	3		10		6				9					8		4	1	7		22
		9			11	5	2		10		6					3				8		4	1	7		23
		9	1		11	5	2		10		6			8		3						4		7		24
		8	1	2	11	5	3		10		6				9							4		7		25
		8	1	2	11	5	3		10		6				9							4		7		26
		8	1	2	11	5	3		10		6				9							4		7		27
7		8	1		11	5	2		10		6				9	3						4				28
		8	1		11	5	2		10		6				7	3			9			4				29
			1		11	5	2		10		6			8	7	3			9			4				30
			1		11	5	2		10		6			8	7	3			9			4				31
			1		11	5	2				6			8	7	3			9	10		4				32
			1		11		2			5	6			8	7	3			9	10		4				33
			1		11	5	2				6			8	7	3			9	10		4				34
			1		11	5	2		10		6			8	7	3			9			4				35
			1		11	5	2		10		6			8	7	3			9			4				36
			1		11	5	2		10		6			8	7	3			9			4				37
			1		11	5	2		10		6			8	7			3	9			4				38
		9	1		11		2		10		6			8	7			3			5	4				39
			1		11	5	2		10		6			8	7	3			9			4				40
	11					5	2		10		6	1		8	7	3			9			4				41
			1		11	5	2		10		6			8	7	3			9			4				42
1	1	24	18	16	41	40	35	2	24	4	37	1	1	13	34	31	2	3	12	23	22	24	23	30		
		11			19	2			10	1					5	9			3	7	7				2		

Bann	Barnett	Bellamy	Blair	Brittan	Clay	Dimmock	Elkes	Forster	Grimsdell	Handley	Lane	Lindsay	Lowe	Nicholls	O'Callaghan	Osborne	Poynton	Richardson	Roe	Sanders	Seed	Skitt	Smith B	Smith J	Thompson	
		9		2	11	5			10		6				3				8		4	1	7		3	
		1	1	1	1				1		1				1				1		1	1	1			
				1					1																	

Bann	Barnett	Bellamy	Blair	Brittan	Clay	Dimmock	Elkes	Forster	Grimsdell	Handley	Lane	Lindsay	Lowe	Nicholls	O'Callaghan	Osborne	Poynton	Richardson	Roe	Sanders	Seed	Skitt	Smith B	Smith J	Thompson	
	11			2	6		8				3			9	10	5			4	1	7				1	
	1			1	1		1				1			1	1	1	1	1	1							
				1																						

Bann	Barnett	Bellamy	Blair	Brittan	Clay	Dimmock	Elkes	Forster	Grimsdell	Handley	Lane	Lindsay	Lowe	Nicholls	O'Callaghan	Osborne	Poynton	Richardson	Roe	Sanders	Seed	Skitt	Smith B	Smith J	Thompson	
2		8			11				10		6				3	9			5	4	1	7				
1		1			1				1		1				1	1			1	1	1	1				
					1											1						1				

1927-28

Manager: Billy Minter

1	Aug	27	(h)	Birmingham	W	1-0	O'Callaghan	37,40
2		31	(a)	Middlesbrough	L	1-3	Dimmock (pen)	29,11
3	Sep	3	(a)	Newcastle U	L	1-4	O'Callaghan	41,03
4		10	(h)	Huddersfield	D	2-2	Lindsay (pen), Dimmock	27,98
5		12	(h)	Middlesbrough	W	4-2	Blair 3, Dimmock (pen)	19,21
6		17	(a)	Portsmouth	L	0-3		26,11
7		22	(h)	Leicester C	W	2-1	Osborne, Blair	9,43
8		24	(a)	Manchester U	L	0-3		13,95
9	Oct	1	(h)	Everton	L	1-3	Townley	7,71
10		8	(a)	Cardiff C	L	1-2	Townley	21,81
11		15	(h)	Blackburn R	D	1-1	Osborne	23,02
12		22	(h)	Sunderland	W	3-1	Osborne, Dimmock 2	19,03
13		29	(a)	Derby C	D	1-1	Grimsdell	15,96
14	Nov	5	(h)	West Ham U	W	5-3	Handley, O'Callaghan 2, Osborne, Elkes	35,09
15		12	(a)	Aston Villa	W	2-1	Osborne 2	30,75
16		19	(h)	Sheffield U	D	2-2	Osborne, Elkes	19,14
17	Dec	3	(h)	Burnley	W	5-0	Handley, O'Callaghan, Osborne 2, Dimmock	20,40
18		10	(a)	Bury	W	2-1	O'Callaghan 2	12,20
19		17	(h)	Liverpool	W	3-1	Osborne, Elkes 2	21,23
20		24	(a)	Leicester C	L	1-6	Handley	19,98
21		26	(a)	Bolton W	L	1-4	Elkes	25,22
22		31	(a)	Birmingham	L	2-3	O'Callaghan, Womack (og)	11,60
23	Jan	2	(a)	Arsenal	D	1-1	O'Callaghan	13,51
24		7	(h)	Newcastle U	W	5-2	Osborne 4, Dimmock	34,73
25		21	(a)	Huddersfield T	L	2-4	O'Callaghan, Osborne	17,89
26	Feb	4	(h)	Manchester U	W	4-0	O'Callaghan, Armstrong 2, Dimmock	23,54
27		6	(h)	Bolton W	L	1-2	Armstrong	18,18
28		11	(a)	Everton	W	5-3	O'Callaghan 4, Dimmock	29,14
29		25	(a)	Blackburn R	L	1-2	O'Callaghan	20,89
30	Mar	5	(h)	Cardiff C	W	1-0	Dimmock	15,55
31		10	(h)	Derby C	L	1-2	Armstrong	22,45
32		17	(a)	West Ham U	D	1-1	Osborne	33,90
33		19	(h)	Portsmouth	L	0-3		12,82
34		24	(h)	Aston Villa	W	2-1	Grimsdell (pen), Lindsay	21,53
35		28	(a)	Sunderland	D	0-0		9,24
36		31	(a)	Sheffield U	L	1-3	Handley	17,49
37	Apr	6	(h)	Sheffield W	L	1-3	Lindsay	26,43
38		7	(h)	Arsenal	W	2-0	O'Callaghan 2	39,19
39		10	(a)	Sheffield W	L	2-4	O'Callaghan, Osborne	15,90
40		14	(a)	Burnley	D	2-2	Osborne, Dimmock	10,90
41		21	(h)	Bury	L	1-4	Lindsay	15,61
42		28	(a)	Liverpool	L	0-2		31,78

FINAL LEAGUE POSITION: 21st in Division One

Appearances
Goals

FA Cup

3	Jan	14	(a)	Bristol C	W	2-1	O'Callaghan, Osborne	36,26
4		28	(h)	Oldham A	W	3-0	Handley, O'Callaghan, Dimmock	36,82
5	Feb	18	(a)	Leicester C	W	3-0	O'Callaghan 2, Dimmock	47,29
6	Mar	3	(a)	Huddersfield T	L	1-6	O'Callaghan	52,39

Appearances
Goals

London FA Charity Cup

1	Oct	17	(a)	Fulham	L	2-6	O'Callaghan, Dimmock (pen)	

Appearances
Goals

London Professional Football Charity Fund

	Nov	7	(h)	Clapton O	W	4-3	O'Callaghan 3, Townley	

Appearances
Goals

Armstrong	Austin	Barnett	Bellamy	Blair	Brittan	Clay	Dimmock	Elkes	Evans	Forster	Grimsdell	Handley	Hartley	Helliwell	Lindsay	Lowdell	Nicholls	O'Callaghan	Osborne	Poynton	Richardson	Sanders	Skitt	Smith	Spiers	Thompson	Townley	No.
							11	10	9	2	6					4	1	8	7	3			5					1
							11	10	9	2	6					4	1	8	7	3			5					2
		7	11					10	9	2	6					4	1	8				3	5					3
				9	1		11	10		2	6	7				4		8		3			5					4
				9	1		11	10		2	6							8	7	3			5	4				5
				9	1		11	10		2	6							8	7	3			5	4				6
				9	1		11	10		2	6							8	7	3			5	4				7
			11	9	1			10		2	6			5				8	7	3				4				8
			11		1					2	6							8	7	3	9		5	4			10	9
			11		1			9		2	6					4		8	7	3			5				10	10
					1	2	11	9			6	10				4		8	7	3			5					11
					1	2	11	10			6	7				4		8	9	3			5					12
					1	2	11	10			6	7				4		8	9	3			5					13
					1	2	11	10			6	7				4		8	9	3			5					14
					1	2	11	10			6	7				4		8	9	3			5					15
					1	2	11	10			6	7				4		8	9	3			5					16
						2	11	10			6	7				4		8	9	3			5		1			17
						2	11	10			6	7				4		8	9	3			5		1			18
						2	11	10			6	7				4		8	9	3			5		1			19
						2	11	10			6	7				4		8	9	3			5		1			20
						2	11	10		3	6	7				4		8	9				5		1			21
10	9					2	11			3	6	7				4		8					5		1			22
10						2	11				6	7			9	4		8		3			5		1			23
10						2	11				6	7				4		8	9	3			5		1			24
						2	11	10		3	6					4		8	9				5		1	7		25
10						2	11			3	6	7				4		8	9				5		1			26
9						2	11	10			6	7				4		8		3			5		1			27
10						2	11				6	7			9	4		8		3			5		1			28
10						2	11				6	7				4		8	9	3			5		1			29
10						2	11			3	6	7				4		8	9	5					1			30
10						2	11			3	6	7				4		8	9	5					1			31
						2	11				6	10			7	4		8	9	3			5		1			32
9						2	11				6	10			7	4		8		3			5		1			33
		7				2	11				6	10			9	4		8		3			5		1			34
		7				2	11				6	10			9	4		8		3			5		1			35
		7				2	11				6	10			9	4		8		3			5		1			36
		7				2	11				6				9	4		8	10	3			5		1			37
						2	11				6	7			10			8	9	3			5	4	1			38
						2	11				6	7			10			8	9	3			5	4	1			39
						2	11				6			5				8	9	3				4	1	7	10	40
						2	11				6				10	4		8	9	3			5		1	7		41
10						2	11				6				9	4		8		3			5		1	7		42
11	1	5	4	5	13	16	38	22	3	32	35	26	2	2	19	34	3	42	31	14	24	1	38	8	26	4	3	
4				4			11	5		2	4				4			19	18				2					

Armstrong	Austin	Barnett	Bellamy	Blair	Brittan	Clay	Dimmock	Elkes	Evans	Forster	Grimsdell	Handley	Hartley	Helliwell	Lindsay	Lowdell	Nicholls	O'Callaghan	Osborne	Poynton	Richardson	Sanders	Skitt	Smith	Spiers	Thompson	Townley	No.
10							11				6	7				4		8	9	3			5		1			3
10						2	11				6	7			3	4		8	9				5		1			4
10						2	11				6	7			9	4		8		3			5		1			5
10						2	11				6	7				4		8	9	3			5		1			6
4						3	4				4	4			2	4		4	3	3			4		4			
						2						1						5	1									

Armstrong	Austin	Barnett	Bellamy	Blair	Brittan	Clay	Dimmock	Elkes	Evans	Forster	Grimsdell	Handley	Hartley	Helliwell	Lindsay	Lowdell	Nicholls	O'Callaghan	Osborne	Poynton	Richardson	Sanders	Skitt	Smith	Spiers	Thompson	Townley	No.
					1	2	11	9	7		6	10						8		3			5	4				1
					1	1	1	1	1		1	1						1		1			1	1				
						1												1										

Armstrong	Austin	Barnett	Bellamy	Blair	Brittan	Clay	Dimmock	Elkes	Evans	Forster	Grimsdell	Handley	Hartley	Helliwell	Lindsay	Lowdell	Nicholls	O'Callaghan	Osborne	Poynton	Richardson	Sanders	Skitt	Smith	Spiers	Thompson	Townley	No.
9					1		11			2	6	7				4		8		5	3						10	1
1					1		1			1	1	1				1		1		1	1						1	
																		3									1	

227

1928-29

Manager: Billy Minter

1	Aug	25	(h)	Oldham A	W	4-1	Elkes, Roberts 2, Osborne	33,173
2		27	(h)	Middlesbrough	L	2-5	Osborne, Dimmock	23,990
3	Sep	1	(a)	Southampton	D	1-1	Galloway	22,574
4		8	(h)	Wolves	W	3-2	Galloway, Hartley, Scott	26,018
5		15	(a)	Notts C	L	0-2		23,304
6		22	(h)	Millwall	W	2-1	Osborne 2	47,073
7		29	(a)	Port Vale	L	1-2	Osborne	12,502
8	Oct	6	(h)	Hull C	W	4-1	Scott, Osborne, Elkes 2	28,737
9		13	(a)	Bradford	L	1-4	Osborne	22,688
10		20	(h)	Grimsby T	W	2-1	Scott, O'Callaghan	22,218
11		27	(a)	Stoke C	L	0-2		15,333
12	Nov	3	(h)	Clapton O	W	2-1	Elkes 2	33,382
13		10	(a)	Swansea T	L	0-4		6,936
14		17	(h)	Nottingham F	W	2-1	Wilding, Osborne	23,384
15		24	(a)	Bristol C	L	1-2	Crompton	13,937
16	Dec	1	(h)	Barnsley	W	2-0	Osborne, Elkes	18,951
17		8	(a)	Chelsea	D	1-1	Armstrong	45,840
18		15	(h)	Blackpool	L	1-2	Dimmock	15,729
19		22	(a)	West Brom A	L	2-3	Crompton, O'Callaghan	12,609
20		25	(h)	Reading	D	2-2	O'Callaghan, Dimmock	28,344
21		26	(a)	Reading	L	3-4	Osborne 2, Dimmock	23,730
22		29	(a)	Oldham A	L	1-3	Osborne	12,833
23	Jan	1	(a)	Middlesbrough	L	0-3		25,145
24		5	(h)	Southampton	W	3-2	Poynton (pen), O'Callaghan, Osborne	15,962
25		19	(a)	Wolves	L	2-4	Osborne, Dimmock	11,956
26		26	(h)	Notts C	W	3-0	O'Callaghan, Elkes 2	16,946
27	Feb	2	(a)	Millwall	L	1-5	Thompson	18,974
28		9	(h)	Port Vale	W	4-2	Barnett, Osborne 2, Dimmock	21,342
29		23	(h)	Bradford	W	3-2	O'Callaghan, Dimmock 2	19,910
30	Mar	2	(a)	Grimsby T	L	0-2		13,850
31		9	(h)	Stoke C	W	1-0	O'Callaghan	26,760
32		16	(a)	Clapton O	W	3-2	Harper, Dimmock 2	37,615
33		23	(h)	Swansea T	D	1-1	Harper	25,109
34		29	(a)	Preston NE	D	2-2	Elkes, Dimmock	19,216
35		30	(a)	Nottingham F	D	2-2	Harper, Elkes	8,504
36	Apr	1	(h)	Preston NE	W	2-0	O'Callaghan, Elkes	23,125
37		6	(h)	Bristol C	D	1-1	Harper	22,396
38		13	(a)	Barnsley	L	1-4	Scott	8,449
39		15	(a)	Hull C	D	1-1	Harper	4,139
40		20	(h)	Chelsea	W	4-1	O'Callaghan, Harper 3	24,356
41		27	(a)	Blackpool	D	2-2	Harper, Dimmock	8,744
42	May	4	(h)	West Brom A	W	2-0	Harper 2	15,789

FINAL LEAGUE POSITION: 10th in Division Two

Appearances
Goals

FA Cup

3	Jan	12	(a)	Reading	L	0-2		26,137

Appearances
Goals

London FA Charity Cup

1	Oct	15	(h)	London Cals	W	2-1	Scott 2	2,000
2		29	(a)	Queen's Park R	D	1-1	Hartley	
R	Nov	5	(h)	Queen's Park R	W	3-1	Helliwell, Hartley, Armstrong	3,371
SF		26	(n*)	Charlton A	W	5-3	Crompton, O'Callaghan, Armstrong 2, Hartley	4,000
F	May	6	(n†)	Millwall	W	5-1	O'Callaghan, Harper 3, Armstrong	5,000

*Played at Upton Park, London. †Played at Arsenal Stadium, Highbury, London.

Appearances
Goals

London Professional Football Charity Fund

	Dec	3	(a)	Clapton O	W	4-2	Skitt, O'Callaghan, Armstrong, Bellamy	

Appearances
Goals

228

Armstrong	Bann	Barnett	Bellamy	Cable	Clay	Crompton	Dimmock	Elkes	Evans A	Forster	Galloway	Grimsdell	Handley	Harper	Hartley	Helliwell	Herod	Knight	Lindsay	Lowdell	Nicholls	O'Callaghan	Osborne	Poynton	Reddish	Richardson	Roberts	Scott	Skitt	Smith	Smy	Spiers	Thompson	Wilding	No.
						11	5			2	6									4		8		10	3			9			1	7			1
						11	5			2	6									4		8		10	3			9			1	7			2
						11				2	9	6		10						4	1	8			3			5				7			3
										2	9	6		10						4	1	8			3			11	5			7			4
	2						5				9	6		10						4	1	8			3			11				7			5
	2						5	8			6			10						4	1		9		3			11				7			6
	2						5				6	10								4	1	8	9		3			11				7			7
		11	5					10		2	6									4	1	8	9		3			7							8
		11	5					10		2	6									4	1	8	9		3			7							9
		11						10		2	5									4	1	8	9		3			7	6						10
		11						10	8	2					5					4	1		9		3			7	6						11
		11						10		2										4	1	8			3			9	7	6			5		12
		11						10		2										4	1	8			3			9	7	6			5		13
										2		11		10						4		8	9	3			6				1	7	5		14
						7				2		11		10						4		8	9	3			6				1		5		15
						7				2		11		10						4		8	9	3			6				1		5		16
9						7				2		11								4		8	10	3			6				1		5		17
9						7				2		11								4		8	10	3			6				1		5		18
9						7				2		11								4		8	10				6				1		5		19
						7				2		11		10						4		8	9	3			6				1		5		20
10										2		11			5					4		8	9	3			6				1	7			21
										2		11		10						4		8	9	3			6				1	7	5		22
										2		11		10				6		4		8	9	3			6				1	7	5		23
9										2		11			5			6				8	10	3			4				1	7			24
						7				2		11		10	5			6		4		8	9	3							1				25
			7							2		11		10	5					4		8	9	3			6				1				26
			7							2		11		10	5					4			9	3			6		1			8			27
			7							2	6	11								4		8	9	3			10		1			5		28
	2	7										11	9						5	4		8			6		3		10		1				29
		7					2					11	9				3			4		8		6			5		10		1				30
		7					2					11					3			4		8	9	6			5		10		1				31
			7				2					11	10							4		8	9	3			6		5		1				32
			7				2					11	10							4		8	9	3			6		5		1				33
												11	10							4		8	7	6				9	3	5	1				34
8												11	10							4			7					9	3		5	6	1		35
			7									11	10							4		8						9	3		5	6	1		36
10							2					11								4		8	7					9	3		5	6	1		37
10										2										4		8	7				11	9	3		5	6	1		38
10										2										4		8	7				11	9	3		5	6	1		39
10										2	11									4		8	7					9	3		5	6	1		40
10										2	11							4				8	7					9	3		5	6	1		41
10						7				2	11							4				8						9	3		5	6	1		42
12	4	6	9	2	5	8	30	27	2	33	3	11	1	11	3	6	13	1	6	39	11	36	33	23	12	4	12	29	10	4	31	13	12		
1		1					2	12		11		2					11	1					9	16	1			2	4			1	1		

Armstrong	Bann	Barnett	Bellamy	Cable	Clay	Crompton	Dimmock	Elkes	Evans A	Forster	Galloway	Grimsdell	Handley	Harper	Hartley	Helliwell	Herod	Knight	Lindsay	Lowdell	Nicholls	O'Callaghan	Osborne	Poynton	Reddish	Richardson	Roberts	Scott	Skitt	Smith	Smy	Spiers	Thompson	Wilding	No.
10										11				2								5		6				8	9	3			4		1	7		3
1										1				1								1		1				1	1	1			1		1	1		

Armstrong	Bann	Barnett	Bellamy	Cable	Clay	Crompton	Dimmock	Elkes	Evans A	Forster	Galloway	Grimsdell	Handley	Harper	Hartley	Helliwell	Herod	Knight	Lindsay	Lowdell	Nicholls	O'Callaghan	Osborne	Poynton	Reddish	Richardson	Roberts	Scott	Skitt	Smith	Smy	Spiers	Thompson	Wilding	No.
		11	5							2							10			4	1	8	9	3			7	6							1
9		11						8		2				10	5					4	1			3			7	6							2
9		11								2				8	5					4	1			3			7	6				10			R
9						7		11		2				10	5					4		8		3				6			1				SF
10						7		11		2			9							4		8		3			5	6		1					F
4		2	1			2		3		5			1	4	3		1			4	3	3	1	3	2		3	5	1		2	1			
4						1								3	3							2					2								

Armstrong	Bann	Barnett	Bellamy	Cable	Clay	Crompton	Dimmock	Elkes	Evans A	Forster	Galloway	Grimsdell	Handley	Harper	Hartley	Helliwell	Herod	Knight	Lindsay	Lowdell	Nicholls	O'Callaghan	Osborne	Poynton	Reddish	Richardson	Roberts	Scott	Skitt	Smith	Smy	Spiers	Thompson	Wilding	No.
9		11				7				2				10	5					4	1	8		3			6								
1		1				1				1				1	1					1	1	1		1			1								
1		1				1				1										1				1											

1929-30

Manager: Billy Minter until November then Percy Smith

1	Aug	31	(a)	Bradford	L 1-2	Dimmock	18,771
2	Sep	2	(a)	Millwall	W 5-2	Osborne, O'Callaghan, Cook, Dimmock 2	22,297
3		7	(h)	Barnsley	W 2-1	O'Callaghan, Cook	26,056
4		14	(a)	Blackpool	L 2-3	O'Callaghan, Smy	14,913
5		21	(h)	Bury	D 2-2	Crompton, Osborne	25,051
6		23	(h)	Millwall	D 1-1	O'Callaghan	16,629
7		28	(a)	Chelsea	L 0-3		46,770
8	Oct	5	(h)	Nottingham F	D 1-1	Cook	22,332
9		9	(h)	Stoke C	W 3-1	Osborne 3	8,545
10		12	(a)	Oldham A	L 0-2		18,265
11		19	(a)	Wolves	L 0-3		26,591
12		26	(h)	Bradford C	D 1-1	Osborne	17,349
13	Nov	2	(a)	Swansea T	W 1-0	Harper	8,961
14		9	(h)	Cardiff C	L 1-2	Meads	23,071
15		16	(a)	Preston NE	L 0-4		10,687
16		23	(h)	Bristol C	W 2-1	Harper, Dimmock	11,863
17		30	(a)	Notts C	W 1-0	Harper	10,294
18	Dec	7	(h)	Reading	D 0-0		11,522
19		14	(a)	Charlton A	L 0-1		17,350
20		21	(h)	Hull C	D 2-2	Harper 2	9,103
21		25	(h)	Southampton	W 3-2	Osborne (pen), Harper 2	26,564
22		26	(a)	Southampton	L 0-1		25,203
23		28	(h)	Bradford	D 1-1	Dimmock	20,726
24	Jan	4	(a)	Barnsley	L 0-2		5,870
25		18	(h)	Blackpool	W 6-1	Meads, Harper 3, Cook, Dimmock	24,956
26		25	(a)	Bury	L 1-2	Cook	13,192
27	Feb	1	(h)	Chelsea	D 3-3	Thompson, Harper, Cook	33,623
28		8	(a)	Nottingham F	D 0-0		9,833
29		15	(h)	Oldham A	W 2-1	Poynton (pen), Cook	35,516
30		22	(h)	Wolves	W 4-2	Thompson, Rowley 3	29,341
31	Mar	1	(a)	Bradford C	W 2-0	Cook, Bellamy	16,642
32		8	(h)	Swansea T	W 3-0	Davies 2, Rowley	30,331
33		15	(a)	Cardiff C	L 0-1		15,404
34		22	(h)	Preston NE	W 1-0	Osborne	29,108
35		29	(a)	Bristol C	L 0-1		10,935
36	Apr	5	(h)	Notts C	W 2-0	Cook, Bellamy	17,848
37		12	(a)	Reading	L 0-3		11,183
38		18	(h)	West Brom A	L 0-2		25,228
39		19	(h)	Charlton A	W 3-0	Harper 2, Smy	15,814
40		21	(a)	West Brom A	L 3-4	Osborne, Harper, Finch (og)	13,989
41		26	(a)	Hull C	L 0-2		6,396
42	May	3	(a)	Stoke C	L 0-1		6,560

FINAL LEAGUE POSITION: 12th in Division Two

Appearances
Goals

FA Cup

3	Jan	11	(h)	Manchester C	D 2-2	Osborne, Cook	37,000
R		15	(a)	Manchester C	L 1-4	Thompson	37,716

Appearances
Goals

London FA Charity Cup

1	Oct	14	(a)	Clapton O	L 1-2	Cook	3,000

Appearances
Goals

London Professional Football Charity Fund

	Nov	4	(h)	Crystal P	W 5-1	O'Callaghan, Garbutt 3, Cook	

Appearances
Goals

Appearances and goals grid (shirt numbers by match). Column headers (left to right):
Armstrong, Bellamy, Cable, Cook, Crompton, Davies, Dimmock, Evans T, Forster, Garbutt, Harper, Hartley, Herod, Illingworth, Lindsay A, Lowdell, Meads, O'Callaghan, Osborne, Poynton, Reddish, Rowley, Scott, Skitt, Smy, Spiers, Taylor, Thompson. Final column = match number.

Arm	Bel	Cab	Coo	Cro	Dav	Dim	Eva	For	Gar	Har	Hrt	Her	Ill	Lin	Low	Mea	OCa	Osb	Poy	Red	Row	Sco	Ski	Smy	Spi	Tay	Tho	#
9			10			11	2				3			4	6	8	7					5		1				1
9			10			11	2				3			4	6	8	7					5		1				2
9			10			11	2				3			4	6	8	7					5		1				3
			9			11					2	6	4			8	7	3				5	10	1				4
			7			11					2	6	4			8	9	3				5		1		10		5
			7			11					2	6	4			8	9	3				5		1		10		6
		9	7			11					2	6	4				3					5	10	1	8			7
		10	7			11					2	6	4	9	8		3					5		1				8
	5	10	7			11	2				3	9	4	6		8								1				9
	5	10	7			11	2				3	9	4	6		8								1				10
	5	10	7			11	2				3	4	6	9	8									1				11
	5	8				11					2	4	6	9	3							10		1		7		12
	5					11					2	4	6	8	10	3								1		7		13
	5	10				11					2	5	8	3								4		1		7		14
	5	10				11					2	6		3								4		1		7		15
	5	10				11					2	6	3		7							4		1	8			16
8	5	10				11					2	6	3		7							4		1				17
8	5	10				11					2	6	3		7							4		1				18
	5	10				11					9	3	2	6	8							4		1	7			19
	5	10				11					9	3	2	6	8							4		1	7			20
7	5	10				11					9	3	2	6	8							4		1				21
7	5	9				11	6				3	2		9								4		1	8			22
7	5	10				11	6	8			3	2		9								4		1				23
7	5					11		9			3	2	6		8							4	10	1				24
	5	10				11		9			3	2		6	7							4		1	8			25
	5	10				11		9			3	2		6	7							4		1	8			26
	5	10				11		9			3	2	6		7							4		1	8			27
	5	10				11		9			2			6	7	3						4		1	8			28
	5	10	7			11					2	6			3	9						4		1	8			29
	5	10	7			11					2	6			3	9						4		1	8			30
11	5	10	7		2						6	8	3	9								4		1				31
11	5	10	7		2					3		6	8	9								4		1				32
11	5	10	7		2					3		6	8	9								4		1				33
11	5	10	7		2					3		6	8	9								4		1				34
11	5	10	7		2	9				3		6				8						4		1				35
11	5	10	7		2					3		6	9			9						4		1	8			36
11	5		7		2					3		6	10			9						4		1	8			37
	5	10	7	11	2					3		6				9						4		1	8			38
	5		7	11	2		9				3	6				8						4	10	1				39
11	5		7		9		2	6			3					8	3					4	10	1				40
	5		7	6	9		2				3					8	3			11		4	10	1				41
	5		7		9		2				3	6				8	3			11		4		1	10			42
5	12	34	32	7	14	32	3	15	19	1	41	9	10	13	33	10	32	16	3	9	5	37	7	42	21			
	2	9	1	2	6			14				2	4	9	1		4					2			2			

I own-goal

	5	10				11						9	3	2	6		7					4		1	8			3
	5	10				11						9	3	2	6		7					4		1	8			R
	2	2				2						2	2	2	2		2					2		2	2			
		1															1							1				

	5	10	7			11	2				3			4	6	9	8							1				I
	1	1	1			1	1				1			1	1	1	1							1				
		1																										

	5	10				11	6	9						2			8	3				4		1	7			I
	1	1				1	1	1			1			1			1	1				1		1	1			
		1						3						1														

231

1930-31

Manager: Percy Smith

					Result	Scorers	Att.
1	Aug	30	(h)	Reading	W 7-1	Harper 5, Cook, Dimmock	25,484
2	Sep	1	(h)	Burnley	W 8-1	Davies, O'Callaghan 2, Harper 2, Cook 3	23,518
3		6	(a)	Wolves	L 1-3	Cook	24,990
4		8	(a)	Preston NE	L 1-2	Harper	17,031
5		13	(h)	Bradford	W 3-2	Harper, Cook, Dimmock	18,828
6		15	(h)	Preston NE	D 0-0		18,793
7		20	(a)	Stoke C	L 1-2	Cook	10,252
8		27	(h)	Millwall	W 4-1	O'Callaghan, Harper, Smy, Dimmock	37,106
9	Oct	4	(a)	Oldham A	W 2-1	Davies, Harper	15,559
10		11	(h)	Nottingham F	W 2-1	O'Callaghan, Harper	34,238
11		18	(h)	Bury	W 3-1	Harper, Cook, Dimmock	32,856
12		25	(a)	Everton	L 2-4	Smy 2	25,265
13	Nov	1	(h)	Charlton A	W 5-0	O'Callaghan, Harper 3, Smy	24,544
14		8	(a)	Bradford C	L 0-2		13,710
15		15	(h)	Swansea T	D 1-1	Lyons (pen)	20,211
16		22	(a)	West Brom A	W 2-0	Harper 2	17,923
17		29	(h)	Port Vale	W 5-0	Harper 4, Cook	23,609
18	Dec	6	(a)	Plymouth A	L 0-2		24,549
19		13	(h)	Bristol C	W 4-1	Messer, Rowley 2, Cook	21,464
20		20	(a)	Barnsley	W 1-0	Bellamy	7,294
21		25	(h)	Southampton	L 1-3	O'Callaghan	36,652
22		26	(a)	Southampton	W 3-0	Davies, O'Callaghan, Rowley	22,408
23		27	(a)	Reading	W 2-1	Davies, O'Callaghan	16,571
24	Jan	3	(h)	Wolves	W 1-0	Cook	26,221
25		17	(a)	Bradford	L 1-4	Harper	15,229
26		26	(h)	Stoke C	W 3-0	Lyons (pen), Messer, Harper	10,927
27		31	(a)	Millwall	W 3-2	Harper, Bellamy 2	27,899
28	Feb	7	(h)	Oldham A	W 4-0	Harper 3, Cook	27,708
29		14	(a)	Nottingham F	D 2-2	Harper 2	14,196
30		21	(a)	Bury	L 0-2		7,776
31	Mar	7	(a)	Charlton A	L 0-1		18,060
32		14	(h)	Bradford C	W 3-1	Harper 2, Smailes	32,976
33		16	(h)	Everton	W 1-0	Harper	30,205
34		21	(a)	Swansea T	W 2-1	Harper, Smailes	9,876
35		28	(h)	West Brom A	D 2-2	O'Callaghan, Smailes	49,921
36	Apr	3	(h)	Cardiff C	D 2-2	Hunt, Cook	41,547
37		4	(a)	Port Vale	L 0-3		14,290
38		6	(a)	Cardiff C	D 0-0		6,666
39		11	(h)	Plymouth A	D 1-1	Hunt	33,546
40		18	(a)	Bristol C	L 1-2	Hunt	15,149
41		25	(h)	Barnsley	W 4-2	Harper 2, Hunt 2	20,762
42	May	2	(a)	Burnley	L 0-1		10,077

FINAL LEAGUE POSITION: 3rd in Division Two

Appearances
Goals

FA Cup

3	Jan	10	(h)	Preston NE	W 3-1	Harper, Cook, Dimmock	36,549
4		24	(a)	West Brom A	L 0-1		40,850

Appearances
Goals

London FA Charity Cup

1	Oct	13	(h)	Charlton A	W 6-0	Davies 2, Harper 3, Cook	2,963
2		27	(a)	Chelsea	W 2-1	Rowley, Hartley	5,000
SF	Nov	17	(n*)	Ilford	W 8-1	Hunt 3, Davies, Thompson, Cook 3	
F	May	4	(n†)	Arsenal	L 1-2	Lyons (pen)	10,160

*Played at Upton Park, London. †Played at Stamford Bridge, London.

Appearances
Goals

London Professional Football Charity Fund

	Nov	3	(a)	Crystal P	D 2-2	Harper 2	

Appearances
Goals

Football appearance/scorer grid (player columns; shirt-number entries; row number at far right).

Alsford	Bellamy	Cable	Cook	Davies	Dimmock	Evans T	Evans W	Harper	Hartley	Herod	Hodgkinson	Howe	Hunt GS	Illingworth	Lyons	Meads	Messer	Nicholls	O'Callaghan	Osborne	Poynton	Rowe	Rowley	Scott	Skitt	Smailes	Smy	Spiers	Taylor	Thompson	#
			10	7	11			9		3					2	6	5	8					4							1	1
			10	7	11			9		3					2	6	5	8					4							1	2
			10	7	11			9		3					2	6	5	8					4							1	3
			10	7	11			9	3						2	6	5	8					4							1	4
		4	10	7	11			9	3						2	6	5	8												1	5
			10	7	11			9		3					2	6	5		8				4							1	6
			10	7						3	9				2	6	5	8			11		4							1	7
				7	11			9		3					2	6	5	8					4			10				1	8
				7	11			9		3					2	6	5	8					4			10				1	9
				7	11			9		3					2	6	5	8					4			10				1	10
			10	7	11			9		3					2	6	5	8					4							1	11
	11			7				9		3					2	6	5	8					4							1	12
	11	5		7				9		3					2	6		8					4							1	13
	11	5		7				9		3					2	6		8					4							1	14
	11	5		7				9		3					2	6		8	10				4							1	15
			10	7	11			9		3					2	6	5	8					4							1	16
			10	7	11			9		3					2	6	5	8					4							1	17
	11		10	7				9		3					2	6	5	8					4							1	18
	11		10	7						3					2	6	5	8					9				4			1	19
	11		10	7						3					2	6	5	8					9				4			1	20
	11		10	7						3					2	6	5	8					9				4			1	21
	11		10	7						3		4			2	6	5	8					9							1	22
4	11		10	7						3						6	5	8		2			9							1	23
	11		10	7				9		3						6	5	8		2			4							1	24
			10	7	11			9		3						6	5	8		2			4							1	25
	11		10	7				9		3		4			2	6	5						8							1	26
	11		10	7				9		3		4			2	6	5						8							1	27
4	11		10	7				9		3					2	6	5	8												1	28
4	11		10	7				9		3					2	6	5	8												1	29
6	11		10	7				9		3					2		5	8					4							1	30
4	11		10	7				9		3					2	6	5	8												1	31
4			10	7				9		3					2	6	5	8								11				1	32
4			10	7				9		3					2	6	5	8								11				1	33
4				7				9		3			10		2	6	5	8								11				1	34
4			10	7						3		9			2	6	5	8								11				1	35
4			10	7						3		9			2	6	5	8								11				1	36
	9			7						3					2	6	5		8		10		4			11				1	37
4	9			7						3		10				6	5	8		2						11				1	38
4				7						3		10			2	6	5	8	9							11				1	39
			10	7						3		8			2	6	5						9		4	11				1	40
4				7				9		3		10				6	5	8		2						11				1	41
4				7				9		3		8				6	5			10						11				1	42
14	17	4	31	42	13			30	3	39	3	9			37	41	39	37	6	5			8	1	24	11	6			42	
	3		13	4	4			36							5		2		2		9			3			3	4				

Alsford	Bellamy	Cable	Cook	Davies	Dimmock	Evans T	Evans W	Harper	Hartley	Herod	Hodgkinson	Howe	Hunt GS	Illingworth	Lyons	Meads	Messer	Nicholls	O'Callaghan	Osborne	Poynton	Rowe	Rowley	Scott	Skitt	Smailes	Smy	Spiers	Taylor	Thompson	#
			10	7	11			9		3					2	6	5	8					4							1	3
			10	7	11			9		3					2	6	5						4						8	1	4
			2	2	2			2		2					2	2	2	1					2						1	2	
			1		1			1																							

Alsford	Bellamy	Cable	Cook	Davies	Dimmock	Evans T	Evans W	Harper	Hartley	Herod	Hodgkinson	Howe	Hunt GS	Illingworth	Lyons	Meads	Messer	Nicholls	O'Callaghan	Osborne	Poynton	Rowe	Rowley	Scott	Skitt	Smailes	Smy	Spiers	Taylor	Thompson	#
	11		10	7				9		3					2	6	5	1					4						8	1	1
6	11								10	3		4	9	2							5	8						1	7		2
6	11		10	7						3	4		2		5	1					9								8		SF
	7	5				6	11				9	8	2				3	4						10		1					F
2	4	1	2	2		1	1	1	1	2	3	2	1	3	1	2	2		1	2	2		1		1	2	3				
			4	3				3	1					3	1				1						1							

Alsford	Bellamy	Cable	Cook	Davies	Dimmock	Evans T	Evans W	Harper	Hartley	Herod	Hodgkinson	Howe	Hunt GS	Illingworth	Lyons	Meads	Messer	Nicholls	O'Callaghan	Osborne	Poynton	Rowe	Rowley	Scott	Skitt	Smailes	Smy	Spiers	Taylor	Thompson	#
4	11			7				9		3	5				2	6										10		1	8		
1	1			1				1		1	1				1	1										1		1	1		
				2																											

1931-32

Manager: Percy Smith

1	Aug	29	(a)	Wolves	L	0-4		23,267
2		31	(h)	Preston NE	W	4-0	Davies, O'Callaghan, Hunt 2	22,104
3	Sep	5	(h)	Bradford	D	3-3	Meads, O'Callaghan, Rowley (pen)	27,108
4		7	(a)	Southampton	L	1-2	O'Callaghan	13,566
5		12	(a)	Manchester U	D	1-1	Rowley	9,557
6		14	(h)	Southampton	W	5-2	Meads 2, Brain, O'Callaghan, Bellamy	19,217
7		19	(h)	Barnsley	W	4-2	Brain, O'Callaghan 2, Bellamy	28,585
8		26	(h)	Nottingham F	L	1-3	Hunt	25,128
9	Oct	3	(a)	Chesterfield	L	2-4	Brain, Bellamy	15,192
10		10	(h)	Burnley	D	1-1	Harper	28,877
11		17	(a)	Notts C	L	1-3	Rowley	13,397
12		24	(h)	Plymouth A	L	0-1		22,863
13		31	(a)	Bristol C	D	1-1	Hunt	9,129
14	Nov	7	(h)	Swansea T	W	6-2	Davies 2, Hunt, O'Callaghan, W.Evans 2	20,834
15		14	(a)	Bury	D	1-1	Mills (og)	7,628
16		21	(h)	Port Vale	W	9-3	Lyons (pen), Colquhoun, Davies 3, Brain 2, Hunt 2	22,226
17		28	(a)	Millwall	W	2-1	Hunt 2	28,424
18	Dec	5	(h)	Bradford C	L	1-5	W.Evans	26,622
19		12	(a)	Leeds U	L	0-1		15,689
20		19	(h)	Oldham A	W	3-2	Hunt, O'Callaghan 2	10,339
21		25	(h)	Charlton A	L	0-1		36,469
22		26	(a)	Charlton A	W	5-2	Davies, Brain, Hunt 3	26,417
23	Jan	2	(h)	Wolves	D	3-3	Hunt 3	25,122
24		16	(a)	Bradford	L	1-2	O'Callaghan	12,596
25		23	(h)	Manchester U	W	4-1	Davies 2, Hunt, O'Callaghan	19,139
26		30	(a)	Barnsley	L	2-3	Hunt, O'Callaghan	5,852
27	Feb	6	(a)	Nottingham F	W	3-1	Brain 2, O'Callaghan	10,487
28		13	(h)	Chesterfield	D	3-3	Davies, Hunt, W.Evans	21,591
29		20	(a)	Burnley	L	0-2		7,517
30		27	(h)	Notts C	W	2-0	O'Callaghan 2	20,481
31	Mar	5	(a)	Plymouth A	L	1-4	Davies	18,903
32		12	(h)	Bristol C	W	2-1	Davies, Greenfield	15,178
33		19	(a)	Swansea T	D	1-1	T.Evans (pen)	11,357
34		25	(h)	Stoke C	D	3-3	T.Evans (pen), Hunt, O'Callaghan	26,503
35		26	(h)	Bury	D	0-0		20,822
36		28	(a)	Stoke C	D	2-2	Greenfield, W.Evans	15,042
37	Apr	2	(a)	Port Vale	W	3-1	Hunt, Greenfield 2	7,682
38		9	(h)	Millwall	W	1-0	T.Evans (pen)	22,495
39		16	(a)	Bradford C	L	0-2		12,740
40		23	(h)	Leeds U	W	3-1	O'Callaghan, Hunt, Greenfield	17,285
41		30	(a)	Oldham A	W	2-1	Hunt 2	5,963
42	May	7	(a)	Preston NE	L	0-2		5,900

FINAL LEAGUE POSITION: 8th in Division Two   Appearances

Goals

FA Cup

3	Jan	9	(h)	Sheffield W	D	2-2	Hunt, W.Evans	41,511
R		13	(a)	Sheffield W	L	1-3	Hunt (pen)	30,000

Appearances

Goals

Alsford	Bellamy	Brain	Cable	Colquhoun	Davies	Evans T	Evans W	Felton	Greenfield	Harper	Hodgkinson	Hunt GS	Lyons	Marshall	Meads	Messer	Moran	Nicholls	O'Callaghan	Poynton	Reddish	Rowe	Rowley	Smailes	Spiers	Taylor	
				4	7				10	9		3			6	5			8	2					11	1	1
	11			4	7							3	9		6	5	2		8	10						1	2
	11			4	7							3	9		6	5	2		8	10						1	3
	11			4	7							3	9		6	5	2		8	10						1	4
	11	8		4	7							3			6	5	2			10			9			1	5
	11	9		4	7							3	8		6	5	2			10						1	6
	11	9		4	7							3	8		6	5	2			10						1	7
	11	8		4	7							3	9		6	5	2			10						1	8
	11	8	5	4	7							3	9		6		2			10						1	9
				4	7				10	9		3	2		6							5	8		11	1	10
				4	7					9		3	2		6	5				10			8		11	1	11
6	9			4	7				10			3	2									5	8		11	1	12
6		8		4	7				10			3	9	2								5			11	1	13
6		8		4	7		11					3	9				2		10			5				1	14
6		8		4	7		11					3	9				2		10			5				1	15
6		8		4	7		11					3	9				2		10			5				1	16
6		8		4	7		11					3	9				2		10			5				1	17
6		8		4	7		11					3	9				2		10			5				1	18
6	7	8		4			11					3	9				2		10			5				1	19
6		8		4	7		11					3	9				2		10			5				1	20
6		8		4	7		11					3	9				2		10			5				1	21
		8		4	7	6	11					3	9				2		10			5				1	22
		8		4	7	6	11					3	9				2		10			5				1	23
		8		4	7		11				1	3	9		6		2		10			5					24
		8		4	7		11				1	3	9		6		2		10			5					25
		8		4	7		11				1	3	9		6		2		10			5					26
		8		4	7		11				1	3	9		6		2		10			5					27
		8		4	7		11				1	3	9		6		2		10			5					28
		8		4	7		11				1	3	9		6		2		10			5					29
		8		4	7		11				1	3	9		6	5	2		10								30
		8		4	7		11				1	3	9		6	5	2		10								31
	11	9	5	4	7				10		1	3			6		2		9								32
	7	8		4		6	11				1	3	9				2		10			5					33
	7	8		4		6	11				1	3	9				2		10			5					34
		8		7	4	11	2	10			1	3	9		6							5					35
		8		7	4	11	2	10			1	3	9		6							5					36
		8		7	4	11	2	10			1	3	9		6							5					37
		8		7	4	11	2	10			1	3	9		6							5					38
		8		7	4	11	2	10			1	3	9		6							5					39
				7	4	11	2	10			1		9		6				8		3	5					40
				7	4	11	2	10					9		6			1	8		3	5					41
				4	7	6	11	2	10				9					1	8		3	5					42
10	12	32	2	36	38	12	28	10	12	3	17	37	17	1	27	11	12	2	34	25	3	29	7	5	17	23	
	3	8		1	12	3	5	5	1			24	1		3				17			3					

1 own-goal

Alsford	Bellamy	Brain	Cable	Colquhoun	Davies	Evans T	Evans W	Felton	Greenfield	Harper	Hodgkinson	Hunt GS	Lyons	Marshall	Meads	Messer	Moran	Nicholls	O'Callaghan	Poynton	Reddish	Rowe	Rowley	Smailes	Spiers	Taylor	
		8		4	7	6	11					3	9				2		10			5				1	3
		8		4	7	6	11					3	9				2		10			5				1	R
		2		2	2	2	2					2	2				1		2	2	1	2				2	
													1						2								

1932-33

Manager: Percy Smith

1	Aug	27	(h)	Charlton A	W 4-1	Hunt 2, W.Evans 2	34,263
2		29	(a)	Nottingham F	L 1-3	Hunt	9,906
3	Sep	3	(a)	Stoke C	L 0-2		12,366
4		5	(h)	Nottingham F	D 0-0		13,757
5		10	(h)	Manchester U	W 6-1	Brain, Hunt 2, O'Callaghan, W.Evans 2 (1 pen)	23,333
6		17	(a)	Bury	L 0-1		11,602
7		24	(a)	Grimsby T	L 2-3	Hunt 2	9,597
8	Oct	1	(h)	Oldham A	D 1-1	Hunt	20,435
9		8	(a)	Preston NE	W 6-2	Colquhoun, O'Callaghan, Hunt, Greenfield, W.Evans 2	6,368
10		15	(h)	Burnley	W 4-1	Howe, Hunt, Greenfield, W.Evans	26,097
11		22	(h)	Southampton	W 5-0	O'Callaghan 3, Hunt, W.Evans	24,778
12		29	(a)	Millwall	W 4-1	Howe, O'Callaghan, Greenfield, W.Evans	32,301
13	Nov	5	(h)	Port Vale	W 4-0	O'Callaghan 2, Hunt, W.Evans (pen)	33,071
14		12	(a)	Lincoln C	D 2-2	Howe, Greenfield	11,654
15		19	(h)	Chesterfield	W 4-1	O'Callaghan, W.Evans 3 (1 pen)	24,584
16		26	(a)	Bradford C	W 1-0	Hunt	18,351
17	Dec	3	(h)	Swansea T	W 7-0	O'Callaghan, Hunt 2, Greenfield 2, W.Evans 2 (1 pen)	31,993
18		10	(a)	Fulham	D 2-2	Hunt 2	42,111
19		17	(h)	West Ham U	D 2-2	O'Callaghan, Hunt	45,129
20		24	(a)	Notts C	L 0-3		16,355
21		26	(a)	Bradford	D 3-3	Howe, O'Callaghan, W.Evans (pen)	25,318
22		27	(h)	Bradford	W 2-0	Hunt, W.Evans	48,478
23		31	(a)	Charlton A	W 3-0	Hunt 2, W.Evans	26,666
24	Jan	7	(h)	Stoke C	W 3-2	Davies, Hunt 2	43,711
25		21	(a)	Manchester U	L 1-2	W.Evans	20,661
26	Feb	1	(h)	Bury	W 2-1	Hunt 2	19,836
27		4	(h)	Grimsby T	W 4-3	O'Callaghan, Hunt, W.Evans 2	33,395
28		11	(a)	Oldham A	W 5-1	O'Callaghan, Hunt 3, Hall	5,412
29		18	(h)	Preston NE	D 1-1	Hunt	41,209
30	Mar	4	(a)	Southampton	D 1-1	Hunt	11,806
31		11	(h)	Millwall	W 2-1	W.Evans 2 (1 pen)	50,299
32		18	(a)	Port Vale	D 1-1	W.Evans (pen)	14,588
33		25	(h)	Lincoln C	W 3-2	Brain, Hunt, W.Evans (pen)	33,930
34	Apr	1	(a)	Chesterfield	D 1-1	Morrison	10,631
35		8	(h)	Bradford C	D 1-1	Allen	32,202
36		14	(h)	Plymouth A	D 0-0		44,483
37		15	(a)	Swansea T	W 2-0	Howe, W.Evans	14,590
38		17	(a)	Plymouth A	D 2-2	Howe 2	21,461
39		22	(h)	Fulham	D 0-0		44,312
40		24	(a)	Burnley	D 1-1	Hunt	11,353
41		29	(a)	West Ham U	L 0-1		31,706
42	May	6	(h)	Notts C	W 3-1	T.Evans, W.Evans 2 (1 pen)	28,015

FINAL LEAGUE POSITION: 2nd in Division Two

Appearances
Goals

FA Cup

3	Jan	14	(a)	Oldham A	W 6-0	O'Callaghan, Hunt 3, W.Evans, Brunskill (og)	16,662
4		28	(a)	Luton T	L 0-2		17,213

Appearances
Goals

236

Player appearance and goals grid. Column headers (left to right): Allen, Alsford, Bellamy, Brain, Colquhoun, Davies, Evans T, Evans W, Felton, Greenfield, Hall GW, Howe, Hunt GS, Levene, McCormick, Meads, Morrison, Nicholls, O'Callaghan, Poynton, Rowe, Taylor, Whatley. Final column = match number.

Allen	Alsford	Bellamy	Brain	Colquhoun	Davies	Evans T	Evans W	Felton	Greenfield	Hall GW	Howe	Hunt GS	Levene	McCormick	Meads	Morrison	Nicholls	O'Callaghan	Poynton	Rowe	Taylor	Whatley	#
				4	7	6	11	2	10			9			1		8			5		3	1
				4	7	6	11	2	10			9			1		8			5		3	2
				4	7	6	11	2	10			9			1		8			5		3	3
			8	4	7		11	2				9		6	1			10		5		3	4
	7		8	4			11	2				9		6	1			10		5		3	5
	7		8	4			11	2				9		6	1			10		5		3	6
			8	4	7		11	2				9		6	1			10		5		3	7
			8	4	7		11	2				9		6	1			10		5		3	8
				4			11	2	10		7	9		6	1		8			5		3	9
				4			11	2	10		7	9		6	1		8			5		3	10
				4			11	2	10		7	9		6	1		8			5		3	11
				4			11	2	10		7	9		6	1		8			5		3	12
				4			11	2	10		7	9		6	1		8			5		3	13
				4			11	2	10		7	9		6	1		8			5		3	14
				4			11	2	10		7	9		6	1		8			5		3	15
				4			11	2	10		7	9		6	1		8			5		3	16
				4			11	2	10		7	9		6	1		8			5		3	17
				4			11	2	10		7	9		6	1		8			5		3	18
10				4			11	2			7	9		6	1		8			5		3	19
				4			11	2			7	9		6	1		8	10		5		3	20
				4			11				7	9		6	1		8	10	2	5		3	21
10				4	7		11	2				9		6	1		8			5		3	22
				4	7		11	2				9		6	1		8	10		5		3	23
				4	7		11	2				9		6	1		8	10		5		3	24
				4	7		11	2				9	5	6	1		8	10				3	25
				4	7		11	2				9		6	1		8	10		5		3	26
				4	7		11	2				9		6	1		8	10		5		3	27
				4	7		11	2				9		6	1		8	10		5		3	28
				4	7		11	2				9		6	1		8	10		5		3	29
		8		4			11	2				9		6	1		7	10		5		3	30
				4			11	2			7	9		6	1		8	10		5		3	31
		8		4			11	2			7	9		6	1			10		5		3	32
		8		4			11	2			7	9		6	1			10		5		3	33
		8		4			11	2			7	9		6	1			10		5		3	34
10		8		4			11	2			7	9		6	1					5		3	35
				4			11	2		8	7	9		6	1			10		5		3	36
				4			11	2		8	7	9		6	1			10		5		3	37
				4	7		11	2		8		9		6				10		5	1	3	38
				4			11	2		8		9		6				10		5	1	3	39
		8		4			11	2			7	9		6				10		5	1	3	40
	7	8		4			11	2				9		6				10		5	1	3	41
				4			11	2		8	7	9		6				10		5	1	3	42
1	2	3	12	29	15	16	42	41	13	21	18	41	5	9	35	1	37	32	4	41	5	39	
1			2	1	1	1	28		6	1	7	33			1			14					

Cup section:

Allen	Alsford	Bellamy	Brain	Colquhoun	Davies	Evans T	Evans W	Felton	Greenfield	Hall GW	Howe	Hunt GS	Levene	McCormick	Meads	Morrison	Nicholls	O'Callaghan	Poynton	Rowe	Taylor	Whatley	#
				4	7		11	2				9	5	6	1		8					3	3
				4	7		11	2				9	5	6	1		8				3		4
				2	2		2	2				2	2	2	2		2				1	1	
							1					3						1					

1 own-goal

237

1933-34

Manager: Percy Smith

1	Aug	26	(a)	Sheffield U	D 0-0	16,583
2		28	(h)	Wolves	W 4-0 O'Callaghan 2, Hunt 2	20,953
3	Sep	2	(h)	Aston Villa	W 3-2 O'Callaghan, Hunt, W.Evans (pen)	44,974
4		4	(a)	Wolves	L 0-1	20,510
5		9	(a)	Leicester C	W 3-1 McCormick 3	26,112
6		16	(h)	Arsenal	D 1-1 Felton (pen)	56,612
7		23	(h)	Liverpool	L 0-3	33,080
8		30	(a)	Chelsea	W 4-0 O'Callaghan, Hunt 3	67,454
9	Oct	7	(h)	Sunderland	W 3-1 Hunt, G.W.Hall, W.Evans	44,235
10		14	(a)	Portsmouth	W 1-0 O'Callaghan	25,679
11		21	(a)	Everton	D 1-1 W.Evans	35,082
12		28	(h)	Middlesbrough	W 2-0 O'Callaghan, Hunt	35,800
13	Nov	4	(a)	West Brom A	W 2-1 Howe, W.Evans	32,292
14		11	(h)	Newcastle U	W 4-0 Hunt 2, W.Evans 2	41,477
15		18	(a)	Leeds U	D 0-0	19,681
16		25	(h)	Derby C	L 1-2 O'Callaghan	41,469
17	Dec	2	(a)	Manchester C	L 0-2	38,021
18		9	(h)	Birmingham	W 3-2 Howe, Hunt 2	26,142
19		16	(a)	Sheffield W	L 1-2 Howe	17,232
20		23	(h)	Blackburn R	W 4-1 Howe, G.W.Hall, W.Evans 2	28,001
21		25	(h)	Huddersfield T	L 1-3 G.W.Hall	53,950
22		26	(a)	Huddersfield T	L 0-2	32,501
23		30	(h)	Sheffield U	W 4-1 Hunt 4	23,894
24	Jan	1	(a)	Blackburn R	L 0-1	19,955
25		6	(a)	Aston Villa	W 5-1 Meads, McCormick 2, Howe, Hunt	35,296
26		20	(h)	Leicester C	L 0-1	31,393
27		31	(a)	Arsenal	W 3-1 Howe, W.Evans 2 (1 pen)	68,674
28	Feb	3	(a)	Liverpool	L 1-3 Hunt	30,809
29		10	(h)	Chelsea	W 2-1 Hunt, W.Evans (pen)	39,652
30		21	(a)	Sunderland	L 0-6	16,105
31		24	(h)	Portsmouth	D 0-0	26,921
32	Mar	3	(h)	Everton	W 3-0 Hunt 3	26,121
33		10	(a)	Middlesbrough	D 1-1 W.Evans	11,832
34		17	(h)	West Brom A	W 2-1 O'Callaghan, W.Evans (pen)	26,393
35		24	(a)	Newcastle U	W 3-1 Hunt 3	25,246
36		30	(h)	Stoke C	D 0-0	32,912
37		31	(h)	Leeds U	W 5-1 McCormick, Hunt 3, W.Evans	29,547
38	Apr	2	(a)	Stoke C	L 0-2	32,665
39		7	(a)	Derby C	L 3-4 McCormick, O'Callaghan, W.Evans (pen)	14,244
40		14	(h)	Manchester C	W 5-1 O'Callaghan 2, Hunt 2, W.Evans	24,576
41		21	(a)	Birmingham	L 0-2	24,576
42		28	(h)	Sheffield W	W 4-3 McCormick 2, Hunt 2	20,322

FINAL LEAGUE POSITION: 3rd in Division One

Appearances
Goals

FA Cup

3	Jan	13	(h)	Everton	W 3-0 Howe, Hunt, W.Evans	45,637
4		27	(h)	West Ham U	W 4-1 Hunt 2, W.Evans 2	51,747
5	Feb	17	(h)	Aston Villa	L 0-1	44,365

Appearances
Goals

Dewar Shield

	May	2	(h)	Corinthians	W 7-4 O'Callaghan 2, Hunt 3, W.Evans 2	5,117

Appearances
Goals

238

Alsford	Bellamy	Bolan	Channell	Colquhoun	Day	Evans T	Evans W	Felton	Hall BAC	Hall GW	Hedley	Howe	Hunt GS	McCormick	Meads	Nicholls	O'Callaghan	Rowe	Whatley	
			4			11	2			10			9	7	6	1	8	5	3	1
6			4			11	2			10			9	7		1	8	5	3	2
			4			11	2			10			9	7	6	1	8	5	3	3
			4			11	2			10			9	7	6	1	8	5	3	4
			4			11	2			10			9	7	6	1	8	5	3	5
			4			11	2			10			9	7	6	1	8	5	3	6
			4			11	2			10			9	7	6	1	8	5	3	7
			4			11	2			10			9	7	6	1	8	5	3	8
			2	4		11				10			9	7	6	1	8	5	3	9
			2	4		11				10			9	7	6	1	8	5	3	10
			4			11	2			10			9	7	6	1	8	5	3	11
			2	4		11				10			9	7	6	1	8	5	3	12
			4			11	2			10		8	9	7	6	1		5	3	13
			3	4		11	2			10			9	7	6	1	8	5		14
6			4			11	2			10			9	7		1	8	5	3	15
6			4			11	2			10			9	7		1	8	5	3	16
			4			11	2			10			9	7	6	1	8	5	3	17
			4			11	2			10		8	9	7	6	1		5	3	18
			4			11	2			10		8	9	7	6	1		5	3	19
			4			11	2			10		8	9	7	6	1		5	3	20
			4			11	2			10		8	9	7	6	1		5	3	21
	11	7	2	4				9		10					6	1	8	5	3	22
	11		4				2			10		8	9	7	6	1		5	3	23
	11		4					2		10		8	9	7	6	1		5	3	24
			2	4		11				10		8	9	7	6	1		5	3	25
			2	4		11				10		8	9	7	6	1		5	3	26
6			4			11	2			10		8	9	7		1		5	3	27
6		7	4			11	2			10			9			1	8	5	3	28
6			2	4		11				10			9	7		1	8	5	3	29
6			2	4		11		9		10				7		1	8	5	3	30
6			2	4		11				10			9	7	3	1	8	5		31
6			2	4		11				10			9	7		1	8	5	3	32
6			2	4		11				10			9	7		1	8	5	3	33
6			2	4		11				10			9	7		1	8	5	3	34
6	11		2	4						10			9	7		1	8	5	3	35
6			2	4		11				10			9	7		1	8	5	3	36
			2	4		11				10			9	7	6	1	8	5	3	37
	11		2	4						10			9	7	6	1	8	5	3	38
			2	4		11				10			9	7	6	1	8	5	3	39
			2		4	11				10			9	7	6	1	8	5	3	40
			2		4	11				10			9	7	6	1	8	5	3	41
			2		4					10	11		9	7	6	1	8	5	3	42
13	5	1	22	13	3	26	36	22	2	42	1	10	40	40	30	42	32	42	40	
						16		1		3		6	32	9	1		11			

Alsford	Bellamy	Bolan	Channell	Colquhoun	Day	Evans T	Evans W	Felton	Hall BAC	Hall GW	Hedley	Howe	Hunt GS	McCormick	Meads	Nicholls	O'Callaghan	Rowe	Whatley	
			2	4		11				10		8	9	7	6	1		5	3	3
6			2	4		11				10		8	9	7		1		5	3	4
6			2	4		11				10		8	9	7		1		5	3	5
2			3	2		1				3		3	3	3	1	3		3	3	
						3							1	3						

Alsford	Bellamy	Bolan	Channell	Colquhoun	Day	Evans T	Evans W	Felton	Hall BAC	Hall GW	Hedley	Howe	Hunt GS	McCormick	Meads	Nicholls	O'Callaghan	Rowe	Whatley	
			2	4		11				10			9	7	6	1	8	5	3	
			1	1		1				1			1	1	1	1	1	1	1	
						2								3			2			

239

1934-35

Manager: Percy Smith

1	Aug	25	(h)	Everton	D 1-1 G.W.Hall	50,586
2		27	(h)	Preston NE	L 1-2 W.Evans	24,961
3	Sep	1	(a)	Huddersfield T	D 0-0	13,941
4		3	(a)	Preston NE	L 0-1	25,936
5		8	(h)	Wolves	W 3-1 McCormick, G.S.Hunt, G.W.Hall	37,114
6		15	(a)	Chelsea	W 3-1 O'Callaghan, G.S.Hunt, W.Evans	46,715
7		22	(h)	Aston Villa	L 0-2	42,088
8		29	(a)	Derby C	L 1-2 G.S.Hunt	15,459
9	Oct	6	(h)	Leicester C	D 2-2 Hedley, Frame (og)	37,409
10		13	(a)	Sunderland	W 2-1 G.S.Hunt, G.W.Hall	28,204
11		20	(a)	Arsenal	L 1-5 G.S.Hunt	70,544
12		27	(h)	Portsmouth	W 4-1 Bolan, Howe, G.S.Hunt 2	33,461
13	Nov	3	(a)	Manchester C	L 1-3 W.Evans	28,802
14		10	(h)	Middlesbrough	W 3-1 Howe, G.S.Hunt, W.Evans	25,761
15		17	(a)	West Brom A	L 0-4	20,416
16		24	(h)	Sheffield W	W 3-2 McCormick, W.Evans 2 (1 pen)	25,103
17	Dec	1	(a)	Birmingham	L 1-2 O'Callaghan	20,546
18		8	(h)	Stoke C	W 3-2 O'Callaghan, G.S.Hunt, Bellamy	31,082
19		15	(a)	Liverpool	L 1-4 O'Callaghan	24,688
20		22	(h)	Leeds U	D 1-1 W.Evans	23,662
21		25	(a)	Grimsby T	L 0-3	19,706
22		26	(h)	Grimsby T	W 2-1 A.G.Hall 2	45,512
23		29	(a)	Everton	L 2-5 McCormick, A.G.Hall	25,851
24	Jan	1	(a)	Blackburn R	L 0-2	12,083
25		5	(h)	Huddersfield T	D 0-0	35,523
26		19	(a)	Wolves	L 2-6 McCormick, W.Evans	28,209
27		30	(h)	Chelsea	L 1-3 D.A.Hunt	28,121
28	Feb	2	(a)	Aston Villa	L 0-1	36,973
29		9	(h)	Derby C	D 2-2 McCormick 2	42,941
30		23	(h)	Sunderland	D 1-1 Channell	44,886
31	Mar	6	(h)	Arsenal	L 0-6	47,714
32		9	(a)	Portsmouth	D 1-1 W.Evans (pen)	11,687
33		16	(h)	Manchester C	D 0-0	43,572
34		23	(a)	Middlesbrough	L 1-3 G.S.Hunt	14,625
35		28	(a)	Leicester C	L 0-6	13,061
36		30	(h)	West Brom A	L 0-1	29,161
37	Apr	6	(a)	Sheffield W	L 0-4	12,158
38		13	(h)	Birmingham	D 1-1 Bell	27,190
39		19	(h)	Blackburn R	W 1-0 Bell	31,101
40		20	(a)	Stoke C	L 1-4 D.A.Hunt	11,574
41		27	(h)	Liverpool	W 5-1 Bolan, D.A.Hunt, W.Evans 3	15,613
42	May	4	(a)	Leeds U	L 3-4 Bolan, Morrison, D.A.Hunt	7,668

FINAL LEAGUE POSITION: 22nd in Division One

Appearances

Goals

FA Cup

3	Jan	12	(h)	Manchester C	W 1-0 W.Evans	48,983
4		26	(h)	Newcastle U	W 2-0 G.S.Hunt 2	61,195
5	Feb	16	(h)	Bolton W	D 1-1 W.Evans	70,347
R		20	(a)	Bolton W	D 1-1 G.S.Hunt	47,453
2R		25	(n*)	Bolton W	L 0-2	26,692

*Played at Villa Park, Birmingham.

Appearances

Goals

Dewar Shield

	Nov	7	(h)	Corinthians	W 7-2 Sargent, A.G.Hall 3, Morrison 2, Hedley

Appearances

Goals

240

Alsford	Bell	Bellamy	Bolan	Brain	Burgon	Channell	Colquhoun	Day	Duncan	Evans T	Evans W	Fullwood	Goldsmith	Greenfield	Hall AG	Hall GW	Hedley	Hooper	Howe	Hunt DA	Hunt GS	Illingworth	Jones	King	Levene	McCormick	Meads	Morrison	Nicholls	O'Callaghan	Phypers	Rowe	Sargent	Taylor	Whatley	#
6						2	4				11					10			9							7			1	8		5			3	1
						2	4				11					10			9							7	6		1	8		5			3	2
						2	4				11					10		8	9							7	6		1			5			3	3
						2	4		6		11					10		8	9							7			1			5			3	4
						2	4		6		11					10			9							7			1	8		5			3	5
			9			2	4		6		11					10									3	7			1	8		5				7
						2	4		6				3		11	10		8	9										1			5	7			8
						2	4								11	10		8	9							7	6		1			5			3	9
						2	4				11					10		8	9							7	6		1			5			3	10
						2	4				11		3			10		8	9							7	6		1			5				11
		7				2	4				11					10		8	9								6		1			5			3	12
		7				2	4				11					10		8	9								6		1			5			3	13
		7				2	4				11							8	9								6		1	10		5			3	14
						2	4				11							8	9							7	6		1	10		5			3	15
						2	4				11							8	9							7	6		1	10		5			3	16
						2	4				11							8	9							7	6		1	10		5			3	17
	11					2	4									10		7	9								6		1	8		5			3	18
	11					2	4									10			5		9					7	6			8				1	3	19
						2	4				11					10			9		5					7	6			8				1	3	20
						2	4				11					10			5		9					7	6			8				1	3	21
6	11					2	4											8	5		9					7	10							1	3	22
6	11					2	4											8			9			5		7	10							1	3	23
6	11					2	4			3						10		8	5		9					7								1		24
6						2	4				11							8			9			5		7				10				1	3	25
6	11					2	4				10							8	5		9					7								1	3	26
6	11					2	4				10							8	5		9					7								1	3	27
6			9			2	4				11							8						5		7				10				1	3	28
6			9			2	4				11							8								7				10				1	3	29
6						2					11							8	5	10				4		7	9							1	3	30
6				11		2												8	5	10	9			4		7								1	3	31
6	8					2	4				11								5		9					7	10							1	3	32
6	8	7				2	4	10											5		9		11											1	3	33
6	8	7				2	4	10			11								5		9													1	3	34
6						2		8		4	11	3				10			5		9					7								1		35
6	7					2	4	10			11							8	5		9								1						3	36
	7					2				10	11								4	8	9	5							1			6			3	37
6	7					2		8			11					10			4		9	5												1	3	38
6	8	7				2					11					10	1		4		9	5													3	39
6		7		11		2										10			4	9	8	2	5												3	40
6	8	7				2					11					10	1		4	9		5													3	41
6		7				2					11					10			4	9		5						8	1						3	42
21	**8**	**7**	**9**	**1**	**4**	**41**	**3**	**9**	**6**	**28**	**32**	**2**	**1**	**6**	**12**	**18**	**3**	**3**	**32**	**12**	**30**	**1**	**8**	**1**	**3**	**28**	**18**	**2**	**21**	**16**	**2**	**18**	**1**	**18**	**37**	
	2	1	3			1					12					3	3	1			2	4	10			6	1			4						

1 own-goal

FA Cup:

Alsford	Bell	Bellamy	Bolan	Brain	Burgon	Channell	Colquhoun	Day	Duncan	Evans T	Evans W	Fullwood	Goldsmith	Greenfield	Hall AG	Hall GW	Hedley	Hooper	Howe	Hunt DA	Hunt GS	Illingworth	Jones	King	Levene	McCormick	Meads	Morrison	Nicholls	O'Callaghan	Phypers	Rowe	Sargent	Taylor	Whatley	#
6	11					2					4					10		8			5	9				7								1	3	3
6	11					2					4					10		8			5	9				7								1	3	4
6	11					2					4					10		8			5	9				7								1	3	5
6						2					4					11		8			5	9				7	10							1	3	R
6						2	4									8		11			5	9				7	10							1	3	2R
5	3					5	1			4	4					5		5			5	2	3			5	1			1				5	5	
											2											3														

										4			3			10	8	11	1		2		5			9			6	7						
										1			1			1	1	1	1		1		1			1			1	1						
													3			1										2				1						

1935-36

Manager: Jack Tresadern

1	Aug	31	(a)	Bradford C	W	1-0	D.A.Hunt	14,359
2	Sep	2	(h)	Hull C	W	3-1	McCormick, Howe, D.A.Hunt	25,603
3		7	(h)	Newcastle U	L	1-2	Howe	47,442
4		9	(a)	Hull C	L	0-1		9,616
5		14	(a)	Sheffield U	D	1-1	Morrison	14,879
6		16	(h)	Barnsley	W	3-0	Duncan, Morrison 2	14,930
7		21	(a)	Manchester U	D	0-0		34,718
8		28	(h)	Port Vale	W	5-2	Howe 2, Morrison 3	32,872
9	Oct	5	(a)	Fulham	W	2-1	Duncan, W.Evans	37,298
10		12	(h)	Burnley	W	5-1	Howe, Morrison 2, G.W.Hall, W.Evans	34,483
11		19	(h)	Bradford	W	4-0	Morrison 2, G.W.Hall, W.Evans	37,796
12		26	(a)	Leicester C	L	1-4	Morrison	24,721
13	Nov	2	(h)	Swansea T	W	7-2	Fullwood (pen), Morrison 2, G.W.Hall 3, W.Evans	36,121
14		9	(a)	West Ham U	D	2-2	Morrison 2	40,245
15		16	(h)	Bury	W	4-3	McCormick, Morrison, G.W.Hall, W.Evans	32,176
16		23	(a)	Southampton	L	0-2		21,333
17		30	(h)	Blackpool	W	3-1	Duncan, Morrison, Cardwell (og)	35,031
18	Dec	7	(a)	Nottingham F	L	1-4	Edrich	9,232
19		14	(h)	Norwich C	W	2-1	McCormick, Morrison	29,204
20		21	(a)	Doncaster R	L	1-2	Morrison	20,131
21		25	(h)	Plymouth A	L	1-2	Morrison	34,510
22		26	(a)	Plymouth A	L	1-2	Bell	34,426
23		28	(h)	Bradford C	W	4-0	Howe (pen), Duncan, W.Evans 2	28,518
24	Jan	4	(a)	Newcastle U	W	4-1	Morrison, Bell, W.Evans 2	35,389
25		18	(h)	Sheffield U	D	1-1	W.Evans	35,534
26	Feb	1	(a)	Port Vale	W	5-1	Sargent, Morrison 3, W.Evans	10,770
27		5	(h)	Manchester U	D	0-0		20,085
28		8	(h)	Fulham	D	2-2	Sargent, W.Evans	45,277
29		22	(a)	Bradford	W	5-2	Sargent 2, Morrison, G.S.Hunt, W.Evans	6,987
30	Mar	4	(h)	Nottingham F	D	1-1	Hunt GS	14,700
31		7	(a)	Bury	D	1-1	Bell	6,012
32		14	(h)	West Ham U	L	1-3	G.S.Hunt	57,417
33		21	(a)	Swansea T	D	1-1	Sargent	12,498
34		28	(h)	Southampton	W	8-0	Meek 3, G.S.Hunt 3 (1 pen), W.Evans 2	28,907
35	Apr	4	(a)	Blackpool	W	4-2	G.S.Hunt 3, Cardwell (og)	11,044
36		10	(h)	Charlton A	D	1-1	Duncan	55,866
37		11	(h)	Leicester C	D	1-1	G.S.Hunt	35,286
38		13	(a)	Charlton A	L	1-2	G.S.Hunt	46,713
39		18	(a)	Norwich C	L	0-1		23,952
40		20	(a)	Burnley	D	0-0		8,567
41		25	(h)	Doncaster R	W	3-1	Meek 2, Duncan	15,093
42	May	2	(a)	Barnsley	D	0-0		9,271

FINAL LEAGUE POSITION: 5th in Division Two

Appearances
Goals

FA Cup

3	Jan	11	(h)	Southend U	D	4-4	Sargent 2, Morrison 2	48,839
R		15	(a)	Southend U	W	2-1	Sargent, W.Evans	23,634
4		25	(h)	Huddersfield T	W	1-0	Howe	64,149
5	Feb	15	(a)	Bradford	D	0-0		24,053
R		17	(h)	Bradford	W	2-1	G.S.Hunt 2	35,492
6		29	(a)	Sheffield U	L	1-3	Morrison	22,295

Appearances
Goals

242

Alsford	Bell	Buckingham	Channell	Day	Duncan	Edrich	Evans T	Evans W	Fullwood	Grice	Hall AE	Hall AG	Hall GW	Hooper	Howe	Hunt DA	Hunt GS	Jones	McCormick	Meek	Morrison	Nicholls	Phypers	Rowe	Sargent	Taylor	Ward	Whatley	
6			2				4	11					10		8	9			7					5		1		3	1
6			2				4	11					10		8	9		5	7							1		3	2
6			2				4	11					10	1	8		9	5	7									3	3
			2	4	10			11	3			8		1		9		5	7				6						4
			2		8		4	11	3				10	1					7		9		6	5					5
			2		8		4	11	3				10	1					7		9		6	5					6
			2		8			11	3				10	1	4				7		9		6	5					7
			2		8			11	3				10	1	4				7		9		6	5					8
			2		8			11	3				10	1	4				7		9		6	5					9
			2		8			11	3				10	1	4			5	7		9		6						10
			2		8			11	3				10	1	4			5	7		9		6						11
			2		8			11	3				10	1	4			5			9		6		7				12
4			2					11	3				10	1			9	5	7		8		6						13
4			2					11					10	1			8	5	7		9		6					3	14
4		5	2		8			11					10	1					7		9		6					3	15
5		4	2		8			11					10	1					7		9		6					3	16
			2		8	11							10	1	4			5	7		9		6					3	17
4			2		8	11							10	1	5				7		9		6					3	18
4			2			11							10		8			5	7		9		6			1		3	19
4			2			11							10		8				7		9		6	5		1		3	20
4			2			11			3				10		8				7		9		6	5		1			21
	10	4	2		8			11	3												9	1	6	5	7				22
	10	3	2		8			11						1	4						9		6	5	7				23
	10	3	2		8			11							4						9		6	5	7	1			24
			2		8			11					10		4						9		6	5	7	1		3	25
			2					11				8	10		4						9		6	5	7	1		3	26
			2			11						8	10		4						9		6	5	7	1		3	27
	8		2					11					10		4						9		6	5	7	1		3	28
6		3	2					11					10		4		9				8			5	7	1			29
6			2		8			11					10		4		9		7					5		1		3	30
	10	3	2					11							4		9				8		6	5	7	1			31
6			2					11					10		4		9				8			5	7	1	3		32
		3						11		6			10		4					8	9	1		5	7		2		33
		3			10			11		6					4		9			8		1		5	7		2		34
		3			10			11		6					4		9			8		1		5	7		2		35
		3			10			11		6					4		9			8		1		5	7		2		36
		3			10			11		6			4		7	5	9			8		1					2		37
								11		6			4		7		9			8	10	1		5			2	3	38
		3						11		6	7		4	1			9			8	10			5			2		39
		3				11	6						10	1	4		7			8	9			5				2	40
		3			10	11	6							1	4		9			8				5	7			2	41
		3			10	11	6					7		1	4					8	9			5				2	42
14	5	16	32	1	24	9	8	33	12	7	1	4	32	21	33	4	15	10	21	10	32	7	26	28	16	14	8	19	
	3				6	1		15	1				6		6	2	11		3	5	25				5				

2 own-goals

Alsford	Bell	Buckingham	Channell	Day	Duncan	Edrich	Evans T	Evans W	Fullwood	Grice	Hall AE	Hall AG	Hall GW	Hooper	Howe	Hunt DA	Hunt GS	Jones	McCormick	Meek	Morrison	Nicholls	Phypers	Rowe	Sargent	Taylor	Ward	Whatley	
	10	3	2		8			11						1	4						9		6	5	7				3
			2		8			11					10		4						9		6	5	7	1		3	R
			2		8			11					10		4						9		6	5	7	1		3	4
6			2					11					10		4		8				9			5	7	1		3	5
6			2					11	3				10		4		8				9			5	7	1			R
		6	2					11					10		4		9				8			5	7	1		3	6
2	1	2	6		3			6	1				5	1	6		3				6		3	6	6	5		4	
								1							1		2				3				3				

1936-37

Manager: Jack Tresadern

1	Aug	29	(a)	West Ham U	L	1-2	Morrison	31,906
2		31	(a)	Blackpool	D	0-0		23,875
3	Sep	5	(h)	Norwich C	L	2-3	G.S.Hunt, Edrich	32,767
4		12	(a)	Newcastle U	W	1-0	Morrison	28,314
5		14	(h)	Leicester C	W	4-2	Morrison 2, Bell, W.Evans	17,913
6		19	(h)	Bradford	W	5-1	Morrison 4, W.Evans	33,177
7		21	(h)	Blackpool	L	1-2	Morrison	16,308
8		26	(a)	Barnsley	L	0-1		12,024
9	Oct	3	(h)	Sheffield U	D	2-2	Morrison, Edrich	34,522
10		10	(a)	Burnley	L	1-3	Morrison	20,447
11		17	(h)	Southampton	W	4-0	McCormick, Morrison 2, G.W.Hall	26,335
12		24	(a)	Swansea T	L	1-2	Meek	15,545
13		31	(h)	Bradford C	W	5-1	Ward, Meek, Morrison 3	16,653
14	Nov	7	(a)	Aston Villa	D	1-1	Morrison	37,220
15		14	(h)	Chesterfield	W	5-1	G.S.Hunt 3 (2 pens), Morrison, Miller	30,054
16		28	(h)	Plymouth A	L	1-3	G.S.Hunt	32,305
17	Dec	5	(a)	Coventry C	L	0-1		27,395
18		12	(h)	Doncaster R	W	2-0	McCormick, G.S.Hunt	16,844
19		19	(a)	Fulham	D	3-3	Ward (pen), Morrison, Miller	20,495
20		25	(a)	Blackburn R	W	4-0	Meek, Morrison 2, Miller	26,756
21		26	(h)	West Ham U	L	2-3	Meek, Miller	34,190
22		28	(h)	Blackburn R	W	5-1	McCormick, Miller 4	16,135
23	Jan	2	(a)	Norwich C	W	3-2	Morrison 3	13,131
24		9	(h)	Newcastle U	L	0-1		30,505
25		23	(a)	Bradford	L	2-3	Meek 2	7,481
26	Feb	3	(h)	Barnsley	W	3-0	Meek, Duncan, Edrich	11,097
27		6	(a)	Sheffield U	L	2-3	McCormick, Morrison	22,838
28		13	(h)	Burnley	W	3-0	McCormick, Morrison, Miller	30,283
29		24	(a)	Southampton	L	0-1		5,226
30		27	(h)	Swansea T	W	3-1	Duncan 3	26,346
31	Mar	10	(a)	Bradford C	D	2-2	Meek, G.S.Hunt	6,050
32		13	(h)	Aston Villa	D	2-2	Meek, Miller	35,652
33		20	(a)	Chesterfield	W	3-1	McCormick 3	13,621
34		26	(a)	Bury	L	3-5	G.S.Hunt, Duncan, Miller	12,748
35		27	(h)	Nottingham F	W	2-1	G.S.Hunt 2	23,801
36		29	(h)	Bury	W	2-0	Duncan, Miller	27,642
37	Apr	3	(a)	Plymouth A	D	2-2	Morrison, Duncan	19,158
38		10	(h)	Coventry C	W	3-1	Ward (pen), Duncan 2	18,515
39		17	(a)	Doncaster R	D	1-1	Morrison	3,560
40		21	(a)	Nottingham F	L	0-3		14,687
41		24	(h)	Fulham	D	1-1	Alexander	21,133
42	May	1	(a)	Leicester C	L	1-4	Morrison	22,761

FINAL LEAGUE POSITION: 10th in Division Two

Appearances

Goals

FA Cup

3	Jan	16	(a)	Portsmouth	W	5-0	Morrison 3, Duncan, Miller	32,665
4		30	(h)	Plymouth A	W	1-0	McCormick	42,430
5	Feb	20	(a)	Everton	D	1-1	McCormick	57,149
R		22	(h)	Everton	W	4-3	Meek, Morrison 3	46,972
6	Mar	6	(h)	Preston NE	L	1-3	Duncan	71,913

Appearances

Goals

244

Football club appearance and goalscoring grid. Columns are player surnames; the final column is the match number. Figures indicate shirt number worn; blank = did not play.

Alexander	Alsford	Bell	Blyth	Brown	Buckingham	Duncan	Edrich	Evans T	Evans W	Fullwood	Grice	Hall AE	Hall GW	Hall J	Hooper	Howe	Hunt DA	Hunt GS	Ludford	McCormick	Meek	Miller	Morrison	Page	Phypers	Ringrose	Rowe	Ward	Whatley	#
8				3			11				6		1			4			10	7			9			5		2		1
	6						11					10	1			4		9		7	8					5		2	3	2
	6				11	4						10	1			5		9		7	8							2	3	3
		10	5		8					3	6		1			4				7		11	9					2		4
7		10	5		8		11			3	6		1			4							9					2		5
7			5	10	8		11			3	6		1			4							9					2		6
7			5		8		11			3	10	4	1			6							9					2		7
7				10			11				6		1			4		9			8					5		2	3	8
7					10	11					6		1			4				8			9			5		2	3	9
					10	11					6			1		4				7	8		9			5		2	3	10
						11					6	10		1		4				7	8		9			5		2	3	11
				10		11					6			1		4				7	8		9			5		2	3	12
			5						11		6	10		1		4				7	8		9					2	3	13
			5	8					11		6	10		1		4				7			9					2	3	14
			5								6	10		1		4		8		7		11	9					2	3	15
			5								6	10		1		4		8		7		11	9					2	3	16
	4		5								6	10		1				8		7		11	9					2	3	17
	4		5								6	10		1		8		9		7		11						2	3	18
	4		5		3	10					6			1						7	8	11						2		19
	4				3	10					6			1						7	8	11	9			5		2		20
	4				3	10					6			1						7	8	11	9			5		2		21
					3	10					6			1		4		9		7	8	11		5				2		22
					6	10								1		4				7	8	11	9		2	5			3	23
8					6	10				3				1		4				7		11	9	5		2				24
					4	10					6			1						7	8	11	9	5				2	3	25
					4	10	11				6			1						7	8		9			5		2	3	26
					4	10	11				6			1						7	8		9			5		2	3	27
					4	10					6			1						7	8	11	9			5		2	3	28
7					4									10		1	8		9			11		5	6				3	29
					4	10					6			1						7	8	11	9			5		2	3	30
					4	10								1				9		7	8	11		5	6			2		31
					4	10					6			1				9		7	8	11		5				2		32
					4	10					6			1				9		7	8	11		5				2		33
					4	10					6			1				9		7	8	11		5				2		34
					4	10					6			1				9		7	8	11		5				2		35
					6	10								1		4				7	8	11	9	5				2	3	36
					6	10	11							1		4				7	8	11	9	5				2	3	37
					6	10								1		4				7	8	11	9	5				2	3	38
					6	10								1		4				7	8	11	9	5				2	3	39
					6	10	11							1		4				7	8		9	5				2	3	40
7					6	8	11						10	1		4							9	5				2	3	41
					6	10							11	1		4				7	8		9	5				2	3	42
9	7	2	11	4	25	29	11	1	7	5	22	1	19	39	3	28	1	13	1	35	28	23	32	15	2	10	15	32	32	
1		1			9	3			2				1						10		8	9	12	29				3			

Alexander	Alsford	Bell	Blyth	Brown	Buckingham	Duncan	Edrich	Evans T	Evans W	Fullwood	Grice	Hall AE	Hall GW	Hall J	Hooper	Howe	Hunt DA	Hunt GS	Ludford	McCormick	Meek	Miller	Morrison	Page	Phypers	Ringrose	Rowe	Ward	Whatley	#
					4	10					6			1						7	8	11	9			5		2	3	3
					4	10					6			1						7	8	11	9			5		2	3	4
					4	10					6			1						7	8	11	9			5		2	3	5
					4	10					6			1						7	8	11	9			5		2	3	R
					4	10					6			1						7	8	11	9			5		2	3	6
					5	5					5			5						5	5	5	5			5	5	5		
					2																2	1	1	6							

245

1937-38

Manager: Jack Tresadern

1	Aug	28	(h)	Coventry C	D	0-0	32,519
2		30	(h)	Burnley	W	4-0 Ward (pen), Morrison 3	13,766
3	Sep	4	(a)	Nottingham F	L	1-3 Sargent	16,478
4		6	(a)	Burnley	L	1-2 Miller	11,287
5		11	(h)	Newcastle U	D	2-2 Sargent, Morrison	25,577
6		16	(a)	Sheffield W	W	3-0 Sargent, Morrison, Gibbons	13,263
7		18	(a)	Luton T	W	4-2 Sargent, Morrison 2, Miller	23,788
8		25	(h)	Barnsley	W	3-0 G.W.Hall, Gibbons, Miller	26,417
9	Oct	2	(a)	Stockport C	L	2-3 G.W.Hall, Morrison	19,069
10		9	(h)	Manchester U	L	0-1	31,189
11		16	(a)	Fulham	L	1-3 Sargent	29,556
12		23	(h)	Plymouth A	W	3-2 Sargent, Morrison, Jeffrey	22,734
13		30	(a)	Chesterfield	D	2-2 Ward (pen), Morrison	16,092
14	Nov	6	(h)	Swansea T	W	2-0 Gibbons 2	22,328
15		13	(a)	Norwich C	L	1-2 Gibbons	19,019
16		20	(h)	West Ham U	W	2-0 Sargent, Gibbons	47,000
17		27	(a)	Bradford	L	1-3 Gibbons	10,794
18	Dec	4	(h)	Aston Villa	W	2-1 G.W.Hall, Morrison	37,238
19		11	(a)	Southampton	L	1-2 Gibbons	17,718
20		18	(h)	Blackburn R	W	3-1 Grice, Lyman 2	20,251
21		25	(a)	Bury	W	2-1 Morrison, Gibbons	13,659
22		27	(h)	Bury	L	1-3 Gibbons	40,901
23	Jan	1	(a)	Coventry C	L	1-2 Duncan	24,336
24		15	(h)	Nottingham F	W	3-0 Sargent, G.W.Hall, Gibbons	21,288
25		29	(h)	Luton T	W	3-0 Morrison, Lyman 2	29,806
26	Feb	2	(a)	Newcastle U	L	0-1	11,249
27		5	(a)	Barnsley	D	1-1 Sargent	13,327
28		19	(a)	Manchester U	W	1-0 Sargent	34,631
29		23	(h)	Stockport C	W	2-0 Howe 2	11,049
30		26	(h)	Fulham	D	1-1 Morrison	34,097
31	Mar	9	(a)	Plymouth A	D	2-2 Morrison, Duncan	15,724
32		12	(h)	Chesterfield	W	2-0 Sargent, Miller	20,915
33		19	(a)	Swansea T	L	2-3 Meek, Gibbons	10,656
34		26	(h)	Norwich C	W	4-0 Ward, Sargent, Morrison 2	18,431
35	Apr	2	(a)	West Ham U	W	3-1 Sargent, Gibbons, Miller	30,031
36		9	(h)	Bradford	W	2-1 Morrison 2	17,967
37		15	(h)	Sheffield U	L	1-2 Howe	23,162
38		16	(a)	Aston Villa	L	0-2	53,730
39		18	(a)	Sheffield U	L	0-1	45,305
40		23	(h)	Southampton	W	5-0 Ward (pen), Sargent, Morrison 3	15,982
41		30	(a)	Blackburn R	L	1-2 Howe	7,088
42	May	7	(h)	Sheffield W	L	1-2 Sargent	13,367

FINAL LEAGUE POSITION: 5th in Division Two

Appearances

Goals

FA Cup

3	Jan	8	(h)	Blackburn R	W	3-2 Sargent, Gibbons 2	35,576
4		22	(a)	New Brighton	D	0-0	13,029
R		26	(h)	New Brighton	W	5-2 Morrison 2, Gibbons 2, Lyman	36,004
5	Feb	12	(a)	Chesterfield	D	2-2 Gibbons, Miller	30,561
R		16	(h)	Chesterfield	W	2-1 Sargent, Morrison	36,994
6	Mar	5	(h)	Sunderland	L	0-1	75,038

Appearances

Goals

Player appearance / batting-position chart (each row is a match; numbers are batting positions).

Buckingham	Duncan	Fullwood	Gibbons	Grice	Hall AE	Hall GW	Hall J	Hitchins	Hooper	Howe	Jeffrey	Ludford	Lyman	McCormick	Meek	Miller	Morrison	Page	Rowe	Sargent	Spelman	Ward	Whatley	#
6	10					8	1							7			9	5		11	4	2	3	1
6	10					8	1						4	7			9	5		11		2	3	2
6	10					8	1						4	7			9	5		11		2	3	3
	10	3	6			8	1						4			11	9	5		7		2		4
6	10	3				8	1						4			11	9	5		7		2		5
6	10	3				8	1						4			11	9	5		7		2		6
6	10	3				8	1						4			11	9	5		7		2		7
6	10	3				8	1						4			11	9	5		7		2		8
6	10	3				8	1						4			11	9	5		7		2		9
6	10	3				8	1						4			11	9	5		7		2		10
6	10	3				8	1						4			11	9	5		7		2		11
		3	6		8		1		5		г		4			11	9			7		2		12
	10	3	6			8			5	1			4			11	9			7		2		13
	10		6			8			5	1			4			11	9			7		2	3	14
	10		6			8			5	1			4			11	9			7		2	3	15
	10		6			8				1			4			11	9	5		7		2	3	16
	10		6			8				1			4			11	9	5		7		2	3	17
	10		6			8				1			4			11	9	5		7		2	3	18
	10		6			8				1			4			11	9	5		7		2	3	19
	10		6			8				1			4			11	9	5		7		2	3	20
	10		6			8				1			4			11	9	5		7		2	3	21
	10		6			8				1			4			11	9	5		7		2	3	22
4	10		6						5	1			11		8		9			7		2	3	23
6	10					8			5	1			4			11	9			7		2	3	24
6	10								5	1			4		8	11	9			7		2	3	25
6	10					8			5	1						11	9			7	4	2	3	26
4	10		6			8				1						11	9	5		7		2	3	27
4	10	3				8			5	1	9					11				7	6	2		28
6						8			5	1		10				11	9			7	4	2	3	29
4	10					8				1						11	9	5		7	6	2	3	30
4	10	3				8				1						11	9	5		7	6	2		31
	10		6							1			4		8	11	9	5		7		2	3	32
		3	9	6						1			4	10	8	11		5		7		2		33
		3	6			8				1			4	10		11	9	5		7		2		34
6	10					8				1			4			11	9	5		7		2	3	35
6	10									1			4		8	11	9	5		7		2	3	36
6	10					8				1			4			11	9	5		7		2	3	37
6	10									1			11		8		9	5		7	4	2	3	38
6	10		9				8			1			11					5		7	4	2	3	39
6	10	3				8				1			4			11	9	5		7		2		40
6	10	3				8				1			4			11	9	5		7		2		41
6	10	3				8				1			4			11	9	5		7		2		42
29	13	15	27	17	7	29	12	10	30	33	1	1	24	3	7	16	39	23	9	42	8	42	25	
	2	13	1			4			4	1			4		1	5	22	15			4			

Buckingham	Duncan	Fullwood	Gibbons	Grice	Hall AE	Hall GW	Hall J	Hitchins	Hooper	Howe	Jeffrey	Ludford	Lyman	McCormick	Meek	Miller	Morrison	Page	Rowe	Sargent	Spelman	Ward	Whatley	#
6	10					8			5	1			4			11	9			7		2	3	3
6	10					8			5	1			4			11	9			7		2	3	4
6	10					8			5	1			4			11	9			7		2	3	R
4	10		6			8				1						11	9	5		7		2	3	5
4	10		6			8				1						11	9	2		7		2	3	R
4	10		6			8				1						11		9		5	7	2	3	6
6		6	3			6			3	6			3			4	2	6		3	6	6	6	
		5											1			1	3			2				

247

1938-39

Manager: Peter McWilliam

1	Aug	27	(a)	Southampton	W	2-1	Sargent, G.W.Hall	22,653
2		29	(h)	Sheffield W	D	3-3	Howe, G.W.Hall 2	28,133
3	Sep	3	(h)	Coventry C	W	2-1	Morrison, Lyman	39,982
4		10	(a)	Nottingham F	L	1-2	G.W.Hall	18,594
5		12	(h)	Sheffield W	D	2-2	Morrison, A.E.Hall	21,323
6		17	(h)	Newcastle U	W	1-0	Whatley (pen)	39,694
7		24	(a)	West Brom A	L	3-4	G.W.Hall, Morrison, A.E.Hall	24,996
8	Oct	1	(h)	Norwich C	W	4-1	G.W.Hall, A.E.Hall 2, Lyman	30,055
9		8	(a)	Luton T	D	0-0		21,061
10		15	(h)	Fulham	W	1-0	Lyman	46,679
11		22	(a)	Blackburn R	L	1-3	Lyman	18,136
12		29	(h)	West Ham U	W	2-1	Lyman 2	51,170
13	Nov	5	(a)	Manchester C	L	0-2		47,998
14		12	(h)	Bradford	D	2-2	Spelman, Ludford	24,132
15		19	(a)	Swansea T	D	1-1	Cox	13,172
16		26	(h)	Chesterfield	D	2-2	Whatley (pen), Ludford	24,434
17	Dec	3	(a)	Tranmere R	W	2-0	A.E.Hall 2	12,043
18		10	(h)	Millwall	W	4-0	Ward (pen), Cox, G.W.Hall, A.E.Hall	47,278
19		17	(a)	Bury	L	1-3	A.E.Hall	5,723
20		24	(h)	Southampton	D	1-1	Ward (pen)	9,454
21		26	(a)	Burnley	L	0-1		15,629
22		27	(h)	Burnley	W	1-0	Duncan	30,276
23		31	(a)	Coventry C	L	0-4		19,499
24	Jan	14	(h)	Nottingham F	W	4-1	Sargent, A.E.Hall, Duncan, Miller	19,091
25		28	(h)	West Brom A	D	2-2	Sargent, Morrison	38,190
26	Feb	4	(a)	Norwich C	W	2-1	Buckingham, Ludford	15,347
27		11	(h)	Luton T	L	0-1		30,704
28		18	(a)	Fulham	L	0-1		26,466
29		25	(h)	Blackburn R	W	4-3	Sargent, Morrison 2, Miller	22,709
30	Mar	1	(a)	Newcastle U	W	1-0	A.E.Hall	18,503
31		4	(a)	West Ham U	W	2-0	G.W.Hall, Duncan	20,832
32		11	(h)	Manchester C	L	2-3	Hitchins, G.W.Hall	27,426
33		18	(a)	Bradford	D	0-0		8,202
34		25	(h)	Swansea T	W	3-0	Burgess, Morrison 2	17,478
35	Apr	1	(a)	Chesterfield	L	1-3	Spelman	15,285
36		7	(h)	Plymouth A	W	1-0	Miller	33,621
37		8	(h)	Tranmere R	W	3-1	Ward (pen), Morrison, Miller	19,229
38		10	(a)	Plymouth A	W	1-0	Ludford	15,230
39		15	(a)	Millwall	L	0-2		33,428
40		22	(h)	Bury	W	4-3	Ludford 2, Duncan 2	16,279
41		29	(a)	Sheffield W	L	0-1		27,639
42	May	6	(a)	Sheffield U	L	1-6	Miller	38,460

FINAL LEAGUE POSITION: 8th in Division Two

Appearances
Goals

FA Cup

3	Jan	7	(h)	Watford	W	7-1	Ward (pen), Sargent, G.W.Hall 2, Duncan, Miller 2	34,896
4		21	(a)	West Ham U	D	3-3	Sargent, Morrison, Duncan	42,716
R		30	(h)	West Ham U	D	1-1*	Sargent	50,798
2R	Feb	2	(n†)	West Ham U	L	1-2	Morrison	50,468

*After extra-time. †Played at Arsenal Stadium, Highbury, London.

Appearances
Goals

Jubilee Trust Fund

Aug	20	(a)	Arsenal	W	2-0	Morrison, Lyman	41,997

Appearances
Goals

248

Buckingham	Burgess	Cox	Duncan	Grice	Hall AE	Hall GW	Hall J	Hitchins	Hooper	Howe	Ludford	Lyman	McCormick	Meek	Miller	Morrison	Nicholson	Page	Sargent	Spelman	Sproston	Tomkin	Ward	Whatley	#
6					10	8			1	4		11				9		5	7		2			3	1
6					10	8			1	4		11				9		5	7		2			3	2
6					10	8			1	4		11				9		5	7		2			3	3
6					10	8			1	4		11				9		5	7		2			3	4
6					10	8			1	4		11				9		5	7		2			3	5
6					10	8			1	4		11				9		5	7		2			3	6
6					10	8	1					11				9		5	7	4	2			3	7
6					10	8			1		9	11						5	7	4			2	3	8
6					10	8			1			11				9		5	7	4			2	3	9
6					10	8			1			11				9		5	7	4	2			3	10
6					10	8			1			11				9	3	5	7	4			2		11
6			10			8			1			11				9		5	7	4	2			3	12
6			10			8			1			11				9		5	7	4			2	3	13
6						10			1		9	11				8	3	5	7	4			2		14
6		7	10			8			1		9	11					3	5		4			2		15
6		7			10	8			1		9	11						5		4			2	3	16
6		7			10	8		5	1							9			11	4			2	3	17
6		7			10	8		5	1			11				9				4			2	3	18
6		7			10	8		5	1			11				9				4			2	3	19
6			10		9	8		5	1			11							7	4			2	3	20
6		7	10		9	8		5	1						11					4			2	3	21
6			10		9	8		5	1			11							7	4			2	3	22
6			10		9	8		5	1						11				7	4			2	3	23
6			10		9	8		5	1						11				7	4			2	3	24
6						8		5	1	10		11				9			7	4			2	3	25
6	4		10			8			1		9						3	5	7			11	2		26
6	4		10		9	8		5	1										7			11	2	3	27
6	4		10		8		1	5				11				9			7				2	3	28
6	4				10	8		5	1						11	9			7				2	3	29
6	4				10	8		5	1						11	9			7				2	3	30
6	4		10			8		5	1						11	9			7				2	3	31
6	4		10			8		5	1						11	9			7				2	3	32
6	4		10			8		5	1						11	9			7				2	3	33
6	4		10			8		5	1						11	9	3		7				2		34
6	4					8		5	1				7		11	9	3			10			2		35
6	4		10			8		5	1						11	9			7				2	3	36
6	4		10			8		5	1						11	9			7				2	3	37
	10			6		8		5	1	4	9				11				7				2	3	38
6	4	8	9					5	1		10				11				7				2	3	39
6	4		10			8		5	1		9				11				7				2	3	40
6	4	7	10			8		5	1		9				11		3						2		41
6	4	7	10			8		5	1		9				11		3						2		42
41	17	9	21	2	24	40	2	25	40	8	10	22	1		17	27	8	17	34	20	9	2	33	34	
1	1	2	5		10	9		1		1	6	6			5	9			4	2			3	2	

Buckingham	Burgess	Cox	Duncan	Grice	Hall AE	Hall GW	Hall J	Hitchins	Hooper	Howe	Ludford	Lyman	McCormick	Meek	Miller	Morrison	Nicholson	Page	Sargent	Spelman	Sproston	Tomkin	Ward	Whatley	#
6			10		9	8		5	1						11				7	4			2	3	3
6			10			8		5	1						11	9			7	4			2	3	4
6						10		5	1			11		8		9			7	4			2	3	R
6					10	8		5	1			11				9			7	4			2	3	2R
4			2		2	4		4	4			2		1	2	3			4	4			4	4	
			2			2									2	2			3				1		

Buckingham	Burgess	Cox	Duncan	Grice	Hall AE	Hall GW	Hall J	Hitchins	Hooper	Howe	Ludford	Lyman	McCormick	Meek	Miller	Morrison	Nicholson	Page	Sargent	Spelman	Sproston	Tomkin	Ward	Whatley
6					10	8			1	4		11				9		5	7		2			3
1					1	1			1	1		1				1		1	1		1			1
												1				1								

1939-40

Manager: Peter McWilliam until September

1	Aug	26	(h)	Birmingham	D 1-1	Sargent	28,366
2		31	(a)	Newport C	D 1-1	Burgess	19,700
3	Sep	2	(a)	West Brom A	W 4-3	Morrison 3, Dix	16,021

FINAL LEAGUE POSITION: 7th in Division Two (League abandoned)

Appearances
Goals

FL South Group 'A'

4	Oct	21	(a)	Southend U	W 2-1	Ludford 2	4,000
5		28	(h)	Millwall	W 3-0	Ludford, Medley 2	4,852
6	Nov	4	(a)	West Ham U	L 1-2	G.W.Hall	7,800
7		11	(h)	Watford	W 8-2	Bennett 3, Morrison 2, Medley 3	4,981
8		18	(a)	Arsenal	L 1-2	Howe	15,000
9		25	(h)	Charlton A	W 4-2	Sargent, Bennett 2, Howe	6,945
10	Dec	2	(a)	Clapton O	L 1-2	Howe	8,000
11		9	(h)	Crystal P	L 1-3	Morrison	4,265
12		16	(a)	Norwich C	L 2-5	Ludford 2	3,000
13		23	(h)	Southend U*	L 3-4	Bennett, A.E.Hall 2	1,008
14		25	(a)	Millwall	L 1-5	Morrison	7,219
15		26	(h)	West Ham U	L 0-1		4,276
16		30	(a)	Watford	L 1-6	A.E.Hall	2,000
17	Jan	13	(a)	Charlton A	W 5-1	Howe, Sargent 2, Morrison, Medley	4,000
18		17	(h)	Southend U	L 2-4	Medley 2	1,000
19		20	(h)	Clapton O	L 2-3	Morrison 2	2,881
20		25	(h)	Arsenal	L 0-1		9,054
21	Feb	28	(a)	Crystal P	D 1-1	Stephens	2,000
22	May	27	(h)	Norwich C	D 2-2	G.W.Hall, Ludford	727

FINAL LEAGUE POSITION: 9th in Group 'A'
*Abandoned after 60 mins — fog.

Appearances
Goals

FL South Group 'C'

23	Feb	10	(a)	West Ham U	L 0-2		7,500
24		17	(h)	Charlton A	W 2-0	Burgess, Ludford	3,531
25		24	(a)	Chelsea	W 2-0	G.W.Hall, Dix	14,073
26	Mar	2	(h)	Southampton	W 4-1	D.A.Hunt, Dix 2, Medley	5,446
27		9	(h)	Brentford	D 1-1	G.W.Hall	9,815
28		16	(a)	Portsmouth	W 2-1	Duncan, Dix	7,000
29		22	(h)	Millwall	L 1-2	Lyman	15,000
30		23	(a)	Fulham	W 3-2	Morrison, Dix 2	8,000
31		25	(a)	Millwall	D 1-1	Ludford	14,624
32		30	(h)	Arsenal	D 1-1	Medley	15,000
33	Apr	6	(h)	West Ham U	L 2-6	Howe, Morrison	15,000
34		10	(h)	Fulham	W 3-1	Cox, Morrison 2	2,000
33		13	(a)	Charlton A	W 4-2	Morrison 3, Medley	5,000
36		24	(n†)	Arsenal	W 4-2	Duncan, Morrison 2, Dix	4,455
37	May	4	(a)	Brentford	W 3-2	Morrison 3	5,000
38		11	(h)	Portsmouth	W 4-1	Morrison 3, Medley	5,301
39		18	(a)	Southampton	D 3-3	Morrison 3	3,000
40		25	(h)	Chelsea	W 3-2	Burgess, Duncan 2	4,824

FINAL LEAGUE POSITION: 1st in Group 'C'
†Away game played at White Hart Lane, London.

Appearances
Goals

League Cup

1	Apr	20	(a)	Crystal P	L 1-4	Cox	15,423
1		27	(h)	Crystal P	W 2-1	Howe, Dix	12,376

Appearances
Goals

Jubilee Trust Fund

1	Aug	19	(h)	Arsenal	L 0-1		32,702

Appearances
Goals

250

Football season appearances and goals grid.

Bennett	Buckingham	Burchell	Burgess	Cox	Ditchburn	Dix	Dorling	Dowers	Duncan	Evans	Hall AE	Hall GW	Hitchins	Hooper	Howe	Hunt DA	Ludford	Lyman	McCormick	McEwan	Medley	Morrison	Nicholson	Ottewell	Page	Piper	Sargent	Spelman	Stephens	Tomkin	Ward	Whatley	Wilbert	Woodley	#
6	4		10								8	5	1			9	11								3		7					2			1
6	4		10								8	5	1			9									3		7		11			2			2
6	4		10								8		1									9			3	5	7		11			2			3
3	3		3								3	2	3			2	1					1			3	1	3		2			3			
			1									1										3			1										

Bennett	Buckingham	Burchell	Burgess	Cox	Ditchburn	Dix	Dorling	Dowers	Duncan	Evans	Hall AE	Hall GW	Hitchins	Hooper	Howe	Hunt DA	Ludford	Lyman	McCormick	McEwan	Medley	Morrison	Nicholson	Ottewell	Page	Piper	Sargent	Spelman	Stephens	Tomkin	Ward	Whatley	Wilbert	Woodley	#
6	4		2			10					8	5	1			9					11					7					3				4
	4					10					8	5	1			9					11			2		7	6				3				5
	4		2			10					8	5	1			9					11					7	6				3				6
8	3					2			10			5	1	4							11	9				7	6								7
						2			10		8	5	1	4							11	9				7	6				3				8
10			4			2					8	5	1	11							9					7	6				3				9
10	4					2					8	5	1	7							9					11	6				3				10
8											5	1	4						10		9			2		7	6		11		3				11
8	6					2						1	4	9					11		10			5		7					3				12
8	6					2	7		10			5	1	4							11	9									3				13
8	6					2			10			1	4	11							9			5		7					3				14
8	6					2			10			5	1	11							9					7	4				3				15
8	6	2					7		10			5	1	11							9					4					3				16
10	6					2					8	5	1	4							11	9				7					3				17
						10					8	5	1	4	6						11	9				2	7				3				18
	6					10					8	5	1	2							11	9				7	4				3				19
	4		10								8	5	1	3			11	7			9				6					2					20
		7									8		1	4							11	9			5	6		10			2	3			21
10		1						6			8	5	4	9							7									2	3	11		22
10	10	1	6	1	1	1	11	2	7	1	4	12	16	18	14	9	1	1	3	9	15			6	1	15	11	1	1	3	17	1			
6									3	2			4			6					8	7			3		1								

Bennett	Buckingham	Burchell	Burgess	Cox	Ditchburn	Dix	Dorling	Dowers	Duncan	Evans	Hall AE	Hall GW	Hitchins	Hooper	Howe	Hunt DA	Ludford	Lyman	McCormick	McEwan	Medley	Morrison	Nicholson	Ottewell	Page	Piper	Sargent	Spelman	Stephens	Tomkin	Ward	Whatley	Wilbert	Woodley	#
6											8		1	4	9			7			11	10			5							2	3			23
	4		10								8	5	1	6		9		7			11										2	3			24
6			10								8	5	1	4							11	9				7					2	3			25
			10									5	1	4	9		7				11	8			6						2	3			26
			10			8					4	5	1	6			7				11	9									2	3			27
			10			8					4	5	1	6				7			11	9									2	3			28
8			10								4	5	1	6			7				11	9									2	3			29
	6		10								8	5	1	4		11	7				9										2	3			30
	6		7				10				8	5	1	4		9	11				7										2	3			31
			7		10	3		8			4	5	1	6		9					11										2				32
	4	7			10						8	5	1	6							11	9									2	3			33
	4	7			10						8	5		6							11	9									2	3	1		34
	4	7			10			8				5	1	6							11	9									2	3			35
	4	7			10			8				5	1	6							11	9									2	3			36
	6	7			10						8	5	1	4							11	9									2	3			37
	6	7					10				8	5	1	4							11	9									2	3			38
					10			8			4	5	1	6		7					11	9									2	3			39
	6	7	1		10			8				5		4							9			11							2	3			40
1	4		8	9	1	14	1		9		15	17	16	18	2	3	5	5		15	15			1	2		1				18	17	1		
			2	1		7			4		2			1	1	2	1				4	18													

Bennett	Buckingham	Burchell	Burgess	Cox	Ditchburn	Dix	Dorling	Dowers	Duncan	Evans	Hall AE	Hall GW	Hitchins	Hooper	Howe	Hunt DA	Ludford	Lyman	McCormick	McEwan	Medley	Morrison	Nicholson	Ottewell	Page	Piper	Sargent	Spelman	Stephens	Tomkin	Ward	Whatley	Wilbert	Woodley	#
	4	7			10						8	5	1	6							11	9									2	3			1
	4	7			10			8				5	1	6							11	9									2	3			1
	2	2		2		1					1	2	2	2							2	2									2	2			
		1		1									1																						

Bennett	Buckingham	Burchell	Burgess	Cox	Ditchburn	Dix	Dorling	Dowers	Duncan	Evans	Hall AE	Hall GW	Hitchins	Hooper	Howe	Hunt DA	Ludford	Lyman	McCormick	McEwan	Medley	Morrison	Nicholson	Ottewell	Page	Piper	Sargent	Spelman	Stephens	Tomkin	Ward	Whatley	Wilbert	Woodley	
6	4		10								8	5	1			9	11								3		7					2			
1	1		1								1	1	1			1	1								1		1					1			

D.A.Hunt (Sheffield Wednesday), S.Ottewell (Chesterfield), V.R.Woodley (Chelsea).

1940-41

Football League South

1	Aug	31	(h)	West Ham U	L	2-3	Burgess 2	2,000
2	Sep	7	(a)	West Ham U*	W	4-1	Burgess 3, Duncan	2,600
3		14	(h)	Chelsea§	W	3-2	Ward, Ludford 2	1,622
4		21	(a)	Chelsea	L	1-4	Duncan	1,756
5		28	(h)	Charlton A	L	1-3	Medley	1,508
6	Oct	5	(a)	Queen's Park R	D	1-1	Ludford	1,800
7		12	(h)	Arsenal†	L	2-3	Skinner, Medley	4,568
8		19	(a)	Charlton A	L	0-4		500
9		26	(h)	Portsmouth	L	1-2	Howe	1,351
10	Nov	2	(a)	Luton T	D	1-1	Ludford	1,100
11		16	(a)	Arsenal	D	1-1	Burgess	1,916
12		23	(h)	Luton T‡	W	2-1	Duncan, Ludford	1,256
13		30	(n¹)	Southend U	L	2-3	White, Ludford	1,000
14	Dec	7	(h)	Queen's Park R	L	2-3	Sargent, Duncan	1,367
15		21	(h)	Clapton O	W	9-0	J.Sperrin 2, Gibbons 3, Duncan 2, Ludford 2	1,290
16		25	(h)	Millwall	D	3-3	Howe, Gibbons, Ludford	5,075
17		28	(n²)	Clapton O	W	7-0	J.Sperrin, O'Callaghan, Gibbons 3, W.Sperrin, Ludford	1,163
18	Mar	15	(n²)	Millwall	L	0-1		4,000
19	Apr	26	(a)	Aldershot	W	3-2	Hall, W.Sperrin, Gibbons	2,841
20	May	10	(h)	Crystal P	D	1-1	W.Sperrin	3,000
21		17	(a)	Leicester C	W	2-1	Burgess 2	3,000
22		24	(h)	Leicester C	W	3-0	Broadis, Gibbons, Ludford	3,000
23	Jun	7	(h)	Fulham	W	2-1	Ward (pen), Broadis	2,815

FINAL LEAGUE POSITION: 10th in Division One

Appearances
Goals

Football League War Cup

1	Feb	15	(h)	Bournemouth	W	4-1	Buckingham, J.Sperrin, Ludford 2	3,413
1		22	(a)	Bournemouth	W	6-1	Ward (pen), Broadis 2, Gibbons 3	1,982
2	Mar	1	(h)	Northampton T	W	4-0	Broadis, Duncan 2, Bedford (og)	4,379
2		8	(a)	Northampton T	W	3-1	W.Sperrin, Broadis, Ludford	5,087
3		22	(h)	Cardiff C	D	3-3	Broadis 3	5,210
3		29	(a)	Cardiff C	W	3-2	Gibbons, Broadis, Ludford	22,000
4	Apr	5	(n²)	Arsenal	L	1-2	Howe	22,107
4		12	(h)	Arsenal	D	1-1	Ludford	25,258

Appearances
Goals

London War Cup Section 'B'

32	Jan	4	(h)	Clapton O	W	3-0	Gibbons 3	1,513
33		11	(a)	Clapton O	W	9-1	Hall, Broadis 2, Gibbons 3, Duncan, Ludford 2	1,013
34		18	(a)	Millwall	W	3-1	Broadis, Gibbons 2	6,000
35		25	(h)	Millwall	W	4-0	Ward (pen), Broadis, Ludford 2	2,280
36	Feb	1	(h)	West Ham U	L	1-2	Broadis	4,691
37		8	(a)	West Ham U	L	2-3	Hall, Gibbons	5,200
38	Apr	14	(h)	Reading	D	2-2	Wallace, Duncan	4,355
39		19	(a)	Reading	D	2-2	Duncan, Ludford	4,000
40	May	3	(h)	Arsenal	D	3-3	Ward (pen), K.Bennett, Gibbons	9,651
41		21	(n²)	Arsenal	W	3-0	Gibbons, Duncan 2	6,673
SF		31	(h)	Brentford	L	0-2		6,495

*Abandoned after 80 mins — air-raid warning. §Match stopped after 15 mins — air-raid warning — restarted after 80 mins. †Abandoned after 47 mins — air-raid warning. ‡Abandoned after 60 mins — air-raid warning. ¹Away match played at Chelmsford. ²Away match played at White Hart Lane, London.

Appearances
Goals

Arnold	Bennett K	Bennett L	Broadis	Browne	Buckingham	Burditt	Burgess	Duncan	Flack	Gibbons	Goodman	Hall	Henley	Hitchins	Hooper	Howe	Ludford	McCarthy	McCormick	Medley	O'Callaghan	Paton	Piper	Sainsbury	Sargent	Saunders	Skinner	Sperrin J	Sperrin W	Wallace	Wallis	Ward	Whatley	White	
					6		9	10				8		5	1		11						4		7							2	3		1
					6		9	10				4		5	1		11		7								8					2	3		2
					6		4					8		5	1		11			10				9	7							2	3		3
	8				6			10	1			4					9			11			5		7							2	3		4
					6		9	10	1			4		5			11			8					7							2	3		5
					6			10	1			8		5		4	9			11					7							2	3		6
	7				6			10	1				4	5			9			11							8					2	3		7
	7				6						10			5	1		9			11			4				8					2	3		8
					6		9		1					5		4	11		7		10	8										2	3		9
					6		4	10						5			9				11	8				1		7				2	3		10
					6		9	10						5			11				8	7				1						2	3	4	11
	7			9	6			10						5			11				8					1					2		3	4	12
	6							11						5	1		9				8	7							10			2	3	4	13
					6			11						5			9	1			8				7				10			2	3	4	14
					3			10		9		6		5	1		11				8							7				2		4	15
								10		9		8		5	1	6	11											7			2	3		4	16
										9		6		5	1	3	11				8							7	10			2		4	17
			8					10		9		6		5	1		11												7			2	3	4	18
								10		9		6		5	1		11											7	8			2	3	4	19
			8					10		9		6		5	1		11												7			2	3	4	20
11						10	9					6		5	1		8													7		2	3	4	21
			8				9			10		6		5	1		11												7			2	3	4	22
			8					10		9		6		5	1		11												7			2	3	4	23
1	5		4	1	14	1	9	17	5	8	1	15	1	22	14	4	23	1	2	6	8	4	3	1	6	3	3	5	8	1	2	22	20	13	
			2				8	6		9		1				2	11			2	1				1		1	3	3			2		1	

Arnold	Bennett K	Bennett L	Broadis	Browne	Buckingham	Burditt	Burgess	Duncan	Flack	Gibbons	Goodman	Hall	Henley	Hitchins	Hooper	Howe	Ludford	McCarthy	McCormick	Medley	O'Callaghan	Paton	Piper	Sainsbury	Sargent	Saunders	Skinner	Sperrin J	Sperrin W	Wallace	Wallis	Ward	Whatley	White	
			8		6			11				10		5	1		9											7				2	3	4	1
			8					10		9		6		5	1		11											7				2	3	4	1
			8					10		9		6		5	1		11											7				2	3	4	2
			8				9	10				6		5	1		11												7			2	3	4	2
			10				8			9		6		5	1		11												7			2	3	4	3
			10				6			9		8		5	1	7	11															2	3	4	3
			10				6			9		8		5	1	7	11															2	3	4	4
			10				6			9		8		5	1		11											7				2	3	4	4
			8		1		5	4		6		8		8	8	2	8											4	2			8	8	8	
			8		1			2		4						1	5											1	1			1			

1 own-goal

Arnold	Bennett K	Bennett L	Broadis	Browne	Buckingham	Burditt	Burgess	Duncan	Flack	Gibbons	Goodman	Hall	Henley	Hitchins	Hooper	Howe	Ludford	McCarthy	McCormick	Medley	O'Callaghan	Paton	Piper	Sainsbury	Sargent	Saunders	Skinner	Sperrin J	Sperrin W	Wallace	Wallis	Ward	Whatley	White	
			8					10		9		6		5	1		11				7											2	3	4	32
			8					10		9		6		5	1		11											7				2	3	4	33
			8					10		9		6		5	1		11											7				2	3	4	34
			8					10		9		6		5	1		11											7				2	3	4	35
		6	8							9		4		5	1		11										10	7			2	3			36
			8		3			10		9		6		5	1		11											7				2		4	37
					5			8		9		6			1		11												10	7		2	3	4	38
					6			10		9		8		5	1		11												7			2	3	4	39
	8							10		9		6		5	1	3	11												7			2		4	40
			8					10		9		6		5	1		11												7			2	3	4	41
			8					10		9		6		5	1		11												7			2	3	4	42
	1	1	8		3			10		11		11		10	11	1	11				1						1	5	5	1	1	11	8	10	
	1		5					5		11		2					5													1		2			

W.Arnold (Leicester City), D.W.Flack (Fulham), L.Henley (Arsenal), E.O'Callaghan (Fulham), T.G.Paton (Bournemouth & Boscombe Athletic), W.Saunders (West Bromwich Albion).

1941-42

London War League

1	Aug	30	(h)	Watford	W	5-0 Gibbons 2, Ludford 3	5,074
2	Sep	6	(a)	Aldershot	L	2-3 Gibbons 2	5,000
3		13	(h)	Millwall	W	3-0 Bennett L, Gibbons, Ludford	6,656
4		20	(a)	Arsenal	L	0-4	17,446
5		27	(h)	Queen's Park R	W	3-1 Ludford 2, Noble	5,955
6	Oct	4	(a)	Reading	D	1-1 Gibbons	5,000
7		11	(h)	Brighton & HA	L	1-2 Broadis	4,542
8		18	(a)	Brentford	W	4-1 Ludford, Duncan 2, Noble	6,000
9		25	(h)	Crystal P	D	1-1 Ludford	4,807
10	Nov	1	(a)	Fulham	D	2-2 Gibbons, Noble	6,000
11		8	(h)	C.Orient	W	2-0 Broadis, Gibbons	5,685
12		15	(a)	Portsmouth	W	2-1 Ludford, Broadis	6,095
13		22	(a)	Chelsea	D	1-1 Duncan	6,718
14		29	(a)	Charlton A	L	1-2 Ludford	4,210
15	Dec	6	(h)	West Ham U	D	1-1 Broadis	8,493
16		13	(a)	Watford	W	2-1 White, Hall	3,000
17		20	(h)	Aldershot	D	1-1 White	4,250
18		25	(a)	Millwall	W	2-1 Broadis 2	
19		27	(h)	Arsenal	L	1-2 Ludford	16,777
20	Jan	3	(a)	Queen's Park R	L	0-1	4,500
21		10	(h)	Reading	W	2-1 Broadis, Burgess	4,418
22		17	(a)	Brighton & HA	L	2-5 Sibley, Burgess	2,000
23		31	(a)	Crystal P	D	2-2 Gibbons, Ludford	5,332
24		14	(a)	C.Orient	W	3-2 Gibbons 3	4,500
25		21	(h)	Portsmouth	D	1-1 Gibbons	4,813
26		28	(h)	Chelsea	W	2-0 Ludford 2	6,558
27	Mar	7	(h)	Charlton A	W	2-0 Gibbons, Revell	4,641
28		14	(a)	West Ham U	W	3-2 Broadis 2, Gibbons	7,986
29	Apr	25	(h)	Brentford	W	2-1 Howe, Broadis	5,131
30	May	2	(h)	Fulham	W	7-1 Broadis, Gibbons 2, Stevens 2, Ludford 2	3,754

FINAL LEAGUE POSITION: 5th in the London War League — Appearances / Goals

London War Cup — Group 3

31	Mar	21	(a)	Reading	W	2-1 Ward (pen), Howe	6,000
32		28	(h)	Watford	W	5-2 Howe, Broadis, Gibbons 2, Ludford	4,627
33	Apr	4	(h)	Reading	W	2-1 Duncan, Ludford	7,526
34		6	(a)	Watford	D	0-0	4,541
35		11	(h)	Charlton A	L	0-3	9,505
36		18	(a)	Charlton A	L	0-4	7,677

Appearances / Goals

254

The following is a player appearance grid (shirt-number chart). Columns are players; the final column is the match number. Values are the shirt numbers worn. Some sparsely-filled cells are difficult to read precisely.

Bennett F	Bennett L	Broadis	Buckingham	Burgess	Cox	Ditchburn	Duncan	Edwards	Finch	Fitzgerald	Gibbons	Gilberg	Hall	Hitchins	Hooper	Howe	Joliffe	Kiernan	Ludford	Mannion	McCormick	McFarlane	Noble	Pearson	Revell	Sainsbury R	Sainsbury W	Sibley	Sperrin J	Sperrin W	Stevens	Trailor	Ward	Whatley	White	Williams	Woodward	#
8		6									9		10	5	1					11												7	2	3	4			1
8								10			9		6	5	1					11												7	2	3	4			2
8	10										9		6	5	1	4				11												7	2	3				3
8		6									9		10	5	1					11												7	2	3	4			4
8							10						6	5	1				7				11										3	2		4	9	5
8							10				9		6	5	1				7				11										3	2		4		6
8							10						6	5	1			9					11		7								3	2		4		7
8							10				9			5	1	6			7				11										3	2		4		8
8							10				9			5	1	6			7				11										3	2		4		9
1		8					10				9			5					7				11										3	2	6	4		10
		7				1	10				9		8	5					11													3	2	6	4		11
		8				1	10				9		4	5					7													3	2	6		11	12
1		8						11					10	5				9											7			3	2	6	4		13
		8				1	10				9		6	5					7													3	2		4	11	14
1		8					10				9	11	6	5					7													3	2		4		15
		8					10				9	11	6	5	1																	3	7	2		4		16
		8				1	10				9		6	5					11										7			3		2		4		17
		8				1	10				9			5					11										7			3	2	6		4		18
		8					10					11	6	5	1		9		7													3	2		4		19
		8	9			1	10						6	5												11			7			3	2		4		20
		8	9				10						6	5	1												11		7			3	2		4		21
			4				10				9		6	5	1				11	8									7			3	2					22
		10				7	1				9		6	5					11	8												3	2		4		23
		8				1	10				9		6	5					11										7			3	2		4		24
		10					11						6	5	1				9	8	7											3	2					25
		10									9		4	5	1				7	8			11		6							3	2					26
		8				1	10				9			5					11					6	7							3	2		4		27
	6	8					10	9					4	5	1	7			11												10	3	2				28
		8				1			7	6	9		4	5					11													3	2					29
3	**1**	**29**	**1**	**5**	**2**	**11**	**24**	**1**	**1**	**1**	**23**	**2**	**29**	**26**	**16**	**4**	**1**		**25**	**4**	**1**		**6**	**2**	**1**	**1**	**2**	**3**	**2**	**8**	**1**	**30**	**1**	**30**	**5**	**24**	**3**	
	1	**11**		**2**			**3**				**17**		**1**		**1**				**16**				**3**				**1**		**1**		**2**				**2**			

Bennett F	Bennett L	Broadis	Buckingham	Burgess	Cox	Ditchburn	Duncan	Edwards	Finch	Fitzgerald	Gibbons	Gilberg	Hall	Hitchins	Hooper	Howe	Joliffe	Kiernan	Ludford	Mannion	McCormick	McFarlane	Noble	Pearson	Revell	Sainsbury R	Sainsbury W	Sibley	Sperrin J	Sperrin W	Stevens	Trailor	Ward	Whatley	White	Williams	Woodward	#
		8				1	11				9		6	5		10													7			3	2		4			31
	6	8					10				9		4	5	1	7			11													3	2					32
		8				1	10				9		6	5		7			11													3	2		4			33
	6	8				1	10						5			11		9		7												3	2		4			34
		10			6				11		9		6	5		7		8	11													3	2					35
		10			6						9		5	1	4	8		7														3	2					36
	6	**2**	**1**	**4**	**4**	**1**			**5**		**5**		**5**	**2**	**6**		**2**	**4**	**1**	**1**									**1**			**6**		**6**	**4**			
		1			**1**				**2**						**2**		**2**																			**1**		

Finch (Fulham), A.Fitzgerald (Queen's Park Rangers), W.J.Mannion (Middlesbrough), T.U.Pearson (Newcastle United), C.H.Revell (Charlton Athletic), C.E.Williams (Bristol City).

1942-43

Football League South

1	Aug	29	(h)	Crystal P	L	1-3	Ludford	5,623
2	Sep	5	(a)	Queen's Park R	W	1-0	Sargent	4,300
3		12	(h)	Charlton A	W	6-1	Martin, Ludford 3, Gibbons, Beasley	7,064
4		19	(a)	West Ham U	L	1-3	Ludford	10,160
5		26	(h)	Southampton	D	1-1	Gibbons	5,678
6	Oct	3	(h)	Aldershot	W	4-0	Gibbons 4	8,132
7		10	(h)	Millwall	W	2-1	Beasley, Martin	5,957
8		17	(a)	Reading	W	6-2	Beasley, O'Callaghan, Gibbons 3, Pattison	5,000
9		24	(a)	Portsmouth	L	0-1		8,500
10		31	(h)	Chelsea	D	1-1	Martin (pen)	12,625
11	Nov	7	(h)	Arsenal	W	1-0	Beasley	21,551
12		14	(a)	Luton T	D	3-3	O'Callaghan, Gibbons, Martin	3,500
13		21	(h)	Watford	W	6-0	Ludford 2, Cox, Beasley, Gibbons, Head (og)	5,459
14		28	(a)	Crystal P	D	0-0		4,893
15	Dec	5	(h)	Queen's Park R	W	6-0	Cox, Martin, Gibbons 2, Ludford, Redyard (og)	8,295
16		12	(a)	Charlton A	W	3-0	Edwards, Ludford 2	7,000
17		19	(h)	West Ham U	W	2-0	Hall, Ludford	9,741
18		25	(h)	Brentford	D	1-1	Broadis	14,621
19		26	(a)	Brentford	L	1-2	Ludford	12,542
20	Jan	2	(a)	Southampton	L	1-2	Beasley	6,700
21		9	(a)	Aldershot	W	3-1	Beasley, Martin, Gibbons	4,000
22		16	(a)	Millwall	W	3-0	Broadis, Pattison 2	6,000
23		23	(h)	Reading	D	2-2	Beasley, Gibbons	7,369
24		30	(h)	Portsmouth	W	5-2	Beasley, Gibbons, Ludford 3	7,146
25	Feb	6	(a)	Chelsea	W	1-0	Gibbons	12,125
26		13	(n*)	Arsenal	L	0-1		30,690
27		20	(h)	Luton T	W	4-1	Sperrin, Martin (pen), Ludford, Beasley	6,868
28		27	(a)	Watford	W	3-0	Ward (pen), Ludford, Sperrin	2,489

FINAL LEAGUE POSITION: 2nd in Division One   Appearances
*Away match played at White Hart Lane, London.   Goals

League Cup

29	Mar	6	(h)	Chelsea	W	2-0	Ludford 2	13,438
30		13	(a)	Reading	D	1-1	Hall	6,000
31		20	(h)	Millwall	W	5-0	Beasley, Martin 2 (1 pen), Nelson, O'Callaghan	8,131
32		27	(a)	Chelsea	W	2-0	Ludford, Broadis	11,707
33	Apr	3	(h)	Reading	L	1-2	Broadis	21,755
34		10	(a)	Millwall	W	1-0	Beasley	6,000

Appearances
Goals

256

Beasley	Briggs	Broadis	Browne	Burgess	Chisholm	Cox	Ditchburn	Edwards	Finlay	Gibbons	Hall	Hooper	Howe	Jackson	Ludford	Martin	McCormick	O'Callaghan	Pattison	Rowley	Sperrin W	Ward	Whatley	White	Match
				6	3		1		7	9	5				8							2		4	1
			6		5		1				3				9			8				2		4	2
11			6		5		1		7	10	3				9	8						2		4	3
			6		5					10	3	1	11		9	8					7	2		4	4
11					5		1		7	10	3		6		9	8						2		4	5
7	1				5					9	6				11	8		10				2	3	4	6
7	1				5					9	6				11	8		10				2	3	4	7
7					5					9	6				10			8	11			2		4	8
8					5		1				10			9			7		11			2		4	9
7					5					9	6	1		10		8			11			2	3	4	10
7				6	5		1			9	10					8			11			2	3	4	11
					5					9	6	1			10	8		7	11			2	3		12
8					5	7				9		1	3		6			10	11			2		4	13
7					5			10			6	1			9				11			2	3	4	14
		10			5	7				9	6	1	3		11	8						2		4	15
		10			5			7		9	3	1			11	8						2		4	16
		10			5			7		9	6	1	3		11	8						2		4	17
8		10			5		1			9	6		7		11							2	3	4	18
7				6	5		1			9	10		2		11	8							3	4	19
7		10			5		1			9	6		3		11	8						2		4	20
7		10			5					9		1	3		6	8			11			2		4	21
7		10			5					9	6	1	3			8			11			2		4	22
8					5	7				9	6	1	3						11			2		4	23
7				6	5					9	2	1	3		10	8			11					4	24
7		10			5					9	6	1	3		11	8						2		4	25
7		10			5					9		1	6		4	8			11			2	3		26
11					5						6	1	4		9	8					7	2	3		27
8					5						10	1	6		9		7				11	2	3	4	28
21	2	9	3	4	28	3	9	3	3	23	25	16	16	2	23	19	2	6	12		3	26	11	25	
10		2				2		1		17	1				17	7		2	3		2	1			

2 own-goals

Beasley	Briggs	Broadis	Browne	Burgess	Chisholm	Cox	Ditchburn	Edwards	Finlay	Gibbons	Hall	Hooper	Howe	Jackson	Ludford	Martin	McCormick	O'Callaghan	Pattison	Rowley	Sperrin W	Ward	Whatley	White	Match
7		8			5						10	1	6		9			11				2	3	4	29
7		8			5						10	1	6		9				11			2	3	4	30
7					5						6	1	4		9	8		11				2	3		31
7		10			5						6	1	4		9	8		11				2	3		32
7		10			5						6	1	4		11	8				9		2	3		33
8					5			7			10	1	4		11					9		2	3		34
6		4			6			1			6	6	6		6	3		3	1	2		6	6	2	
2		2									1				3	2		1							

Barron played number 1 in Match 8; Bennett played number 6 in Match 16; Buckingham played number 6 in Match 34; Chapman played number 8 in Match 14; Dix played number 10 in Match 27; Duncan played number 10 in Match 1; Eastham played number 4 in Match 12; Gurr played number 10 in Match 23; Hores played number 10 in Match 2; Marshall played number 6 in Match 9; Muir played number 3 in Match 8; Nelson played number 10 in Match 31 and scored 1; Nicholson played number 3 in Match 9; Sainsbury played number 11 in Match 1; Sargent played number 7 in Match 2 and scored 1; Staley played number 11 in Match 2.

A.A.Beasley (Huddersfield Town), C.Briggs (Halifax Town), R.Brown (Leeds United), E.Chapman (West Ham United), S.Eastham (Liverpool), W.Hores (Newport County), H.Jackson (Burnley), E.Marshall (Sheffield United), J.R.Martin (Aston Villa), A.Muir (Albion Rovers), D.Nelson (Arsenal), E.O'Callaghan (Fulham), J.M.Pattison (Queen's Park Rangers), J.F.Rowley (Manchester United), R.Staley (Derby County).

1943-44

Football League South

1	Aug	28	(h)	Crystal P	D 1-1	Clayton	8,189
2	Sep	4	(a)	Queen's Park R	L 0-1		10,770
3		11	(h)	Charlton A	W 4-2	Beasley, Rowley 2, Mosley	9,950
4		18	(a)	West Ham U	D 3-3	O'Donnell 2, Rowley	12,148
5		25	(h)	Southampton	D 2-2	Bennett, O'Donnell	8,485
6	Oct	2	(h)	Aldershot	W 5-2	White, Martin, Rowley 2, Jones	13,159
7		9	(h)	Brighton & HA	W 2-0	Martin, Rowley	10,668
8		16	(a)	Reading	W 3-2	Burgess, Beasley, Jones	10,000
9		23	(a)	Luton T	L 2-4	O'Donnell 2	3,000
10		30	(h)	Chelsea	W 5-1	Beasley, Rowley 2, Smith, Jones	10,375
11	Nov	6	(a)	Brentford	W 2-0	Rowley 2	9,560
12		13	(a)	Clapton O	W 4-0	Burgess 2, O'Donnell, Jones	4,000
13		20	(h)	Watford	W 4-2	Burgess 3, Jobling (og)	8,499
14		27	(a)	Crystal P	L 0-3		6,138
14	Dec	4	(h)	Queen's Park R	D 2-2	Beasley, Jones	12,485
16		11	(a)	Charlton A	W 2-0	Beasley, Rowley	3,500
17		18	(h)	Arsenal	W 2-1	Beasley, Rowley	22,683
18		25	(h)	Fulham	W 2-0	Walters, Jones	16,629
19		27	(a)	Fulham	W 2-0	Ludford, Jones	13,200
20	Jan	1	(h)	West Ham U	W 1-0	Cox	40,997
21		8	(h)	Brentford	W 1-0	Burgess	16,922
22		15	(a)	Southampton	W 3-2	Burgess, Beasley, O'Donnell	13,000
23		22	(a)	Aldershot	W 1-0	Howe	6,000
24		29	(a)	Brighton & HA	W 2-0	Ward, Walters	6,000
25	Feb	5	(h)	Reading	D 2-2	Walters 2	14,937
26		12	(h)	Luton T	W 8-1	Beasley, Rowley 7	11,468
27	Apr	8	(a)	Chelsea	D 1-1	Russell (og)	25,000
28		22	(n*)	Arsenal	D 3-3	Burgess, Beasley, Martin	26,330
29		29	(h)	Clapton O	W 1-0	Whent	7,952
30	May	6	(a)	Watford	D 1-1	Bryant	2,655

*Away match played at White Hart Lane, London.

Appearances

Goals

League South Cup Section 2

31	Feb	19	(n‡)	Millwall	W 1-0	Beasley	4,000
32		26	(h)	Portsmouth	W 1-0	Rowley	15,224
33	Mar	4	(a)	Aldershot	L 1-2	Bryant	10,000
34		11	(h)	Millwall	W 1-0	Cox	15,319
35		18	(a)	Portsmouth	W 2-1	Rowley 2	15,000
36		25	(h)	Aldershot	W 2-0	Burgess, Martin	39,266
37	Apr	1	(n†)	Charlton A	L 0-3		35,000

†Semi-final, played at Stamford Bridge, London.

‡Away match played at Selhurst Park, London.

Appearances

Goals

Adams	Beasley	Browne	Bryant	Buckingham	Burgess	Chisholm	Clayton	Cox	Ditchburn	Dix	Flack	Gibbins	Gilberg	Hall	Harris	Hooper	Howe	Jones	Ludford	Martin	Mogford	Mosley	O'Callaghan	O'Donnell	Page	Rowley	Smith T	Walters	Ward	Whatley	Whent	White	Willis	Young	
	7		4		5	8			10					1	9				11										2	3		6			1
	8				5									1	7				10		4			9	11				2	3		6			2
	7				5	10								1				11	6	8	4			9					2	3					3
	7				5									1				11	8		4			9		10			2	3		6			4
	7				5									1	6			11						9		10			2	3		4			5
	7				5								6					11	8					9		10			2	3		4			6
	7			6	5				1									11	8							9			2	3		4			7
	7			6	5				1							10		11	8							9			2	3		4			8
	7			6	5				1									11	10	8				9					2	3		4			9
	7			6	5				1									11	8					9	10				2	3		4			10
	7		4		5				1				6					11	8					9	10				2	3					11
	8			6	5	7		1								10		11						9					2	3		4			12
	8			6	5	7		1								10		11						9					2	3		4			13
	7			5	6			1	8							10			11					9					2	3		4			14
	7			5			10	1								11	6	8					9					2	3		4			15
	7			6	5	11		1								3		9	8					10				2							16
	7			6	5			1								11	4	8					9		10			2	3						17
	10			6	5			1								11	9	8								7	2		4		3				18
	10			6	5			1								11	9		8						7	2		4		3				19
	10			6	5	11		1								9			8						7	2	3		4					20
3	10			6				1								11		8						5	9	7	2		4					21
	8			6	5	11		1								9									10	7	2	3		4				22
	8	9			5			6						1	10	11						6				7	2				3			23
	9		10	6	5	11		1								4						7	2		8		3							24
11				6	5			1		4												8			10	7	2			3					25
	8			6	5	11		1													10	9	7	2	3			4							26
11	7	9			5			1							8	6										2	3		4					27
	7			5	6			1		11							8						9		2	3		4							28
11	7	9		6						5						1			6		10	9		2		8	4	3							29
	4	7				11					5						1	6		10	9		2		8	3									30
4	28	2	3	6	19	24	2	9	21	2	2	2	1	6	1	8	5	16	14	14	4	3	2	11	2	18	2	9	30	21	2	22	6	2	
	9	1		9		1	1			1	7	1	3	1	7	19	1		4														1	1	1	

2 own-goals

Adams	Beasley	Browne	Bryant	Buckingham	Burgess	Chisholm	Clayton	Cox	Ditchburn	Dix	Flack	Gibbins	Gilberg	Hall	Harris	Hooper	Howe	Jones	Ludford	Martin	Mogford	Mosley	O'Callaghan	O'Donnell	Page	Rowley	Smith T	Walters	Ward	Whatley	Whent	White	Willis	Young	
	8	9				10	5		11										1									7	2	3		4	6			31
	8				6	5		11	1							10					4						9	7	2	3		4				32
	8	9			6	5		11	1							10											7	2	3		4				33
	8	9			5			11	1									10										2	3		4				34
	7	9			6	5		11	1						8											10		2	3		4				35
	7				6	5			1								10			8								2	3	4						36
11	10	9			5	7										1	6			1	6						2	3		4						37
1	7	1	4		6	6		6	5		1		2	2	2		1	1				2		3	7	7		3	3							
	1	1	1					1					1									3														

Bennett played number 8 in Match 5 and scored 1; Briggs played number 1 in Match 6; Davie played number 9 in Match 25; Edwards played number 10 in Match 27; Evans played number 6 in Match 34; Hunt played number 9 in Match 36; Manley played number 4 in Match 23; Nelson played number 10 in Match 33; Parker played number 11 in Match 36; Sainsbury played number 4 in Match 16; Sargent played number 8 in Match 37; JR Smith played number 4 in Match 36; Sperrin played number 7 in Match 34; Wilson played number 10 in Match 28.

A.A.Beasley (Huddersfield Town), C.Briggs (Halifax Town), B.L.Bryant (Chelsea), S.Clayton (Notts County), J.Davie (Brighton & Hove Albion), F.Edwards (Luton Town), J.L.Evans (Fulham), W.L.W.Flack (Norwich City), A.Harris (Belfast Distillery), D.A.Hunt (Sheffield Wednesday), E.N.Jones (West Bromwich Albion), T.Manley (Brentford), J.R.Martin (Aston Villa), R.Mogford (Newport County), D.Nelson (Arsenal), E.O'Callaghan (Fulham), F.O'Donnell (Aston Villa), C.Parker (Portsmouth), J.F.Rowley (Manchester United), J.C.R.Smith (Millwall), T.Smith (Crystal Palace), J.R.Whent (Canadian Army), J.Wilson (Brighton & Hove Albion), A.E.Young (Arsenal).

259

1944-45

Football League South

1	Aug	26	(h)	West Ham U	D	2-2	O'Donnell, Stevens	14,379
2	Sep	2	(h)	Arsenal	W	4-0	Broadis 2, Ludford 2	13,625
3		9	(a)	Reading	D	0-0		9,060
4		16	(h)	Portsmouth	D	1-1	Walters	14,167
5		23	(a)	Southampton	W	3-1	Burgess, Stevens, Walters	12,600
6		30	(h)	Charlton A	W	2-1	Stevens, Beasley	15,768
7	Oct	7	(a)	Crystal P	W	3-1	Ludford, Gilberg 2	9,000
8		14	(h)	Chelsea	L	1-5	Stevens	21,087
9		21	(a)	Luton T	W	9-1	Walters 2, Howe, Foreman, Burgess 4, Ludford	7,000
10		28	(h)	Brentford	D	2-2	Gilberg 2	23,207
11	Nov	4	(h)	Aldershot	W	7-0	Walters, Beasley 3, Foreman 3	14,768
12		11	(a)	Millwall	W	4-3	Beasley, Foreman 2, Stevens	6,964
13		18	(a)	Clapton O	W	2-0	Foreman 2	7,500
14		25	(h)	Fulham	W	2-1	Walters, Beasley	14,300
15	Dec	2	(a)	West Ham U	W	1-0	Gilberg	23,000
16		9	(n*)	Arsenal	W	3-2	Gibbons 3	29,432
17		16	(h)	Reading	W	3-2	Burgess, Gibbons 2	9,938
18		23	(a)	Queen's Park R	D	0-0		13,011
19		25	(h)	Queen's Park R	W	4-2	Burgess, Gibbons, Gilberg, Mallett (og)	16,958
20		30	(a)	Portsmouth	D	0-0		15,000
21	Jan	6	(h)	Southampton	W	4-0	Ward (pen), Burgess, Gibbons 2	16,727
22		13	(a)	Charlton A	W	2-1	Walters, Gibbons	7,000
23		20	(h)	Crystal P	W	3-1	Ward 2, Rowley	11,105
24		27	(a)	Chelsea	W	2-1	Walters, Rowley	20,540
25	Mar	24	(a)	Brentford	W	2-0	Burgess, Whittingham	16,750
26		31	(a)	Aldershot	W	2-1	Burgess, Henley	6,000
27	Apr	14	(h)	Millwall	W	4-0	Ward (pen), Beasley, Gibbons, Hall AE	13,597
28		21	(h)	Clapton O	W	4-0	Beasley, Burnett 2, Medley	10,317
29		28	(a)	Fulham	W	4-2	Ward (pen), Ludford, A.E.Hall, Freeman (og)	8,000
30	May	5	(h)	Luton T	W	1-0	Beasley	5,984

*Away match played at White Hart Lane, London.

Appearances
Goals

League South Cup Group 3

31	Feb	3	(h)	Queen's Park R	D	1-1	Burgess	20,331
32		10	(a)	West Ham U	L	0-1		21,000
33		17	(h)	Aldershot	W	6-1	Walters 2, Gibbons 4	15,616
34		24	(a)	Queen's Park R	L	0-1		20,000
35	Mar	3	(h)	West Ham U	W	4-0	Burgess, Martin, Gibbons 2	29,838
36		10	(a)	Aldershot	W	2-0	Flavell, Medley	6,000

Appearances
Goals

260

Adams	Beasley	Broadis	Brown	Burgess	Burke	Chisholm	Duke	Flavell	Foreman	Gibbons	Gilberg	Hall AE	Hall F	Howe	Hughes	Jackson	Ludford	Martin	Medley	Mogford	O'Donnell	Page	Rowley	Stevens	Wallis	Walters	Ward	White	Willis	
11				6											1			8			9	5	10			7	2	4	3	1
10	8			6											1	9					6					7	2	4	3	2
11				6		1									4		9			8				3		7	2			3
11													8		1	6					9	5	10	3		7	2	4		4
11				6											1	9					10	3				7	2		4	5
11				6	5			9							1					8			10	3		7	2		4	6
				6	5		8			11					1	9					10					7	2		3	7
				6						5	11				9			8			10					7	2	4	3	8
	10	6					9			5	8	1	11													7	2	4	3	9
8		9					10	5	6	1		11														7	2	4	3	10
8	1	6					9	10	5		11															7	2	4	3	11
8		6					9		5	1		11							10						7	2	4	3	12
8	1	6					9		5		11														7	2	4	3	13
8	1						9		5	6		11							10						7	2	4	3	14
10		6					8	9	11	5	1															7	2	4	3	15
10		6					8	9		5	1	11														7	2	4	3	16
10		6					8	9	11	5	1															7	2	4	3	17
8		6					9		5	1	11								10						7	2	4	3	18
	10	6	5				8	9	11	1															7	2	4	3	19
11	8	10		6	5			9		1															7	2	4	3	20
11	10			6	5		8	9		1															7	2	4	3	21
11		10		6	4		8	9		5															7	2		3	22
6				5			8	9		1											10	11	7	2	4	3			23
11	8	6					9		5	1														10	7	2	4	3	24
10		6	5				8			1		11													7	2	4		25
10		6	5					9		1	11													7	2	4	3	26
8		6		5			9	11	10	1														7	2	4	3	27
8			4	1			10	5				6	11											7	2		3		28
8		6	5				10		9		11													7	2	4	3		29
8		9	5				10		1	6	11													7	2	4	3		30
4	24	6	3	23	10	6	2	10	5	11	8	5	14	5	21	2	12	1	7	3	2	3	2	12	4	30	30	24	27	
	9	2	10					8	10	6	2	1			5			1	1			2	5			8	5			

2 own-goals

Adams	Beasley	Broadis	Brown	Burgess	Burke	Chisholm	Duke	Flavell	Foreman	Gibbons	Gilberg	Hall AE	Hall F	Howe	Hughes	Jackson	Ludford	Martin	Medley	Mogford	O'Donnell	Page	Rowley	Stevens	Wallis	Walters	Ward	White	Willis	
11				6			8	9					5										10			7	2	4	3	31
10	8	6					9		5	1		11													7	2	4	3	32
		6			10	9			5		8	11													7	2	4	3	33
10		6	4	5	1		9			8	11														7	2		3	34
		6		5	10	9			1	4	8														7	2			35
		6	5		10		9	1			8	11													7	2	4		36
3	1	6	2	2	1	4	5	3	1	3	1	4	4	1	6							1		6	6	4	5			
	2		1	6					1	1		2																		

Anderson played number 1 in Match 22; Boulton played number 1 in Match 8; Burnett played number 9 in Match 28 and scored 2; Dix played number 10 in Match 13; Dunn played number 10 in Match 3; Goodman played number 11 in Match 2; Henley played number 8 in Match 26 and scored 1; Hooper played number 1 in Match 33; Lyman played number 11 in Match 35; Moodie played number 1 in Match 31; Muir played number 4 in Match 7; Oakes played number 5 in Match 2; Smith played number 8 in Match 5; Swift played number 5 in Match 5; Tunney played number 3 in Match 36; Whatley played number 3 in Match 25; Whittingham played number 9 in Match 25 and scored 1.

A.Anderson (Heart of Midlothian), A.A.Beasley (Huddersfield Town), F.P.Boulton (Derby County), H.J.Brown (Queen's Park Rangers), C.Burke (Bournemouth & Boscombe Athletic), J.Burnett (Tooting), H.P.Duke (Norwich City), R.Dunn (West Ham United), R.Flavell (Arsenal), G.A.Foreman (West Ham United), F.W.Hall (Blackburn Rovers), W.A.Hughes (Huddersfield Town), J.Jackson (Chelsea), J.R.Martin (Aston Villa), R.Mogford (Newport County), J.Moodie (Airdrieonians), W.Muir (Rochdale), J.Oakes (Charlton Athletic), F.O'Donnell (Aston Villa), R.I.Pryde (Blackburn Rovers), J.F.Rowley (Manchester United), K.Smith (Bolton Wanderers), E.Tunney (Wrexham), A.Whittingham (Bradford City).

261

1945-46

Football League South

1	Aug	25	(h)	Wolves	L	1-4 Broadis	33,852
2	Sep	1	(a)	Wolves	L	2-4 Ward (pen), Lyman	24,899
3		8	(a)	West Ham U	D	1-1 Burgess	26,437
4		12	(h)	Leicester C	W	6-2 Burgess 2, McCormick, A.E.Hall, Ludford 2	13,294
5		15	(h)	West Ham U	L	2-3 Gibbons 2	34,342
6		22	(a)	West Brom A	L	0-5	24,433
7		29	(h)	West Brom A	W	4-2 Acquroff 2, Lyman 2	31,403
8	Oct	6	(a)	Birmingham C	L	0-8	21,608
9		13	(h)	Birmingham C	L	0-1	30,589
10		20	(a)	Swansea T	L	2-4 Stevens, Gibbons	16,985
11		27	(h)	Swansea T	W	3-1 A.E.Hall, Gibbons 2	20,407
12	Nov	3	(h)	Brentford	W	1-0 Gibbons	28,603
13		10	(a)	Brentford	W	3-1 A.E.Hall 2, Gibbons	19,270
14		17	(a)	Chelsea	W	2-1 Dix, Lyman	35,343
15		24	(h)	Chelsea	W	3-2 Broadis 2, Gibbons	43,717
16	Dec	1	(h)	Millwall	W	5-1 Ward (pen), Gibbons 3, Dix	34,807
17		8	(a)	Millwall	L	2-3 Burgess, Gibbons	24,143
18		15	(a)	Southampton	L	2-3 Ward (pen), Lyman	13,935
19		22	(h)	Southampton	W	4-3 Ward (pen), Gibbons 2, Lyman	17,932
20		25	(h)	Derby C	L	2-5 Broadis 2	33,700
21		26	(a)	Derby C	L	0-2	30,823
22		29	(a)	Leicester C	L	0-4	15,330
23	Jan	12	(a)	Luton T	L	1-3 Skinner	9,528
24		19	(h)	Luton T	L	2-3 Burgess, Lyman	13,108
25		26	(h)	Coventry C	W	2-0 Burgess, Whitchurch	17,632
26	Feb	2	(a)	Aston Villa	L	1-5 Burgess	30,736
27		9	(n*)	Arsenal	D	1-1 Blair	38,927
28		16	(h)	Arsenal	W	2-0 A.E.Hall, Whitchurch	44,510
29		20	(h)	Aston Villa	W	3-0 Jinks 2, Whitchurch	19,300
30		23	(h)	Charlton A	W	2-1 Skinner, Dix	37,743
31	Mar	9	(a)	Fulham	D	1-1 Whitchurch	30,000
32		16	(h)	Fulham	L	1-3 Dix (pen)	23,211
33		23	(h)	Plymouth A	W	2-0 Foreman 2	20,789
34		30	(a)	Plymouth A	W	1-0 Foreman	25,000
35	Apr	6	(a)	Portsmouth	W	1-0 Medley	22,000
36		13	(h)	Portsmouth	W	2-0 Foreman 2	23,000
37		17	(a)	Charlton A	L	0-1	10,000
38		19	(h)	Nottingham F	W	3-2 Ludford, Foreman, Medley	23,955
39		20	(a)	Newport C	W	4-1 Foreman 4	16,000
40		22	(a)	Nottingham F	W	2-0 Foreman, Medley	18,474
41		27	(h)	Newport C	W	1-0 Foreman	15,223
42	May	4	(a)	Coventry C	W	1-0 Foreman	11,446

    * Away match played at White Hart Lane   Appearances
                                                                                    Goals

FA Cup

3	Jan	5	(h)	Brentford	D	2-2 Burgess, A.E.Hall	30,202
3		10	(a)	Brentford	L	0-2	21,050

                                                                 Appearances
                                                                  Goals

Acquroff	Adams	Beasley	Bennett	Blair	Broadis	Buckingham	Burgess	Ditchburn	Dix	Ford	Foreman	Gibbons	Hall AE	Hall F	Hall J	Hughes	Joslin	Ludford	Lyman	McCormick	Medley	Nicholson	Page	Rundle	Sargent	Skinner	Smith	Stevens	Walters	Ward	Whitchurch	White	Willis	Match
		7				8	6					9	10			1					11									2		4	3	1
		7				8	6					9	10			1					11		5							2			3	2
							6						10	8		1	4	9					5	7						2			3	3
							6						10	8		1		9	7				5			11				2		4	3	4
							6						10	8		1		9	7				5			11				2		4	3	5
			7				6						10	8		1		9	11				5							2		4	3	6
9							6		5			10				1					11	7						8		2		4		7
							6	10	5			9				1					11	7						8		2		4	3	8
9							6	10	5			8				1					11	7								2		4	3	9
											10	9				1		6	11	7						5		8		2		4	3	10
			7				6		10			9	8			1	4	11					5							2			3	11
			7				6		10			9	8			1	4	11					5							2			3	12
									10			9	8			1	4	11			5					6	7			2			3	13
							6		10			9	8			1	4	11			5						7			2			3	14
			7				6		10			9	8			1	4	11			5									2			3	15
			7				6		10			9	8			1	4	11			5									2			3	16
							6		10			9	8			1	4	11			5						7			2			3	17
			7				6		10			9	8			1	4	11			5									2			3	18
							6		10			9	8			1	4	11	7		5									2			3	19
			8	7			6					9				1		4			11		5					10		2			3	20
			8				6		10							1		4	9		11		5	7						2			3	21
									10				8			1		4	11	7		5								2	6		3	22
		3							10							1		6	9		11					8		7		5		4	2	23
							6		10						5	1		9	11							8				2	7	4	3	24
						5	6		10							1		4								8				2	11			25
						5	6		10							1		4	7							8				2	11		3	26
			9		3		6		10						7	5	1									8					11	4	2	27
			9		3		6		10						7	5	1									8					11	4	2	28
					3		6								7	5	1									8					11	4	2	29
					3		6		10						7	5	1		9							8					11	4	2	30
			9		3		6		10								1				5					8		7			11	4	2	31
		9			3		6		10						7		1				5					8					11	4	2	32
		8			3		6		10	9					7		1	4					5								11		2	33
		8			3		6			9						1	4				7		5	10							11		2	34
		8			3		6			9						1	4				11	5				10					7		2	35
		8			3		6		10	9						1	4				11	5						7			7		2	36
		8			3		6			9						1	4				11	5			10						7		2	37
		8			3		6		10	9						1	4				11	5						7			7		2	38
		8			3		6			9						1	4				11	5			10			7			7		2	39
		8			3		6		10	9						1	4				11	5	7										2	40
		8			3		6	1	10	9							4				11	5						7					2	41
		8			3			1		9						6					11	5			10								2	42
2	1	2	11	2	9	19	37	2	26	3	10	21	24	6	9	27	4	30	21	3	17	11	16	3	2	11	4	14	2	26	17	25	32	
2			1	5		7			4		13	14	5			3	7	1	3			2	1			2	1			4	4			

Acquroff	Adams	Beasley	Bennett	Blair	Broadis	Buckingham	Burgess	Ditchburn	Dix	Ford	Foreman	Gibbons	Hall AE	Hall F	Hall J	Hughes	Joslin	Ludford	Lyman	McCormick	Medley	Nicholson	Page	Rundle	Sargent	Skinner	Smith	Stevens	Walters	Ward	Whitchurch	White	Willis	Match
							6		10						8	1		9	11	7		5								2		4	3	3
		7				5	6		10						8	1		9	11											2		4	3	3
1						1	2		2						2	2	2	2		1		1					2				2	2			
									1																									

Baily played number 10 in Match 29; Chisholm played number 5 in Match 1; Cox played number 7 in Match 42; Duquemin played number 9 in Match 31; Ferrier played number 3 in Match 25; Fletcher played number 9 in Match 26; Garwood played number 4 in Match 42; Gilberg played number 11 in Match 3; Howe played number 4 in Match 2; Howshall played number 6 in Match 25; Jinks played number 9 in Match 29 and scored 2; Morrison played number 9 in Match 22; Young played number 3 in Match 7.

J.Acquroff (Norwich City), A.A.Beasley (Huddersfield Town), H.Ferrier (Barnsley), F.Ford (Charlton Athletic), F.W.Hall (Blackburn Rovers), T.Howshall (Clapton Orient), W.A.Hughes (Huddersfield Town until October 1945 when he signed for Spurs), J.Jinks (Millwall), P.J.Joslin (Torquay United), G.H.Smith (Charlton Athletic), A.E.Young (Arsenal).

263

1946-47

Manager: Joe Hulme

1	Aug	31	(h)	Birmingham C	L	1-2	Foreman	51,256
2	Sep	7	(a)	West Brom A	L	2-3	Bennett, Medley	34,970
3		9	(h)	Southampton	W	2-1	Rundle, Bennett	22,153
4		14	(h)	Newcastle U	D	1-1	Bennett	52,213
5		19	(a)	Newport C	W	4-2	Ludford, Whitchurch, Bennett, Dix	18,169
6		21	(a)	Swansea T	W	2-0	Bennett 2	22,934
7		28	(h)	Manchester C	D	0-0		55,253
8	Oct	5	(h)	Burnley	D	1-1	Medley	44,351
9		7	(h)	Newport C	W	3-1	Foreman 2, Medley	14,540
10		12	(a)	Barnsley	W	3-1	Burgess, Foreman, Medley	24,494
11		19	(a)	West Ham U	D	2-2	Bennett, Foreman	34,341
12		26	(h)	Sheffield W	W	2-0	Cox, Bennett	33,251
13	Nov	2	(a)	Fulham	D	1-1	Foreman	40,762
14		9	(h)	Bury	W	2-1	Burgess, Stevens	38,764
15		16	(a)	Luton T	L	2-3	Bennett, Foreman	26,362
16		23	(h)	Plymouth A	W	2-1	Bennett, Foreman	40,795
17		30	(a)	Leicester C	D	1-1	Foreman	34,543
18	Dec	7	(h)	Chesterfield	L	3-4	Bennett, Cox 2	38,654
19		14	(a)	Millwall	W	3-0	Rundle 2, Foreman	20,937
20		21	(h)	Bradford	D	3-3	Foreman 2, Dix (pen)	24,779
21		25	(a)	Coventry C	L	1-3	Burgess	23,307
22		26	(h)	Coventry C	D	0-0		44,311
23		28	(a)	Birmingham C	L	0-1		44,171
24	Jan	4	(h)	West Brom A	W	2-0	Burgess, Walters	40,537
25		18	(a)	Newcastle U	L	0-1		62,876
26		27	(h)	Swansea T	W	3-1	Bennett, Dix, Whitchurch	6,292
27	Feb	1	(a)	Manchester C	L	0-1		41,645
28		18	(a)	Burnley	D	0-0		28,462
29	Mar	1	(a)	Sheffield W	L	1-5	Rundle	23,144
30		8	(h)	Fulham	D	1-1	Bennett	27,715
31		22	(h)	Luton T	W	2-1	Cox, Dix	36,160
32		29	(a)	Plymouth A	W	4-3	Bennett 2, Foreman 2	22,525
33	Apr	4	(h)	Nottingham F	W	2-0	Burgess, Rundle	29,176
34		5	(h)	Leicester C	W	2-1	Rundle 2	37,843
35		7	(a)	Nottingham F	D	1-1	Bennett	30,656
36		12	(a)	Chesterfield	D	0-0		14,802
37		19	(h)	Millwall	W	2-1	Rundle, Brolly (og)	34,311
38		26	(a)	Bradford	L	1-2	Rundle	11,371
39	May	3	(a)	Bury	W	2-1	Cox, Rundle	13,063
40		10	(a)	Southampton	L	0-1		12,884
41		17	(h)	West Ham U	D	0-0		37,503
42	Jun	7	(h)	Barnsley	D	1-1	Dix (pen)	17,575

FINAL LEAGUE POSITION: 6th in Division Two

Appearances
Goals

FA Cup

3	Jan	11	(h)	Stoke C	D	2-2	Ludford, Bennett	65,681
R		15	(a)	Stoke C	L	0-1		38,631

Appearances
Goals

Norwich Hospital Charity Cup

	May	12	(a)	Norwich C	W	2-0	Bennett 2	

Appearances
Goals

	Baily	Bennett	Buckingham	Burgess	Cox	Ditchburn	Dix	Foreman	Gilberg	Hall AE	Hughes	Jones	Joseph	Ludford	Medley	Nicholson	Rundle	Skinner	Stevens	Tickridge	Trailor	Walters	Whitchurch	Willis	Woodward	
	8	2	6	7	1		9							4	11	5	10							3		1
	8	3	6		1		9							4	11	5		10					7	2		2
	8	3	6		1		9							4	11	5	7	10					2			3
	8		6		1	10	9							4	11	5	7			3				2		4
	8		6		1	10	9							4	11					3			7	2	5	5
	8		6		1	10	9							4	11					3			7	2	5	6
	8		6		1	10	9							4	11					3			7	2	5	7
	8	4	6		1	10	9		7						11	5				3				2		8
	8		6		1	10	9							4	11	5				3			7	2		9
10			6	7	1	8	9							4	11	5				3				2		10
	8			7	1	10	9							4		6			11	3				2	5	11
	8		6	7	1	10	9							4		3			11					2	5	12
	8		6	7	1	10	9							4		3			11					2	5	13
	8		6	7	1	10	9							4		3			11					2	5	14
	8		6	7	1	10	9							4		3			11					2	5	15
	8		6	7	1	10	9							4		3			11					2	5	16
	8		6	7	1	10	9							4		3			11					2	5	17
	8		6	7	1	10	9							4		3			11					2	5	18
		3	6	7	1	10	9							4		5	8		11					2		19
	8	3	6	7	1	10	9							4		5			11					2		20
	8	3	6	7	1	10	9							4		5			11					2		21
		3	6		1	10	9		7					4		5	8		11	2				2		22
		3	6		1	10	9		8					4		5			11	2		7		2		23
10		3	6		1	8	9							4		5			11	2	7			2		24
	8		6		1		9	11	7					4		5	10			3				2		25
	8	3	6		1	10	9		7					4		5							11	2		26
	8	3	6		1	10	9		7					4		5							11	2		27
	8	3	6		1	10	9		7			11		4		5								2		28
	8	3	6	7	1	10								4		5	9		11					2		29
	8	3	6	7	1	10								4		5	9		11					2		30
	8	3	6	7	1	10								4		5	9		11					2		31
	8	2	6	7	1		10							4		5	9		11					3		32
	8	3	6	7	1	10								4		5	9		11					2		33
	8	3	6	7	1	10								4		5	9		11	2				2		34
	8	3	6	7		10							1	4		5	9		11					2		35
	8	3	6	7	1	10								4		5	9		11					2		36
	8	3	6	7	1	10								4		5	9		11					2		37
	8	3	6	7	1	10								4		5	9		11					2		38
	8	3	6	7	1	10								4		5	9		11					2		39
	8	3		7	1	10								4		5	9		11		6			2		40
	8	3	6	7	1	10	9							4		5			11					2		41
	8	3	6		1	10						7		4		5	9		11					2		42
1	38	27	40	25	41	31	36	1	8	1	1	1	1	41	10	39	18	1	30	14	1	1	8	37	11	
	16			5	5			5	14					1	4		10		1			1	2			

1 own-goal

	Baily	Bennett	Buckingham	Burgess	Cox	Ditchburn	Dix	Foreman	Gilberg	Hall AE	Hughes	Jones	Joseph	Ludford	Medley	Nicholson	Rundle	Skinner	Stevens	Tickridge	Trailor	Walters	Whitchurch	Willis	Woodward	
	8	3	6		1	10	9							4		5			11				7	2		3
	8	3	6		1	10	9							4		5			11				7	2		R
	2	2	2		2	2	2							2		2			2				2	2		
	1													1												

	Baily	Bennett	Buckingham	Burgess	Cox	Ditchburn	Dix	Foreman	Gilberg	Hall AE	Hughes	Jones	Joseph	Ludford	Medley	Nicholson	Rundle	Skinner	Stevens	Tickridge	Trailor	Walters	Whitchurch	Willis	Woodward	
	8	3		7	1	10								4		5	9		11		6			2		
	1	1		1	1	1								1		1	1		1		1			1		
	2																									

1947-48

1	Aug	23	(a)	West Brom A	L 0-1	32,521
2		27	(a)	Bury	L 0-2	16,391
3		30	(h)	Sheffield W	W 5-1 Jordan 2, Duquemin, Bennett 2	36,751
4	Sep	1	(h)	Bury	D 2-2 Duquemin, Jones	29,635
5		6	(a)	Cardiff C	W 3-0 Duquemin 2, Bennett	48,894
6		8	(a)	West Ham U	D 1-1 Jordan	25,732
7		13	(h)	Bradford	W 3-1 Jordan, Duquemin 2	44,004
8		15	(h)	West Ham U	D 2-2 Jordan, Bennett	33,415
9		20	(a)	Nottingham F	L 0-1	26,202
10		27	(h)	Doncaster R	W 2-0 Jordan 2	46,011
11	Oct	4	(a)	Southampton	D 1-1 Duquemin	23,860
12		11	(a)	Barnsley	L 1-2 Duquemin	24,715
13		18	(h)	Plymouth A	W 2-0 Duquemin, Bennett	35,249
14		25	(a)	Luton T	D 0-0	26,496
15	Nov	1	(h)	Brentford	W 4-0 Baily, Duquemin 3	42,362
16		8	(a)	Leicester C	W 3-0 Cox, Stevens 2	34,426
17		15	(h)	Leeds U	W 3-1 Burgess, Baily, Duquemin	41,563
18		22	(a)	Fulham	W 2-0 Duquemin, Stevens	36,147
19		29	(h)	Coventry C	W 2-1 Bennett, Stevens	41,843
20	Dec	6	(a)	Newcastle U	L 0-1	57,950
21		13	(h)	Birmingham C	L 1-2 Baily	53,730
22		20	(h)	West Brom A	D 1-1 Cox	40,219
23		25	(h)	Chesterfield	W 3-0 Baily, Duquemin, Bennett	44,863
24		27	(a)	Chesterfield	L 1-3 Burgess	19,495
25	Jan	3	(a)	Sheffield W	L 0-1	47,902
26		17	(h)	Cardiff C	W 2-1 Cox (pen), Jordan	57,386
27		31	(a)	Bradford	W 2-0 Cox, Jordan	20,807
28	Feb	14	(a)	Doncaster R	D 1-1 Woodward	24,033
29		21	(h)	Southampton	D 0-0	29,784
30	Mar	6	(a)	Plymouth A	D 1-1 Bennett	32,049
31		15	(h)	Barnsley	L 0-3	31,969
32		20	(a)	Brentford	L 0-2	31,297
33		26	(a)	Millwall	D 0-0	42,288
34		27	(h)	Leicester C	D 0-0	33,108
35		29	(h)	Millwall	W 3-2 Jordan (pen), Duquemin, Jones	31,339
36	Apr	3	(a)	Leeds U	W 3-1 Rundle, Baily, Flint	24,891
37		7	(h)	Luton T	L 0-1	23,807
38		10	(h)	Fulham	L 0-2	32,490
39		12	(h)	Nottingham F	L 0-3	18,569
40		17	(a)	Coventry C	D 1-1 Barratt (og)	18,262
41		24	(h)	Newcastle U	D 1-1 Opp own goal	44,164
42	May	1	(a)	Birmingham C	D 0-0	35,569

FINAL LEAGUE POSITION: 8th in Division Two

Appearances
Goals

FA Cup

3	Jan	10	(a)	Bolton W	W 2-0* Duquemin 2	37,075
4		24	(h)	West Brom A	W 3-1 Cox, Duquemin 2	71,853
5	Feb	7	(h)	Leicester C	W 5-2 Cox (pen), Jordan 3, South (og)	69,049
6		28	(a)	Southampton	W 1-0 Bennett	28,425
SF	Mar	13	(n†)	Blackpool	L 1-3* Duquemin	70,687

*After extra-time. †Played at Villa Park, Birmingham.

Appearances
Goals

Player appearances and goals grid (shirt numbers by match).

Baily	Bennett	Buckingham	Burgess	Chisholm	Cox	Ditchburn	Dix	Duquemin	Flint	Gilberg	Hughes	Jones	Jordan	Ludford	Medley	Nicholson	Rundle	Stevens	Tickridge	Trailor	Walters	Willis	Withers	Woodward	
8	3	6	5			1	10					7				4	9	11	2						1
8	3	6	5			1	10					7				4	9	11	2						2
10	3	6			7	1		9				11	8			4			2					5	3
	3				7	1	10	9				11	8			4			2	6				5	4
10	3	6			7	1		9				11	8			4			2					5	5
10	3	6			7	1		9				11	8			4			2					5	6
10	3	6				1		9				7	8			4		11	2					5	7
10	3	6				1						7	8			4	9	11	2					5	8
10	3	6				1						7	8			4	9	11	2					5	9
	3	6			7	1	10						8			4	9	11	2					5	10
	3	6			7	1	10	9					8			4		11	2					5	11
10	3	6			7	1		9					8			4		11	2					5	12
10	3				7	1		9					8			4		11	2	6				5	13
10	3	6			7	1		9					8			4		11	2					5	14
8	10	3	6		7	1		9								4		11	2					5	15
8	10	3	6		7	1		9								4		11	2					5	16
8	10	3	6		7	1		9								4		11	2					5	17
8	10	3	6		7	1		9								4		11	2					5	18
8	10	3	6		7	1		9								4		11	2					5	19
8	10	3	6		7	1		9								4		11	2					5	20
8	10	3	6		7	1		9								4		11	2					5	21
8	10	3	6		7	1		9								4		11	2					5	22
8	10	3	6		7	1		9								4		11	2					5	23
8	10	3	6		7	1		9						4				11	2					5	24
8	10	3	6		7	1		9						4				11	2					5	25
8		3	6		7	1		9					10			4		11	2					5	26
10		3	6		7	1		9				11	8			4			2					5	27
10		3	6		7	1		9				11	8			4			2					5	28
10		3			7	1		9				11	8			4			2	6				5	29
10	8	3			7	1		9				11				4			2	6				5	30
10	8	6				1		9				11				4			2	7		3		5	31
10	8	3			7	1		9				11				4			2	6				5	32
10	3	6			7	1		9	11				8			4			2					5	33
10	3				7	1		9				11	8			4			2	6				5	34
10	3					1		9			7	11	8			4			2	6				5	35
10		6	3		7	1							8			4	9	11	2					5	36
10		6	3		7	1		9	11				8			4			2					5	37
10	4	3	6		7	1		9	11				8						2					5	38
10	8	3	6		7	1		9		7		11				4			2					5	39
10	3	6			7	1		9				11	8			4			2					5	40
10	3	6			7	1		9				11	8			4			2					5	41
10	3	6			7	1		9				11	8			4			2					5	42
22	35	41	32	2	34	41	5	36	5	1	1	19	24	8	2	38	6	22	38	10	1	3	1	35	
5	8		2		4			16	1			2	10				1	4						1	

2 own-goals

Baily	Bennett	Buckingham	Burgess	Chisholm	Cox	Ditchburn	Dix	Duquemin	Flint	Gilberg	Hughes	Jones	Jordan	Ludford	Medley	Nicholson	Rundle	Stevens	Tickridge	Trailor	Walters	Willis	Withers	Woodward	
10		3	6		7	1		9					8			4		11	2					5	3
10		3	6		7	1		9					8			4		11	2					5	4
10		3	6		7	1		9					8			4		11	2					5	5
8	10	3			7	1		9				11			4				2	6					6
10	8	3	6		7	1		9								4		11	5		2				SF
5	2	5	4		5	5		5				1	3	2	1	5		3	5	1				3	
	1												3												

1 own-goal

1948-49

Manager: Joe Hulme

1	Aug	21	(h)	Sheffield W	W 3-2	Baily, Duquemin, Jones	51,265
2		23	(a)	Coventry C	L 0-2		21,110
3		28	(a)	Lincoln C	D 0-0		19,540
4		30	(h)	Coventry C	W 4-0	Cox, Duquemin 2, Jones	31,768
5	Sep	4	(h)	Chesterfield	W 4-0	Cox, Baily 2, Jones	46,804
6		8	(a)	Leeds U	D 0-0		33,793
7		11	(a)	West Brom A	D 2-2	Duquemin, Bennett	32,279
8		13	(h)	Leeds U	D 2-2	Cox, Jones	37,640
9		18	(h)	Bury	W 3-1	Duquemin, Bennett, Jones	60,442
10		25	(a)	West Ham U	L 0-1		38,132
11	Oct	2	(h)	Blackburn R	W 4-0	Baily, Bennett 2, Jones	53,721
12		9	(a)	Cardiff C	W 1-0	Jones	56,018
13		16	(h)	Queen's Park R	W 1-0	Baily	69,718
14		23	(a)	Luton T	D 1-1	Baily	24,859
15		30	(h)	Bradford	W 5-1	Burgess 2, Duquemin, Bennett, Jones	47,955
16	Nov	6	(a)	Southampton	L 1-3	Jones	28,800
17		13	(h)	Barnsley	W 4-1	Bennett, Duquemin, Baily 2	48,989
18		20	(a)	Grimsby T	D 1-1	Cox	15,863
19		27	(h)	Nottingham F*	D 0-0		31,989
20	Dec	4	(a)	Fulham	D 1-1	Nicholson	36,444
21		11	(h)	Plymouth A	W 3-0	Baily, Duquemin, Boyd (og)	41,910
22		18	(a)	Sheffield W	L 1-3	Baily	40,256
23		25	(a)	Leicester C	W 2-1	Burgess, Bennett	30,949
24		27	(h)	Leicester C	D 1-1	Rundle	49,411
25	Jan	1	(h)	Lincoln C	L 1-2	Jones	33,218
26		15	(a)	Chesterfield	L 0-1		15,861
27		22	(h)	West Brom A	W 2-0	Baily, Jones	62,566
28	Feb	5	(a)	Bury	D 1-1	Bennett	17,679
29		12	(h)	Nottingham F	W 2-1	Duquemin, Bennett	37,599
30		19	(h)	West Ham U	D 1-1	Bennett	62,980
31		26	(a)	Blackburn R	D 1-1	Jones	20,262
32	Mar	5	(h)	Cardiff C	L 0-1		51,183
33		12	(a)	Queen's Park R	D 0-0		25,416
34		19	(h)	Luton T	W 2-1	Bennett 2	41,839
35		26	(a)	Bradford	D 1-1	Duquemin	13,304
36	Apr	2	(h)	Southampton	L 0-1		69,265
37		9	(a)	Barnsley	L 1-4	Bennett	16,796
38		15	(h)	Brentford	W 2-0	Bennett, Medley	39,050
39		16	(h)	Grimsby T	W 5-2	Bennett 2, Duquemin 2, Medley	29,808
40		18	(a)	Brentford	D 1-1	Walters	19,004
41		23	(a)	Nottingham F	D 2-2	Nicholson, Duquemin	27,126
42		30	(h)	Fulham	D 1-1	Duquemin	50,133
43	May	7	(a)	Plymouth A	W 5-0	Duquemin, Bennett 3, Medley	23,927

FINAL LEAGUE POSITION: 5th in Division Two
*Abandoned 17 minutes — fog.

Appearances
Goals

FA Cup

3	Jan	8	(a)	Arsenal	L 0-3		47,314

Appearances
Goals

Baily	Bennett	Buckingham	Burgess	Clarke	Cox	Ditchburn	Duquemin	Garwood	Gilberg	Jones	Ludford	Medley	Nicholson	Rundle	Stevens	Tickeridge	Toulouse	Walters	Willis	Withers	Woodward	#
8	10	3	6		7	1	9			11			4			2					5	1
8	10	3	6			1	9			7			4	5	11	2						2
8	10	3	6		7	1	9			11			4			2					5	3
8	10	3	6		7	1	9			11			4			2					5	4
8	10	3	6		7	1	9			11			4			2					5	5
8	10	3	6		7	1	9			11			4			2					5	6
8	10	3	6		7	1	9			11			4			2	5					7
8	10	3	6		7	1	9			11			4			2	5					8
8	10	3	6		7	1	9			11			4	5		2						9
8	10	3	6		7	1	9			11			4	5		2						10
8	10	3	6		7	1	9			11			4	5		2						11
8	10	5	6		7	1	9			11			4			2			3			12
8	10	5	6		7	1	9			11			4			2			3			13
8	10	5			7	1	9	6					4		11	2			3			14
8	10	5	6		7	1	9			11			4			2			3			15
8	10	5	6		7	1	9			11			4			2			3			16
10	8	5	6		7	1	9			11			4			2			3			17
8	10	5	6		7	1	9			11			4			2			3			18
8	10	5	6			1	9			11			4			2		7		3		19
8	10	5	6		7	1	9			11			4			2			3			20
8	10	3	6		7	1	9			11			4			2					5	21
8	10	3	6		7	1	9			11			4			2					5	22
8	10	3	6		7	1	9			11			4			2					5	23
8	10	3	6		7	1				11		9	4			2					5	24
8	10	5	6		7	1				11		9	4			2			3			25
8	10		6		7	1				11		9	4			2				3	5	26
8	10		6			1	9			11			4			2		7		3	5	27
8	10		6			1	9			11			4			2		7		3	5	28
8	10		6			1	9			11			4			2		7		3	5	29
8	10		6			1	9			11			4			2		7		3	5	30
8	10		6			1	9			11			4			2		7		3	5	31
8	10	3	6			1	9			11			4			2		7			5	32
	10		6		7	1	9			11	3		4	8		2					5	33
8	10		6	5	7	1	9			11	3		4			2						34
8	10		6	5	7	1	9			11	3		4			2						35
8	10		6	5	7	1	9			11	3		4			2						36
10	8		6	5	7	1	9			11	3		4			2						37
10	8		6	5		1	9			11			4			2		7		3		38
10	8		6	5		1	9			11			4			2		7		3		39
10	8		6	5		1	9			11			4			2		7		3		40
10	8			5		1	9	6		11			4			2		7		3		41
10	8		6	5		1	9			11			4			2		7		3		42
8	10		6	5		1	9			11			4			2		7		3		43
42	43	26	41	10	31	43	38	2		36	10	6	42	4	2	42	2	13	11	12	17	
11	19	3			4		15			12		3	2	1				1				

1 own-goal

Baily	Bennett	Buckingham	Burgess	Clarke	Cox	Ditchburn	Duquemin	Garwood	Gilberg	Jones	Ludford	Medley	Nicholson	Rundle	Stevens	Tickeridge	Toulouse	Walters	Willis	Withers	Woodward	#
	10	3	6		7	1	8			11			4	9		2					5	3
	1	1	1		1	1	1			1			1	1		1					1	

1949-50

Manager: Arthur Rowe

#	Month	Date		Opponent	Result	Scorers	Attendance
1	Aug	20	(a)	Brentford	W 4-1	Bennett, Duquemin, Medley 2	32,702
2		22	(h)	Plymouth A	W 4-1	Ramsey (pen), Bennett, Baily, Medley	41,882
3		27	(h)	Blackburn R	L 2-3	Walters 2	53,016
4		31	(a)	Plymouth A	W 2-0	Bennett, Baily	24,828
5	Sep	3	(a)	Cardiff C	W 1-0	Medley	42,649
6		5	(h)	Sheffield W	W 1-0	Duquemin	37,697
7		10	(h)	Leeds U	W 2-0	Bennett, Baily	48,274
8		17	(h)	Bury	W 3-1	Nicholson, Duquemin, Baily	54,438
9		24	(a)	Leicester C	W 2-1	Walters, Duquemin	36,846
10	Oct	1	(h)	Bradford	W 5-0	Ramsey (pen), Walters, Bennett, Medley 2	54,905
11		8	(a)	Southampton	D 1-1	Walters	30,240
12		15	(h)	Coventry C	W 3-1	Bennett, Duquemin 2	54,375
13		22	(a)	Luton T	D 1-1	Walters	27,319
14		29	(h)	Barnsley	W 2-0	Duquemin, Baily	54,856
15	Nov	5	(a)	West Ham U	W 1-0	Walters	31,734
16		12	(h)	Sheffield U	W 7-0	Walters 3, Duquemin 2, Medley 2	54,193
17		19	(a)	Grimsby T	W 3-2	Ramsey, Bennett, Medley	22,482
18		26	(h)	Queen's Park R	W 3-0	Nicholson, Bennett 2	62,783
19	Dec	3	(a)	Preston NE	W 3-1	Bennett, Duquemin, Medley	35,501
20		10	(h)	Swansea T	W 3-1	Bennett, Duquemin 2	50,758
21		17	(h)	Brentford	D 1-1	Baily	49,297
22		24	(a)	Blackburn R	W 2-1	Scarth, Medley	33,078
23		26	(h)	Chesterfield	W 1-0	Ramsey (pen)	61,879
24		27	(a)	Chesterfield	D 1-1	Scarth	26,341
25		31	(h)	Cardiff C	W 2-0	Rees, Baily	59,780
26	Jan	14	(a)	Leeds U	L 0-3		50,476
27		21	(a)	Bury	W 2-1	Walters, Bennett	27,386
28	Feb	4	(h)	Leicester C	L 0-2		60,595
29		18	(a)	Bradford	W 3-1	Duquemin 2, Rees	20,287
30		25	(h)	Southampton	W 4-0	Rees, Duquemin, Medley 2	70,302
31	Mar	4	(a)	Coventry C	W 1-0	Medley	36,320
32		11	(h)	Luton T	D 0-0		53,145
33		18	(a)	Barnsley	L 0-2		22,346
34		25	(h)	West Ham U	W 4-1	Walters 2, Bennett, Medley	51,124
35	Apr	1	(a)	Queen's Park R	W 2-0	Baily, Medley	29,771
36		7	(h)	Hull C	D 0-0		66,889
37		8	(h)	Preston NE	W 3-2	Walters, Bennett, Medley	49,170
38		10	(a)	Hull C	L 0-1		38,345
39		15	(a)	Sheffield U	L 1-2	Medley	41,419
40		22	(h)	Grimsby T	L 1-2	Duquemin	46,423
41		29	(a)	Swansea T	L 0-1		16,417
42	May	6	(a)	Sheffield W	D 0-0		50,777

FINAL LEAGUE POSITION: 1st in Division Two

Appearances
Goals

FA Cup

3	Jan	7	(a)	Stoke C	W 1-0	Baily	47,000
4		28	(h)	Sunderland	W 5-1	Walters 2, Bennett 2, Medley	66,246
5	Feb	11	(a)	Everton	L 0-1		72,921

Appearances
Goals

Norwich Hospital Charity Cup

	May	8	(a)	Norwich C	D 2-2	Duquemin, Scarth	15,000

Appearances
Goals

Baily	Bennett	Burgess	Clarke	Cook	Ditchburn	Duquemin	Gilberg	Ludford	Marchi	Medley	Nicholson	Ramsey	Rees	Rundle	Scarth	Tickeridge	Walters	Willis	Withers	No.
10	8	6	5		1	9			11	4	2					7		3		1
10	8	6	5		1	9			11	4	2					7		3		2
10	8	6	5		1	9			11	4	2					7		3		3
10	8	6	5		1	9			11	4	2					7		3		4
10	8	6	5		1	9			11	4	2					7		3		5
10	8	6	5		1	9			11	4	2					7		3		6
10	8	6	5		1	9			11	4	2					7		3		7
10	8	6	5		1	9			11	4	2					7		3		8
10	8	6	5		1	9			11	4	2					7		3		9
10	8	6	5		1	9			11	4	2					7		3		10
10	8	6	5		1	9			11	4	2					7		3		11
10	8		5		1	9	6		11	4	2					7		3		12
10	8	6	5		1	9			11	4	2					7		3		13
10	8	6	5		1	9			11	4	2					7		3		14
10	8	6	5		1	9			11	4	2					7		3		15
10	8	6	5		1	9			11	4	2					7		3		16
10	8	6	5		1	9			11	4	2					7		3		17
10	8	6	5	7	1	9			11	4	2							3		18
10	8	6	5	7	1	9			11	4	2							3		19
10	8	6	5	7	1	9			11	4	2							3		20
10	8	6	5		1	9			11	4	2				7			3		21
10	8	6	5		1	9			11	4	2				7			3		22
10	8	6	5		1	9			11	4	2					7		3		23
10		6	5		1	9			11	4	2	8			7			3		24
10			5		1	9	6		11	4	2	8				7		3		25
10		6	5		1	9			11	4	2	8				7		3		26
10	8	6	5		1				11	4	2	9				7		3		27
10	8	6	5		1				11	4	2	9				7		3		28
	8	6	5		1	9		4	11		2	10				7		3		29
10			5		1	9	6		11	4	2	8				7		3		30
10		6	5		1	9			11	4	2	8				7		3		31
10		6	5		1	9			11	4	2	8				7		3		32
10	8	6	5		1	9			11	4	2					7		3		33
10	8	6	5		1	9			11	4	2					7		3		34
10	8	6	5		1	9			11	4	2					7		3		35
10	8	6	5		1	9			11	4	2					7		3		36
10	8	6	5		1	9			11	4	2					7		3		37
10	8	6	5		1	9			11	4	2			7				3		38
10	8	6	5		1	9			11	4					2	7		3		39
10		4	5		1	9	6		11		2	8				7		3		40
	8	4	5		1	9	6		11		2	10				7	3			41
10	8	6	5		1	9			11	4	2					7		3		42
40	35	39	42	3	42	40	4	2	42	39	41	11		4	1	35	2	40		
8	14					16			18	2	4	3				2		14		

Baily	Bennett	Burgess	Clarke	Cook	Ditchburn	Duquemin	Gilberg	Ludford	Marchi	Medley	Nicholson	Ramsey	Rees	Rundle	Scarth	Tickeridge	Walters	Willis	Withers	No.
10		6	5		1	9			11	4	2	8				7		3		3
10	8	6	5		1				11	4	2	9				7		3		4
10	8	6	5		1	9			11	4	2					7		3		5
3	2	3	3		3	2			3	3	3	2				3		3		
1	2				1						1					2				

Baily	Bennett	Burgess	Clarke	Cook	Ditchburn	Duquemin	Gilberg	Ludford	Marchi	Medley	Nicholson	Ramsey	Rees	Rundle	Scarth	Tickeridge	Walters	Willis	Withers
	8	6	5		1	9	4		10	11	2					7		3	
	1	1	1		1	1	1		1	1	1					1		1	
					1					1									

271

1950-51

Manager: Arthur Rowe

1	Aug	19	(h)	Blackpool	L	1-4	Baily	64,978
2		23	(a)	Bolton W	W	4-1	Walters, Murphy, Duquemin, Medley	21,745
3		26	(a)	Arsenal	D	2-2	Burgess, Walters	64,638
4		28	(h)	Bolton W	W	4-2	Opp own goal, Duquemin 2, Baily	44,246
5	Sep	2	(a)	Charlton A	D	1-1	Ramsey (pen)	61,480
6		6	(a)	Liverpool	L	1-2	Medley	39,015
7		9	(h)	Manchester U	W	1-0	Walters	60,621
8		16	(a)	Wolves	L	1-2	Chatham (og)	55,364
9		23	(h)	Sunderland	D	1-1	Baily	59,190
10		30	(a)	Aston Villa	W	3-2	Murphy, Duquemin, Medley	36,538
11	Oct	7	(h)	Burnley	W	1-0	Medley	46,518
12		14	(a)	Chelsea	W	2-0	Walters, Duquemin	65,992
13		21	(h)	Stoke C	W	6-1	Walters, Bennett 2, Duquemin 2, Medley	54,124
14		28	(a)	West Brom A	W	2-1	Walters, Medley	44,543
15	Nov	4	(h)	Portsmouth	W	5-1	Walters, Duquemin, Baily 3	66,402
16		11	(a)	Everton	W	2-1	Baily, Medley	47,125
17		18	(h)	Newcastle U	W	7-0	Ramsey (pen), Walters, Bennett, Baily, Medley 3	70,336
18		25	(a)	Huddersfield T	L	2-3	Nicholson, Walters	39,519
19	Dec	2	(h)	Middlesbrough	D	3-3	Ramsey (pen), Walters, Duquemin	61,148
20		9	(a)	Sheffield W	D	1-1	Bennett	44,367
21		16	(a)	Blackpool	W	1-0	Duquemin	22,203
22		23	(h)	Arsenal	W	1-0	Baily	54,898
23		25	(a)	Derby C	D	1-1	Murphy	32,301
24		26	(h)	Derby C	W	2-1	McClellan 2	59,885
25		30	(h)	Charlton A	W	1-0	Walters	54,667
26	Jan	13	(a)	Manchester U	L	1-2	Baily	45,104
27		20	(h)	Wolves	W	2-1	Walters, McClellan	66,796
28	Feb	3	(a)	Sunderland	D	0-0		56,817
29		17	(h)	Aston Villa	W	3-2	Ramsey (pen), Baily, Medley	47,842
30		24	(a)	Burnley	L	0-2		33,047
31	Mar	3	(h)	Chelsea	W	2-1	Burgess, Wright	59,449
32		10	(a)	Stoke C	D	0-0		24,236
33		17	(h)	West Brom A	W	5-0	Bennett, Duquemin 3, Baily	45,353
34		23	(a)	Fulham	W	1-0	Murphy	47,391
35		24	(a)	Portsmouth	D	1-1	Uphill	49,716
36		26	(h)	Fulham	W	2-1	Bennett, Murphy	51,862
37		31	(h)	Everton	W	3-0	Walters, Bennett, Murphy	46,651
38	Apr	7	(a)	Newcastle U	W	1-0	Walters	41,241
39		14	(h)	Huddersfield T	L	0-2		55,014
40		21	(a)	Middlesbrough	D	1-1	Murphy	36,689
41		28	(h)	Sheffield W	W	1-0	Duquemin	46,645
42	May	5	(h)	Liverpool	W	3-1	Walters, Murphy 2	49,072

FINAL LEAGUE POSITION: 1st in Division One

Appearances
Goals

FA Cup

3	Jan	6	(a)	Huddersfield T	L	0-2		25,390

Appearances
Goals

Festival of Britain

May	7	(h)	FC Austria	L	0-1		30,000
	12	(h)	Borussia Dortmund	W	2-1	Baily, Murphy	29,000

Appearances
Goals

Football appearances and goals grid.

Baily	Bennett	Brittan	Burgess	Clarke	Ditchburn	Duquemin	Marchi	McClellan	Medley	Murphy	Nicholson	Ramsey	Scarth	Tickridge	Uphill	Walters	Willis	Withers	Wright	No.
10	8		6	5	1	9			11		4	2				7		3		1
10			6	5	1	9			11	8	4	2				7		3		2
10			6	5	1	9			11	8	4	2				7	3			3
10	8		6	5	1	9			11		4	2				7	3			4
10	8		6	5	1	9			11		4	2				7	3			5
10			6	5	1	9			11	8	4	2				7	3			6
10	8		6	5	1	9				11	4	2				7	3			7
10	8		6	5	1	9			11		4	2				7	3			8
10			6	5	1			9	11		4	2			8	7	3			9
10			6	5	1	9			11	8	4	2				7	3			10
	10	6		5	1	9			11	8	4		2			7	3			11
10	8		6	5	1	9			11		4	2				7	3			12
10	8	6		5	1	9			11		4	2				7	3			13
10	8		6	5	1	9			11		4	2				7	3			14
10	8		6	5	1	9			11		4	2				7	3			15
10	8		6	5	1	9			11		4	2				7	3			16
10	8	6		5	1	9			11		4	2				7	3			17
10	8	6		5	1	9			11		4	2				7	3			18
10	8		6	5	1	9			11		4	2				7	3			19
10	8		6	5	1	9			11		4	2				7	3			20
10	8	6		5	1	9			11		4	2				7	3			21
10	8		6	5	1	9			11		4	2				7	3			22
	8	6		5	1	9			11	10	4	2				7	3			23
10			6	5	1			9	11	8	4	2				7	3			24
10	8		6	5	1	9			11		4	2				7	3			25
10		4		5	1			9	11	8	6	2				7	3			26
10			6	5	1			9	11	8	4	2				7	3			27
10			6	5	1			9	11	8	4	2				7	3			28
10		4	6	5	1			9	11	8		2				7	3			29
10			6	5	1			9	11	8	4	2				7	3			30
10			6	5	1				11	8	4	2				7	3	9		31
10			6	5	1				11	8	4	2				7	3	9		32
10	8		6	5	1	9			11		4	2				7	3			33
10	8		6	5	1	9			11		4	2				7	3			34
10			6	5	1	9			11		4	2			8	7	3			35
10	8		6	5	1	9			7	11	4	2					3			36
10	8		6	5	1	9			11		4	2				7	3			37
10	8		6	5	1	9			11		4	2				7	3			38
10	8		6	5	1	9			11		4					7	2	3		39
10			6	5	1	9			11	8	4	2				7	3			40
10			6	5	1	9			11	8	4	2				7	3			41
10			6	5	1	9			11	8	4	2				7	3			42
40	25	8	35	42	42	33		7	35	25	41	40	1	1	2	40	39	4	2	
12	7		2			14		3	11	9	1	4			1	15	1			

2 own-goals

Baily	Bennett	Brittan	Burgess	Clarke	Ditchburn	Duquemin	Marchi	McClellan	Medley	Murphy	Nicholson	Ramsey	Scarth	Tickridge	Uphill	Walters	Willis	Withers	Wright	
10	8		6	5	1	9			11		4	2				7	3			3
1	1		1	1	1	1			1		1	1				1	1			

Baily	Bennett	Brittan	Burgess	Clarke	Ditchburn	Duquemin	Marchi	McClellan	Medley	Murphy	Nicholson	Ramsey	Scarth	Tickridge	Uphill	Walters	Willis	Withers	Wright	
10			6	5	1	9			11	8	4					7	3	2		
10	8	4		5	1*		6	9		11		2				7	3	12		
2	1	1	1	2	2	1	1	1	1	2	1	1				2	2	1		
1									1											

1951-52

Manager: Arthur Rowe

1	Aug	18	(a)	Middlesbrough	L	1-2	Bennett	44,004
2		20	(h)	Fulham	W	1-0	Medley	48,766
3		25	(h)	West Brom A	W	3-1	Bennett 2, Medley	51,544
4		29	(a)	Fulham	W	2-1	Bennett, McClellan	33,920
5	Sep	1	(a)	Newcastle U	L	2-7	Scarth, Bennett	52,541
6		3	(a)	Burnley	D	1-1	Bennett	27,045
7		8	(h)	Bolton W	W	2-1	Bennett, Edwards (og)	61,838
8		10	(h)	Burnley	D	1-1	Ramsey (pen)	35,948
9		15	(a)	Stoke C	W	6-1	Ramsey (pen), Walters, Bennett, McClellan, Medley 2	27,154
10		22	(h)	Manchester U	W	2-0	Bennett, Medley	70,882
11		29	(a)	Arsenal	D	1-1	Murphy	72,164
12	Oct	6	(h)	Manchester C	L	1-2	Bennett	58,163
13		13	(a)	Derby C	L	2-4	Bennett, McClellan	27,495
14		20	(h)	Aston Villa	W	2-0	Bennett, Duquemin	49,026
15		27	(a)	Sunderland	W	1-0	Walters	50,513
16	Nov	3	(h)	Wolves	W	4-2	Ramsey (pen), Walters, Bennett, Duquemin	61,626
17		10	(a)	Huddersfield T	D	1-1	Duquemin	30,259
18		17	(h)	Chelsea	W	3-2	Nicholson, Bennett, Duquemin	48,985
19		24	(a)	Portsmouth	L	0-2		46,815
20	Dec	1	(h)	Liverpool	L	2-3	Walters, Bennett	51,342
21		8	(a)	Blackpool	L	0-1		14,821
22		15	(h)	Middlesbrough	W	3-1	Bennett, Murphy 2	37,781
23		22	(a)	West Brom A	L	1-3	Murphy	29,962
24		25	(a)	Charlton A	W	3-0	Medley, Bennett, Robb	37,711
25		26	(h)	Charlton A	L	2-3	Walters, Murphy	49,350
26		29	(h)	Newcastle U	W	2-1	Walters, Medley	55,219
27	Jan	5	(a)	Bolton W	D	1-1	Harmer	46,354
28		19	(h)	Stoke C	W	2-0	Duquemin, Harmer	45,976
29		26	(a)	Manchester U	L	0-2		42,668
30	Feb	9	(h)	Arsenal	L	1-2	Walters	66,438
31		16	(a)	Manchester C	D	1-1	Walters	39,080
32		23	(h)	Preston NE	W	1-0	Harmer	49,193
33	Mar	1	(h)	Derby C	W	5-0	Walters, Bennett, Duquemin, Adams, Mozley (og)	44,388
34		8	(a)	Aston Villa	W	3-0	Walters, Duquemin 2	56,475
35		15	(h)	Sunderland	W	2-0	Bennett, Duquemin	51,745
36		22	(a)	Wolves	D	1-1	Baily	45,343
37	Apr	2	(h)	Huddersfield T	W	1-0	Duquemin	22,396
38		12	(h)	Portsmouth	W	3-1	Duquemin, Baily 2	66,988
39		14	(a)	Preston NE	D	1-1	Ramsey (pen)	36,525
40		19	(a)	Liverpool	D	1-1	Duquemin	36,898
41		26	(h)	Blackpool	W	2-0	Ramsey, Baily	45,991
42		30	(a)	Chelsea	W	2-0	Bennett, Medley	46,574

FINAL LEAGUE POSITION: 2nd in Division One

Appearances
Goals

FA Cup

3	Jan	12	(a)	Scunthorpe U	W	3-0	Baily, Duquemin 2	22,652
4	Feb	2	(h)	Newcastle U	L	0-3		69,009

Appearances
Goals

FA Charity Shield

	Sep	24	(h)	Newcastle U	W	2-1	Bennett, Murphy	27,760

Appearances
Goals

Ipswich Hospital Charity Cup

	May	5	(a)	Ipswich T	D	2-2	Bennett, Meadows	

Appearances
Goals

274

Player appearance / shirt-number grid (columns are players; cells give the shirt number worn; final column is the match number). This is a dense historical statistics grid and some cell placements are approximate.

Adams	Baily	Bennett	Brittan	Burgess	Clarke	Ditchburn	Duquemin	Farley	Harmer	King	McClellan	Meadows	Medley	Murphy	Nicholson	Ramsey	Robb	Robshaw	Scarth	Uphill	Walters	Wetton	Willis	Withers	No.
	10	8		6		1	9	5				11		7	4	2							3		1
	10	8		6	5	1	9					11		7	4	2							3		2
		8		6	5	1	9		10			11			4	2				7			3		3
		8	4	6		1	9		10			11	5				2				7			3		4
		8	4	6		1	9		10			11	5				2				7			3		5
		8	4	6		1	9		10			11	5				2				7			3		6
		8	4	6		1	9		10			11	5				2				7			3		7
		8	4	6		1	9	9				11	5				2				7			3		8
		8	4	6		1			10			11	5				2				7			3		9
		8		6	5	1			10			11			4		2				7			3		10
				6	5	1			10			11	8		4		2				7			3		11
	10	8		6	5	1	9					11			4		2				7			3		12
	10	8		6	5	1	9					11			4		2				7			3		13
		8			5	1	9		10			11		4							7	6	3	2		14
	10	8		6	5	1	9					11			4		2				7			3		15
	10	8			5	1	9					11			4		2				7	6	3			16
	10	8		6	5	1	9					11			4		2				7			3		17
	10	8		6	5	1	9					11			4		2				7			3		18
	10	8		6	5	1	9					11			4		2				7			3		19
	10	8		6	5	1	9					11			2		4				7			3		20
	8			6	5	1	9					11	10				2				7	4	3			21
	8	9		6	5	1						11	10	4		2					7		3			22
	8	9		6	5	1						11	10	4		2					7		3			23
	8	9		6	5	1		10				7			2	11						4	3			24
	8	9		6	5	1						11	10			2					7	4	3			25
	8			6	5	1	9		10			11			2						7	4	3			26
	8			6	5	1	9		10			11		4	2						7		3			27
	8			6	5	1	9		10			11		4	2						7		3			28
	8			6	5	1	9		10			11		4	2						7		3			29
	8			6	5	1	9		10			11		4	2						7		3			30
	9			6	5	1		10				11		4	2				8	7		3				31
	9	11		5	1			10						4	2				8	7	6		3			32
11	10	8		6	5	1	9							4	2					7			3		33
11	10	8		6	5	1	9							4	2					7			3		34
11	10	8		6	5	1	9							4	2					7			3		35
11	10	8		6	5	1	9							4						7		2	3		36
11	10	8		6	5	1	9							4						7		2	3		37
	10	8		6	5	1	9					11		4	2					7			3		38
	10	8		6	5	1	9					11		4	2					7			3		39
	10	8		6	5	1	9			11				4	2					7			3		40
	10	8		6	5	1						9	11	4	2					7			3		41
	10	8		6	5	1						9	11	4						7		2	3		42
5	30	35	6	40	33	42	25	1	13	2	12	34	13	37	38	1	1	2	2	37	7	17	29		
1	4	20					12		3		3		8	5	1	5	1			1			10		

2 own-goals

Adams	Baily	Bennett	Brittan	Burgess	Clarke	Ditchburn	Duquemin	Farley	Harmer	King	McClellan	Meadows	Medley	Murphy	Nicholson	Ramsey	Robb	Robshaw	Scarth	Uphill	Walters	Wetton	Willis	Withers	No.
	8			6	5	1	9		10			11		4	2					7			3		3
	8			6	5	1	9		10			11		4	2					7			3		4
	2			2	2	2	2		2			2		2	2					2			2		
	1						2																		

Adams	Baily	Bennett	Brittan	Burgess	Clarke	Ditchburn	Duquemin	Farley	Harmer	King	McClellan	Meadows	Medley	Murphy	Nicholson	Ramsey	Robb	Robshaw	Scarth	Uphill	Walters	Wetton	Willis	Withers
	8			6	5	1	9					11	10	4						7		3	2	
	1			1	1	1	1					1	1	1						1		1	1	
	1						1																	

Adams	Baily	Bennett	Brittan	Burgess	Clarke	Ditchburn	Duquemin	Farley	Harmer	King	McClellan	Meadows	Medley	Murphy	Nicholson	Ramsey	Robb	Robshaw	Scarth	Uphill	Walters	Wetton	Willis	Withers
10	8			6	5	1						9	11		2		4			7			3	
1	1			1	1	1						1	1		1		1			1			1	
	1											1												

1952-53

Manager: Arthur Rowe

1	Aug	23	(h)	West Brom A	L	3-4	Ramsey (pen), Bennett, Duquemin	56,552
2		27	(a)	Manchester C	W	1-0	Duquemin	33,621
3		30	(a)	Newcastle U	D	1-1	McClellan	59,629
4	Sep	1	(h)	Manchester C	D	3-3	Ramsey (pen), McClellan, Robb	41,113
5		6	(h)	Cardiff C	W	2-1	McClellan, Duquemin	62,150
6		10	(a)	Liverpool	L	1-2	Baily	49,869
7		13	(a)	Sheffield W	L	0-2		42,136
8		15	(h)	Liverpool	W	3-1	Groves 2, Harmer	37,319
9		20	(h)	Arsenal	L	1-3	Harmer	69,247
10		27	(h)	Burnley	W	2-1	Duquemin, Medley	43,031
11	Oct	4	(a)	Preston NE	L	0-1		28,108
12		11	(a)	Derby C	D	0-0		27,696
13		18	(h)	Blackpool	W	4-0	Ramsey (pen), Duquemin, Baily 2	53,928
14		25	(a)	Chelsea	L	1-2	Ramsey (pen)	62,688
15	Nov	1	(h)	Manchester U	L	1-2	Walters	44,285
16		8	(a)	Portsmouth	L	1-2	Uphill	40,462
17		15	(h)	Bolton W	D	1-1	Bennett	31,442
18		22	(a)	Aston Villa	W	3-0	Bennett, Duquemin, Dicker	32,265
19		29	(h)	Sunderland	D	2-2	Bennett, Duquemin	45,980
20	Dec	6	(a)	Wolves	D	0-0		37,062
21		13	(h)	Charlton A	W	2-0	Walters, Bennett	35,684
22		20	(a)	West Brom A	L	1-2	Dicker	18,698
23		25	(h)	Middlesbrough	W	7-1	Bennett 4, Duquemin 2, Baily	36,102
24		27	(a)	Middlesbrough	W	4-0	Walters, Bennett, Duquemin, Bilciss (og)	23,265
25	Jan	3	(h)	Newcastle U	W	3-2	Burgess 2, Duquemin	52,648
26		17	(a)	Cardiff C	D	0-0		36,423
27		24	(h)	Sheffield W	W	2-1	Walters, Baily	43,241
28	Feb	7	(a)	Arsenal	L	0-4		69,051
29		17	(a)	Burnley	L	2-3	Baily, Duquemin	13,771
30		21	(h)	Preston NE	D	4-4	Walters, Duquemin 3	50,070
31	Mar	7	(a)	Blackpool	L	0-2		26,796
32		12	(h)	Derby C	W	5-2	Bennett, Hollis, McClellan 2, Robb	13,933
33		14	(h)	Chelsea	L	2-3	Willis (pen), Bennett	47,903
34		25	(a)	Manchester U	L	2-3	Walters, McClellan	20,215
35		28	(h)	Portsmouth	D	3-3	Duquemin 2, Harmer	38,636
36	Apr	3	(h)	Stoke C	W	1-0	Harmer	35,606
37		4	(a)	Bolton W	W	3-2	McClellan, Stokes, Duquemin	40,185
38		6	(a)	Stoke C	L	0-2		25,346
39		11	(h)	Aston Villa	D	1-1	McClellan	39,217
40		18	(a)	Sunderland	D	1-1	Walters	24,953
41		25	(h)	Wolves	W	3-2	Ramsey (pen), Bennett 2	48,136
42		30	(a)	Charlton A	L	2-3	Ramsey, Walters	9,269

FINAL LEAGUE POSITION: 10th in Division One

Appearances
Goals

FA Cup

3	Jan	10	(a)	Tranmere R	D	1-1	Bennett	21,537
R		12	(h)	Tranmere R	W	9-1	McClellan 3, Duquemin 2, Hollis 2, Baily 2	31,541
4		31	(a)	Preston NE	D	2-2	Withers 2	34,956
R	Feb	4	(h)	Preston NE	W	1-0	Duquemin	55,601
5		14	(a)	Halifax T	W	3-0	Bennett 2, Duquemin	36,995
6		28	(a)	Birmingham C	D	1-1	Bennett	52,348
R	Mar	4	(h)	Birmingham C	D	2-2*	Bennett, Duquemin	59,543
2R		9	(n†)	Birmingham C	W	1-0	Walters	50,801
SF		21	(n‡)	Blackpool	L	1-2	Duquemin	68,221

*After extra-time. †Played at the Molineux Grounds, Wolverhampton. ‡Played at Villa Park, Birmingham.

Appearances
Goals

Coronation Cup

SF	May	11	(n[1])	Hibernian	D	1-1*	Walters	43,000
R		12	(n[2])	Hibernian	L	1-2	McClellan	13,000

*After extra-time. [1]Played at Ibrox Park, Glasgow. [2]Played at Hampden Park, Glasgow.

Appearances
Goals

Appearance and goalscoring chart (shirt numbers shown per match).

Football League

Adams	Baily	Baker	Bennett	Brittan	Brooks	Burgess	Clarke	Dicker	Ditchburn	Duquemin	Gibbins	Groves	Grubb	Harmer	Hollis	Hopkins	King	Marchie	McClellan	Medley	Nicholson	Ramsey	Reynolds	Robb	Stokes	Uphill	Walters	Wetton	Willis	Withers	#
	10		8			6	5	11	1	9				7							4	2								3	1
	10		8			6	5		1	9				7							4	2		11			4	3			2
	10		8			6	5		1	9							11		7		4	2					4		3		3
	10		8			6	5		1	9									7		4	2		11			4		3		4
	10		8			6	5	11	1	9									7		4	2					4	3			5
	10		8			6	5	11	1	9									7		4	2					4	3			6
	10		8			6	5	11	1	9									7		4	2					4		3		7
	10						5		1	9			7	8							4	2		11				6	3		8
	10					6	5		1	9				8					7		4	2		11				3			9
	10		8				5		1	9									11		4	2					7	6		3	10
11			8			6	5		1	9				10							2						7	4		3	11
	10		8			6	5		1	9								3		11	4	2					7				12
	10		8				5		1	9										11	4	2					7	6	3		13
	10		8				5		1	9										11	4	2					7		3		14
	10					6	5		1	9										11	4	2			8		7		3		15
	10					6	5		1	9										11	4	2			8		7		3		16
	10		8			6	5	11	1								9				4	2					7		3		17
			8			6	5	11	1	9				10							4	2					7		3		18
			8			6	5	11	1	9				10							4	2					7		3		19
			8			6	5	11	1	9				10							4	2					7		3		20
		8	6				5	11	1	9				10							4	2					7		3		21
		8	6				5	11	1	9				10							4	2					7		3		22
	10		8	6			5		1	9										11	4	2					7		3		23
	10		8	6			5		1	9										11	4	2					7		3		24
	10		8		6		5	7	1	9										11	4	2							3		25
	10			6			5		1	8							9			7	11	4							3	2	26
	10		8			6	5		1	9										11	4	2					7		3		27
	10		8	6			5		1	9										11	4	2					7		3		28
	8					6	5		1	9				10					11		4	2					7			3	29
	10		8			6	5		1	9										11	4	2					7		3		30
	8								1			5	7	10	9				4	11		2						6		3	31
		8							1				7		9		5	4	10					11				6	3	2	32
	10		8	4		6			1	9							5		11								7		3	2	33
	10					6			1	9							5		8		4	2		11			7			3	34
	8					6			1	9				10			5			11	4	2					7			3	35
	8					6			1	9				10			5		7	11	4	2								3	36
						6			1	9				10			5	4	7	11		2			8				3		37
	8		9	6	10		5		1								4	7	11		2								3		38
						6			1	9				10			5		11		4	2			8		7		3		39
	2	8				6			1	9				10			5		11	4							7	3			40
	8					6			1	9				10			5	4	11	3	2						7				41
	8					6			1	9				10			3	5	11		4	2					7				42
1	30	1	30	9	1	30	31	10	42	38	1	3	2	17	3	2	10	5	17	21	31	37		6	2	2	26	12	27	15	
6	14		2		2	18		2		4	1							8	1		6		2	1	1	8		1			

1 own-goal

FA Cup

Adams	Baily	Baker	Bennett	Brittan	Brooks	Burgess	Clarke	Dicker	Ditchburn	Duquemin	Gibbins	Groves	Grubb	Harmer	Hollis	Hopkins	King	Marchie	McClellan	Medley	Nicholson	Ramsey	Reynolds	Robb	Stokes	Uphill	Walters	Wetton	Willis	Withers	Rd
	10		8			6	5		1	9										11	4	2					7		3		3
	10			6				1	8	5						9			7	11	4	2						3			R
	10		8			6	5		1	9										4	2						7		3	11	4
	10		8			6	5		1	9										4	2						7		3	11	R
	10		8	6			5		1	9										11	4	2					7		3		5
	10		8			6	5		1	9										11	4	2					7		3		6
	10		8	4		6			1	9	5									11		2					7		3		R
	10		8	4		6			1	9	5									11		2					7		3		2R
	10		8			6	5		1	9									11		4	2					7		3		SF
	9		8	4		7	6		9	9	3						1		2	6	7	9						8	5	6		
	2		5				6										2			3								1		2		

Adams	Baily	Baker	Bennett	Brittan	Brooks	Burgess	Clarke	Dicker	Ditchburn	Duquemin	Gibbins	Groves	Grubb	Harmer	Hollis	Hopkins	King	Marchie	McClellan	Medley	Nicholson	Ramsey	Reynolds	Robb	Stokes	Uphill	Walters	Wetton	Willis	Withers	Rd
	10	2	8	6						9							5	4	11		3			1				7				SF
	10	2	8	6						9							5	4	11		3			1				7				R
	2	2	2	2						2							2	2	2		2			2				2				
	1																		1													

277

1953-54

Manager: Arthur Rowe

#					Result	Scorers	Attendance
1	Aug	15	(h)	Aston Villa	W 1-0	Parkes (og)	50,202
2		22	(a)	Sheffield W	L 1-2	Walters	38,114
3		26	(h)	Charlton A	W 3-1	Baily, Robb 2	48,035
4		29	(h)	Middlesbrough	W 4-1	Walters, Bennett, Duquemin, Robb	44,911
5	Sep	3	(a)	Charlton A	W 1-0	Groves	37,609
6		5	(a)	West Brom A	L 0-3		42,959
7		7	(a)	Burnley	L 2-4	Walters, Robb	34,280
8		12	(h)	Liverpool	W 2-1	Ramsey, Walters	47,535
9		16	(h)	Burnley	L 2-3	Duquemin 2	30,472
10		19	(a)	Newcastle U	W 3-1	Walters, Baily, Robb	53,056
11		26	(h)	Manchester U	D 1-1	Duquemin	52,837
12	Oct	3	(a)	Bolton W	L 0-2		39,842
13		10	(h)	Arsenal	L 1-4	Robb	69,821
14		17	(a)	Cardiff C	L 0-1		41,083
15		24	(h)	Manchester C	W 3-0	Duquemin, Robb 2	37,577
16		31	(a)	Sunderland	L 3-4	Walters, Duquemin, Robb	38,345
17	Nov	7	(h)	Chelsea	W 2-1	Walters, Baily	44,795
18		14	(a)	Blackpool	L 0-1		19,667
19		21	(h)	Huddersfield T	W 1-0	Duquemin	42,503
20		28	(a)	Sheffield U	L 2-5	Walters, Bennett	31,337
21	Dec	5	(h)	Wolves	L 2-3	Bennett, Duquemin	48,164
22		12	(a)	Aston Villa	W 2-1	Walters, Baily	27,480
23		19	(h)	Sheffield W	W 3-1	Baker, Duquemin, Curtis (og)	25,957
24		25	(h)	Portsmouth	D 1-1	Brooks	36,502
25		26	(a)	Portsmouth	D 1-1	Walters	36,677
26	Jan	2	(a)	Middlesbrough	L 0-3		35,141
27		16	(h)	West Brom A	L 0-1		48,812
28		23	(a)	Liverpool	D 2-2	Walters, Lock (og)	43,592
29	Feb	6	(h)	Newcastle U	W 3-0	Walters, Robb 2	35,798
30		13	(a)	Manchester U	L 0-2		37,289
31		27	(a)	Arsenal	W 3-0	Walters, Robb 2	64,311
32	Mar	3	(h)	Bolton W	W 3-2	Walters, Stokes, Dunmore	16,720
33		6	(h)	Cardiff C	L 0-1		45,248
34		17	(a)	Manchester C	L 1-4	Marchi	9,984
35		20	(h)	Sunderland	L 0-3		39,393
36		27	(a)	Chelsea	L 0-1		49,315
37	Apr	3	(h)	Blackpool	D 2-2	Baily, Robb	43,870
38		10	(a)	Huddersfield T	W 5-2	Hutchinson, Brooks, Harmer, Robb 2	26,232
39		16	(a)	Preston NE	L 1-2	Harmer	24,521
40		17	(h)	Sheffield U	W 2-1	Ramsey (pen), Brittan	35,105
41		19	(h)	Preston NE	L 2-6	Bennett, Dunmore	30,206
42		24	(a)	Wolves	L 0-2		44,055

FINAL LEAGUE POSITION: 16th in Division One

Appearances
Goals

FA Cup

					Result	Scorers	Attendance
3	Jan	9	(a)	Leeds U	D 3-3	Walters, Bennett 2	41,645
R		13	(h)	Leeds U	W 1-0	Bennett	35,023
4		30	(a)	Manchester C	W 1-0	Bennett	51,182
5	Feb	20	(a)	Hull C	D 1-1	Bennett	46,839
R		24	(h)	Hull C	W 2-0	Walters, Baily	52,934
6	Mar	13	(a)	West Brom A	L 0-3		51,049

Appearances
Goals

278

Baily	Baker	Bennett	Brittan	Brooks	Burgess	Clarke	Ditchburn	Dunmore	Duquemin	Groves	Harmer	Hopkins	Hutchinson	King	Marchi	McClellan	Nicholson	Owen	Ramsey	Reynolds	Robb	Stokes	Walters	Wetton	Willis	Withers	
10		8			6	5	1		9								4		2		11		7			3	1
10		8			6	5	1								4	9			2		11		7			3	2
10		8			6	5	1		9								4		2		11		7			3	3
10		8			6	5	1		9								4		2		11		7			3	4
10		8			6	5	1		9								4		2		11		7			3	5
10				8	6	5	1		9								4		2		11		7			3	6
10					6	5	1				8				9		4		2		11		7			3	7
10		8			6	5	1		9										2		11		7	4		3	8
10		8			6	5	1		9										2		11		7	4		3	9
10		8	6			5	1		9						2						11		7	4		3	10
10		8			6	5	1		9			7					4		2		11					3	11
		8			6	5	1		9		10	7					4		2		11					3	12
		8				5	1		9		10						4		2		11		7	6		3	13
10				8	6	5	1		9								4		2		11		7			3	14
10	2			8		5	1		9								4				11		7	6		3	15
10				8	6	5	1		9								4		2		11		7			3	16
10				8	6	5	1		9										2		11		7	4		3	17
10				8	6	5	1		9								4		2		11		7			3	18
10				8	6	5	1		9								4		2		11		7			3	19
10	9			8	6	5	1										4		2		11		7			3	20
10		8			6	5	1		9							11	4		2				7			3	21
10		8	6			5	1		9								4		2		11		7			3	22
10	2	8			6	5	1		9								4				11		7			3	23
10				8		5	1		9								4		2		11		7	6		3	24
				10		5	1		9	3							4		2		11	8	7	6			25
		8		10		5	1		9				3				4		2		11		7	6			26
10		8			6	5	1		9								4		2		11		7			3	27
10		8			6	5	1		9								4		2		11		7			3	28
10		8				5	1		9								4		2		11		7	6		3	29
10		8				5	1		9								4		2		11		7	6		3	30
10		8				5	1		9								4		2		11		7	6		3	31
10					6	5	1		9								4		2		11	8	7			3	32
10		8			6	5	1		9								4		2		11		7			3	33
		8				5	1		9					10			4		2		11		7	6	3		34
		8		10		5			9						4	7			2	1	11			6	3		35
10	9	8				5									4	7			2	1	11			6	3		36
10				8					9					5			4		2	1	11		7	6	3		37
		8				5	1		9		10	7					4		2		11			6	3		38
		8				5	1		9		10	7					4		2		11			6	3		39
8			4		6	5	1		9		10		11						2				7		3		40
	2	8		10		5	1		9								4	11					7	6	3		41
10	2	8				5	1		9							11	4						7	6	3		42
33	4	26	3	18	24	41	39	10	27	1	6	2	5	2	8	5	30	1	37	3	37	2	37	21	9	31	—
5	1	4	1	2				2	9	1	2		1		1				2		16	1	14				—

3 own-goals

Baily	Baker	Bennett	Brittan	Brooks	Burgess	Clarke	Ditchburn	Dunmore	Duquemin	Groves	Harmer	Hopkins	Hutchinson	King	Marchi	McClellan	Nicholson	Owen	Ramsey	Reynolds	Robb	Stokes	Walters	Wetton	Willis	Withers	
10		8			6	5	1		9								4		2		11		7			3	3
10		8			6	5	1		9								4		2		11		7			3	R
10		8			6	5	1		9								4		2		11		7			3	4
10		8			6	5	1		9								4		2		11		7			3	5
10		8				5	1		9								4		2		11		7	6		3	R
10		8			6	5	1		9								4		2		11		7			3	6
6	6			5	6	6		6									6		6		6		6	1		6	—
1		5																					2				—

279

1954-55

Manager: Arthur Rowe

1	Aug	21	(a)	Aston Villa	W	4-2	Dowsett, Bennett 2, Baily	44,193
2		25	(h)	Wolves	W	3-2	Dunmore 3	47,776
3		28	(h)	Sunderland	L	0-1		53,646
4		30	(a)	Wolves	L	2-4	Walters, Robb	37,384
5	Sep	4	(a)	Arsenal	L	0-2		53,971
6		8	(h)	Manchester U	L	0-2		35,162
7		11	(a)	Sheffield W	D	2-2	McClellan, Baily	34,047
8		15	(a)	Manchester U	L	1-2	McClellan	31,041
9		18	(h)	Portsmouth	D	1-1	McClellan	37,404
10		25	(a)	Blackpool	L	1-5	Ramsey (pen)	34,626
11	Oct	2	(h)	Charlton A	L	1-4	Brooks	33,105
12		9	(h)	West Brom A	W	3-1	Ramsey (pen), McClellan 2	45,547
13		16	(a)	Newcastle U	D	4-4	Baily 2, McClellan 2	45,306
14		23	(h)	Preston NE	W	3-1	Ramsey (pen), McClellan, Dunmore	42,863
15		30	(a)	Sheffield U	L	1-4	Dunmore	24,084
16	Nov	6	(h)	Cardiff C	L	0-2		38,805
17		13	(a)	Chelsea	L	1-2	Gavin	52,961
18		20	(h)	Leicester C	W	5-1	Gavin 2, Baily, Robb 2	27,874
19		27	(a)	Burnley	W	2-1	Gavin, Baily	21,973
20	Dec	4	(h)	Everton	L	1-3	Baily	31,554
21		11	(a)	Manchester C	D	0-0		27,052
22		18	(h)	Aston Villa	D	1-1	Baily	28,131
23		25	(a)	Bolton W	W	2-1	Dunmore, Robb	25,978
24		26	(h)	Bolton W	W	2-0	Baily, Brooks	41,063
25	Jan	1	(a)	Sunderland	D	1-1	Dunmore	49,884
26		15	(h)	Arsenal	L	0-1		36,263
27		22	(h)	Sheffield W	W	7-2	Gavin 2, Brooks 2, Duquemin, Baily, Robb	26,315
28	Feb	5	(a)	Portsmouth	W	3-0	Gavin 2, Duquemin	27,539
29		12	(h)	Blackpool	W	3-2	Baily, Robb 2	47,386
30	Mar	5	(h)	Manchester C	D	2-2	Duquemin 2	35,358
31		12	(a)	Preston NE	L	0-1		24,344
32		19	(h)	Sheffield U	W	5-0	Gavin 4, Brooks	26,678
33		26	(a)	Cardiff C	W	2-1	Duquemin, Robb	14,461
34	Apr	2	(h)	Chelsea	L	2-4	Duquemin 2	53,159
35		9	(a)	Everton	L	0-1		42,219
36		11	(h)	Huddersfield T	D	1-1	Brooks	23,332
37		12	(a)	Huddersfield T	L	0-1		23,580
38		16	(h)	Burnley	L	0-3		23,555
39		23	(a)	Leicester C	L	0-2		23,908
40		27	(a)	West Brom A	W	2-1	Brooks, Baily	16,617
41		30	(h)	Newcastle U	W	2-1	Gavin, Stokoe (og)	37,262
42	May	5	(a)	Charlton A	W	2-1	Walters, Duquemin	12,318

FINAL LEAGUE POSITION: 16th in Division One

Appearances
Goals

FA Cup

3	Jan	8	(a)	Gateshead	W	2-0	Brooks 2	18,842
4		29	(h)	Port Vale	W	4-2	Gavin, Duquemin, Brooks 2	50,684
5	Feb	19	(a)	York C	L	1-3	Robb	21,000

Appearances
Goals

280

Appearances and goals grid (shirt numbers shown per match). Players across the top; match numbers down the right-hand side.

Baily	Baker	Bennett	Blanchflower	Brittan	Brooks	Clarke	Ditchburn	Dowsett	Dunmore	Duquemin	Dyson	Gavin	Harmer	Henry	Hopkins	King	Marchi	McClellan	Nicholson	Ramsey	Reynolds	Robb	Walters	Wetton	Withers	Woods	#
10		8	6			5	1	7	9											2		11		4	3		1
10		8	6			5	1		9											2		11	7	4	3		2
10		8	6			5	1		9											2		11	7	4	3		3
10		8	6			5	1		9											2		11	7	4	3		4
10		8	6			5	1		9											2		11	7	4	3		5
10			6			5	1		9				8		3					2		11	7		4		6
10			6				1		9				8		3	5				2		11	7		4		7
10			6				1		9			7	8		3	5				2		11			4		8
10			6				1		9			7	8		3	5				2		11			4		9
10		8	6				1		9			7		3		5				2		11			4		10
8					10	5	1		9			7			3		6		4	2		11					11
8					10	5	1		9			7					6		4	2		11			3		12
10					8	5	1		9			7					6		4	2		11			3		13
8					10	5	1		9			7			3		6		4	2		11					14
8					10	5	1		9			7			3		6		4	2		11					15
8					10	5	1		9			7			3		6		4	2		11					16
8					10	5			9			7					6		4	2	1	11			3		17
8					10	5			9			7			3		6		4	2	1	11					18
8					10	5			9			7			3		6		4	2	1	11					19
8					10	5			9			7			3		6		4	2	1	11					20
8			4		10	5			9			7			3		6			2	1	11					21
8			4		10	5			9			7			3		6			2	1	11					22
8			4		10	5				9		7			3		6			2	1	11					23
8			4		10	5				9		7			3		6			2	1	11					24
8			4		10	5				9		7			3		6			2	1	11					25
8			4		10	5				9		7			3		6			2	1	11					26
8			4		10	5				9		7			3		6			2	1	11					27
8			4		10	5				9		7			3		6			2	1	11					28
8			4		10	5				9		7			3		6			2	1	11					29
8			4		10	5				9		7			3		6			2	1	11					30
			4		10	5				9	11	7	8		3		6			2	1						31
10	2		4	8		5				9		7			3		6	11			1						32
8	2		4		10	5				9		7			3		6				1	11					33
8	2		4		10	5				9		7			3		6				1	11					34
8	2		4		10	5				9		7			3		6				1	11					35
8	2		4		10	5				9		7			3		6				1	11					36
8	2		4		10					9		7			3	5	6				1	11					37
10			4			5				9		7			3		6	11		2	1					8	38
10			4	8		5				9		7			3		6			2	1	11					39
10			4	8		5				9		7			3		6				1	11			2		40
10	2		4	8		5				9		7					6				1	11			3		41
10	2		4	8		5				9							6				1	11	7		3		42
41	8	6	22	10	31	36	16	1	22	19	1	29	5	1	32	5	32	11	10	33	26	36	7	5	11	6	—
12	2		7					1	7	8		13					8			3		8			2		—

1 own-goal

Baily	Baker	Bennett	Blanchflower	Brittan	Brooks	Clarke	Ditchburn	Dowsett	Dunmore	Duquemin	Dyson	Gavin	Harmer	Henry	Hopkins	King	Marchi	McClellan	Nicholson	Ramsey	Reynolds	Robb	Walters	Wetton	Withers	Woods	#
8			4		10	5			9			7			3		6			2	1	11					3
8			4		10	5			9			7			3		6			2	1	11					4
8			4		10	5			9						3		6			2	1	11	7				5
3			3	3	3	3			1	2		2			3		3			3	3	3	1				—
			4						1			1										1					—

1955-56

Manager: Jimmy Anderson

1	Aug	20	(h)	Burnley	L	0-1		33,178
2		24	(a)	Manchester U	D	2-2	Gavin (pen), Stokes	28,713
3		27	(a)	Luton T	L	1-2	Gavin	21,143
4		31	(h)	Manchester U	L	1-2	Clarke	27,453
5	Sep	3	(h)	Charlton A	L	2-3	Clarke, Brooks	33,198
6		5	(a)	Sheffield U	L	0-2		19,692
7		10	(h)	Arsenal	W	3-1	Stokes 2, Baily	51,029
8		17	(a)	Everton	L	1-2	Walters	42,851
9		24	(h)	Newcastle U	W	3-1	Clarke, Stokes 2	41,096
10	Oct	1	(a)	Birmingham C	L	0-3		31,320
11		8	(h)	Bolton W	L	0-3		35,237
12		15	(a)	Chelsea	L	0-2		48,195
13		22	(h)	Sunderland	L	2-3	Brooks, Robb	36,396
14		29	(a)	Portsmouth	L	1-4	Robb	26,018
15	Nov	5	(h)	Cardiff C	D	1-1	Brooks (pen)	34,368
16		12	(a)	Manchester C	W	2-1	McClellan, Dunmore	24,094
17		19	(h)	Wolves	W	2-1	McClellan, Robb	51,363
18		26	(a)	Aston Villa	W	2-0	Clarke, McClellan	23,836
19	Dec	3	(h)	Blackpool	D	1-1	Brooks	51,336
20		10	(a)	Huddersfield T	L	0-1		11,094
21		17	(a)	Burnley	L	0-2		20,346
22		24	(h)	Luton T	W	2-1	Brooks, Duquemin	41,168
23		26	(h)	West Brom A	W	4-1	Norman, Brooks, Duquemin 2	32,430
24		27	(a)	West Brom A	L	0-1		31,381
25		31	(a)	Charlton A	W	2-1	Duquemin, Robb	37,872
26	Jan	14	(a)	Arsenal	W	1-0	Robb	60,606
27		21	(h)	Everton	D	1-1	Smith	37,119
28	Feb	4	(a)	Newcastle U	W	2-1	Robb, Duquemin	29,597
29		11	(h)	Birmingham C	L	0-1		26,141
30		25	(h)	Chelsea	W	4-0	Marchi, Brooks 2, Smith	46,767
31	Mar	10	(h)	Portsmouth	D	1-1	Smith	44,314
32		21	(a)	Bolton W	L	2-3	Smith, Robb	10,942
33		24	(h)	Manchester C	W	2-1	Brooks (pen), Smith	31,622
34		30	(h)	Preston NE	L	0-4		39,441
35		31	(a)	Sunderland	L	2-3	McClellan 2	22,311
36	Apr	2	(a)	Preston NE	D	3-3	Harmer 2 (1 pen), Ryden	26,699
37		7	(h)	Aston Villa	W	4-3	McClellan, Harmer, Smith, Brooks	36,235
38		14	(a)	Blackpool	W	2-0	McClellan, Smith	19,257
39		18	(a)	Wolves	L	1-5	Harmer (pen)	29,890
40		21	(h)	Huddersfield T	L	1-2	Harmer (pen)	36,387
41		23	(a)	Cardiff C	D	0-0		19,684
42		28	(h)	Sheffield U	W	3-1	Smith 3	32,612

FINAL LEAGUE POSITION: 18th in Division One

Appearances
Goals

FA Cup

3	Jan	7	(h)	Boston U	W	4-0	Duquemin, Smith 2, Robb	46,185
4		28	(h)	Middlesbrough	W	3-1	Norman, Dunmore, Robb	41,895
5	Feb	18	(a)	Doncaster R	W	2-0	Brooks, Smith	30,436
6	Mar	3	(h)	West Ham U	D	3-3	Harmer (pen), Duquemin, Robb	69,118
R		8	(a)	West Ham U	W	2-1	Harmer, Duquemin	34,911
SF		17	(n*)	Manchester C	L	0-1		69,788

*Played at Villa Park, Birmingham.

Appearances
Goals

Football appearances / goals grid (positions worn by each player per match).

Baily	Baker	Blanchflower	Brittan	Brooks	Clarke	Ditchburn	Dulin	Dunmore	Duquemin	Dyson	Gavin	Harmer	Henry	Hopkins	Marchi	McClellan	Norman	Reynolds	Robb	Ryden	Smith	Stokes	Walley	Walters	Withers	#
10		4		8	5	1						7		3	6				11			9		2		1
10		4		8	5	1						7		3	6				11			9		2		2
10		4		8	5	1						7		3	6				11			9		2		3
				8	5	1			10					3	6				11			9	4	7	2	4
10	2	4		8	5	1								3	6				11			9		7		5
10	2	4		8	5	1								3	6				11			9		7		6
10		4		8	5	1								3	6				11			9		7	2	7
10		4		8	5	1								3	6				11			9		7	2	8
10		4		8	5	1								3	6				11			9		7	2	9
		4		8	5	1					10			3	6				11			9		7	2	10
10				8	5	1								3	6				11			9	4	7	2	11
	2	4		8	5	1		9	11					3	6	10								7		12
10	2	4		8	5	1		9						3	6				11					7		13
10	2	4		8	5	1		9						3	6				11					7		14
10		4		8	5				9				3		6		2	1	11					7		15
10		4		8	5				9					3	6	7	2	1	11							16
10		4		8	5				9					3	6	7	2	1	11							17
10		4		8	5				9					3	6	7	2	1	11							18
10		4		8	5				9					3	6	7	2	1	11							19
10		4		8	5				9					3	6	7	2	1	11							20
10		4		8	5		7		9					3	6		2	1	11							21
		4		8	5		7		9					3	6		2	1	11		10					22
		4		8	5		7		9					3	6		2	1	11		10					23
		4		8	5		7		9					3	6		2	1	11		10					24
		4		8	5		7		9					3	6		2	1	11		10					25
		4		8	5		7		9					3	6		2	1	11		10					26
		4		8	5				9					3	6		2	1	11		10			7		27
		4		8	5			9	11					3	6		2	1	7		10					28
		4		8	5			9	11					3	6		2	1	7		10					29
		4		8	5				9					3	6	7	2	1	11		10					30
		4		8	5				9					3	6	7	2	1	11		10					31
		4		8	5			9						3	6	7	2	1	11		10					32
		4		8	5			9						3	6	7	2	1	11		10					33
		4		8	5			9						3	6	7	2	1	11		10					34
		4		8	5			9						3	6	7	2	1	11		10					35
		4						9				8		3	6	7	2	1	11	5	10				2	36
		4		10								8		3	6	7	2	1	11	5	9					37
		4		10	5							8		3	6	7	2	1	11		9					38
		4		10	5							8		3	6	7	2	1	11		9					39
		4		10	5							8		3	6	7	2	1	11		9					40
		4		10				9				8		3	6		2	1	11		10			7		41
		4		10								8		3	6	7	2	1	11	5	9					42
18	5	40	1	39	39	14	6	10	17	3	3	10	1	41	42	16	27	28	41	3	21	11	2	14	10	
1				10	4			1	5		2	5			1	7	1		7	1	10	5			1	

Baily	Baker	Blanchflower	Brittan	Brooks	Clarke	Ditchburn	Dulin	Dunmore	Duquemin	Dyson	Gavin	Harmer	Henry	Hopkins	Marchi	McClellan	Norman	Reynolds	Robb	Ryden	Smith	Stokes	Walley	Walters	Withers	#
		4		8	5		7		9					3	6		2	1	11		10					3
		4		8	5		7		9					3	6		2	1	11		10					4
		4		7	5				9			8		3	6		2	1	11		10					5
		4		8	5				9			7		3	6		2	1	11		10					6
		4		8	5				9			7		3	6		2	1	11		10					R
		4		8	5		7		9					3	6		2	1	11		10					SF
		6		6	6		1	2	6			3		6	6		6	6	6		6					
				1	1			3	2			1			3				3							

1956-57

Manager: Jimmy Anderson

1	Aug	18	(a)	Preston NE	W 4-1 Medwin 2, Brooks 2	22,752
2		22	(a)	Manchester C	D 2-2 Medwin, Brooks	32,718
3		25	(h)	Leeds U	W 5-1 Blanchflower, Medwin, Smith, Brooks, Robb	51,212
4		29	(h)	Manchester C	W 3-2 Medwin, Harmer (pen), Smith	33,443
5	Sep	1	(a)	Bolton W	L 0-1	30,889
6		3	(a)	Blackpool	L 1-4 Brooks	28,460
7		8	(h)	Wolves	W 4-1 Smith 2, Brooks 2	62,592
8		15	(a)	Aston Villa	W 4-2 Harmer, Smith, Stokes, Robb	43,947
9		22	(h)	Luton T	W 5-0 Harmer (pen), Stokes, Robb 2, Dunne (og)	58,960
10		29	(a)	Sunderland	W 2-0 Smith, Stokes	41,657
11	Oct	6	(a)	Chelsea	W 4-2 Stokes 3, Robb	55,788
12		13	(h)	Cardiff C	W 5-0 Stokes 2, Robb 3	52,429
13		20	(a)	Arsenal	L 1-3 Smith	60,588
14		27	(h)	Burnley	W 2-0 Medwin, Harmer (pen)	49,154
15	Nov	3	(a)	Portsmouth	W 3-2 Smith, Brooks, Wilson (og)	31,903
16		10	(h)	Newcastle U	W 3-1 Smith 2, Robb	51,722
17		17	(a)	Sheffield W	L 1-4 Harmer (pen)	32,115
18		24	(h)	Manchester U	D 2-2 Harmer (pen), Robb	57,724
19	Dec	1	(a)	Birmingham C	D 0-0	38,035
20		8	(h)	West Brom A	D 2-2 Harmer, Smith	36,098
21		15	(h)	Preston NE	D 1-1 Medwin	29,748
22		25	(h)	Everton	W 6-0 Medwin 2, Harmer (pen), Smith 2, Stokes	27,761
23		26	(a)	Everton	D 1-1 Robb	20,172
24		29	(h)	Bolton W	W 4-0 Dyson, Harmer (pen), Smith, Robb	42,030
25	Jan	12	(a)	Wolves	L 0-3	42,416
26		19	(h)	Aston Villa	W 3-0 Smith, Stokes 2	38,934
27	Feb	2	(a)	Luton T	W 3-1 Duquemin, Stokes, Robb	22,586
28		9	(h)	Sunderland	W 5-2 Harmer, Smith, Stokes 2, Anderson (og)	52,104
29		20	(h)	Chelsea	L 3-4 Medwin, Harmer (pen), Stokes	20,849
30	Mar	2	(a)	Leeds U	D 1-1 Stokes	33,895
31		9	(a)	West Brom A	D 1-1 Stokes	30,602
32		13	(h)	Arsenal	L 1-3 Medwin	64,555
33		16	(h)	Portsmouth	W 2-0 Smith, Mansell (og)	36,110
34		23	(a)	Newcastle U	D 2-2 Medwin, Stokes	37,955
35		30	(h)	Sheffield W	D 1-1 Harmer	34,485
36	Apr	6	(a)	Manchester U	D 0-0	60,583
37		13	(h)	Birmingham C	W 5-1 Medwin, Harmer (pen), Dunmore 2, Dyson	33,512
38		19	(a)	Charlton A	D 1-1 Brooks	27,793
39		20	(a)	Cardiff C	W 3-0 Dunmore, Brooks, Dyson	25,181
40		22	(h)	Charlton A	W 6-2 Medwin, Harmer 2, Smith, Brooks, Robb	25,579
41		27	(h)	Blackpool	W 2-1 Harmer 2 (1 pen)	49,878
42		29	(a)	Burnley	L 0-1	12,048

FINAL LEAGUE POSITION: 2nd in Division One

Appearances
Goals

FA Cup

3	Jan	5	(h)	Leicester C	W 2-0 Blanchflower, Robb	56,492
4		26	(h)	Chelsea	W 4-0 Medwin, Harmer, Smith, Stokes	66,398
5	Feb	16	(a)	Bournemouth	L 1-3 Medwin	25,892

Appearances
Goals

Anglo-Scottish Floodlit Tournament

Sep	17	(a)	Hibernian	W 5-1 Blanchflower, Harmer, Smith 2, Dyson	15,000
	26	(h)	Partick Thistle	W 4-1 Medwin, Smith, Stokes 2	26,210
Oct	15	(a)	Hearts	L 2-3 Harmer (pen), Dyson	17,000
	31	(h)	Hibernian	D 3-3 Hopkins, Medwin, Brooks	16,561
Nov	12	(h)	Hearts	W 4-2 Smith 3, Stokes	17,542
	26	(a)	Partick Thistle	L 0-2	9,000

Appearances
Goals

Appearance and goals grid (player shirt numbers per match).

Baker	Blanchflower	Brittan	Brooks	Clarke	Ditchburn	Dulin	Dunmore	Duquemin	Dyson	Harmer	Henry	Hollowbread	Hopkins	Marchi	Medwin	Norman	Reynolds	Robb	Ryden	Smith	Stokes	Walley	Wilkie	#
	4		10	5	1				8	3	6	7	2			11				9				1
	4		10	5	1				8	3	6	7	2			11				9				2
	4		10	5	1				8	3	6	7	2			11				9				3
	4		10	5	1				8	3	6	7	2			11				9				4
2	4		10	5	1				8	3	6	7				11				9				5
2	4		10	5	1				8	3	6	7				11				9				6
2	4		10	5	1				8	3	6	7				11				9				7
2	4			5	1				8	3	6	7				11				9	10			8
2	4			5	1				8	3	6	7				11				9	10			9
2	4			5	1				8	3	6	7				11				9	10			10
2		4		5	1				8	3	6	7				11				9	10			11
2	4			5	1				8	3	6	7				11				9	10			12
2	4			5	1	7			8	3	6					11				9	10			13
2	4			5	1				8	3	6	7				11				9	10			14
2	4		10	5	1				8	3	6	7				11				9				15
2	4		10	5	1				8	3	6	7				11				9				16
2	4		10	5	1				8	3	6	7				11				9				17
2	4		10	5	1				8	3	6	7				11				9				18
2	4		10	5	1				8	3	6	7				11				9				19
2	4		10	5	1				8	3	6	7				11				9				20
2	4			5	1				8	3	6	7				11				9	10			21
2	4				1				8	3	6	7				11	5			9	10			22
2	4				1		7		8	3	6					11	5			9	10			23
2	4				1		7		8	3	6					11	5			9	10			24
2	4				1		7		8	3	6					11	5			9	10			25
2	4				1		7		8	3	6					11	5			9	10			26
2					1			9	8	3	6	7				11	5				10	4		27
2	4				1				8	3	6	7				11	5			9	10			28
2	4		10		1				8	3	6	7				11	5			9				29
2	4		10						8		6	7	3	1		11	5			9				30
2	4								8		6	7	3	1		11	5			9	10			31
2	4		10						8		6	7	3	1		11	5			9				32
2	4								8		6	7	3	1		11	5			9	10			33
2	4							9	8		6	7	3	1		11	5				10			34
2	4								8		6	7	3	1		11	5			9	10			35
2	4		10					9	11	8	3	6	7	5	1									36
2	4		10					9	11	8	3	6	7	5	1									37
2	4		10					9	11	8	3	6	7	5	1									38
2	4		10					9	11	8	3	6	7	5	1									39
2	4		10						8	3	6	7	5	1		11				9				40
2	4		10					9	8	3	6	7	5	1		11								41
2			10						8	3	6	7		1		5	9			4	11			42
38	39	1	23	21	29	1	5	2	8	42	1	35	42	37	16	13	37	15	33	21	2	1		
	1		11				3	1	3	17				14			14	18	18					

4 own-goals

Baker	Blanchflower	Brittan	Brooks	Clarke	Ditchburn	Dulin	Dunmore	Duquemin	Dyson	Harmer	Henry	Hollowbread	Hopkins	Marchi	Medwin	Norman	Reynolds	Robb	Ryden	Smith	Stokes	Walley	Wilkie	#
2	4				1		7		8	3	6					11	5			9	10			3
2	4				1				8	3	6	7				11	5			9	10			4
2	4				1				8	3	6	7				11	5			9	10			5
3	3				3		1	3		3	3	2				3	3	3	3					
	1							1				2				1		1	1					

Baker	Blanchflower	Brittan	Brooks	Clarke	Ditchburn	Dulin	Dunmore	Duquemin	Dyson	Harmer	Henry	Hollowbread	Hopkins	Marchi	Medwin	Norman	Reynolds	Robb	Ryden	Smith	Stokes	Walley	Wilkie	#
2	4			5	1				11	8	3	6	7							9	10			
2	4			5	1					8	3	6	7			11				9	10			
2	4			5	1				11	8	3	6	7							9	10			
2	4		10	5	1					8	3	6	7			11				9				
2	4						7	8	1		6		3			11	5			9	10			
	4						11	8		3	6	7	2	1			5	9	10					
5	6		1	4	4		4	6		1	5	6	5	2	1	3	2	6	5					
	1		1				2	2		1		2				6	3							

1957-58

Manager: Jimmy Anderson

1	Aug	24	(h)	Chelsea	D 1-1	Stokes	52,580
2		28	(a)	Portsmouth	L 1-5	Smith	33,479
3		31	(a)	Newcastle U	L 1-3	Smith	37,742
4	Sep	4	(h)	Portsmouth	L 3-5	Harmer (pen), Brooks, Dulin	35,813
5		7	(h)	Burnley	W 3-1	Dunmore 2, Dulin	40,108
6		11	(a)	Birmingham C	D 0-0		26,485
7		14	(a)	Preston NE	L 1-3	Stokes	23,364
8		18	(h)	Birmingham C	W 7-1	Harmer (pen), Stokes 5, Dyson	35,292
9		21	(h)	Sheffield W	W 4-2	Medwin, Smith 2, Dyson	39,954
10		28	(a)	Manchester C	L 1-5	Brannigan (og)	22,497
11	Oct	2	(a)	Wolves	L 0-4		36,024
12		5	(h)	Nottingham F	L 3-4	Medwin, Harmer, Brooks	51,429
13		12	(h)	Arsenal	W 3-1	Medwin 2, Smith	60,671
14		19	(a)	Bolton W	L 2-3	Smith, Robb	20,381
15		26	(h)	Leeds U	W 2-0	Medwin, Smith	33,860
16	Nov	2	(a)	Sunderland	D 1-1	Brooks	36,091
17		9	(h)	Everton	W 3-1	Brooks, Smith, Harmer (pen)	39,999
18		16	(a)	Aston Villa	D 1-1	Smith	28,390
19		23	(h)	Luton T	W 3-1	Medwin 2, Brooks	41,242
20		30	(a)	Manchester U	W 4-3	Smith 3, Blanchflower (og)	43,307
21	Dec	7	(h)	Leicester C	L 1-4	Brooks	27,855
22		14	(a)	Blackpool	W 2-0	Smith 2	14,938
23		21	(a)	Chelsea	W 4-2	Medwin, Harmer, Smith 2	39,747
24		26	(h)	Wolves	W 1-0	Smith	58,393
25		28	(h)	Newcastle U	D 3-3	Norman, Harmer (pen), Stokes	51,649
26	Jan	11	(a)	Burnley	L 0-2		25,927
27		18	(h)	Preston NE	D 3-3	Medwin, Brooks (pen), Smith	43,941
28	Feb	1	(a)	Sheffield W	L 0-2		22,966
29		8	(h)	Manchester C	W 5-1	Smith 3, Brooks, Robb	37,539
30		15	(a)	Nottingham F	W 2-1	Brooks, Robb	32,334
31		22	(a)	Arsenal	D 4-4	Harmer 2 (1 pen), Smith 2	59,116
32	Mar	8	(a)	Leeds U	W 2-1	Smith 2	23,429
33		12	(h)	Bolton W	W 4-1	Brooks, Smith 3	22,978
34		15	(h)	Sunderland	L 0-1		40,751
35		22	(a)	Luton T	D 0-0		22,384
36		29	(h)	Aston Villa	W 6-2	Medwin 2, Smith 4	34,102
37	Apr	4	(h)	West Brom A	D 0-0		56,166
38		5	(a)	Everton	W 4-3	Smith 2, Clayton 2	30,149
39		7	(a)	West Brom A	W 2-0	Medwin, Clayton	26,556
40		12	(h)	Manchester U	W 1-0	Harmer (pen)	59,836
41		19	(a)	Leicester C	W 3-1	Medwin, Smith, Jones	37,234
42		26	(h)	Blackpool	W 2-1	Medwin, Smith	37,632

FINAL LEAGUE POSITION: 3rd in Division One

Appearances
Goals

FA Cup

3	Jan	4	(h)	Leicester C	W 4-0	Medwin, Smith 2, Stokes	42,716
4		25	(h)	Sheffield U	L 0-3		51,136

Appearances
Goals

286

Baker	Bing	Blanchflower	Brittan	Brooks	Clayton	Ditchburn	Dulin	Dunmore	Dyson	Harmer	Henry	Hills	Hopkins	Iley	Ireland	Jones	Medwin	Norman	Reynolds	Robb	Ryden	Smith	Stokes	Walley	
		4	6							8			3				7	2	1	11	5	9	10		1
		4	6							8			3				7	2	1	11	5	9	10		2
		4								8			3	6			7	2	1	11	5	9	10		3
2		4		10					11	8			3	6			7		1		5	9			4
2		4						9	11	8			3	6			7		1		5		10		5
2		4						9	11	8			3	6			7		1		5		10		6
2		4						9	11	8			3	6			7		1		5		10		7
2		4							11	8			3	6			7		1		5	9	10		8
2		4							11	8			3	6			7		1		5	9	10		9
2		4						9	11	8			3	6			7		1		5		10		10
2		4							11	8			3	6			7		1		5	9	10		11
2									11	8			3	6			7	5	1		4	9	10		12
2		4				1			11	8			3	6			7	5				9	10		13
2	7	4				1				8			3	6						11	5	9	10		14
2		4		8		1		9					3				7	5		11	6		10		15
2		4	6	8		1				10			3				7	5		11		9			16
2		4		8		1				10			3				7	5		11	6	9			17
2		4		8		1				10			3				7	5		11	6	9			18
2		4		8		1				10			3				7	5		11	6	9			19
2		4		8		1				10			3				7	5		11	6	9			20
2		4		8		1				10			3				7	5		11	6	9			21
		4		8		1			11	10		2	3				7	5			6	9			22
		4		10		1			11	8		2	3				7	5			6	9			23
		4		10		1			11	8		2	3				7	5			6	9			24
		4				1			11	8		2	3				7	5			6	9	10		25
		4				1			11	10		2	3				7	5			6	9	8		26
		4		8		1			11			2	3			10	7	5			6	9			27
		4		10		1			11	8		2	3				7	5			6	9			28
		4		10		1				8	3	2					7	5		11	6	9			29
		4		10		1				8	3	2					7	5		11	6	9			30
		4		10		1				8	3	2				11	7	5			6	9			31
		4		8		1				10	3	2				11	7	5			6	9			32
		4		8		1			11	10	3	2					7	5			6	9			33
				8		1				10	3	2				11	7	5			6	9		4	34
		4		8		1				10	3	2				11	7	5			6	9			35
		4		8		1				10	3	2				11	7	5			6	9			36
		4		8		1				10	3	2		6		11	7	5				9			37
		4		10		1				8	3	2		6		11	7	5				9			38
		4		10						8	3	2		6		11	7	5	1			9			39
		4		10						8	3	2		6		11	7	5	1			9			40
		4		8						10	3	2		6		11	7	5	1			9			41
		4		10						8	3	2		6		11	7	5	1			9			42
18	1	40	3	25	5	26	3	5	12	40	15	21	26	19	1	10	39	33	16	15	35	38	15	1	
		10		3				2	2	2				9		1	14	1		3		36	8		

2 own-goals

Baker	Bing	Blanchflower	Brittan	Brooks	Clayton	Ditchburn	Dulin	Dunmore	Dyson	Harmer	Henry	Hills	Hopkins	Iley	Ireland	Jones	Medwin	Norman	Reynolds	Robb	Ryden	Smith	Stokes	Walley	
		4				1			11	8		2	3				7	5			6	9	10		3
		4		10		1			11	8		2	3				7	5			6	9			4
		2		1		2			2	2		2	2				2	2			2	2	1		
																	1					2	1		

1958-59

Manager: Jimmy Anderson until October, then Bill Nicholson

1	Aug	23	(h)	Blackpool	L	2-3	Smith, Brooks	57,043
2		27	(a)	Chelsea	L	2-4	Medwin, Smith	59,203
3		30	(a)	Blackburn R	L	0-5		41,830
4	Sep	3	(h)	Chelsea	W	4-0	Medwin 3, Robb	50,299
5		6	(h)	Newcastle U	L	1-3	Medwin	41,805
6		10	(a)	Nottingham F	D	1-1	Smith	26,097
7		13	(a)	Arsenal	L	1-3	Clayton	65,565
8		17	(h)	Nottingham F	W	1-0	Sharpe	39,431
9		20	(a)	Manchester U	D	2-2	Smith 2	62,277
10		27	(h)	Wolves	W	2-1	Smith, Clayton	48,563
11	Oct	4	(a)	Portsmouth	D	1-1	Stokes	26,402
12		11	(h)	Everton	W	10-4	Ryden, Medwin, Harmer, Smith 4, Stokes 2, Robb	37,794
13		18	(a)	Leicester C	W	4-3	Harmer (pen), Smith, Stokes 2	31,509
14		25	(h)	Leeds U	L	2-3	Iley, Smith	38,691
15	Nov	1	(a)	Manchester C	L	1-5	Smith	30,601
16		8	(h)	Bolton W	D	1-1	Smith	39,820
17		15	(a)	Luton T	W	2-1	Dunmore, Medwin	23,592
18		22	(h)	Birmingham C	L	0-4		28,708
19		29	(a)	West Brom A	L	3-4	Dunmore, Smith 2	21,753
20	Dec	6	(h)	Preston NE	L	1-2	Smith	31,806
21		13	(a)	Burnley	L	1-3	Stokes	17,047
22		20	(a)	Blackpool	D	0-0		12,939
23		25	(a)	West Ham U	L	1-2	Smith	26,178
24		26	(h)	West Ham U	L	1-4	Stokes	43,817
25	Jan	3	(h)	Blackburn R	W	3-1	Harmer (pen), Smith, Dunmore	39,552
26		17	(a)	Newcastle U	W	2-1	Dunmore 2	32,503
27		31	(h)	Arsenal	L	1-4	Smith	60,241
28	Feb	7	(h)	Manchester U	L	1-3	Norman	48,401
29		21	(h)	Portsmouth	D	4-4	Smith 2, Clayton, Jones (pen)	27,237
30		28	(a)	Everton	L	1-2	Jones	36,782
31	Mar	2	(a)	Wolves	D	1-1	Harmer	30,437
32		7	(h)	Leicester C	W	6-0	Blanchflower, Medwin 4, Dunmore	30,561
33		14	(a)	Leeds U	L	1-3	Norman	17,010
34		21	(h)	Manchester C	W	3-1	Medwin, Smith, Jones (pen)	34,493
35		27	(h)	Aston Villa	W	3-2	Medwin, Smith, Jones	45,059
36		28	(a)	Bolton W	L	1-4	Clayton	21,384
37		30	(a)	Aston Villa	D	1-1	Norman	34,354
38	Apr	4	(h)	Luton T	W	3-0	Medwin, Smith, Brooks	37,093
39		8	(h)	Burnley	D	2-2	Smith 2	32,296
40		11	(a)	Birmingham C	L	1-5	Jones (pen)	20,557
41		18	(h)	West Brom A	W	5-0	Smith 4, Brooks	36,805
42		25	(a)	Preston NE	D	2-2	Smith, Brooks	20,323

FINAL LEAGUE POSITION: 18th in Division One

Appearances
Goals

FA Cup

3	Jan	10	(h)	West Ham U	W	2-0	Smith, Jones	56,252
4		24	(h)	Newport C	W	4-1	Smith 2, Dunmore 2	50,561
5	Feb	14	(h)	Norwich C	D	1-1	Jones	67,633
R		18	(a)	Norwich C	L	0-1		38,000

Appearances
Goals

288

Football appearance grid (shirt numbers by player and match). Last column is the match number.

Baker	Blanchflower	Brooks	Clayton	Ditchburn	Dodge	Dunmore	Dyson	Harmer	Henry	Hills	Hollowbread	Hopkins	Iley	Ireland	Jones	Mackay	Medwin	Norman	Robb	Ryden	Sharpe	Smith	Stokes	#
	4	10		1			11	8	3	2			6				7	5				9		1
	4	10		1			11	8	3	2			6				7	5				9		2
2	4	8				9	11				1	3	6				7	5					10	3
2	4	10						8			1	3	6				7	5	11			9		4
	4	10					11	8		2	1	3	6				7	5				9		5
2	4	10						8			1	3	6				7	5	11			9		6
2	4	10						8			1	3	6				7	5	11			9		7
2		10									1	3	6				7		11	5	4	9	8	8
2	4	10									1	3	6				7		11	5		9	8	9
2	4	10									1	3	6				7		11	5		9	8	10
2		10						4			1	3	6				7		11	5		9	8	11
2	4	8									1	3	6				7		11	5		9	10	12
2	4	8							3		1		6				7		11	5		9	10	13
2	4						11	8			1	3	6				7	5				9	10	14
	4						11	8		2	1	3	6				7	5				9	10	15
2	4		7			9		8			1	3	6		11			5				10		16
2	4		7			9		8			1	3	6		11			5				10		17
2	4		7			9		8			1	3	6		11			5				10		18
2	4					9	11	8			1	3	6				7	5				10		19
	4		7			9		8	3	2	1		6		11			5				10		20
	4							8	3	2	1		6		11		7	5				9	10	21
2	4							8	3		1		6		11		7	5				9	10	22
2	4							8	3		1		6		11		7	5				9	10	23
2	4		7					8	3		1		6		11			5				9	10	24
2			7		4	10		8			1	3	6		11			5				9		25
2			7		4	10		8			1	3	6		11			5				9		26
2			7		4	10		8			1	3	6		11			5				9		27
2			7		4	10		8			1	3	6		11			5				9		28
2	4	8						10			1	3	6		11		7	5				9		29
2	4	10						8			1	3	6		11		7	5				9		30
2	4	8						10			1	3	6		11		7	5				9		31
2	4	8						10			1	3	6		11		7	5				9		32
2	4	8						10			1	3	6		11		7	5				9		33
2	4	10						8			1	3			11	6	7	5				9		34
2	4	10						8			1	3	6		11		7	5				9		35
2	4	10	7								1	3	6		11			5				9	8	36
2	4	10						8			1	3	6		11		7	5				9		37
2	4	10						8			1	3	6		11		7	5				9		38
2	4	10						8			1	3	6		11		7	5				9		39
2	4	10						8			1	3	6		11		7	5				9		40
2	4	10						8			1	3			11	6	7	5				9		41
2	4	10						8			1	3			11	6	7	5				9		42
36	36	25	11	2	5	13	7	35	8	7	40	34	34	2	22	4	35	35	9	10	2	36	14	
1	4	4				6		4						1	5		14	3	2	1	1	32	7	

Baker	Blanchflower	Brooks	Clayton	Ditchburn	Dodge	Dunmore	Dyson	Harmer	Henry	Hills	Hollowbread	Hopkins	Iley	Ireland	Jones	Mackay	Medwin	Norman	Robb	Ryden	Sharpe	Smith	Stokes	#
2			7		4	10		8			1	3	6		11			5				9		3
2			7		4	10		8			1	3	6		11			5				9		4
2			7		4	10		8			1	3	6		11			5				9		5
2	4	8						10			1	3	6		11		7	5				9		R
4	1	3	1		4	3		3			4	4	4		4		1	4				4		
		2													2							3		

289

1959-60

1	Aug	22	(a)	Newcastle U	W	5-1	Brooks 2, Jones 3	40,782
2		26	(h)	West Brom A	D	2-2	Medwin, R.Smith	54,114
3		29	(h)	Birmingham C	D	0-0		45,243
4	Sep	2	(a)	West Brom A	W	2-1	Harmer, R.Smith	35,924
5		5	(a)	Arsenal	D	1-1	Medwin	60,791
6		9	(h)	West Ham U	D	2-2	R.Smith, Jones	58,909
7		12	(a)	Manchester U	W	5-1	Mackay, Harmer, R.Smith 2, Dunmore	55,641
8		14	(a)	West Ham U	W	2-1	Marchi, R.Smith	36,831
9		19	(h)	Preston NE	W	5-1	Mackay, R.Smith, Dunmore, Jones 2	51,776
10		26	(a)	Leicester C	D	1-1	Jones (pen)	34,445
11	Oct	3	(h)	Burnley	D	1-1	Medwin	42,717
12		10	(h)	Wolves	W	5-1	R.Smith 4, Jones	59,344
13		17	(a)	Sheffield W	L	1-2	White	37,623
14		24	(h)	Nottingham F	W	2-1	R.Smith 2	52,002
15		31	(a)	Manchester C	W	2-1	Mackay, Jones	45,506
16	Nov	7	(h)	Bolton W	L	0-2		41,909
17		14	(a)	Luton T	L	0-1		22,528
18		21	(h)	Everton	W	3-0	Jones (pen), Harris (og), King (og)	39,432
19		28	(a)	Blackpool	D	2-2	Mackay, R.Smith	17,085
20	Dec	5	(h)	Blackburn R	W	2-1	Medwin, Bray (og)	37,130
21		12	(a)	Fulham	D	1-1	Jones (pen)	36,772
22		19	(h)	Newcastle U	W	4-0	Blanchflower, Norman, White, Jones	32,824
23		26	(a)	Leeds U	W	4-2	Harmer, R.Smith, Allen 2	36,037
24		28	(h)	Leeds U	L	1-4	Mackay	54,170
25	Jan	2	(a)	Birmingham C	W	1-0	Allen	27,558
26		16	(h)	Arsenal	W	3-0	R.Smith, Allen 2	58,962
27		23	(h)	Manchester U	W	2-1	R.Smith 2	62,602
28	Feb	6	(a)	Preston NE	D	1-1	Mackay	33,039
29		13	(h)	Leicester C	L	1-2	R.Smith	33,504
30		27	(a)	Blackburn R	W	4-1	Mackay, R.Smith, Allen, Jones	29,228
31	Mar	1	(a)	Burnley	L	0-2		32,992
32		5	(h)	Sheffield W	W	4-1	White, Jones 3	53,822
33		12	(a)	Nottingham F	W	3-1	Mackay, White, Allen	35,291
34		19	(h)	Fulham	D	1-1	Mackay	52,189
35		26	(a)	Bolton W	L	1-2	Mackay	31,106
36	Apr	2	(h)	Luton T	D	1-1	Jones	39,462
37		9	(a)	Everton	L	1-2	Jones	57,959
38		15	(a)	Chelsea	W	3-1	R.Smith 3	67,819
39		16	(h)	Manchester C	L	0-1		49,767
40		18	(h)	Chelsea	L	0-1		37,200
41		23	(a)	Wolves	W	3-1	Jones, R.Smith, Mackay	56,283
42		30	(h)	Blackpool	W	4-1	Blanchflower, Jones, White, R.Smith	49,823

FINAL LEAGUE POSITION: 3rd in Division One

Appearances

Goals

FA Cup

3	Jan	9	(a)	Newport C	W	4-0	Blanchflower, R.Smith, Allen 2	22,655
4		30	(a)	Crewe A	D	2-2	Allen, Jones	20,000
R	Feb	3	(h)	Crewe A	W	13-2	Harmer, R.Smith 4, Allen 5, Jones 3 (1 pen)	64,365
5		20	(h)	Blackburn R	L	1-3	Jones	54,745

Appearances

Goals

Appearance and goalscoring grid (player columns left to right: Allen, Baker, Blanchflower, Brooks, Brown, Clayton, Dodge, Dunmore, Dyson, Harmer, Henry, Hills, Hollowbread, Hopkins, Jones, Mackay, Marchi, Medwin, Norman, Smith J, Smith R, White, Worley; final column = match number).

Allen	Baker	Blanchflower	Brooks	Brown	Clayton	Dodge	Dunmore	Dyson	Harmer	Henry	Hills	Hollowbread	Hopkins	Jones	Mackay	Marchi	Medwin	Norman	Smith J	Smith R	White	Worley	#
	2	4	10	1					8				3	11	6		7	5		9			1
	2	4	10	1					8				3	11	6		7	5		9			2
	2	4	10	1					8				3	11	6		7	5		9			3
	2	4		1			10		8				3	11	6		7	5		9			4
	2	4		1			10		8				3	11		6	7	5		9			5
	2			1			10		8				3	11	6	4	7	5		9			6
	2	4		1			10		8				3	11	6		7	5		9			7
	2	4		1			10	11					3		6	8	7	5		9			8
	2	4		1			10		8				3	11	6		7	5		9			9
	2	4		1			10		8				3	11	6		7	5		9			10
	2				4		10		8			1	3	11		6	7	5		9			11
	2	4		1			10		8				3	11	6		7	5		9			12
	2	4		1				11	8	3					6			5		9	10	7	13
	2	4		1					8				3	11	6		7	5		9	10		14
	2	4		1					8				3	11	6		7	5		9	10		15
	2	4		1					8	3				11	6		7	5		9	10		16
	2	4	11	1					8	3					6		7	5		9	10		17
	2	4		1					8	3				11	6		7	5		9	10		18
	2	4		1					8	3				11	6		7	5		9	10		19
	2	4		1					8	3				11	6		7	5		9	10		20
	2	4		1					8	3				11	6		7	5		9	10		21
10	2	4		1					8	3				11	6			5		9	7		22
10	2	4		1					8	3				11	6			5		9	7		23
10	2	4		1					8	3				11	6			5		9	7		24
10	2	4		1					8	3				11	6			5		9	7		25
10	2	4		1					8	3				11	6			5		9	7		26
10	2	4		1					8	3				11	6			5		9	7		27
10		4		1				9	8	3	2			11	6		7	5					28
10	2	4		1					8	3				11	6			5		9	7		29
10	2	4		1					8	3				11	6			5		9	7		30
10	2	4		1					8	3				11	6		7	5		9			31
10	2	4		1					8	3				11	6			5		9	7		32
10	2	4		1				11	8	3					6			5		9	7		33
10	2	4		1					8	3				11	6			5		9	7		34
10	2	4							8	3		1		11	6	5				9	7		35
10	2	4		1					8	3				11	6	5				9	7		36
	2	4		1					8	3				11	6			5	10	9	7		37
	2	4		1					8	3				11	6		7	5		9	10		38
	2	4		1					8	3				11	6		7	5		9	10		39
	2	4		1					11	3				10	6		7	5		9	8		40
	2	4		1					11	3				7	10	6		5		9	8		41
	2	4		1					11	3				7	10	6		5		9	8		42
15	41	40	4	40	1	1	10	6	37	25	1	2	14	38	38	14	26	39	1	40	28	1	
7		2	2			2		3						20	11	1	4	1		25	5		

3 own-goals

Allen	Baker	Blanchflower	Brooks	Brown	Clayton	Dodge	Dunmore	Dyson	Harmer	Henry	Hills	Hollowbread	Hopkins	Jones	Mackay	Marchi	Medwin	Norman	Smith J	Smith R	White	Worley	#
10	2	4		1					8	3				11	6			5		9	7		3
10	2	4		1					8	3				11	6			5		9	7		4
10		4		1					8	3	2			11	6			5		9	7		R
10	2	4		1					8	3				11	6			5		9	7		5
4	3	4		4					4	4	1			4	3	1		4		4	4		
8									1					1						5	5		

1960-61

Manager: Bill Nicholson

1	Aug	20	(h)	Everton	W 2-0	R.Smith, Allen	50,393
2		22	(a)	Blackpool	W 3-1	Medwin, Dyson 2	27,656
3		27	(a)	Blackburn R	W 4-1	R.Smith 2, Allen, Dyson	26,819
4		31	(h)	Blackpool	W 3-1	R.Smith 3	45,684
5	Sep	3	(h)	Manchester U	W 4-1	R.Smith 2, Allen 2	55,442
6		7	(a)	Bolton W	W 2-1	White, Allen	41,565
7		10	(a)	Arsenal	W 3-2	Saul, Allen, Dyson	59,868
8		14	(h)	Bolton W	W 3-1	Blanchflower (pen), R.Smith 2	43,559
9		17	(a)	Leicester C	W 2-1	R.Smith 2	30,129
10		24	(h)	Aston Villa	W 6-2	Mackay, White 2, R.Smith, Allen, Dyson	61,356
11	Oct	1	(a)	Wolves	W 4-0	Blanchflower, Jones, Allen, Dyson	52,829
12		10	(h)	Manchester C	D 1-1	R.Smith	58,916
13		15	(a)	Nottingham F	W 4-0	Mackay, Jones 2, White	37,248
14		29	(a)	Newcastle U	W 4-3	Norman, Jones, White, R.Smith	51,369
15	Nov	2	(h)	Cardiff C	W 3-2	Blanchflower (pen), Medwin, Dyson	47,605
16		5	(h)	Fulham	W 5-1	Jones 2, White, Allen 2	56,270
17		12	(a)	Sheffield W	L 1-2	Norman	53,988
18		19	(h)	Birmingham C	W 6-0	Jones 2, White, R.Smith (pen) Dyson 2	46,010
19		26	(a)	West Brom A	W 3-1	R.Smith 2, Allen	39,017
20	Dec	3	(h)	Burnley	D 4-4	Norman, Mackay, Jones 2	58,737
21		10	(a)	Preston NE	W 1-0	White	21,657
22		17	(a)	Everton	W 3-1	Mackay, White, Allen	61,052
23		24	(h)	West Ham U	W 2-0	White, Dyson	54,930
24		26	(a)	West Ham U	W 3-0	White, Allen, Brown (og)	34,351
25		31	(h)	Blackburn R	W 5-2	Blanchflower, R.Smith 2, Allen 2	48,742
26	Jan	16	(a)	Manchester U	L 0-2		65,535
27		21	(h)	Arsenal	W 4-2	Blanchflower (pen), R.Smith, Allen 2	65,251
28	Feb	4	(h)	Leicester C	L 2-3	Blanchflower (pen), Allen	53,627
29		11	(a)	Aston Villa	W 2-1	R.Smith, Dyson	50,786
30		22	(h)	Wolves	D 1-1	R.Smith	62,261
31		25	(a)	Manchester C	W 1-0	Medwin	40,278
32	Mar	11	(a)	Cardiff C	L 2-3	Allen, Dyson	45,463
33		22	(h)	Newcastle U	L 1-2	Allen	46,470
34		25	(a)	Fulham	D 0-0		38,536
35		31	(h)	Chelsea	W 4-2	Jones 2, Saul, Allen	65,032
36	Apr	1	(h)	Preston NE	W 5-0	Jones 3, White, Saul	46,325
37		3	(a)	Chelsea	W 3-2	Norman, R.Smith, Medwin	57,101
38		8	(a)	Birmingham C	W 3-2	White, R.Smith, Allen	40,961
39		17	(h)	Sheffield W	W 2-1	R.Smith, Allen	61,205
40		22	(a)	Burnley	L 2-4	Baker, R.Smith	28,991
41		26	(h)	Nottingham F	W 1-0	Medwin	35,743
42		29	(h)	West Brom A	L 1-2	R.Smith	52,054

FINAL LEAGUE POSITION: 1st in Division One

Appearances
Goals

FA Cup

3	Jan	7	(h)	Charlton A	W 3-2	Allen 2, Dyson	54,969
4		28	(h)	Crewe A	W 5-1	Mackay, Jones, R.Smith, Allen, Dyson	53,721
5	Feb	18	(a)	Aston Villa	W 2-0	Jones, Neil (og)	65,474
6	Mar	4	(a)	Sunderland	D 1-1	Jones	61,236
R		8	(h)	Sunderland	W 5-0	Mackay, R.Smith, Allen, Dyson 2	64,797
SF		18	(n*)	Burnley	W 3-0	Jones, R.Smith 2	69,968
F	May	6	(n†)	Leicester C	W 2-0	R.Smith, Dyson	100,000

*Played at Villa Park, Birmingham. †Played at Wembley Stadium.

Appearances
Goals

Allen	Baker	Barton	Blanchflower	Brown	Dyson	Henry	Hollowbread	Jones	Mackay	Marchi	Medwin	Norman	Saul	Smith J	Smith R	White	
10	2		4	1	11	3		7	6			5			9	8	1
10	2		4	1	11	3			6		7	5			9	8	2
10	2		4	1	11	3			6		7	5			9	8	3
10	2		4	1	11	3			6		7	5			9	8	4
10	2		4	1	11	3			6		7	5			9	8	5
10	2		4	1	11	3			6		7	5	9			8	6
10	2		4	1	11	3			6		7	5	9			8	7
10	2		4	1	11	3		7	6			5			9	8	8
10	2		4	1	11	3		7	6			5			9	8	9
10	2		4	1	11	3		7	6			5			9	8	10
10	2		4	1	11	3		7		6		5			9	8	11
10	2		4	1	11	3		7	6			5			9	8	12
10	2		4	1	11	3		7	6			5			9	8	13
10	2		4	1	11	3		7	6			5			9	8	14
10	2		4	1	11	3			6		7	5			9	8	15
10	2		4	1	11	3		7	6			5			9	8	16
10	2		4	1	11	3		7	6			5			9	8	17
10	2		4	1	11	3		7	6			5			9	8	18
10	2		4	1	11	3		7	6			5			9	8	19
10	2		4	1	11	3		7	6			5			9	8	20
10	2		4	1	11	3		7	6			5	9			8	21
10	2		4	1	11	3		7	6			5			9	8	22
10	2		4	1	11	3		7	6			5			9	8	23
10	2		4		11	3	1		6		7	5			9	8	24
10	2		4	1	11	3			6		7	5			9	8	25
10		2	4	1	11	3			6			5		7	9	8	26
10	2		4	1	11	3		7	6			5			9	8	27
10	2		4	1	11	3		7	6			5			9	8	28
10	2		4	1	11	3		7	6			5			9	8	29
10	2		4	1	11	3		7	6			5			9	8	30
10	2		4	1	11	3			6	5	7				9	8	31
10	2		4	1	11	3		7	6			5			9	8	32
10	2		4	1	11	3		7	6			5			9	8	33
10	2		4	1	11	3		7		6		5	9			8	34
10	2		4	1	11	3		7		6		5	9			8	35
10	2		4	1		3		7		6	11	5	9			8	36
10	2		4	1		3		7	6		11	5			9	8	37
10	2		4	1	11	3		7	6			5			9	8	38
10	2		4	1	11	3		7	6			5			9	8	39
10	2		4	1	11	3			6		7	5			9	8	40
10	2		4	1	11	3			6		7	5			9	8	41
10	2		4	1	11	3		7	6			5			9	8	42
42	41	1	42	41	40	42	1	29	37	6	14	41	6	1	36	42	
23	1		6		12			15	4		5	4	3		28	13	

1 own-goal

Allen	Baker	Barton	Blanchflower	Brown	Dyson	Henry	Hollowbread	Jones	Mackay	Marchi	Medwin	Norman	Saul	Smith J	Smith R	White	
10	2		4	1	11	3			6		7	5			9	8	3
10	2		4	1	11	3		7	6			5			9	8	4
10	2		4	1	11	3		7	6			5			9	8	5
10	2		4	1	11	3		7	6			5			9	8	6
10	2		4	1	11	3		7	6			5			9	8	R
10	2		4	1	11	3		7	6			5			9	8	SF
10	2		4	1	11	3		7	6			5			9	8	F
7	7		7	7	7	7		6	7		1	7			7	7	
4					5			4	2						5		

1 own-goal

293

1961-62

Manager: Bill Nicholson

1	Aug	19	(a)	Blackpool	W 2-1	Jones, R.Smith	29,023
2		23	(h)	West Ham U	D 2-2	Dyson 2	50,434
3		26	(h)	Arsenal	W 4-3	Allen, Dyson 3	59,371
4		28	(a)	West Ham U	L 1-2	Allen	36,274
5	Sep	2	(h)	Cardiff C	W 3-2	Blanchflower (pen), Jones, R.Smith	37,834
6		4	(a)	Sheffield U	D 1-1	White	32,902
7		9	(a)	Manchester U	L 0-1		57,135
8		16	(h)	Wolves	W 1-0	Mackay	45,334
9		23	(a)	Nottingham F	L 0-2		40,875
10		30	(h)	Aston Villa	W 1-0	Dyson	38,099
11	Oct	9	(a)	Bolton W	W 2-1	Allen, Clayton	24,726
12		14	(h)	Manchester C	W 2-0	Medwin, White	40,561
13		21	(a)	Ipswich T	L 2-3	Jones 2	28,778
14		28	(h)	Burnley	W 4-2	Jones 2, Saul, Clayton	56,771
15	Nov	4	(a)	Everton	L 0-3		54,234
16		11	(h)	Fulham	W 4-2	Jones, White 2, Mackay	35,662
17		18	(a)	Sheffield W	D 0-0		43,085
18		25	(h)	Leicester C	L 1-2	White	41,745
19	Dec	2	(a)	West Brom A	W 4-2	Medwin, White, Allen, Howe (og)	28,701
20		9	(h)	Birmingham C	W 3-1	Allen 2, Mackay	32,509
21		16	(h)	Blackpool	W 5-2	Allen 2, Greaves 3	42,734
22		23	(a)	Arsenal	L 1-2	Mackay	63,440
23		26	(a)	Chelsea	W 2-0	Greaves, Jones	51,282
24		30	(h)	Chelsea	W 5-2	Mackay, Allen, Jones 3	44,630
25	Jan	13	(a)	Cardiff C	D 1-1	Mackay	33,606
26		20	(h)	Manchester U	D 2-2	Greaves 2	55,225
27	Feb	3	(a)	Wolves	L 1-3	White	45,687
28		10	(h)	Nottingham F	W 4-2	Medwin, R.Smith, Jones 2	42,710
29		21	(a)	Aston Villa	D 0-0		49,892
30		24	(h)	Bolton W	D 2-2	R.Smith, Greaves	36,470
31	Mar	3	(a)	Manchester C	L 2-6	Greaves 2	31,706
32		14	(h)	Ipswich T	L 1-3	Greaves	51,098
33		17	(a)	Burnley	D 2-2	Greaves, Jones	46,810
34		24	(h)	Everton	W 3-1	Jones, White, Greaves	47,343
35	Apr	7	(h)	Sheffield W	W 4-0	Clayton, Saul, Greaves 2	40,856
36		9	(h)	Sheffield U	D 3-3	Blanchflower (pen), R.Smith, Greaves	49,030
37		17	(a)	Fulham	D 1-1	Greaves	43,355
38		20	(h)	Blackburn R	W 4-1	Medwin, R.Smith, Greaves, Jones	55,183
39		21	(h)	West Brom A	L 1-2	Saul	53,512
40		23	(a)	Blackburn R	W 1-0	Greaves	23,301
41		28	(a)	Birmingham C	W 3-2	Mackay, Greaves 2	29,614
42		30	(a)	Leicester C	W 3-2	Mackay, Medwin, Greaves	23,929

FINAL LEAGUE POSITION: 3rd in Division One

Appearances
Goals

FA Cup

3	Jan	6	(a)	Birmingham C	D 3-3	Greaves 2, Jones	46,096
R		10	(h)	Birmingham C	W 4-2	Medwin 2, Allen, Greaves	62,917
4		27	(a)	Plymouth A	W 5-1	Medwin, White, Greaves 2, Jones	40,040
5	Feb	17	(a)	West Brom A	W 4-2	R.Smith 2, Greaves 2	53,539
6	Mar	10	(h)	Aston Villa	W 2-0	Blanchflower, Jones	64,000
SF		31	(n*)	Manchester U	W 3-1	Medwin, Greaves, Jones	65,000
F	May	5	(n†)	Burnley	W 3-1	Blanchflower (pen), R.Smith, Greaves	100,000

*Played at Hillsborough, Sheffield. †Played at Wembley Stadium.

Appearances
Goals

FA Charity Shield

Aug	12	(h)	FA XI	W 3-2	R.Smith, Allen 2	36,593

Appearances
Goals

Allen	Baker	Barton	Blanchflower	Brown	Clayton	Collins	Dyson	Greaves	Henry	Hollowbread	Hopkins	Jones	Mackay	Marchi	Medwin	Norman	Saul	Smith J	Smith R	White	No.
10	2		4	1			11		3			7	6			5			9	8	1
10	2		4	1	8		11		3			7		6		5			9		2
10	2		4	1			11		3			7		6		5	8		9		3
10	2		4	1			11		3			7		6		5	8		9		4
10	2		4	1			11		3			7	6			5			9	8	5
10	2		4	1			11		3			7	6			5			9	8	6
10	2		4	1			11		3			7		6		5			9	8	7
	2		4	1			11		3			7	6			5	10		9	8	8
10	2		4	1			11		3			7	6			5			9	8	9
10	2		4	1			11		3			7	6			5			9	8	10
9	2		4		10		11		3	1		7	6			5				8	11
10	2		4	1			11		3				6	7		5			9	8	12
10	2		4	1			11		3			7	6			5			9	8	13
	2		4	1	10		11		3			7		6		5	9			8	14
	2		4			10	11		3	1		7		6		5	9			8	15
	2		4	1			11		3			7	10	6		5	9			8	16
10	2		4	1			11		3			7		6		5			9	8	17
10	2		4				11		3	1		7		6		5			9	8	18
9	2		4	1					3			11	6	7		5			10	8	19
9	2		4	1					3			11	10	6	7	5				8	20
9	2		4	1			10		3			11	6	7		5				8	21
9	2		4	1			10		3			11	6	7		5				8	22
9	2		4	1			10		3			11	6	7		5				8	23
9			4	1			10		3		2	11	6	7		5				8	24
9			4	1		10		9	3		2	11	6	7		5					25
9	2		4	1			11	10	3			7	8	6		5					26
9	2		4	1			10		3			11	6	7		5				8	27
	2		4	1			10		3			11	6	7		5			9	8	28
	2		4	1			11	10	3				6		7	5			9	8	29
							11	10	3	1	2		6	7		5	4		9	8	30
	2		4				10		3	1		11	6	7		5			9	8	31
	2		4	1			10		3			11	6	7		5			9	8	32
	2		4	1			10		3			11	6	7		5			9	8	33
	2		4	1			11	10	3			7		6		5			9	8	34
	2		4	1	7		10		3			11	6			5			9	8	35
	2		4	1	7		10		3			11	6			5			9	8	36
	2		4	1	7		10		3			11	6			5			9	8	37
	2		4	1			10		3			11	6	7		5			9	8	38
	2		4	1	8		10		3			11	6	7		5	9				39
	2					10			3	1		11	6	5	7		9		4	8	40
	2		4	1			10		3			11	6	7		5			9	8	41
	2			1			11	10	3		2		6	7		5	9		4	8	42
23	36	2	39	35	7	2	23	22	41	7	5	38	26	21	20	40	8	5	26	36	
9			2	3		6	21					16	8		5		3		6	8	

1 own-goal

Allen	Baker	Barton	Blanchflower	Brown	Clayton	Collins	Dyson	Greaves	Henry	Hollowbread	Hopkins	Jones	Mackay	Marchi	Medwin	Norman	Saul	Smith J	Smith R	White	
9	2		4	1			10		3			11	6	7		5				8	3
9	2		4	1			10		3			11	6	7		5				8	R
9	2		4	1			10		3			11	6	7		5				8	4
	2		4	1			10		3			11	6	7		5			9	8	5
	2		4	1			10		3			11	6	7		5			9	8	6
	2		4	1			10		3			11	6	7		5			9	8	SF
	2		4	1			10		3			11	6	7		5			9	8	F
3	7		7	7			7		7			7	7	7		7			4	7	
1			2				9					4			4				3	1	

Allen	Baker	Barton	Blanchflower	Brown	Clayton	Collins	Dyson	Greaves	Henry	Hollowbread	Hopkins	Jones	Mackay	Marchi	Medwin	Norman	Saul	Smith J	Smith R	White	
10	2		4	1			11		3			7	6			5			9	8	
1	1		1	1			1		1			1	1			1			1	1	
2																1					

295

1962-63

Manager: Bill Nicholson

1	Aug	18	(h)	Birmingham C	W 3-0	Blanchflower (pen), Greaves, Jones	51,140
2		20	(a)	Aston Villa	L 1-2	Medwin	55,630
3		25	(a)	West Ham U	W 6-1	Medwin, White, Greaves 2, Jones, Lyall (og)	32,527
4		29	(h)	Aston Villa	W 4-2	White, Greaves 2, Jones	55,650
5	Sep	1	(h)	Manchester C	W 4-2	Blanchflower (pen), Medwin, Greaves, Jones	48,758
6		8	(a)	Blackpool	W 2-1	Norman, Allen	31,786
7		12	(h)	Wolves	L 1-2	White	61,412
8		15	(h)	Blackburn R	W 4-1	Medwin, White, Allen, Taylor (og)	43,014
9		19	(a)	Wolves	D 2-2	Greaves 2	48,166
10		22	(a)	Sheffield U	L 1-3	Greaves	38,355
11		29	(h)	Nottingham F	W 9-2	Medwin, White, Allen (pen), Greaves 4, Jones 2	49,075
12	Oct	6	(h)	Arsenal	D 4-4	Mackay, White, Jones 2	61,749
13		13	(a)	West Brom A	W 2-1	Marchi, Jones	32,753
14		24	(h)	Manchester U	W 6-2	Medwin 2, Greaves 3, Jones	51,314
15		27	(a)	Leyton O	W 5-1	Medwin, White, Allen, Jones, Bishop (og)	30,967
16	Nov	3	(h)	Leicester C	W 4-0	Blanchflower (pen), Medwin, Greaves 2	52,361
17		10	(a)	Fulham	W 2-0	Mackay, Jones	39,961
18		17	(h)	Sheffield W	D 1-1	Mackay	42,390
19		24	(a)	Burnley	L 1-2	Greaves	44,478
20	Dec	1	(h)	Everton	D 0-0		60,626
21		8	(a)	Bolton W	L 0-1		20,737
22		15	(a)	Birmingham C	W 2-0	R.Smith, Greaves	36,623
23		22	(h)	West Ham U	D 4-4	J.Smith, Mackay 3	44,650
24		26	(h)	Ipswich T	W 5-0	R.Smith, Greaves 3, Jones	34,822
25	Jan	19	(h)	Blackpool	W 2-0	Greaves 2	25,710
26	Feb	23	(a)	Arsenal	W 3-2	Marchi, R.Smith, Jones	59,980
27	Mar	2	(h)	West Brom A	W 2-1	R.Smith 2	41,193
28		9	(a)	Manchester U	W 2-0	Saul, Jones	53,416
29		16	(a)	Ipswich T	W 4-2	Saul, Greaves 2 (1 pen), Jones	23,679
30		23	(a)	Leicester C	D 2-2	R.Smith, Greaves	41,622
31		27	(h)	Leyton O	W 2-0	R.Smith, Greaves (pen)	40,260
32		30	(h)	Burnley	D 1-1	Greaves	46,536
33	Apr	8	(a)	Sheffield W	L 1-3	McAnearney (og)	43,368
34		12	(a)	Liverpool	L 2-5	Jones, Dyson	54,463
35		13	(h)	Fulham	D 1-1	Greaves	45,951
36		15	(h)	Liverpool	W 7-2	Jones 2, Saul, Greaves 4 (1 pen)	53,727
37		20	(a)	Everton	L 0-1		67,650
38		27	(h)	Bolton W	W 4-1	Marchi, Greaves, White, R.Smith	40,965
39	May	4	(h)	Sheffield U	W 4-2	Jones, Saul, Greaves, Dyson	42,886
40		11	(a)	Manchester C	L 0-1		27,784
41		18	(a)	Nottingham F	D 1-1	Allen	27,995
42		20	(a)	Blackburn R	L 0-3		22,867

FINAL LEAGUE POSITION: 2nd in Division One

Appearances
Goals

FA Cup

3	Jan	16	(h)	Burnley	L 0-3		32,756

Appearances
Goals

FA Charity Shield

1	Aug	11	(a)	Ipswich T	W 5-1	Medwin, White, Smith, Greaves 2	20,179

Appearances
Goals

Allen	Baker	Blanchflower	Brown	Clayton	Dyson	Greaves	Henry	Hollowbread	Jones	Mackay	Marchi	Medwin	Norman	Piper	Saul	Smith J	Smith R	White	
	2	4	1			10	3		11	6		7	5				9	8	1
	2	4	1			10	3		11	6		7	5				9	8	2
9	2	4	1			10	3		11	6		7	5					8	3
9	2	4	1			10	3		11	6		7	5					8	4
9	2	4	1			10	3		11	6		7	5					8	5
9	2	4	1			10	3		11	6		7	5					8	6
9	2	4	1			10	3		11	6		7	5					8	7
9	2	4	1		11	10	3			6		7	5					8	8
9	2	4	1		11	10	3			6		7	5					8	9
9	2	4	1			10	3		11	6		7	5					8	10
9	2	4	1			10	3		11	6		7	5					8	11
9	2	4	1	10			3		11	6		7	5					8	12
9	2		1			10	3		11	6	4	7	5					8	13
9	2	4	1			10	3		11	6		7	5					8	14
9	2	4	1			10	3		11		6	7	5					8	15
9	2	4	1		11	10	3			6		7	5					8	16
9	2	4	1			10	3		11	6		7	5					8	17
9	2	4	1		11	10	3			6		7	5					8	18
9	2	4	1			10	3		11	6		7	5					8	19
9	2	4	1	7		10	3		11	8	6		5						20
9	2	4	1	8		10	3		11	6		7	5						21
	2		1			10	3		11	6	4	7	5				9	8	22
	2		1			10	3		11	6	5	7		4			9	8	23
	2		1			10	3		11	6		7	5	4			9	8	24
	2		1			10	3		11	6	4	7	5				9	8	25
	2		1			10	3		11	6	4	7	5				9	8	26
	2		1			10	3		11	6	4	7	5				9	8	27
			1			10	3	2	11	6	4		5	7			9	8	28
9						10	3	1	2	11	6	4	5	7				8	29
			1			10	3	2	11	6	4		5	7			9	8	30
						10	3	1	2	11	6	4	5	7			9	8	31
			1			10	3	2	11	6	4		5	7			9	8	32
9			1			10	3	2	11	6	4		5	7				8	33
9			1		11	10	3	2	7	6	4		5					8	34
	2		1		11	10	3		7	6			5		9	4		8	35
			1		11	10	3	2	7	6			5		9	4		8	36
	2		1		11	10	3		7	6			5		4		9	8	37
10	2	4	1		11	7	3			6			5				9	8	38
	2	4	1		11	10	3		7	6			5				9	8	39
	2	4	1		11	10	3		7	6			5				8	9	40
9		4	1		11	10	3	2	7	6			5					8	41
9	2		1		11	10	3		7	6			5		4			8	42
25	33	24	40	3	13	41	42	2	37	37	22	26	38	1	10	7	15	37	
5		3			2	37			20	6	3	9	1		4	1	8	8	

4 own-goals

Allen	Baker	Blanchflower	Brown	Clayton	Dyson	Greaves	Henry	Hollowbread	Jones	Mackay	Marchi	Medwin	Norman	Piper	Saul	Smith J	Smith R	White	
	2		1		11	10	3		7	6			5		4		9	8	3
	1		1		1	1	1		1	1			1		1		1	1	

Allen	Baker	Blanchflower	Brown	Clayton	Dyson	Greaves	Henry	Hollowbread	Jones	Mackay	Marchi	Medwin	Norman	Piper	Saul	Smith J	Smith R	White	
	2	4	1			10	3		11	6		7	5				9	8	
	1	1	1			1	1		1	1		1	1				1	1	
			2						1								1	1	

1963-64

Manager: Bill Nicholson

1	Aug	24	(a)	Stoke C	L	1-2	R.Smith	40,638
2		28	(a)	Wolves	W	4-1	R.Smith 2, Greaves 2 (1 pen)	41,488
3		31	(h)	Nottingham F	W	4-1	Jones, Greaves 3	49,407
4	Sep	4	(h)	Wolves	W	4-3	Norman, White, Dyson 2	51,851
5		7	(a)	Blackburn R	L	2-7	Mackay, Greaves	20,949
6		14	(h)	Blackpool	W	6-1	Jones, White, R.Smith, Greaves 3	38,138
7		16	(a)	Aston Villa	W	4-2	Jones, Greaves 2, Dyson	36,643
8		21	(a)	Chelsea	W	3-0	Baker, R.Smith, Shellito (og)	57,401
9		28	(h)	West Ham U	W	3-0	Mackay, Jones, Brown (og)	51,667
10	Oct	2	(h)	Birmingham C	W	6-1	White, R.Smith, Greaves 3 (1 pen), Dyson	37,649
11		5	(a)	Sheffield U	D	3-3	R.Smith, Greaves, Dyson	33,606
12		15	(a)	Arsenal	D	4-4	Mackay, R.Smith 2, Greaves	67,857
13		19	(h)	Leicester C	D	1-1	Jones	50,521
14		26	(a)	Everton	L	0-1		65,386
15	Nov	2	(h)	Fulham	W	1-0	Greaves	42,023
16		9	(a)	Manchester U	L	1-4	Gregg (og)	57,513
17		16	(h)	Burnley	W	3-2	Norman, R.Smith 2	42,222
18		23	(a)	Ipswich T	W	3-2	Marchi, Dyson 2	25,014
19		30	(h)	Sheffield W	D	1-1	R.Smith	39,378
20	Dec	7	(a)	Bolton W	W	3-1	Greaves, Dyson, Farrimond (og)	18,394
21		14	(h)	Stoke C	W	2-1	Greaves 2	36,776
22		21	(a)	Nottingham F	W	2-1	Jones, Greaves	23,888
23		26	(a)	West Brom A	D	4-4	Jones, R.Smith, Greaves 2	37,189
24		28	(h)	West Brom A	L	0-2		47,863
25	Jan	11	(h)	Blackburn R	W	4-1	Greaves 3, Dyson	43,953
26		18	(a)	Blackpool	W	2-0	Greaves, Martin (og)	13,955
27		25	(h)	Aston Villa	W	3-1	Possee, Greaves, Dyson	36,394
28	Feb	1	(h)	Chelsea	L	1-2	Greaves	51,007
29		8	(a)	West Ham U	L	0-4		36,838
30		15	(h)	Sheffield U	D	0-0		30,833
31		22	(h)	Arsenal	W	3-1	Jones 2, Greaves (pen)	57,261
32		29	(a)	Birmingham C	W	2-1	Jones, Greaves (pen)	28,433
33	Mar	7	(h)	Everton	L	2-4	Allen, Dyson	41,926
34		21	(h)	Manchester U	L	2-3	L.Brown, Greaves (pen)	56,292
35		27	(h)	Liverpool	L	1-3	Norman	57,022
36		28	(a)	Fulham	D	1-1	Greaves	30,388
37		30	(a)	Liverpool	L	1-3	Mullery	52,904
38	Apr	4	(h)	Ipswich T	W	6-3	Jones 3, White 2, Robertson	25,115
39		13	(a)	Sheffield W	L	0-2		26,628
40		18	(h)	Bolton W	W	1-0	Greaves	32,507
41		21	(a)	Burnley	L	2-7	Jones, Greaves	16,660
42		25	(a)	Leicester C	W	1-0	White	26,441

FINAL LEAGUE POSITION: 4th in Division One

Appearances
Goals

FA Cup

3	Jan	4	(h)	Chelsea	D	1-1	Dyson	49,382
R		8	(a)	Chelsea	L	0-2		70,123

Appearances
Goals

298

The table records the shirt number (1–11) worn by each player in each league match (1–42), with appearance and goal totals below.

Allen	Baker	Barton	Beal	Blanchflower	Brown L	Brown W	Clayton	Dyson	Greaves	Henry	Hollowbread	Hopkins	Jones	Mackay	Marchi	Mullery	Norman	Possee	Robertson	Saul	Smith J	Smith R	White	No.
	2			4		1		11	10	3			7	6			5					9	8	1
	2			4		1		11	10	3			7				5				6	9	8	2
	2		4					11	10		1	3	7				5				6	9	8	3
	2			4		1		11	10	3			7				5				6	9	8	4
	2			4		1		11	10	3				6			5		7			9	8	5
	2			4		1		11	10	3			7	6			5					9	8	6
9	2			4		1		11	10	3			7	6			5						8	7
	2			4		1		11	10	3			7	6			5					9	8	8
				4		1		11	10	3		2	7	6			5					9	8	9
				4				11	10	3	1	2	7	6			5					9	8	10
				4		1		11	10	3		2	7	6			5					9	8	11
	2			4		1		11	10	3			7	6			5					9	8	12
	2			4		1		11	10	3			7	6			5					9	8	13
	2			4		1		11	10	3			7	6			5					9	8	14
	2			4		1		11	10	3			7	6			5					9	8	15
	2			4		1		11	10	3			7	6			5					9	8	16
	2					1		11	10	3			7	6	4		5					9	8	17
9	2					1		11	10	3			7	6	4		5						8	18
	2					1		11	10	3			7	6	4		5					9	8	19
	2					1		11	10	3			7	6	4		5					9	8	20
	2					1		11	10	3			7		4		5				6	9	8	21
	2					1		11	10			3	7		4		5				6	9	8	22
	2					1		11	10			3	7		4		5				6	9	8	23
	2					1	8	11	10			3	7		4		5				6	9		24
9	2		4					11	10		1	3	7	6			5						8	25
9	2		4					11	10		1	3	7	6			5						8	26
9	2		4					11	10		1	3		6			5		7				8	27
9	2		4					11	10		1	3	7	6			5						8	28
	2		4					11	10		1	3	7	6			5					9	8	29
	2		4					11	10		1	3	7	6			5					9	8	30
	2		4		9			11	10		1	3	7	6			5						8	31
	2		4		9			11	10		1	3	7	6			5						8	32
10	2		4		9			11			1	3	7	6			5						8	33
	2				9			11	10	3	1		7	6		4	5						8	34
	2				9			11	10	3	1		7	6		4	5						8	35
			6		9	1		11	10	3		2	7			4	5						8	36
10			6		9					3	1	2	7			4	5	11					8	37
			6		9				10	3	1	2	7			4	5	11					8	38
	2		6		9	1			10	3			7			4	5	11					8	39
	2		6			1		11	10	3			7			4	5					9	8	40
	2	6				1		11	10	3			7			4	5					9	8	41
	2					1		11	10	3			7	6		4	5					9	8	42
8	**35**	**1**	**16**	**15**	**9**	**27**	**1**	**39**	**41**	**29**	**15**	**19**	**39**	**17**	**21**	**9**	**42**	**1**	**3**	**2**	**7**	**26**	**40**	
1	1				1			11	35				14	3	1	1	3	1	1			13	6	

5 own-goals

Allen	Baker	Barton	Beal	Blanchflower	Brown L	Brown W	Clayton	Dyson	Greaves	Henry	Hollowbread	Hopkins	Jones	Mackay	Marchi	Mullery	Norman	Possee	Robertson	Saul	Smith J	Smith R	White	
	2		6				8	11	10		1	3	7				5			4	9			3
9	2		4				8	11	10		1	3	7	6			5							R
1	2	2				2	2	2	2	2	2		2	1			2			1	1			
						1																		

1964-65

Manager: Bill Nicholson

1	Aug	22	(h)	Sheffield U	W	2-0 Greaves, Saul	45,724
2		25	(a)	Burnley	D	2-2 Greaves, Saul	21,661
3		29	(a)	Everton	L	1-4 Jones	55,148
4	Sep	2	(h)	Burnley	W	4-1 Saul 3, Dyson	42,326
5		5	(h)	Birmingham C	W	4-1 Robertson, Greaves, Dyson, Foster (og)	34,809
6		9	(a)	Stoke C	L	0-2	36,329
7		12	(a)	West Ham U	L	2-3 Greaves 2 (1 pen)	36,730
8		16	(h)	Stoke C	W	2-1 Greaves, Saul	34,821
9		19	(h)	West Brom A	W	1-0 Greaves	36,993
10		26	(a)	Manchester U	L	1-4 Robertson	53,362
11		28	(a)	Blackpool	D	1-1 Jones	26,436
12	Oct	5	(h)	Fulham	W	3-0 Norman, Greaves, Saul	32,908
13		10	(h)	Arsenal	W	3-1 Robertson, Greaves, Saul	55,959
14		17	(a)	Leeds U	L	1-3 Greaves	41,464
15		24	(h)	Chelsea	D	1-1 Jones	52,927
16		31	(a)	Leicester C	L	2-4 Greaves, Allen	29,167
17	Nov	7	(h)	Sunderland	W	3-0 Robertson, Greaves, Jones	36,677
18		14	(a)	Wolves	L	1-3 L.Brown	28,728
19		21	(h)	Aston Villa	W	4-0 Mullery, Robertson, Greaves, Dyson	29,724
20		28	(a)	Liverpool	D	1-1 Greaves	41,198
21	Dec	5	(h)	Sheffield W	W	3-2 Greaves 2 (1 pen), Megson (og)	24,019
22		12	(a)	Sheffield U	D	3-3 Greaves, Saul 2	19,325
23		19	(h)	Everton	D	2-2 Greaves 2	41,994
24		26	(a)	Nottingham F	W	2-1 Gilzean, Jones	42,056
25		28	(h)	Nottingham F	W	4-0 Robertson, Greaves, Gilzean, Dyson	56,693
26	Jan	2	(a)	Birmingham C	L	0-1	33,833
27		16	(h)	West Ham U	W	3-2 Greaves 2, Dyson	50,054
28		23	(a)	West Brom A	L	0-2	23,718
29	Feb	6	(h)	Manchester U	W	1-0 Henry	58,639
30		13	(a)	Fulham	L	1-4 Greaves	27,708
31		23	(a)	Arsenal	L	1-3 Gilzean	48,367
32		27	(h)	Leeds U	D	0-0	42,350
33	Mar	10	(a)	Chelsea	L	1-3 Gilzean	51,390
34		13	(h)	Blackpool	W	4-1 Mullery, Robertson, Greaves, Jones	27,257
35		20	(a)	Sunderland	L	1-2 Greaves	44,394
36		27	(h)	Wolves	W	7-4 Clayton, Allen, Gilzean 2, Jones 3	25,974
37	Apr	3	(a)	Aston Villa	L	0-1	24,930
38		9	(h)	Liverpool	W	3-0 Saul, Low, Gilzean	28,441
39		16	(h)	Blackburn R	W	5-2 Greaves 2, Gilzean 3	36,497
40		17	(a)	Sheffield W	L	0-1	21,843
41		19	(a)	Blackburn R	L	1-3 Jones	14,026
42		24	(h)	Leicester C	W	6-2 Greaves 2 (1 pen), Gilzean, Jones 3	32,427

FINAL LEAGUE POSITION: 6th in Division One

Appearances
Goals

FA Cup

3	Jan	9	(a)	Torquay U	D	3-3 Norman, Gilzean 2	20,000
R		18	(h)	Torquay U	W	5-1 Robertson, Greaves 3, Gilzean	55,081
4		30	(h)	Ipswich T	W	5-0 Greaves 3 (1 pen), Gilzean 2	43,992
5	Feb	20	(a)	Chelsea	L	0-1	63,205

Appearances
Goals

Glasgow Charity Cup

1	Aug	5	(n*)	Glasgow XI	L	2-4 Saul, Robertson	58,768

*Played at Hampden Park, Glasgow.

Appearances
Goals

300

Allen	Baker	Beal	Brown L	Brown W	Clayton	Dyson	Gilzean	Greaves	Henry	Jennings	Jones	Knowles	Low	Mackay	Marchi	Mullery	Norman	Possee	Robertson	Saul	Weller	
		6				11		8	3	1	10	2				4	5		7	9		1
		6				11		8	3	1	10	2				4	5		7	9		2
		6				11		8	3	1	10	2				4	5		7	9		3
		6				11		8	3	1	10	2				4	5		7	9		4
		6				11		8	3	1	10	2				4	5		7	9		5
	2	6				11		8	3	1	10					4	5		7	9		6
		6				11		8	3	1	10	2				4	5		7	9		7
	2	6				11		8	3	1	10					4	5		7	9		8
						11		8	3	1	10	2			6	4	5		7	9		9
			5			11		8	3	1	10	2			6	4			7	9		10
			5			11		8	3	1	10	2			6	4			7	9		11
						11		8	3	1	10	2			6	4	5		7	9		12
						11		8	3	1	10	2			6	4	5		7	9		13
9						11		8	3	1	10	2			6	4	5		7			14
9						11		8	3	1	10	2			6	4	5		7			15
9						11		8	3	1	10	2			6	4	5		7			16
9						11		8	3	1	10	2			6	4	5		7			17
			4	1				8	3		11	2			6	10	5		7	9		18
				1		11		8	3		10	2			6	4	5		7	9		19
						11		8	3	1	10	2			6	4	5		7	9		20
						11		8	3	1	10	2	6			4	5		7	9		21
						11		8	3	1	10	2	6			4	5		7	9		22
				1		11	9	8	3		10	2			6	4	5		7			23
				1		11	9	8	3		10	2			6	4	5		7			24
						11	9	8	3	1	10	2			6	4	5		7			25
			5	1		11	9	8	3		10	2			6	4			7			26
				1	6	11	9	8	3		10	2				4	5		7			27
			5	1	6	11	9	8	3		10	2				4			7			28
				1	6	11	9	8	3		10	2				4	5		7			29
				1	6	11	9	8	3		10	2				4	5		7			30
				1	10		9	8	3		11	2			6	4	5		7			31
			5	1	6		10	8	3		11	2				4			7	9		32
			5	1	6	11	9	8	3		10	2				4			7			33
	2		5	1	6	11	9	8	3		10					4			7			34
			5	1	6	11	9	8	3		10	2				4			7			35
9			5	1	6		10	8	3		11	2				4					7	36
9			6	1			10	8	3			2				4	5	7			11	37
			5		6		10		3	1	11	2	9			4				8	7	38
			5		6		10	7	3	1		2	8			4				9	11	39
			5	1	6		10	7				2	9			4	3			8	11	40
			5	1	6		10	8	3		11		9			4	2		7			41
			5	1	6		10	8	3		11	2				4				9	7	42
6	3	8	16	19	15	32	20	41	41	23	39	38	6		17	42	30	1	36	23	6	
2			1		1	5	11	29	1		13		1			2	1		7	11		

2 own-goals

				1		11	9	8	3		10	2			6	4	5		7			3
				1	6	11	9	8	3		10	2				4	5		7			R
				1	6	11	9	8	3		10	2				4	5		7			4
				1	10		9	8	3		11	2			6	4	5		7			5
				4	3	3	4	4	4		4	4			2	4	4		4			
							5	6									1		1			

		6		1				8	3		7	2		10		4	5		11	9		
		1		1				1	1		1	1		1		1	1		1	1		
																			1	1		

1965-66

Manager: Bill Nicholson

1	Aug	25	(h)	Leicester C	W	4-2	Knowles, Possee, Greaves, Robertson	39,876
2		27	(h)	Blackpool	W	4-0	Clayton, Gilzean, Greaves 2	36,882
3	Sep	1	(a)	Leicester C	D	2-2	Possee, Greaves (pen)	28,463
4		4	(a)	Fulham	W	2-0	Mackay, Clayton	28,718
5		8	(h)	Leeds U	W	3-2	Mackay, Greaves 2	48,156
6		11	(h)	Arsenal	D	2-2	Gilzean, Saul	53,962
7		15	(a)	Leeds U	L	0-2		41,920
8		18	(h)	Liverpool	W	2-1	Clayton, Gilzean	46,925
9		25	(a)	Aston Villa	L	2-3	Norman, Robertson	29,856
10	Oct	6	(h)	Sunderland	W	3-0	Mackay, Clayton, Greaves	37,364
11		9	(a)	Everton	L	1-3	Mullery	40,022
12		16	(h)	Manchester U	W	5-1	Johnson, Clayton, Gilzean, Greaves, Robertson	58,051
13		23	(a)	Newcastle U	D	0-0		42,430
14		30	(h)	West Brom A	W	2-1	Greaves 2	43,658
15	Nov	6	(a)	Nottingham F	L	0-1		29,611
16		13	(h)	Sheffield W	L	2-3	Mackay (pen), Saul	30,422
17		20	(a)	Northampton	W	2-0	Mackay, Saul	17,611
18		27	(h)	Stoke C	D	2-2	Gilzean, Robertson	26,406
19	Dec	4	(a)	Burnley	D	1-1	Clayton	19,509
20		11	(h)	Chelsea	W	4-2	Gilzean 2, Jones 2	42,299
21		18	(a)	Manchester U	L	1-5	Jones	39,511
22		27	(h)	Sheffield U	W	1-0	Gilzean	45,766
23		28	(a)	Sheffield U	W	3-1	Saul, Jones 2	24,787
24	Jan	1	(h)	Everton	D	2-2	Knowles, Saul	34,953
25		8	(a)	Chelsea	L	1-2	Mackay (pen)	48,529
26		15	(h)	Newcastle U	D	2-2	Knowles, Weller	27,490
27		29	(h)	Blackburn R	W	4-0	Saul, Gilzean 2, Greaves (pen)	34,573
28	Feb	5	(a)	Blackpool	D	0-0		13,103
29		19	(h)	Fulham	W	4-3	Saul, Jones 3	32,244
30	Mar	8	(a)	Arsenal	D	1-1	Possee	51,824
31		12	(a)	Liverpool	L	0-1		50,760
32		19	(h)	Aston Villa	D	5-5	L.Brown, Robertson, Greaves, Saul, Gilzean	28,371
33		26	(a)	Sunderland	L	0-2		27,828
34	Apr	2	(h)	Nottingham F	L	2-3	Robertson, Clayton	27,593
35		8	(h)	West Ham U	L	1-4	Gilzean	50,635
36		9	(a)	Sheffield W	D	1-1	Clayton	17,456
37		16	(h)	Northampton	D	1-1	Greaves (pen)	29,749
38		23	(a)	Stoke C	W	1-0	Greaves (pen)	19,112
39		25	(a)	West Ham U	L	0-2		32,232
40		30	(h)	Burnley	L	0-1		29,337
41	May	7	(a)	West Brom A	L	1-2	Clayton	22,586
42		9	(a)	Blackburn R	W	1-0	Greaves	7,256

FINAL LEAGUE POSITION: 8th in Division One

Appearances
Sub Appearances
Goals

FA Cup

3	Jan	22	(h)	Middlesbrough	W	4-0	Mackay 2 (1 pen), Saul 2	37,349
4	Feb	12	(h)	Burnley	W	4-3	Gilzean 3, Saul	50,611
5	Mar	5	(a)	Preston NE	L	1-2	Greaves	36,792

Appearances
Goals

302

Football appearances grid (shirt number worn by each player per match).

Beal	Brown L	Brown W	Clayton	Collins	Gilzean	Greaves	Henry	Hoy	Jennings	Johnson	Jones	Kinnear	Knowles	Low	Mackay	Mullery	Norman	Pitt	Possee	Robertson	Saul	Venables	Weller	No.
	5	1	8	9	10								3		6	4	2		7	11				1
	5	1	8	9	10								3		6	4	2		11	7				2
	5	1	8	9	10								3		6	4	2		7			11		3
	5	1	8	10	7								3		6	4	2			11	9			4
	5	1	8	9	7								3		6	4	2			11	10			5
	5	1	8	9	7						12		3		6	4	2			11*	10			6
	5	1	8	9	10								3		6	4	2		7			11		7
	5	1	8	9	10								3		6	4	2		7			11		8
	5	1	8	9	10								3		6	4	2		7			11		9
	5	1	8	9	10						7		3		6	4	2			11				10
	5	1	8	9	10						7		3		6	4	2			11				11
	5		8	9	10				1		7		3		6	4	2			11				12
	5		8	9	10				1		7		3		6	4	2			11				13
4	5		8	9	10				1		7		3		6		2			11				14
	5	1	8	9							7		3		6	4	2			11	10			15
	5		8	9					1		7		3		6	4	2			11	10			16
2	5		8		10				1		11		3		6	4			7		9			17
2	5		8		10				1				3		6	4			7	11	9			18
2	5		8		10				1		11		3		6	4			7		9			19
2	5		8		10				1		11		3		6	4			7		9			20
2	5		8		10				1		11		3		6	4			7		9			21
2	5		8		10				1		11		3		6	4			7		9			22
2	5		8		10				1		11	3			6	4			7		9			23
2	5		8		10				1		11		3		6	4			7		9			24
2	5		8		10				1		11		3		6	4			7		9			25
2	5		8		10				1				3		6	4			11	7	9			26
2	5		8		10	11			1		12		3		6	4*			7		9			27
2	5		4		10	11			1	6	8		3						7		9			28
2	5				10	8			1		11		3		6	4			7		9			29
	5		4		10	8			1			2	3		6				11	7	9			30
	5		4		10	8			1			2	3		6				11	7	9			31
	5		4		10	8			1			2	3		6				11	7	9			32
			10		9	8	3	5	1			2			6	4			7	11				33
		1	10		9	8		5				2	3		6	4			7	11				34
		1	10			8		5				2	3		6	4			11	7	9			35
6	5	1	8									2	3		10	4			11	7	9			36
6	5	1	8		9							2	3		10	4			7	11				37
6	5	1	8									2	3		10	4			7	11	9			38
6	5		8		9				1			2	3		10	4			7	11				39
6	5	1	8									2	3		10	4			7	11	9			40
6	5	1	8		9							2	3		10	4			7	11				41
6	5	1			9							2	3		10	4			7	11			8	42
21	37	20	38	2	40	29	1	5	22	9	9	8	41		41	40	16	1	17	33	26	1	5	
											1						1							
	1		9	12	15					1	8		3		6	1	1		3	6	8		1	

Beal	Brown L	Brown W	Clayton	Collins	Gilzean	Greaves	Henry	Hoy	Jennings	Johnson	Jones	Kinnear	Knowles	Low	Mackay	Mullery	Norman	Pitt	Possee	Robertson	Saul	Venables	Weller	No.
2	5		8		10				1		11		3		6	4			7		9			3
2	5		6		9	8			1		11		3			4			7		10			4
2	5		8		10	11			1				3		6	4			7		9			5
3	3		3		3	2			3		2		3		2	3			3		3			
			3		1								2								3			

1966-67

Manager: Bill Nicholson

1	Aug	20	(h)	Leeds U	W	3-1	Mullery, Greaves, Gilzean	43,844
2		24	(a)	Stoke C	L	0-2		34,683
3		27	(a)	Newcastle U	W	2-0	Mackay, Robertson	35,780
4		31	(h)	Stoke C	W	2-0	Greaves (pen), Gilzean	37,908
5	Sep	3	(h)	Arsenal	W	3-1	Greaves 2, Jones	56,271
6		6	(a)	Sheffield U	L	1-2	Greaves (pen)	21,650
7		10	(h)	Manchester U	W	2-1	Greaves, Gilzean	56,295
8		17	(a)	Burnley	D	2-2	Greaves, Saul	25,184
9		24	(h)	Nottingham F	W	2-1	Mullery, Greaves	34,405
10	Oct	1	(a)	Fulham	W	4-3	Robertson, Greaves, Gilzean, Venables	28,628
11		8	(a)	Manchester C	W	2-1	Gilzean 2	32,551
12		15	(h)	Blackpool	L	1-3	Knowles	36,459
13		26	(a)	Chelsea	L	0-3		54,191
14		29	(h)	Aston Villa	L	0-1		31,014
15	Nov	5	(a)	Blackpool	D	2-2	Gilzean 2	16,524
16		12	(h)	West Ham U	L	3-4	Greaves (pen), Gilzean, Venables	57,157
17		19	(a)	Sheffield W	L	0-1		32,376
18		26	(h)	Southampton	W	5-3	Mullery, Mackay, Greaves (pen), Jones 2	35,736
19	Dec	3	(a)	Sunderland	W	1-0	Greaves	32,733
20		10	(h)	Leicester C	W	2-0	Greaves, Rodrigues (og)	41,089
21		17	(a)	Leeds U	L	2-3	Greaves, Gilzean	29,852
22		26	(a)	West Brom A	L	0-3		37,969
23		27	(h)	West Brom A	D	0-0		39,129
24		31	(h)	Newcastle U	W	4-0	Mackay, Greaves 2, Venables	27,948
25	Jan	7	(a)	Arsenal	W	2-0	Robertson, Gilzean	49,851
26		14	(a)	Manchester U	L	0-1		57,365
27		21	(h)	Burnley	W	2-0	Greaves, Jones	42,187
28	Feb	4	(a)	Nottingham F	D	1-1	Greaves	41,822
29		11	(h)	Fulham	W	4-2	Greaves, Gilzean, Jones 2	43,961
30		25	(h)	Manchester C	D	1-1	Robertson	33,832
31	Mar	4	(a)	Aston Villa	D	3-3	Mullery, England, Gilzean	31,718
32		18	(h)	Chelsea	D	1-1	Greaves	49,553
33		22	(a)	Everton	W	1-0	Greaves	50,108
34		25	(a)	Leicester C	W	1-0	Robertson	27,711
35		27	(h)	Everton	W	2-0	Mullery, Gilzean	46,917
36	Apr	1	(h)	Liverpool	W	2-1	Greaves 2	53,135
37		15	(h)	Sheffield W	W	2-1	Saul 2	36,062
38		22	(a)	Southampton	W	1-0	Gilzean	30,285
39	May	3	(h)	Sunderland	W	1-0	Greaves (pen)	33,936
40		6	(a)	Liverpool	D	0-0		40,845
41		9	(a)	West Ham U	W	2-0	Greaves, Gilzean	35,758
42		13	(h)	Sheffield U	W	2-0	Greaves, Saul	44,912

FINAL LEAGUE POSITION: 3rd in Division One

Appearances
Sub Appearances
Goals

FA Cup

3	Jan	28	(a)	Millwall	D	0-0		41,260
R	Feb	1	(h)	Millwall	W	1-0	Gilzean	58,189
4		18	(h)	Portsmouth	W	3-1	Greaves, Gilzean 2	57,910
5	Mar	11	(h)	Bristol C	W	2-0	Greaves 2 (1 pen)	54,610
6	Apr	8	(a)	Birmingham C	D	0-0		51,500
R		12	(h)	Birmingham C	W	6-0	Greaves 2, Gilzean, Venables 2, Saul	52,304
SF		29	(n*)	Nottingham F	W	2-1	Greaves, Saul	55,000
F	May	20	(n†)	Chelsea	W	2-1	Robertson, Saul	100,000

*Played at Hillsborough, Sheffield. †Played at Wembley Stadium.

Appearances
Sub Appearances
Goals

FL Cup

2	Sep	14	(a)	West Ham U	L	0-1		34,068

Appearances
Sub Appearances
Goals

Football appearance and scoring grid.

Beal	Bond	Brown R	Clayton	England	Gilzean	Greaves	Jennings	Jones	Kinnear	Knowles	Low	Mackay	Mullery	Robertson	Saul	Venables	Weller	Match
2				5	9	8	1	11		3		6	4	7		10		1
2				5	9	8	1	11		3		6	4	7		10		2
2				5	9	8	1	11		3		6	4	7		10		3
4				5	9	8	1	11	2	3		6		7		10		4
4				5	9	8	1	11	2	3		6		7		10		5
4		11		5	9	8	1		2	3		6*		7		10	12	6
6*		12		5	9	8	1		2	3			4	7		10	11	7
				5	9	8	1		2	3		6	4	7	11	10		8
				5	9	8	1	11	2	3		6	4	7		10		9
				5	9	8	1		2	3		6	4	7	11	10		10
2*		12		5	9	8	1			3		6	4	7	11	10		11
	1	2		5		8		11		3		6	4	7	9	10		12
2				5	9	8	1	11		3		6	4	7		10		13
2				5	9	8	1			3		6	4	7	11	10		14
2				5	9	8	1	11		3		6	4	7		10		15
2				5	9	8	1	11		3		6	4	7		10		16
2				5	9	8	1	11		3		6	4	7		10		17
2				5	9	8	1	11		3		6	4	7		10		18
2				5	9	8	1	11		3		6	4	7		10		19
2				5	9	8	1	11*		3	12	6	4	7		10		20
2		11*		5	9	8	1			3		6	4	7		10	12	21
2				5	9	8	1			3		6	4		11	10	7	22
2				5	9	8	1			3		6	4	7		10	11	23
2		12		5	9	8	1			3		6*	4	7		10	11	24
2		6		5	9*	8	1			3			4	7	12	10	11	25
2		6		5		8	1			3			4	7	9	10	11	26
2				5	9	8	1	11		3		6	4	7		10		27
2				5	9	8	1	11*		3		6	4	7	12	10		28
2				5	9	8	1	11		3		6	4	7		10		29
2*				5	9		1		12	3		6	4	7	8	10	11	30
				5	9		1	11	2	3		6	4	7		10	8	31
		10		5	9	8	1		2	3		6	4	7	11			32
				5	9	8	1		2	3		6	4	7	11	10		33
				5	9	8	1		2	3		6	4	7	11	10		34
				5	9	8	1		2	3		6	4	7	11	10		35
		12		5	9	8	1		2	3		6*	4	7	11	10		36
				5	9		1	11	2	3		6	4	7	8	10		37
				5	9		1	11	2	3		6	4	7	8	10		38
				5	9	8	1		2	3		6	4	7	11	10		39
				5	9	8	1		2	3		6	4	7	11	10		40
				5	9	8	1		2	3		6	4	7	11	10		41
				5	9	8	1		2	3		6	4	7	11	10		42
26	1	6		42	40	38	41	20	19	42		39	39	40	20	41	8	
		1	3					1	1						2		2	
				1	17	25		6		1		3	5	5		4	3	

1 own-goal

Beal	Bond	Brown R	Clayton	England	Gilzean	Greaves	Jennings	Jones	Kinnear	Knowles	Low	Mackay	Mullery	Robertson	Saul	Venables	Weller	Round
				5	9	8	1	11	2	3		6	4	7		10		3
				5	9	8	1	11	2	3		6	4	7		10		R
2				5	9	8	1	11		3		6	4	7		10		4
				5	9	8	1	11	2	3		6	4	7		10		5
				5	9	8	1		2	3		6	4	7	11	10		6
				5	9	8	1		2	3		6	4	7	11	10		R
				5	9	8	1		2	3	12	6*	4	7	11	10		SF
				5	9	8	1		2	3		6	4	7	11	10		F
1				8	8	8	8	4	7	8		8	8	8	4	8		
											1							
					4	6						1	3	2				

Beal	Bond	Brown R	Clayton	England	Gilzean	Greaves	Jennings	Jones	Kinnear	Knowles	Low	Mackay	Mullery	Robertson	Saul	Venables	Weller	
5		6			9	8	1		2	3			4	7	11	10		2
1		1			1	1	1		1	1			1	1	1	1		

1967-68

Manager: Bill Nicholson

1	Aug	19	(a)	Leicester C	W 3-2	Kinnear, England, Saul	32,552
2		23	(h)	Everton	D 1-1	Gilzean	53,809
3		26	(h)	West Ham U	W 5-1	Mullery, Greaves 2 (1 pen), Saul, Jones	55,831
4		29	(a)	Everton	W 1-0	Saul	57,790
5	Sep	2	(a)	Burnley	L 1-5	Greaves	23,337
6		6	(h)	Wolves	W 2-1	Robertson, Greaves	44,408
7		9	(h)	Sheffield W	W 2-1	Gilzean, Saul	43,317
8		16	(a)	Arsenal	L 0-4		62,936
9		23	(a)	Manchester U	L 1-3	Gilzean	58,779
10		30	(h)	Sunderland	W 3-0	Greaves 2, Todd (og)	36,017
11	Oct	7	(h)	Sheffield U	D 1-1	Greaves	33,233
12		14	(a)	Coventry C	W 3-2	Greaves 2, Jones	38,008
13		25	(h)	Nottingham F	D 1-1	Greaves	40,928
14		28	(a)	Stoke C	L 1-2	Venables	27,144
15	Nov	4	(h)	Liverpool	D 1-1	Jones	47,682
16		11	(a)	Southampton	W 2-1	Robertson, Gilzean	29,902
17		18	(h)	Chelsea	W 2-0	Gilzean, Jones	53,981
18		25	(a)	West Brom A	L 0-2		29,033
19	Dec	2	(h)	Newcastle U	D 1-1	Gilzean	34,494
20		9	(a)	Manchester C	L 1-4	Greaves	35,792
21		16	(h)	Leicester C	L 0-1		26,036
22		23	(a)	West Ham U	L 1-2	Robertson	32,122
23		26	(h)	Fulham	D 2-2	Jones 2	36,274
24		30	(a)	Fulham	W 2-1	Robertson, Jones	30,051
25	Jan	17	(a)	Sheffield W	W 2-1	Chivers, Greaves	31,610
26		20	(h)	Arsenal	W 1-0	Gilzean	57,885
27	Feb	3	(h)	Manchester U	L 1-2	Chivers	57,690
28		10	(a)	Sunderland	W 1-0	Jones	31,735
29		26	(a)	Sheffield U	L 2-3	Greaves, Chivers	27,008
30	Mar	1	(h)	West Brom A	D 0-0		31,318
31		16	(a)	Nottingham F	D 0-0		37,707
32		23	(h)	Stoke C	W 3-0	England, Robertson, Jones	29,530
33		30	(h)	Burnley	W 5-0	England, Greaves 2, Venables, Jones	26,494
34	Apr	6	(h)	Southampton	W 6-1	Mullery, Greaves 2 (1 pen), Chivers, Jones, Hollywood (og)	41,834
35		12	(h)	Leeds U	W 2-1	Greaves, Chivers	56,587
36		13	(a)	Chelsea	L 0-2		53,049
37		17	(a)	Leeds U	L 0-1		48,933
38		20	(h)	Coventry C	W 4-2	Mackay, Greaves 2, Jones	36,175
39		27	(a)	Newcastle U	W 3-1	Gilzean, Chivers 2	30,281
40		29	(a)	Liverpool	D 1-1	Greaves	41,688
41	May	4	(h)	Manchester C	L 1-3	Greaves (pen)	51,242
42		11	(a)	Wolves	L 1-2	Greaves	40,929

FINAL LEAGUE POSITION: 7th in Division One

Appearances
Sub Appearances
Goals

FA Cup

3	Jan	27	(a)	Manchester U	D 2-2	Chivers 2	63,500
R		31	(h)	Manchester U	W 1-0*	Robertson	57,200
4	Feb	17	(h)	Preston NE	W 3-1	Greaves 2, Chivers	47,088
5	Mar	9	(h)	Liverpool	D 1-1	Greaves	54,005
R		12	(a)	Liverpool	L 1-2	Jones	53,658

*After extra-time

Appearances
Sub Appearances
Goals

FA Charity Shield

	Aug	12	(a)	Manchester U	D 3-3	Jennings, Robertson, Saul	54,106

Appearances
Goals

Appearances and goals

Beal	Bond	Chivers	Clayton	England	Gilzean	Greaves	Hoy	Jennings	Jones	Kinnear	Knowles	Mackay	Mullery	Robertson	Saul	Venables	Want	No.
4				5	9	8		1		2	3	6		7	11	10		1
				5	9	8		1		2	3	6	4	7	11	10		2
12				5		8		1	11	2	3	6*	4	7	9	10		3
6				5		8		1	11	2	3		4	7	9	10		4
6				5		8		1	11	2	3		4	7	9	10		5
6				5	9	8		1		2	3		4	7	11	10		6
6				5	9	7		1	12	2	3		4	7	11*	10		7
6				5	9	8		1		2	3		4	7	11	10		8
6	10			5	9	8		1		2	3		4	7	11			9
6				5*	9	8		1	11	2	3		4	7	12	10		10
6				5	9	8		1	11*	2	3		4	7	12	10		11
6				5	9	8		1	11	2	3		4	7		10		12
6	12			5	9	8		1		2	3		4	7	11*	10		13
6		12		5	9	8*		1		2	3		4	7	11	10		14
				5	9	8		1	11	2	3	6	4	7		10		15
2					9	8	5	1	11		3	6	4	7		10		16
				5	9	8		1	11	2	3	6	4	7		10		17
					9	8	5	1	11	2	3	6	4	7		10		18
	10				9	8	5	1	11	2	3	6	4		7			19
					9	8	5	1	11	2	3	6	4		7	10		20
						8	5	1	11	2	3	6	4	7	9	10		21
5	10			8*				1	11	2	3	6	4	7	9	12		22
5	10			8				1	11	2	3	6	4	7	9			23
5	10			8				1	11	2	3	6	4	7	9			24
5	8	9		10	11			1		2	3	6	4	7				25
5		9				8		1	11	2	3	6	4	7		10		26
6		9		5		8		1	11	2	3		4	7		10		27
11		9		5		8		1	7	2	3	6	4			10		28
8		9		5	7			1	11	2	3	6	4			10		29
10		9		5		8		1	11	2		6	4	7			3	30
11		9		5	10	8		1	12	2		6	4	7*			3	31
3		9*		5	12	8		1	11	2		6	4	7		10		32
2		9		5	7	8		1	11		3	6	4			10		33
2		9		5	7	8		1	11		3	6	4			10		34
2		9		5	7	8		1	11		3	6*	4	12		10		35
2		9		5	7	8		1	11		3	6	4			10		36
2		9		5	7	8		1	11		3	6	4			10		37
2		9*		5	12	8		1	11		3	6	4	7		10		38
2		9		5	7	8		1	12	3*		6	4	11		10		39
2		9		5	11	8		1			3	6	4	7		10		40
2		9		5	11	8		1			3	6	4	7		10		41
2		9		5	11	8		1	12		3	6*	4	7		10		42
34	5	18	1	31	32	39	5	42	27	29	42	29	41	33	17	35	2	
1	1		1		2				3	1				1	2	1		
	7			3	8	23				12	1		1	2	5	4	2	

2 own-goals

Beal	Bond	Chivers	Clayton	England	Gilzean	Greaves	Hoy	Jennings	Jones	Kinnear	Knowles	Mackay	Mullery	Robertson	Saul	Venables	Want	No.
11		9		5		8		1	12	2	3	6	4	7		10*		3
11		9		5		8*	10	1		2	3	6	4	7		12		R
		9		5		8	7	1	11	2	3	6	4			10		4
11		9		5	10	8		1	12	2		6	4	7*			3	5
11		9		5	10	8		1	12	2		6*	4		7		3	R
4		5		5		5	4	5	1	3	5	5	5	3		3	2	
									3							1		
		3				3			1					1			1	

Beal	Bond	Chivers	Clayton	England	Gilzean	Greaves	Hoy	Jennings	Jones	Kinnear	Knowles	Mackay	Mullery	Robertson	Saul	Venables	Want
				5	9	8		1		2	3	6	4	7	11	10	
				1	1	1		1		1	1	1	1	1	1	1	
					1										1	1	

1968-69

Manager: Bill Nicholson

1	Aug	10	(h)	Arsenal	L 1-2	Greaves	56,280
2		17	(a)	Everton	W 2-0	Greaves, Chivers	56,570
3		21	(h)	West Brom A	D 1-1	Gilzean	35,746
4		24	(h)	Sheffield W	L 1-2	England	30,542
5		28	(a)	Manchester U	L 1-3	Greaves	62,649
6		31	(a)	Chelsea	D 2-2	Jones, Greaves	48,412
7	Sep	7	(h)	Burnley	W 7-0	Jones 2, Robertson, Greaves 3 (1 pen), Chivers	30,167
8		14	(a)	West Ham U	D 2-2	Greaves, Gilzean	35,802
9		17	(a)	Coventry C	W 2-1	Chivers, Gilzean	40,950
10		21	(h)	Nottingham F	W 2-1	Jones, Greaves	37,386
11		28	(a)	Newcastle U	D 2-2	Mullery, Pearce	30,469
12	Oct	5	(h)	Leicester C	W 3-2	Greaves 3	36,622
13		9	(h)	Manchester U	D 2-2	Jones, Gilzean	56,205
14		12	(a)	Manchester C	L 0-4		38,019
15		19	(h)	Liverpool	W 2-1	Greaves 2	44,122
16		26	(a)	Ipswich T	W 1-0	Gilzean	30,251
17	Nov	2	(h)	Stoke C	D 1-1	Greaves	33,308
18		9	(a)	Leeds U	D 0-0		38,995
19		16	(h)	Sunderland	W 5-1	Greaves 4, England	29,072
20		23	(a)	Southampton	L 1-2	Greaves	27,384
21	Dec	7	(a)	Wolves	L 0-2		30,846
22		14	(h)	Manchester C	D 1-1	England	28,462
23		21	(a)	Liverpool	L 0-1		43,843
24	Jan	11	(a)	Stoke C	D 1-1	Jenkins	21,729
25		18	(h)	Leeds U	D 0-0		42,396
26		29	(h)	Queen's Park R	W 3-2	Beal, Gilzean, Jenkins	38,766
27	Feb	1	(a)	Sunderland	D 0-0		22,251
28		15	(a)	Queen's Park R	D 1-1	Greaves	30,013
29		22	(h)	Wolves	D 1-1	Morgan	35,912
30	Mar	8	(h)	Everton	D 1-1	Morgan	44,882
31		18	(a)	Ipswich T	D 2-2	Knowles, Greaves (pen)	21,608
32		22	(h)	Chelsea	W 1-0	Johnson	47,349
33		24	(a)	Arsenal	L 0-1		43,972
34		29	(a)	Burnley	D 2-2	Johnson, Pearce	14,547
35	Apr	2	(h)	Newcastle U	L 0-1		22,528
36		4	(h)	Coventry C	W 2-0	Johnson, Pearce	35,034
37		7	(a)	West Brom A	L 3-4	Knowles, Greaves 2 (1 pen)	24,173
38		12	(a)	Nottingham F	W 2-0	Greaves, Gilzean	22,920
39		19	(h)	West Ham U	W 1-0	Greaves	50,970
40		22	(h)	Southampton	W 2-1	Greaves, Morgan	29,201
41		29	(a)	Leicester C	L 0-1		35,833
42	May	12	(a)	Sheffield W	D 0-0		28,582

FINAL LEAGUE POSITION: 6th in Division One

Appearances
Goals

FA Cup

3	Jan	4	(a)	Walsall	W 1-0	Greaves	18,779
4		25	(h)	Wolves	W 2-1	Johnson, Greaves	48,985
5	Feb	12	(a)	Aston Villa	W 3-2	England, Greaves 2 (1 pen)	49,986
6	Mar	1	(a)	Manchester C	L 0-1		48,872

Appearances
Sub Appearance
Goals

FL Cup

2	Sep	4	(a)	Aston Villa	W 4-1	Jones, Chivers 3	24,775
3		25	(h)	Exeter C	W 6-3	Greaves 3, Pearce 2, Venables	25,798
4	Oct	16	(h)	Peterborough U	W 1-0	Greaves	28,378
5		30	(h)	Southampton	W 1-0	Collins	35,198
SF	Nov	20	(a)	Arsenal	L 0-1		55,237
SF	Dec	4	(h)	Arsenal	D 1-1	Greaves	55,923

Appearances
Sub Appearance
Goals

Appearances / line-up grid (numbers = shirt number worn; * = substituted). Player columns left→right: Beal, Bond, Chivers, Collins, England, Evans, Gilzean, Greaves, Jenkins, Jennings, Johnson, Jones, Kinnear, Knowles, Morgan, Mullery, Pearce, Pratt, Robertson, Venables, Want.

Beal	Bond	Chivers	Collins	England	Evans	Gilzean	Greaves	Jenkins	Jennings	Johnson	Jones	Kinnear	Knowles	Morgan	Mullery	Pearce	Pratt	Robertson	Venables	Want	#
2		9	6	5			8		1				3		4	11		7	10		1
6		9		5		11	8		1			2	3		4			7	10		2
6		9		5		11	8*		1			2	3		4	12		7	10		3
6		9		5		11	8		1			2	3		4			7	10		4
6		9		5		11*	8		1	12		2	3		4			7	10		5
6		9		5		11	8		1	7		2	3		4			12	10*		6
6	10	9		5		11	8		1	7*		2	3		4			12			7
6		9		5		11	8		1			2	3		4			7	10		8
6		9		5		11	8		1	7		2	3		4				10		9
6		9*		5		11	8		1	7		2	3		4	12			10		10
6				5		11	8		1	7		2	3		4	9			10		11
6				5		11	8		1			2			4	9		7	10	3	12
6				5		11	8		1	7		2			4	9			10	3	13
6				5*		7	8		1			2	12		4	9		11	10	3	14
6				5		11	8	7	1			2	3		4	9			10		15
6				5		11	8	7	1			2	3		4	9			10		16
6	10	12		5		11	8	7*	1			2	3		4	9					17
6		7		5		11	8		1			2	3		4	9			10		18
6			9	5		11	8		1			2	3		4	7			10		19
6		5*	9			11	8		1			2	3		4	7			10	12	20
6			9	5		11	8	7	1			2	3*		4	12			10		21
6			9	5		11	8	7	1			2	3		4				10		22
6			9	5		11	8	7	1			2	3		4				10		23
6				5		11	8	7	1			2	3		4	9			10		24
6		12		5		11	8	7	1			2*	3		4	9			10		25
2			6	5		9	8	11	1	7			3		4				10		26
2			6	5		9	8		1	7			3		4	11			10		27
2			6	5			8	9	1				3	11	4	7			10		28
2			6	5		9	8		1	12			3	11	4	7*			10		29
2			6	5*		9	8		1	12			3	11	4	7			10		30
2			6	5		9	8		1	12			3	11	4	7			10*		31
2			6	5		9	8		1	7			3		4	11			10		32
			6		2	9	8	12	1	11					4	7*	5		10	3	33
			6	5	2	8			1	7				11	9	4			10	3	34
			6	5	2	8			1	7				11	4	9*	12		10	3	35
6				5	2	8			1	7			3	11	4	9	10				36
6			5	2	9	8			1	7			3	11	4				10		37
2		5			9	8			1	7			3	11*	4	12	6		10		38
2		12	5*		9	8			1	7			3	11	4	10	6				39
2			5		9	8			1	7			3	11	4		6		10		40
2		5*	12		9	8			1	7			3	11	4		6		10		41
2		5			9	8			1	7			3	11	4		6		10		42
39	2	10	22	36	5	37	42	10	42	13	6	24	36	13	41	24	8	8	37	7	
		3		1			3	1		1		3	1	3		1			1		
1		3		3		7	27	2		3	5		2	3	1	3		1			

Beal	Bond	Chivers	Collins	England	Evans	Gilzean	Greaves	Jenkins	Jennings	Johnson	Jones	Kinnear	Knowles	Morgan	Mullery	Pearce	Pratt	Robertson	Venables	Want	#
6			9	5		11	8	7	1			2	3		4				10		3
2			6	5		9	8	11	1	7			3		4				10		4
2			6	5		9*	8	12	1	7			3		4	11			10		5
2			6	5		9	8		1	7			3		4	11			10		6
4			4	4		4	4	2	4	3		1	4		4	2			4		
								1													
			1			4				1											

Beal	Bond	Chivers	Collins	England	Evans	Gilzean	Greaves	Jenkins	Jennings	Johnson	Jones	Kinnear	Knowles	Morgan	Mullery	Pearce	Pratt	Robertson	Venables	Want	#
6	10	9		5		11	8		1	7		2	3		4						2
6				5		11	8		1	7		2	3		4	9			10		3
6	12		5			11	8		1			2			4	9		7	10*	3	4
6	7*	12	5			11	8		1			2	3		4	9			10		5
6			5	9		11	8		1			2	3		4	7			10		SF
6			5	9		11	8		1			2	3		4	7			10		SF
6	2	1	3	5		6	6		6	2		6	5		6	5		1	5	1	
	1		1																		
	3	1				5			1						2			1			

1969-70

Manager: Bill Nicholson

1	Aug	9	(a)	Leeds U	L	1-3	Greaves	35,804
2		13	(h)	Burnley	W	4-0	Collins, Pearce, Greaves, Chivers	35,920
3		16	(h)	Liverpool	L	0-2		50,474
4		19	(a)	Burnley	W	2-0	Collins, Pearce	19,485
5		23	(a)	Crystal P	W	2-0	Pearce, Chivers	39,494
6		27	(h)	Chelsea	D	1-1	Pearce	47,661
7		30	(h)	Ipswich T	W	3-2	Mullery, Greaves, Gilzean	33,333
8	Sep	6	(a)	West Ham U	W	1-0	Pearce	40,561
9		13	(h)	Manchester C	L	0-3		41,644
10		16	(a)	Arsenal	W	3-2	Chivers, Gilzean, Pratt	55,280
11		20	(a)	Derby C	L	0-5		41,826
12		27	(h)	Sunderland	L	0-1		30,523
13	Oct	4	(a)	Southampton	D	2-2	Greaves, Gilzean	23,901
14		7	(a)	Liverpool	D	0-0		46,518
15		11	(h)	Wolves	L	0-1		36,736
16		18	(h)	Newcastle U	W	2-1	Greaves 2	33,287
17		25	(a)	Stoke C	D	1-1	Gilzean	19,569
18	Nov	1	(h)	Sheffield W	W	1-0	Morgan	31,656
19		8	(a)	Nottingham F	D	2-2	Pearce, Greaves	24,034
20		15	(h)	West Brom A	W	2-0	Chivers, Morgan	28,340
21		22	(a)	Manchester U	L	1-3	Chivers	53,053
22	Dec	6	(a)	Coventry C	L	2-3	England, Gilzean	28,443
23		13	(a)	Manchester C	D	1-1	Johnson	29,216
24		17	(h)	Everton*	D	0-0		28,494
25		20	(h)	West Ham U	L	0-2		28,375
26		26	(h)	Crystal P	W	2-0	Mullery, Perryman	32,845
27		27	(a)	Ipswich T	L	0-2		24,658
28	Jan	10	(h)	Derby C	W	2-1	Greaves, Morgan	38,645
29		17	(a)	Sunderland	L	1-2	Morgan	13,993
30		31	(h)	Southampton	L	0-1		27,693
31	Feb	7	(a)	Wolves	D	2-2	Chivers 2	27,295
32		14	(h)	Leeds U	D	1-1	Cooper (og)	41,723
33		21	(h)	Stoke C	W	1-0	Mullery	29,976
34		28	(a)	Newcastle U	W	2-1	Pearce, Chivers	34,827
35	Mar	11	(h)	Everton	L	0-1		27,764
36		14	(a)	Everton	L	2-3	Gilzean, Bond (pen)	51,533
37		21	(h)	Coventry C	L	1-2	Peters	34,942
38		27	(h)	Nottingham F	W	4-1	Gilzean 2, Chivers 2	36,947
39		28	(a)	West Brom A	D	1-1	Peters	24,890
40		30	(a)	Sheffield W	W	1-0	Mullery	30,340
41	Apr	4	(a)	Chelsea	L	0-1		44,925
42		13	(h)	Manchester U	W	2-1	Gilzean, Chivers	41,808
43	May	2	(h)	Arsenal	W	1-0	Gilzean	46,969

FINAL LEAGUE POSITION: 11th in Division One
*Abandoned after 29 minutes — floodlight failure.

Appearances
Sub Appearance
Goals

FA Cup

3	Jan	3	(a)	Bradford C	D	2-2	Greaves, Morgan	23,000
R		7	(h)	Bradford C	W	5-0	Pearce 2, Greaves 2, Morgan	36,039
4		24	(h)	Crystal P	D	0-0		43,948
R		28	(a)	Crystal P	L	0-1		45,980

Appearances
Sub Appearance
Goals

FL Cup

2	Sep	3	(a)	Wolves	L	0-1		34,017

Appearances
Sub Appearance
Goals

Beal	Bond	Chivers	Collins	England	Evans	Gilzean	Greaves	Hancock	Jenkins	Jennings	Johnson	Kinnear	Knowles	Morgan	Mullery	Naylor	Pearce	Perryman	Peters	Pratt	Want	Woolcott	
2		9	6	5			10	8		1			3	11	4					7			1
		9	6	5			10	8		1			3	11	4		7				2		2
		9	6	5			10	8		1			3	11	4		7				2		3
		9	6	5			10	8		1			3	11	5		7				2		4
12		9	6	5			10	8		1			3	11	4		7*				2		5
		9	6	5			10	8		1			3	11	4		7				2		6
12		9*	6	5			10	8		1			3	11	4		7				2		7
2			6	5		9	8			1			3	11	4*		7	10		12			8
2	12		6	5		9	8			1			3	11	4		7	10*					9
2	7*		6	5		9	8			1			3	11	4			10		12			10
2			6	5		9	8			1			3	11*	4		7	10		12			11
2	10		6	5		9	8			1			3		4		7	11					12
6	10			5		9	8			1			3	7	4*		12	11			2		13
6	10	9		5			8			1			3	7	4			11			2		14
	10	9	6	5		7	8			1			3		4			11			2		15
6	7			5		9	8			1			3	10	4			11			2		16
6	7*			5		9	8			1			3	10	4		12	11			2		17
6				5		9	8			1			3	10	4		7	11			2		18
6				5		9	8			1			3	10	4		7	11			2		19
6*		12		5		9	8			1			3	10	4		7	11			2		20
		9		5		10	8			1			3	7	4		11	6			2		21
	10	12	5			9	8			1	7*		3		4		11	6		2			22
	9*		5	6	10	8			1	7	2	3		4		12	11						23
			5		6		8		10	1	7	2	3		4	9	11						24
5				6			8			1	7	2	3	10	4	9	11						25
5				6	9	8			1	7	2	3	10	4*	12	11							26
5				6	11	8			1	7	2	3		4	12	10			9*				27
6			5			9	8			1		2	3	11	4		7	10					28
6	12	5				9	8	1			2	3	11	4	7*	10							29
6	10	7		5	2					1			11	4	9		8	3					30
6	10	7		5	2	12				1			11	4	9		8*	3					31
6	10	9		5	2					1			11	4	7		8	3					32
6	10	9		5	2	12				1			11	4*	7		8	3					33
6	10	9*		5	2			12		1			11	4	7		8	3					34
6	10*	9		5	2			12		1			11	4	7		8	3					35
6	10*		12	5	2	9				1			11		7	4	8	3					36
6	10	12		5	2	9		7*		1			11	4			8	3					37
6		9	5		2	7				1			11	4		10	8	3					38
	9*	5		7						1	2	3	11	4	6	12	8	10					39
	9		5	12	7					1	2	3	11*	4	6		10	8					40
6	9		5		7					1	2	3	11	4			8	10					41
	9		5	2	7					1		3	11	4	6		8	10					42
6		9	5	2	7					1		3	11	4		8	10						43
29	12	27	17	36	16	34	29	1	2	42	6	10	34	37	42	3	26	24	7	12	26	1	
2		4	2		1	2				2								6			3		
	1	11	2	1		10	8			1			4	4			7	1	2	1			

1 own-goal

Beal	Bond	Chivers	Collins	England	Evans	Gilzean	Greaves	Hancock	Jenkins	Jennings	Johnson	Kinnear	Knowles	Morgan	Mullery	Naylor	Pearce	Perryman	Peters	Pratt	Want	Woolcott	
6			5			9	8			1	7*	2	3	11	4		12	10					3
6		12	5*			9	8			1		2	3	11	4		7	10					R
6		12	5			9	8			1		2	3	11	4		7*	10					4
6		7	5			9	8			1		2	3	11	4		12	10*					R
4		1	4		4	4	4			4	1	4	4	4	4		2	4					
		2															2	2					
						3							2		2			2					

Beal	Bond	Chivers	Collins	England	Evans	Gilzean	Greaves	Hancock	Jenkins	Jennings	Johnson	Kinnear	Knowles	Morgan	Mullery	Naylor	Pearce	Perryman	Peters	Pratt	Want	Woolcott	
2		9*	6	5			8			1			3	11	4		7		12	10			2
1		1	1	1			1			1			1	1	1		1		1				
																	1						

1970-71

Manager: Bill Nicholson

1	Aug	15	(h)	West Ham U	D	2-2	Gilzean 2	53,640
2		19	(h)	Leeds U	L	0-2		39,927
3		22	(a)	Wolves	W	3-0	Mullery, Chivers, Morgan	23,896
4		25	(a)	Southampton	D	0-0		27,149
5		29	(h)	Coventry C	W	1-0	Chivers	27,103
6	Sep	1	(a)	Huddersfield T	D	1-1	Chivers	26,701
7		5	(a)	Arsenal	L	0-2		48,931
8		12	(h)	Blackpool	W	3-0	Mullery (pen), Peters 2	19,894
9		19	(a)	Crystal P	W	3-0	Mullery, Chivers 2	41,308
10		26	(h)	Manchester C	W	2-0	Gilzean, Chivers	42,490
11	Oct	3	(a)	Derby C	D	1-1	Peters	36,007
12		10	(h)	Liverpool	W	1-0	Peters	44,547
13		17	(a)	West Ham U	D	2-2	Mullery, England	42,322
14		24	(h)	Stoke C	W	3-0	Gilzean, Chivers 2	36,238
15		31	(a)	Nottingham F	W	1-0	Chivers	25,301
16	Nov	7	(h)	Burnley	W	4-0	Gilzean, Perryman, Chivers 2	30,524
17		14	(a)	Chelsea	W	2-0	Mullery, Pearce	61,277
18		21	(h)	Newcastle U	L	1-2	Chivers	38,873
19		28	(a)	Everton	D	0-0		44,301
20	Dec	5	(h)	Manchester U	D	2-2	Gilzean, Peters	55,693
21		12	(a)	West Brom A	L	1-3	Chivers	26,584
22		19	(h)	Wolves	D	0-0		30,544
23	Jan	9	(a)	Leeds U	W	2-1	Chivers 2	43,867
24		16	(h)	Southampton	L	1-3	Chivers	39,486
25		30	(h)	Everton	W	2-1	Gilzean, Chivers	42,105
26	Feb	6	(a)	Manchester U	L	1-2	Peters	48,416
27		17	(h)	West Brom A	D	2-2	Mullery (pen), Gilzean	22,695
28		20	(a)	Newcastle U	L	0-1		31,718
29	Mar	10	(h)	Nottingham F	L	0-1		21,697
30		13	(h)	Chelsea	W	2-1	Chivers, Peters	49,292
31		20	(a)	Burnley	D	0-0		16,376
32		23	(a)	Ipswich T	W	2-1	Gilzean, Peters	21,718
33	Apr	3	(a)	Coventry C	D	0-0		22,947
34		7	(h)	Derby C	W	2-1	Chivers, Pearce	25,627
35		10	(a)	Ipswich T	W	2-0	Chivers, Morris (og)	28,708
36		12	(a)	Blackpool	D	0-0		16,541
37		17	(a)	Liverpool	D	0-0		46,363
38		24	(h)	Crystal P	W	2-0	Perryman, Blyth (og)	28,619
39		28	(h)	Huddersfield T	D	1-1	Chivers	18,959
40	May	1	(a)	Manchester C	W	1-0	Perryman	19,761
41		3	(h)	Arsenal	L	0-1		51,992
42		5	(a)	Stoke C	W	1-0	Peters	14,019

FINAL LEAGUE POSITION: 3rd in Division One

Appearances
Sub Appearances
Goals

FA Cup

3	Jan	2	(h)	Sheffield W	W	4-1	Mullery (pen), Gilzean 2, Peters	34,170
4		23	(a)	Carlisle U	W	3-2	Gilzean, Peters, Neighbour	25,369
5	Feb	13	(h)	Nottingham F	W	2-1	Gilzean, Chivers	46,366
6	Mar	6	(a)	Liverpool	D	0-0		54,731
R		16	(h)	Liverpool	L	0-1		56,283

Appearances
Sub Appearances
Goals

FL Cup

2	Sep	9	(h)	Swansea C	W	3-0	Perryman, Peters, Morgan	15,848
3	Oct	7	(h)	Sheffield U	W	2-1	Chivers, Pearce	23,559
4		28	(h)	West Brom A	W	5-0	Gilzean 2, Peters 3	31,598
5	Nov	18	(h)	Coventry C	W	4-1	Gilzean, Chivers 3	31,864
SF	Dec	16	(a)	Bristol C	D	1-1	Gilzean	30,201
SF		23	(h)	Bristol C	W	2-0*	Chivers, Pearce	29,982
F	Feb	27	(n†)	Aston Villa	W	2-0	Chivers 2	100,000

*After extra-time. †Played at Wembley Stadium.

Appearances
Sub Appearances
Goals

Texaco Cup

1	Sep	16	(h)	Dunfermline A	W	4-0	England, Chivers 3	16,388
1		29	(a)	Dunfermline A	W	3-0	Chivers, Peters 2	9,000
2	Oct	21	(h)	Motherwell	W	3-2	Chivers, Peters 2	19,670
2	Nov	3	(a)	Motherwell	L	1-3	Pearce	22,688

Appearances
Sub Appearances
Goals

Player appearance / shirt-number grid.

Beal	Bond	Chivers	Collins	England	Evans	Gilzean	Hancock	Jennings	Johnson	Kinnear	Knowles	Morgan	Mullery	Naylor	Neighbour	Pearce	Perryman	Peters	Pratt	Want	No.
	6	9		5	2	7		1			3		4			11	8	10			1
		9	6	5	2	7		1			3		4			11	8	10			2
		9	6	5		7		1		2	3	11	4				8	10			3
12		9	6	5				1		2	3	11	4			7*	8	10			4
		9	6	5		7		1		2	3	11*	4			12	8	10			5
		9	6*	5		7		1		2	3	11	4			12	8	10			6
6		9		5		7		1		2		11	4				8	10	3		7
6		9		5	2	7		1			3	11	4				8	10			8
6		9		5		7		1	12	2	3		4			11*	8	10			9
6		9		5		7		1		2	3	11*	4			12	8	10			10
6		9		5				1		2	3	11	4			7	8	10			11
6		9		5		7		1		2	3		4			11	8	10			12
6		9		5		7		1		2	3		4			11	8	10			13
6		9		5		7*		1		2	3		4		12	11	8	10			14
6		9		5		7		1		2	3		4	12		11	8*	10			15
6		9		5		7		1		2	3		4			11	8	10			16
6		9		5		7		1	12	2	3		4			11	8*	10			17
		9	6	5		7		1		2	3		4		12	11*	8	10			18
		9	6	5		7		1		2	3		4			11	8	10			19
8		9		5		7		1		2	3		4		12	11	8*	10			20
6		9		5		7		1		2	3		4			11	8	10			21
6		9		5		7		1		2	3		4		12	11*	8	10			22
		9		5	6	7		1		2	3		4		11*	12	8	10			23
		9		5*	6	7		1	12	2	3		4			11	8	10			24
6		9	5			7		1		2	3		4			11	8	10			25
6		9	5		2	7		1			3		4			11	8	10			26
6		9	5			7		1		2	3		4			11	8	10			27
6		9	5			7		1		2	3		4			11*	12	8	10		28
6		9	5					1		2	3		4			11	7	8	10		29
6		9	5			7*		1		2	3		4		12		8	10	11		30
6		9	5*					1		2	3		4		11	12	8	10	7		31
6		9				7		1		2	3*		4	5	11	8	10	12			32
6		9	5			7		1		2			4		11	8	10		3		33
6		9	5			7		1		2			4		11	8	10		3		34
6		9	5			7		1		2	3		4		11	8	10				35
6		9	5		2	7*		1			3		4		11	8	10	12			36
6		9	5			7		1		2*	3		4		12	8	10	11			37
6		9	5		2	7		1			3*		4		11	12	8	10			38
6		9	5			7		1		2	3		4		11		8	10			39
6		9	5			7		1		2	3				11		8	10	4		40
6		9	5			7*		1		2	3		4		11	12	8	10			41
6		9	5		2	7*		1					4		11	12	8	10	3		42
32	1	42	26	22	7	38	2	40		35	38	8	41	3	12	23	42	42	4	4	—
	1							3						1	5	10			2		—
		21		1		9							1	6			2	3	9		—

2 own-goals

Beal	Bond	Chivers	Collins	England	Evans	Gilzean	Hancock	Jennings	Johnson	Kinnear	Knowles	Morgan	Mullery	Naylor	Neighbour	Pearce	Perryman	Peters	Pratt	Want	No.
		9		5		7		1		2	3		4	6	11		8	10			3
6		9				7		1		2	3		4	5	11		8	10			4
6		9	5			7		1		2	3		4		11		8	10			5
6		9	5					1		2	3		4		11		8	10	7		6
6		9	5					1		2	3		4		11		8	10	7		R
4		5	4		3		5			5	5		5	2	5		5	5	2		—
		1			4								1	1			2				—

Beal	Bond	Chivers	Collins	England	Evans	Gilzean	Hancock	Jennings	Johnson	Kinnear	Knowles	Morgan	Mullery	Naylor	Neighbour	Pearce	Perryman	Peters	Pratt	Want	No.
6		9		5		7		1		2		11	4*		12		8	10	3			2
6		9		5		7		1		2	3	11*	4		12		8	10				3
6		9		5		7		1		2	3		4		11		8	10				4
6*		9		5		7		1		2	3		4	12	11			10	8			5
6		9		5		7		1		2	3		4		11		8	10				SF
6		9		5*		7		1		2	3		4	11	12		8	10				SF
6		9	5			7		1		2	3		4	11			8	10				F
7		7	1	6		7	1	6		7	6	2	7	2	3	6	7	1	1		—
		7			4							1		2	1	4					—

Beal	Bond	Chivers	Collins	England	Evans	Gilzean	Hancock	Jennings	Johnson	Kinnear	Knowles	Morgan	Mullery	Naylor	Neighbour	Pearce	Perryman	Peters	Pratt	Want	No.
6		9		5		7		1		2		11*	4		12		8	10	3			1
6		9		5		7*		1		2	3	11	4		12		8	10				1
		9		5		7		1		2	3		4	6	11		8	10				2
6		9		5		7		1		2	3		4	8*	12	11		10				2
3		4		4		4	2	2		4	3	2	4	2		2	3	4	1			—
		5		1										1	2			1	4			—

1971-72

Manager: Bill Nicholson

1	Aug	14	(a)	Wolves	D	2-2	Chivers, Gilzean	30,495
2		18	(h)	Newcastle U	D	0-0		42,715
3		21	(h)	Huddersfield T	W	4-1	Chivers 2, Gilzean 2	33,260
4		25	(n*)	Leeds U	D	1-1	Gilzean	25,099
5		28	(a)	Manchester C	L	0-4		33,683
6	Sep	4	(h)	Liverpool	W	2-0	Chivers, Peters	50,124
7		11	(a)	Sheffield U	D	2-2	Peters, Gilzean	41,663
8		18	(h)	Crystal P	W	3-0	Mullery, Chivers, Peters (pen)	37,239
9		25	(a)	Coventry C	L	0-1		26,517
10	Oct	2	(h)	Ipswich T	W	2-1	Chivers, Peters	33,562
11		9	(a)	Derby C	D	2-2	Pearce, Chivers	35,744
12		16	(h)	Wolves	W	4-1	Neighbour, Chivers 2, Gilzean	36,582
13		23	(h)	Nottingham F	W	6-1	Mullery, Chivers, Peters 2 (1 pen), Pearce 2	35,846
14		30	(a)	Stoke C	L	0-2		28,540
15	Nov	6	(h)	Everton	W	3-0	Pratt, Chivers 2	40,005
16		13	(a)	Manchester U	L	1-3	Chivers	54,058
17		20	(h)	West Brom A	W	3-2	England, Gilzean 2	31,895
18		24	(h)	Arsenal	D	1-1	Chivers	52,884
19		27	(a)	Chelsea	L	0-1		52,581
20	Dec	4	(h)	Southampton	W	1-0	Gilzean	31,351
21		11	(a)	Leicester C	W	1-0	Peters	30,721
22		18	(a)	Liverpool	D	0-0		43,409
23		27	(h)	West Ham U	L	0-1		53,868
24	Jan	1	(a)	Crystal P	D	1-1	Chivers	35,571
25		8	(h)	Manchester C	D	1-1	Peters	36,470
26		22	(a)	Newcastle U	L	1-3	Gilzean	30,113
27		29	(h)	Leeds U	W	1-0	Chivers	46,774
28	Feb	12	(a)	Nottingham F	W	1-0	Peters	20,209
29		19	(h)	Stoke C	W	2-0	Chivers 2	32,841
30	Mar	1	(a)	Everton	D	1-1	Peters	21,601
31		4	(h)	Manchester U	W	2-0	Perryman, Chivers	54,814
32		11	(h)	Derby C	L	0-1		36,310
33		25	(h)	Sheffield U	W	2-0	Gilzean, Chivers	30,984
34		28	(a)	Huddersfield T	D	1-1	Pearce	16,123
35		31	(h)	Coventry C	W	1-0	Chivers	32,542
36	Apr	1	(a)	West Ham U	L	0-2		30,763
37		3	(a)	Ipswich T	L	1-2	Chivers	24,302
38		8	(a)	West Brom A	D	1-1	Chivers	20,862
39		15	(h)	Chelsea	W	3-0	Chivers 2, Coates	45,799
40		22	(a)	Southampton	D	0-0		24,914
41		29	(h)	Leicester C	W	4-3	Knowles 2 (1 pen), England, Pearce	19,631
42	May	11	(a)	Arsenal	W	2-0	Mullery, Coates	42,038

FINAL LEAGUE POSITION: 6th in Division One

Appearances
Sub Appearances
Goals

*Away match played at Boothferry Park, Hull.

FA Cup

3	Jan	15	(h)	Carlisle U	D	1-1	Gilzean	33,702
R		18	(a)	Carlisle U	W	3-1	Gilzean, Chivers 2	21,560
4	Feb	5	(h)	Rotherham U	W	2-0	Gilzean, Peters	36,903
5		26	(a)	Everton	W	2-0	Gilzean, Peters	50,511
6	Mar	18	(a)	Leeds U	L	1-2	Pratt	43,937

Appearances
Sub Appearances
Goals

FL Cup

2	Sep	8	(a)	West Brom A	W	1-0	Pearce	26,185
3	Oct	6	(a)	Torquay U	W	4-1	Pearce, Chivers 2, Peters (pen)	20,213
4		27	(h)	Preston NE	D	1-1	Chivers	30,338
R	Nov	8	(a)	Preston NE	W	2-1†	Perryman, Chivers	27,239
5		17	(h)	Blackpool	W	2-0	Chivers, Peters	30,099
SF	Dec	22	(a)	Chelsea	L	2-3	Naylor, Chivers	43,330
SF	Jan	5	(h)	Chelsea	D	2-2	Chivers, Peters (pen)	52,755

†After extra-time

Appearances
Sub Appearance
Goals

Anglo-Italian League Cup-winners' Cup

	Sep	1	(a)	AC Torino	W	1-0	Chivers	28,000
		22	(h)	AC Torino	W	2-0	Chivers, Gilzean	34,103

Appearances
Sub Appearance
Goals

Beal	Chivers	Coates	Collins	Daines	England	Evans	Gilzean	Holder	Jennings	Kinnear	Knowles	Morgan	Mullery	Naylor	Neighbour	Pearce	Perryman	Peters	Pratt	Want	No.
6	9	7			5		11		1	2	3		4				8	10			1
6	9	7			5		11		1	2			4		12		8	10*	3		2
	9	7			5		11		1	2			4	6			8	10	3		3
	9	7	12		5		11*		1	2			4	6			8	10	3		4
	9	7			5		11		1	2			4	6			8	10	3		5
6	9	7*			5		11		1	2	3		4				8	10	12		6
6	9	7			5		11		1	2	3		4				8*	10	12		7
6	9	7			5		11		1	2	3		4				8	10			8
6	9	7			5		11		1	2	3*		4		12		8	10			9
6	9	7			5		11		1	2	3		4				8	10			10
6	9				5	2	11		1		3*		4		7		8	10	12		11
6	9				5		11		1	2	3		4		7		8	10			12
6	9				5		11*		1	2	3		4		7	12	8	10			13
6	9				5	2			1		3		4*	11	7		8	10	12		14
6	9				5	2	11		1		3				7		8	10	4		15
6	9				5	2	7*		1		3			11	12		8	10	4		16
6	9	4		1	5	2	11				3				7		8	10			17
6	9	4			5	2	11		1		3				7		8	10			18
6	9	4			5	2	11*		1		3				7		8	10	12		19
6	9	4			5	2	11		1		3				7		8	10			20
6	9	4	5			2	11		1		3						8	10	7		21
6	9	4			5	2		12	1			8		11*				10	7	3	22
6	9	4*			5	2	11		1		3				12		8	10	7		23
6	9	4			5	2	11		1		3						8	10	7		24
6	9	4			5	2	7*		1					11	12		8	10		3	25
6	9	4			5		7		1	2	3	12		11			8	10*			26
6	9	4			5	2	7		1		3	11					8	10			27
6	9	4			5	2	7	8	1		3	11						10			28
6	9	4			5	2	7*	12	1		3	11					8	10			29
	9				5	2	7		1		3		6	11			8	10	4		30
6	9*				5	2	7	4	1		3	11					8	10	12		31
6	9				5	2	7	4	1		3	11					8	10			32
	9	4			5	2	7	10	1		3*	11	6				8		12		33
		4			5		7		1	2	3		6			9	8	10	11		34
6*	9	4			5		7		1	2	3	11				12	8	10			35
	9				5	2	7		1		3	12	6*	11			8	10	4		36
	9	4	5			2			1		12	11	6			7	8	10*	3		37
	9	4			5		7		1	2	3	11	6				8	10			38
	9	11	6		5		7		1	2	3*		4		12		8	10			39
3	9	7*	6		5				1	2			4	11			10	8	12		40
6		4			5		9		1	2	3				11	7	8	10			41
6		11			5		7		1	2	3		4			9	8	10			42
32	39	32	6	1	38	22	38	4	41	20	34	8	18	12	12	9	39	39	35	15	7
	1								2		1		2			2	6			8	
	25	2			2		11			2		3		1	5	1	10	1			

Beal	Chivers	Coates	Collins	Daines	England	Evans	Gilzean	Holder	Jennings	Kinnear	Knowles	Morgan	Mullery	Naylor	Neighbour	Pearce	Perryman	Peters	Pratt	Want	No.
6	9	4			5	2	7		1						11		8	10	3		3
6	9	4	12		5		7*		1	2	3	11					8	10			R
6	9	4			5	2	7		1		3			11*	12		8	10			4
6	9				5	2	7		1		3	11					8	10	4		5
6	9	12			5	2	7		1		3	11					8	10*	4		6
5	5	3			5	4	5		5	1	4	2		1	2		5	5	2	1	
		1	1												1						
	2					4												2	1		

Beal	Chivers	Coates	Collins	Daines	England	Evans	Gilzean	Holder	Jennings	Kinnear	Knowles	Morgan	Mullery	Naylor	Neighbour	Pearce	Perryman	Peters	Pratt	Want	No.
6	9	7			5				1	2	3		4		11		8	10			2
6	9	7*			5		11		1	2	3		4		12		8	10			3
6	9				5	2			1		3		4		7	11	8	10			4
6	9	12			5	2	7*		1		3				11		8	10	4		R
6	9	7*			5	2	11		1		3				12		8	10	4		5
6	9	4			5	2			1		3	8		11				10	7		SF
6	9	7			5	2	11		1		3				12		8	10	4*		SF
7	7	5			7	5	4		7	2	7	3	1	2	3		6	7	4		
		1											1	2							
	7											1			2	1	3				

Beal	Chivers	Coates	Collins	Daines	England	Evans	Gilzean	Holder	Jennings	Kinnear	Knowles	Morgan	Mullery	Naylor	Neighbour	Pearce	Perryman	Peters	Pratt	Want	No.
6	9	7			5		11		1	2			4				8	10	3		1
6	9	7			5		11		1	2	3		4				8	10			1
2	2	2			2		2		2	2	1		2				2	2	1		
	2						1														

1972-73

Manager: Bill Nicholson

1	Aug	12	(h)	Coventry C	W 2-1 Peters 2	33,884
2		16	(a)	West Brom A	W 1-0 Peters	19,175
3		19	(a)	Wolves	L 2-3 Pratt, Peters	24,237
4		23	(h)	Birmingham C	W 2-0 Chivers, Coates	30,798
5		26	(h)	Leeds U	D 0-0	41,191
6		30	(a)	Newcastle U	W 1-0 Kinnear	27,912
7	Sep	2	(a)	Ipswich T	D 1-1 Peters (pen)	23,140
8		9	(h)	Crystal P	W 2-1 England, Peters (pen)	28,545
9		16	(a)	Manchester C	L 1-2 Peters	31,755
10		23	(h)	West Ham U	W 1-0 Lampard (og)	51,291
11		30	(a)	Derby C	L 1-2 Perryman	32,133
12	Oct	7	(h)	Stoke C	W 4-3 Pratt 2, Gilzean, Coates	31,951
13		14	(a)	Norwich C	L 1-2 Chivers	34,445
14		21	(h)	Chelsea	L 0-1	47,429
15		28	(a)	Manchester U	W 4-1 Peters 4	52,497
16	Nov	4	(a)	Birmingham C	D 0-0	38,504
17		11	(h)	West Brom A	D 1-1 Chivers	25,875
18		18	(a)	Leicester C	W 1-0 Chivers	22,707
19		25	(h)	Liverpool	L 1-2 Chivers	45,497
20	Dec	2	(a)	Southampton	D 1-1 Chivers	16,486
21		9	(h)	Arsenal	L 1-2 Peters	47,515
22		16	(a)	Everton	L 1-3 Neighbour	31,129
23		23	(h)	Sheffield U	W 2-0 Perryman, Chivers	19,877
24		26	(a)	West Ham U	D 2-2 Peters, Pearce	37,397
25	Jan	6	(a)	Leeds U	L 1-2 Gilzean	32,404
26		20	(h)	Ipswich T	L 0-1	33,014
27		27	(a)	Crystal P	D 0-0	44,536
28	Feb	10	(h)	Manchester C	L 2-3 Chivers 2	30,944
29		17	(a)	Coventry C	W 1-0 Pratt	26,854
30		24	(h)	Everton	W 3-0 Gilzean, Chivers, Pearce	27,427
31	Mar	10	(h)	Norwich C	W 3-0 Chivers 2 (1 pen), Pearce	25,088
32		14	(a)	Stoke C	D 1-1 Pearce	23,351
33		24	(h)	Manchester U	D 1-1 Chivers	50,017
34		31	(a)	Liverpool	D 1-1 Gilzean	48,477
35	Apr	3	(a)	Chelsea	W 1-0 Pratt	25,536
36		7	(h)	Southampton	L 1-2 Peters	23,693
37		14	(a)	Arsenal	D 1-1 Chivers	50,863
38		18	(h)	Derby C	W 1-0 McFarland (og)	22,659
39		21	(h)	Leicester C	D 1-1 Gilzean	23,312
40		28	(h)	Newcastle U	W 3-2 Chivers 2 (1 pen), Peters	21,721
41		30	(h)	Wolves	D 2-2 Coates, Collins	16,942
42	May	2	(a)	Sheffield U	L 2-3 Collins, Chivers (pen)	20,716

FINAL LEAGUE POSITION: 8th in Division One

Appearances
Sub Appearances
Goals

FA Cup

3	Jan	13	(a)	Margate	W 6-0 Knowles, Pratt, Pearce, Chivers 2, Peters	8,500
4	Feb	3	(a)	Derby C	D 1-1 Chivers	37,895
R		7	(h)	Derby C	L 3-5* England (pen), Gilzean, Chivers	52,736

*After extra-time

Appearances
Sub Appearances
Goals

FL Cup

2	Sep	6	(h)	Huddersfield T	W 2-1 Gilzean, Chivers	21,422
3	Oct	3	(a)	Middlesbrough	D 1-1 Pearce	23,822
R		11	(h)	Middlesbrough	D 0-0*	19,256
2R		30	(h)	Middlesbrough	W 2-1* Gilzean, Peters	19,287
4	Nov	1	(h)	Millwall	W 2-0 Perryman, Peters	28,904
5	Dec	4	(a)	Liverpool	D 1-1 Peters	48,677
R		6	(h)	Liverpool	W 3-1 Pratt, Chivers 2	34,565
SF		20	(a)	Wolves	W 2-1 Pratt, Peters	28,327
SF		30	(h)	Wolves	D 2-2* Chivers, Peters	41,653
F	Mar	3	(n†)	Norwich C	W 1-0 Coates	100,000

*After extra-time. †Played at Wembley Stadium.

Appearances
Sub Appearances
Goals

Squad appearance / scorer grid.

Beal	Chivers	Clarke	Coates	Collins	Daines	Dillon	England	Evans	Gilzean	Jennings	Kinnear	Knowles	Naylor	Neighbour	Pearce	Perryman	Peters	Pratt	No.
6	9	11				5		7		1	2	3				8	10	4	1
6	9	11				5		7		1	2	3				8	10	4	2
6	9	11				5		7		1	2	3				8	10	4	3
6	9	11				5		7		1	2*	3			12	8	10	4	4
6	9	11*				5	2	7		1		3			12	8	10	4	5
6	9					5		7*		1	2	3		11	12	8	10	4	6
6	9					5		7		1	2	3		11		8	10	4	7
	9	11				5		7		1	2*	3	6		12	8	10	4	8
6		11				5	2	7		1		3			9	8	10	4	9
6	9	12				5	2	7		1		3		11		8	10*	4	10
6	9	11				5		7*		1	2	3		10	12	8		4	11
6	9	11				5		7		1	2	3				8	10	4	12
6	9	11				5		7		1	2	3	4		12	8	10*		13
6	9	11				5		7		1	2	3			12	8	10	4*	14
	9	11*		6		5	2			1		3		7	12	8	10	4	15
	9	11*				5	2	7		1		3	6		4	8	10	12	16
	9				1	5	2	7				3	6	11		8	10	4	17
	9					5	2	7		1		3	6	11		8	10	4	18
	9					5	2	7		1		3	6	11		8	10	4	19
	9					5	2	7		1		3	6	11		8	10	4	20
	9	12				5	2			1		3	6	7*	11	8	10	4	21
		6				5	2	7		1		3		11	9	8	10	4	22
	9	11				5	2	7		1		3	6			8	10	4	23
	9	7	5				2			1		3	6	11		8	10	4	24
	9					5	2	7		1		3	6	11		8	10	4	25
	9	11				5	2	7		1		3	6			8	10	4	26
	9	11				5	2	7		1		3	6*		12	8	10	4	27
6	9	12				5		7		1	2	3		11		8	10	4*	28
6	9					5		7		1	2	3		11		8	10	4	29
6	9					5		7		1	2	3		11		8	10	4	30
6	9	4	5							1	2	3		7	11	8	10		31
6	9	4	5							1	2	3		7	11	8	10		32
6	9	4	5					7		1	2	3			11	8	10		33
6	9	4	5					7*		1	2	3			12	8	10	11	34
6	9	4	5				3			1	2			11		8	10	7	35
6	9	4			1	5		7			2*	3			12	8	10	11	36
6	9	4*				5	12	7		1	2	3				8	10	11	37
6		4				5	3	7		1	2				9	8	10	11	38
	12		5	6			3	7*		1	2			11	9	8	10	4	39
	9	4	5	6			3	7		1				11		8	10	2	40
	9	4	5	6			3	7		1				11		8	10	2	41
	9	4	5	6			2			1				7	11	8	10	3	42
24	38	29	7	2	8	31	23	35	40	24	35	14	6	27	41	41	41	37	
		1	3				1						2	1	8				
17		3	2				1		5			1			1	4	2	15 5	

2 own-goals

Beal	Chivers	Clarke	Coates	Collins	Daines	Dillon	England	Evans	Gilzean	Jennings	Kinnear	Knowles	Naylor	Neighbour	Pearce	Perryman	Peters	Pratt	No.
	9	11				5	2	7		1		3	6		12	8*	10	4	3
6	9	11				5		7*		1	2	3			12	8	10	4	4
6	9	11*				5	2	7		1		3			12	8	10	4	R
2	3	3				3	2	3		3	1	3	1		3	3	3	3	
															3				
	4					1		1				1			1		1	1	

Beal	Chivers	Clarke	Coates	Collins	Daines	Dillon	England	Evans	Gilzean	Jennings	Kinnear	Knowles	Naylor	Neighbour	Pearce	Perryman	Peters	Pratt	No.
6*	9	11				5		7		1	2	3			12	8	10	4	2
6	9	11				5				1	2	3	10	7		8		4	3
	9	11				5		7		1	2	3	6	11	12	8	10	4*	R
	9	11		6		5	2	12		1		3		7		8	10	4*	2R
	9	12				5	2	7*		1		3	6		4	8	10	11	4
	9					5	2	7		1		3	6	11		8	10	4	5
	9					5	2	7*		1		3	6	11	12	8	10	4	R
	9					5	2	7		1		3	6	11		8	10	4	SF
	9	12				5	2	7*		1		3	6	11		8	10	4	SF
6	9	12				5		7		1	2	3		11		8	10	4*	F
3	10	4		1		10	6	8	10	4	10	7		9	10	8	10		
	3						1				1	1	1						
	4	1					2								1	1	5	2	

1973-74

Manager: Bill Nicholson

1	Aug	25	(a)	Coventry C	L	0-1	25,094
2		28	(a)	Birmingham C	W	2-1 Peters 2	37,754
3	Sep	1	(h)	Leeds U	L	0-3	42,091
4		5	(h)	Burnley	L	2-3 Knowles, Chivers	25,543
5		8	(a)	West Ham U	W	1-0 Chivers	30,888
6		11	(a)	Burnley	D	2-2 Holder, Peters	25,158
7		15	(h)	Sheffield U	L	1-2 Chivers	26,350
8		22	(a)	Liverpool	L	2-3 Chivers, Peters	42,901
9		29	(h)	Derby C	W	1-0 Coates	31,408
10	Oct	6	(a)	Ipswich T	D	0-0	23,903
11		13	(h)	Arsenal	W	2-0 Gilzean, Chivers	41,856
12		20	(a)	Norwich C	D	1-1 Gilzean	24,819
13		27	(h)	Newcastle U	L	0-2	31,259
14	Nov	3	(a)	Everton	D	1-1 Perryman	37,827
15		10	(h)	Manchester U	W	2-1 Knowles, Chivers	42,756
16		17	(a)	Southampton	D	1-1 Chivers	22,882
17		24	(h)	Wolves	L	1-3 Chivers (pen)	22,541
18	Dec	1	(a)	Leicester C	L	0-3	22,088
19		8	(h)	Stoke C	W	2-1 Evans, Pratt	14,034
20		15	(h)	Manchester C	L	0-2	17,066
21		22	(a)	Derby C	L	0-2	23,672
22		26	(h)	Queen's Park R	D	0-0	30,762
23		29	(h)	West Ham U	W	2-0 Pratt, Chivers	33,176
24	Jan	1	(a)	Leeds U	D	1-1 McGrath	46,545
25		12	(a)	Sheffield U	D	2-2 McGrath, Coates	20,367
26		19	(h)	Coventry C	W	2-1 Peters 2	20,985
27	Feb	2	(a)	Manchester C	D	0-0	24,652
28		6	(h)	Birmingham C	W	4-2 Chivers 3, Dillon	14,345
29		16	(a)	Arsenal	W	1-0 McGrath	38,892
30		23	(h)	Ipswich T	D	1-1 Pratt	26,289
31	Mar	2	(a)	Queen's Park R	L	1-3 Chivers (pen)	25,775
32		16	(h)	Norwich C	D	0-0	18,476
33		23	(a)	Manchester U	W	1-0 Coates	36,278
34		30	(h)	Everton	L	0-2	19,839
35	Apr	3	(h)	Chelsea	L	1-2 Evans	23,646
36		6	(a)	Wolves	D	1-1 McGrath	24,073
37		13	(h)	Southampton	W	3-1 Pratt, Chivers 2	21,456
38		15	(a)	Chelsea	D	0-0	26,258
39		20	(a)	Stoke C	L	0-1	20,189
40		27	(h)	Leicester C	W	1-0 Chivers	20,110
41	May	8	(h)	Liverpool	D	1-1 McGrath	24,618
42		11	(a)	Newcastle U	W	2-0 Chivers, Gilzean	21,601

FINAL LEAGUE POSITION: 11th in Division One

Appearances
Sub Appearances
Goals

FA Cup

3	Jan	5	(a)	Leicester C	L	0-1	28,280

Appearances
Sub Appearances
Goals

FL Cup

2	Oct	8	(a)	Queen's Park R	L	0-1	23,353

Appearances
Sub Appearances
Goals

318

Beal	Chivers	Coates	Daines	Dillon	England	Evans	Gilzean	Holder	Jennings	Kinnear	Knowles	Lee	McGrath	McNab	Naylor	Neighbour	Osgood	Perryman	Peters	Pratt	No.
6	9	4		5		2	7	12	1		3					11*		8	10		1
6	9	11		5		2	4		1		3					7		8	10		2
6	9	4		5		2	7		1		3					11		8	10		3
6	9	11		5		2	7		1		3							8	10	4	4
6	9	4		5		2	7*		1	12	3					11		8	10		5
6	9	4		5		2		7	1	12	3					11*		8	10		6
6	9	4		5		2	7		1		3					11		8	10		7
6	9			5		2	7*	11	1	12	3							8	10	4	8
6	9	11	1	5		2	7				3							8	10	4	9
6	9	11	1	5		2	7				3							8	10	4	10
6	9		1	5		2	7				3		11					8	10	4	11
	9	11	1	5		2	7*				3		12	6				8	10	4	12
6		11	1	5		2	7				3		9*	12				8	10	4	13
6		11		5		2	7		1		3		9					8	10	4	14
6	9*			5		2	12		1		3		11	7				8	10	4	15
6	9	11		5		2			1		3			7				8	10	4	16
6	9	11		5		2	7		1		3			12				8	10	4*	17
6	9	11		5		2			1		3			7				8	10	4	18
6	9	11		5		2			1		3*			7	12	10		8		4	19
6	9	11		5		2	12		1					7	3			8	10	4*	20
6	9	11		5		2	7		1						3			8	10	4	21
6	12	11		5		2	7		1					9*	3			8	10	4	22
6	9	11*		5		2	7		1						12	3		8	10	4	23
6	9		7	5		2			1				11	3*	12			8	10	4	24
6	9	11*	12	5		2			1					7	3			8	10	4	25
6	9	11		5		2			1					7	3	12		8	10	4*	26
6	9	11		5		2			1					7	3			8	10	4	27
6	9	11	12	5		2			1					7	3			8	10*	4	28
6	9	11		5		2	10		1					7	3			8		4	29
6	9	11		5		2			1					7	3			8	10	4	30
6	9	11*	5			2	12		1					7	3			8	10	4	31
6	9	11	12	5		2			1					7*	3			8	10	4	32
6	9	11		5		2			1					7	3			8	10	4	33
6	9	11	5*			2	12		1					7	3			8	10	4	34
6	9	11	5			2	10		1	8			7	12	3*					4	35
6	9	8		5		2			1	12			7	3		11*			10	4	36
6	9			5		2	11	10	1				3	7				8		4	37
6	9		11	5		2	10		1				3	7				8		4	38
6	9	7	10	5		12	1	2					3	11				8		4*	39
6	9	11		5		4	1	2					7	3				8	10	4	40
6	9	11		5		2			1				7	3				8	10	4	41
6*	9	7	3	5		2	11					8	1		10		12			4	42
41	39	36	5	13		33	40	21	5	36	3	20	1	22	27	11		39	35	35	
	1			3		4	2		4			3	1	1	3	1					
	17	3		1		2	3	1			2		5					1	6	4	

Beal	Chivers	Coates	Daines	Dillon	England	Evans	Gilzean	Holder	Jennings	Kinnear	Knowles	Lee	McGrath	McNab	Naylor	Neighbour	Osgood	Perryman	Peters	Pratt	No.
6	9			3		5	2	7			1					11		8	10	4	3
1	1			1		1	1	1			1					1		1	1	1	

Beal	Chivers	Coates	Daines	Dillon	England	Evans	Gilzean	Holder	Jennings	Kinnear	Knowles	Lee	McGrath	McNab	Naylor	Neighbour	Osgood	Perryman	Peters	Pratt	No.
6	9	11*	1	5		2	7				3			4				8	10	12	2
1	1	1	1	1		1	1				1			1				1	1		
																				1	

1974-75

Manager: Bill Nicholson until September, then Terry Neill

1	Aug	17	(h)	Ipswich T	L	0-1		26,444
2		21	(a)	Manchester C	L	0-1		31,549
3		24	(a)	Carlisle U	L	0-1		18,426
4		28	(h)	Manchester C	L	1-2	Peters	20,079
5		31	(h)	Derby C	W	2-0	Neighbour 2	20,670
6	Sep	7	(a)	Liverpool	L	2-5	Perryman, Chivers	47,538
7		14	(h)	West Ham U	W	2-1	England, Chivers	27,959
8		21	(a)	Wolves	W	3-2	Chivers 2, Peters	20,647
9		28	(h)	Middlesbrough	L	1-2	Neighbour	23,282
10	Oct	5	(h)	Burnley	L	2-3	Pratt, England	18,441
11		12	(a)	Chelsea	L	0-1		32,660
12		16	(h)	Carlisle U	D	1-1	Chivers	12,813
13		19	(h)	Arsenal	W	2-0	Perryman, Chivers	36,294
14		26	(a)	Luton T	D	1-1	Chivers	22,420
15	Nov	2	(a)	Stoke C	D	2-2	Duncan 2	24,667
16		9	(h)	Everton	D	1-1	Chivers	29,052
17		16	(a)	Leicester C	W	2-1	Coates, Peters	23,244
18		23	(h)	Birmingham C	D	0-0		27,761
19		30	(a)	Sheffield U	W	1-0	Duncan	20,289
20	Dec	4	(a)	Leeds U	L	1-2	Duncan	25,832
21		7	(h)	Newcastle U	W	3-0	Knowles 2, Chivers	23,422
22		14	(a)	Ipswich T	L	0-4		20,812
23		21	(h)	Queen's Park R	L	1-2	Duncan	21,150
24		26	(a)	West Ham U	D	1-1	Peters	37,682
25		28	(h)	Coventry C	D	1-1	Smith (og)	20,307
26	Jan	11	(a)	Newcastle U	W	5-2	Knowles, Conn 3, Duncan	39,679
27		18	(h)	Sheffield U	L	1-3	Duncan	15,812
28	Feb	1	(a)	Everton	L	0-1		40,912
29		8	(h)	Stoke C	L	0-2		22,941
30		15	(a)	Coventry C	D	1-1	Duncan	15,227
31		18	(a)	Birmingham C	L	0-1		24,240
32		22	(h)	Leicester C	L	0-3		20,937
33	Mar	1	(a)	Derby C	L	1-3	Jones	22,995
34		15	(a)	Middlesbrough	L	0-3		25,637
35		22	(h)	Liverpool	L	0-2		34,331
36		28	(h)	Wolves	W	3-0	Perryman 2, Duncan	27,238
37		29	(a)	Queen's Park R	W	1-0	Duncan	25,461
38	Apr	5	(h)	Luton T	W	2-1	Conn, Duncan	25,796
39		12	(a)	Burnley	L	2-3	Perryman, Duncan	17,865
40		19	(h)	Chelsea	W	2-0	Conn, Perryman	50,998
41		26	(a)	Arsenal	L	0-1		43,762
42		28	(h)	Leeds U	W	4-2	Knowles 2 (1 pen), Conn, Chivers	49,886

FINAL LEAGUE POSITION: 19th in Division One

Appearances
Sub Appearanc
Goals

FA Cup

3	Jan	4	(a)	Nottingham F	D	1-1	Chivers	23,355
R		8	(h)	Nottingham F	D	0-1		27,996

Appearances
Sub Appearanc
Goals

FL Cup

2	Sep	11	(h)	Middlesbrough	L	0-4		15,216

Appearances
Sub Appearanc
Goals

320

Appearance grid (shirt numbers by player and match). Players left-to-right: Beal, Chivers, Coates, Conn, Daines, Duncan, England, Evans, Jennings, Jones, Kinnear, Knowles, McAllister, McGrath, McNab, Naylor, Neighbour, Osgood, Perryman, Peters, Pratt.

Beal	Chivers	Coates	Conn	Daines	Duncan	England	Evans	Jennings	Jones	Kinnear	Knowles	McAllister	McGrath	McNab	Naylor	Neighbour	Osgood	Perryman	Peters	Pratt	#
6						4	2	1	9		7				3	11	5	8	10		1
6	4						2	1	9		7				3	11	5	8	10		2
4	6					5	2	1	9*				12		3	11		8	10	7	3
6	9	4				5	2	1			7				3	11		8	10		4
6	9	11				5	2	1			3					7		8	10	4	5
6	9	11			12	5*	2	1			3					7		8	10	4	6
6	9	11				5	2	1			3					7		8	10	4	7
6	9	11				5	2	1			3				12	7		8	10*	4	8
6	9	11				5	2	1			3					7		8	10	4	9
6	9	11				5	2	1			3	10				7		8		4	10
6	9					5	2	1	10		3				11	7		8		4	11
	9	11				5	2	1	10		3				6	7		8		4	12
	9	12				5	2	1	11		3				6	7		8*	10	4	13
	9	12			11	5	2	1			3				6	7*		8	10	4	14
3	9	7			11	5	2	1							6			8	10	4	15
3*	9	7			11	5	2	1							6	12		8	10	4	16
3	9	7			11	5	2	1							6			8	10	4	17
3	9	7			11	5	2	1						12	6			8	10	4*	18
	9	7			11	5	2	1			3				6			8	10	4	19
	9	7			11	5	2	1			3				6			8	10	4	20
2	9*	7	12		11	5		1			3	4			6			8	10		21
2		7			11	5		1			3	4*	9		6			8	10	12	22
2*	9	7			11	5		1			3				6	12		8	10	4	23
	9	7			11	5		1		2	3				6			8	10	4	24
	9*	7			11	5		1		2	3				6	12		8	10	4	25
4		9			11	5	12	1		2	3				6	7*		8	10		26
4		9			11	5		1		2	3				6	7		8	10		27
4	9	7			11	5		1		2					6			8	10	3	28
4	9	12	7	1	11	5					3				6			8	10*	2	29
	9	7			11	5		1		2	3	4			6			8	10		30
	9	12	7		11	5		1		2	3	4			6			8	10		31
	9	7			11	5		1		2	3	4			6	12		8	10		32
	10	7			11			1	9	2	3	4			6		5	8			33
	10	7			11			1	9	2	3	4			6		5	8			34
	10	7			11			1	9	2	3*	4	12		6		5	8			35
4		7			10			1	9	2	3				6	11	5	8			36
4					10			1	9	2*	3	12			6	11	5	8		7	37
4	12	7			10			1	9	2	3				6	11*	5	8		6	38
4	10	7			11			1	9	2	3				6		5	8			39
4		7			10			1	9	2	3				6	11	5	8			40
4		7			10			1	9	2	3				6	11*	5	8		12	41
4	9	7						1	10	2	3				6		5	8		11	42
28	27	26	16	1	28	31	20	41	16	17	31	7	5	2	37	21	10	42	29	27	—
	1	4	1			1						1	4		1	4			2		—
10	1	6		12	2			1		5					3			6	4	1	—

1 own-goal

Beal	Chivers	Coates	Conn	Daines	Duncan	England	Evans	Jennings	Jones	Kinnear	Knowles	McAllister	McGrath	McNab	Naylor	Neighbour	Osgood	Perryman	Peters	Pratt	#
	9	7			11	5		1		2	3				6			8	10	4	3
	7	9			11	5		1		2	3				6	12		8	10*	4	R
1	2	1			2	2				2	2				2			2	2	2	
1																					

Beal	Chivers	Coates	Conn	Daines	Duncan	England	Evans	Jennings	Jones	Kinnear	Knowles	McAllister	McGrath	McNab	Naylor	Neighbour	Osgood	Perryman	Peters	Pratt	#
6	9	11	12				2	1				10	3	7	5*	8			4		2
1	1	1					1	1				1	1	1	1	1			1		
		1																			

1975-76

Manager: Terry Neill

					Result	Scorers	Attendance
1	Aug	16	(h)	Middlesbrough	W 1-0	Perryman	25,502
2		20	(h)	Ipswich T	D 1-1	Duncan	28,351
3		23	(a)	Liverpool	L 2-3	Jones, Duncan	42,729
4		25	(a)	West Ham U	L 0-1		36,567
5		30	(h)	Norwich C	D 2-2	Pratt, Duncan	23,140
6	Sep	6	(a)	Manchester U	L 2-3	Chivers, Jones	51,641
7		13	(h)	Derby C	L 2-3	Chivers, Duncan	28,455
8		20	(a)	Leeds U	D 1-1	Pratt	27,372
9		27	(h)	Arsenal	D 0-0		37,064
10	Oct	4	(a)	Newcastle U	D 2-2	Pratt, Duncan	33,290
11		11	(a)	Aston Villa	D 1-1	Pratt	40,048
12		18	(h)	Manchester C	D 2-2	Jones 2	30,554
13		25	(a)	Leicester C	W 3-2	Coates, Perryman, Chivers	22,088
14	Nov	1	(h)	Wolves	W 2-1	Young, Neighbour	26,102
15		8	(a)	Queen's Park R	D 0-0		28,434
16		15	(h)	Stoke C	D 1-1	Jones	25,698
17		22	(a)	Manchester C	L 1-2	Osgood	31,457
18		29	(h)	Burnley	W 2-1	Duncan 2	21,222
19	Dec	6	(a)	Sheffield U	W 2-1	Duncan 2	22,949
20		10	(h)	Everton	D 2-2	Pratt, Duncan	18,638
21		13	(h)	Liverpool	L 0-4		29,891
22		20	(a)	Middlesbrough	L 0-1		22,046
23		26	(h)	Birmingham C	L 1-3	Chivers (pen)	21,651
24		27	(a)	Coventry C	D 2-2	Duncan 2	21,125
25	Jan	10	(a)	Derby C	W 3-2	McAllister, Perryman, Neighbour	28,085
26		17	(h)	Manchester U	D 1-1	Duncan	49,189
27		31	(a)	Ipswich T	W 2-1	Osgood (pen), Coates	24,049
28	Feb	7	(h)	West Ham U	D 1-1	Duncan	32,832
29		14	(h)	Queen's Park R	L 0-3		28,190
30		21	(a)	Stoke C	W 2-1	Hoddle, Duncan	17,110
31		24	(a)	Everton	L 0-1		18,126
32		28	(h)	Leicester C	D 1-1	Chivers	21,427
33	Mar	6	(a)	Norwich C	L 1-3	Chivers	20,460
34		13	(h)	Aston Villa	W 5-2	McAllister, Perryman, Duncan, Robinson, Nicholl (og)	24,169
35		16	(a)	Wolves	W 1-0	Pratt	21,544
36		20	(a)	Burnley	W 2-1	Pratt, Duncan	15,490
37		27	(h)	Sheffield U	W 5-0	Young, Perryman 2, Chivers, Duncan	21,370
38	Apr	3	(a)	Arsenal	W 2-0	Pratt, Duncan	42,031
39		10	(h)	Leeds U	D 0-0		40,365
40		17	(a)	Birmingham C	L 1-3	Pratt	30,616
41		19	(h)	Coventry C	W 4-1	Pratt, Osgood, Duncan, Neighbour	21,107
42		24	(h)	Newcastle U	L 0-3		29,649

FINAL LEAGUE POSITION: 9th in Division One

Appearances
Sub Appearances
Goals

FA Cup

3	Jan	3	(h)	Stoke C	D 1-1	Duncan	26,715
R		24	(a)	Stoke C	L 1-2	Perryman	29,751

Appearances
Sub Appearances
Goals

FL Cup

2	Sep	9	(a)	Watford	W 1-0	Jones	14,997
3	Oct	8	(a)	Crewe A	W 2-0	Pratt, Conn	10,561
4	Nov	12	(h)	West Ham U	D 0-0		49,161
R		24	(a)	West Ham U	W 2-0*	Young, Duncan	38,443
5	Dec	3	(h)	Doncaster R	W 7-2	Pratt, Chivers 2, Duncan 3, Chappell (og)	25,702
SF	Jan	14	(h)	Newcastle U	W 1-0	Pratt	40,215
SF		21	(a)	Newcastle U	L 1-3	McAllister	49,657

*After extra-time

Appearances
Sub Appearances
Goals

322

Brotherston	Chivers	Coates	Conn	Daines	Duncan	Hoddle	Jennings	Jones	Kinnear	Knowles	McAllister	McGrath	McNab	Naylor	Neighbour	Osgood	Perryman	Pratt	Robinson	Smith	Stead	Walford	Young	No.
	9			1	10	2		6		7	3	11	5	8	4									1
	9			12		1	10		3	6		7	2*	11	5	8	4							2
	9	7		11		1	10		3	6			2		5	8	4							3
	9	7		11*		1	10		3	6		12	2		5	8	4							4
				11	12	1	10	3*	6		7	8	9	5		4		2							5
	12			11		1	10		6		7	3	9	5	8	4	2*							6
	4			9		1	10		6		7	3	11	5	8	2								7
				9		1	10	3		7	2	11	6	8	4							5		8
	12			9*		1	10	3		7	2	11	6	8	4							5		9
		12		9		1	10	3*		7	2	11	6	8	4							5		10
	10		7	9*		1	12		3		2	11	6	8	4							5		11
	9		7			1	10	3	2			11	6	8	4							5		12
	9	3	7			1	10		2			11	6	8	4							5		13
	9	4	7*			1	10		3		12	11	6	8	2							5		14
	9*	7		12		1	10		3		2	11	6	8	4							5		15
		7	11	9		1	10		3*	12	2		6	8	4							5		16
		7	12	9*		1	10		3		2	11	6	8	4							5		17
		7		9		1	10	3		12	2	11*	6	8	4							5		18
		7		9		1	10	3	8	2	11	6		4								5		19
		7*		9		1	10	3		12	2	11	6	8	4							5		20
				9		1	10*		3	7	2	11	6	8	4				12	5				21
	9			10		1		3	7	2	11	6	8	4							5			22
	9			10		1	12	3	7*	11	2		6	8	4							5		23
	9			10		1	12	3	7*		2	11	6	8	4							5		24
	9	7		10		1		3		2	11	6	8	4							5			25
	9	7		10		1		3		2	11	6	8	4							5			26
		7		9		1	10	3		11	6	8	4					2	5					27
	12	7		9		1	10	3		2	11*	6	8	4							5			28
	12	7*		9		1	10	3		2	11	6	8	4							5			29
	10			9*	7	1	12	3		11	6	8	4		2				5					30
	10			9	7	1		3		11	6	8	4		2				5					31
	9	12			7	1		3		2	11	6	8	4*	10	3		5						32
	9	7		10		1	12	3		2*	11	6	8	4					5					33
11*	9	7		10	4	1		3		2		6	8		12				5					34
	9	7		10	11	1		3		2		6	8	4					5					35
	9	7	1	10	11		3		2		6	8	4					5						36
	9	7*	1	10		12	3		2	11	6	8	4					5						37
	9			10	1	7	3		2	11	6	8	4					5						38
	9	12		10	1	7*	3		2	11	6	8	4					5						39
	9	7		10	1	12	3		2	11*	6	8	4					5						40
	9*	7		10	1	12	3		2	11	6	8	4					5						41
	9*	7		10	1	12		3		2	11	6	8	4					5					42
1	28	21	7	2	35	6	40	25	1	10	35	3	11	36	35	42	40	41	1	2	4	1	35	
	4	3	1		2	1		9			1	4				1			1					1	
	7	2			20	1		5			2				3	3	6	10	1					2	

I own-goal

Brotherston	Chivers	Coates	Conn	Daines	Duncan	Hoddle	Jennings	Jones	Kinnear	Knowles	McAllister	McGrath	McNab	Naylor	Neighbour	Osgood	Perryman	Pratt	Robinson	Smith	Stead	Walford	Young	
	9	7*			10		1	12		3		2	11	6	8	4						5		3
	7				9		1	10		3		2	11	6	8	4						5		R
	1	2			2		2	1		2		2	2	2	2	2						2		
								1																
					1							1												

Brotherston	Chivers	Coates	Conn	Daines	Duncan	Hoddle	Jennings	Jones	Kinnear	Knowles	McAllister	McGrath	McNab	Naylor	Neighbour	Osgood	Perryman	Pratt	Robinson	Smith	Stead	Walford	Young	
	4			1	9			10			6		11	3	7	5	8	2						2
	10	8	7		9		1			3		2	11	6		4						5		3
		7	12		9*		1	10		3		2	11	6	8	4						5		4
		7			9		1	10	12	3*		2	11	6	8	4						5		R
	9	7			10		1		3		12	2	11	6	8	4*						5		5
	9	7			10		1		3			2	11	6	8	4						5		SF
	9	7			10		1		3			2	11	6*	8	4						5		SF
	5	6	1	1	7		6	3	1	6		1	7	7	7	6	7					6		
		1					1	1	1		1													
	2		1		4			1			1						3					1		

I own-goal

1976-77

Manager: Keith Burkinshaw

1	Aug	21	(a)	Ipswich T	L	1-3	Jones	28,490
2		25	(h)	Newcastle U	L	0-2		24,022
3		28	(h)	Middlesbrough	D	0-0		21,721
4	Sep	4	(a)	Manchester U	W	3-2	Coates, Pratt, Moores	60,723
5		11	(h)	Leeds U	W	1-0	Jones	34,725
6		18	(a)	Liverpool	L	0-2		47,421
7		25	(h)	Norwich C	D	1-1	Hoddle	22,440
8	Oct	2	(a)	West Brom A	L	2-4	Jones, Taylor	23,461
9		16	(a)	Derby C	L	2-8	Osgood (pen), Perryman	24,216
10		20	(h)	Birmingham C	W	1-0	Osgood (pen)	20,193
11		23	(h)	Coventry C	L	0-1		21,877
12		30	(h)	Everton	D	3-3	McAllister, Osgood (pen), Pratt	26,047
13	Nov	6	(a)	West Ham U	L	3-5	Hoddle, Osgood (pen), Duncan	28,997
14		13	(h)	Bristol C	L	0-1		28,795
15		20	(a)	Sunderland	L	1-2	Moores	30,325
16		27	(h)	Stoke C	W	2-0	Osgood 2 (1 pen)	22,500
17	Dec	11	(h)	Manchester C	D	2-2	Taylor 2	24,608
18		18	(a)	Leicester C	L	1-2	Coates	16,397
19		27	(h)	Arsenal	D	2-2	Young, Duncan	47,751
20	Jan	1	(h)	West Ham U	W	2-1	Osgood (pen), Duncan	44,972
21		11	(a)	Queen's Park R	L	1-2	Duncan	24,266
22		22	(h)	Ipswich T	W	1-0	Taylor	35,126
23	Feb	5	(a)	Middlesbrough	L	0-2		21,231
24		12	(h)	Manchester U	L	1-3	Jones	46,946
25		19	(a)	Leeds U	L	1-2	Armstrong	26,858
26		26	(a)	Newcastle U	L	0-2		30,236
27	Mar	5	(a)	Norwich C	W	3-1	Pratt, Armstrong, Taylor	22,949
28		9	(h)	Liverpool	W	1-0	Coates	32,098
29		12	(h)	West Brom A	L	0-2		28,834
30		19	(a)	Birmingham C	W	2-1	Jones, Hoddle	23,398
31		23	(h)	Derby C	D	0-0		27,359
32		26	(a)	Everton	L	0-4		32,549
33	Apr	2	(a)	Coventry C	D	1-1	Taylor	16,210
34		9	(h)	Queen's Park R	W	3-0	Jones 2, Taylor	32,680
35		11	(a)	Arsenal	L	0-1		47,432
36		12	(a)	Bristol C	L	0-1		27,568
37		16	(h)	Sunderland	D	1-1	Jones	34,155
38		20	(a)	Aston Villa	L	1-2	Armstrong	42,047
39		23	(a)	Stoke C	D	0-0		15,644
40		30	(h)	Aston Villa	W	3-1	Hoddle, Jones, Taylor	30,690
41	May	7	(a)	Manchester C	L	0-5		37,919
42		14	(h)	Leicester C	W	2-0	Pratt, Holmes	26,094

FINAL LEAGUE POSITION: 22nd in Division One

Appearances
Sub Appearance
Goals

FA Cup

3	Jan	8	(a)	Cardiff C	L	0-1		27,868

Appearances
Sub Appearance
Goals

FL Cup

2	Aug	31	(a)	Middlesbrough	W	2-1	Moores, Neighbour	19,042
3	Sep	22	(h)	Wrexham	L	2-3	Hoddle, Moores	19,156

Appearances
Sub Appearance
Goals

324

Armstrong	Coates	Conn	Daines	Duncan	Gorman	Hoddle	Holmes	Jennings	Jones	Keeley	McAllister	McNab	Moores	Naylor	Neighbour	Osgood	Perryman	Pratt	Stead M	Taylor	Young	
9	7							1	10		3			2	11	6	8	4			5	1
9	7*	12						1	10		3			2	11	6	8	4			5	2
9	7				4			1	10		3			2	11	6	8				5	3
	7*				4			1	10		3		9	2	11	6	8	12			5	4
	7				4			1	10		3		9	2	11	6*	8	12			5	5
	7				4			1	10		3		9	2	11	6	8				5	6
	7				4			1	10				9	2	11	6	8	5	3			7
12	7				4			1	10				9	2		6	8	5	3*	11		8
	7				4			1	10				9	2		3	8	6		11	5	9
					4			1	10	2	3	12	9			6	8	7*		11	5	10
	7				4			1	10	2	3	12	9*			6	8			11	5	11
	10			9*	4			1			3	12		2		6	8	7		11	5	12
12	10			9	4			1			3			2		6	8	7		11*	5	13
	7			9	3	4		1						2		6	8	10		11	5	14
	7				3	4		1					9	2		6	8	10		11	5	15
10	7				3	4		1					9	2		6	8			11	5	16
10	7				3	4		1					9	2		6	8			11	5	17
10	7*				3	4		1					9	2		6	8	12		11	5	18
10	7			9	3	4*		1						2		6	8	12		11	5	19
10	7			9	3	4		1						2		6	8	5		11		20
10*				9	3	4		1	7			12		2		6	8	5		11		21
				9	3	4		1	7	5	10			2		6	8			11		22
				9	3	4		1	7	5	10			2		6	8			11		23
			1	9	3	4			7	5	10			2		6	8			11		24
9	12		1		3	4*			7		10			2		6	8			11	5	25
9	10		1		3	7			11					2		6	8	4			5	26
9	10		1		3	5			8					2		6	7	4		11		27
9	10		1		3*	6			7			12		2		5	8	4		11		28
9	10		1			6	3		7			12		2		5	8*	4		11		29
9	10		1			8	3		7					2		5	6	4		11		30
9	10		1			8	3		7					2		5	6	4		11		31
9	10		1			8	3		7					2		5	6	4		11		32
9	10		1			8	3		7					2		5	6	4		11		33
9	10		1			8	3		7					2		5	6	4		11		34
9	10		1			8	3		7					2		5	6	4		11		35
9			1			8	3*		7	12	10			2		5	6	4		11		36
9	10		1			8			7					2		5	6	4	3	11		37
12	10		1			8			7				9	2		5	6	4	3	11*		38
11	10		1			8	7						9	2		5	6	4	3			39
11	10		1			8			7				9*	2		5	6	4	3	12		40
9	10		1			8			7				12	2		5	6	4	3	11*		41
11	10		1			8							9	2		5	6	4	3	7		42
20	28	12	19	9	15	39	10	23	31	5	10	6	16	40	7	42	42	30	8	31	19	
1	3	1								1	2	4	1					4		1		
3	3			4		4	1		9		1		2			7	1	4		8	1	

Armstrong	Coates	Conn	Daines	Duncan	Gorman	Hoddle	Holmes	Jennings	Jones	Keeley	McAllister	McNab	Moores	Naylor	Neighbour	Osgood	Perryman	Pratt	Stead M	Taylor	Young	
10*	7			9	3	4		1				12		2		6	8	5		11		3
1	1			1	1	1		1				1		1		1	1	1		1		
									1													

Armstrong	Coates	Conn	Daines	Duncan	Gorman	Hoddle	Holmes	Jennings	Jones	Keeley	McAllister	McNab	Moores	Naylor	Neighbour	Osgood	Perryman	Pratt	Stead M	Taylor	Young	
	7				4				10		3		9	2	11	6	8*	12			5	2
	7*				4			1	10		3		9	2	11	6	8	12			5	3
	2				1			2	2		2		2	2	2	2	2	2			2	
																		2				
						1			2		1											

1977-78

Manager: Keith Burkinshaw

1	Aug	20	(h)	Sheffield U	W	4-2	Osgood 2 (2 pens), Duncan, Jones	27,673
2		24	(a)	Blackburn R	D	0-0		9,540
3		27	(h)	Notts C	W	2-1	Duncan 2	25,839
4	Sep	3	(a)	Cardiff C	D	0-0		8,880
5		10	(h)	Fulham	W	1-0	Jones	31,939
6		17	(a)	Blackpool	W	2-0	Hoddle, Duncan	16,910
7		24	(h)	Luton T	W	2-0	Osgood (pen), Jones	32,814
8	Oct	1	(a)	Orient	D	1-1	Taylor	24,131
9		4	(a)	Hull C	L	0-2		10,966
10		8	(h)	Oldham A	W	5-1	Duncan 2, Robinson, Taylor 2	24,636
11		15	(a)	Charlton A	L	1-4	Taylor	30,706
12		22	(h)	Bristol R	W	9-0	Hoddle, Moores 3, Lee 4, Taylor	26,571
13		29	(a)	Stoke C	W	3-1	Pratt, Armstrong 2	21,012
14	Nov	5	(h)	Burnley	W	3-0	Hoddle, McNab, Taylor	30,634
15		12	(a)	Crystal P	W	2-1	Moores, Duncan	40,522
16		19	(h)	Brighton & HA	D	0-0		48,613
17		26	(a)	Bolton W	L	0-1		34,290
18	Dec	3	(h)	Southampton	D	0-0		37,873
19		10	(a)	Sunderland	W	2-1	Duncan 2	31,960
20		17	(h)	Crystal P	D	2-2	Hoddle 2	34,211
21		26	(a)	Millwall	W	3-1	Duncan, Lee, Taylor	14,644
22		27	(h)	Mansfield T	D	1-1	Duncan	36,288
23		31	(h)	Blackburn R	W	4-0	Hoddle, Pratt, Lee 2	30,520
24	Jan	2	(a)	Sheffield U	D	2-2	Duncan, Taylor	31,207
25		14	(a)	Notts C	D	3-3	Pratt 2, Lee	15,709
26		21	(h)	Cardiff C	W	2-1	Duncan 2	29,104
27	Feb	4	(a)	Fulham	D	1-1	Taylor	24,763
28		11	(h)	Blackpool	D	2-2	McAllister, Pratt	28,707
29		22	(a)	Luton T	W	4-1	Hoddle 2, McAllister, Duncan	17,024
30		25	(h)	Orient	D	1-1	Lee	32,869
31	Mar	4	(a)	Oldham A	D	1-1	McNab	14,122
32		11	(h)	Charlton A	W	2-1	Hoddle (pen), Pratt	34,511
33		18	(a)	Bristol R	W	3-2	Pratt, McNab, Jones	17,708
34		22	(h)	Stoke C	W	3-1	McAllister, Lee 2	30,646
35		25	(a)	Mansfield T	D	3-3	Hoddle 2 (1 pen), Jones	12,144
36		27	(h)	Millwall	D	3-3	Hoddle, Jones 2	33,074
37	Apr	1	(a)	Burnley	L	1-2	Taylor	16,916
38		8	(h)	Bolton W	W	1-0	McAllister	50,097
39		15	(a)	Brighton & HA	L	1-3	Jones	32,647
40		22	(h)	Sunderland	L	2-3	Duncan, Taylor	38,220
41		26	(h)	Hull C	W	1-0	Perryman	36,913
42		29	(a)	Southampton	D	0-0		28,846

FINAL LEAGUE POSITION: 3rd in Division Two

Appearances
Sub Appearances
Goals

FA Cup

3	Jan	7	(h)	Bolton W	D	2-2	Hoddle, Duncan	43,731
R		10	(a)	Bolton W	L	1-2*	Taylor (pen)	31,314

*After extra-time

Appearances
Sub Appearances
Goals

FL Cup

2	Aug	31	(h)	Wimbledon	W	4-0	Osgood (pen), Duncan 3	22,807
3	Oct	26	(h)	Coventry C	L	2-3	Pratt, Armstrong	35,099

Appearances
Sub Appearances
Goals

Armstrong	Coates	Daines	Duncan	Hoddle	Holmes	Jones	Lee	McAllister	McNab	Moores	Naylor	Osgood	Perryman	Pratt	Robinson	Stead	Taylor	
		1	9	4	3	10		8	2		5		6	7			11	1
4		1	9		3	10		8	2		5		6	7			11	2
		1	9	4	3	10		8	2		5		6	7			11	3
		1	9	4	3	10		8	2		5		6	7			11	4
		1	9	4	3	10		8	2		5		6	7			11	5
		1	9	4	3	10		8	2		5		6	7			11	6
12		1	9*	4	3	10		8	2		5		6	7			11	7
9		1		4	3			8	2		5		6	7	10		11	8
9	12	1		4	3			8	2		5		6	7*	10		11	9
12		1	9	4	3			8	2		5		6	7	10*		11	10
12		1		4	3		5	8	9	2			6	7	10*		11	11
		1		4	3	10	5	8	9	2			6	7			11	12
10		1		4	3		5	8	9	2			6	7			11	13
12		1		4	3	10	5*	8	9	2			6	7			11	14
12		1		4	3	10		8*	9	2	5		6	7			11	15
		1		4	3	10*	12	8	9	2	5		6	7			11	16
		1		4	3	10		8	9	2	5		6	7			11	17
12		1	9	4	3	10		8	2		5*		6	7			11	18
12		1	9	4	3*	10		8	2		5		6	7			11	19
		1	9	4	3	10		8	2		5		6	7			11	20
		1	9	4	3	10		8	2		5		6	7			11	21
		1	9	4	3	10		8	2		5		6	7			11	22
12		1	9*	4	3	10	5	8	2				6	7			11	23
12		1	9	4	3	10	5*	8	2				6	7			11	24
11		1	9	4	3	10	5	8	2				6	7				25
		1	9	4	3	10	5	8	2				6	7			11	26
		1	9	4	3	10	5	8	2				6	7			11	27
		1	9	4	3	10	5	8	2				6	7			11	28
12		1	9	4	3	10	5*	8	2				6	7			11	29
5		1	9	4	3	10		8	2				6	7			11	30
5		1	9	4	3	10		8	2				6	7			11	31
		1	9	4	3	10	5	8	2				6	7			11	32
12		1	9	4	3	10	5	8	2*				6	7			11	33
		1		4	3	10	5	8	9				6	7		2	11	34
		1		4	3	10	5	8	9				6	7		2	11	35
2		1		4	3	10	5	8	9				6	7			11	36
2		1		4	3	10	5	8	9				6	7			11	37
2		1		4	3	10*	5	8	9			12	6	7			11	38
12		1	9	4	3	10*	5	8	2				6	7			11	39
5		1	9	4	3	10	12	8	2				6	7*			11	40
		1	9	4	3	10	5	8	2				6	7			11	41
12		1	9	4	3	10*	5	8	2				6	7			11	42
10	1	42	27	41	38	20	23	25	42	7	37	18	42	42	4	2	41	
9	2					2				3						1		
2			16	12		8	11	4	3	4		3	1	7	1		11	

Armstrong	Coates	Daines	Duncan	Hoddle	Holmes	Jones	Lee	McAllister	McNab	Moores	Naylor	Osgood	Perryman	Pratt	Robinson	Stead	Taylor	
12		1	9	4	3	10	5	8	2				6	7*			11	3
12		1	9	4	3	10	5	8*	2				6	7			11	R
2		2	2	2	2	2	2	2	2				2	2			2	
		1	1														1	

Armstrong	Coates	Daines	Duncan	Hoddle	Holmes	Jones	Lee	McAllister	McNab	Moores	Naylor	Osgood	Perryman	Pratt	Robinson	Stead	Taylor	
		1	9	4	3	10		8	2		5		6	7			11	2
10		1		4	3		5	8	9	2			6	7			11	3
1		2	1	2	2	1	1	2	1	2	1		2	2			2	
1			3										1	1				

1978-79

Manager: Keith Burkinshaw

1	Aug	19	(a)	Nottingham F	D	1-1 Villa	41,223
2		23	(h)	Aston Villa	L	1-4 Hoddle (pen)	47,892
3		26	(h)	Chelsea	D	2-2 Armstrong, Duncan	40,632
4	Sep	2	(a)	Liverpool	L	0-7	50,705
5		9	(h)	Bristol C	W	1-0 Rodgers (og)	34,035
6		16	(a)	Leeds U	W	2-1 Lee, Taylor	36,062
7		23	(a)	Manchester C	L	0-2	43,471
8		30	(h)	Coventry C	D	1-1 Hoddle	35,806
9	Oct	7	(a)	West Brom A	W	1-0 Taylor	33,068
10		14	(h)	Birmingham C	W	1-0 Ainscow (og)	41,230
11		21	(a)	Derby C	D	2-2 McAllister, Taylor	26,181
12		28	(h)	Bolton W	W	2-0 Pratt, Lee	37,337
13	Nov	4	(a)	Norwich C	D	2-2 Lee, Taylor	27,031
14		11	(h)	Nottingham F	L	1-3 Pratt	50,494
15		18	(a)	Chelsea	W	3-1 Lee 2, Hoddle	42,328
16		22	(h)	Liverpool	D	0-0	50,393
17		25	(h)	Wolves	W	1-0 Taylor	35,430
18	Dec	9	(h)	Ipswich T	W	1-0 Pratt	33,882
19		16	(a)	Manchester U	L	0-2	52,026
20		23	(h)	Arsenal	L	0-5	42,273
21		26	(a)	Queen's Park R	D	2-2 Lee, Taylor (pen)	24,845
22		30	(a)	Everton	D	1-1 Taylor	44,572
23	Jan	13	(a)	Bristol C	D	0-0	29,122
24		20	(h)	Leeds U	L	1-2 Hoddle	36,838
25	Feb	3	(h)	Manchester C	L	0-3	32,037
26		10	(a)	Coventry C	W	3-1 Lee, Taylor 2	25,071
27		24	(a)	Birmingham C	L	0-1	20,980
28	Mar	3	(h)	Derby C	W	2-0 Ardiles 2	28,089
29		17	(h)	Norwich C	D	0-0	24,982
30		24	(a)	Aston Villa	W	3-2 Jones, Hoddle 2	35,486
31		28	(h)	Southampton	D	0-0	23,570
32		31	(a)	Middlesbrough	L	0-1	19,172
33	Apr	3	(a)	Wolves	L	2-3 Jones 2	19,819
34		7	(h)	Middlesbrough	L	1-2 Taylor (pen)	21,580
35		10	(a)	Arsenal	L	0-1	53,896
36		14	(h)	Queen's Park R	D	1-1 Perryman	28,854
37		16	(a)	Southampton	D	3-3 Pratt, Jones, Taylor	22,096
38		21	(h)	Manchester U	D	1-1 Jones	36,665
39		28	(a)	Ipswich T	L	1-2 Hoddle (pen)	28,179
40	May	5	(h)	Everton	D	1-1 Ardiles	26,077
41		8	(a)	Bolton W	W	3-1 Holmes, Falco, Villa	17,879
42		14	(h)	West Brom A	W	1-0 Villa	24,789

FINAL LEAGUE POSITION: 11th in Division One

Appearances
Sub Appearances
Goals

FA Cup

3	Jan	10	(h)	Altrincham	D	1-1 Taylor (pen)	31,081
R		16	(n*)	Altrincham	W	3-0 Lee 3	27,878
4	Feb	12	(h)	Wrexham	D	3-3 Hoddle, Jones, Roberts (og)	27,120
R		21	(a)	Wrexham	W	3-2† Jones 3	16,050
5		28	(a)	Oldham A	W	1-0 Perryman	16,097
6	Mar	10	(h)	Manchester U	D	1-1 Ardiles	51,800
R		14	(a)	Manchester U	L	0-2	54,510

*Played at Maine Road, Manchester. †After extra-time.

Appearances
Sub Appearances
Goals

League Cup

2	Aug	29	(a)	Swansea C	D	2-2 Hoddle (pen), Armstrong	24,335
R	Sep	6	(h)	Swansea C	L	1-3 Villa	33,672

Appearances
Sub Appearances
Goals

Tottenham Hotspur — appearances and goals grid (shirt numbers per match). Column headers read vertically.

Aleksic	Ardiles	Armstrong	Beavon	Daines	Duncan	Falco	Galvin	Gorman	Hoddle	Holmes	Jones	Kendall	Lacy	Lee	McAllister	McNab	Miller	Moores	Naylor	Perryman	Pratt	Smith	Taylor	Villa	Match
	8	9						3	10	4			5		2					6	12		11*	7	1
	8	9						3	10	4			5		2					6			11	7	2
	8	9						3	10	4			5		2					6			11	7	3
	8			1				3	10	4			5	9	2					6			11	7	4
	8			1				3	10	4			5	9	2					6			11	7	5
	8	12		1				3	10	4			5	9	2					6			11	7*	6
	8	12		1				3	10	4			5	9	2					6*			11	7	7
	8	7*		1				3	10	4	12		5	9	2					6			11		8
	8	5		1			7	3	10	4				9	2					6			11		9
	8			1					10	4			5	9	3				2	6	7		11		10
	8			1					10	4			5	9	3				2	6	7		11		11
	8			1					10*				5	9	3				2	6	7		11	12	12
	8*			1					10	4			5	9	3				2	6	7		11	12	13
	8*			1					10	4			5	9	3				2	6	7		11	12	14
	8								10	4		1	5	9	3				2	6	7		11		15
	8							3	10*	4		1	5	9	2					6	7		11	12	16
	8							3	10*	4		1	5	9	2					6	7		11	12	17
	8							3	10	4		1	5	9	2					6	7		11		18
	8							3	10	4*		1	5	9	2					6	7		11	12	19
	8							3	10	4	12	1	5	9	2					6	7*		11		20
	8							3	10			1	5	9	2					6	7		11	4	21
	8							3	10			1	5	9	2					6	7		11	4	22
	8							3	10			1	5	9	2					6	7		11	4	23
1	8							3	10	4			5	9	2					6	7		11		24
	8	9	10				7	3		4		1	5		2					6			11		25
	8*		12					3	10	4		1	5	9	2					6	7		11		26
	8							3	10	4		1	5	9	2					6	7		11		27
	8							3	10	4		1	5	9						6	7		11		28
	8*								10	4		1	5	9	3				2	6	7		11	12	29
	8								10	4		1	5	9	3				2	6	7		11		30
	8								10	4		1	5	9	3				2	6	7		11		31
	8*								10	4	12	1	5	9	3				2	6	7		11		32
	8								10	4		1	5	9	3				2	6	7		11		33
	7								10	4		1	5	9	3				2	6		8	11		34
		1							10	4				9	3		5		2	6	7	8	11		35
		1							10	4				9	3		5	8	2	6	7		11		36
	10									4	9	1			3		5	8	2	6	7		11		37
	10									4	9	1	5	8	3		4			2	6		11	7	38
1	8								10	4			5	9	3				2	6	7		11		39
1	8								10	4			5	9	3				2	6	7		11		40
1	8						9		10	4			5		3*				2	6	7	12	11		41
1	8								10	4	9		5		3				2	6	7		11		42
5	**38**	**7**	**1**	**14**	**2**	**1**	**1**	**15**	**34**	**33**	**18**	**23**	**35**	**26**	**38**	**2**	**7**	**2**	**22**	**42**	**37**	**1**	**32**	**26**	
		3						1					1		1						1	1	1	6	
	3	1			1	1		7	1	5			7	1					1	4			11	3	

2 own-goals

Aleksic	Ardiles	Armstrong	Beavon	Daines	Duncan	Falco	Galvin	Gorman	Hoddle	Holmes	Jones	Kendall	Lacy	Lee	McAllister	McNab	Miller	Moores	Naylor	Perryman	Pratt	Smith	Taylor	Villa	Match
	8	12						3	10	1			5	9*	2					6	7		11	4	3
1	8							3	10				5	9	2				12	6	7		11	4*	R
		9*					8	4	3	12		1	5	10						2	6	7	11		4
		12						4	3	10		1	5	9*						2	6	7	11	8	R
	8*							4	3	10		1	5	12	9					2	6	7	11		5
	8								10	4	9	1	5		3					2	6	7	12	11*	6
	8								10	4	9	1	5		3					2	6	7*	12	11	R
1	**5**	**1**					**1**	**5**	**7**	**6**	**6**	**7**	**4**	**5**				**5**	**7**	**7**	**5**	**5**			
		2							1				1							1		2			
	1								1	4			3							1		1			

1 own-goal

Aleksic	Ardiles	Armstrong	Beavon	Daines	Duncan	Falco	Galvin	Gorman	Hoddle	Holmes	Jones	Kendall	Lacy	Lee	McAllister	McNab	Miller	Moores	Naylor	Perryman	Pratt	Smith	Taylor	Villa	Match
	7*	12		1			9	4					5		2	10			3	6			11	8	2
	8	5		1			9	4						3	10				2	6			11	7	R
	2	1	2	2			2	2					1		2	2			2	2			2	2	
	1	1																							
		1						1																1	

1979-80

Manager: Keith Burkinshaw

1	Aug	18	(h)	Middlesbrough	L	1-3	Hoddle	32,743
2		22	(a)	Norwich C	L	0-4		16,647
3		25	(a)	Stoke C	L	1-3	Perryman	22,832
4	Sep	1	(h)	Manchester C	W	2-1	Jones, Hoddle	30,901
5		8	(h)	Brighton & HA	W	2-1	Armstrong, Hoddle (pen)	34,107
6		15	(a)	Southampton	L	2-5	Jones, Hoddle	22,573
7		22	(h)	West Brom A	D	1-1	Hoddle (pen)	29,914
8		29	(a)	Coventry C	D	1-1	Jones	20,085
9	Oct	6	(a)	Crystal P	D	1-1	Villa	45,274
10		10	(h)	Norwich C	W	3-2	Hoddle 2, Villa	26,488
11		13	(h)	Derby C	W	1-0	Armstrong	33,269
12		20	(a)	Leeds U	W	2-1	Jones, Armstrong	25,203
13		27	(h)	Nottingham F	W	1-0	Hoddle	49,038
14	Nov	3	(a)	Middlesbrough	D	0-0		19,557
15		10	(h)	Bolton W	W	2-0	Yorath, Hoddle (pen)	33,155
16		17	(a)	Liverpool	L	1-2	Jones	51,092
17		24	(a)	Everton	D	1-1	Jones	31,079
18	Dec	1	(h)	Manchester U	L	1-2	Hoddle	51,389
19		8	(a)	Bristol C	W	3-1	Miller, Hoddle 2 (1 pen)	25,090
20		15	(h)	Aston Villa	L	1-2	Ardiles	30,555
21		21	(a)	Ipswich T	L	1-3	McAllister	18,945
22		26	(a)	Arsenal	L	0-1		44,560
23		29	(h)	Stoke C	W	1-0	Pratt	28,810
24	Jan	12	(a)	Manchester C	D	1-1	Hoddle	34,837
25		19	(a)	Brighton & HA	W	2-0	Hughton, Villa	29,406
26	Feb	2	(h)	Southampton	D	0-0		37,155
27		9	(a)	West Brom A	L	1-2	Hoddle	26,319
28		23	(a)	Derby C	L	1-2	Galvin	21,183
29		27	(h)	Coventry C	W	4-3	Falco, Hoddle 3 (2 pens)	22,536
30	Mar	1	(h)	Leeds U	W	2-1	Falco, Hoddle	35,331
31		11	(a)	Nottingham F	L	0-4		25,633
32		15	(h)	Crystal P	D	0-0		28,419
33		22	(a)	Bolton W	L	1-2	Jones	14,474
34		29	(h)	Liverpool	W	2-0	Pratt, Hoddle (pen)	32,114
35	Apr	2	(h)	Ipswich T	L	0-2		26,423
36		5	(a)	Wolves	W	2-1	Jones, Galvin	30,713
37		7	(h)	Arsenal	L	1-2	Jones	41,365
38		12	(a)	Manchester U	L	1-4	Ardiles	53,151
39		19	(h)	Everton	W	3-0	Miller, Ardiles, Galvin	25,245
40		23	(h)	Wolves	D	2-2	Armstrong, Galvin	19,843
41		26	(a)	Aston Villa	L	0-1		29,549
42	May	3	(h)	Bristol C	D	0-0		23,585

FINAL LEAGUE POSITION: 14th in Division One

Appearances
Sub Appearances
Goals

FA Cup

3	Jan	5	(h)	Manchester U	D	1-1	Ardiles	45,207
R		9	(a)	Manchester U	W	1-0*	Ardiles	53,762
4		26	(a)	Swindon T	D	0-0		26,000
R		30	(h)	Swindon T	W	2-1	Armstrong 2	46,707
5	Feb	16	(h)	Birmingham C	W	3-1	Armstrong, Hoddle 2 (1 pen)	49,936
6	Mar	8	(h)	Liverpool	L	0-1		48,033

*After extra-time

Appearances
Sub Appearances
Goals

FL Cup

2	Aug	29	(h)	Manchester U	W	2-1	Pratt, Hoddle	29,163
2	Sep	5	(a)	Manchester U	L	1-3	Armstrong	48,292

Appearances
Sub Appearances
Goals

Appearance grid (shirt numbers by player and match). Columns are players; final column is the match number.

Aleksic	Ardiles	Armstrong	Beavon	Daines	Falco	Galvin	Gibson	Hazard	Hoddle	Hughton	Jones	Kendall	Lacy	Lee	McAllister	Miller	Naylor	Perryman	Pratt	Smith	Southey	Taylor	Villa	Yorath	No.
	8			1		9			10		12		5	2				6	7*	3			11	4	1
	8			1		7			10		9		5	2				6		3			11	4	2
	8			1		9*			10		11		5	2	12			6	7	3				4	3
	8*			1		12			10	3	9			11	2	5		6	7					4	4
	9	12		1					10	2	8			11		5		6	7*	3				4	5
	9	11		1					10	2	8		5					6	7	3				4	6
	7	9		1					10	2	8				3	5		6					11	4	7
	7	9		1					10	2	8				3	5		6					11	4	8
	7*	9		1					10	2	8				3	5		6	12				11	4	9
	7	9		1					10	2	8				3	5		6	12				11	4*	10
	7	9*		1					10	2	8			12	3	5		6	4				11		11
	7	9		1*					10	2	8				3	5		6	12				11	4	12
1	7	9*							10	2	8			12		5		6		3			11	4	13
1	7	9							10	2	8				3			6		5			11	4	14
1	7	9							10	2	8				3			6		5			11	4	15
1	7	9							10	2	8				3			6		5			11	4	16
1	7	9							10	2	8				3			6		5			11	4	17
1	7	9							10	2	8				3			6	4	5			11		18
	7			1					10	2	8			9	3			6	4	5			11		19
	7			1					10	2	8			9	3			6	4	5			11		20
	7			1					10	2	8			9	5	3		6					11	4	21
1	7	9*		12					10	2	8				3			6	11	5				4	22
1	7			12		9*			10	2	8				5			6	11	3				4	23
	7	9		1					10	2	8*				3	5		6	12				11	4	24
	7	9		1					10	2					5	3		6	12			8*	11	4	25
	7	9		1					10	2					5	3		6				8	11	4	26
	7	9		1					10	2	8				5	3		6					11	4	27
	7	9	11*			8	12		10	2		1			5	3		6	4						28
	7	9	8						10	2		1			5	3		6	4				11		29
	7	9		1		8			10	2					5	3		6				4	11		30
	7	9		1					10	2	8				5	3	12	6					11	4*	31
	7	9		1					10	3	8				5		2	6				4	11		32
	7	9		1					10	3	8				5	4	2	6					11		33
	7	12		1					10	3	8				5		2	6	9				11*	4	34
	7			1					10	3	8				5		2	6	9				11	4	35
	7			1	9				10	3	8				5	4		6	11			2			36
	7			1	11				10	3	8				5		2	6	9					4	37
	7	12		1	11*				10	3	8				5		2	6	9					4	38
	7	9		1	11			4*	10	3	8				5		2	6					12		39
	7	9		1	11				10	3	8*				5		2	6					12	4	40
	7	11*		1	12	9			10	2	8				3	5	4	6							41
	7			1	9	11		4	10	3	8				5		2	6							42
8	**40**	**28**	**2**	**32**	**7**	**7**	**1**	**3**	**41**	**39**	**36**	**2**	**4**	**8**	**35**	**27**	**6**	**40**	**19**	**14**	**1**	**7**	**22**	**33**	
	2	1			2	3					1			2	1			1					5		2
	3	4			2	4			19	1	9				1	2		1	2				3	1	

(The last three rows are season totals, substitute appearances, and goals.)

Aleksic	Ardiles	Armstrong	Beavon	Daines	Falco	Galvin	Gibson	Hazard	Hoddle	Hughton	Jones	Kendall	Lacy	Lee	McAllister	Miller	Naylor	Perryman	Pratt	Smith	Southey	Taylor	Villa	Yorath	No.
1	7				9				10	2	8*				5	3		6	12				11	4	3
1*	7	8			9				10	2					5	3		6	12				11	4	R
	7	9		1					10	2	8				3	5		6	12				11*	4	4
	7	9		1					10	2	8*				5	3		6	4				12	11	R
	7	9		1		8			10	2					5	3		6	12				11*	4	5
	7	9		1		8			10	2					5	3		6	12				4*	11	6
2	**6**	**5**		**4**	**2**	**2**			**6**	**6**	**3**				**5**	**6**	**1**	**6**	**1**				**6**	**5**	
											2								3					2	

Aleksic	Ardiles	Armstrong	Beavon	Daines	Falco	Galvin	Gibson	Hazard	Hoddle	Hughton	Jones	Kendall	Lacy	Lee	McAllister	Miller	Naylor	Perryman	Pratt	Smith	Southey	Taylor	Villa	Yorath	No.
	8			1		12			10	3	9			11	2	5		6	7*					4	2
	9*	12		1					10	2	8			11		5		6	7	3				4	2
	1	**1**		**2**		**2**	**1**		**1**	**2**	**1**		**2**		**2**	**2**	**1**	**2**	**2**	**1**				**2**	
	1					1																		1	

1980-81

Manager: Keith Burkinshaw

1	Aug	16	(h)	Nottingham F	W	2-0	Hoddle (pen), Crooks	43,398
2		19	(a)	Crystal P	W	4-3	Archibald, Hoddle, Crooks 2	27,841
3		23	(h)	Brighton & HA	D	2-2	Hoddle, Crooks	39,763
4		30	(a)	Arsenal	L	0-2		54,045
5	Sep	6	(h)	Manchester U	D	0-0		40,995
6		13	(a)	Leeds U	D	0-0		21,947
7		20	(h)	Sunderland	D	0-0		32,030
6		27	(a)	Leicester C	L	1-2	Villa	22,616
7	Oct	4	(a)	Stoke C	W	3-2	Hughton, Archibald, Taylor (pen)	18,614
10		11	(h)	Middlesbrough	W	3-2	Archibald, Villa, Crooks	27,380
11		18	(a)	Aston Villa	L	0-3		30,940
12		22	(a)	Manchester C	L	1-3	Hoddle	28,788
13		25	(h)	Coventry C	W	4-1	Archibald 2, Hoddle 2	25,484
14	Nov	1	(a)	Everton	D	2-2	Archibald 2	26,223
15		8	(h)	Wolves	D	2-2	Hoddle (pen), Crooks	29,244
16		12	(h)	Crystal P	W	4-2	Archibald, Crooks 3	25,777
17		15	(a)	Nottingham F	W	3-0	Ardiles, Archibald 2	25,400
18		22	(a)	Birmingham C	L	1-2	Ardiles	24,817
19		29	(h)	West Brom A	L	2-3	Lacy, Perryman	27,372
20	Dec	6	(a)	Liverpool	L	1-2	Hoddle	39,545
21		13	(h)	Manchester C	W	2-1	Archibald, Hoddle	23,883
22		17	(h)	Ipswich T	W	5-3	Perryman, Ardiles, Archibald, Hoddle, Crooks	22,741
23		20	(a)	Middlesbrough	L	1-4	Lacy	15,990
24		26	(h)	Southampton	D	4-4	Brooke 2, Archibald, Crooks	28,792
25		27	(a)	Norwich C	D	2-2	Archibald, Hoddle	23,145
26	Jan	10	(h)	Birmingham C	W	1-0	Crooks	24,909
27		17	(h)	Arsenal	W	2-0	Archibald 2	32,944
28		31	(a)	Brighton & HA	W	2-0	Ardiles, Crooks	23,610
29	Feb	7	(h)	Leeds U	D	1-1	Archibald	32,372
30		17	(a)	Manchester U	D	0-0		40,642
31		21	(h)	Leicester C	L	1-2	Archibald	27,326
32		28	(a)	Sunderland	D	1-1	Crooks	22,382
33	Mar	11	(h)	Stoke C	D	2-2	Ardiles, Brooke	28,742
34		14	(a)	Ipswich T	L	0-3		32,044
35		21	(h)	Aston Villa	W	2-0	Archibald, Crooks	35,091
36		28	(a)	Coventry C	W	1-0	Roberts (og)	18,654
37	Apr	4	(a)	Everton	D	2-2	Galvin, Crooks	27,208
38		18	(h)	Norwich C	L	2-3	Miller, Hoddle (pen)	34,413
39		20	(a)	Southampton	D	1-1	Miller	23,735
40		25	(h)	Liverpool	D	1-1	Hoddle	35,334
41		30	(a)	Wolves	L	0-1		18,350
42	May	2	(a)	West Brom A	L	2-4	Smith, Falco	20,549

FINAL LEAGUE POSITION: 10th in Division One

Appearances
Sub Appearances
Goals

FA Cup

3	Jan	3	(a)	Queen's Park R	D	0-0		28,829
R		7	(h)	Queen's Park R	W	3-1	Galvin, Hoddle, Crooks	36,294
4		24	(h)	Hull C	W	2-0	Archibald, Brooke	37,532
5	Feb	14	(h)	Coventry C	W	3-1	Hughton, Ardiles, Archibald	36,688
6	Mar	7	(h)	Exeter C	W	2-0	Miller, Roberts	40,629
SF	Apr	11	(n*)	Wolves	D	2-2†	Archibald, Hoddle	50,174
R		15	(n‡)	Wolves	W	3-0	Villa, Crooks 2	52,539
F	May	9	(n§)	Manchester C	D	1-1†	Hutchinson (og)	100,000
R		14	(n§)	Manchester C	W	3-2	Villa 2, Crooks	96,000

*Played at Hillsborough, Sheffield. ‡Played at Arsenal Stadium, Highbury, London. §Played at Wembley Stadium. †After extra-time.

Appearances
Sub Appearances
Goals

FL Cup

2	Aug	27	(a)	Orient	W	1-0	Lacy	20,087
2	Sep	3	(h)	Orient	W	3-1	Archibald 2, Crooks	25,806
3		24	(h)	Crystal P	D	0-0		29,654
R		30	(a)	Crystal P	W	3-1†	Villa, Hoddle, Crooks	26,885
4	Nov	4	(h)	Arsenal	W	1-0	Ardiles	42,511
5	Dec	2	(a)	West Ham U	L	0-1		36,003

†After extra-time.

Appearances
Sub Appearances
Goals

Player appearances and goals chart.

League

Aleksic	Archibald	Ardiles	Armstrong	Brooke	Crooks	Daines	Falco	Galvin	Hazard	Hoddle	Hughton	Kendall	Lacy	Mazzon	McAllister	Miller	O'Reilly	Perryman	Roberts	Smith	Taylor	Villa	Yorath	#
	8	7*	12		11					10	3	1	5					6		2		9	4	1
	8	7			11					10	3	1	5					6		2		9	4	2
	8	7			11					10	3	1	5					6		2		9	4	3
	8	7			11					10	3	1	5					6		2*	12	9	4	4
	8	7*			11	1				10	3		5					6		2	12	9	4	5
	8	7			11	1				10	3		5					6		2	4	9		6
	8	7	12		11	1				10	3		5					6		2	4*	9		7
	8	7			11	1				10	3		5					6		2		9	4	8
	8	7			11*	1					3		5					6	12	2	10	9	4	9
	8	7*			11	1				10	3		5					6		2	12	9	4	10
	8		12		11	1				10	3		5					6		2	7	9	4*	11
	8	7	12		11*	1				10	3		5					6		2	4	9		12
	8	7			11	1				10	3		5			4		6		2		9		13
	8	7			11	1				10	3		5			4		6		2		9		14
	8	7			11	1				10	3*		5			4		6	12	2		9		15
	8	7			11	1				10	3		5		2*	4		6	12		9		16
	8	7			11	1				10	3		5		2	4		6				9		17
	8	7			11	1				10	3		5		2	4		6				9		18
	8	7*	12		11	1				10	3		5		2	4		6				9		19
	8	7			11	1				10	3		5		2			6	4			9		20
	8	7*			11	1				10	3		5		2			6	4		9	12	21
	8	7			11	1				10	3		5		2			6	4		9*	12	22
1	8	7			11					10	3		5		2			6	4*		9	12	23
1	8		7		11					10	3*		5				12	6	4		9	2	24
1	8		7		11					10			5			12	3	6		2		9*	4	25
	8		7*		11	1		9		10			5		12	2	3	6	4				26
	8		7		11	1		9		10			5*			2	3	6	4		12		27
	8		7*	12	11	1		9		10			5			2	3	6	4				28
	8		7	12	11*	1		9		10			5			2	3	6	4				29
	8		7		11	1		9		10	2		5				3	6	4				30
	8		7	12	11*	1		9		10	2		5				3	6	4				31
	8*		7		11	1		9		10	2				5		3	6	4	12			32
	8		7	12	11	1		9		10	2*				5		3	6	4				33
	8		7*	12	11	1		9		10	2				5		3	6	4				34
1	8		7	5	11			9		10	2						3	6	4				35
1	8		7	5*	11			9		10	2						3	6	4	12			36
1	8		7	5*	11			9		10	2						3	6	4		12		37
1	8		7	5*	11			9	12	10	2						3	6	4				38
1			7	12	11*		8	9		10				2	5	4	3	6					39
1	8		7	12	11			9		10						4	3	6		2	5*		40
	8	7		5	11	1		9	12	10	3*							6	4	2	5		41
1	12		7			11	9	8								4	3	6	10*	2		5	42
10	40	36		10	40	28	3	17	2	38	34	4	31	1	18	24	1	42	21	18	5	28	11	
1			4	8			2					1		1	1			3	2	3	1	4		
	20	5			3	16			1	1	12	1			2	2	2		2		1	1	2	

I own-goal

Cup

Aleksic	Archibald	Ardiles	Armstrong	Brooke	Crooks	Daines	Falco	Galvin	Hazard	Hoddle	Hughton	Kendall	Lacy	Mazzon	McAllister	Miller	O'Reilly	Perryman	Roberts	Smith	Taylor	Villa	Yorath	#
	8		7		11	1			12	10			5				3	6	4		9*	2		3
	8		7		11	1		9		10			5		2		3	6	4					R
	8	7*		12	11	1		9		10					2		3	6	4		5			4
	8	7*		12	11	1		9		10	2				5		3	6	4					5
	8	7			11	1		9		10	2				5		3	6	4					6
1	8	7		12	11			9		10	2						3	5	4	6*				SF
1	8	7*		12	11			9		10	2						3	5	4		5			R
1	8	7		12	11			9		10	2						3	5	4	6*				F
1	8	7			11			9		10	2						3	6	4	5				R
4	9	7		2	9	5		8		9	6				3	1	2	9	9	9	5	2		
				5				1																
	3	1		1	4			1		2	1				1			1		3				

I own-goal

League Cup

Aleksic	Archibald	Ardiles	Armstrong	Brooke	Crooks	Daines	Falco	Galvin	Hazard	Hoddle	Hughton	Kendall	Lacy	Mazzon	McAllister	Miller	O'Reilly	Perryman	Roberts	Smith	Taylor	Villa	Yorath	#
	8	7			11					10	3	1	5					6		2		9	4	2
	8	7*			11	1				10	3		5					6		2	12	9	4	2
	8	7			11	1				10	3		5					6		2		9	4	2
	8	7*			11	1				10	3		5					6		2	12	9	4	R
	8	7*			11	1				10	3		5			4		6	12	2		9	4	4
	8	7			11	1				10	3		5		2			6				9	4	5
	6	6			6	5				6	6	1	6		1	1		6		5	2	6	5	
																	1			2				
	2	1			2					1			1					1						

1981-82

Manager: Keith Burkinshaw

1	Aug	29	(a)	Middlesbrough	W	3-1	Villa, Hoddle, Falco	20,490
2	Sep	2	(h)	West Ham U	L	0-4		41,200
3		5	(h)	Aston Villa	L	1-3	Villa	31,265
4		12	(a)	Wolves	W	1-0	Galvin	18,675
5		19	(h)	Everton	W	3-0	Hughton, Roberts, Hoddle (pen)	31,219
6		22	(a)	Swansea C	L	1-2	Hoddle (pen)	22,352
7		26	(a)	Manchester C	W	1-0	Falco	39,085
8	Oct	3	(h)	Nottingham F	W	3-0	Hazard, Falco 2	34,870
9		10	(h)	Stoke C	W	2-0	Ardiles, Crooks	30,520
10		17	(a)	Sunderland	W	2-0	Hazard, Archibald	25,317
11		24	(h)	Brighton & HA	L	0-1		37,294
12		31	(a)	Southampton	W	2-1	Roberts, Corbett	24,131
13	Nov	7	(h)	West Brom A	L	1-2	Crooks	32,436
14		21	(h)	Manchester U	W	3-1	Roberts, Hazard, Archibald	35,534
15		28	(a)	Notts C	D	2-2	Crooks 2	15,550
16	Dec	5	(h)	Coventry C	L	1-2	Hazard	27,972
17		12	(a)	Leeds U	D	0-0		28,780
18	Jan	27	(h)	Middlesbrough	W	1-0	Crooks	22,819
19		30	(a)	Everton	D	1-1	Villa	30,709
20	Feb	6	(h)	Wolves	W	6-1	Villa 3, Falco, Hoddle (pen), Crooks	29,960
21		17	(a)	Aston Villa	D	1-1	Crooks	23,877
22		20	(h)	Manchester C	W	2-0	Hoddle 2 (1 pen)	46,181
23		27	(a)	Stoke C	W	2-0	Crooks 2	20,592
24	Mar	9	(a)	Brighton & HA	W	3-1	Ardiles, Archibald, Crooks	27,082
25		20	(h)	Southampton	W	3-2	Roberts 3	46,827
26		23	(a)	Birmingham C	D	0-0		17,708
27		27	(a)	West Brom A	L	0-1		20,151
28		29	(h)	Arsenal	D	2-2	Hughton, Archibald	40,940
29	Apr	10	(a)	Ipswich T	W	1-0	Hoddle	45,215
30		12	(a)	Arsenal	W	3-1	Hazard, Crooks 2	48,897
31		14	(h)	Sunderland	D	2-2	Galvin, Hoddle	39,898
32		17	(a)	Manchester U	L	0-2		50,724
33		24	(h)	Notts C	W	3-1	Villa, Archibald, Galvin	38,017
34		28	(h)	Birmingham C	D	1-1	Villa	25,470
35	May	1	(a)	Coventry C	D	0-0		15,408
36		3	(h)	Liverpool	D	2-2	Perryman, Archibald	38,091
37		5	(h)	Swansea C	W	2-1	Brooke 2 (1 pen)	26,348
38		8	(h)	Leeds U	W	2-1	Brooke, Burns (og)	35,020
39		10	(a)	West Ham U	D	2-2	Hoddle (pen), Brooke	27,667
40		12	(a)	Nottingham F	L	0-2		15,273
41		15	(a)	Liverpool	L	1-3	Hoddle	48,122
42		17	(a)	Ipswich T	L	1-2	Crooks	21,202

FINAL LEAGUE POSITION: 4th in Division One

Appearances
Sub Appearances
Goals

FA Cup

3	Jan	2	(h)	Arsenal	W	1-0	Crooks	38,421
4		23	(h)	Leeds U	W	1-0	Crooks	46,126
5	Feb	13	(h)	Aston Villa	W	1-0	Falco	43,419
6	Mar	6	(a)	Chelsea	W	3-2	Hazard, Archibald, Hoddle	42,557
SF	Apr	3	(n*)	Leicester C	W	2-0	Crooks, Wilson (og)	46,606
F	May	22	(n†)	Queen's Park R	D	1-1‡	Hoddle	100,000
R		27	(n†)	Queen's Park R	W	1-0	Hoddle (pen)	92,000

*Played at Villa Park, Birmingham. †Played at Wembley Stadium. ‡After extra-time.

Appearances
Sub Appearances
Goals

FL Cup

2	Oct	7	(h)	Manchester U	W	1-0	Archibald	39,333
2		28	(a)	Manchester U	W	1-0	Hazard	55,890
3	Nov	11	(h)	Wrexham	W	2-0	Hughton, Hoddle	24,084
4	Dec	2	(h)	Fulham	W	1-0	Hazard	30,214
5	Jan	18	(h)	Nottingham F	W	1-0	Ardiles	31,192
SF	Feb	3	(a)	West Brom A	D	0-0		32,238
SF		10	(h)	West Brom A	W	1-0	Hazard	47,241
F	Mar	13	(n†)	Liverpool	L	1-3‡	Archibald	100,000

†Played at Wembley Stadium. ‡After extra-time.

Appearances
Sub Appearances
Goals

FA Charity Shield

	Aug	22	(n†)	Aston Villa	D	2-2	Falco 2	92,500

†Played at Wembley Stadium.

Appearances
Sub Appearances
Goals

Tottenham Hotspur appearances and goals grid (shirt numbers by match).

Aleksic	Archibald	Ardiles	Brooke	Clemence	Corbett	Crook	Crooks	Dick	Falco	Galvin	Gibson	Hazard	Hoddle	Hughton	Jones	Lacy	Mazzon	Miller	O'Reilly	Parks	Perryman	Price	Roberts	Smith	Villa	
	7	8	1							11	9		10	2				3			6	4			5	1
		8	1							11	9	7	10	2				3			6	4*	2	12	5	2
	7	8	1							11			10	9	12			3*			6		2	4	5	3
	7	8*	1							11	9		10	2	12			3			6		4		5	4
8	7		1							11	9		10	2				3			6		4		5	5
8	7		1							11	9		10	2				3			6		4		5	6
8	7		1							11	9		10	2				3			6		4		5	7
8	7		1							11	9	5	10	2				3			6		4			8
8	7		1				11				9	12	10	2				3			6		4	5*		9
8	7		1				11				9	5*	10	2	12			3			6		4			10
8	7		1				11				9	5	10	2				3			6		4			11
8	7		1	12		11*					9	5	10	2				3			6		4			12
8	7*		1			11					9	5		2	12			3			6	10	4			13
8	7		1			11					9	5	10	2				3			6		4			14
8	7		1			11					9	5	10	2				3			6		4			15
8	7		1			11					9	5	10	2*				3			6		4	12		16
	7		1			11					9	5*	10	2	12			3			6		4	8		17
	7		1			11	8	9				10	2					3			6		4		5	18
	7	12	1			11	8*	9				10	2					3			6	4			5	19
	7		1			11*	8	9			12	10	2					3			6	4			5	20
12	7		1			11	8				5	10	2					3			6	9	4*			21
8	7		1			11	9*				5	10	2					3			6	4	12			22
8	7*		1			11		9			5	10	2					3			6	4	12			23
8	7		1			11		9			5		2					3			6	4	10			24
8			1					9			5	10	2					3			6	4	7	11		25
	7		1				10	9	8*	5		2			12			3			6		4	11		26
8	7	12	1				10*	9				2						3			6	5	4	11		27
8	7		1					9	11	10	2										6	4	3	5		28
8*		12	1			11		9			5	10	2					3			6		4	7		29
			1			11		9			5	10		8				3			6		4	2	7	30
		12	1			11		9*			5	10		8				3			6		4	2	7	31
8			1			11		9			5	10	2					3*			6	12	4	7		32
8			1			11		9			5	10	2								6	3	4	7		33
8			1			11		9			10	2	5								6	3	4	7		34
8		11	1		12		10	9*			2	5						3			6	4	7			35
1	8			10		11		9			2	12	5	3	7				6		4*					36
1	8			10	3	11*		9			2	12	5		7			6			4					37
		4	1	3	8*	11		9			10	2	12	5	7			6								38
	8		2*		11		9			7	10				5			3	12	1	6	4				39
	7	1		11		8					10	2	5							6	3	4	9			40
	7	1		11*		8			5	10	2						3			6	12	4	9			41
8	7		1			11				5	10*	2						3			6	12	4				42
2	26	26	12	38	3	3	27	1	21	32	1	26	34	37	3	7		35	4	2	42	18	35	1	26	
	1		4		1	1			2				4	5				1				3	2	1	1	
	6	2	4			1		13		5	3		5	10	2						1		6		8	

1 own-goal

Aleksic	Archibald	Ardiles	Brooke	Clemence	Corbett	Crook	Crooks	Dick	Falco	Galvin	Gibson	Hazard	Hoddle	Hughton	Jones	Lacy	Mazzon	Miller	O'Reilly	Parks	Perryman	Price	Roberts	Smith	Villa	
	7		1			11	8	9				10	2					3			6		4		5	3
	7		1			11	8*	9			12	10	2					3			6		4		5	4
12	7		1			11*	8	9				10	2					3			6	4	5			5
8	7		1			11		9			5	10	2					3			6	4				6
8	7		1			11		9			5	10	2					12			6	4	3*			SF
8		12	1			11		9			5*	10	2					3			6	4	7			F
8		12	1			11		9			5*	10	2					3			6	4	7			R
4	5		7			7		3	7	4	7	7						6			7	5	6	2		
1		2							1								1								
1						3		1			1	3													

1 own-goal

Aleksic	Archibald	Ardiles	Brooke	Clemence	Corbett	Crook	Crooks	Dick	Falco	Galvin	Gibson	Hazard	Hoddle	Hughton	Jones	Lacy	Mazzon	Miller	O'Reilly	Parks	Perryman	Price	Roberts	Smith	Villa	
8	7		1			11*	9				10	2			12	3					6		4		5	2
8	7		1			11		9			5	10	2					3			6		4			2
8	7		1			11		9			5	10	2					3			6		4			3
8	7		1			11		9			5	10	2					3			6		4			4
	7		1			11	8*	9			12	10	2					3			6		4		5	5
	7		1			11	8	9				10	2					3			6		4		5	SF
	7		1			11	8	9			5	10	2					3			6		4			SF
8	7		1			11		9			5*	10	2					3			6	4		12		F
5	8		8			7		4	8	5	8	8						8			8	3	5	3		
								1				1											1			
	2	1						3	1	1																

Aleksic	Archibald	Ardiles	Brooke	Clemence	Corbett	Crook	Crooks	Dick	Falco	Galvin	Gibson	Hazard	Hoddle	Hughton	Jones	Lacy	Mazzon	Miller	O'Reilly	Parks	Perryman	Price	Roberts	Smith	Villa	
8	7		1			11	9				10	2						3			6		4		5	
1	1		1			1	1				1	1						1			1		1		1	
						2																				

1982-83

Manager: Keith Burkinshaw

1	Aug	28	(h)	Luton T	D	2-2 Hazard, Mabbutt	35,195
2		31	(a)	Ipswich T	W	2-1 Archibald, Crooks	23,224
3	Sep	4	(a)	Everton	L	1-3 Archibald	30,563
4		8	(h)	Southampton	W	6-0 Brooke (pen), Perryman, Galvin 2, Villa, Crooks	26,579
5		11	(h)	Manchester C	L	1-2 Mabbutt	32,483
6		18	(a)	Sunderland	W	1-0 Brooke	21,137
7		25	(h)	Nottingham F	W	4-1 Mabbutt 2, Crooks 2	30,662
8	Oct	2	(a)	Swansea C	L	0-2	16,381
9		9	(h)	Coventry C	W	4-0 Crooks, Brooke 3 (1 pen)	25,188
10		16	(a)	Norwich C	D	0-0	21,668
11		23	(h)	Notts C	W	4-2 Brooke, Mabbutt, Crooks 2	26,183
12		30	(a)	Aston Villa	L	0-4	25,992
13	Nov	6	(h)	Watford	L	0-1	42,634
14		13	(a)	Manchester U	L	0-1	47,869
15		20	(h)	West Ham U	W	2-1 Archibald 2	41,960
16		27	(a)	Liverpool	L	0-3	40,691
17	Dec	4	(h)	West Brom A	D	1-1 Wile (og)	26,608
18		11	(a)	Stoke C	L	0-2	15,849
19		18	(h)	Birmingham C	W	2-1 Mabbutt 2	20,946
20		27	(a)	Arsenal	L	0-2	51,497
21		28	(h)	Brighton & HA	W	2-0 Villa, Hughton	23,994
22	Jan	1	(a)	West Ham U	L	0-3	33,383
23		3	(h)	Everton	W	2-1 Gibson 2	28,455
24		15	(a)	Luton T	D	1-1 Hoddle	21,231
25		22	(h)	Sunderland	D	1-1 Gibson	25,250
26	Feb	5	(a)	Manchester C	D	2-2 Gibson, Brooke (pen)	26,357
27		12	(h)	Swansea C	W	1-0 Crooks	24,632
28		26	(h)	Norwich C	D	0-0	23,342
29	Mar	5	(a)	Notts C	L	0-3	11,841
30		12	(a)	Coventry C	D	1-1 Miller	11,027
31		19	(a)	Watford	W	1-0 Falco	27,373
32		23	(h)	Aston Villa	W	2-0 Falco 2	22,455
33	Apr	2	(a)	Brighton & HA	L	1-2 Roberts	20,341
34		4	(h)	Arsenal	W	5-0 Hughton 2, Brazil, Falco 2	43,642
35		9	(a)	Nottingham F	D	2-2 Mabbutt, Brazil	18,265
36		16	(h)	Ipswich T	W	3-1 Mabbutt, Brazil 2	30,587
37		23	(a)	West Brom A	W	1-0 Archibald	14,879
38		30	(h)	Liverpool	W	2-0 Archibald 2	44,907
39	May	3	(a)	Southampton	W	2-1 Mabbutt, Brazil	21,602
40		7	(a)	Birmingham C	L	0-2	18,947
41		11	(h)	Manchester U	W	2-0 Roberts, Archibald	32,803
42		14	(h)	Stoke C	W	4-1 Brazil, Archibald 3	33,691

FINAL LEAGUE POSITION: 4th in Division One

Appearances
Sub Appearances
Goals

FA Cup

3	Jan	8	(h)	Southampton	W	1-0 Hazard	38,040
4		29	(h)	West Brom A	W	2-1 Gibson, Crooks	38,208
5	Feb	19	(a)	Everton	L	0-2	42,995

Appearances
Sub Appearances
Goals

FL Cup

2	Oct	6	(h)	Brighton & HA	D	1-1 Brooke (pen)	20,416
2		26	(a)	Brighton & HA	W	1-0 Crooks	20,755
3	Nov	9	(a)	Gillingham	W	4-2 Archibald 2, Crooks 2	14,366
4	Dec	1	(h)	Luton T	W	1-0 Villa	27,861
5	Jan	19	(h)	Burnley	L	1-4 Gibson	30,771

Appearances
Sub Appearances
Goals

FA Charity Shield

	Aug	21	(n*)	Liverpool	L	0-1	82,500

*Played at Wembley Stadium.

Appearances
Sub Appearances
Goals

Football season appearance & goals grid (shirt numbers per player per match; * = substituted, † = see note, subscript/small numbers = substitute appearances).

Archibald	Ardiles	Brazil	Brooke	Clemence	Corbett	Crook	Crooks	Dick	Falco	Galvin	Gibson	Hazard	Hoddle	Hughton	Lacy	Mabbutt	Mazzon	Miller	O'Reilly	Parks	Perryman	Price	Roberts	Villa	Webster	No.
8*		12		1		11		9				5	10	2		4	7		3		6					1
8		5		1		11		9					10	2		4	7		3		6					2
8		5		1		11		9				12	10	2		4	7		3*		6					3
8		5		1		11		9				7	10*	2		4					6	3		12		4
8		5		1		11		9				7*		2		4					6	3	12	10		5
8		5		1		11		9						2		4	7				6	3		10		6
		5		1	12	11		9		8*				2		4	7				6	3		10		7
8		5*		1		11		9						2	3	7				12	6	4		10		8
8*		5				11	12	9						2	3	4	7			1	6			10		9
8		5		1		11		9							3	4	7				6		2	10		10
		7		1	12	11	8	6				5	9			4			3	2				10*		11
		7		1		11	8	6			3	5	9			4				2				10		12
8		4		1		11		12				10	2	5		2		3			6			9*		13
8		9		1		11						10	2	5		7		3	4		6					14
8		12		1		11						5	10	2			7		4	6*	3			9		15
8				1		11		9				5*		2		10		4		6	3	12	7			16
8				1		11		9						10	2		7			4		3	6	5		17
8				1	12	11*		9						10	2	4	7				3	6	5			18
		12		1		11		9		8			10	2	3	7					6		4	5*		19
8		12		1		11		9*				5	10	2		7				3	6		4			20
8		7		1	12	11						5	10	2					3		6		4*	9		21
8		9		1		11							10	2				3			7		6	4	5	22
8		7		1				11					9	10	2				4		3		6		5	23
8	7	5		1				9*					12	2		11					3		6	4	10	24
8				1				7					9	10	2	3	11				6		4	5		25
	7*	10		1		11		12		9				2	3	8					6		4	5		26
		10		1		11	12	7	9				2*	3	8						6	4		5		27
				1		11		7	9	5*			2	3	8						6	4	12	10		28
				1		11	10	7	9				2	3	8						6	4	12	5*		29
		1				11*	10	7	9				2	8	5	3					6	4		12		30
	10	1				9	8	11					2	7	5	3					6	4				31
	8	1				9	11	12	10*	2			7	5	3						6	4				32
8	10	1				9	11	6*	12			2	5	7		3					4					33
8	10	1				11	9	6				2	7	5	3						4					34
8	10	1				11	9	6				2	7	5	3*	12					4					35
8	10	1				11	9		12			2	7	5	3*	6					4					36
8	11*	1				9	12			10	2		7	5	3						6	4				37
8	11	1				9				10	2		7	5	3						6	4				38
8	11	1				9				10	2		7	5	3						6	4				39
8	11	1				12	9	6*		10	2		7	5	3							4				40
8	11	1				9				10	2	7	5	3						6	4					41
8	11	1				12	9			10	2	4	7	5	3*		6									42

31	2	12	19	41		1	26	2	11	26	14	15	22	38	22	38	2	23	25	1	32	16	20	21	1	
	4		1	3			5			2	3	2						1		1		4	1	1		
11		6	7				8		5	2	4	1	1	3			10			1			2	2		

1 own-goal

Archibald	Ardiles	Brazil	Brooke	Clemence	Corbett	Crook	Crooks	Dick	Falco	Galvin	Gibson	Hazard	Hoddle	Hughton	Lacy	Mabbutt	Mazzon	Miller	O'Reilly	Parks	Perryman	Price	Roberts	Villa	Webster	No.
8		7		1		11						9*	5	2		12			3		6		4	10		3
	7	12		1		11	10*		9				2	3	8						6		4	5		4
				1		11		7	9	10	12	2	3	8							6	4		5*		5
1	1		1	3		2	2		1	3	2		3	2	2		1		3	1	2	3				
		1							1					1					1							
		1				1			1																	

8		5		1		11*		12		9			2	3	7					6		4	10			2
	7			1		11	8*		6		5	9	12	4	3					2			10			2
8		9		1		11				4	10	2	5	7		3			6							3
8				1		11		9				10	2	7			4		3	6	5					4
8	7	12		1		11				9		10	2	11			3		6	4	5*					5
4	1	3	5	4		1	1	1	3	3	4	3	5	2	4	2	3	2	4							
		1					1												1							
2		1		3			1				1												1			

| 8 | | | | 1 | | 11 | 13 | 9 | 5† | 10 | 2 | 6 | 7 | | 3 | 4* | | 12 | | | | | | | | |
| 1 | | 1 | | 1 | | 1 | | 1 | 1 | 1 | 1 | 1 | 1 | | 1 | 1 | | | | | | | | | | |

1983-84

Manager: Keith Burkinshaw

					Result		Attendance
1	Aug	27	(a)	Ipswich T	L	1-3 Archibald	26,562
2		29	(h)	Coventry C	D	1-1 Hoddle (pen)	35,454
3	Sep	3	(h)	West Ham U	L	0-2	38,042
4		7	(a)	West Brom A	D	1-1 Roberts	14,830
5		10	(a)	Leicester C	W	3-0 Stevens, Mabbutt, Crooks	15,886
6		17	(h)	Everton	L	1-2 Falco	29,125
7		24	(a)	Watford	W	3-2 Hughton, Hoddle, Archibald	21,056
8	Oct	2	(h)	Nottingham F	W	2-1 Stevens, Archibald	30,596
9		15	(a)	Wolves	W	3-2 Archibald 2, Falco	12,523
10		22	(h)	Birmingham C	W	1-0 Archibald	18,937
11		29	(h)	Notts C	W	1-0 Archibald	29,198
12	Nov	5	(a)	Stoke C	D	1-1 Falco	14,726
13		12	(h)	Liverpool	D	2-2 Archibald, Hoddle (pen)	44,348
14		19	(a)	Luton T	W	4-2 Dick, Archibald 2, Cooke	17,275
15		26	(h)	Queen's Park R	W	3-2 Archibald, Falco 2	38,789
16	Dec	3	(a)	Norwich C	L	1-2 Dick	21,987
17		10	(h)	Southampton	D	0-0	29,711
18		16	(a)	Manchester U	L	2-4 Brazil, Falco	33,616
19		26	(h)	Arsenal	L	2-4 Roberts, Archibald	38,756
20		27	(a)	Aston Villa	D	0-0	30,125
21		31	(a)	West Ham U	L	1-4 Stevens	30,939
22	Jan	2	(h)	Watford	L	2-3 Hughton, Hoddle (pen)	32,495
23		14	(h)	Ipswich T	W	2-0 Roberts, Falco	25,832
24		21	(a)	Everton	L	1-2 Archibald	17,990
25	Feb	4	(a)	Nottingham F	D	2-2 Hughton, Falco	21,482
26		8	(h)	Sunderland	W	3-0 Perryman, Archibald 2	19,327
27		11	(a)	Leicester C	W	3-2 Archibald, Falco, Galvin	28,410
28		21	(a)	Notts C	D	0-0	7,943
29		25	(h)	Birmingham C	L	0-1	23,564
30	Mar	3	(h)	Stoke C	W	1-0 Falco (pen)	18,271
31		10	(a)	Liverpool	L	1-3 Stevens	36,718
32		17	(h)	West Brom A	L	0-1	22,385
33		24	(a)	Coventry C	W	4-2 Roberts, Hazard, Brazil 2 (1 pen)	12,847
34		31	(h)	Wolves	W	1-0 Hazard	19,296
35	Apr	7	(a)	Sunderland	D	1-1 Falco	15,433
36		14	(h)	Luton T	W	2-1 Roberts, Falco	25,390
37		18	(h)	Aston Villa	W	2-1 Roberts (pen), Mabbutt	18,668
38		21	(a)	Arsenal	L	2-3 Archibald 2	48,831
39		28	(a)	Queen's Park R	L	1-2 Archibald	24,937
40	May	5	(h)	Norwich C	W	2-0 Archibald, Falco	18,874
41		7	(a)	Southampton	L	0-5	21,141
42		12	(h)	Manchester U	D	1-1 Archibald	39,790

FINAL LEAGUE POSITION: 8th in Division One

Appearances
Sub Appearances
Goals

FA Cup

					Result		Attendance
3	Jan	7	(a)	Fulham	D	0-0	23,398
R		11	(h)	Fulham	W	2-0 Roberts, Archibald	32,898
4		28	(h)	Norwich C	D	0-0	37,792
R	Feb	1	(a)	Norwich C	L	1-2 Falco	26,811

Appearances
Sub Appearances
Goals

FL Cup

					Result		Attendance
2	Oct	5	(h)	Lincoln C	W	3-1 Galvin, Archibald, Houghton (og)	20,241
2		26	(a)	Lincoln C	L	1-2 Falco	12,239
3	Nov	9	(h)	Arsenal	L	1-2 Hoddle (pen)	48,200

Appearances
Sub Appearances
Goals

338

Player appearance and goalscoring grid (shirt numbers per match). Columns left-to-right: Archibald, Ardiles, Bowen, Brace, Brazil, Brooke, Clemence, Cockram, Cooke, Crook, Crooks, Culverhouse, Dick, Falco, Galvin, Hazard, Hoddle, Hughton, Mabbutt, Miller, O'Reilly, Parks, Perryman, Price, Roberts, Stevens, Thomas, Webster.

Arch	Ard	Bow	Brc	Brz	Brk	Clem	Cck	Cke	Crk	Crks	Culv	Dick	Falc	Galv	Haz	Hod	Hug	Mab	Mil	O'R	Park	Perr	Pri	Rob	Stev	Thom	Web	#
8					11	1						12	9	7*		10		3				6		4	5	2		1
8	2	11*				1						12	9			10	7					6		4	5	3		2
8						1					11		8	9	10*	2	7	12				6		4	5	3		3
					10	1					11		8	9		2	7	3				6		4	5			4
	12				10*	1					11		8	9		2	7	3				6		4	5			5
					12 10	1					11*		8	9		2	7	3				6	5	4				6
12					9	11*	1						8	3		10	2	7				6		4	5			7
8					11*	12	1						9	3		10	2	7				6		4	5			8
8					11	1							9	3		10	2	7				6	12	4*	5			9
8						1	11*						9	3		10	2	7	12			6		4	5			10
8					11*	1					12		9	3		10	2	7				6		4	5			11
8						1							9	11		10	2	7*	12			6		4	5	3		12
8		12				1				7*		9	11		10	2					6		4	5	3			13
8						1	11			7		9		10	2					6		4	5	3				14
8						1	7			11		9		10	2					6		4	5	3				15
8						1	7*			11		9		10	2				12		6		4	5	3			16
8*					11	12	1		7				9			10			2			6		4	5	3		17
	12				8	1					11	9	7*		10				2			6		4	5	3		18
8	7				9	1			3		11	12		10	2*						6		4	5			19
8					9	1					12	7*		10	11		2				6		4	5	3		20
8	7	3				1					11	9			2					6			5	10	4		21
8	2				12	1	11*					9		10	3		5			6		4	7				22
8	3						7	12				9	11	10*			5		1	6		4	2				23
8	3											9	11	10		7	5		1	6		4	2				24
8	10											9	11		3	7	5*		1	6		4	2	12			25
8	7											9	11	10	3		5		1	6		4	2				26
8	7*									12		9	11	10	3		5		1	6		4	2				27
	7			8							12	9	11*	10	3		4		1	6			5	2			28
8				9			7					11*	12	10	3		5		1	6		4	2				29
	7			8	12							11*	9	10	3		5		1	6		4	2				30
8				9					12			11*		10	3		5*			6		4	7	2			31
8	7			9		1				12			3	11	5*					6		4	10	2			32
8				9		1				11			7		3		5			6		4	10	2			33
				8						9			11	7	3		5		1	6		4	10	2			34
				10	12					9			11	7	3		5		1	6		4	8*	2			35
8				9						11*		7		3	10	5		1	6		4	12	2				36
8				9						11		7*		3	10	5		1	6		4	12	2				37
8									10* 11			9		3	7	5		1	6		4	2					38
8				9						11		7		3	10	5		1	6		4	2					39
8						7			12			9*	11		3	10	5		1	6		4	2				40
	3	12	10	8*	1		9	7	6	11		2						5	4				4				41
8				9						11			3	7	5			1	6		4	10	2				42
31	**8**	**6**		**17**	**7**	**26**	**2**	**9**	**3**	**6**	**1**	**10**	**32**	**30**	**9**	**24**	**34**	**21**	**20**	**9**	**16**	**41**	**1**	**35**	**37**	**26**	**1**	
1	1	1	1	2	5					4	1	1	4		2				1	3		1			3	1		
21				3				1		1		2	13	1	2	4	3	2				1		6	4			

Arch	Ard	Bow	Brc	Brz	Brk	Clem	Cck	Cke	Crk	Crks	Culv	Dick	Falc	Galv	Haz	Hod	Hug	Mab	Mil	O'R	Park	Perr	Pri	Rob	Stev	Thom	Web	#
	3			8	7	1*				12			9		11	10			5		6		4	2				3
8	3						7						9	11		10			5		1	6		4	2			R
8	3												9*	11	12	10		7	5		1	6		4	2			4
8	10												9*	11	12		3	7	5		1	6		4	2			R
3	1	3			1	1	1			1			4	3	1	3	1	2	3	1	3	4		4	4			
						1										2												
1													1									1						

Arch	Ard	Bow	Brc	Brz	Brk	Clem	Cck	Cke	Crk	Crks	Culv	Dick	Falc	Galv	Haz	Hod	Hug	Mab	Mil	O'R	Park	Perr	Pri	Rob	Stev	Thom	Web	#
8					11*	1							9	3	12	10	2	7				6		4	5			2
8						1				11* 12			9	3		10	2	7				6		4	5			2
8		12				1							9	11		10	2					6	4*	7	5	3		3
3					1	3		1					3	3		3	3	2				3	1	3	3	1		
					1											1								1				
1													1	1		1												

I own-goal

1984-85

Manager: Peter Shreeve

1	Aug	25	(a)	Everton	W 4-1	Falco, Allen 2, Chiedozie	35,630
2		27	(h)	Leicester C	D 2-2	Roberts 2 (1 pen)	30,046
3	Sep	1	(h)	Norwich C	W 3-1	Chiedozie, Falco, Galvin	24,947
4		4	(a)	Sunderland	L 0-1		18,895
5		8	(a)	Sheffield W	L 1-2	Falco	33,421
6		15	(h)	Queen's Park R	W 5-0	Falco 2, Allen 2, Hazard	31,655
7		22	(a)	Aston Villa	W 1-0	Chiedozie	22,409
8		29	(h)	Luton T	W 4-2	Roberts (pen), Perryman, Falco, Hazard	30,204
9	Oct	6	(a)	Southampton	L 0-1		21,825
10		12	(h)	Liverpool	W 1-0	Crooks	28,599
11		20	(a)	Manchester U	L 0-1		54,516
12		27	(h)	Stoke C	W 4-0	Roberts (pen), Chiedozie, Allen 2	23,477
13	Nov	3	(h)	West Brom A	L 2-3	Chiedozie, Hazard	24,494
14		10	(a)	Nottingham F	W 2-1	Hazard, Galvin	21,306
15		17	(a)	Ipswich T	W 3-0	Mabbutt, Allen, Hoddle	21,894
16		24	(h)	Chelsea	D 1-1	Falco	31,197
17	Dec	1	(a)	Coventry C	D 1-1	Falco	14,518
18		8	(h)	Newcastle U	W 3-1	Roberts (pen), Falco 2	29,695
19		15	(a)	Watford	W 2-1	Falco, Crooks	24,225
20		22	(a)	Norwich C	W 2-1	Galvin, Crooks	17,682
21		26	(h)	West Ham U	D 2-2	Mabbutt, Crooks	37,186
22		29	(h)	Sunderland	W 2-0	Hoddle, Crooks	26,930
23	Jan	1	(a)	Arsenal	W 2-1	Falco, Crooks	48,714
24		12	(a)	Queen's Park R	D 2-2	Falco, Crooks	27,404
25	Feb	2	(a)	Luton T	D 2-2	Roberts, Falco	17,511
26		23	(a)	West Brom A	W 1-0	Falco	15,418
27	Mar	2	(a)	Stoke C	W 1-0	Crooks	12,552
28		12	(h)	Manchester U	L 1-2	Falco	42,918
29		16	(a)	Liverpool	W 1-0	Crooks	43,852
30		23	(h)	Southampton	W 5-1	Ardiles, Falco, Hoddle, Crooks, Brooke	33,772
31		30	(h)	Aston Villa	L 0-2		27,971
32	Apr	3	(h)	Everton	L 1-2	Roberts	48,108
33		6	(a)	West Ham U	D 1-1	Ardiles	24,435
34		13	(a)	Leicester C	W 2-1	Falco, Hoddle	15,609
35		17	(h)	Arsenal	L 0-2		40,399
36		20	(h)	Ipswich T	L 2-3	Leworthy 2	20,348
37		27	(a)	Chelsea	D 1-1	Galvin	26,310
38	May	4	(h)	Coventry C	W 4-2	Falco 2, Hoddle, Hughton	16,711
39		6	(a)	Newcastle U	W 3-2	Leworthy, Hoddle, Crook	29,702
40		11	(h)	Watford	L 1-5	Hoddle (pen)	23,167
41		14	(h)	Sheffield W	W 2-0	Falco, Hoddle (pen)	15,669
42		17	(h)	Nottingham F	W 1-0	Falco	20,075

FINAL LEAGUE POSITION: 3rd in Division One

Appearances
Sub Appearances
Goals

FA Cup

3	Jan	5	(h)	Charlton A	D 1-1	Crooks	29,029
R		23	(a)	Charlton A	W 2-1	Falco, Galvin	21,409
4		27	(a)	Liverpool	L 0-1		27,905

Appearances
Sub Appearances
Goals

FL Cup

2	Sep	26	(a)	Halifax T	W 5-1	Falco 2, Crooks 3	7,027
2	Oct	9	(h)	Halifax T	W 4-0	Hughton, Hazard 2, Crooks	14,802
3		31	(h)	Liverpool	W 1-0	Allen	38,690
4	Nov	21	(a)	Sunderland	D 0-0		27,421
R	Dec	5	(h)	Sunderland	L 1-2	Roberts (pen)	25,835

Appearances
Sub Appearances
Goals

340

Main table

Allen	Ardiles	Bowen	Brooke	Chiedozie	Clemence	Crook	Crooks	Dick	Falco	Galvin	Hazard	Hoddle	Hughton	Leworthy	Mabbutt	Miller	Perryman	Roberts	Stevens	Thomas	#
9				7	1				8	11		10*	3		12	5	6	4	2		1
9				7	1				8	11		10*	3		12	5	6	4	2		2
9				7*	1				8	11		10	3		12	5	6	4	2		3
9				7	1				8	11		10*	3			5	6	4	2	12	4
9				7	1				8*	11		10	3		12	5	6	4	2		5
9				7	1				8*	11		10	3		12	5	6	4	2		6
				7	1		11		8	9		10	3		4	5	6		2		7
				7	1		11		8	9		10	3			5	6	4	2		8
				7	1		11		8	9		10	3*		12	5	6	4	2		9
				7*	1		11		8	9		10	3		12	5	6	4	2		10
					1		11*		8	9		10	12	3	7	5	6	4	2		11
9				7	1				8	11	12	10	3			5*	6	4	2		12
9				7	1				8	11	10	12	3			5	6	4	2*		13
9				7*	1				8	11	10	12	3			5	6	4	2		14
9				7	1				8		11	10	3			5	6	4	2		15
9				7	1				8	11	10		3			5	6	4	2		16
9				7	1				8	11*		10	3			5	6	4	2		17
				7	1				8	9*		10	3			5	6	4	2		18
				7	1		11*		8	9		10	3			5	6	4	2	12	19
				7	1		11*		8	9	12	10	3			5	6	4	2		20
				7	1		11		8	9	12	10	3*			5	6	4	2		21
				7	1		11		8	9*		10	12	3		5	6	4	2		22
12				7	1		11		8	9		10*	3			5	6	4	2		23
	12			7*	1		11		8	9		10	3			5	6	4	2		24
				7*	1		11		8	9	12	10	3			5	6	4	2		25
				7	1		11	9	8		12	10	3			5*	6	4	2		26
				7	1		11	9	8			10	3			5	6	4	2		27
			7		1		11		8	9	12	10	3			5	6	4	2*		28
				7*	1		11		8	9	12	10	3			5	6	4	2		29
	7*			12	1		11		8	9		10	3			5	6	4	2		30
	7*	3		12	1	4	11		8	9		10				5	6		2		31
	7	3		12	1		11*		8	9		10				5	6	4	2		32
	7	3		12	1				8	9*		10				5	6	4	2		33
	7	3		12	1		11*		8	9		10				5	6	4	2		34
	7	3		5	1				8	11*	12	10		9			6	4	2		35
	7	3		12	1				8	11		10		9		5*	6	4	2		36
	7	3*		12	1				8	11		10		9		5	6	4	2		37
	7				1				8	11		10	3	9		5	6	4	2		38
	7*			12	1				8	11		10	3	9		5	6	4	2		39
	7				1				8	11		10	3	9	12	5*	6	4	2		40
	7*			12	1				8	11		10	3	9		5	6	4	2		41
					1	7			8	11		10	3	9		5	6	4	2		42
12	**10**	**6**	**1**	**31**	**42**	**2**	**22**	**2**	**42**	**38**	**15**	**26**	**29**	**6**	**15**	**39**	**42**	**40**	**28**	**14**	
1	1	3	3	3							8	2	2		10					2	
7	2			1			5	1	10	22	4	4	8	1	3	2		1	7		

Lower table (cup)

Allen	Ardiles	Bowen	Brooke	Chiedozie	Clemence	Crook	Crooks	Dick	Falco	Galvin	Hazard	Hoddle	Hughton	Leworthy	Mabbutt	Miller	Perryman	Roberts	Stevens	Thomas	#
				7	1		11		8	9*		10	12	3		5	6	4	2		3
				7	1		11		8	9		10	3			5	6	4	2		R
				7	1		11		8	9		10*	3		12	5	6	4	2		4
				3	3		3		3	3		3	2	1		3	3	3	3		
													1		1						
												1					1	1			

Lower table (cup)

Allen	Ardiles	Bowen	Brooke	Chiedozie	Clemence	Crook	Crooks	Dick	Falco	Galvin	Hazard	Hoddle	Hughton	Leworthy	Mabbutt	Miller	Perryman	Roberts	Stevens	Thomas	#
				7	1		11		8	9		10	3			5	6	4	2		2
				7	1		11		8	9	10		3		12	5	6*	4	2		2
9				7	1				8	11	12	10*	3			5	6	4	2		3
9				7	1				8		11	10	3			5	6	4	2		4
9*				7	1				8	11		10	3		12	5	6	4	2		R
3				5	5		2		5	3	3	3	4		2	5	5	4	5	1	
												1			2						
1									4	2		2	1					1			

1985-86

Manager: Peter Shreeve

1	Aug	17	(h)	Watford	W 4-0	P.Allen, Falco, Waddle 2		29,884
2		21	(a)	Oxford U	D 1-1	Thomas		10,634
3		24	(a)	Ipswich T	L 0-1			17,758
4		26	(h)	Everton	L 0-1			29,720
5		31	(a)	Manchester C	L 1-2	Miller		27,789
6	Sep	4	(h)	Chelsea	W 4-1	Roberts, Miller, Falco, Chiedozie		23,642
7		7	(h)	Newcastle U	W 5-1	Falco, Chiedozie 2, Hoddle, Hazard		23,883
8		14	(a)	Nottingham F	W 1-0	Hughton		17,554
9		21	(h)	Sheffield W	W 5-1	Falco 2, Hoddle, Waddle 2		23,601
10		28	(a)	Liverpool	L 1-4	Chiedozie		41,521
11	Oct	5	(a)	West Brom A	D 1-1	Waddle		12,040
12		20	(a)	Coventry C	W 3-2	Falco, Hoddle (pen), Chiedozie		13,545
13		26	(h)	Leicester C	L 1-3	Falco		17,944
14	Nov	2	(a)	Southampton	L 0-1			17,440
15		9	(h)	Luton T	L 1-3	Cooke		19,163
16		16	(a)	Manchester U	D 0-0			54,575
17		23	(h)	Queen's Park R	D 1-1	Mabbutt		20,334
18		30	(a)	Aston Villa	W 2-1	Mabbutt, Falco		14,099
19	Dec	7	(h)	Oxford U	W 5-1	Falco, C.Allen 2, Hoddle, Waddle		17,698
20		14	(a)	Watford	L 0-1			16,327
21		21	(h)	Ipswich T	W 2-0	C.Allen, Hoddle		18,845
22		26	(h)	West Ham U	W 1-0	Perryman		33,835
23		28	(a)	Chelsea	L 0-2			37,115
24	Jan	1	(a)	Arsenal	D 0-0			45,109
25		11	(h)	Nottingham F	L 0-3			19,043
26		18	(h)	Manchester C	L 0-2			17,009
27	Feb	1	(a)	Everton	L 0-1			33,178
28		8	(h)	Coventry C	L 0-1			13,135
29		22	(a)	Sheffield W	W 2-1	Chiedozie, Howells		23,232
30	Mar	2	(h)	Liverpool	L 1-2	Waddle		16,436
31		8	(h)	West Brom A	W 5-0	Mabbutt, Falco 2, Galvin, Waddle		10,841
32		15	(a)	Birmingham C	W 2-1	Stevens, Waddle		9,394
33		22	(a)	Newcastle U	D 2-2	Hoddle, Waddle		30,615
34		29	(h)	Arsenal	W 1-0	Stevens		33,427
35		31	(a)	West Ham U	L 1-2	Ardiles		27,497
36	Apr	5	(a)	Leicester C	W 4-1	Bowen, Falco 3		9,574
37		12	(a)	Luton T	D 1-1	C.Allen		13,141
38		16	(h)	Birmingham C	W 2-0	Chiedozie, Falco		9,359
39		19	(h)	Manchester U	D 0-0			32,357
40		26	(a)	Queen's Park R	W 5-2	Falco 2, C.Allen 2, Hoddle		17,768
41	May	3	(h)	Aston Villa	W 4-2	Falco 2, C.Allen 2		14,854
42		5	(h)	Southampton	W 5-3	Galvin 3, C.Allen, Waddle		13,036

FINAL LEAGUE POSITION: 10th in Division One

Appearances
Sub Appearances
Goals

FA Cup

3	Jan	4	(a)	Oxford U	D 1-1	Chiedozie		10,638
R		8	(h)	Oxford U	W 2-1*	Waddle, C.Allen		19,136
4		25	(a)	Notts C	D 1-1	C.Allen		17,546
R		29	(h)	Notts C	W 5-0	Chiedozie, Falco, C.Allen, Hoddle, Waddle		17,393
5	Mar	4	(h)	Everton	L 1-2	Falco		23,338

*After extra-time

Appearances
Sub Appearances
Goals

FL Cup

2	Sep	23	(a)	Orient	L 0-2			13,828
2	Oct	30	(h)	Orient	W 4-0	Roberts 2, Galvin, Waddle		21,046
3	Nov	6	(h)	Wimbledon	W 2-0	Leworthy, Mabbutt		16,899
4		20	(h)	Portsmouth	D 0-0			28,619
R		27	(a)	Portsmouth	D 0-0*			28,100
2R	Dec	10	(a)	Portsmouth	L 0-1			26,306

*After extra-time

Appearances
Sub Appearances
Goals

Screen Sport Super Cup

A	Oct	2	(h)	Southampton	W 2-1	Falco 2		11,549
A	Dec	3	(a)	Liverpool	L 0-2			14,855
A		17	(a)	Southampton	W 3-1	Falco, C.Allen, Leworthy		4,680
A	Jan	14	(h)	Liverpool	L 0-2			10,078
SF	Feb	5	(h)	Everton	D 0-0			7,548
SF	Mar	19	(a)	Everton	L 1-3*	Falco		12,008

*After extra-time

Appearances
Sub Appearances
Goals

Season appearance and scoring grid. Shirt numbers per match; `*` = substituted, `†` = sent off/other, sub numbers 12–14.

League (Matches 1–42)

Allen C	Allen P	Ardiles	Bowen	Chiedozie	Clemence	Cooke	Crook	Dick	Falco	Galvin	Hazard	Hoddle	Howells	Hughton	Jennings	Leworthy	Mabbutt	Miller	Perryman	Roberts	Stevens	Thomas	Waddle	#
4	7				1				8	11	10			3			12		5	6*		2	9	1
4	7				1				8	11	10			3					5	6		2	9	2
6	7				1				8	11*	10			3			12		5		4	2	9	3
6	7*				1		12		8	11		10		3					5		4	2	9	4
6	7		12		1				8	11*		10		3					5		4	2	9	5
6	7		9		1				8			10*		3			12		5		4	2	11	6
6	7		9		1				8*		12	10		3					5		4	2	11	7
6*	7		9		1				8			10		3					5	12	4	2	11	8
6	7*		9		1				8			10		3			12		5		4	2	11	9
5	7*		9		1				8			10		3			12		5	6	4	2	11	10
9	7				1				8*			10		3			12		5	6	4	2	11	11
	7*		12		1				8		9	10		3					5	6	4	2	11	12
	7				1				8		9	10		3					5	6	4	2	11	13
		7			1		12		8	9*				3		10			5	6	4	2	11	14
					1		12	7*	8			10		3		9			5	6	4	2	11	15
	7				1				8		9	10		3					5	6	4	2	11	16
	7				1				8		9	10		3					5	6	4	2	11	17
9	7				1				8			10		3					5	6	4	2	11	18
9	12	7			1				8			10		3					5	6	4*	2	11	19
9*	7	12			1				8	11		10		3					5	6	4	2		20
9	12				1				8			10*		3					5	6	4	2	11	21
9	12	7*			1				8			10		3					5	6	4	2	11	22
9	7	12			1				8			10		3					5	6	4	2*	11	23
9		7			1				8			10		3					5	6	4	2	11	24
12	8	7	9		1							10		3					5	6	4	2	11*	25
9*	7				1				8					3		10			5	6	4	2	11	26
9*	12		7		1				8			10		3			4	5	6			2	11	27
8		7			1		12	9				10					4	5	6	3*	2		11	28
	2	7			1				8				9				4	5	6		10	3	11	29
	2	7			1				8			10					4	5	6	9	3		11	30
12	2				1				8	9*		10					7	5	4	6	3		11	31
	2				1				8	9		10					7	5	4	6	3		11	32
	2*	12			1				8	9		10					7	5	4	6	3		11	33
	2				1				8	9		10					7	5	4	6	3		11	34
12	2	10*			1				8	9							7	5	4	6	3		11	35
10	2	7*	6	12	1				8	9							4	5				3	11	36
10	2				1				8	9							4	5			6		11	37
9	2		12		1				8*	11				3			4	5	10	6				38
9*			12		1				8	11				3			7	5	4	6	2			39
9			12		1				8	6				10			7	5		4	2	3	11*	40
9					1				8	6				10			7	5		4		2	11	41
9					1				8	6			10*				7	5		4	12	2	11	42
16	29	20	1	13	42		1	1	40	23	3	31	1	33		2	29	29	22	32	28	27	39	—
3	4	3	1	5		2	3				1						3	3		1		1		—
9	1	1	1	7		1			19	4	1	7	1	1			3	2	1	1	2	1	11	—

League Cup

Allen C	Allen P	Ardiles	Bowen	Chiedozie	Clemence	Cooke	Crook	Dick	Falco	Galvin	Hazard	Hoddle	Howells	Hughton	Jennings	Leworthy	Mabbutt	Miller	Perryman	Roberts	Stevens	Thomas	Waddle	Rd
9*	8	7			1		12					10		3					5	6	4	2	11	3
12	8	7*	9		1							10		3					5	6	4	2	11	R
8	7*			12	1			9				10		3			4	5	6			2	11	4
9*	12	7			1				8			10		3			4	5	6			2	11	R
	2			12	1				8			10				7	5*	6	4	9	3		11	5
3	4	2		2	5			3				5		4	5		3	5	3	5	1	5	5	—
1	1			3																				—
3				2				2			1							2						—

FA Cup

Allen C	Allen P	Ardiles	Bowen	Chiedozie	Clemence	Cooke	Crook	Dick	Falco	Galvin	Hazard	Hoddle	Howells	Hughton	Jennings	Leworthy	Mabbutt	Miller	Perryman	Roberts	Stevens	Thomas	Waddle	Rd
6	7		9		1				8			10		3					5		4	2	11	2
	12				1			7*	8	9		10		3					5	6	4	2	11	2
					1			7*	8			10		3	12	9		5	6	4	2		11	3
	7				1		12		8	9*		10		3					5	6	4	2	11	4
	7	10*			1				8	9				3					5	6	4	2	11	R
9	12	7*			1				8			10		3					5	6	4	2	11	2R
1	3	3		2	6		1		6	3		5		6			5	2	4	6	5	2	6	—
1	1							1							1							1		—
								1									1		2			1		—

A / SF

Allen C	Allen P	Ardiles	Bowen	Chiedozie	Clemence	Cooke	Crook	Dick	Falco	Galvin	Hazard	Hoddle	Howells	Hughton	Jennings	Leworthy	Mabbutt	Miller	Perryman	Roberts	Stevens	Thomas	Waddle	Rd
9*	5	7†		13	1				8			10		3			12			6	4	2	11	A
9	7†	13			1				8			10		3			12		5	6*	4	2	11	A
9†	11	7*			1		12					3		13		5			6	4	10	2		A
9	7			8			12			11*				3	1	10	5	6	4	2				A
9	13				1		7		8†						12		4	5	6	3*	2		11	SF
13	4		12		1		10†		8	9							7	5		6	2*		11	SF
5	5	2		3	5		1		5	2		2		5	1		5	3	5	5	5	3	4	—
1	1	1	1	1		2									1	1					1			—
1									4						1									—

1986-87

Manager: David Pleat

1	Aug	23	(a)	Aston Villa	W 3-0	C.Allen 3	24,712
2		25	(h)	Newcastle U	D 1-1	C.Allen	25,381
3		30	(h)	Manchester C	W 1-0	Roberts	23,164
4	Sep	2	(a)	Southampton	L 0-2		17,911
5		6	(a)	Arsenal	D 0-0		44,703
6		13	(h)	Chelsea	L 1-3	C.Allen (pen)	28,202
7		20	(a)	Leicester C	W 2-1	C.Allen 2	13,141
8		27	(h)	Everton	W 2-0	C.Allen 2	28,007
9	Oct	4	(h)	Luton T	D 0-0		22,738
10		11	(a)	Liverpool	W 1-0	C.Allen	43,139
11		18	(h)	Sheffield W	D 1-1	C.Allen	26,876
12		25	(a)	Queen's Park R	L 0-2		18,579
13	Nov	1	(h)	Wimbledon	L 1-2	M.Thomas	21,820
14		8	(a)	Norwich C	L 1-2	Claesen	22,019
15		15	(h)	Coventry C	W 1-0	C.Allen	20,255
16		22	(a)	Oxford U	W 4-2	C.Allen 2, Waddle 2	12,143
17		29	(h)	Nottingham F	L 2-3	C.Allen 2	30,042
18	Dec	7	(a)	Manchester U	D 3-3	Mabbutt, C.Allen, Moran (og)	35,267
19		13	(h)	Watford	W 2-1	Gough, Hoddle	23,137
20		20	(a)	Chelsea	W 2-0	C.Allen 2	21,576
21		26	(h)	West Ham U	W 4-0	Hodge, C.Allen 2, Waddle	39,019
22		27	(a)	Coventry C	L 3-4	C.Allen 2, Claesen	22,175
23	Jan	1	(a)	Charlton A	W 2-0	Claesen, Galvin	19,744
24		4	(h)	Arsenal	L 1-2	M.Thomas	37,723
25		24	(h)	Aston Villa	W 3-0	Hodge 2, Claesen	19,121
26	Feb	14	(h)	Southampton	W 2-0	Hodge, Gough	22,066
27		25	(h)	Leicester C	W 5-0	C.Allen 2 (1 pen), P.Allen, Claesen 2	16,038
28	Mar	7	(h)	Queen's Park R	W 1-0	C.Allen (pen)	21,071
29		22	(h)	Liverpool	W 1-0	Waddle	32,763
30		25	(a)	Newcastle U	D 1-1	Hoddle	30,836
31		28	(a)	Luton T	L 1-3	Waddle	13,447
32	Apr	4	(h)	Norwich C	W 3-0	C.Allen 3	22,400
33		7	(a)	Sheffield W	W 1-0	C.Allen	19,488
34		15	(a)	Manchester C	D 1-1	Claesen	21,460
35		18	(h)	Charlton A	W 1-0	C.Allen	26,926
36		20	(a)	West Ham U	L 1-2	C.Allen	23,972
37		22	(a)	Wimbledon	D 2-2	Claesen, Bowen	7,917
38		25	(h)	Oxford U	W 3-1	P.Allen, Waddle, Hoddle	20,064
39	May	2	(a)	Nottingham F	L 0-2		19,837
40		4	(h)	Manchester U	W 4-0	M.Thomas 2, C.Allen (pen), P.Allen	36,692
41		9	(a)	Watford	L 0-1		20,024
42		11	(a)	Everton	L 0-1		28,287

FINAL LEAGUE POSITION: 3rd in Division One

Appearances
Sub Appearances
Goals

FA Cup

3	Jan	10	(h)	Scunthorpe U	W 3-2	Mabbutt, Waddle, Claesen	19,339
4		31	(h)	Crystal P	W 4-0	Mabbutt, C.Allen (pen), Claesen, O'Reilly (og)	29,603
5	Feb	21	(h)	Newcastle U	W 1-0	C.Allen (pen)	38,033
6	Mar	15	(a)	Wimbledon	W 2-0	Waddle, Hoddle	15,636
SF	Apr	11	(n*)	Watford	W 4-1	Hodge 2, C.Allen, P.Allen	46,151
F	May	16	(n†)	Coventry C	L 2-3‡	C.Allen, Mabbutt	98,000

*Played at Villa Park, Birmingham. †Played at Wembley Stadium. ‡After extra-time.

Appearances
Sub Appearances
Goals

FL Cup

2	Sep	23	(a)	Barnsley	W 3-2	Roberts, C.Allen, Waddle	10,079
2	Oct	8	(h)	Barnsley	W 5-3	Close, Hoddle 2, Galvin, C.Allen	12,299
3		29	(h)	Birmingham C	W 5-0	Roberts, C.Allen 2, Hoddle, Waddle	15,542
4	Nov	26	(a)	Cambridge U	W 3-1	C.Allen, Close, Waddle	10,033
5	Jan	27	(a)	West Ham U	D 1-1	C.Allen	28,648
R	Feb	2	(h)	West Ham U	W 5-0	C.Allen 3 (1 pen), Hoddle, Claesen	41,995
SF		8	(a)	Arsenal	W 1-0	C.Allen	41,256
SF	Mar	1	(h)	Arsenal	L 1-2‡	C.Allen	37,099
R		4	(h)	Arsenal	L 1-2	C.Allen	41,005

‡After extra-time.

Appearances
Sub Appearances
Goals

Squad appearance and scoring grid (shirt numbers by match; `*` / `†` denote substitutions).

Competition 1

Allen C	Allen P	Ardiles	Bowen	Chiedozie	Claesen	Clemence	Close	Falco	Galvin	Gough	Gray	Hoddle	Hodge	Howells	Hughton	Mabbutt	Miller	Moncur	Moran	O'Shea	Parks	Polston	Roberts	Ruddock	Samways	Stevens	Stimson	Thomas D	Thomas M	Waddle	No.
7	12					1		8	11	5		10*				6							4			2			3	9	1
7						1		8	11	5		10				6							4			2			3	9	2
7			8			1			11	5		10				6							4			2			3	9	3
7						1		8	11	5		10				6							4*			2		12	3	9	4
7	12					1		8*	11	5		10				6							4			2			3	9	5
7	12					1		8	11	5*		10				6							4			2			3	9	6
7	11	12				1				5		10				6							4			2*		8	3	9	7
7	8					1		12	11*	5		10				6							4			2			3	9	8
	8*	12				1			11	5		10		7		6							4			2			3	9	9
7	12				8	1			11*	5		10				6							4			2			3	9	10
7	11				8	1				5		10				6							4			2			3	9	11
7	11	12			8	1				5		10				6							4			2*			3	9	12
7	11	12			8	1				5		10				6							4			2*			3	9	13
7	11				8	1				5		10			2*	6							4						3	9	14
7	11	12			8	1				5		10				6							4						3	9	15
7	2	11			8*	1				5		10				6							4					12	3	9	16
7	2	11*				1	8					10				6						5	4					12	3	9	17
7	2	11*				1		8		5		10				6							4					12	3	9	18
7	8	12				1			11*	5		10				6							4			2			3	9	19
7	8	4				1			11	5		10				6	1									2			3	9	20
7	8	12				1			11	5		10	4			6										2			3*	9	21
7	8	3*			12	1			11	5		10	4			6										2				9	22
7	8				11	1			12	5		10	4*			6	3									2				9	23
7	8	4*			12	1			11	5		10				6										2			3	9	24
7	8				11*	1			12	5		10	4			6										2			3	9	25
7	8	11*			12	1				5		10	4			6										2			3	9	26
7	8				11	1				5			4			6									10	2			3	9	27
7	8				12	1			11	5			4			6									10	2*			3	9	28
7	8	11				1				5		10	4			6										2			3	9	29
7	8	11				1				5		10	4			6										2			3	9	30
7	8	12			11	1				5		10	4*			6										2			3	9	31
7	8*				11	1			12	5		10	4		2	6													3	9	32
7	8				11*	1				5		10	4			6		12								2			3	9	33
7	8			12	11	1				5			4			6										2*			3	9	34
7	8	9*			11	1			12	5			4		2							6							3		35
7	8				12	1			11*	5		10	4		2							6							3	9	36
12	8	4	10		9*	1			11	5								7		2		6							3		37
7*	8	11			12	1				5		10	4		2	6													3	9	38
	8	11			10	1			7*	5			4		2	6								6	12				3	9*	39
7	8	11			12	1				5		10	4		2	6													3	9	40
7	8	11*			12	1				5		10	4			6									2				3	9	41
		9			12					8			2			10	7*			10	7*	1	5	6	11	4	3				42
38	34	15	1	1	18	40	1	5	20	40	1	35	19	1	9	37	2	1	1	1	2	6	17	4	1	20	1	13	39	39	—
1	3	9	1		8				1	1			4				1					1			1			1		4	—
33	3				1	8			1	2		3	4			1						1			1				4	6	—

1 own-goal

Competition 2

Allen C	Allen P	Ardiles	Bowen	Chiedozie	Claesen	Clemence	Close	Falco	Galvin	Gough	Gray	Hoddle	Hodge	Howells	Hughton	Mabbutt	Miller	Moncur	Moran	O'Shea	Parks	Polston	Roberts	Ruddock	Samways	Stevens	Stimson	Thomas D	Thomas M	Waddle	Rd
7	8				11	1				5		10	4			6										2			3	9	3
7	8*				13	1			11†	5		10	4			6									12	2			3	9	4
7	8	11			13	1				5		10	4*			6									12	2			3	9†	5
7	8	11†			12	1				5		10	4			6									13	2*			3	9	6
7*	8†	11			12	1				5		10	4		2	6									13			3	9	SF
7	8	11†			12	1				5		10	4		2*	6									13			3	9	F
6	6	4			1	6			1	6		6	6		2	6									1	4		3	6	6	—
					5																				1	4					—
4	1				2				1	2		3																	2		—

1 own-goal

Competition 3

Allen C	Allen P	Ardiles	Bowen	Chiedozie	Claesen	Clemence	Close	Falco	Galvin	Gough	Gray	Hoddle	Hodge	Howells	Hughton	Mabbutt	Miller	Moncur	Moran	O'Shea	Parks	Polston	Roberts	Ruddock	Samways	Stevens	Stimson	Thomas D	Thomas M	Waddle	Rd
7	11					1		12		5		10*				8	6						4			2			3	9	2
13	12	7				1	8		11†	5*		10				6							4			2			3	9	2
7	11				8	1				5		10				6	12						4			2			3*	9	3
7†	2	11				1	8			5*		10				6						12	4			13			3	9	4
7	8	4				1			11	5		10				6										2			3	9	5
7	8	4			11	1				5		10				6										2			3	9	R
7	8	4			11*	1			12	5		10				6										2			3	9	SF
7	8	4*			11†	1			13	5		10				6									12	2			3	9	SF
7	8	4			11*	1			12	5						6									10	2			3	9	R
8	8	7			5	9	2		2	9		8				8	2						4			2	7		9	9	9	—
1	1						1	3							1						1	1				1			1		—
12					1		2	1		4												2							3		—

1987-88

Manager: David Pleat until October, Terry Venables from December

1	Aug	15	(a)	Coventry C	L	1-2 Mabbutt	23,947
2		19	(h)	Newcastle U	W	3-1 C.Allen, Waddle, Hodge	26,261
3		22	(h)	Chelsea	W	1-0 Claesen	37,079
4		29	(a)	Watford	D	1-1 C.Allen (pen)	19,073
5	Sep	1	(h)	Oxford U	W	3-0 C.Allen, Claesen 2	21,811
6		5	(a)	Everton	D	0-0	32,389
7		12	(h)	Southampton	W	2-1 C.Allen (pen), Claesen	24,728
8		19	(a)	West Ham U	W	1-0 Fairclough	27,750
9		26	(a)	Manchester U	L	0-1	47,601
10	Oct	3	(h)	Sheffield W	W	2-0 P.Allen, Claesen	24,311
11		10	(a)	Norwich C	L	1-2 Claesen	18,669
12		18	(h)	Arsenal	L	1-2 Claesen	36,680
13		24	(a)	Nottingham F	L	0-3	23,543
14		31	(h)	Wimbledon	L	0-3	22,282
15	Nov	4	(a)	Portsmouth	D	0-0	15,302
16		14	(h)	Queen's Park R	D	1-1 P.Allen	28,113
17		21	(a)	Luton T	L	0-2	10,091
18		28	(h)	Liverpool	L	0-2	47,362
19	Dec	13	(h)	Charlton A	L	0-1	20,392
20		20	(a)	Derby C	W	2-1 C.Allen, Claesen	17,593
21		26	(a)	Southampton	L	1-2 Fairclough	18,456
22		28	(h)	West Ham U	W	2-1 Fairclough, Waddle	39,456
23	Jan	1	(h)	Watford	W	2-1 C.Allen, Moran	25,235
24		2	(a)	Chelsea	D	0-0	29,317
25		16	(h)	Coventry C	D	2-2 C.Allen 2	25,650
26		23	(a)	Newcastle U	L	0-2	24,616
27	Feb	13	(a)	Oxford U	D	0-0	9,906
28		23	(h)	Manchester U	D	1-1 C.Allen	25,731
29		27	(a)	Sheffield W	W	3-0 C.Allen, P.Allen, Claesen	18,046
30	Mar	1	(h)	Derby C	D	0-0	15,986
31		6	(a)	Arsenal	L	1-2 C.Allen	37,143
32		9	(h)	Everton	W	2-1 Fairclough, Walsh	18,662
33		12	(h)	Norwich C	L	1-3 Claesen	19,322
34		19	(a)	Wimbledon	L	0-3	8,616
35		26	(h)	Nottingham F	D	1-1 Foster (og)	25,306
36	Apr	2	(h)	Portsmouth	L	0-1	18,616
37		4	(a)	Queen's Park R	L	0-2	14,738
38		23	(a)	Liverpool	L	0-1	44,798
39	May	2	(a)	Charlton A	D	1-1 Hodge	13,977
40		4	(h)	Luton T	W	2-1 Mabbutt, Hodge	15,437

FINAL LEAGUE POSITION: 13th in Division One

Appearances
Sub Appearances
Goals

FA Cup

3	Jan	9	(a)	Oldham A	W	4-2 Thomas, C.Allen 2, Waddle	16,931
4		30	(a)	Port Vale	L	1-2 Ruddock	20,045

Appearances
Sub Appearances
Goals

FL Cup

2	Sep	23	(a)	Torquay U	L	0-1	5,000
	Oct	7	(h)	Torquay U	W	3-0 Claesen 2, Cole (og)	20,970
3		28	(a)	Aston Villa	L	1-2 Ardiles	29,114

Appearances
Sub Appearances
Goals

Player appearance / shirt-number grid (values are shirt numbers worn in each match; final column is the match number).

Allen C	Allen P	Ardiles	Claesen	Clemence	Close	Fairclough	Fenwick	Gough	Gray	Hodge	Howells	Hughton	Mabbutt	Metgod	Mimms	Moncur	Moran	O'Shea	Parks	Polston	Ruddock	Samways	Statham	Stevens	Thomas	Waddle	Walsh	No.
7	8*	13	11†	1		5		4		10			6	12										2	3	9		1
7	8			1		5		4		10			6	11								12		2*	3	9		2
7	8	2	12	1		5		4		10			6	11*											3	9		3
7	8	2	11	1		5		4		10			6												3	9		4
7	8†	2	11	1		5		4		10			6	13								12			3*	9		5
7	8	2	11	1		5		4		10*			6	12											3	9		6
7	8	9	11	1		5		4		10			6	12										2*	3			7
7†	8	9	11	1		5		4		10				12			6*					13		2	3			8
	8	9†	11	1		5		4		10			6	13			7*					12		2	3			9
7*	8	9	11	1	12	5				10			6									4		2	3			10
	8	9*	11	1	7	5				10	12		6									4		2	3			11
13	8	4	11		7*	5				10†			6						1			12		2	3	9		12
7	8	9	11		12	5							6	13		2*			1			4†	10		3			13
7	8	9	11		12	5							6			2			1		13	4†	10		3*			14
12	8	9	11			5						3	6				7*		1			4	10	2				15
7	8	9	11*			5				10		3	6						1			4	12	2				16
7	8†	9				5	13			10		11	6						1			4		2*	12			17
7	8		12			5				10			6			2*			1		13	4†		11	3	9		18
7	8		11			5							6			2			1			4	10	3	9			19
7	8†	10	11			5						12	6*	13					1			4		2	3	9		20
7†		10				5				8	13	2		11					1		4*	12	6		3	9		21
	8	10	13			5		4		11		2	7†						1			12	6*		3	9		22
7	8	10				5	2	4		12			6	11*					1						3	9		23
7*	8†					5		4		10	12	2	6	11					1		13				3	9		24
7	8	10*				5		4			13	2	6	11†					1			12			3	9		25
7	8	10				5		4			13	2*	6	11†					1			12			3	9		26
7	8	11				5		4					6						1				10	2	3	9		27
7	8	10				5		4					6		1									2	3	9	11	28
7	8	12				5		4					6		1		9						10	2	3		11*	29
7	8	12				5		4					6		1		9*						10	2	3		11	30
7	8	9				5		4					6		1								10	2	3		11	31
7	8	9				5		4					6		1							12	10*	2	3		11	32
7	8	9	12			5		4					6		1								10*	2	3		11	33
7	8	9*				5		4		12			6		1								10	2	3		11	34
	8	11†				5		4*		9	13		6		1							12	10	2	3		7	35
	8	11				5		4		9†	12		6		1		3*					13	10	2			7	36
	8					5		4		9*	11†	3	6		1							12	10	2		13	7	37
12	8					5		4*		11			6		1								10	2	3	9	7	38
7*	8	12				5		4		11			6	13	1								10†	2	3	9		39
7†	8					5		4*			13	11	6	10	1							12		2	3	9		40
31	**39**	**26**	**19**	**11**	**2**	**40**	**17**	**9**		**25**	**3**	**12**	**37**	**5**	**13**	**3**	**9**		**16**		**3**	**21**	**14**	**18**	**35**	**21**	**11**	
3		2	5		5					1	1	8	1				7				2	4	1	2	2	5	4	
11	3		10			4				3			2				1								2	1		

I own-goal

Allen C	Allen P	Ardiles	Claesen	Clemence	Close	Fairclough	Fenwick	Gough	Gray	Hodge	Howells	Hughton	Mabbutt	Metgod	Mimms	Moncur	Moran	O'Shea	Parks	Polston	Ruddock	Samways	Statham	Stevens	Thomas	Waddle	Walsh	No.
7		10				5	8			4*	13	2	6				11†		1			12			3	9		3
7	8					5		10		12	2*	6					11		1			4			3	9		4
2	1	1				2	2	1		2	2	2	2				2		2			1			2	2		
										2													1					
2																	1								1	1		

Allen C	Allen P	Ardiles	Claesen	Clemence	Close	Fairclough	Fenwick	Gough	Gray	Hodge	Howells	Hughton	Mabbutt	Metgod	Mimms	Moncur	Moran	O'Shea	Parks	Polston	Ruddock	Samways	Statham	Stevens	Thomas	Waddle	Walsh	No.
	8	2		1		5		4		10	7		6	11*					12						3	9		2
	8	9	11	1	7	5				10			6	12							4*			2	3			
7	8	9	11			5				13	6	10†		12	1							4†		2	3			3
1	3	3	2	2	1	3		1		2	1	3	2	1			2		2			3		1	2	2	3	
												1										3						
		1	2											3														

I own-goal

1988-89

Manager: Terry Venables

1	Sep	3	(a)	Newcastle U	D 2-2	Fenwick, Waddle	32,977
2		10	(h)	Arsenal	L 2-3	Gascoigne, Waddle	32,621
3		17	(a)	Liverpool	D 1-1	Fenwick	40,929
4		24	(h)	Middlesbrough	W 3-2	Fenwick (pen), Waddle, Howells	23,427
5	Oct	1	(h)	Manchester U	D 2-2	Walsh, Waddle	29,318
6		8	(a)	Charlton A	D 2-2	Fenwick (pen), Allen	14,384
7		22	(a)	Norwich C	L 1-3	Fairclough	20,330
8		25	(h)	Southampton	L 1-2	Ray Wallace (og)	19,517
9		29	(a)	Aston Villa	L 1-2	Fenwick (pen)	26,238
10	Nov	5	(h)	Derby C	L 1-3	Stewart	22,868
11		12	(h)	Wimbledon	W 3-2	Butters, Fenwick (pen), Samways	23,589
12		20	(a)	Sheffield W	W 2-0	Stewart 2	15,386
13		23	(h)	Coventry C	D 1-1	Stewart	21,961
14		26	(h)	Queen's Park R	D 2-2	Gascoigne, Waddle	26,698
15	Dec	3	(a)	Everton	L 0-1		29,657
16		10	(h)	Millwall	W 2-0	Gascoigne, Waddle	27,660
17		17	(a)	West Ham U	W 2-0	Thomas, Mabbutt	28,365
18		26	(h)	Luton T	D 0-0		27,337
19		31	(h)	Newcastle U	W 2-0	Walsh, Waddle	27,739
20	Jan	2	(a)	Arsenal	L 0-2		45,129
21		15	(h)	Nottingham F	L 1-2	Waddle	16,903
22		21	(a)	Middlesbrough	D 2-2	Stewart 2	23,692
23	Feb	5	(a)	Manchester U	L 0-1		41,423
24		11	(h)	Charlton A	D 1-1	Stewart	22,803
25		21	(h)	Norwich C	W 2-1	Gascoigne, Waddle	19,120
26		25	(a)	Southampton	W 2-0	Nayim, Waddle	16,702
27	Mar	1	(h)	Aston Villa	W 2-0	Waddle 2	19,090
28		11	(a)	Derby C	D 1-1	Gascoigne	18,206
29		18	(a)	Coventry C	D 1-1	Waddle	17,156
30		22	(a)	Nottingham F	W 2-1	Howells, Samways	23,098
31		26	(h)	Liverpool	L 1-2	Fenwick (pen)	30,012
32		28	(a)	Luton T	W 3-1	Howells, Walsh, Gascoigne	11,146
33	Apr	1	(h)	West Ham U	W 3-0	Fenwick (pen), Nayim, Stewart	28,375
34		12	(h)	Sheffield W	D 0-0		17,270
35		15	(a)	Wimbledon	W 2-1	Waddle, Stewart	12,366
36		22	(h)	Everton	W 2-1	Walsh 2	28,568
37		29	(a)	Millwall	W 5-0	Walsh, Stewart 3, Samways	16,551
38	May	13	(a)	Queen's Park R	L 0-1		21,873

FINAL LEAGUE POSITION: 6th in Division One

Appearances
Sub Appearanc
Goals

FA Cup

3	Jan	7	(a)	Bradford C	L 0-1		15,917

Appearances
Sub Appearanc
Goals

League Cup

2	Sep	27	(a)	Notts C	D 1-1	Samways	9,269
	Oct	11	(h)	Notts C	W 2-1	Fenwick (pen), Gascoigne	14,953
3	Nov	1	(h)	Blackburn R	D 0-0		18,814
R		9	(a)	Blackburn R	W 2-1*	Thomas, Stewart	12,961
4		29	(a)	Southampton	L 1-2	Osman (og)	17,357

* After extra-time

Appearances
Sub Appearanc
Goals

Tottenham Hotspur — Football League appearances and goals

Allen	Bergsson	Butters	Fairclough	Fenwick	Gascoigne	Gray	Howells	Hughton	Mabbutt	Mimms	Moncur	Moran	Nayim	Polston J	Robson	Samways	Statham	Stevens	Stewart	Stimson	Thomas	Thorstvedt	Waddle	Walsh	No.
11			5	4	8†		13	3	6	1			12			2			10				9	7*	1
11			5	4	8		12		6	1			13		10†	2*					3		9	7	2
11			5	4	8		13	12	6	1					10	2					3		9†	7*	3
11			5	4	8		12		6	1			13		10	2*					3		9	7†	4
11				4	8*		12	5	6	1					10	2			13		3		9†	7	5
5				4	8		12		6	1					10	2			11*		3		9	7*	6
11			5	4	8				6	1					10*	2	7				3		9		7
11			5	4	8				6	1						2			10		3		9	7	8
11†			5	4	8		7*		6	1			12			2			10	13	3		9		9
11†			5	4	8		12		6	1		7*	13			2			10		3		9		10
	12		5	4	8				6	1		7	11			2*			10		3		9		11
13		2	5	4	8†		12		6	1		7*	11						10		3		9		12
13		2	5	4	8				6	1		7*	11†						10		3		9	12	13
11		2	5	4	8		13		6	1			12						10		3*		9	7†	14
11		2	5	4	8				6	1		7*							10		3		9	12	15
11		2	5	4	8				6	1									10		3		9	7	16
11		2	5	4	8†				6	1		13	12						10		3		9	7*	17
11		2	5	4	8†		13		6	1			12						10		3		9	7*	18
11	8	2	5	4			12		6	1									10		3		9	7*	19
11	8	2	5	4					6	1									10		3		9	7	20
11	8	2	5	4	13		12	3*	6										10			1	9	7†	21
11		2	5	4	8†		7*	3	6				13						10			1	9	12	22
11		2	5*	4	8		7†	3	6				12						10			1	9	13	23
11		2	5	4	8		7*	3	6										10			1	9	12	24
11		2			8		12	3	6			4	10*					5				1	9	7	25
11		2	5				12	3	6			4	10*						8			1	9	7	26
11		2	5	4				3	6				8						10			1	9	7	27
11		2		4	8			3	6			5*	13						10		12	1	9	7†	28
11		2		4	8*		12	3	6			5							10			1	9	7	29
11		2		4	8			3	6			5*	12						10			1	9	7	30
11		2		4	8			3	6			5*	12		13				10			1	9	7†	31
11		2	5	4	8			3	6										10			1	9	7	32
11		2	5	4	8		12	3	6										10			1	9	7	33
11	4	2	5		8			3	6										10			1	9	7	34
11		2	5	4	8			3	6										10			1	9	7	35
11†		2	5	4	8*		13	3	6				12						10			1	9	7	36
11		2	5	4*	8		13	3	6				12						10			1	9†	7	37
11†		2	5	4	8*			3	6				12		13				10			1	9	7	38
35	8	27	20	34	31		12	20	38	20		4	8		3	12	6	5	29		22	18	38	28	
2	1		1	1			15	1				1	4		3	3	2	7			1	1	3		
1				1	1		8	6					3		1				2		3		12	1	14 6	

1 own-goal

F.A. Cup

Allen	Bergsson	Butters	Fairclough	Fenwick	Gascoigne	Gray	Howells	Hughton	Mabbutt	Mimms	Moncur	Moran	Nayim	Polston J	Robson	Samways	Statham	Stevens	Stewart	Stimson	Thomas	Thorstvedt	Waddle	Walsh	
11	8†	2	5	4			13	6	1				12						10		3*		9	7	3
1	1	1	1	1				1	1										1		1		1	1	
							1						1												

Football League Cup

Allen	Bergsson	Butters	Fairclough	Fenwick	Gascoigne	Gray	Howells	Hughton	Mabbutt	Mimms	Moncur	Moran	Nayim	Polston J	Robson	Samways	Statham	Stevens	Stewart	Stimson	Thomas	Thorstvedt	Waddle	Walsh	
11			5	4	8				6	1					10	2					3		9	7	2
5			4		8		12		6	1					10	2			11*		3		9	7	
11			5	4	8*				6	1		7			12	2		2	10		3		9		3
11	12	5*	4	8					6	1			13			2		2	10		3		9†	7	R
5	1	4	5	5				5	5	1					3	2	2	4	5		5	3			4
	1						1						1						2						
												1													

1 own-goal

349

1989-90

Manager: Terry Venables

1	Aug	19	(h)	Luton T	W	2-1	Stewart, Allen	17,668
2		22	(a)	Everton	L	1-2	Allen	34,402
3		26	(a)	Manchester C	D	1-1	Gascoigne	32,004
4	Sep	9	(a)	Aston Villa	L	0-2		24,769
5		16	(h)	Chelsea	L	1-4	Gascoigne	16,260
6		23	(a)	Norwich C	D	2-2	Gascoigne, Lineker	20,095
7		30	(h)	Queen's Park R	W	3-2	Lineker 3	23,781
8	Oct	14	(a)	Charlton A	W	3-1	Gascoigne, Lineker, Thomas	17,692
9		18	(h)	Arsenal	W	2-1	Walsh, Samways	33,944
10		21	(h)	Sheffield W	W	3-0	Lineker 2, Moran	26,909
11		29	(a)	Liverpool	L	0-1		36,550
12	Nov	4	(a)	Southampton	D	1-1	Gascoigne	19,601
13		11	(h)	Wimbledon	L	0-1		26,855
14		18	(a)	Crystal P	W	3-2	Howells, Samways, Lineker (pen)	26,366
15		25	(h)	Derby C	L	1-2	Stewart	28,075
16	Dec	2	(a)	Luton T	D	0-0		12,620
17		9	(h)	Everton	W	2-1	Stewart, Lineker	29,374
18		16	(a)	Manchester U	W	1-0	Lineker	36,230
19		26	(h)	Millwall	W	3-1	Samways, Lineker, McLeary (og)	26,874
20		30	(h)	Nottingham F	L	2-3	Lineker 2	33,401
21	Jan	1	(a)	Coventry C	D	0-0		19,599
22		13	(h)	Manchester C	D	1-1	Howells	26,384
23		20	(a)	Arsenal	L	0-1		46,132
24	Feb	4	(h)	Norwich C	W	4-0	Lineker 3 (1 pen), Howells	19,599
25		10	(a)	Chelsea	W	2-1	Howells, Lineker	29,130
26		21	(h)	Aston Villa	L	0-2		32,472
27		24	(a)	Derby C	L	1-2	Moncur	19,676
28	Mar	3	(h)	Crystal P	L	0-1		26,181
29		10	(h)	Charlton A	W	3-0	J.Polston, Lineker, Howells	21,104
30		17	(a)	Queen's Park R	L	1-3	Walsh	16,691
31		21	(h)	Liverpool	W	1-0	Stewart	25,656
32		31	(a)	Sheffield W	W	4-2	Allen, Lineker 2, Stewart	26,582
33	Apr	7	(a)	Nottingham F	W	3-1	Stewart, Allen 2	21,669
34		14	(h)	Coventry C	W	3-2	Lineker 2, Stewart	23,317
35		16	(a)	Millwall	W	1-0	Lineker	10,573
36		21	(h)	Manchester U	W	2-1	Gascoigne, Lineker	33,317
37		28	(a)	Wimbledon	L	0-1		12,800
38	May	5	(h)	Southampton	W	2-1	Stewart, Allen	31,038

FINAL LEAGUE POSITION: 3rd in Division One

Appearances
Sub Appearan
Goals

FA Cup

3	Jan	6	(h)	Southampton	L	1-3	Howells	33,134

Appearances
Sub Appearan
Goals

League Cup

2	Sep	20	(h)	Southend U	W	1-0	Fenwick	15,734
	Oct	4	(a)	Southend U	L	2-3*	Allen, Nayim	10,400
3		25	(a)	Manchester U	W	3-0	Lineker, Samways, Nayim	45,759
4	Nov	22	(a)	Tranmere R	D	2-2	Gascoigne, Higgins (og)	13,789
R		29	(h)	Tranmere R	W	4-0	Allen, Howells, Mabbutt, Stewart	22,720
5	Jan	17	(a)	Nottingham F	D	2-2	Lineker, Sedgley	30,044
R		24	(h)	Nottingham F	L	2-3	Nayim, Walsh	32,357

*After extra-time — Tottenham won on away-goals rule.

Appearances
Sub Appearan
Goals

Tottenham Hotspur — appearances and goals grid

Allen	Bergsson	Butters	Fenwick	Gascoigne	Howells	Hughton	Lineker	Mabbutt	Mimms	Moncur	Moran	Nayim	Polston A	Polston J	Robson	Samways	Sedgley	Stevens	Stewart	Thomas	Thorstvedt	Van den Hauwe	Walsh	
11	3	2	4	8†	5		10	6							7*	13		9			1		12	1
11		2	4	8†	5		10	6							12	7*	3	9			1		13	2
11†		2	4	8	5*		10	6							13	7	3	9			1		12	3
11	2*	4	8	5			10	6							7*		12	9			1	3	13	4
11		4	8	5†			10	6							13		3*	9	12		1	2	7	5
	2	4	8				10†	6							12	7*	11	9	5		1	3	13	6
12	2	4	8				10	6				7					11	9	5*		1	3		7
5	2*	4	8				10	6				7†		13			11	9	12		1	3		8
5		4	8	12			10	6							9*	11			2		1	3	7	9
5		4	8*	7			10	6				12			9	11			2		1	3		10
5*	4			7			10	6	12	8†					9	11			2		1	3	13	11
5	4		8	7			10	6							9*	11			2		1	3	12	12
13	4		8	5			10	6							9†	11	12		2		1	3	7*	13
	4		8	5			10*	6		11					7		3	9	2		1		12	14
11			8	5*			10	6		13					7†	4	9		2		1	3	12	15
4	3		8	5			10*	6							7		11	9	2		1		12	16
4	12		8	5			10	6							7*		11	9	2		1	3		17
4			8	5			10	6	1						7		11	9	2			3		18
4	3		8	5			10	6	1						7	11	12	9	2*					19
4	2*		8	5			10	6	1						7†	11	12	9				3	13	20
4	2		8*	5			10	6	1			12			7	11		9				3		21
4				5	6		10								8	7	11	9	2		1	3		22
4					5		10	6					13		8	7†	11	9	2		1	3*	12	23
		8	5	2			10*	6				12			9	4	11				1	3	7	24
		8	5	2			10†	6		13		12			9	4	11				1	3	7*	25
		8*	5	2			10	6		12		13			9†	4	11				1	3	7	26
12			5	2*			10	6				8			9	4	11†		13		1	3	7	27
		8*	5	2			10	6		11†		9			13	4	12				1	3	7	28
11		8	5	2			10	6							9	4					1	3	7	29
11		8	5	2*			10	6				13			9	4†	12				1	3	7	30
11	2		8	5*			10	6								4	13		12		1	3	7†	31
11	2		8	5			10	6								4	12		13		1	3	7*	32
11	2		8	5*			10	6							7†	4	12				1	3		33
11	2		8				10	6								4	7	5			1	3		34
11	2		8*	5			10	6								4	7		12		1	3	13	35
11	2		8	5			10	6				9*		12		4	7				1	3		36
11	2*		8	5			10	6				9			12	4	7		13		1	3†		37
11	2*		8	5			10	6				9				4	7		12		1	3		38
29	17	7	10	34	33	8	38	36	4	2		18		11		18	31	4	24	17	34	31	12	
3	1			1					3	5	1	1	2	3	5	1	3	4	9				14	
6				6	5		24			1	1			1		3			8	1			2	

1 own-goal

Allen	Bergsson	Butters	Fenwick	Gascoigne	Howells	Hughton	Lineker	Mabbutt	Mimms	Moncur	Moran	Nayim	Polston A	Polston J	Robson	Samways	Sedgley	Stevens	Stewart	Thomas	Thorstvedt	Van den Hauwe	Walsh	
4	8				5	3	10	6	1						7*	11		9	2				12	3
1	1				1	1	1	1	1						1	1		1	1				1	
																						1		
			1																					

Allen	Bergsson	Butters	Fenwick	Gascoigne	Howells	Hughton	Lineker	Mabbutt	Mimms	Moncur	Moran	Nayim	Polston A	Polston J	Robson	Samways	Sedgley	Stevens	Stewart	Thomas	Thorstvedt	Van den Hauwe	Walsh	
		2	4	8				6				11	12	10			9	5*		1	3	7		2
5†		4	8	12			10	6				7				11	9	2*		1	3	13		3
5		4*		7			10	6			12	8			9	11		2		1	3			3
11	4*		8	5			10	6				3		7		12	9†		2	1		13		4
4			8	5			10	6				7			11	9		2	1		3			R
4			5				10	6			12		8*	7	11	9	2		1	3				5
4			5	12			10	6				7	8	11	9†	2		1	3*	13				R
6	1	1	3	4	5			6			7	3	3	1	4	6		6	7	7	6	1		
1	1										1	1				1	1					3		
2		1	1					1			3		3		1	4	6		6	7	7	6	1	

1 own-goal

1990-91

Manager: Terry Venables

1	Aug	25	(h)	Manchester C	W 3-1	Gascoigne, Lineker 2	33,501
2		28	(a)	Sunderland	D 0-0		30,214
3	Sep	1	(a)	Arsenal	D 0-0		40,009
4		8	(h)	Derby C	W 3-0	Gascoigne 3	23,614
5		15	(a)	Leeds U	W 2-0	Howells, Lineker	31,342
6		22	(h)	Crystal P	D 1-1	Gascoigne	34,859
7		29	(h)	Aston Villa	W 2-1	Lineker, Allen	34,939
8	Oct	6	(a)	Queen's Park R	D 0-0		21,405
9		20	(h)	Sheffield U	W 4-0	Nayim, Walsh 3	34,612
10		27	(a)	Nottingham F	W 2-1	Howells 2	27,347
11	Nov	4	(h)	Liverpool	L 1-3	Lineker	35,003
12		10	(h)	Wimbledon	W 4-2	Mabbutt, Stewart, Lineker (pen), Walsh	28,769
13		18	(a)	Everton	D 1-1	Howells	23,716
14		24	(h)	Norwich C	W 2-1	Lineker 2	33,942
15	Dec	1	(a)	Chelsea	L 2-3	Gascoigne, Lineker	33,478
16		8	(h)	Sunderland	D 3-3	Lineker, Walsh 2	30,431
17		15	(a)	Manchester C	L 1-2	Gascoigne	31,236
18		22	(h)	Luton T	W 2-1	Stewart 2	27,007
19		26	(a)	Coventry C	L 0-2		22,731
20		29	(a)	Southampton	L 0-3		21,405
21	Jan	1	(h)	Manchester U	L 1-2	Lineker (pen)	29,399
22		12	(h)	Arsenal	D 0-0		34,753
23		20	(a)	Derby C	W 1-0	Lineker	17,747
24	Feb	2	(h)	Leeds U	D 0-0		32,253
25		23	(a)	Wimbledon	L 1-5	Bergsson	10,500
26	Mar	2	(h)	Chelsea	D 1-1	Lineker (pen)	26,168
27		16	(a)	Aston Villa	L 2-3	Samways, Allen	32,638
28		23	(h)	Queen's Park R	D 0-0		30,860
29		30	(h)	Coventry C	D 2-2	Nayim 2	29,033
30	Apr	1	(a)	Luton T	D 0-0		11,322
31		6	(h)	Southampton	W 2-0	Lineker 2	24,291
32		10	(a)	Norwich C	L 1-2	Hendry	19,014
33		17	(a)	Crystal P	L 0-1		26,285
34		20	(a)	Sheffield U	D 2-2	Edinburgh, Walsh	25,706
35		24	(h)	Everton	D 3-3	Allen, Mabbutt, Nayim	21,675
36	May	4	(h)	Nottingham F	D 1-1	Nayim	30,891
37		11	(a)	Liverpool	L 0-2		36,192
38		20	(a)	Manchester U	D 1-1	Hendry	46,791

FINAL LEAGUE POSITION: 11th in Division One

Appearances
Sub Appearanc
Goals

FA Cup

3	Jan	5	(a)	Blackpool	W 1-0	Stewart	9,563
4		26	(h)	Oxford U	W 4-2	Mabbutt, Gascoigne 2, Lineker	31,665
5	Feb	16	(a)	Portsmouth	W 2-1	Gascoigne 2	26,049
6	Mar	10	(h)	Notts C	W 2-1	Nayim, Gascoigne	29,686
SF	Apr	14	(n*)	Arsenal	W 3-1	Gascoigne, Lineker 2	77,893
F	May	18	(n*)	Nottingham F	W 2-1†	Stewart, Walker (og)	80,000

*Played at Wembley Stadium. †After extra-time.

Appearances
Sub Appearanc
Goals

League Cup

2	Sep	26	(h)	Hartlepool U	W 5-0	Gascoigne 4 (1 pen), Lineker	19,760
	Oct	9	(a)	Hartlepool U	W 2-1	Stewart 2	9,631
3		30	(h)	Bradford C	W 2-1	Stewart, Gascoigne	25,451
4	Nov	27	(a)	Sheffield U	W 2-0	Gascoigne, Stewart	25,852
5	Jan	16	(a)	Chelsea	D 0-0		34,178
R		23	(h)	Chelsea	L 0-3		33,861

Appearances
Sub Appearanc
Goals

Allen	Bergsson	Dearden	Edinburgh	Fenwick	Garland	Gascoigne	Gray	Hendon	Hendry	Howells	Lineker	Mabbutt	Moncur	Moran	Nayim	Samways	Sedgley	Stewart	Thomas	Thorstvedt	Tuttle	Van den Hauwe	Walker	Walsh	№
11*	2					8				5	10	6			9	12	4	7		1		3			1
11	2					8				5	10	6			9†	13	4	7*		1		3		12	2
11	2					8*				5	10	6			9		4	7	12	1		3			3
11	2					8				5	10	6			9†	13	4	7*		1		3		12	4
11	2					8				5	10	6			9		4	7		1		3			5
11	2					8				5	10	6			9		4	7		1		3			6
11	2*					8				5†	10	6			9		4	7	13	1		3		12	7
11						8				5	10	6			9†	12	4	7*	13	1		3		2	8
11						8*				5		6	12		9		4	7	2	1		3		10	9
11						8				5	10	6			9		4*	7	2	1		3		12	10
11	2*					8				5	10	6			9†		4	7	12	1		3		13	11
11			12			8				5	10	6			9		4†	7	2	1		3*		13	12
11						8				5	10*	6			9		4	7	2	1		3		12	13
11						8				5	10	6			9		4	7	2	1		3			14
11			12			8				5	10	6			9†			7	2	1	4*	3		13	15
11	4*					8				5	10	6			9	13		7†	2	1		3		12	16
13						8				5*	10	6			9†	12	4	7	2	1		3		11	17
13						8				5	10*	6			9	12	4	7	2	1		3		11†	18
9						8				5	10	6			12	13	4*	7	2	1		3		11†	19
11	12									5*	10	6			9†	8	4	7	2	1		3		13	20
11						8				5	10	6	12		9		4*	7	2	1		3			21
11			3	4		8				5	10	6						7	2	1				9	22
11			3	2						5	10†	6*				8	4	7	12	1		13		9	23
11	2										10	6			5*	12	4	7	8	1		3		9	24
11	2		3			12					10	6	9		5*	7	4		8	1					25
11	2					8*	9†				10	6	12		5		4	7	13	1		3			26
11	2*						13	12			10†	6	9		8		4	7	5	1		3			27
11	2						9†				10	6	12		5*	8	4	7	3	1				13	28
11	2						9†					6	12		5	8	4*	7	13	1		3		10	29
11												6	9		5	8		7	2	1	4	3		10	30
11	2									12	10	6	13		8†		4	7	5*	1		3		9	31
				13	8†	12	10	2		11			7	4	5			6			3*		1	9	32
11					8†		13					6			5	9	4	7	2	1	12	3*		10	33
11	12		2							5					8	9*	4	7	3	1	6			10	34
11	2									5	10†	6			4	9	13	7	3	1	12			8*	35
11	2					8				5	10	6			7	9	4			1		3*		12	36
11	2					8			13	5*	10†	6			9		4	7		1		3		12	37
12			2	3					11	5	10†	6*			9		4	7	13	1				8	38
34	9		14	4		26	3		2	29	32	35	4		32	14	33	35	23	37	4	31	1	16	
2	3		2	1		3	2	2			5	1	1		9	1			8		2	1		13	
3	1			1		7				2	15	2			4	5								7	

Allen	Bergsson	Dearden	Edinburgh	Fenwick	Garland	Gascoigne	Gray	Hendon	Hendry	Howells	Lineker	Mabbutt	Moncur	Moran	Nayim	Samways	Sedgley	Stewart	Thomas	Thorstvedt	Tuttle	Van den Hauwe	Walker	Walsh	№
11			3	2		8				5	10	6			9		4	7		1					3
11				2		8				5*	10	6				12	4	7		1		3		9	4
11				2		8	12				10	6	5		7*		4	9		1		3			5
11				2		8					10	6			5*	12	4	7	9†	1		3		13	6
11				2		8*				5	10	6	12		9†		4	7		1		3		13	SF
11				2		8*				5	10	6	12		9†		4	7		1		3		13	F
6			5	2		6				4	6	6	1		3	4	4	5	2	6		5		1	
						1							2		1	1								3	
						6					3	1			1									2	

1 own-goal

Allen	Bergsson	Dearden	Edinburgh	Fenwick	Garland	Gascoigne	Gray	Hendon	Hendry	Howells	Lineker	Mabbutt	Moncur	Moran	Nayim	Samways	Sedgley	Stewart	Thomas	Thorstvedt	Tuttle	Van den Hauwe	Walker	Walsh	№
11	2*					8				5	10	6			9		4	7†	12	1		3		13	2
11		1	3			12				5*		6	8†		13	10	4	7	2					9	
11						8				5	10†	6	12		9*		4	7	2	1		3		13	3
11			3			8				5	10	6			9†		4*	7	2	1	12			13	4
11			3	4						5	10	6	12		8†	13		7	2*	1				9	5
11			3	2*		8				5	10	6	12		13		4†	7		1				9	R
6		1	5	2		4				6	5	6	1		2	4	4	6	4	5		2		3	
						1							1		1						1			3	
											6				1									4	

1991-92

Manager: Peter Shreeve

#	Month	Date		Opponent	Result	Scorers	Attendance
1	Aug	17	(a)	Southampton	W 3-2	Durie, Lineker 2	18,581
2		24	(h)	Chelsea	L 1-3	Lineker	34,645
3		28	(a)	Nottingham F	W 3-1	Durie, Lineker, Bergsson	24,018
4		31	(a)	Norwich C	W 1-0	Lineker	19,460
5	Sep	7	(a)	Aston Villa	D 0-0		33,096
6		14	(h)	Queen's Park R	W 2-0	Lineker 2	30,059
7		21	(a)	Wimbledon	W 5-3	Samways, Lineker 4 (1 pen)	11,927
8		28	(h)	Manchester U	L 1-2	Durie	35,087
9	Oct	5	(a)	Everton	L 1-3	Lineker	29,505
10		19	(h)	Manchester C	L 0-1		30,502
11		26	(a)	West Ham U	L 1-2	Lineker	23,946
12	Nov	2	(a)	Sheffield W	D 0-0		31,573
13		16	(h)	Luton T	W 4-1	Lineker 2, Houghton 2	27,543
14		23	(h)	Sheffield U	L 0-1		28,168
15	Dec	1	(a)	Arsenal	L 0-2		38,892
16		7	(h)	Notts C	W 2-1	Mabbutt, Walsh	23,364
17		14	(a)	Leeds U	D 1-1	Howells	31,404
18		18	(h)	Liverpool	L 1-2	Walsh	27,434
19		22	(a)	Crystal P	W 2-1	Walsh, Lineker	22,491
20		26	(h)	Nottingham F	L 1-2	Stewart	31,079
21		28	(h)	Norwich C	W 3-0	Nayim, Lineker, Allen	27,969
22	Jan	1	(a)	Coventry C	W 2-1	Stewart, Lineker	19,639
23		11	(a)	Chelsea	L 0-2		28,628
24		18	(h)	Southampton	L 1-2	Mabbutt	23,191
25		25	(h)	Oldham A	D 0-0		20,843
26	Feb	1	(a)	Manchester C	L 0-1		30,123
27		16	(h)	Crystal P	L 0-1		19,834
28		22	(h)	Arsenal	D 1-1	Stewart	33,124
29	Mar	7	(h)	Leeds U	L 1-3	Allen	27,622
30		11	(a)	Luton T	D 0-0		11,494
31		14	(h)	Sheffield W	L 0-2		23,027
32		21	(a)	Liverpool	L 1-2	Stewart	39,968
33		28	(h)	Coventry C	W 4-3	Durie 3, Lineker	22,744
34	Apr	1	(h)	West Ham U	W 3-0	Lineker 3	31,809
35		4	(h)	Aston Villa	L 2-5	Lineker, Teale (og)	26,370
36		7	(a)	Notts C	W 2-0	Lineker 2	9,205
37		11	(a)	Queen's Park R	W 2-1	A.Gray, Durie	20,678
38		14	(a)	Sheffield U	L 0-2		21,526
39		18	(h)	Wimbledon	W 3-2	Lineker 2, Hendry	23,934
40		20	(a)	Oldham A	L 0-1		15,443
41		25	(h)	Everton	D 3-3	Stewart, Minton, Allen	36,340
42	May	2	(a)	Manchester U	L 1-3	Lineker	44,595

FINAL LEAGUE POSITION: 15th in Division One

Appearances
Sub Appearance
Goals

FA Cup

3	Jan	5	(a)	Aston Villa	D 0-0		29,316
R		14	(h)	Aston Villa	L 0-1		25,462

Appearances
Sub Appearance
Goals

League Cup

2	Sep	25	(a)	Swansea C	L 0-1		11,416
	Oct	9	(h)	Swansea C	W 5-1	Stewart, Samways, Lineker, Allen, Brazil (og)	20,198
3	Oct	29	(a)	Grimsby T	W 3-0	Howells, Durie, Lineker	17,017
4	Dec	4	(a)	Coventry C	W 2-1	Durie, Allen	20,095
5	Jan	8	(h)	Norwich C	W 2-1	Walsh, Lineker	29,471
SF	Feb	9	(a)	Nottingham F	D 1-1	Lineker (pen)	21,402
	Mar	1	(h)	Nottingham F	L 1-2	Lineker	28,216

Appearances
Sub Appearance
Goals

FA Charity Shield

	Aug	19	(n*)	Arsenal	D 0-0		65,483

*Played at Wembley Stadium.

Appearances
Sub Appearance
Goals

Football appearance and scoring grid (shirt numbers per match; * and † denote substitutions). Players across the top, match numbers (1–42) down the right.

Allen	Bergsson	Cundy	Durie	Edinburgh	Fenwick	Gray A	Hendon	Hendry	Houghton	Howells	Lineker	Mabbutt	Minton	Moncur	Nayim	Samways	Sedgley	Stewart	Thorstvedt	Tuttle	Van den Hauwe	Walker	Walsh	No.
11†	13		8		2						5*	10	6		12	9	4	7	1		3			1
11	12		8		2*						5	10	6			9	4	7	1		3			2
11†	13		8*		2					12	5	10	6			9	4	7	1		3			3
11			8		2						5	10	6			9	4	7	1		3			4
11			8		2						5	10	6			9	4	7	1		3			5
12	11		8		2						5*	10	6			9†	4	13	7		1		3	6
11†	2		8							12		10	6			4	9	5	7		3		1	7
11	2†		8							13	12	10	6			4*	9	3	7	5			1	8
11	2		8							13	12	10	6			4*	9†	3	7	1	5			9
11	5		8	2								13	10	6		4*	9	7	1		3†		12	10
11	13		8	2							12		10	6		4*	9	5	7	1	3†			11
11	113		8	2							5	10*	6		9		4†		1	3			12	12
11†	7			2						13	5*	10	6		12	9	4		1	3			8	13
	7		8	2						13	5*	10	6		4†	9	12		1	3			11	14
11	4		8	2							5		6		12	9*		7	1	3			10	15
11	4		8	2							5*		6		12	9†	13	7	1	3			10	16
11	4		8†	2							5		6		12	9*	13	7	1	3			10	17
11	4			2							5*	10	6		12	9		7	1	3			8	18
11	4	3†		2							5	10*	6		12	9	13	7	1				8	19
11	4†			2							5	10	6		12	9*	13	7	1	3			8	20
11				2							12	10	6		5	9	4	7	1	3			8*	21
11		13		2							12	5	10	6		9†	4	7	1	3			8*	22
11	12			2							13	5†			10	9	4	7*	1	3			8	23
11	12	8		2							13		10	6		9†	4	7	3*	1			5	24
11		8		2							12		10	6	5*		4	7	3	1			9	25
11	6	8		2	3						5*	10			13	9†	4	7	1				12	26
11	13	8		2							5†	10	6			9*	4	7	1	3			12	27
11		8		2							5	10	6		9*		4	7	1	3			12	28
11	13	8		2	9						5	10*	6				4	7	1	3†			12	29
11	12	8	3	2	9						5		6				4	7	1		10*			30
11	13	8	3	2†	5							12	6		9*		4	7	1		10			31
11		8	3	2	9						5*		6				4	7	1	10			12	32
11	5	8	3		4*							10†	6		9	13		7	1	2			12	33
11	5	8	3		4*							10	6		9	13		7	2†	1			12	34
11	2	5	8*	3	4						7	10	6		9				1				12	35
11	5		3		4	13					9	10†	6			12		7	2	1			8*	36
11	5	8	3		4						9*	10	6†		13			7	2	1			12	37
11	5		3	13	4				12		9*	10		8†			6	7	2	1				38
11	5		3		4†				12			10	6		9	13		7	2	1			8*	39
11	5		3		4	8*						10	6		9	13	12	7	2†	1				40
11	5	8	3		4†							10	6	9*		12		7	2	1			13	41
11	5	8	3		4						12	10	6	9*				7	2	1				42
38	17	10	31	22	22	14			1		27	35	40	2	22	26	21	38	24	2	35	18	17	
1	11			1	1		2	4	10	4					9	1	13					12		
3	1		7			1		1	2	1	28	2	1		1	1		5			3			

1 own-goal

Allen	Bergsson	Cundy	Durie	Edinburgh	Fenwick	Gray A	Hendon	Hendry	Houghton	Howells	Lineker	Mabbutt	Minton	Moncur	Nayim	Samways	Sedgley	Stewart	Thorstvedt	Tuttle	Van den Hauwe	Walker	Walsh	
11				2							5	10	6			9	4	7	1		3		8	3
11	12		8†		2*							10	6		13	9	4	7	1		3		5	R
2			1		2						1	2	2			2	2	2	2		2		2	
	1															1								

Allen	Bergsson	Cundy	Durie	Edinburgh	Fenwick	Gray A	Hendon	Hendry	Houghton	Howells	Lineker	Mabbutt	Minton	Moncur	Nayim	Samways	Sedgley	Stewart	Thorstvedt	Tuttle	Van den Hauwe	Walker	Walsh	
11		8*			2	12						10		6	13	4	9	5	7		3†	1		2
11	2	8									12		10	6		4	9	3	7	1	5*			3
11*	13	8		2							5†	10	6			9	4	7	1		3		12	3
11	4	8		2							5		6		12	9†	13	7	1		3		10*	4
11	12			2*								13		10	6	5	9†	4	7	1	3		8	5
11	6	8	12	2							5	10*			13	9†	4	7	1		3			SF
11		8	13	2†							5	10	6		9*	12	4	7	1		3			
7	3		6	1	4	1					5	5	6		4	6	6	7	6	1	6	1	2	
	2				2					1	2				1	2	1	1					1	
2		2									1	5				1		1			1			

1 own-goal

Allen	Bergsson	Cundy	Durie	Edinburgh	Fenwick	Gray A	Hendon	Hendry	Houghton	Howells	Lineker	Mabbutt	Minton	Moncur	Nayim	Samways	Sedgley	Stewart	Thorstvedt	Tuttle	Van den Hauwe	Walker	Walsh	
11				2							5	10	6		8	9	4	7	1		3			
1				1							1	1	1		1	1	1	1	1		1			

1992-93

First Team Coaches: Doug Livermore and Ray Clemence

1	Aug	15	(a)	Southampton	D	0-0		19,654
2		19	(h)	Coventry C	L	0-2		24,388
3		22	(h)	Crystal P	D	2-2	Durie, Sedgley	25,237
4		25	(a)	Leeds U	L	0-5		28,218
5		30	(a)	Ipswich T	D	1-1	Cundy	20,100
6	Sep	2	(h)	Sheffield U	W	2-0	Sheringham, Durie	21,322
7		5	(h)	Everton	W	2-1	Allen, Turner	26,503
8		14	(a)	Coventry C	L	0-1		15,348
9		19	(h)	Manchester U	D	1-1	Durie	33,296
10		27	(a)	Sheffield W	L	0-2		24,895
11	Oct	3	(a)	Queen's Park R	L	1-4	Sheringham	19,845
12		17	(h)	Middlesbrough	D	2-2	Sheringham (pen), Barmby	24,735
13		25	(a)	Wimbledon	D	1-1	Barmby	8,628
14		31	(h)	Liverpool	W	2-0	Nayim, Ruddock	32,917
15	Nov	7	(a)	Blackburn R	W	2-0	Howells, Sheringham (pen)	17,305
16		21	(h)	Aston Villa	D	0-0		32,852
17		28	(a)	Manchester C	W	1-0	Watson	25,496
18	Dec	5	(h)	Chelsea	L	1-2	Campbell	31,540
19		12	(h)	Arsenal	W	1-0	Allen	33,707
20		19	(a)	Oldham A	L	1-2	Sheringham	11,735
21		26	(a)	Norwich C	D	0-0		19,413
22		28	(h)	Nottingham F	W	2-1	Barmby, Mabbutt	32,118
23	Jan	9	(a)	Manchester U	L	1-4	Barmby	35,648
24		16	(h)	Sheffield W	L	0-2		25,702
25		27	(h)	Ipswich T	L	0-2		23,738
26		30	(a)	Crystal P	W	3-1	Sheringham 2, Gray	20,937
27	Feb	7	(h)	Southampton	W	4-2	Sheringham 2, Anderton, Barmby	20,098
28		10	(a)	Everton	W	2-1	Mabbutt, Allen	16,164
29		20	(h)	Leeds U	W	4-0	Ruddock, Sheringham 3 (1 pen)	32,040
30		27	(h)	Queen's Park R	W	3-2	Sheringham 2, Anderton	32,341
31	Mar	2	(a)	Sheffield U	L	0-6		16,654
32		10	(a)	Aston Villa	D	0-0		37,727
33		20	(a)	Chelsea	D	1-1	Sheringham (pen)	25,157
34		24	(h)	Manchester C	W	3-1	Anderton, Nayim, Turner	27,247
35	Apr	9	(h)	Norwich C	W	5-1	Sheringham 2, Allen, Nayim, Ruddock	31,425
36		12	(a)	Nottingham F	L	1-2	Sedgley	25,682
37		17	(h)	Oldham A	W	4-1	Sheringham 2 (2 pens), Turner, Anderton	26,663
38		20	(a)	Middlesbrough	L	0-3		13,472
39	May	1	(h)	Wimbledon	D	1-1	Anderton	24,473
40		5	(h)	Blackburn R	L	1-2	Anderton	23,097
41		8	(a)	Liverpool	L	2-6	Sedgley, Sheringham	43,385
42		11	(a)	Arsenal	W	3-1	Sheringham, Hendry 2	26,393

FINAL LEAGUE POSITION: 8th in FA Premier League

Appearances
Sub Appearanc
Goals

FA Cup

3	Jan	2	(a*)	Marlow	W	5-1	Barmby 2, Samways 2, Sheringham	26,636
4		24	(a)	Norwich C	W	2-0	Sheringham 2	15,005
5	Feb	14	(h)	Wimbledon	W	3-2	Anderton, Sheringham, Barmby	26,529
6	Mar	7	(a)	Manchester C	W	4-2	Nayim 3, Sedgley	34,050
SF	Apr	4	(n†)	Arsenal	L	0-1		76,263

*Played at White Hart Lane. †Played at Wembley Stadium

Appearances
Sub Appearanc
Goals

League Cup

2	Sep	21	(h)	Brentford	W	3-1	Sheringham, Watson, Durie	19,365
	Oct	7	(a)	Brentford	W	4-2	Sheringham 2 (1 pen), Turner, Anderton	11,445
3		28	(a)	Manchester C	W	1-0	Samways	18,399
4	Dec	2	(a)	Nottingham F	L	0-2		22,812

Appearances
Sub Appearanc
Goals

Appearances / shirt-number grid (shirt number worn shown in each player's column; final column = match number).

Allen	Anderton	Austin	Barmby	Bergsson	Campbell	Cundy	Dearden	Durie	Edinburgh	Fenwick	Gray	Hendry	Hill	Hodges	Howells	McDonald	Mabbutt	Minton	Moran	Nayim	Nethercott	Ruddock	Samways	Sedgley	Sheringham	Thorstvedt	Turner	Tuttle	Van den Hauwe	Walker	Watson	No.
11	10							5	8	3	2	12			4								6	9			7*			1		1
11	10				5*				8	3	2	12			4								6	9		13	7			1†		2
11	10	13							8	3	2†	12	7*										6	9	4			1	5			3
11	10	2						5	8	3					4								6	9	7			1				4
11*	7*	2						5	8	3		12											6	9	4	10			1			5
11	7*	2						5	8			12											6	9†	4	10	13	3	1			6
11	7*	2						5	8					4										9	10	12	6	3	1			7
11		2						5	8					4									6	9†	13	10	12	3	1			8
11	9	2*						5	8		4†	13										6		7	10	9	12	3	1			9
11	9	2*	8					5			12											7	10	4†	6	3	1		13				10
11	9†		8					5		2*	12										6	4	7†	10	13	3	1					11
11			12						8	2									13			6	4	7	10	12	5*	3	1				12
11		3	13						8†	2								5		9		6	4	7	10	12		1*					13
11		3*	4†						8	2				12			5		9		6		7	10	1	13						14
11		3							8	2				7			5		9		6	4	10	1								15
11†		3	12				13	8*	2					7			5		9		6	4	10	1								16
	13	3	8			12			2					7*			5	13	9		6	4	10	1			11†					17
	2	8*	12	7					3								5		9		6	4	10	1			11†					18
11		2	12					8*	3					7			5		9		6	4	10	1								19
11	9	2	12					8	3					7			5		9*		6	4	10	1								20
11	9*	2	8†						3					7			5		12		6	4	10	1								21
11	12	2	8†	13					3					7			5		12		6	4	10	1								22
11	9	2†	8	13					3					7			5		9*		6	4	10	1								23
11	9	2	8	12				3†			13		7*			5				6	4	10	1								24
11	9	2†	7				8*		3					12			5				6	4	10	1			13					25
11	9	2							3		8*			7			5				6	4	10	1			12					26
11	9	2	8†						3		12			7*			5				6	4	10	1			13					27
11	9	2†							3		8*			7			5		12		6	4	10	1			13					28
11	9	2	8†						3		12			7*			5				6	4	10	1			13					29
11	9	2	8*		6				3		7						5		12			4	10	1								30
11	9	2			6						7*	13					5				8†		4	12	10	1		3				31
	9	2							3		11*						5				8	6	4	7	10	1	12					32
	9†	2		12					3		4	13							8	5	6			10	1	11†			7*			33
11	9†	2		12					3								5				8	6*	4	7	10	1	13	3				34
11	9	2	4*						3								5				8	12	6	7	10	1	13					35
11	9	2	4				12		3								5				8†	6	4	7	10	1*	13					36
11	9	2	8						3								5				6	4*	7	10	12			1				37
11	9	2†	8						3	13							5				6	4	7	10	12			1				38
11	9										12						5				2†	6	4	7	10	8	3	1				39
11	9										12	13					5				2*	6	4	7	10	8†	3	1				40
11	9										4	13			2	5					12	6		7	10		3*	1	8†			41
11	9										8	4	12		2	5						6		7	10		3	1				42
38	32	33	17			13		17	31	3	9	2	2		16	2	29			15	3	38	34	20	38	25	7	4	13	17	4	
	2	1	5	5	1	2	1		1	2	8	3	2	4	2			3	3	2		2			2		11	1	5		1	
5	5		5			1	1		3		1	2		1	2			3		3		3	21		3			1				

Allen	Anderton	Austin	Barmby	Bergsson	Campbell	Cundy	Dearden	Durie	Edinburgh	Fenwick	Gray	Hendry	Hill	Hodges	Howells	McDonald	Mabbutt	Minton	Moran	Nayim	Nethercott	Ruddock	Samways	Sedgley	Sheringham	Thorstvedt	Turner	Tuttle	Van den Hauwe	Walker	Watson	No.
11*	12	2	8						3					7			5				9		6	4†	10	1			13			3
11	9	2	7					8*	3					12			5				6	4	10	1								4
11	9	2	8						3					7			5				6	4	10	1								5
11	9*	2							3								5		8	6	4*	7†	10	1	12							6
11	9	2	12	13					3								5		8	6	4*	7†	10	1								SF
5	4	5	3			1		5						2			5		3	5	5	2	5	5								
	1		1	1										1								1			1							
	1		3																2	1	4											

Allen	Anderton	Austin	Barmby	Bergsson	Campbell	Cundy	Dearden	Durie	Edinburgh	Fenwick	Gray	Hendry	Hill	Hodges	Howells	McDonald	Mabbutt	Minton	Moran	Nayim	Nethercott	Ruddock	Samways	Sedgley	Sheringham	Thorstvedt	Turner	Tuttle	Van den Hauwe	Walker	Watson	No.
11	9*				5			8	13								12					6		7	10			2	3	1	4†		2
11	9	13	8*						2								6	4†	10		12	5	3	1									3
11		3	8						2			13		5			9†		6	4*	7	10	1	12								3
11†		3	12				7	8*	2								5				9	6	4	10					13				4
4	2	2	2			2		2	3			2		2			4	3	3	4	2		2	2	2	1							
	1	1							1					1			1				2			1									
	1	1							1								1		3		1											

357

Spurs Against Other League Clubs

Tottenham Hotspur have played 71 clubs in the Football League since 1908-09. Below is their record against each club. Some clubs changed their names (eg Clapton Orient became Leyton Orient then Orient and then Leyton Orient again) and some clubs modified their titles (eg Swansea Town became Swansea City). In all cases the current name used by each club cover all games under previous names.

	P	W	D	L	F	A
ARSENAL	112	42	24	46	162	170
ASTON VILLA	100	43	21	36	176	158
BARNSLEY	26	13	4	9	47	34
BIRMINGHAM CITY	69	33	13	23	111	77
BLACKBURN ROVERS	62	29	11	22	120	97
BLACKPOOL	50	26	13	11	103	63
BOLTON WANDERERS	62	29	8	25	99	85
BRADFORD	32	16	8	8	75	50
BRADFORD CITY	28	11	7	10	39	38
BRENTFORD	6	3	2	1	12	5
BRIGHTON & HOVE ALBION	10	5	2	3	15	10
BRISTOL CITY	20	10	5	5	28	18
BRISTOL ROVERS	2	2	0	0	12	2
BURNLEY	88	32	22	34	159	138
CARDIFF CITY	40	20	10	10	60	37
CARLISLE UNITED	2	0	1	1	1	2
CHARLTON ATHLETIC	30	16	4	10	58	36
CHELSEA	90	40	18	32	152	118
CHESTERFIELD	20	9	6	5	45	28
COVENTRY CITY	66	30	19	17	110	79
CRYSTAL PALACE	22	12	7	3	39	21
DERBY COUNTY	50	16	14	20	71	86
DONCASTER ROVERS	6	3	2	1	10	5
EVERTON	113	38	34	41	176	162
FULHAM	44	22	18	4	78	49
GAINSBOROUGH TRINITY	2	1	1	0	3	1
GATESHEAD	2	2	0	0	5	0
GLOSSOP	2	0	2	0	4	4
GRIMSBY TOWN	14	8	1	5	27	24
HUDDERSFIELD TOWN	36	9	13	14	44	50
HULL CITY	14	5	4	5	18	13
IPSWICH TOWN	42	19	6	17	67	63
LEEDS UNITED	68	26	20	22	99	91

	P	W	D	L	F	A
LEICESTER CITY	72	36	14	22	143	120
LEYTON ORIENT	0	6	3	1	20	8
LINCOLN CITY	6	2	3	1	13	8
LIVERPOOL	100	29	24	47	115	158
LUTON TOWN	46	21	17	8	75	46
MANCHESTER CITY	98	30	26	42	129	156
MANCHESTER UNITED	112	32	32	48	159	175
MANSFIELD TOWN	2	0	2	0	4	4
MIDDLESBROUGH	52	17	10	25	86	101
MILLWALL	18	13	3	2	43	24
NEWCASTLE UNITED	96	42	23	31	165	133
NEWPORT COUNTY	3	2	1	0	8	4
NORTHAMPTON TOWN	2	1	1	0	3	1
NORWICH CITY	42	18	11	13	74	55
NOTTINGHAM FOREST	97	47	24	26	167	125
NOTTS COUNTY	35	16	8	11	53	48
OLDHAM ATHLETIC	35	20	4	11	72	42
OXFORD UNITED	6	4	2	0	16	5
PLYMOUTH ARGYLE	22	10	6	6	39	29
PORTSMOUTH	26	7	11	8	41	44
PORT VALE	12	9	1	2	40	15
PRESTON NORTH END	53	22	14	17	96	79
QUEEN'S PARK RANGERS	36	14	12	10	53	45
READING	6	2	2	2	14	11
ROTHERHAM UNITED	2	1	1	0	3	1
SHEFFIELD UNITED	78	31	22	25	144	131
SHEFFIELD WEDNESDAY	80	33	15	32	141	123
SOUTHAMPTON	74	31	21	22	134	93
STOCKPORT COUNTY	6	4	1	1	11	5
STOKE CITY	66	35	15	16	109	71
SUNDERLAND	76	23	23	30	92	109
SWANSEA CITY	26	15	5	6	56	28
TRANMERE ROVERS	2	2	0	0	5	1
WATFORD	12	6	1	5	18	17
WEST BROMWICH ALBION	108	39	23	46	163	173
WEST HAM UNITED	84	31	23	30	136	130
WIMBLEDON	14	5	3	6	23	29
WOLVERHAMPTON WANDERERS	74	36	14	24	146	125

Spurs in Europe

European Cup

1961-62
Preliminary Round (1st leg)
Sep 13 v Górnik Zabrze (a) 2-4
Jones, Dyson
Brown; Baker, Henry, Blanchflower, Norman,
Mackay, Jones, White, R.Smith, Allen, Dyson.
Att: 70,000
Preliminary Round (2nd leg)
Sep 20 v Górnik Zabrze (h) 8-1 (agg 10-5)
Blanchflower, Jones 3, White, R.Smith 2, Dyson
Brown; Baker, Henry, Blanchflower, Norman,
Mackay, Jones, White, R.Smith, Allen, Dyson.
Att: 56,737
Round 1 (1st leg)
Nov 1 v Feyenoord (a) 3-1
Saul 2, Dyson
Brown; Baker, Henry, Blanchflower, Norman, Marchi,
Jones, White, Saul, Clayton, Dyson.
Att: 64,000
Round 1 (2nd leg)
Nov 15 v Feyenoord (h) 1-1 (agg 4-2)
Dyson
Brown; Baker, Henry, Blanchflower, Norman, Marchi,
Jones, White, Saul, Mackay, Dyson.
Att: 62,144

Round 2 (1st leg)
Feb 14 v Dukla Prague (a) 0-1
Brown; Baker, Henry, Marchi, Norman, Mackay,
Medwin, White, R.Smith, Blanchflower, Jones.
Att: 64,000
Round 2 (2nd leg)
Feb 26 v Dukla Prague (h) 4-1 (agg 4-2)
Mackay 2, R.Smith 2
Brown; Baker, Henry, Blanchflower, Norman, Marchi,
Medwin, White, R.Smith, Mackay, Jones.
Att: 55,388
Semi-final (1st leg)
Mar 21 v Benfica (a) 1-3
R.Smith
Brown; Baker, Henry, Marchi, Norman, Mackay,
Greaves, White, R.Smith, Blanchflower, Jones.
Att: 86,000
Semi-final (2nd leg)
Apr 5 v Benfica (h) 2-1 (agg 3-4)
Blanchflower (pen), R.Smith
Brown; Baker, Henry, Blanchflower, Norman,
Mackay, Medwin, White, R.Smith, Greaves, Jones.
Att: 64,448

European Cup-winners' Cup

1962-63
Round 1 (1st leg)
Oct 31 v Glasgow Rangers (h) 5-2
Norman, White 2, Allen, Shearer (og)
Brown; Baker, Henry, Blanchflower, Norman,
Mackay, Medwin, White, Allen, Greaves, Jones.
Att: 58,859
Round 1 (2nd leg)
Dec 11 v Glasgow Rangers (a) 3-2 (agg 8-4)
R.Smith 2, Greaves
Brown, Baker, Henry, Blanchflower, Norman,
Mackay, Medwin, White, R.Smith, Greaves, Jones.
Att: 80,000
Round 2 (1st leg)
Mar 5 v Slovan Bratislava (a) 0-2
Brown; Baker, Henry, Marchi, Norman, Mackay, Saul,
White, R.Smith, Greaves, Jones.
Att: 32,000
Round 2 (2nd leg)
Mar 14 v Slovan Bratislava (h) 6-0 (agg 6-2)
Mackay, White, R.Smith, Greaves 2, Jones
Brown; Hopkins, Henry, Marchi, Norman, Mackay,
Saul, White, R.Smith, Greaves, Jones.
Att: 61,504
Semi-final (1st leg)
Apr 24 v OFK Belgrade (a) 2-1
White, Dyson
Brown; Baker, Henry, Marchi, Norman, Mackay,
Greaves, J.Smith, R.Smith, White, Dyson.
Att: 45,000

Semi-final (2nd leg)
May 1 v OFK Belgrade (h) 3-1 (agg 5-2)
Mackay, Jones, R.Smith
Brown; Baker, Henry, Blanchflower, Norman, Marchi,
Jones, White, R.Smith, Mackay, Dyson.
Att: 59,736
Final
May 15 v Atlético Madrid (Rotterdam) 5-1
White, Greaves 2, Dyson 2
Brown; Baker, Henry, Blanchflower, Norman, Marchi,
Jones, White, R.Smith, Greaves, Dyson.
Att: 40,000

1963-64
Round 1 (1st leg)
Dec 3 v Manchester United (h) 2-0
Mackay, Dyson
W.Brown; Baker, Henry, Marchi, Norman, Mackay,
Jones, White, R.Smith, Greaves, Dyson.
Att: 57,447
Round 1 (2nd leg)
Dec 10 v Manchester United (a) 1-4 (agg 3-4)
Greaves
W.Brown; Baker, Henry, Marchi, Norman, Mackay,
Jones, White, R.Smith, Greaves, Dyson.
Att: 48,639

1967-68
Round 1 (1st leg)
Sep 20 v Hajduk Split (a) 2-0
Robertson, Greaves
Jennings; Kinnear, Knowles, Mullery, England, Beal,
Robertson, Greaves, Gilzean, Venables, Saul.
Att: 25,000
Round 1 (2nd leg)
Sep 27 v Hajduk Split (h) 4-3 (agg 6-3)
Robertson 2, Gilzean, Venables
Jennings; Kinnear, Knowles, Mullery, England, Beal,
Robertson, Greaves, Gilzean, Venables, Jones.
Att: 38,623
Round 2 (1st leg)
Nov 29 v Olympique Lyonnais (a) 0-1
Jennings; Kinnear, Knowles, Mullery, Hoy, Mackay,
Robertson, Greaves, Gilzean, Venables, Jones.
Att: 10,997
Round 2 (2nd leg)
Dec 13 v Olympique Lyonnais (h) 4-3 (agg 4-4)
Spurs lost on away-goals rule
Greaves 2 (1 pen), Gilzean, Jones
Jennings; Kinnear, Knowles, Bond, Hoy, Mackay,
Robertson, Greaves, Gilzean, Venables, Jones.
Att: 41,895

1981-82
Round 1 (1st leg)
Sep 16 v Ajax Amsterdam (a) 3-1
Villa, Falco 2
Clemence; Hughton, Miller, Roberts, Villa, Perryman,
Ardíles, Archibald, Galvin, Hoddle, Falco.
Att: 21,742
Round 1 (2nd leg)
Sep 29 v Ajax Amsterdam (h) 3-0 (agg 6-1)
Ardíles, Galvin, Falco
Clemence; Hughton, Miller, Roberts(Lacy), Villa,
Perryman, Ardíles, Archibald, Galvin, Hoddle, Falco.
Att: 34,606
Round 2 (1st leg)
Oct 21 v Dundalk (a) 1-1
Crooks
Clemence; Hughton, Miller, Roberts, Hazard,
Perryman, Ardíles, Archibald, Galvin(Smith), Hoddle,
Crooks.
Att: 17,500
Round 2 (2nd leg)
Nov 4 v Dundalk (h) 1-0 (agg 2-1)
Crooks
Clemence; Hughton, Miller, Roberts, Hazard,
Perryman, Ardíles, Archibald, Galvin, Hoddle,
Crooks.
Att: 33,455
Round 3 (1st leg)
Mar 3 v Eintracht Frankfurt (h) 2-0
Miller, Hazard
Clemence; Hughton, Miller, Price, Hazard, Perryman,
Ardíles, Archibald, Galvin, Hoddle, Crooks(Falco).
Att: 38,172
Round 3 (2nd leg)
Mar 17 v Eintracht Frankfurt (a) 1-2 (agg 3-2)
Hoddle
Clemence; Hughton, Miller, Price, Hazard, Perryman,
Ardíles(Roberts), Archibald, Galvin, Hoddle,
Falco(Villa).
Att: 45,000

Semi-final (1st leg)
Apr 7 v Barcelona (h) 1-1
Roberts
Clemence; Hughton, Miller(Jones), Price, Hazard,
Perryman, Roberts, Villa, Galvin, Hoddle, Crooks.
Att: 41,545
Semi-final (2nd leg)
Apr 21 v Barcelona (a) 0-1 (agg 1-2)
Clemence; Hughton, Price(Falco), Roberts, Hazard,
Perryman, Villa, Archibald, Galvin, Hoddle, Crooks.
Att: 80,000

1982-83
Round 1 (1st leg)
Sep 15 v Coleraine (a) 3-0
Archibald, Crooks 2
Clemence; Hughton, Price, Lacy, Brooke, Perryman,
Mabbutt(Hazard), Archibald, Galvin, Villa, Crooks.
Att: 12,000
Round 1 (2nd leg)
Sep 28 v Coleraine (h) 4-0 (agg 7-0)
Brooke, Mabbutt, Crooks, Gibson
Clemence(Parks); Hughton, Price, Lacy, Brooke,
Perryman, Mabbutt, Archibald, Hazard, Villa,
Crooks(Gibson).
Att: 20,925
Round 2 (1st leg)
Oct 20 v Bayern Munich (h) 1-1
Archibald
Clemence; Price, O'Reilly(Gibson), Miller, Lacy,
Hazard, Brooke, Archibald(Falco), Mabbutt, Villa,
Crooks.
Att: 36,488
Round 2 (2nd leg)
Nov 3 v Bayern Munich (a) 1-4 (agg 2-5)
Hughton
Clemence; Price, Hughton, Miller(Perryman), Lacy,
Hazard, Mabbutt, Archibald, Brooke(Hoddle), Villa,
Crooks.
Att: 55,000

1991-92
Preliminary Round (1st leg)
Aug 21 v Sparkasse Stockerau (Vienna) 1-0
Durie
Thorstvedt; Fenwick, Van den Hauwe, Nayim,
Howells, Mabbutt, Stewart, Durie, Samways
(Hendon), Lineker, Allen.
Att: 17,700
Preliminary Round (2nd leg)
Sep 4 v Sparkasse Stockerau (h) 1-0
Mabbutt
Walker; Fenwick, Van den Hauwe, Nayim,
Howells(Sedgley), Mabbutt, Stewart, Durie, Samways,
Lineker(Moran), Bergsson.
Att: 28,072
Round 1 (1st leg)
Sep 17 v Hadjuk Split (Linz, Austria) 0-1
Walker; Fenwick, Van den Hauwe, Nayim,
Howells(Allen), Mabbutt, Stewart, Durie, Samways,
Lineker(Sedgley), Bergsson.
Att: 7,000
Round 1 (2nd leg)
Oct 2 v Hadjuk Split (h) 2-0
Tuttle, Durie

Thorstvedt; Bergsson, Sedgley, Nayim, Tuttle, Mabbutt, Stewart, Durie, Samways, Lineker(Hendon), Allen.
Att: 24,297
Round 2 (1st leg)
Oct 23 v Porto (h) 3-1
Durie, Lineker 2
Thorstvedt; Edinburgh, Van den Hauwe, Sedgley, Walsh(Houghton), Mabbutt, Stewart, Durie, Samways(Bergsson), Lineker, Allen.
Att: 23,621
Round 2 (2nd leg)
Nov 7 v Porto (a) 0-0
Thorstvedt; Edinburgh, Van den Hauwe, Bergsson, Howells, Mabbutt, Stewart, Durie (Sedgley), Samways, Lineker(Walsh), Allen.
Att: 55,000

Round 3 (1st leg)
Mar 4 v Feyenoord (a) 0-1
Thorstvedt; Fenwick, Van den Hauwe, Sedgley, Howells(Samways), Mabbutt, Stewart, Durie, Nayim, Lineker(Walsh), Allen.
Att: 48,000
Round 3 (2nd leg)
Mar 18 v Feyenoord (h) 0-0
Thorstvedt; Bergsson, Edinburgh, Sedgley, Howells(Houghton), Mabbutt, Stewart, Durie, Nayim(Walsh), Lineker, Allen.
Att: 29,834

UEFA Cup

1971-72
Round 1 (1st leg)
Sep 14 v Keflavik (a) 6-1
Mullery 2, Coates, Gilzean 3
Jennings; Kinnear, Knowles, Mullery(Souness), England, Beal, Coates(Pearce), Perryman, Chivers, Peters, Gilzean.
Att: 18,000
Round 1 (2nd leg)
Sep 28 v Keflavik (h) 9-0 (agg 15-1)
Knowles, Coates, Perryman, Chivers 3, Holder, Gilzean 2
Jennings; Evans, Knowles, Mullery(Pearce), England, Beal, Coates, Perryman, Chivers, Peters(Holder), Gilzean.
Att: 23,818
Round 2 (1st leg)
Oct 20 v FC Nantes (a) 0-0
Jennings; Kinnear, Knowles, Mullery, England, Beal, Neighbour, Perryman, Chivers, Peters, Gilzean(Morgan).
Att: 20,033
Round 2 (2nd leg)
Nov 2 v FC Nantes (h) 1-0 (agg 1-0)
Peters
Jennings; Evans, Knowles, Pratt, England, Beal, Neighbour, Perryman, Chivers, Peters, Gilzean(Pearce).
Att: 32,630
Round 3 (1st leg)
Dec 8 v Rapid Bucharest (h) 3-0
Chivers 2, Peters
Jennings; Evans, Knowles, Coates(Pearce), England, Beal, Gilzean, Perryman, Chivers, Peters, Neighbour.
Att: 30,702
Round 3 (2nd leg)
Dec 15 v Rapid Bucharest (a) 2-0 (agg 5-0)
Chivers, Pearce
Jennings; Evans, Knowles, Coates, Collins, Beal, Pratt, Perryman(Naylor), Chivers, Peters, Gilzean(Pearce).
Att: 12,000
Round 4 (1st leg)
Mar 7 v Unizale Textile Arad (a) 2-0
England, Morgan
Jennings; Evans, Knowles, Pratt, England, Beal, Gilzean(Collins), Perryman, Chivers, Peters, Morgan.
Att: 20,000

Round 4 (2nd leg)
Mar 21 v Unizale Textile Arad (h) 1-1 (agg 3-1)
Gilzean
Jennings; Evans, Knowles, Coates, England, Naylor, Gilzean, Perryman, Pratt, Peters, Morgan.
Att: 30,253
Semi-final (1st leg)
Apr 5 v AC Milan (h) 2-1
Perryman 2
Jennings; Kinnear, Knowles, Coates(Neighbour), England, Naylor, Gilzean, Perryman, Chivers, Peters, Mullery.
Att: 42,064
Semi-final (2nd leg)
Apr 19 v AC Milan (a) 1-1 (agg 3-2)
Mullery
Jennings; Kinnear, Knowles, Mullery, England, Beal, Coates, Perryman, Chivers, Peters, Pratt (Naylor).
Att: 68,482
Final (1st leg)
May 3 v Wolverhampton Wanderers (a) 2-1
Chivers 2
Jennings; Kinnear, Knowles, Mullery, England, Beal, Gilzean, Perryman, Chivers, Peters, Coates(Pratt).
Att: 38,362
Final (2nd leg)
May 17 v Wolverhampton Wanderers (h) 1-1 (agg 3-2)
Mullery
Jennings; Kinnear, Knowles, Mullery, England, Beal, Gilzean, Perryman, Chivers, Peters, Coates.
Att: 54,303
1972-73
Round 1 (1st leg)
Sep 13 v Lyn Oslo (a) 6-3
Pratt, Gilzean 2, Chivers 2, Peters
Jennings; Evans, Knowles, Pratt, England, Naylor, Gilzean, Perryman, Chivers, Peters, Pearce.
Att: 10,770
Round 1 (2nd leg)
Sep 27 v Lyn Oslo (h) 6-0 (agg 12-3)
Chivers 3, Pearce, Coates 2
Jennings; Kinnear, Knowles, Pratt(Holder), England, Beal(Naylor), Gilzean, Perryman, Chivers, Pearce, Coates.
Att: 21,109

Round 2 (1st leg)
Oct 25 v Olympiakos Pireus (h) 4-0
Pearce 2, Chivers, Coates
Jennings; Evans, Knowles, Pearce, England, Beal(Naylor), Gilzean(Neighbour), Perryman, Chivers, Peters, Coates.
Att: 27,815
Round 2 (2nd leg)
Nov 8 v Olympiakos Pireus (a) 0-1 (agg 4-1)
Jennings; Evans, Knowles, Pearce, England, Dillon, Gilzean, Perryman, Chivers, Naylor, Pratt.
Att: 35,000
Round 3 (1st leg)
Nov 29 v Red Star Belgrade (h) 2-0
Gilzean, Chivers
Jennings; Evans, Knowles, Pratt, England, Naylor, Gilzean, Perryman, Chivers, Peters, Pearce.
Att: 23,958
Round 3 (2nd leg)
Dec 13 v Red Star Belgrade (a) 0-1 (agg 2-1)
Jennings; Evans, Knowles, Pratt, England, Kinnear, Coates, Perryman, Chivers, Peters, Pearce.
Att: 70,000
Round 4 (1st leg)
Mar 7 v Vitória Setúbal (h) 1-0
Evans
Jennings; Kinnear, Knowles, Coates, England, Beal, Gilzean(Evans), Perryman, Chivers, Peters, Pearce.
Att: 30,469
Round 4 (2nd leg)
Mar 21 v Vitória Setúbal (a) 1-2 (agg 2-2)
Spurs won on away-goals rule
Chivers
Jennings; Kinnear, Knowles, Coates, England, Beal, Gilzean (Naylor), Perryman, Chivers, Peters, Pearce.
Att: 30,000
Semi-final (1st leg)
Apr 10 v Liverpool (a) 0-1
Jennings; Kinnear, Knowles, Coates(Pearce), England, Beal, Gilzean, Perryman, Chivers(Evans), Peters, Pratt.
Att: 42,174
Semi-final (2nd leg)
Apr 25 v Liverpool (h) 2-1 (agg 2-2)
Spurs lost on away-goals rule
Peters 2
Jennings; Kinnear(Evans), Knowles(Pearce), Coates, England, Beal, Gilzean, Perryman, Chivers, Peters, Pratt.
Att: 46,919

1973-74
Round 1 (1st leg)
Sep 19 v Grasshopper Zürich (a) 5-1
Evans, Chivers 2, Gilzean 2
Jennings; Evans, Knowles, Coates(Holder), England, Beal, Pratt, Perryman, Chivers, Peters, Neighbour (Gilzean).
Att: 11,200
Round 1 (2nd leg)
Oct 3 v Grasshopper Zürich (h) 4-1 (agg 9-2)
England, Peters 2, Lador (og)
Daines; Evans, Knowles, Pratt, England, Beal, Gilzean, Perryman, Chivers, Peters, Coates.
Att: 18,105

Round 2 (1st leg)
Oct 24 v Aberdeen (a) 1-1
Coates
Daines; Evans, Kinnear(Naylor), Pratt, England, Beal, Gilzean, Perryman, McGrath, Peters, Coates (Neighbour).
Att: 30,000
Round 2 (2nd leg)
Nov 7 v Aberdeen (h) 4-1 (agg 5-2)
Peters, Neighbour, McGrath 2
Jennings; Evans, Knowles, Pratt, England, Beal, Gilzean, Perryman, Chivers, Peters, Neighbour(McGrath).
Att: 21,785
Round 3 (1st leg)
Nov 28 v Dinamo Tbilisi (a) 1-1
Coates
Jennings; Evans, Knowles, Pratt, England, Beal, Naylor, Perryman, Chivers, Peters, Coates.
Att: 45,000
Round 3 (2nd leg)
Dec 12 v Dinamo Tbilisi (h) 5-1 (agg 6-2)
McGrath, Chivers 2, Peters 2
Jennings; Evans, Naylor, Pratt, England, Beal, McGrath, Perryman, Chivers, Peters, Coates
Att: 18,602
Round 4 (1st leg)
Mar 6 v 1.FC Cologne (a) 2-1
McGrath, Peters
Jennings; Evans, Naylor, Pratt, England, Beal, McGrath, Perryman, Chivers, Peters, Dillon.
Att: 28,000
Round 4 (2nd leg)
Mar 20 v 1.FC Cologne (h) 3-0 (agg 5-1)
Chivers, Peters, Coates
Jennings; Evans, Naylor, Pratt, England, Beal, McGrath, Perryman, Chivers, Peters, Coates.
Att: 40,968
Semi-final (1st leg)
Apr 10 v 1.FC Lokomotive Leipzig (a) 2-1
Peters, Coates
Jennings; Evans, Naylor, Pratt, England, Beal, Neighbour, Perryman, Chivers, Peters, Coates(Holder).
Att: 74,000
Semi-final (2nd leg)
Apr 24 v 1.FC Lokomotive Leipzig (h) 2-0 (agg 4-1)
McGrath, Chivers
Jennings; Kinnear, Naylor, Pratt(Holder), England, Beal, McGrath, Perryman, Chivers, Peters, Coates
Att: 41,280
Final (1st leg)
May 21 v Feyenoord (h) 2-2
England, Van Deele (og)
Jennings; Evans, Naylor, Pratt, England, Beal(Dillon), McGrath, Perryman, Chivers, Peters, Coates.
Att: 46,281
Final (2nd leg)
May 29 v Feyenoord (a) 0-2 (agg 2-4)
Jennings; Evans, Naylor, Pratt(Holder), England, Beal, McGrath, Perryman, Chivers, Peters, Coates.
Att: 68,000

1983-84
Round 1 (1st leg)
Sep 14 v Drogheda (a) 6-0
Mabbut 2, Falco 2, Galvin, Crooks
Clemence; Hughton, O'Reilly, Roberts, Price, Perryman, Mabbutt, Falco, Galvin, Brooke, Crooks.
Att: 7,000

Round 1 (2nd leg)
Sep 28 v Drogheda (h) 8-0 (agg 14-0)
Hughton, Roberts 2, Archibald, Falco 2, Brazil 2
Clemence; Hughton(O'Reilly), Galvin, Roberts, Price,
Perryman, Mabbutt, Archibald, Falco, Hoddle, Brazil
Att: 19,831
Round 2 (1st leg)
Oct 19 v Feyenoord (h) 4-2
Galvin 2, Archibald 2
Clemence; Hughton, Galvin, Roberts, Stevens,
Perryman, Mabbutt, Archibald, Falco, Hoddle,
Brooke(Crook).
Att: 35,404
Round 2 (2nd leg)
Nov 2 v Feyenoord (a) 2-0 (agg 6-2)
Hughton, Galvin
Clemence; Hughton, Thomas, Roberts, Stevens,
Perryman, Mabbutt, Archibald, Falco(Brazil),
Hoddle, Galvin.
Att: 45,061
Round 3 (1st leg)
Nov 23 v Bayern Munich (a) 0-1
Clemence; Hughton, Thomas, Roberts, Stevens,
Perryman, Hazard(Brooke), Archibald, Falco,
Hoddle, Dick(Brazil).
Att: 20,000
Round 3 (2nd leg)
Dec 7 v Bayern Munich (h) 2-0 (agg 2-1)
Archibald, Falco
Clemence; Hughton(O'Reilly), Thomas, Roberts,
Stevens, Perryman, Cooke, Archibald, Falco, Hoddle,
Dick(Brooke).
Att: 41,977
Round 4 (1st leg)
Mar 7 v FK Austria Vienna (h) 2-0
Archibald, Brazil
Parks; Stevens, Hughton, Roberts, Miller, Perryman,
Ardíles, Archibald, Brazil, Hazard (Hoddle), Dick.
Att: 34,069
Round 4 (2nd leg)
Mar 21 v FK Austria Vienna (a) 2-2 (agg 4-2)
Ardíles, Brazil
Clemence; Stevens, Hughton, Roberts(Thomas),
Miller, Perryman, Ardíles, Archibald, Brazil (Falco),
Mabbutt, Galvin.
Att: 21,000
Semi-final (1st leg)
Apr 11 v Hajduk Split (a) 1-2
Falco
Parks; Thomas, Hughton, Roberts, Miller, Perryman,
Hazard, Archibald, Falco, Mabbutt (Crook), Galvin.
Att: 40,000
Semi-final (2nd leg)
Apr 25 v Hajduk Split (h) 1-0 (agg 2-2)
Spurs won on away-goals rule
Hazard
Parks; Thomas, Hughton, Roberts, Miller, Perryman,
Hazard, Archibald, Falco, Stevens (Mabbutt), Galvin.
Att: 43,969
Final (1st leg)
May 9 v Anderlecht (a) 1-1
Miller
Parks; Thomas, Hughton, Roberts, Miller, Perryman,
Hazard, Archibald, Falco, Stevens (Mabbutt), Galvin.
Att: 38,000

Final (2nd leg)
May 23 v Anderlecht (h) 1-1 a.e.t. (agg 2-2)
Spurs won 4-3 on penalties
*Roberts (penalties scored by Roberts, Falco, Stevens,
Archibald)*
Parks; Thomas, Hughton, Roberts, Miller(Ardíles),
Mabbutt(Dick), Hazard, Archibald, Falco, Stevens,
Galvin.
Att: 46,258

1984-85
Round 1 (1st leg)
Sep 19 v SC Braga (a) 3-0
Falco 2, Galvin
Clemence; Mabbutt, Hughton, Roberts, Miller,
Perryman, Chiedozie, Falco, Allen(Crooks),
Hazard(Thomas), Galvin.
Att: 30,000
Round 1 (2nd leg)
Oct 3 v SC Braga (h) 6-0 (agg 9-0)
Stevens, Hughton, Falco, Crooks 3
Clemence; Stevens, Hughton, Roberts, Miller
(Hoddle), Perryman, Chiedozie, Falco(Cooke), Galvin,
Hazard, Crooks.
Att: 22,478
Round 2 (1st leg)
Oct 24 v Club Brugge KV (a) 1-2
Allen
Clemence; Stevens, Hughton, Roberts, Miller,
Perryman, Chiedozie, Falco, Galvin, Hazard (Hoddle),
Crooks (Allen).
Att: 27,000
Round 2 (2nd leg)
Nov 7 v Club Brugge KV (h) 3-0 (agg 4-2)
Roberts, Allen, Hazard
Clemence; Stevens, Mabbutt, Roberts, Miller,
Perryman, Chiedozie(Brooke), Falco(Thomas), Allen,
Hazard, Galvin.
Att: 34,356
Round 3 (1st leg)
Nov 28 v Bohemians Prague (h) 2-0
Stevens, Ondrá (og)
Clemence; Stevens, Mabbutt(Hughton), Roberts,
Miller, Perryman, Chiedozie, Falco, Allen, Hoddle,
Hazard(Cooke).
Att: 27,971
Round 3 (2nd leg)
Dec 12 v Bohemians Prague (a) 1-1 (agg 3-1)
Falco
Clemence; Stevens, Hughton, Roberts, Miller,
Perryman, Chiedozie, Falco, Galvin, Hoddle
(Mabbutt), Crooks(Thomas).
Att: 17,500
Round 4 (1st leg)
Mar 6 v Real Madrid (h) 0-1
Clemence; Stevens, Hughton, Hazard, Miller(Dick),
Perryman, Chiedozie(Brooke), Falco, Galvin, Hoddle,
Crooks.
Att: 39,914
Round 4 (2nd leg)
Mar 20 v Real Madrid (a) 0-0 (agg 0-1)
Clemence; Thomas, Hughton, Roberts, Miller,
Perryman, Hazard, Falco, Galvin(Dick), Hoddle,
Crooks(Brooke).
Att: 95,000

Spurs in Pre-League Days

BEFORE they joined the Southern League in 1896-7, apart from the 1892-3 season when they competed in the Southern Alliance, all Tottenham Hotspurs' fixtures consisted of Cup and Friendly matches. What details are known of these pre-League matches are listed below.

1882-83
FRIENDLIES
Aug 30 v Radicals (venue unknown) 0-2
Team unknown.
Jan 6 v Latymer (a) 1-8
Scorer unknown.
Team unknown.

1883-84
FRIENDLIES
Oct 6 v Brownlow Rovers (h) 9-0
Scorers unknown.
Leaman; Tyrell, Dexter, Casey, Lovis, Lomas, Cottrell, Watson, Fisher, Harston, Buckle.
(Jull mentioned in match report but not line-up)
Oct 13 v Evelyn (h) 6-1
Scorer unknown.
Team unknown.
(One Spurs goal disputed)
Oct 20 v Grange Park (h) 1-3 (60 minutes only played).
Buckle
Team unknown.
Oct 27 v Leyton Rovers (h) 1-0
Buckle
Team unknown.
Nov 10 v Brownlow Rovers (a) 1-0 (abandoned after 55 minutes because ball burst)
Jull
Team unknown.
Nov 24 v Sekforde Rovers (a) 2-0
Scorers unknown.
Team unknown but included Watson, Baillie and Buckle.
Dec 1 v Sekforde Rovers (a) 1-0
Scorer unknown.
Team unknown.
Dec 8 v Leyton Rovers (a) 1-3
Buckle
Team unknown but Spurs fielded only ten players.
Dec 15 v Claremont (h) 2-0 (60 minutes only played)
Scorers unknown.
Team unknown.
Dec 22 v Latymer (h) 2-0
Buckle, Scorer unknown.
Team unknown.
Jan 12 v Woodgrange (a) 0-1
Team unknown but included Jull, Hartson and Buckle.
Jan 19 v Grafton (a) 1-0
Scorer unknown.
Team unknown.
Jan 26 v Albion (h) 0-1
Team unknown.
Feb 2 v Clarence (a) 1-0
Scorer unknown.
Team unknown.
Feb 9 v Albion (a) 3-0 (50 minutes only played)
Jull 3
Team unknown.
Feb 16 v Hanover Utd 2nd XI (h) 1-2 (80 minutes only played)

Jull
Team unknown.
Feb 23 v Grange Park (h) 1-0 (60 minutes only played)
Buckle
Team unknown.
Mar 8 v Hanover Utd 2nd XI (a) 2-0
Scorers unknown.
Team unknown.
Mar 15 v Latymer (a) 2-0
Watson, Randall
Team unknown but also included Jull, Tyrell and Baillie.
Mar 22 v Remington (h) 2-0 (80 minutes only played)
Jull, Watson.
Team unknown.

1884-85
FRIENDLIES
Oct 4 v Remington (h) 4-0
Amos 2, Buckle 2
Team unknown but also included Jull and Bull.
Oct 11 v Abbey (h) 1-0
Amos
Team unknown but also included Jull, Tyrell, Buckle and Harston.
Oct 18 v Woodgrange (h) 4-5
Mason, Scorers unknown 3
Team unknown but also included Jull, Bull, Amos, Tyrell and Buckle.
Oct 25 v Grange Park (h) 4-0 (60 minutes only played)
Scorers unknown.
Team unknown but included Jull, Tyrell and Randall.
Nov 1 v Sekforde Rovers (a) 4-0
Scorers unknown.
Team unknown.
Nov 8 v Marlborough Rovers (h) 1-0
Scorers unknown.
Team unknown.
Nov 15 v Latymer (a) 2-1
Scorers unknown.
Team unknown.
Nov 22 v St Peter's 2nd XI (h) 3-2
Scorers unknown.
Team unknown.
Nov 29 v Hadley (h) 0-1
Team unknown.
Dec 6 v Tottenham (h) 4-0
Scorers unknown.
Team unknown.
Dec 13 v Woodgrange (a) 0-0 (40 minutes only played)
Team unknown.
Dec 20 v Sekforde Rovers (h) 5-0
Scorers unknown.
Team unknown but included Jull, Amos, Cawkill, Tyrell and Buckle.
Dec 26 v Grove (h) score unknown
Scorers unknown.
Team unknown.
Dec 27 v Enfield (h) 3-0
Scorers unknown.
Team unknown.

Jan 3 v Hadley (a) score unknown
Scorers unknown.
Team unknown.
Jan 10 v Abbey (a) 1-1
Scorer unknown.
Team unknown but Spurs fielded only nine players.
(Both goals disputed)
Jan 17 v Grange Park (a) 0-1
Team unknown but included Bumberry, Cawkill,
Mason and Lomas.
Jan 24 v Victoria Wanderers (h) 4-0 (60 minutes only played)
Scorers unknown.
Team unknown.
Jan 31 v St Martin's (h) 1-0
Scorer unknown.
Team unknown.
Feb 7 v Fillebrook (h) 3-0
Scorers unknown.
Team unknown but Spurs fielded only ten players.
Feb 14 v Latymer (h) 0-0 (75 minutes only played)
Team unknown.
Feb 21 v St Peter's (h) 1-1
Scorer unknown.
Team unknown.
Feb 28 v Bedford Rovers (a) 1-1
Scorer unknown.
Team unknown but Spurs fielded only ten players.
Mar 7 v Marlborough Rovers (a) 1-0
Scorer unknown.
Team unknown.
Mar 14 v Victoria Wanderers (a) score unknown
Scorers unknown.
Team unknown.
Mar 21 v Remington (a) score unknown
Scorers unknown.
Team unknown.
Mar 28 v St Martin's (a) score unknown
Scorers unknown.
Team unknown.
Apr 4 v Mars (h) score unknown
Scorers unknown.
Team unknown.
Apr 11 v Grove (a) score unknown
Scorers unknown.
Team unknown.

1885-86
LONDON ASSOCIATION CUP
Round 1
Oct 17 v St Albans (h) 5-2
Scorers unknown.
Bumberry; Jull, Tyrell, Bull, Lovis, Casey, Buckle,
Harston, Mason, Amos, Cottrell.
Round 2
Nov 7 v Casuals (a) 0-8
Bumberry; Jull, Tyrell, Bull, Conu, Casey, Buckle,
Harston, Mason, Amos, Cottrell.

FRIENDLIES
Oct 3 v Silesia College (a) 4-3
Scorers unknown.
Team unknown.
Oct 10 v Grange Park (a) 0-3
Scorers unknown.
Team unknown.
Oct 24 v Westminster Rovers (h) 3-1

Scorers unknown.
Team unknown.
Nov 14 v Rutland (a) 0-3
Team unknown but Spurs fielded only ten players
including Bull, Harston, Jull and Adellington).
Nov 21 v South Hackney (a) 3-1
Scorers unknown.
Team unknown.
Nov 28 v Dalston Rovers (h) 3-0
Scorers unknown.
Team unknown.
Dec 26 v Edmonton Independent (a) 2-1
Scorers unknown.
Team unknown.
Jan 2 v St Martin's (h) 3-0
Scorers unknown.
Team unknown.
Jan 9 v Dalston Rovers (a) won but scoreline unknown.
Scorers unknown.
Team unknown.
Jan 16 v Woodgrange (a) 0-3
Team unknown but Spurs fielded only ten players.
Feb 6 v Edmonton Independent (h) 4-1
Scorers unknown.
Team unknown.
Feb 13 v Grange Park 2nd XI (h) 0-3
Team unknown.
Feb 20 v South Hackney (h) 8-0
Scorers unknown.
Team unknown.
Feb 27 v Silesia College (h) 1-2
Scorer unknown.
Team unknown.
Mar 6 v Ilford (h) 6-1
Scorers unknown.
Team unknown.
Mar 13 v Rutland (h) 5-0
Mason, Randall 4
Team unknown.
Mar 20 v Upton Excelsior (h) won but score unknown
Scorers unknown.
Team unknown.
Mar 27 v Enfield Lock (h) 7-0
Scorers unknown.
Team unknown.
(One Spurs goal disputed).
Apr 10 v Park (h) 8-0
Scorers unknown.
Anderson; Jull, Tyrell, Bull, Casey, Lovis, Buckle,
Harston, Mason, Cottrell, Randall.
Apr 17 v Hermitage (h) 3-0
Scorers unknown.
Team unknown.

1886-87
LONDON ASSOCIATION CUP
Round 1
Oct 16 v Upton Park (a) 0-6
Lomas; Jull, Tyrell, Bull, Casey, Lovis, Cottrell,
Randall, Buckle, Harston, Mason.

EAST END CUP
Round 1
Dec 18 v Phoenix (h) 6-0
Buckle 2, Mason 2, Harston 2
Anderson; Jull, Tyrell, Bull, Casey, Lovis, Buckle,
Mason, Cottrell, Harston, Randall.

366

Round 2
Jan 15 v Park (h) 2-0
Mason, Scorer unknown.
Anderson; Jull, Tyrell, Bull, Casey, Lovis, Buckle,
Cottrell, Mason, Harston, Randall.
Round 3
Feb 19 v St Luke's (h) 2-1
Buckle, Mason
Anderson; Jull, Tyrell, Bull, Casey, Lovis, Buckle,
Harston, Mason, Cottrell, Randall.
Semi-final
Mar 26 v London Caledonians (h) 1-0
Scorer unknown.
Team unknown.
London Caledonians failed to attend. Spurs kicked
off, scored and claimed the match but a further match
was ordered.
Replay
Apr 16 v London Caledonians (h) 0-1
Anderson; Jull, Tyrell, Bull, Casey, Lovis, Buckle,
Harston, Mason, Cottrell, Randall.

FRIENDLIES
Oct 2 v South Hackney (h) 13-1
Scorers unknown.
Team unknown.
Oct 9 v Woodford Bridge (h) 2-0
Scorers unknown.
Team unknown.
Oct 30 v Old St Paul's (h) 1-1
Scorer unknown.
Team unknown.
Nov 13 v Silesia College (a) 2-3
Buckle, Scorer unknown
Team unknown but also included Bull. Spurs fielded
eight players and two subs at start until a further player
arrived late.
Nov 27 v Fillebrook (a) 1-4
Buckle
Team unknown but also included Jull and Mason.
Dec 4 v Iona (a) 5-0
Cottrell, Harston, Randall, Purdie 2
Team unknown.
Dec 27 v Dreadnought (h) 6-0
Scorers unknown.
Team unknown.
Jan 22 v Foxes (a) 2-1 (80 minutes only played)
Scorers unknown.
Team unknown.
Feb 5 v Park (h) 4-1
Scorers unknown.
Team unknown but Spurs fielded only ten players.
Feb 12 v Fillebrook (h) 3-0
Scorers unknown.
Team unknown.
Mar 5 v Edmonton Association (a) 3-1
Scorers unknown.
Team unknown.
(One Spurs goal disputed)
Mar 19 v London Caledonians (North Greenwich) 0-2
Anderson; Jull, Tyrell, Lovis, Casey, Bull, Randall,
Harston, Mason, Cottrell, Buckle.
This match should have been the semi-final of the East
End Cup but as the pitch was in such a bad state
the teams agreed to play a friendly.
Apr 23 v Enfield Lock (h) 7-1
Scorers unknown.

Team unknown.
(One Spurs goal disputed)

1887-88
LONDON SENIOR CUP
Round 1
Oct 8 v Hendon (a) 0-6
Anderson; Jull, Tyrell, Bull, Lovis, Baldock, Buckle,
Harston, Mason, Cottrell, Bird.

FRIENDLIES
Oct 1 v Buckhurst Hill (h) 6-1
Scorers unknown.
Team unknown.
Nov 12 v Nondescripts (h) 6-1
Scorers unknown.
Team unknown.
**Nov 19 v Royal Arsenal (h) 2-1 (abandoned after 75
minutes because of bad light)**
Scorers unknown.
Team unknown.
Dec 3 v Luton Town (a) 2-1
Mason, Harston
Team unknown.
Dec 10 v Priory (a) 3-0
Scorers unknown.
Team unknown but Spurs fielded only nine players
until half-time and ten thereafter.
Dec 24 v Balmoral (h) 1-1
Scorer unknown.
Team unknown.
Dec 31 v St Martin's (h) 3-0
Scorers unknown.
Team unknown.
Jan 7 v St Bride's (h) 3-2
Cottrell, Buckle, Mason
Team unknown.
Jan 14 v Bowes Park (a) 2-2
Scorers unknown.
A.N.Other; Jull, Tyrell, Bull, Lovis, Casey, Hudson,
Baldock, Mason, Harston, Adellington.
Jan 21 v Old St Paul's (a) 2-1
Scorers unknown.
Team unknown.
Feb 4 v Royal Arsenal (a) 2-6
Scorers unknown.
Team unknown but Spurs fielded only nine players.
Feb 18 v Olympic (a) 5-1
Scorers unknow.
Team unknown.
Mar 17 v St Bride's (h) 3-0
Buckle, Scorers unknown 2
Team unknown.
Apr 2 v Clapton (a)1-6
Scorer unknown.
Team unknown.

1888-89
LONDON SENIOR CUP
Round 1
Oct 13 v Old Etonians (h) 2-8
Buckle, Purdie
Baldock; Jull, Crossley, Bull, Casey, Tyrell, Buckle,
Harston, Purdie, Mason, Cottrell.

MIDDLESEX SENIOR CUP
Round 1

Jan 10 v Civil Engineers (h) 0-0
Team unknown.
Replay
Jan 19 v Civil Engineers (a) 1-4
Scorer unknown.
Team unknown but included Buckle and Harston.

FRIENDLIES
Sep 22 v Royal Arsenal (a) 1-0
Baldock
Team unknown but also included Jull and Casey.
Oct 20 v Clapton (h) 2-5
Scorers unknown.
Team unknown
Nov 17 v Millwall Rovers (h) 1-1 (60 minutes only played)
Scorer unknown.
Team unknown.
Nov 24 v Plaistow (h) 4-0
Scorers unknown.
Team unknown but included Jull.
Dec 1 v Old St Mark's (h) 5-1
Scorers unknown.
Team unknown but Spurs fielded only ten players including Bull.
Dec 8 v Upton Excelsior (h) 3-3
Scorers unknown.
Team unknown.
Dec 15 v Plaistow (a) 2-1 (40 minutes only played)
Payne, Buckle
Team unknown but Spurs fielded only ten players.
Dec 22 v Bowes Park (a) 4-0
Jull 2, Buckle., Cottrell
Team unknown but also included Bull.
Dec 26 v Orion Gymnasium (h) score unknown
Scorers unknown.
Team unknown.
Jan 16 v Windsor Phoenix (a) 1-2
Buckle
Adellington; Jull, Crossley, Casey, Simpson, Latymer, Buckle, Harston. Parker, Mason, Goddard.
Mar 2 v Windsor Phoenix (a) 1-2
Buckle
Team unknown
Mar 9 v Royal Arsenal (h) 0-1
Team unknown.
Mar 16 v Edmonton (h) 1-1
Harston
Team unknown.
Apr 13 v Orion Gymnasium (h) 6-1
Scorers unknown.
Team unknown.

1889-90
LONDON SENIOR CUP
Round 1
Bye
Round 2
Nov 2 v Old St Mark's (a) 0-4
Walford; Jull, Littleford, Casey, Davies, Baldock, Buckle, Harston, Marpole, Cottrell, S.Lovis.

MIDDLESEX SENIOR CUP
Round 1
Jan 18 v Old St Stephen's (a) 4-2
Lovis, Harston, Humber 2
Team unknown but also included Jull, Casey and Littleford.

Round 2
Feb 11 v Clapton (h) 2-4
Scorers unknown.
Team unknown.

FRIENDLIES
Sep 21 v Royal Arsenal (a) 1-10
Parker
Anderson; Griffith, Jull, Baldock, Pracey, Ayres, Cottrell, Cadman, Tyrell, Buckle, Parker.
Sep 28 v Westminster (h) 13-0
Buckle, Harston, Cottrell, Tyrell, Scorers unknown 9.
Team unknown but also included Cadman and Lovis.
Oct 5 v Vulcan (h) 5-1
Lovis, Jull, Scorers unknown 3.
Walford; Marpole, Jull, Casey, Baldock, Leaman, Buckle, Harston, Mason, Cottrell, Lovis.
Oct 12 v Iona (h) 10-0
Jull 5, Scorers unknown 5
Team unknown but included Littleford, Davies and Lovis.
Oct 19 v Edmonton (a) 2-3
Scorers unknown.
Team unknown.
Nov 9 v Clapton (h) 5-3
Scorers unknown.
Team unknown.
Nov 16 v Finchley (a) 1-1
Scorer unknown.
Team unknown.
Nov 23 v Hampstead (h) 1-0
Scorer unknown.
Team unknown.
Nov 30 v Foxes (h) 1-0
Scorer unknown.
Team unknown.
Jan 4 v Foxes (h) 1-1
Scorer unknown
Team unknown.
Jan 11 v Romford (a) 0-0 (40 minutes only played)
Team unknown.
Feb 1 v Robin Hood (h) 1-0
Scorer unknown.
Team unknown.
Feb 8 v Vulcan (h) 2-1
Buckle, Bassett
Team unknown but also included Casey.
Mar 1 v Swindon Town (a) 1-2
Perry.
Walford; Jull, Littleford, Casey, Simpson, Bassett, Buckle, Perry, Humber, Cottrell, Harston.
(One Swindon goal disputed)
Mar 8 v Unity (h) 3-1
Scorers unknown.
Team unknown but included Jull and Bassett.
Mar 15 v Edmonton (h) 1-4
Scorer unknown.
Walford; Littleford, Jull, Casey, Cadman, Bassett, Lovis, Cottrell, Humber, Harston, Buckle.
Apr 4 v Dreadnought (h) 0-1
Team unknown.
Apr 5 v Uxbridge (a) 2-2
Scorers unknown.
Team unknown.
Apr 7 v Maidenhead (a) 3-2
Scorers unknown.
Team unknown.

Date unknown v Foxes (h) 2-2
Bumberry, Scorer unknown.
Team unknown.

Note: It is also known that matches were arranged against Acton, Luton Town, Old St Stephen's, Olympic, Wolverton and Woodford. However, no records remain of results, dates, scorers or teams.

1890-91
LONDON SENIOR CUP
Preliminary Round 1
Bye
Preliminary Round 2
Nov 1 v Queen's Park Rangers (a) 1-1
Cottrell
Team unknown but also included Walford, Jull, Simpson, Baxter, Buckle.
Replay
Nov 8 v Queen's Park Rangers (h) 2-1
Buckle, Harston
Team unknown but included Baxter.
Preliminary Round 3
Nov 22 v Barking (h) 2-0
Baxter, Buckle
Team unknown but included Walford, Jull, Casey and Harston.
Round 1
Jan 24 v Barnes (a) 1-0
Cottrell
Team unknown but also included Simpson.
Round 2
Jan 31 v Millwall Athletic (a) 1-5
Harston
Walford; Jull, Bassett, Simpson, Cadman, Drysdale, Baxter, Cottrell, Perry, Harston, Buckle.

MIDDLESEX SENIOR CUP
Round 1
Feb 7 v Orion Gymnasium (h) 7-1
Scorers unknown.
Team unknown.
Round 2
Feb 14 v Clapton (h) lost but score unknown
Scorers unknown.
Team unknown.

FRIENDLIES
Sep 27 v Hampstead (h) 6-3
Scorers unknown.
Team unknown.
Oct 4 v Grove House (h) score unknown
Scorers unknown.
Team unknown.
Oct 11 v Edmonton (a) 4-6
Scorers unknown.
Team unknown.
Oct 18 v Luton Town (a) 1-4
Baxter
Team unknown.
Oct 25 v Northumberland Fusiliers (h) 1-0
Scorer unknown.
Team unknown.
Nov 15 v City Ramblers (h) 1-0
Buckle
Team unknown but also included Cottrell.
Dec 6 v Unity (a) 1-1
Pilbrow
Team unknown but Spurs fielded only nine players including Jull.
Feb 21 v Vulcan (h) 6-0
Scorers unknown.

Team unknown.
Feb 28 v Old St Stephen's (h) 3-0
Buckle 2, Scorer unknown
Team unknown but also included Jull.
Mar 7 v 1st Scots Guards (h) score unknown
Scorers unknown.
Team unknown.

1891-92
LONDON SENIOR CUP
Round 1
Oct 10 v Caledonian Athletic (h) 4-3
Cottrell, Bassett 2, H.Leese
Team unknown but included Jull, Cadman, Lovis and Millard.
Round 2
Oct 31 v Hampstead (a) 3-2
Lovis, Cottrell, Buckle
Anderson; Jull, Bassett, Casey, Monk, Simpson, Lovis, Harston, Cottrell, Buckle, Leese H.
Round 3
Nov 21 v City Ramblers (a) 1-4
H.Leese (pen)
Monk; Jull, Bassett, Casey, Bull, Simpson, Lovis, Harston, Cottrell, Buckle, H.Leese.

MIDDLESEX SENIOR CUP
Round 1
Bye
Round 2
Dec 5 v Minerva (a) 0-2
Team unknown but included Monk, Jull, Bassett, Lovis, Miller, H.Leese.

LUTON CHARITY CUP
Round 1
Nov 7 v Coldstream Guards (h) 3-3
Harston, Cottrell, Opp own-goal
Team unknown but also included Anderson, Dingwell, Fox and H.Leese.
Replay
Nov 14 v Coldstream Guards (h) 7-2
Cottrell 5, Millard, Weston
Team unknown but also included Monk and H.Leese. (Played at home by mutual consent).
Round 2
Dec 19 v 1st Btn Scots Guards (a) 0-4
Team unknown but included Monk.

FRIENDLIES
Sep 26 v Hampstead (h) 6-2
Scorers unknown.
Team unknown but included Jull, Bull and H.Leese.
Oct 3 v Grange Park (h) 4-2
Scorers unknown.
Team unknown but Spurs fielded only ten players, nine at the start.
Oct 24 v Clapton (h) 1-2
Millard
Team unknown but included Anderson, Jull, Fox, Lovis, Bassett, Cottrell and H.Leese.
Nov 28 v Old St Stephen's (h) 0-0
Monk; Jull, Dingwell, Bull, Casey, Bassett, Lovis, Fox, Cottrell, Buckle. (10 men only).
Dec 12 v Forest Swifts (h) 1-1 (abandoned after 60 minutes because of bad light)
H.Leese
Monk; Jull, Casey, Shillingworth, Miller, H.Leese, Harkins, Lovis, Weston, Shepherd. (10 men only).
Jan 2 v Uxbridge (h) 3-0
Weston, Tyler, H.Leese
Monk; Jull, Coulson, Bassett, F.Leese, Casey, Sykes,

Weston, Tyler, Miller, H.Leese.
Jan 9 v Queen's Park Rangers (h) 1-2
Tyler
Monk; Jull, F.Leese, Casey, Crossley, Bull, Cottrell, Weston, Tyler, Joel, H.Leese.
Jan 23 v Westminster Criterion (h) 2-2
Sykes, Tyler
Monk; Jull, Casey, Bull, Briggs, Miller, Sykes, Weston, Tyler, Bridgen, Ellis.
Jan 30 v Old St Luke's (h) 3-1
Scorers unknown.
Team unknown.
Feb 6 v St Albans (a) 1-2
Tyler
Team unknown but also included Monk, Jull, Briggs, Sykes, Hepburn, Buckle, and Hurry.
Feb 13 v Clapton (a) 2-0
Miller, Weston
Team unknown but also included Monk, Jull, Briggs, Sykes, Hepburn, Tyler, Buckle and Hurry.
Feb 20 v City Ramblers (h) score unknown
Scorers unknown.
Team unknown.
Feb 27 v Grenadier Guards (h) 9-0
Barnes, Tyler, Barber, Sykes 2, Scorers unknown 4
Team unknown but also included Briggs and Weston.
Mar 12 v Casuals (h) 3-1
Lovis 2, Hepburn
Monk; Jull, Coulson, Casey, Briggs, Bull, Lovis, Harston, Tyler, Hepburn, H.Leese.
Mar 26 v Luton Town (a) 1-3
Scorer unknown.
Monk; Coulson, J.Jull, Casey, Briggs, H.Jull, Sykes, Harston, Tyler, Hepburn, Williams.

It is known that matches were arranged against Carpenters Institute, Gresham, Maidenhead, Orion Gymnasium and Shalford St Peter's but no records survive of dates, results, scorers or teams.

1892-93
SOUTHERN ALLIANCE
Sep 24 v Polytechnic (a) 2-1
Sykes, Brigden
Team unknown but also included Monk, Jull, Moody, Welham, Cottrell and Cubberley.
Oct 15 v Old St Stephen's (a) 0-3
Monk; Moody, Welham, Jull, Simpson, Briggs, Brigden, Ellis, Cottrell, Harston, Sykes.
Nov 5 v Windsor and Eton (a) 2-1
Weston, Scorer unknown
Monk; Moody, Welham, Jull, Briggs, Simpson, Weston, Cottrell, Brigden, Ellis, Sykes.
Nov 19 v Erith (h) 3-2
Briggs, Jull 2
Monk; Moody, Welham, Casey, Briggs, Simpson, Sykes, Cottrell, Jull, Brigden, Ellis.
Jan 14 v Erith (a) 1-2
Sykes
Team unknown but also included Monk, Welham, Jull, Brigden and Casey.
Jan 21 v Slough (a) 3-3
H.Lovis, Bell 2
Monk; Moody, Jull, Baldock Casey, J.Lovis, Sykes, Bell, S.Lovis, Ellis, H.Lovis.
Feb 4 v Slough (h) 5-2
Bell 2, Jull 2, Opp own-goal
Monk; Moody, Welham, P.Lovis, Briggs, Bull, Sykes, Baxter, Bell, S.Lovis, Jull.
Feb 11 v Polytechnic (h) 2-2
Sykes 2
Monk; Moody, Welham, Casey, Briggs, Jull, Sykes,

Bell, Cottrell, Brigden, Ellis.
Feb 25 v Upton Park (h) 1-0
Bell
Hart; Moody, Jull, Casey, Briggs, Bull, Cubberley, Sykes, Bell, Brigden, Ellis.
Mar 4 v Windsor & Eton (h) 5-2
Baxter 2, Gilderson, Fortnam, Cattell
Hart; Moody, F.Markham, W.Markham, Jull, E.Markham, Sykes, Baxter, Gilderson, Fortnam, Cattell.
Mar 25 v Old St Stephen's (h) 1-2
Brigden
Monk; Rose, Welham, Jull, Gamble, Bull, Sykes, Cubberley, Cattell, Brigden, Ellis.
Apr 8 v Upton Park (a) 4-1
Scorers unknown.
Team unknown but included Briggs and Sykes.

LONDON SENIOR CUP
Round 1
Bye
Round 2
Minerva (h) scratched
Round 3
Dec 3 v Polytechnic (a) 2-2
Scorers unknown.
Monk; Jull, Welham, Casey, Briggs, Simpson, Sykes, Bull, Cottrell, Brigden, Ellis.
Replay
Dec 17 v Polytechnic (h) 3-0
Jull 3
Team unknown but also included Moody and Welham.
Round 4
Jan 28 v Casuals (h) 0-1
Monk; Moody, Welham, Casey, Briggs, Simpson, Sykes, Cottrell, Jull, Brigden, P.Lovis.

WOLVERTON & DISTRICT CHARITY CUP
Apr 15 v Smethwick (Wolverton) 0-2
Hart; Jull, Moody, Gamble, Briggs, Thornley, Sykes, Meggs, Cattell, Brigden, Ellis.

FRIENDLIES
Sep 17 v Paddington (h) 10-0
Scorers unknown.
Team unknown but included Monk, Jull, Moody, Welham, Sykes, Cottrell, Brigden and Lomas.
Oct 1 v Royal Arsenal Athletic (h) 3-0
Jull, Harston 2
Monk; Moody, Welham, Jull, Briggs, Simpson, Sykes, Lomas, Cottrell, Harston, Ellis.
Oct 8 v 2nd Coldstream Guards (h) 6-0
Scorers unknown.
Team unknown.
Oct 15 v University (h) 5-4
Scorers unknown.
Team unknown.
Oct 22 v Coldstream Guards (h) 3-2
Baxter, Cottrell 2
Monk; Moody, Welham, Jull, Briggs, Simpson, Sykes, Cottrell, Baxter, Brigden, Ellis.
Oct 29 v 2nd Scots Guards (h) 2-4
Baxter 2
Team unknown but also included Monk, Moody, Briggs, Cottrell and Brigden.
Nov 12 v Clapton (h) 1-2 (70 minutes only played)
Scorer unknown.
Team unknown.
Nov 26 v Caledonian Athletic (h) 5-0
Scorers unknown.
Team unknown.
Dec 10 v Hampstead (h) 1-1

Scorers unknown.
Team unknown.
Dec 24 v Coldstream Guards (h) score unknown
Scorers unknown.
Team unknown.
Dec 26 v Edmonton (h) score unknown
Scorers unknown.
Team unknown.
Feb 18 v London Welsh (h) 2-2
Briggs, Fortnam
Team unknown but also included Hart, Jull and Sykes.
Mar 11 v Queen's Park Rangers (h) 1-0
Brigden
Team unknown but also included Hart, Jull, Ellis, Briggs, Bull and Cubberley.
Apr 1 v City Ramblers (h) 1-0
Palmer
Monk; Moody, Jull, Baldock, Tyrell, Bull, Meggs, Fortnam, Palmer, Brigden, Ellis.
Apr 22 v London Welsh (h) 4-1
Sykes 2, Cottrell 2
Moody; Rose, Jull, F.Markham, Briggs, Bull, Sykes, Baxter, Cottrell, Brigden, Ellis.

1893-94
FA AMATEUR CUP
Round 1
Nov 11 v Vampires (h) 3-1
Briggs, Mills, Taylor
Monk; Moody, Welham, Shepherd, Briggs, Jull, Sykes, Cubberley, Mills, Taylor, Ellis.

LONDON SENIOR CUP
Round 1
Oct 21 v Old St Mark's (h) 0-0
Monk; Jull, Welham, Shepherd, Briggs, Newby, Sykes, Cubberley, Tyler, Hepburn, Burton.
Replay
Oct 28 v Old St Mark's (h) 1-6
Briggs
Monk; Jull, Welham, Shepherd, Briggs, Newby, Sykes, Cubberley, Bowyer, Brigden, Ellis.
(Played at home by mutual consent)

MIDDLESEX SENIOR CUP
Round 1
Jan 13 v 3rd Grenadier Guards (h) 1-1
Cubberley
Monk; Rose, Welham, Shepherd, Briggs, Jull, Sykes, Cubberley, Shaw, Coleman, Renals.
Replay
Jan 20 v 3rd Grenadier Guards (h) 0-2
Monk; Jull, Rose, Shepherd, Casey, Newby, Sykes, Cubberley, Briggs, Renals, Shearing.
(Played at home by mutual consent)

LONDON CHARITY CUP
Round 1
Dec 9 v Crusaders (h) 2-5
Sykes, Taylor
Monk; Moody, Welham, Shepherd, Briggs, Jull, Sykes, Cubberley, Mills, Taylor, Renals.

WOLVERTON & DISTRICT CHARITY CUP
Round 1
Jan 27 v Chesham (h) 2-2
Sykes, Jull
Monk; Moody, Welham, Shepherd, Briggs, Newby, Sykes, Cubberley, Milne, MacDonald, Jull.
Replay
Feb 24 v Chesham (a) 3-1
Cubberley, MacLachlan, Payne

Monk; Jull, Welham, Shepherd, Briggs, Newby, Sykes, Cubberley, Milne, MacLachlan, Payne.
Semi-final
Mar 10 v Smethwick (Wolverton) 0-1
Monk; Jull, Welham, Shepherd, Briggs, Newby, Shaw, Cubberley, Milne, MacLachlan, Payne.

FRIENDLIES
Sep 16 v Enfield (a) 1-5
Hepburn
Team unknown but also included Sykes, Baker, Newby, Welham, Moody, Ellis and Monk.
Sep 23 v Romford (h) 2-2
Sykes, Meggs
Monk; Jull, Welham, Kingan, Newby, Briggs, Sykes, Griffiths, Meggs, Brigden, Ellis.
Sep 30 v Casuals (h) 0-1
Monk; Jull, Welham, Shepherd, Briggs, Newby, Sykes, Meggs, Cottrell, Hepburn, Ellis.
Oct 7 v City Ramblers (h) 2-0
Briggs, Hepburn
Monk; Jull, Welham, Shepherd, Briggs, Newby, Sykes, Baxter, Tyler, Hepburn, Ellis.
Oct 14 v London Welsh (h) 1-0
Cubberley
Monk; Jull, Welham, Shepherd, Briggs, Newby, Sykes, Cubberley, Tyler, Brigden, Ellis.
Nov 4 v 1st Scots Guards (h) 1-2
Mills
Monk; Moody, Welham, Shepherd, Briggs, Jull, Cubberley, Renals, Mills, Taylor, Ellis.
Nov 18 v London Welsh (h) 2-1
Sykes, Cubberley
Monk; Rose, Welham, Jull, Casey, Shepherd, Sykes, Cubberley, Mills, Taylor, Renals.
Dec 16 v Erith (h) 0-1
Monk; Moody, Welham, Shepherd, Casey, Jull, Sykes, Cubberley, Mills, MacLachlan, Renals.
Dec 19 v Friars (h) 2-1
Hepburn 2
Perrin; Rose, Welham, Tarbolton, Casey, Jull, Sykes, Bannerman, Hepburn, Newbury, Renals.
Dec 23 v Wolverton (h) 2-2
Briggs, Renals
Monk; Rose, Moody, Shepherd, Briggs, Jull, Sykes, Cubberley, Mills, Taylor, Renals.
Dec 26 v Southampton St Mary's (a) 0-1
Monk; Moody, Welham, Shepherd, Briggs, Jull, Casey, Cubberley, Mills, Jones, Renals.
Dec 30 v Uxbridge (a) 0-1
Monk; Jull, Rose, Shepherd, Briggs, Casey, Sykes, Cubberley, Mills, Coleman, Renals.
Feb 3 v City Ramblers (h) 0-0
Monk; Jull, Welham, Shepherd, Briggs, Newby, Sykes Cubberley, Milne, MacLachlan, Aitken.
Feb 8 v London Hospital (h) 1-1
Nesbit
Wood; McGahey, Briggs, Mordin, Mills, E.Markham, Baxter, Nisbit, King, MacLachlan, Jull.
Feb 10 v Polytechnic (h) 5-0
Milne, Payne 4
Monk; Jull, Welham, Shepherd, Briggs, Newby, Shaw, Cubberley, Milne, MacLachlan, Payne.
Feb 17 v Highland Light Infantry (h) 2-2
Briggs, Milne
Monk; Jull, Welham, Shepherd, Briggs, Newby, Sykes, Cubberley, Milne, MacClachlan, Payne.
Mar 3 v Uxbridge (h) 1-1
Shaw
Monk; Jull, Welham, Shepherd, Briggs, Newby, Shaw, Cubberley, Milne, MacLachlan, Payne.
Mar 23 v 2nd Scots Guards (h) 3-1

371

Simmonds 2, Payne
Monk; Jull, Shepherd, Jackson, Fincham, Milne, Cubberley, Bannerman, Simmonds, Payne, MacLachlan.
Mar 24 v Slough (h) 2-0
Bannerman, Payne
Monk; Jull, Shepherd, Fincham, Milne, Newby, Sykes, Cubberley, Bannerman, MacLachlan, Payne.
Mar 26 v New Brompton (a) 3-3
Newby, Fincham, Payne
Monk; Shepherd, Jull, Newby, Milne, Fincham, Sykes, Cubberley, Gilderson, Payne, MacLachlan.
Mar 31 v Polytechnic (h) 0-0
Monk; Shepherd, Jull, Newby, Lovis, Fincham, Sykes, Cubberley, Bannerman, MacLachlan, Ellis.
Apr 7 v Old St Stephen's (h) 1-1
Simmonds
Monk; Gorman, Welham, Shepherd, Milne, Fincham, Sykes, Cubberley, Simmonds, MacLachlan, Jull.
Apr 14 v Ilford (h) 0-1
Monk; Gorman, Welham, Shepherd, Briggs, Jull, Sykes, Cubberley, Simmonds, MacLachlan, Payne.
Apr 21 v Crouch End (a) 2-2
Cubberley, MacLachlan
Monk; Gorman, Welham, Shepherd, Briggs, Jull, Sykes, Cubberley, Edwards, MacLachlan, Payne.

1894-95
FA CUP
Round 1 (Qualifying)
Oct 13 v West Herts (h) 3-2
Hunter, Goodall 2
Monk; Jull, Welham, Shepherd, Briggs, Julian, Cubberley, Goodall, Hunter, Eccles, Payne.
Round 2 (Qualifying)
Nov 3 v Wolverton (h) 5-3
Goodall, Hunter 2, Payne 2
Ambler; Burrows, Jull, Shepherd, Briggs, Julian, Cubberley, Goodall, Hunter, Eccles, Payne.
Round 3 (Qualifying)
Nov 24 v Clapton (a) 4-0
Eccles 2, Hunter, Goodall
Ambler; Jull, Burrows, Shepherd, Briggs, Julian, Payne, Eccles, Hunter, Goodall, Cubberley.
Round 4 (Qualifying)
Dec 15 v Luton Town (h) 2-2
Eccles, Cubberley
Ambler; Jull, Burrows, Welham, Julian, Shepherd, Payne, Eccles, Hunter, Goodall, Cubberley.
Replay
Dec 19 v Luton Town (a) 0-4
Ambler; Jull, Burrows, Welham, Julian, Shepherd, Payne, Eccles, Hunter, Coleman, Cubberley.

FA AMATEUR CUP
Round 1 (Qualifying)
Oct 20 v Old Harrovians (h) 7-0
Julian, Simpson, Eccles, Edwards, Hunter, Goodall, Cubberley
Monk; Welham, Sullivan, Shepherd, Julian, Simpson, Eccles, Edwards, Hunter, Goodall, Cubberley.
Round 2 (Qualifying)
Nov 10 v City Ramblers (h) 6-1
Shepherd, Goodall, Hunter 2, Payne 2
Ambler; Burrows, Jull, Shepherd, Briggs, Julian, Cubberley, Goodall, Hunter, Eccles, Payne.
Round 3 (Qualifying)
Dec 1 v Romford (a) 8-0
Payne 2, Eccles, Hunter 3, Goodall 2
Ambler; Jull, Burrows, Shepherd, Briggs, Julian, Payne, Eccles, Hunter, Goodall, Cubberley.
Divisional Final

Dec 22 v London Welsh (h) 1-1
Payne
Ambler; Jull, Burrows, Welham, Julian, Shepherd, Payne, Eccles, Hunter, Goodall, Cubberley.
Replay
Jan 5 v London Welsh (a) 3-3
Shaw, Hunter, Eccles
Ambler; Burrows, Jull, Shepherd, Simpson, Welham, Shaw, Goodall, Hunter, Eccles, Payne.
2nd Replay
Jan 19 v London Welsh (Spotted Dog) 4-2
Jull, Welham, Payne, Hunter
Ambler; Burrows, Jull, Julian, Welham, Shepherd, Payne, Eccles, Hunter, Rose, Nixon.
Round 1
Feb 23 v Beeston (h) 2-0
Julian, Hunter
Ambler; Burrows, Welham, Shepherd, Collins, Julian, Cubberley, Goodall, Hunter, Eccles, Payne.
Round 2
Mar 16 v Old Carthusians (h) 0-5
Ambler; Burrows, Markham, Jull, Collins, Shepherd, Clements, Rose, Hunter, Eccles, Payne.

LONDON SENIOR CUP
Round 1
Jan 26 v London Welsh (h) 5-0
Hunter, Eccles, Payne 3
Ambler; Burrows, Jull, Shepherd, Welham, Julian, Bailey, Collins, Hunter, Eccles, Payne.
Round 2
Mar 2 v Old Westminsters (a) 3-3
Rose, Goodall 2
Ambler; Burrows, Hay, Julian, Collins, Shepherd, Payne, Rose, Hunter, Goodall, Bailey.
Replay
Mar 9 v Old Westminsters (h) 4-5
Bailey, Hunter, Reynolds, Payne
Ambler; Burrows, Jull, Shepherd, Collins, Julian, Bailey, Hunter, Reynolds, Clements, Payne.

LONDON CHARITY CUP
Round 1
Dec 8 v Crusaders (h) 4-2
Goodall 2, Welham, Eccles
Ambler; Bull, Burrows, Shepherd, Welham, Julian, Payne, Eccles, Hunter, Goodall, Cubberley.
Round 2
Mar 21 v Old Carthusians (a) 0-3
Ambler; Burrows, Barker, Smith, Collins, Julian, Reynolds, Hunter, Eccles, Payne, Clements.

FRIENDLIES
Sep 15 v Uxbridge (a) 0-2
Monk; Jull, Welham, Shepherd, Briggs, Dickie, Cubberley, Eccles, Hunter, Goodall, Payne.
Sep 22 v Casuals (h) 3-1
Hunter 2, Payne
Monk; Jull, Welham, Shepherd, Briggs, Dickie, Cubberley, Goodall, Hunter, Eccles, Payne.
Sep 29 v London Caledonians (a) 1-3
Hunter
Monk; Jull, Welham, Julian, Briggs, Dickie, Payne, Eccles, Hunter, Cubberley, Shepherd.
Oct 6 v 3rd Grenadier Guards (h) 1-1
Payne
Monk; Burrows, Welham, Julian, Briggs, Shepherd, Payne, Eccles, Goodall, Cubberley, Elliott.
Oct 27 v Crouch End (a) 2-2
Julian, Goodall
Fenn; Burrows, Caldecott, Julian, Newby, Shepherd, Eccles, Cubberley, Hunter, Goodall, Payne.

Nov 17 v Highland Light Infantry (h) 1-1
Hunter
Ambler; Burrows, Jull, Shepherd, Briggs, Julian, Cubberley, Goodall, Hunter, Eccles, Payne.
Dec 25 v Sheffield & District League (h) 7-1
Goodall, Hunter 3, Jones, Payne 2
Ambler; Burrows, Jull, Shepherd, Smith, McKenzie, Cubberley, Goodall, Hunter, Jones, Payne.
Dec 26 v West Liverpool (h) 3-0
Hunter, Payne Jnr, Payne Snr
Ambler; Burrows, Jull, Shepherd, Oliver, McKenzie, Sykes, Goodall, Hunter, Payne Jnr, Payne Snr.
Dec 29 v Vampires (h) 4-1
Goodall 2, Hunter, Jones
Ambler; Burrows, Jull, Shepherd, Simmonds, Simpson, Shaw, Goodall, Hunter, Jones, Payne.
Mar 23 v London Caledonians (h) 5-1
Stirling, Collins, Goodall, Hunter 2
Ambler; Burrows, Jull, Stirling, Collins, Julian, Clements, Goodall, Hunter, Eccles, Payne.
Mar 30 v City Ramblers (h) 2-0
Hunter, Carver
Ambler; Burrows, Jull, Shepherd, Collins, Julian, Sykes, Brennan, Hunter, Carver, Clements.
Apr 6 v Casuals (h) 1-2 (60 minutes only played)
Clements
Ambler; Burrows, Jull, Shepherd, Collins, Julian, Clements, Cottrell, Hunter, Newman, Payne.
Apr 12 v Liverpool Casuals (h) 6-0
Wilkinson, Laycock, Hunter 2, McElhaney 2
Ambler; Burrows, Barker, Stirling, Collins, Julian, Wilkinson, Laycock, Hunter, McElhaney, Payne.
Apr 13 v 2nd Scots Guards (h) 1-1
Shepherd
Ambler; Burrows, Jull, Shepherd, Collins, Julian, Clements, Sykes, Hunter, Simmonds, Pryor.
Apr 15 v Southampton St Mary's (h) 0-0
Ambler; Burrows, Jull, Stirling, Collins, Julian, Pryor, Ward-Leaver, Hunter, McElhaney, Payne.
Apr 16 v Bristol South End (a) 7-0
Pryor, Clements, Hunter 2, McElheney, Payne 2
Ambler; Burrows, Jull, Shepherd, Stirling, Julian, Pryor, Clements, Hunter, McElhaney, Payne.
Apr 25 v London Caledonians (h) 2-0 (70 minutes only played)
Pryor 2
Ambler; Burrows, Jull, Stirling, Collins, Julian, Pryor, Mayor, Hunter, McElhaney, Payne.
Apr 27 v Brimsdown (a) 2-0
Hunter, Monk
Monk; Godfrey, T.E.Jull, Risley, Casey, J.Jull, Everdell, Payne, Buckle, Hunter, Hurry.

1895-96
FA CUP
Round 1 (Qualifying)
Oct 12 v Luton Town (a) 2-1
Hunter, Owen
Ambler; Briggs, Burrows, McKenzie, Collins, Shepherd, Payne, Clements, Hunter, Owen, Pryor.
Round 2 (Qualifying)
Nov 2 v Vampires (a) 2-4
Pryor, Clements
Ambler; Shepherd, Williams, Burne, Briggs, Collins, Pryor, Cottrell, Hunter, Clements, Payne.
(Pitch wrongly marked so replay ordered)
Replay
Nov 16 v Vampires (h) 2-1
Pryor, Hunter
Monk; Burrows, Jull, Collins, Almond, Briggs, Pryor, Gilmore, Hunter, Clements, Payne.
Round 3 (Qualifying)

Nov 23 v Ilford (a) 5-1
Almond, Pryor 2, Payne 2
Ambler; Burrows, Jull, Collins, Almond, Briggs, Pryor, Gilmore, Hunter, Clements, Payne.
Round 4 (Qualifying)
Dec 14 v Old St Stephen's (h) 2-1
Clements, O'Sullivan (og)
Ambler; Collins, Jull, Shepherd, Almond, Briggs, Pryor, Eccles, Hunter, Clements, Payne.
Round 1
Feb 1 v Stoke (a) 0-5
Ambler; Hay, Montgomery, Collins, Almond, Briggs, Pryor, Lanham, Hunter, Clements, Payne.

LONDON CHARITY CUP
Round 1
Nov 9 v London Westminsters (h) 2-1
Pryor, Hunter
Ambler; Burrows, McGahey, Collins, Almond, Briggs, Pryor, Brown, Hunter, Clements, Payne.

FRIENDLIES
Sep 7 v Royal Engineers (a) 3-0
Pryor, Eccles, Payne
Ambler; Burrows, Jull, F.Markham, Briggs, McKenzie, Pryor, Clements, Hunter, Eccles, Payne.
Sep 14 v 1st Royal Scots Greys (h) 3-2
Clements, Payne 2
Ambler; Burrows, Jull, F.Markham, Briggs, McKenzie, Pryor, Clements, Hunter, Eccles, Payne.
Sep 21 v Casuals (h) 3-2
Pryor, Clements, Payne
Ambler; Burrows, Jull, Collins, Briggs, McKenzie, Pryor, Eccles, Hunter, Clements, Payne.
Sep 28 v Royal Ordnance (h) 2-0
Hunter, Burne
Ambler; Burrows, Jull, Clements, Collins, McKenzie, Pryor, Eccles, Hunter, Burne, Payne.
Oct 5 v Clapton (a) 4-5
Clements 3, Payne
Ambler; Burrows, Jull, Collins, Briggs, McKenzie, Pryor, Goodall, Hunter, Clements, Payne.
Oct 19 v Ilford (a) 2-0
Hunter 2
Ambler; Burrows, Williams, McKenzie, Briggs, Collins, Pryor, Butler, Hunter, Clements, Payne.
Oct 26 v Royal Artillery (h) 1-2
Burton
Ambler; Burrows, Williams, Shepherd, Briggs, Collins, Pryor, Burton, Hunter, Clements, Payne.
Nov 7 v Luton Town (h) 0-2
Ambler; Burrows, 'Bach'*, Collins, Briggs, Julian, Pryor, Brown, Hunter, Clements, Payne.
* Pseudonym of A.E.Marjoram who was playing for Swanscombe at the time.
Nov 30 v London Welsh (h) 3-2
Hunter 2, Payne
Ross; Dawson, Jull, Collins, Almond, Briggs, Pryor, Gilmore, Hunter, Clements, Payne.
Dec 7 v London Caledonians (h) 0-3
Ambler; Jull, Marjoram, Shepherd, Almond, Collins, Sykes, Gilmore, Hunter, Clements, Payne.
Dec 21 v Casuals (h) 3-1
Hunter, Clements, Payne
Ambler; McGahey, Marjoram, Shepherd, Almond, Collins, Pryor, Lindsay, Hunter, Clements, Payne.
Dec 25 v Millwall Athletic (a) 3-5
Hunter 2, Clements
Ambler; E.Markham, McGahey, Regan, Collins, McKenzie, Pryor, Lindsay, Hunter, Clements, Payne.
Dec 26 v Accrington (h) 3-0
Briggs, Lindsay, Clements

Ambler; Jull, Dawson, Briggs, Collins, F.Markham, Pryor, Lindsay, Hunter, Clements, Payne.
Dec 28 v Freemantle (h) 2-2
Clements, Hunter (pen)
Ambler; Jull, Collins, Shepherd, Almond, Briggs, Payne, Clements, Hunter, Lindsay, Pryor.
Jan 4 v Reading (h) 2-1
Lanham, Payne
Ambler; Burrows, Montgomery, Collins, Almond, Briggs, Pryor, Logan, Lanham, Clements, Payne.
Jan 11 v Millwall Athletic (h) 1-1
Lanham
Ambler; McGahey, Jull, Collins, Almond, Briggs, Pryor, Logan, Lanham, Clements, Payne.
Jan 18 v Ilford (h) 2-1
Russell, Payne
Ambler; Dawson, Montgomery, Collins, Almond, Briggs, Pryor, Clements, Russell, Lanham, Payne.
Jan 25 v Notts County (h) 1-5
Clements
Ambler; Stark, Montgomery, Collins, Almond, Briggs, Pryor, Lanham, Hunter, Clements, Payne.
Feb 8 v Royal Scots Greys (h) 2-1
Logan 2
Ambler; McGahey, Montgomery, Collins, Almond, Briggs, Pryor, Logan, Lanham, Clements, Payne.
Feb 10 v Luton Town (a) 0-9
Ambler; Beveridge, Montgomery, Collins, Buchan, Briggs, Lanham, McInroy, Hunter, Clements, Payne.
Feb 14 v Royal Ordnance (a) 1-2
Clements
Ambler; McGahey, Montgomery, Collins, Almond, Hughes, Pryor, Lanham, Hunter, Clements, Payne.
Feb 22 v Clapton (h) 4-0
Lanham, Clements 2, Payne
Ambler; McGahey, Montgomery, Collins, Almond, Briggs, Logan, Lanham, Hunter, Clements, Payne.
Feb 29 v Burslem Port Vale (h) 4-0
Logan 2, Hunter, Clements
Ambler; McGahey, Montgomery, Collins, Almond, Briggs, Lanham, Logan, Hunter, Clements, Payne.
Mar 4 v Gravesend (a) 1-1
Scorer unknown.
Monk; Buist, Montgomery, Collins, Almond, Julian, Lanham, Logan, Hunter, Clements, Payne.
Mar 7 v 1st Scots Guards (h) 8-0
Lanham 4, Logan 4
Ambler; Burrows, Montgomery, Shepherd, Almond, Collins, Lanham, Logan, Brown, Clements, Payne.
Mar 9 v Royal Ordnance (a) 1-3
Logan
Ambler; McGahey, Montgomery, E.Markham, Johnson, Julian, Lanham, Logan, Brown, Clements, Payne.
Mar 14 v Uxbridge (h) 4-0
Burrows, Almond 2, Logan
Ambler; Burrows, Montgomery, Collins, Almond, Shepherd, Lanham, Logan, Brown, Clements, Payne.
Mar 16 v Woolwich Arsenal (a) 3-1
Hunter, Brown, Gilmer (og)

Ambler; McGahey, Montgomery, Collins, Briggs, F.Markham, Lanham, Hunter, Brown, Clements, Logan.
Mar 19 v Royal Ordnance (h) 2-2
Clements 2
Jull; E.Markham, Montgomery, Collins, Julian, F.Markham, Pryor, Lanham, Brown, Clements, Payne.
Mar 21 v Manchester Regiment (h) 8-0
Almond, Logan, Hunter 2 (1 pen), Clements 2, Payne 2
Ambler; Hay, Montgomery, Collins, Almond, F.Markham, Logan, Hunter, Brown, Clements, Payne.
Mar 26 v Woolich Arsenal (h) 1-3
Clements
Ambler; Hay, Montgomery, Collins, Almond, F.Markham, Logan, Hunter, Brown, Clements, Payne.
Mar 28 v London Caledonians (a) 5-0
Hunter 2, Brown, Clements, Payne
Ambler; McGahey, Collins, Shepherd, Almond, Smith, Logan, Hunter, Brown, Clements, Payne.
Apr 3 v Reading (a) 3-2
Lanham, Hunter 2
Ambler; McGahey, Montgomery, Smith, Almond, Collins, Lanham, Hunter, Brown, Clements, Payne.
Apr 4 v Oswaldtwistle Rovers (h) 4-0
Logan 2, Brown 2
Ambler; McGahey, Owen, F.Markham, Almond, Collins, Logan, Hunter, Brown, Clements, Payne.
Apr 6 v Middlesbrough (h) 5-0
Brown 2, Clements 2, Payne
Ambler; Montgomery, McGahey, Smith, Almond, Collins, Logan, Hunter, Brown, Clements, Payne.
Apr 7 v Swindon Town (h) 2-3
Clements 2
Ambler; Montgomery, E.Markham, Shepherd (McGahey), Collins, F.Markham, Lanham, Hunter, Brown, Clements, Logan.
Apr 11 v Aston Villa (h) 1-3
Logan
Ambler; Owen, Montgomery, Collins, Almond, F.Markham, Logan, Hunter, Brown, Clements, Payne.
Apr 15 v Swindon Town (a) 2-0
Clements, Payne
Ambler; McGahey, Montgomery, Collins, Buist, Welch, Pryor, Logan, Brown, Clements, Payne.
Apr 18 v Southampton St Mary's (a) 1-4
Lanham
Ambler; Owen, Montgomery, Collins, Almond, Smith, Lanham, Hunter, Brown, Clements, Payne.
Apr 22 v Gravesend (a) 1-1
Clements
Ambler; Montgomery, Flowers, Collins, Cherrie, Crump, Lanham, Hunter, Brown, Clements, Buist.
Apr 25 v Wellingborough (h) 3-0
Almond, Lanham, Brown
Ambler; Collins, Montgomery, Cherrie, Almond, Crump, Lanham, Hunter, Brown, Clements, Payne.
Apr 30 v Woolwich Arsenal (h) 3-2
Almond, Clements, Payne
Ambler; McGahey, Montgomery, Collins, Almond, Crump, Lanham, Logan, Brown, Clements, Payne.

Spurs On Tour

THE following section covers Spurs matches played abroad outside what is regarded as the normal Football League season, details of which can be found in the section on friendly games. It does not include pre-season or end-of-season matches, nor matches against foreign opposition during the League season. Unless otherwise stated, matches below are friendly games. Full details are given where known.

1905 (TO AUSTRIA, HUNGARY AND CZECHOSLOVAKIA)
May 4 v Homen Wart Club (Vienna) 6-0
McNaught, Glen 3, O'Hagan 2
Eggett; Watson, Tait, Bull, McNaught, Hughes, Glen, O'Hagan, Woodward, Copeland, Kirwan.
May 7 v Everton (Vienna) 0-2
Team unknown but included Woodward.
May 10 v Vienna Athletic Club (Vienna) 4-1
Morris, Woodward 2, Murray
Team unknown.
May 12 v Buda Pesth Thorna (Budapest) 7-1
Morris 2, Walton, Stansfield, Cameron 3
Team unknown.
May 14 v Testgyakorborora (Budapest) 12-1
Bull, Stansfield, Cameron, Woodward 4, Glen 2, O'Hagan 3
Team unknown.
May 16 v Everton (Prague) 0-1
Team unknown.
May 21 v Slavia (Prague) 8-1
Bull 2, Walton 2, Cameron 2, Glen, O'Hagan
Team unknown.

1907 (TO BELGIUM)
May 20 v Fulham (Ostend) 2-1
Whyman, Bull
Team unknown but also included Woodward and Darnell.
May 26 v Ostend (Ostend) 8-1
Seeburg 3, Woodward 2, Payne 2, Whyman
Manning; Burton, J.Watson, Walker, Morris, Bull, Darnell, Seeburg, Woodward, Payne, Whyman.

1909 (TO ARGENTINA AND URUGUAY)
Jun 5 v Everton (Palermo) 2-2
Tull, Middlemiss
Boreham; Coquet, Wilkes, Bull, D.Steel, McFarlane, Curtis, Minter, Tull, Clark, Middlemiss.
Jun 10 v Uruguay League (Montevideo) 8-0
Curtis 2, Minter 2, McConnor, Clark 3
Boreham; Coquet, Wilkes, Morris, D.Steel, Bull, Curtis, Minter, McConnor, Clark, Middlemiss.
Jun 13 v Argentinos (Palermo) 1-0
McConnor
Boreham; Coquet, Wilkes, Morris, D.Steel, McFarlane, Curtis, Minter, McConnor, Clark, Middlemiss.
Jun 16 v Liga Argentina (Palermo) 4-1
Bull, Minter, Clark, McFarlane
Boreham; Coquet, Wilkes, Bull, D.Steel, McFarlane, Curtis, Minter, Tull, Clark, Middlemiss.
Jun 19 v Everton (Palermo) 0-4
Boreham; Coquet, Wilkes, Bull, D.Steel, Morris, Curtis, Minter, Tull, Clark, Middlemiss.
Jun 20 v Rosario (Rosario) 9-0
Scorers unknown.
Team unknown.
Jun 24 v Alumini (Alumini) 5-0
Morris, Curtis, Minter 2, McFarlane
Boreham; Coquet, Wilkes, Morris, D.Steel, Bull, Curtis, McFarlane, Minter, Tull, Middlemiss.

1911 (TO GERMANY)
May 7 v North German Combined XI (Hamburg) 4-1
Scorers unknown.
Team unknown.
May 13 v Preussen (Berlin) 7-0
Scorers unknown.
Team unknown.
May 14 v Hertha FC (Berlin) 4-1
Scorers unknown.
Team unknown.
May 20 v Wacker FC (Leipzig) 8-1
Scorers unknown.
Team unknown.
May 21 v Eintracht FC (Brunswick) 4-1
Scorers unknown.
Team unknown.
May 25 v Kickers-Victoria FC (Frankfurt) 6-0
Scorers unknown.
Team unknown.

1912 (TO BELGIUM, GERMANY, AUSTRIA AND HUNGARY)
May 12 v Hull C (Brussels) 0-2
Lunn; Norris, Gliddow, Darnell, D.Steel Lightfoot, Curtis, Minter, Elliott, R.Steel(Bliss), Middlemiss.
Above game was for the Decker Cup.
May 16 v Bewegungs Spiele (Leipzig) 3-1
Grimsdell, Tattersall, Bliss
Team unknown.
May 18 v Sports Athletic Club (Vienna) 5-2
Scorers unknown.
Team unknown.
May 24 v Woolwich Arsenal (Vienna) 0-4
Team unknown but included Lightfoot.
May 27 v Ferencvárosi Torna (Budapest) 4-1
Scorers unknown.
Team unknown but included Darnell, Bliss, Middlemiss, Lunn and Minter.
May 28 v Olympic Players (Budapest) 2-2
Scorers unknown.
Team unknown but included Bliss and Middlemiss.
May 30 v Olympic Players (Budapest) 4-3
Scorers unknown.
Team unknown but included Bliss.
Jun 2 v Olympic Players (Vienna) 0-3
Team unknown but included Curtis.

1913 (TO FRANCE)
May 1 v Red Star Amical (Paris) 2-1
Minter, Bliss
Team unknown but also included Tate, R.Steel and Walden.
May 4 v Red Star Amical (Paris) 9-0
Grimsdell 3, Fleming 3, Minter 2, Bliss
Team unknown.

1914 (TO GERMANY, ITALY AND SWITZERLAND)
May 3 v Hanover FC (Hanover) 6-3
Banks, Elliott, Bliss, Middlemiss 3
Team unknown.
May 6 v 1st Club of Nuremberg (Nuremberg) 1-1
Sparrow

Team unknown but also included Joyce and Middlemiss.
May 9 v Bayern Munich (Munich) 6-0
Joyce (pen), Banks 2, Sparrow 3
Joyce; Clay, Cartwright, Fleming, Elliott, Lightfoot, Tattersall, Banks, Sparrow, Bliss, Middlemiss.
May 10 v Furth FC (Furth) 2-2
Bliss 2 (1 pen)
Joyce; Clay, Cartwright, Weir, Steel, Grimsdell, Tattersall, Banks, Sparrow, Bliss, Middlemiss.
May 13 v Milan (Milan) 5-0
Fleming, Elliott 2, Bliss 2
Joyce; Clay, Pearson, Fleming, Steel, Lightfoot, Tattersall, Banks, Elliott, Bliss, Middlemiss.
May 17 v Zürich (Zürich) 6-0
Tattersall 2, Elliott, Bliss 3
Joyce; Clay, Cartwirght, Fleming, Weir, Lightfoot, Tattersall, Banks, Elliott, Bliss, Middlemiss.
May 21 v St Gallen (St Gallen) 3-0
Scorers unknown.
Team unknown but included Steel.
May 23 v Pforzhiem (Pforzhiem) 4-0
Scorers unknown.
Team unknown but included Joyce, Fleming, Steel, Pearson and Tattersall.
May 24 v Stuttgart (Stuttgart) 1-0
Scorer unknown.
Team unknown.

1925 (TO SWITZERLAND)
May 9 v Basel Old Boys 3-0
Thompson, Lane, Dimmock
Team unknown.
May 10 v Zürich Young Fellows 2-0
Seed, Handley
Team unknown.
May 17 v Winterthur 4-0
Seed 2, Lane, Dimmock
Team unknown.
May 18 v Lausanne 6-1
Handley 3, Dimmock 3 (1 pen)
Hinton; Clay, Grimsdell, Smith, Skitt, White, Thompson, Seed, Lane, Handley, Dimmock.
May 20 v La Chaux de Fonds 8-1
Richardson, Smith, White, Lindsay, Handley 3, Dimmock
Team unknown.
May 21 v Berne 5-0
Clay, Lindsay 3, Dimmock
Team unknown.
May 24 v Basel 1-0
Lindsay
Team unknown.

1928 (TO HOLLAND)
May 6 v Olympic 'A' Team (Amsterdam) 5-2
Grimsdell, Thompson, O'Callaghan 2, Dimmock
Spiers; Forster, Poynton, Lowdell, Skitt, Grimsdell, Thompson, O'Callaghan, Lindsay, Armstrong, Dimmock.
May 9 v Den Haag (The Hague) 6-2
Skitt 2, Thompson, Dimmock 3
Team unknown.
May 13 v All Holland (Almelo) 3-0
Thompson, Townley, Dimmock
Team unknown but also included Spiers, Poynton, Lindsay and O'Callaghan.
May 16 v Rotterdam (Rotterdam) 3-0
Thompson, O'Callaghan, Dimmock
Team unknown.

1929 (TO MALTA)
May 11 v Sliema Wanderers 7-1
Harper 3, Armstrong 2, Crompton, Lindsay
Spiers; Forster(Illingworth), Herod, Lindsay, Skitt, Smith, Crompton, O'Callaghan, Harper, Armstrong, Dimmock.
May 12 v Valetta United 2-1
Harper, Crompton
Spiers; Illingworth, Herod, Lindsay, Skitt, Smith, Crompton, O'Callaghan, Harper, Armstrong, Dimmock.
May 16 v British Army 5-0
Thompson, Armstrong, Garbutt, Crompton 2
Spiers; Illingworth, Herod, Lindsay, Skitt, Smith, Crompton, O'Callaghan, Garbutt, Thompson, Armstrong.
May 18 v Royal Navy 1-0
Harper (pen)
Spiers; Illingworth, Herod, Lindsay, Skitt, Smith, O'Callaghan, Crompton, Harper, Thompson, Garbutt.
May 19 v Floriana 2-1
Harper 2
Spiers; Illingworth, Herod, Lindsay, Skitt, Smith, Crompton, O'Callaghan, Harper, Armstrong, Dimmock.
May 21 v Pick of Malta 5-1
Garbutt 3, Harper 2
Spiers; Illingworth, Herod, Lindsay, Skitt, Smith, Thompson, O'Callaghan, Harper, Armstrong, Garbutt.
Above game was for Valetta Cup.

1932 (TO CHANNEL ISLANDS)
May 12 v Guernsey 2-1
Greenfield 2
Spiers; Felton, Poynton, Colquhoun, Rowe, T.Evans, Davies, O'Callaghan, Hunt, Greenfield, W.Evans.
May 16 v Jersey 9-0
Colquhoun, Davies, O'Callaghan, Hunt 6
Spiers; T.Evans, Poynton, Colquhoun, Rowe, Day, Davies, O'Callaghan, Hunt, Greenfield, W.Evans.

1933 (TO CHANNEL ISLANDS)
May 11 v Channel Islands (Guernsey) 6-0
T.Evans, Hall 2, W.Evans 2 (1 pen), Opp own-goal
Taylor; Felton, Whatley, T.Evans, Rowe, Alsford, McCormick, O'Callaghan, Brain, Hall, W.Evans.
May 13 v Guernsey 8-0
McCormick, O'Callaghan, Hall 2, W.Evans 4
Taylor; T.Evans, Whatley, Colquhoun, Rowe, Alsford, McCormick, O'Callaghan, Brain, Hall, W.Evans.
May 18 v Jersey 5-1
Alsford, Colquhoun 2, W.Evans 2
Taylor; Felton, Whatley, T.Evans, Rowe, Alsford, McCormick, O'Callaghan, Colquhoun, Hall, W.Evans.

1935 (TO GUERNSEY)
May 16 v Channel Islands (Guernsey) 5-0
Alsford, A.G.Hall, D.A.Hunt 2, G.W.Hall
Nicholls; Channell, Fullwood, Howe, Jones, Alsford, Bolan, A.G.Hall, D.A.Hunt, G.W.Hall, Hedley.
May 18 v Guernsey (Guernsey) 5-0
A.G.Hall, D.A.Hunt 4
Nicholls; Channell, Fullwood, Phypers, Howe, Alsford, Bolan, A.G.Hall, D.A.Hunt, G.W.Hall, Hedley.

1947 (TO FRANCE)
Jun 13 v Olympique de Marseilles 1-2
Gilberg
Ditchburn; Willis, Buckingham, Ludford, Nicholson, Burgess, Jones, Bennett, Rundle, Stevens, Gilberg.
Jun 15 v Toulouse 1-2

Rundle
Ditchburn; Tickridge, Buckingham, Ludford, Woodward, Nicholson, Jones, Bennett, Rundle, Dix, Stevens.
Jun 19 v Olympique de Montpéllier 1-0
Duquemin
Ditchburn; Willis, Tickridge, Trailor, Woodward, Burgess, Jones, Bennett, Duquemin, Foreman, Stevens.
Jun 21 v Saint-Etienne 2-0
Rundle, Bennett
Ditchburn; Tickridge, Buckingham, Ludford, Woodward, Burgess, Rundle, Bennett, Duquemin, Dix, Stevens.

1948 (TO CHANNEL ISLANDS)
May 8 v Jersey 3-0
Baily, Duquemin, Bennett
Ditchburn; Tickridge, Buckingham, Ludford, Woodward, Burgess, Cox, Baily, Duquemin, Bennett, Jones.
May 11 v Guernsey 7-0
Cox 2, Duquemin 3 (1 pen), Bennett 2
Ditchburn; Tickridge, Withers, Gilberg, Woodward, Burgess, Cox, Jordan, Duquemin, Bennett, Jones.

1950 (TO GERMANY AND BELGIUM)
May 14 v Hanover Arminia (Hanover) 3-0
Willis (pen), Harmer, Scarth
Ditchburn; Tickridge, Willis, Gilberg, Clarke, Burgess, Walters, Bennett, Duquemin, Harmer, Scarth.
May 18 v Tennis-Borussia (Berlin) 2-0
Gilberg, Walters
Ditchburn; Willis, Withers, Gilberg, Clarke, Burgess, Walters, Bennett, Duquemin, Scarth, Adams.
May 21 v Wacker Club (Berlin) 5-2
Bennett, Duquemin, Baily 2, Opp own-goal
Ditchburn; Ramsey, Withers, Nicholson, Farley, Burgess, Walters, Bennett, Duquemin, Baily, Scarth.
May 24 v Borussia Dortmund (Dortmund) 4-0
Walters, Duquemin, Baily, Gilberg
Ditchburn; Ramsey, Withers, Nicholson, Clarke, Burgess, Walters, Bennett, Duquemin, Baily, Gilberg.
May 27 v Royal Beerschot (Antwerp) 1-2
Duquemin
Ditchburn; Ramsey, Willis, Nicholson, Clarke, Burgess, Walters, Bennett, Duquemin, Baily, Gilberg.

1951 (TO DENMARK)
May 29 v Combined Copenhagen XI (Copenhagen) 4-2
Walters, Bennett, Duquemin 2
Reynolds; Ramsey, Willis, Nicholson, Clarke, Burgess, Walters, Bennett, Duquemin, Baily, Murphy.
May 30 v Combined Copenhagen XI (Copenhagen) 2-2
Walters, McClellan
Reynolds; Withers, Willis, Nicholson, Clarke, Brittan, Walters, Bennett, McClellan, Murphy, Medley.
May 31 v Combined Copenhagen XI (Copenhagen) 2-0
Nicholson, Duquemin
Reynolds; Ramsey, Withers, Nicholson, Clarke, Burgess, Walters, Murphy, Duquemin, Baily, Medley.

1952 (TO NORTH AMERICA)
May 22 v Toronto & District FA (Toronto) 7-0
Walters 2, Bennett, Duquemin 2, Harmer 2
Ditchburn; Willis, Withers, Wetton, Clarke, Burgess, Walters, Bennett, Duquemin, Harmer, Medley.
May 28 v Saskatchewan FA (Saskatoon) 18-1
McClellan 9, Bennett 3, Duquemin 2, Uphill, Adams 3
Squad: Ditchburn(Hayes); Willis, Withers, Gibbons, Clarke, Burgess, Duquemin, Bennett(Harmer),

Walters, Medley, Wetton, Uphill, McClellan, Adams.
May 31 v British Columbia FA (Vancouver) 9-2
Ramsey (pen), Walters 2, Bennett 4, Duquemin 2
Team unknown but also included Ditchburn, Clarke, Harmer and Medley.
Jun 2 v Victoria & District FA (Victoria) 7-0
Walters, Adams, Baily 4, Medley
Team unknown.
Jun 4 v British Columbia FA (Vancouver) 8-2
Walters 2, Duquemin, Baily 2, Bennett 3
Team unknown but also included Ditchburn, Clarke, Burgess and Medley.
Jun 7 v Alberta FA (Calgary) 11-0
Wetton, McClellan 2, Baily, Duquemin 2, Harmer 3, Uphill 2
Team unknown but also included Ditchburn.
Jun 9 v Manitoba FA (Winnipeg) 5-0
Walters, Bennett 3, Duquemin
Ditchburn; Ramsey, Willis, Nicholson, Clarke, Wetton, Walters, Bennett, Duquemin, Baily, Medley.
Jun 14 v Manchester U (Toronto) 5-0
Walters, Bennett, Duquemin, Baily, Medley
Ditchburn; Ramsey, Willis, Nicholson, Clarke, Wetton, Walters, Bennett, Duquemin, Baily, Medley.
Jun 15 v Manchester U (New York) 7-1
McClellan, Bennett 2, Duquemin 4
Ditchburn; Ramsey, Withers, Wetton, Clarke, Burgess, McClellan, Bennett, Duquemin, Baily, Medley.
Jun 18 v Quebec FA (Montréal) 8-0
Wetton, McClellan 3, Bennett 3, Medley
Ditchburn; Ramsey, Willis, Wetton, Clarke, Burgess, Walters, Bennett, Duquemin(McClellan), Baily, Medley.

1954 (TO AUSTRIA AND WEST GERMANY)
Apr 28 v Austrian State XI (Vienna) 0-2
Ditchburn; Withers, Willis, Nicholson, Clarke, Burgess, Walters, Bennett, Dunmore, Baily, Robb.
May 1 v VfB Stuttgart (Stuttgart) 1-3
Duquemin
Reynolds; Ramsey, Willis, Burgess, Marchi, Wetton, Walters, Brooks, Duquemin, Harper, Baily(Withers).
May 5 v Eintracht Brunswick (Brunswick) 0-1
Reynolds; Baker, Withers, Marchi, Clarke, Wetton, Walters, Brooks, Duquemin, Harmer, Dunmore.
May 8 v SV Hamburg (Hamburg) 2-2
Walters, Bennett
Reynolds; Ramsey(Withers), Willis, Nicholson, Marchi, Wetton, Walters, Bennett, Duquemin, Baily, Dunmore.

1955 (TO AUSTRIA, HUNGARY AND FRANCE)
May 11 v FC Austria (Vienna) 2-6
Duquemin 2
Reynolds; Baker, Hopkins, Blanchflower, Clarke, Marchi, Gavin, Brooks, Duquemin, Baily, Robb.
May 15 v FC Kinizsi (Budapest) 1-4
Brooks
Reynolds; Baker, Hopkins, Blanchflower, Clarke, Marchi, Walters, Brooks, Duquemin, Baily, Robb.
May 18 v FC Vasas (Budapest) 2-4
Brooks 2
Reynolds; Withers, Hopkins(Baker), Blanchflower, Clarke, Marchi, Walters, Brooks, Duquemin, Baily, Gavin.
May 20 v Pécs Dozsa (Pécs) 1-0
Gavin
Reynolds; Nicholson, Withers, Blanchflower, Clarke, Marchi, Walters, Brooks, Duquemin, Baily, Gavin.
May 25 v Racing Club de Paris (Paris) 0-0
Reynolds; Baker, Withers, Blanchflower, Clarke,

Marchi, Walters, Brooks, Duquemin, Harmer, Gavin.

1957 (TO NORTH AMERICA)
May 19 v Glasgow Celtic (New York) 4-3
Dulin, Smith 3
Reynolds; Baker, Henry, Blanchflower, Ryden, Marchi, Dulin, Harmer, Smith, Brooks, Dyson.
May 22 v Essex Cty All Stars (Windsor) 8-1
Walley, Harmer (2 pens), Smith 4, Wilkie
Reynolds; Hills, Henry, Blanchflower(Walley), Ryden, Marchi, Dulin(Bing), Harmer, Smith, Stokes, Wilkie.
May 25 v Ontario All Stars (Ontario) 7-0
Harmer, Smith 5, Stokes
Reynolds; Baker, Henry, Blanchflower, Ryden, Marchi, Dulin, Harmer, Smith, Stokes, Dyson(Wilkie).
May 29 v Alberta All Stars (Calgary) 6-1
Blanchflower, Dulin, Smith, Dunmore, Stokes 2
Reynolds; Baker, Henry, Blanchflower, Ryden, Marchi, Dulin, Harmer, Smith(Dunmore), Stokes, Brooks.
Jun 1 v Glasgow Celtic (Vancouver) 6-3
Blanchflower, Smith 2, Stokes 2, Brooks
Reynolds; Baker, Henry, Blanchflower, Ryden, Marchi, Dulin, Harmer, Smith, Stokes, Brooks.
Jun 3 v British Columbia All Stars (Vancouver) 0-2
Reynolds; Baker, Henry, Blanchflower, Ryden, Marchi, Dulin, Harmer, Smith, Stokes, Brooks. (subs used but not identified).
Jun 5 v Manitoba All Stars (Winnipeg) 12-0
Dulin 2, Harmer, Dunmore, Stokes 5, Dyson 3
Reynolds; Hills, Henry, Blanchflower(Baker), Ryden, Walley, Dulin(Bing), Harmer, Dunmore, Stokes, Dyson.
Jun 8 v Glasgow Celtic (Toronto) 3-1
Smith 3
Reynolds, Hills, Henry, Blanchflower, Ryden, Walley, Dulin, Harmer, Smith, Brooks, Dyson.
Jun 9 v Glasgow Celtic (Montréal) 0-2
Reynolds; Baker, Henry, Walley(Blanchflower), Ryden, Marchi, Dulin, Harmer, Smith(Dunmore), Stokes, Brooks.

1959 (TO RUSSIA)
May 27 v Torpedo Moscow (Moscow) 1-0
Medwin
Hollowbread; Baker, Hopkins, Blanchflower, Norman, Mackay, Medwin, Harmer(Clayton), Smith, Brooks, Jones.
Jun 1 v Dynamo Kiev (Kiev) 2-1
Brooks 2
Reynolds; Baker, Henry, Blanchflower, Norman, Mackay, Medwin(Clayton), Harmer, Dunmore(Smith), Brooks, Jones.
Jun 4 v CCCP Select XI (Leningrad) 1-3
Brooks
Reynolds; Baker, Henry, Blanchflower(Mackay), Norman, Iley, Harmer, Brooks(Dunmore), Smith, Clayton, Jones.

1961 (TO HOLLAND)
May 15 v Feyenoord 2-1
Medwin, Allen
Brown; Baker, Henry, Blanchflower, Norman, Mackay, Medwin, White, Saul, Allen, Dyson.
May 17 v Amsterdam Select XI 3-0
White, Allen, Dyson
Brown; Baker, Henry, Blanchflower, Norman, Marchi, Medwin, White, Saul, Allen, Dyson.
1962 (TO ISRAEL)
May 26 v Tel Aviv Select XI 2-1

Mackay, Clayton
Brown; Baker, Henry, Blanchflower, Marchi, Mackay, Medwin, White, R.Smith, Clayton, Dyson.
May 30 v Haifa Select XI 5-0
Mackay, White, Saul, Allen, Clayton
Brown; Baker, Henry, Blanchflower(J.Smith), Marchi, MacKay, Medwin(Dyson), White, Saul, Allen, Clayton.

1963 (TO SOUTH AFRICA)
May 31 v NSAFL Invitation XI (Cape Town) 5-1
Saul, Allen 3, Jones
Brown; Baker, Hopkins, Blanchflower, Marchi, J.Smith, Medwin(Dyson), White, Saul, Allen, Jones.
Jun 5 v NFL Select XI (Durban) 5-2
Jones 2, Greaves 2, Dyson
Brown; Baker, Henry, J.Smith, Norman, Marchi, Jones, White, R.Smith, Greaves, Dyson.
Jun 8 v South African XI (Johannesburg) 3-1
Clayton, Smith R, Greaves
Hollowbread; Hopkins, Henry, Blanchflower, Norman, Marchi, Clayton, White, R.Smith, Greaves, Dyson.

1965 (TO HOLLAND)
May 18 v DWS Club (Amsterdam) 0-1
Jennings; Norman, Henry, Mullery, L.Brown, Clayton, Robertson, Saul, Mackay(Low), Gilzean, Jones.
May 22 v Telstar Club (Ukjmuiden) 3-2
Saul, Jones 2
Jennings; Knowles, Henry, Mullery, Norman, Beal, Weller, Clayton, Saul, Mackay, Jones.

1965 (TO ISRAEL)
Jun 21 v Hakoah (Haifa) 3-1
Greaves 2 (1 pen), Jones
Jennings; Knowles, Henry, Mullery, Norman, Mackay, Weller, Greaves, Saul, Gilzean, Jones.
Jun 24 v Maccabi Tel Aviv (Tel Aviv) 3-2
Muller, MacKay, Gilzean
W.Brown, Norman, Knowles, Mullery, L.Brown, Mackay, Pitt, Greaves, Saul(Clayton), Gilzean, Jones (Weller).
Above game for John White Cup.

1965 (TO SPAIN)
Costa Del Sol Tournament
Semi-final
Aug 14 v Valencia (Costa Del Sol) 2-1
Clayton, Jones
W.Brown; Norman, Knowles, Mullery, L.Brown, Mackay, Possee, Clayton, Gilzean, Greaves, Jones (Robertson).
Final
Aug 15 v Standard Liège (Costa Del Sol) 1-0
Mullery
W.Brown; Norman, Knowles, Mullery, L.Brown, Mackay, Possee, Clayton(Saul), Gilzean, Greaves, Robertson(Beal).

1966 (TO BERMUDA & THE AMERICAS)
May 19 v Bermuda Select XI (Hamilton) 3-2
Gilzean 2, Venables
W.Brown(Jennings); Kinnear, Knowles(Henry), Mullery, Hoy(L.Brown), Beal, Possee(Clayton), Mackay, Gilzean(Saul), Venables, Robertson.
May 21 v Glasgow Celtic (Toronto) 0-1
W.Brown; Kinnear, Knowles, Mullery, Hoy, Mackay, Possee, Gilzean, Venables, Saul, Robertson.
May 25 v Hartford Select XI (Hartford) 3-0
Weller 2, Saul

Jennings; Beal, Knowles, Mullery, L.Brown, Clayton, Weller, Gilzean, Venables, Saul, Possee.

May 29 v Bologna (Jersey City) 0-1
Jennings; Kinnear, Knowles, Mullery, L.Brown, Mackay, Possee(Weller), Gilzean, Venables, Saul, Robertson.

Jun 1 v Glasgow Celtic (San Francisco) 1-2
Mackay (pen)
W.Brown; Kinnear(Henry), Knowles, Mullery, L.Brown, MacKay, Possee, Gilzean, Venables, Saul, Robertson.

Jun 4 v Glasgow Celtic (Vancouver) 1-1
Venables
Jennings; Beal, Knowles, Mullery, L.Brown, Mackay, Possee, Clayton, Weller, Venables, Robertson(Gilzean).

Jun 8 v British Columbia XI (Vancouver) 3-0
Mullery, MacKay, Saul
W.Brown; Beal, Henry, Mullery, L.Brown, Mackay, Possee, Gilzean, Venables, Saul, Weller.

Jun 12 v Mexican National XI (Mexico City) 1-0
Gilzean
Jennings; Beal, Knowles, Mullery, L.Brown, Mackay, Weller(Gilzean), Clayton(Henry), Saul, Venables, Robertson(Possee).

Jun 15 v America Club of Mexico (Mexico City) 2-0
Weller, Gilzean
Jennings; Beal, Henry, Mullery, L.Brown, Mackay, Weller(Possee), Clayton, Saul(Gilzean), Venables, Robertson.

Jun 17 v Bayern Munich (Detroit) 3-0
Weller, Saul, Venables
W.Brown; Beal, Knowles, Mullery, L.Brown, Henry, Weller, Clayton, Saul, Venables, Robertson.

Jun 19 v Bayern Munich (Chicago) 1-1
Henry
Jennings; Beal, Knowles, Mullery, L.Brown, Henry, Weller(Possee), Clayton, Saul(Gilzean), Venables, Robertson.

1966 (TO SPAIN)
Costa Del Sol Tournament
Semi-final
Aug 14 v Malaga CD (Costa Del Sol) 2-1
Mullery, Gilzean
Jennings; Kinnear, Knowles, Mullery, Henry, Mackay, Robertson, Greaves, Gilzean, Venables, Jones(Weller).
Final
Aug 15 v Benfica (Costa Del Sol) 2-1
Robertson, Greaves
Jennings; Kinnear, Knowles, Mullery, Henry, Mackay, Robertson(Weller), Beal, Gilzean, Venables, Greaves.

1967 (TO SWITZERLAND)
May 30 v FC Zürich 2-0
Robertson 2
Jennings; Kinnear, Want, Mullery, England, Mackay, Robertson, Greaves, Gilzean, Venables, Saul. (Substitutes Johnson and Jones used but not specified whom they replaced.)

Jun 1 v BSC Young Boys 3-2
Greaves 2, Bond
Jennings; Kinnear, Want, Clayton, England, Mackay, Robertson, Greaves, Gilzean, Bond, Jones. (Substitutes Johnson and Saul used but not specified whom they replaced.)

Jun 7 v FC Servette 4-1
Greaves 2, Venables, Saul
Jennings; Kinnear, Want, Mullery, England, Mackay, Robertson, Greaves, Gilzean, Venables, Saul. (Sub-

stitutes Johnson and Jones used but not specified whom they replaced.)

1968 (TO GREECE AND CYPRUS)
May 15 v Panathinaikos (Athens) 2-2
Gilzean 2
Jennings; Beal, Want, Mullery, England, Mackay, Jones(Robertson), Greaves, Chivers, Venables, Gilzean.

May 19 v Anorthosis (Famagusta) 5-0
Robertson 3, Greaves 2
Jennings; Kinnear, Want, Collins, Beal, Venables, Robertson, Pearce, Bond, Greaves, Gilzean.

May 22 v AEL (Limassol) 7-1
Jones 2, Bond, Robertson, Gilzean 3
Jennings; Kinnear, Want, Collins, England, Pearce, Jones, Venables, Bond, Greaves(Robertson), Gilzean.

May 25 v Cyprus International XI (Nicosia) 3-0
Robertson 2, Gilzean
Jennings; Kinnear, Want, Collins, England, Mackay, Jones(Pratt), Bond, Beal, Robertson, Gilzean.

May 29 v Apoel (Nicosia) 3-0
Robertson, Pearce, Jones
Jennings; Kinnear, Want, Beal, Collins, Mackay, Robertson, Bond(Pearce), Gilzean(Pratt), Venables, Jones(Johnson).

1969 (TO NORTH AMERICA)
May 15 v West Ham U (Baltimore) 4-3
Greaves 2, Pearce, Morgan
Jennings; Want, Knowles, Perryman, Collins, Beal, Johnson, Greaves, Pearce, Venables, Morgan.

May 17 v Aston Villa (Atlanta) 2-2
Greaves 2
Hancock; Want, Knowles, Perryman(Pratt), Evans, Beal, Jenkins(Johnson), Greaves, Pearce, Venables, Morgan.

May 28 v Fiorentina (Toronto) 0-3
Jennings; Want(Evans), Knowles, Perryman, Collins, Beal, Pearce, Greaves, Gilzean(Johnson), Venables, Morgan.
Above game was for Toronto Cup.

Jun 1 v Glasgow Rangers (Toronto) 4-3
Greaves 3 (2 pen), Morgan
Hancock; Want, Knowles, Perryman, Evans, Beal, Johnson(Venables), Greaves, Pearce, Pratt, Morgan.
Above game was for Toronto Cup.

1970 (TO MALTA)
May 13 v Valetta U 3-0
Gilzean, Pratt, Morgan
Jennings; Evans, Want, Pearce, England, Beal, Gilzean, Bond, Chivers, Pratt, Morgan.

May 16 v Sliema Wanderers 2-1
Pearce, Chivers
Jennings; Evans, Knowles, Pearce(Johnson), England, Beal, Gilzean, Bond, Chivers, Perryman, Morgan(Pratt).

May 17 v Maltese Select XI 0-1
Jennings; Evans, Want, Perryman, Collins, Beal, Gilzean, Bond, Chivers(Pearce), Pratt, Johnson.

1970 (TO SPAIN)
Palma de Mallorca Tournament
Aug 7 v FC Cologne (Palma) 0-1
Jennings; Evans, Knowles, Mullery, England, Beal, Gilzean, Perryman, Chivers, Peters, Pearce(Collins).

Aug 8 v Atletico Madrid (Palma) 0-1
Jennings; Kinnear, Knowles, Mullery(Bond), Collins, Beal, Gilzean, Perryman, Chivers, Peters, Pearce.

1971 (TO JAPAN)

379

May 27 v All Japan XI (Kōbe) 6-0
Kinnear, Collins, Gilzean, Chivers 2, Pratt
Jennings; Kinnear, Knowles(Want), Mullery, Collins,
Beal, Gilzean, Perryman, Chivers, Pratt, Neighbour
(Morgan).
Jun 3 v All Japan XI (Tōkyō) 7-2
Mullery, Gilzean 2, Chivers 2, Pratt 2
Jennings; Kinnear, Knowles, Mullery, Collins, Beal,
Gilzean, Perryman, Chivers, Pratt, Neighbour(Morgan).
Jun 9 v All Japan XI (Tōkyō) 3-0
Mulley 2 (1 pen), Chivers
Jennings; Want, Knowles, Mullery, Collins, Beal,
Gilzean, Perryman, Chivers, Pratt, Morgan(Pearce).

1972 (TO ISRAEL)
Jun 7 v Maccabi Tel Aviv (Tel Aviv) 3-2
Pearce, Gilzean, Peters
Jennings; Evans, Knowles, Mullery, England, Beal,
Pearce(Naylor), Pratt, Gilzean, Peters, Coates
(Neighbour).

1974 (TO MAURITIUS)
Jun 8 v Mauritius Select XI (Curepipe) 5-0
Chivers 3, Gilzean 2
Jennings; Evans, Knowles(Naylor), Beal, Dillon, Pratt,
Coates, Perryman, Chivers, Gilzean, McGrath.
Jun 13 v Mauritius Select XI (Curepipe) 6-3
Knowles (pen), Gilzean 2, Perryman 2, Peters
Jennings; Kinnear(Pratt), Knowles, Naylor, Beal,
Holder, Neighbour(McGrath), McNab(Coates),
Gilzean, Perryman, Peters.
Jun 16 v Mauritius Select XI (Curepipe) 6-0
Coates, Perryman, Gilzean 3, Peters
Jennings; Evans, Knowles, Beal, Naylor, Pratt, Coates,
Perryman, Gilzean, Peters, McGrath.

1975 (TO WEST GERMANY AND HOLLAND)
Jul 23 v Rot-Weiss Essen 1-1
Jones
Jennings; Kinnear, Pratt, Coates, Osgood, McAllister,
Conn, Perryman, Chivers, Jones, McNab(Neighbour).
Jul 25 v Karlsruher SC 1-2
Kinnear (pen)
Jennings; Kinnear, McAllister(McNab), Pratt,
Osgood, Naylor, McGrath(Conn), Perryman, Chivers,
Duncan (Jones), Neighbour(Coates).
Jul 29 v Hannover 96 1-1
Jones
Jennings; Kinnear, McAllister, Pratt, Osgood, Naylor,
Coates, Perryman, Chivers, Jones, Neighbour.
Aug 3 v NAC Breda 1-0
Kinnear (pen)
Jennings; Osgood, Knowles, Pratt, McAllister, Naylor,
Coates(McNab[Kinnear]), Perryman, Chivers, Jones,
McGrath(Neighbour).

1976 (TO CANADA, FIJI AND AUSTRALASIA)
Apr 27 v Toronto Metros-Croatia (Toronto) 1-0
Coates
Jennings(Daines); Naylor, Stead, Hoddle(Pratt),
Young, Osgood, Jones(Armstrong), Perryman,
Chivers, Coates, Neighbour.
May 1 v Fijian Select XI (Lautoka) 4-0
Chivers, Duncan, Armstrong, Jones
Daines(Kendall); Stead, Naylor, Pratt, Young(Walford),
Osgood, Hoddle, Coates, Chivers(Duncan), Armstrong,
Jones.
May 3 v Auckland FA XI (Auckland) 5-3
Pratt, Osgood (pen), Neighbour, Duncan 2

Daines; Stead, Walford, Pratt, Young, Osgood,
Neighbour, Armstrong, Duncan, Perryman, Coates.
May 5 v Wellington FA XI (Wellington) 3-2
Pratt, Armstrong, Duncan
Daines; Stead, McAllister(Coates), Pratt, Young,
Osgood, Neighbour, Naylor, Armstrong, Duncan,
Hoddle.
May 9 v Victoria (Victoria) 3-1
Pratt, Perryman, Jones
Daines(Kendall); Osgood, Naylor(Stead), Pratt
(Hoddle), Young, Walford, Pratt, Neighbour, Perryman,
Jones, Armstrong(Duncan), Coates.
May 12 v Northern New South Wales (Newcastle) 5-1
Young, Hoddle, Chivers, Osgood (pen), Smythe (og)
Kendall; Naylor(Neill), Stead, Pratt(Neighbour),
Young, Walford, Hoddle, Perryman(Armstrong),
Jones, Chivers, Osgood.
May 16 v Australian National XI (Sydney) 3-2
Neighbour, Jones, Coates
Daines; Naylor, Stead, Pratt, Young, Osgood,
Neighbour, Perryman, Chivers, Jones, Coates.
May 17 v South Australia (Adelaide) 5-2
Osgood 2, Jones, Chivers, Coates
Kendall; Naylor(Armstrong), Stead, Pratt, Young,
Walford, Neighbour, Osgood, Jones, Chivers,
Coates.
May 23 v Western Australia (Perth) 4-0
Chivers 3, Jones
Daines(Kendall); Naylor, Stead(Armstrong), Pratt
(Hoddle), Young, Osgood(Walford), Neighbour,
Perryman, Chivers, Jones, Coates.

1976 (TO WEST GERMANY)
Jul 24 v VFL Osnabrück 3-1
Armstrong, Jones 2
Jennings; Naylor, McAllister, Pratt, Young, Osgood,
Coates, Perryman(Holder), Armstrong(Conn), Jones,
Neighbour.
Jul 28 v Eintracht Frankfurt 1-4
Young
Jennings; Naylor, McAllister, Pratt, Young, Osgood,
Coates, Perryman, Armstrong(Conn), Jones, Neighbour.
Jul 31 v 1.FC Cologne 1-3
Jones
Daines; Naylor, Stead, Pratt, Young, Osgood, Coates,
Perryman, Hoddle, Jones, Neighbour(Robinson).
Aug 4 v KSV Baunatal 2-1
Jones 2
Daines; Stead(Naylor), McAllister, Pratt, Young,
Walford(Osgood), Coates, Perryman, Hoddle
(Robinson), Jones, Conn.
Aug 6 v FV Bad Honnef 2-0
Conn, Armstrong
Jennings(Daines); Naylor, McAllister, Pratt, Young,
Walford(Stead), Robinson(Conn), Perryman,
Armstrong, Osgood, Neighbour.

1977 (TO NORWAY)
May 17 v Stord FC 5-0
Osgood, Armstrong, Jones, Moores, Taylor
Jennings(Daines); Naylor, Stead, Pratt, Osgood,
Perryman, Holmes, Hoddle, Armstrong(Jones),
Moores, Taylor.
May 19 v Sogndal FC 6-0
Pratt, Perryman, Armstrong 2, Jones, Taylor
Jennings(Daines); Naylor(Jennings), Stead, Pratt
(Coates), Osgood, Perryman, Jones, Hoddle
(Armstrong), Moores, Holmes, Taylor.

1977 (TO SWEDEN)
Nolia Cup
Semi-final
Aug 7 v Royale Union (Umea) 2-0
Duncan, Moores
Daines; Naylor(Stead), Holmes, Hoddle, Armstrong,
Perryman, Coates, McNab(Gorman), Duncan(Moores),
Jones, Pratt.
Final
Aug 10 v Leicester City (Umea) 2-1
Moores, Opp own-goal
Daines; Naylor, Holmes, Hoddle, Armstrong,
Perryman, Coates, McNab, Duncan, Moores, Pratt.
Aug 12 v Norsjo IF 3-2
Armstrong, Duncan, Jones
Kendall; Stead, Holmes, Naylor, Armstrong, Perryman,
Coates, McNab, Moores(Duncan[Moores]), Jones,
Pratt.

1978 (TO SYRIA)
May 8 v Aleppo FC (Aleppo) 1-0
Jones
Daines(Kendall); Naylor, Holmes(Stead), Hoddle,
McAllister, Perryman, Pratt, McNab, Jones, Duncan
(Moores[Falco]), Taylor.
May 10 v Syrian Police (Damascus) 4-0
Holmes, Falco, Taylor 2
Daines(Kendall); Naylor, Holmes, Hoddle, McAllister,
Perryman, Pratt, McNab, Duncan(Falco), Stead,
Taylor.

1978 (TO NORWAY AND SWEDEN)
May 15 v FC Hamar 0-3
Daines(Kendall); Naylor, Holmes, Sloan(McNab),
McAllister, Perryman(Gorman), Pratt(Stead), McNab
(Hoddle), Jones(Moores), Duncan(Perryman), Taylor.
May 17 v Kvik Halden 2-0
McNab, Taylor (pen)
Daines(Kendall); Naylor, Stead(Gorman), Sloan
(Hoddle), McAllister, Holmes, Pratt, McNab, Jones,
Duncan(Moores), Taylor.
May 18 v FC Karlstad 4-1
Pratt, Moores, Duncan 2
Daines(Kendall) Naylor, Holmes(Gorman), Hoddle,
McAllister, Perryman, Pratt, McNab, Moores(Stead),
Duncan, Taylor.

**1979 (TO KUWAIT, MALAYSIA, JAPAN AND
BERMUDA)**
May 16 v Kuwait Army XI 2-1
Falco, Villa
Aleksic; Lee, Smith, McAllister(Naylor), Lacy,
Perryman, Pratt(Beavon), Ardiles(Galvin), Jones
(Falco), Hoddle, Villa.
May 23 v Malaysia Select XI (Kuala Lumpar) 4-0
Lee, Falco 3 (1 pen)
Aleksic; Lee, Smith(McAllister), Miller, Lacy,
Perryman (Beavon), Pratt, Naylor, Falco, Galvin,
Villa.

Japan Cup
Group A
May 27 v Indonesia (Yokohama) 6-0
Lee 2, McAllister, Galvin, Villa 2
Aleksic; Lee, McAllister, Miller, Lacy(Naylor),
Perryman, Pratt, Beavon, Galvin, Falco(Jones), Villa.
May 29 v Japan 'A' (Tōkyō) 2-0
Jones, Ardiles
Aleksic; Lee, Smith, Miller, McAllister, Perryman,

Pratt(Beavon), Naylor, Jones, Ardiles, Villa.
May 31 v Fiorentina (Nishigaoka) 1-1
Lee
Daines; Lee, Smith, McAllister, Lacy, Beavon, Pratt,
Naylor, Jones, Galvin, Villa.
Semi-final
**Jun 2 v San Lorenzo (Tōkyō) 3-3 (Spurs won 5-3 on
penalties)**
*Lee, Pratt, Galvin. Penalties scored by Lee, Smith,
Pratt, Falco, Villa*
Aleksic; Lee, Smith, Miller, Lacy, Perryman, Pratt,
Ardiles(Falco), Galvin, Jones, Villa.
Jun 4 v Dundee U (Tōkyō) 2-0
Smith, Ardiles
Aleksic; Lee, Smith, McAllister, Lacy, Perryman,
Pratt, Naylor, Jones(Falco), Ardiles, Villa.
Jun 6 v Bermuda Select XI (a) 3-1
Lee, Bean, Jones
Daines; Lee(Simmonds), Day(Marshall), McAllister,
Lacy, Pratt, Aleksic(Bean), Naylor, Jones, Smith,
Varney(Astwood).

1980 (TO AUSTRIA)
May 11 v Rapid/FC Austria XI (Vienna) 0-3
Daines; Miller, Hughton, Naylor, McAllister,
Perryman, Ardiles, Jones, Falco(Roberts), Taylor,
Galvin.
May 13 v Gais/Sturm Select XI (Graz) 0-2
Kendall; Lacy, Hughton, Naylor, McAllister(Miller),
Perryman, Roberts(Falco), Jones, Hazard, Taylor,
Galvin.

1981 (TO BAHRAIN AND KUWAIT)
May 10 v Syrian Police (Damascus) 4-0
Holmes, Falco, Taylor 2
Daines(Kendall); Naylor, Holmes, Hoddle, McAllister,
Perryman, Pratt, McNab, Duncan(Falco), Stead,
Taylor.
May 24 v Bahrain Select XI 3-0
Miller, Galvin, Brooke
Aleksic; McAllister, Miller(Cooper), Roberts, Villa,
Perryman(Mazzon), Ardiles, Hazard(Crook), Galvin,
Brooke, Crooks(Falco).
May 26 v Kuwait Army XI 2-1
Brooke, Crooks
Daines; McAllister(Cooper), Miller, Roberts, Villa,
Perryman, Ardiles, Hazard(Crook), Galvin, Brooke
(Mazzon), Crooks(Falco).
May 28 v Bahrain Select XI 5-3
Miller, Galvin, Falco 2, Crooks
Daines; McAllister, Miller(Mazzon), Roberts, Villa
(Cooper[Crook]), Perryman, Ardiles, Hazard, Galvin,
Falco, Crooks.

1981 (TO TURKEY)
Jun 19 v Trabzonspor 4-0
Villa, Ardiles, Falco, Crooks
Aleksic; Hughton, Miller, Roberts, Villa, Perryman,
Ardiles, Falco(Smith), Galvin, Hoddle(Mazzon),
Crooks(Hazard).
Jun 13 v Fenerbahçe 5-1
Villa, Falco, Galvin, Hoddle, Crooks
Daines; Smith, Miller(Mazzon), Roberts, Villa(Falco),
Perryman, Ardiles(Hazard), Archibald, Galvin,
Hoddle, Crooks.

1982 (TO HOLLAND)
Amsterdam 707 Tournament
Round 1

Aug 13 v Ajax (Amsterdam) 2-3
Roberts 2
Clemence; Hughton, Miller, Roberts(Brooke), Hazard, Mabbutt, Archibald, Galvin, Hoddle, Crooks, Lacy.
Third/Fourth Place Play-off
Aug 15 v 1.FC Cologne (Amsterdam) 0-0
Spurs lost 1-3 on penalties
Penalty scored by Archibald
Clemence; Hughton, Miller, Hazard, Mabbutt, O'Reilly, Archibald, Falco, Lacy, Gibson, Brooke.

1983 (TO SWAZILAND)
Royal Swazi Hotel Tournament
Jun 4 v Manchester Utd (Swaziland) 1-2
Archibald
Clemence; Hughton, O'Reilly, Roberts, Miller, Perryman(Hazard), Mabbutt, Archibald(Falco), Galvin, Hoddle, Brazil(Crooks).
Jun 11 v Manchester Utd (Swaziland) 2-0
Perryman, Mabbutt.
Clemence; Hughton, Price, Roberts, Miller, Perryman, Mabbutt, Falco(Crooks), Galvin, Hoddle(Hazard), Brazil.
Spurs won the tournament 3-2 on penalties, Brazil, Price and Perryman scoring.

1984 (TO SWAZILAND)
Royal Swazi Sun Challenge
Jun 2 v Liverpool (Swaziland) 2-5
Thomas, Falco
Parks; Thomas, Hughton, Galvin, Miller, Perryman, Ardiles, Hazard(Brooke) Falco, Brazil(Crook), Crooks.
Jun 9 v Liverpool (Swaziland) 1-1
Brazil
Clemence; Thomas, Hughton, O'Reilly, Miller, Perryman(Crook), Ardiles(Bowen), Hazard, Falco (Crooks), Brazil, Galvin.

1984 (TO SWEDEN AND NORWAY)
Jul 27 v St Jordal Blink 9-0
Kempes 3, Falco, Galvin, Ardiles, Hoddle, Crooks, Opp own-goal
Clemence; Thomas(Mabbutt), Hughton, Roberts, Stevens, Perryman, Ardiles, Kempes(Miller) Falco (Crooks), Hazard,(Hoddle), Galvin.
Jul 29 v Ostersund 4-0
Galvin, Stevens, Crooks, Hoodle (pen)
Parks; Thomas, Hughton, Roberts(Hoddle), Miller, Perryman, Ardiles, Kempes, Falco(Crooks), Stevens, Galvin.
Jul 30 v Viking 1-0
Crooks
Clemence; Thomas, Hughton, Roberts, Stevens, Perryman, Ardiles(Hoddle) Kempes, Falco(Crooks), Hazard(Miller), Galvin.

1985 (TO HONG KONG AND AUSTRALIA)
May 23 v Seiko FC (Hong Kong) 4-0
Mabbutt 2, Falco, Dick
Clemence; Thomas, Hughton, Roberts(Culverhouse), Miller, Mabbutt, Ardiles, Falco, Crook(Dick), Hazard (Leworthy), Galvin.
$200,000 Tournament
May 29 v Australia Soccer Federation (Melbourne) 0-1
Clemence; Thomas, Bowen, Roberts, Miller (Culverhouse), Mabbutt, Ardiles, Falco, Leworthy, Hazard(Crook), Dick.
Jun 1 v Udinese (Sydney) 0-2
Clemence; Thomas(Culverhouse), Bowen, Roberts,

Miller, Mabbutt, Ardiles, Falco, Crook(Leworthy), Hazard, Dick.
Jun 5 v Vasco da Gama (Adelaide) 1-1
Falco
Clemence; Thomas, Hughton, Roberts, Miller (Culverhouse), Mabbutt, Ardiles, Falco, Dick, Hazard (Leworthy), Galvin(Crook).
Third/Fourth Place Play-off
Jun 9 v Udinese (Melbourne) 4-1
Miller, Falco, Leworthy, Opp own-goal
Clemence; Thomas, Hughton, Roberts, Miller, Mabbutt, Ardiles(Crook), Falco, Leworthy, Chiedozie (Hazard), Galvin(Dick).

1987 (TO SWEDEN AND FINLAND)
Jul 30 v Örebro SK (Örebro)1-3
Mabbutt
Parks; Polston(Fairclough), Mabbutt, Gough, Ruddock(Stevens), Metgod(Ardiles), C.Allen(Thomas), P.Allen, Waddle, Hodge(Galvin), Samways(Claesen).
Aug 1 v Lansi Uudenmaan Dist (Karjaa) 7-1
Fairclough, C.Allen 2, Close 4
Clemence; Polston(Ruddock), Thomas, Gough, Fairclough, Mabbutt, Robson(C.Allen), Close, Waddle, Ardiles(Metgod), Galvin.
Aug 3 v IFK/VSK Västerås Select XI (Västerås) 4-2
Waddle, C.Allen, Close 2
Clemence; Thomas, Ruddock(Samways), Ardiles, Fairclough, Mabbutt, C.Allen, P.Allen, Waddle, Hodge(Galvin), Metgod(Close).
Aug 5 v Marsta IK (Marsta) 5-0
Claesen 2, Metgod, Mabbutt, Stevens
Clemence; Stevens, Thomas(Samways), Gough, Fairclough, Mabbutt, Claesen, P.Allen(C.Allen), Galvin(P.Allen), Ardiles(Metgod), Samways(Hodge).
Aug 6 v Swedish Div 1 North Select XI (Gavle) 0-1
Parks; Stevens(Metgod), Polston, Metgod(Samways), Fairclough, Ruddock, Robson(Mabbutt), Close (Ardiles), Cleasen, Hodge, Galvin.

1988 (TO SWEDEN)
Jul 26 v Vederslav/Danningelanda IF 4-1
Walsh 3, Stewart (pen)
Mimms(Guthrie); Statham, Thomas(Stimson), Fenwick, Fairclough, Mabbutt, Walsh(Gray), Gascoigne(Howells), Waddle(Robson), Samways, Stewart(Moran).
Jul 28 v Trelleborgs FF 3-0
Fenwick 2 (1 pen), Moran
Mimms; Stimson, Fenwick, Fairclough, Mabbutt, Allen, Walsh(Moran), Gascoigne(Howells), Waddle, Stewart(Gray), Samways(Robson).
Jul 31 v GAIS 1-1
Walsh
Mimms(Guthrie); Mabbutt, Stimson, Fenwick, Fairclough, Allen(Howells[Robson]), Walsh(Gray), Gascoigne, Waddle, Stewart, Samways.
Aug 2 v Jönköpings Sodra IF 1-1
Waddle
Guthrie; Statham, Stimson(Fairclough), Fenwick, Mabbutt, Robson(Howells), Walsh(Gray), Gascoigne, Waddle, Stewart(Allen), Samways(Moran).

1989 (TO IRELAND, SCOTLAND, NORWAY AND SPAIN)
Jul 23 v Bohemians 2-0
Stewart, Walsh
Thorstvedt; Butters, Hughton, Sedgley(Thomas), Bergsson(A.Polston), Mabbutt, Samways(Robson), Gascoigne(Howells), Stewart(Hendon), Lineker

(Walsh), Nayim.
Jul 25 v Cork City 3-0
Mabbutt, Gascoigne, Lineker
Thorstvedt; Butters(Stevens), Hughton(Hendon), Sedgley, Bergsson(A.Polston), Mabbutt, Samways (Robson), Gascoigne(Thomas), Stewart(Walsh), Lineker, Nayim(Howells).
Aug 6 v Rangers 0-1
Thorstvedt; Butters, Hughton(Bergsson), Fenwick, Nayim(Allen), Mabbutt, Sedgley, Gascoigne, Stewart(Moran), Lineker(Walsh), Samways(Howells).
Aug 8 v Viking (Stavanger) 5-1
Stewart, Fenwick (pen), Gascoigne, Lineker 2
Thorstvedt; Butters, Bergsson, Fenwick, Allen, Mabbutt, Sedgley(Robson), Samways(Gascoigne), Stewart, Lineker, Howells.
Aug 10 v Brann (Bergen) 2-0
Lineker 2
Thorstvedt; Butters(Mabbutt), A.Polston, Fenwick (Hendon), Stevens(Bergsson), Allen, Howells (Gascoigne), Samways(Sedgley), Walsh, Lineker(Moran), Robson.
Aug 11 v Dinamo Bucharest (Madrid) 1-3
Howells
Thorstvedt; Butters, Bergsson, Fenwick, Allen(Robson), Mabbutt, Sedgley, Gascoigne(Moran), Stewart, Walsh, Howells(Hendon).
Aug 13 v Atletico Madrid 0-1
Thorstvedt; Butters, Bergsson(A.Polston), Fenwick, Howells, Mabbutt, Robson(Sedgley), Gascoigne, Walsh, Lineker, Allen.

1990 (TO IRELAND, NORWAY AND SCOTLAND)
Aug 1 v Shelbourne 3-0
Gascoigne 2, Lineker
Thorstvedt(Mimms); Bergsson, Van Den Hauwe (Edinburgh), Sedgley(Butters), Howells(Moncur), Mabbutt, Stewart(Lineker), Thomas(Gascoigne), Nayim, Walsh(Moran), Allen.
Aug 3 v Derry City 3-0 *Stewart 2, Lineker*
Thorstvedt(Mimms); Bergsson(Thomas), Edinburgh (Butters), Sedgley, Howells, Mabbutt, Stewart(Walsh), Gascoigne(Moncur), Nayim, Lineker(Moran), Allen.
Aug 7 v Brann (Bergen) 1-0
Howells
Thorstvedt(Mimms); Bergsson, Edinburgh, Sedgley, Howells, Mabbutt, Stewart(Moran), Gascoigne (Thomas), Nayim, Lineker(Walsh), Allen.
Aug 9 v Viking 1-1
Walsh
Thorstvedt; Polston(Bergsson), Edinburgh(Sedgley), Thomas, Butters, Mabbutt, Walsh, Gascoigne(Nayim), Moncur, Lineker(Moran), Allen(Howells).
Aug 11 v Sogndal 1-0
Moran
Mimms(Thorstvedt); Bergsson(Butters), Edinburgh, Sedgley, Howells, Mabbutt(Polston), Walsh(Stewart), Gascoigne(Lineker), Moncur, Moran, Allen(Nayim).

Aug 13 v Heart of Midlothian 1-1
Howells
Thorstvedt; Bergsson, Edinburgh, Sedgley, Howells, Mabbutt, Stewart(Walsh), Gascoigne(Moncur), Nayim, Lineker(Moran), Allen.

1991 (TO JAPAN)
Kirin Cup
Jun 2 v Vasco Da Gama (Kobe) 0-0
Walker; Edinburgh, Thomas, Sedgley, Howells, Tuttle, Stewart, Walsh, Samways, Hendry, Allen.
Jun 5 v Thailand (Nagoya) 2-1
Hendry, Edwards
Walker; Edinburgh(Edwards), Thomas, Sedgley, Hendon, Tuttle, Stewart, Walsh, Samways, Houghton(Hendry), Allen.
Jun 9 v Japan (Tokyo) 0-4
Walker; Edinburgh, Thomas(Edwards), Sedgley, Howells(Garland), Tuttle, Stewart, Hendry, Samways, Lineker, Allen.

1991 (TO EIRE, NORWAY, SCOTLAND, ITALY)
Jul 23 v Sligo Rovers (a) 4-0
Mabbutt, Stewart (pen), Samways, Thomas
Thorstvedt(Walker); Edinburgh, Van den Hauwe(Bergsson), Sedgley, Nayim, Mabbutt, Stewart, Walsh, Samways(Moncur), Lineker(Thomas (Tuttle)), Allen(Fenwick).
Jul 25 v Drogheda United (a) 2-0
Mabbutt, Lineker
Thorstvedt; Edinburgh(Edwards), Fenwick, Sedgley, Nayim, Mabbutt, Stewart, Moncur, Samways(Walsh), Lineker(P.Gray), Bergsson.
Jul 27 v Shelbourne (a) 3-1
Samways, Walsh, P.Gray
Thorstvedt; Edinburgh, Fenwick, Sedgley(Moncur), Nayim, Mabbutt, Stewart(P.Gray), Edwards, Samways(Tuttle), Lineker(Walsh), Bergsson.
Jul 30 v Brann (Bergen) 1-1
Stewart
Thorstvedt; Edinburgh(Hendon), Fenwick(Bergsson), Sedgley, Nayim(Edwards), Mabbutt(Moncur), Stewart, Walsh, Samways, Lineker(P.Gray), Allen.
Aug 4 v Celtic (a) 0-1
Thorstvedt; Fenwick, Van den Hauwe(Edinburgh), Sedgley(Bergsson), Howells(Hendon), Mabbutt, Stewart, Nayim, Samways, Lineker(Walsh), Allen(Moncur).
Aug 11 v Messina (Catanzaro) 0-2
Thorstvedt; Edinburgh, Statham(Sedgley), Hendon, Tuttle, Bergsson, Garland, Walsh(Robson), Hendry, P.Gray, Moncur(Edwards).
Aug 13 v Catanzaro (a) 1-0
Bergsson
Thorstvedt(Walker); Bergsson, Van den Hauwe, Sedgley(Tuttle), Hendon, Mabbutt, Stewart(Hendry), Nayim, Samways, Lineker(P.Gray), Allen.

Friendly Spurs

THIS section contains all the details it has been possible to trace of friendly games played by Spurs since 1896-97. It does not include testimonial matches where the beneficiary was associated with Spurs, or tour matches, but testimonial matches where the beneficiary was not associated with the club are included as are friendly matches played abroad during the course of a normal League season. Also excluded are matches played 'behind closed doors' and training games played against other clubs.

1896-97

Sep 3 v Rossendale (h) 7-0
Crump, McElhaney, Newbigging 2, Clements 2, Payne
Ambler; Burrows, Montgomery, Briggs, Devlin, Crump, McElhaney, McDermott, Newbigging, Clements, Payne.

Sep 10 v London Caledonians (h) 3-3
Devlin, Milliken, Clements
Sunderland; Burrows, Montgomery, Briggs, Devlin, Crump, McDermott, Milliken, Newbigging, Clements, Payne.

Sep 17 v Casuals (h) 4-0
McElhaney, Newbigging 3
Sunderland; Burrows, Montgomery, Crump, Briggs, Devlin, McElhaney, Milliken, Newbigging, Clements, Payne.

Sep 24 v Luton Town (h) 0-0 (abandoned after 75 minutes because of rain)
Ambler; Burrows, Montgomery, Devlin, Briggs, Crump, Thorburn, McElhaney, Newbigging, Clements, Milliken.

Sep 26 v Casuals (a) 4-1
McElhaney, Newbigging 2, Clements
Ambler; Burrows, Montgomery, Devlin, Briggs, Collins, McElhaney, Milliken, Newbigging, Clements, Payne.

Oct 1 v 1st Coldstream Guards (h) 4-0
Milliken, Newbigging, Clements (pen), Scorer unknown
Hatfield; Collins, Montgomery, Devlin, Briggs, Crump, Thorburn, Milliken, Newbigging, Clements, Payne.

Oct 8 v Royal Scots Greys (h) 5-0
Newbigging 2, Clements 2, Payne
Hatfield; Collins, Scott, Devlin, Briggs, Crump, McElhaney, Milliken, Newbigging, Clements, Payne.

Oct 29 v Southampton St Mary's (h) 3-1
Brown, Newbigging, Crump
Hatfield; Hay, Montgomery, Devlin, Briggs, Collins, Lanham, Brown, Newbigging, Clements, Crump.

Nov 16 v Luton T (a) 0-3
Hatfield; Goodman, Milarvie, Devlin, Collins, Crump, McElhaney, Milliken, Fleming, Clements, Newbigging.

Nov 21 v Blackpool (h) 0-2
Ambler; Burrows, Montgomery, Briggs, Almond, Mair, McElhaney, Milliken, Fleming, Newbigging, Payne.

Dec 19 v Clapton (a) 2-1
Hunter, Payne
Ambler; Burrows, Montgomery, Devlin, Almond, Mair, McElhaney, Milliken, Hunter, Payne, Crump.

Dec 26 v Vampires (h) 4-0
Montgomery, Clements Jnr, Clements Snr, Payne
Hatfield; Burrows, T.E.Jull, Regan, Mair, Oates, Milliken, Clements Jnr, Montgomery, Clements Snr, Payne.

Dec 26 v 3rd Grenadier Guards (h) 2-3
Clements, Payne
Ambler; Mair, Montgomery, Regan, Almond, Crump, McElhaney, Devlin, Milliken, Clements, Payne.

Dec 29 v Northfleet (h) 4-0
McElhaney 2, Milliken, Allen
Gardiner; Mair, Montgomery, Devlin, Keith, Crump,

McElhaney, Milliken, Allen, Clements, Newbigging.

Jan 11 v Chatham (a) 1-2
Newbigging
Gardiner; Scott, Montgomery, Devlin, Regan, Crump, McElhaney, Allen, Newbigging, Clements, Craig.

Jan 23 v Aston Villa (h) 2-2
Lanham 2
Ambler; Burrows, Montgomery, Devlin, Almond, Crump, McElhaney, Lanham, Newbigging, Clements, Payne.

Jan 28 v Chatham (h) 2-2
Lanham, Clements
Gardiner; Mair, Montgomery, Devlin, Coe, Crump, McElhaney, Lanham, Allen, Clements, Hobson.

Feb 6 v 3rd Grenadier Guards (h) 9-3
Almond 2, McElhaney, Milliken 2, Robertson, Clements, Payne 2
Gardiner; Burrows, Montgomery, Devlin, Almond, Crump, McElhaney, Milliken, Robertson, Clements, Payne.

Feb 10 v Gravesend (a) 3-1
Gardiner, McElhaney, Robertson
Gardiner; Scott, Montgomery, Devlin, Newbigging, Crump, McElhaney, Lanham, Robertson, Milliken, Clements.

Feb 13 v Northfleet (h) 5-0
Milliken, Robertson, Clements 2, Scorer unknown
Ambler; Burrows, Montgomery, Devlin, Almond, Crump, Milliken, McElhaney, Robertson, Clements, Payne.

Feb 15 v Southampton St Mary's (a) 0-2
Ambler; Montgomery, Marjoram, Crump, Mair, Devlin, Lanham, Newbigging, Robertson, Milliken, McElhaney.

Mar 9 v Eastbourne (a) 1-0
Allen
Hatfield; Burrows, Montgomery, Devlin, Newbigging, F.Markham, Lanham, Brown, Allen, Clements, Crump.

Mar 22 v Gravesend (h) 3-2
McElhaney, Wilson, Crump
Hatfield; F.Markham, Montgomery, Devlin, Allen, Briggs, McElhaney, Milliken, Wilson, Clements, Crump.

Apr 16 v Nottingham F (h) 1-1
Crump
Latham; Montgomery, Mair, Clements Snr, Allen, Crump, Lanham, Payne, Newbigging, Clements Jnr, Edwards.

Apr 20 v Blackburn R (h) 1-2
Lanham
Ambler; Allen, Montgomery, Mair, W.Markham, E.Markham, Lanham, Clements Jnr, Newbigging, Clements Snr, Edwards.

Apr 22 v Everton (h) 2-1
Lanham, Newbigging
Ambler; Milligan, Montgomery, Shepherd, Allen, Crump, Lanham, Brown, Newbigging, Clements, Edwards.

Apr 26 v London Caledonians (a) 1-1 (abandoned after 45 minutes because an opponent broke a leg)
Newbigging

Hatfield; T.E.Jull, Montgomery, F.Markham, Allen, Crump, Janes, Brown, Newbigging, Gair, Hobson.

1897-98
Sep 2 v Glossop North End (h) 3-2
Hartley, Joyce, Black
Cullen; Knowles, Montgomery, Hall, Jones, Stormont, Tannahill, Meade, Hartley, Joyce, Black.
Sep 9 v Royal Scots Fusilliers (h) 12-0
Tannahill, Davidson 4, Joyce 3, Meade 3, Black
Cullen; Knowles, Montgomery, Hall, Jones, Stormont, Tannahill, Davidson, Joyce, Meade, Black.
Sep 11 v Chorley (h) 3-1
Jones, Joyce, Meade
Cullen; Burrows, Montgomery, Hall, Jones, Stormont, Tannahill, Davidson, Joyce, Meade, Black.
Sep 23 v 2nd Scots Guards (h) 4-1
Davidson, Meade, Joyce, Black
Cullen; Burrows, Montgomery, Hall, Jones, Stormont, Tannahill, Davidson, Meade, Joyce, Black.
Oct 7 v 3rd Grenadier Guards (h) 4-0
Davidson, Hartley 2, Joyce
Cullen; Knowles, Crump, Hall, Jones, Stormont, Tannahill, Davidson, Hartley, Joyce, Hargreaves.
Oct 20 v Reading (h) 2-1
Hartley, Black
Cullen; Knowles, Montgomery, Hall, Jones, Crump, Hartley, Davidson, Joyce, Meade, Black.
Nov 2 v Eastbourne (a) 2-0
Joyce 2
Cullen; Burrows, Montgomery, Hall, Briggs, Jones, Tannahill, Meade, Joyce, Stormont, Black.
Nov 9 v New Brompton (h) 3-0
Tannahill, Hartley, Joyce
Cullen; Knowles, Montgomery, Hall, Briggs, Crump, Tannahill, Hartley, Joyce, Stormont, Black.
Dec 1 v Gravesend U (a) 0-3
Ambler; Knowles, Montgomery, Hall, Jones, Crump, Tannahill, Davidson, Joyce, Clements, Black.
Dec 11 v Kettering (h) 1-0
Black
Ambler; Downie, Knowles, Hall, Crump, Clements, Meade, Davidson, Joyce, Stormont, Black.
Dec 27 v Ilkeston T (h) 4-2
Joyce 2, Black 2
Cullen; Burrows, Downie, Hall, Jones(Knowles), Crump, Meade, Davidson, Joyce, Stormont, Black.
Dec 28 v Stockton (h) 3-0
Joyce 2, Clements
Ambler; Knowles, Montgomery, Hartley, Crump, Stormont, Payne, Davidson, Joyce, Clements, Black.
Jan 27 v Gravesend U (h) 1-2
Davidson
Cullen; Montgomery, Knowles, Hall, Jones, Stormont, Tannahill, Davidson, Joyce, Hartley, Crump.
Feb 9 v Sussex (a) 2-1
Hartley, Meade
Cullen; Knowles, Montgomery, Hall Jones, Downie, Hartley, Davidson, Meade, Stormont, Black.
Feb 12 v Sheffield U (h) 1-1
Davidson
Cullen; Knowles, Montgomery, Hall, Jones, Crump, Hartley, Davidson, Joyce, Stormont, Black.
Feb 15 v St Barnard's (h) 4-0
Hartley 3, Black
Cullen; Knowles, Montgomery, Hall, Jones, Crump, Hartley, Davidson, Joyce, Stormont, Black.
Feb 28 v Chesham (a) 4-2
Jones, Hartley, Joyce, Clements

Cullen; Montgomery, Monk, Hall, Jones, Downie, Hartley, Madden, Joyce, Clements, Black.
Mar 9 v Tunbridge Wells (a) 5-0
Davidson, Stormont, Joyce 3
Cullen; Knowles, Montgomery, Hall, Downie, Crump, Hartley, Davidson, Meade, Stormont, Joyce.
Mar 26 v Sunderland (h) 0-2
Cullen; Burrows, Knowles, Hall, Jones, Downie, Hartley, Madden, Joyce, Stormont, Black.
Apr 12 v Lincoln C (h) 2-1
Tannahill, Clements
Cullen; Knowles, Montgomery, Stormont, Jones, Downie, Tannahill, Hartley, Meade, Clements, Black.
Apr 18 v Reading (a) 3-3
Clements, Hartley 2
Cullen; Knowles, Burrows, Downie, Jones, Hall, Black, Stormont, Joyce, Clements, Hartley.
Apr 25 v Aston Villa (h) 2-3
Hartley, Black
Cullen; Burrows, Downie, Hall, Jones, Crump, Hartley, Meade, Joyce, Stormont, Black.
Apr 28 v Woolwich Arsenal (a) 0-3
Cullen; Burrows, Montgomery, Hall, Jones, Downie, Hartley, Davidson, Joyce, Stormont, Crump.
Apr 30 v Bolton W (h) 2-2
Joyce, Crump
Cullen; Monk, Montgomery, Hall, Jones, Downie, Hartley, Davidson, Joyce, Stormont, Crump.
1898-99
Sep 1 v Gainsborough T (h) 6-2
Smith 2 (1 pen), McKay 3, Joyce
Cullen; Melia, Cain, Jones, McNaught, Stormont, Smith, McKay, Joyce, Cameron, Bradshaw.
Sep 12 v Surrey Wanderers (h) 5-0
McKay, Joyce 2, Cameron, Bradshaw
Cullen; Erentz, Cain, Jones, Hall, Stormont, Smith, McKay, Joyce, Cameron, Bradshaw.
Oct 1 v Burton W (h) 5-2
Hartley, McKay, Meade, Payne, Widden (og)
Cullen; McGahey, Cain, Jones, Downie, Stormont, Hartley, McKay, Meade, Bradshaw, Payne.
Dec 21 v Surrey Wanderers (a) 1-1
Leach
Cullen; Melia, Markham, Hall, Downie, Kerry, Smith, Atherton, Hartley, Hickson, Leach.
Dec 27 v Ilkeston T (a) 1-0
Leach
Cullen; Melia, Erentz, Jones, Hall, Stormont, Hartley, McKay, Cameron, Hickson, Leach.

1899-1900
Sep 4 v Notts C (h) 4-1
Pratt, Copeland 3
Clawley; Erentz, Tait, Jones, McNaught, Morris, Smith, Pratt, Copeland, Cameron, Kirwan.
Sep 13 v Richmond (a) 3-1
Copeland, Pratt, Raby
Clawley; Erentz, Tait, Hughes, McNaught, Morris, Smith, Pratt, Copeland, Kirwan, Raby.
Sep 27 v Clapton (a) 4-1
Hyde 2, Pratt, Raby
Clawley; Erentz, Tait, Morris, McNaught, Stormont, Smith, Pratt, Raby, Hyde, Kirwan.
Sep 30 v Southampton (a) 1-1
Smith
Clawley; Erentz, Tait, Morris, McNaught, Jones, Smith, Pratt, Copeland, Cameron, Kirwan.
Oct 28 v Southampton (h) 4-3
Stormont, Cameron, Copeland, Kirwan

Meates; Melia, Tait, Jones, Morris, Stormont, Smith, Pratt, Copeland, Cameron, Kirwan.
Nov 11 v Ilkeston T (h) 7-0
Melia, Smith, Rule 2, Copeland 2, Pratt
Haddow; Melia, Tait, Jones, Morris, Stormont, Smith, Rule, Copeland, Pratt, Kirwan.
Nov 18 v Bolton W (h) 4-0
Rule, Pratt, Cameron 2
Haddow; Melia, Tait, Hughes, Morris, Stormont, Smith, Rule, Pratt, Cameron, Kirwan.
Nov 25 v Corinthians (h) 5-1
Cameron 2, Copeland, Kirwan 2
Haddow; Melia, Tait, Jones, Morris, Stormont, Smith, Cameron, Pratt, Copeland, Kirwan.
Nov 27 v The Kaffirs (h) 6-4
Kirwan 2, Melia, Raby 2, Stormont
Haddow; Melia, Tait, Hughes, McNaught, Stormont, Kirwan, Raby, Erentz, Copeland, Hyde.
Dec 18 v H.R.Burkes XI (h) 12-2
Cameron 2, Copeland 4, Kirwan 4, Pratt, Smith
Haddow; Erentz, Crump, Hughes, McNaught, Stormont, Smith, Cameron, Pratt, Copeland, Kirwan.
Jan 1 v Middlesborough (a) 2-2
Raby, Pratt
Haddow; Erentz, Stevens, Crump, McNaught, Hughes, Smith, Raby, Pratt, Kirwan, Hyde.
Jan 2 v Sunderland (a) 3-1
Hughes, Pratt 2
Haddow; Erentz, Tait, Jones, McNaught, Hughes, Smith, Cameron, Pratt, Kirwan, Hyde.
Feb 5 v Oxford University (h) 6-0
Smith 2, Cameron, Pratt 3
Haddow; Erentz, Tait, Morris, McNaught, Stormont, Smith, Cameron, Pratt, Copeland, Kirwan.
Feb 12 v Chesterfield (h) 7-2
Raby, Pratt 4, Copeland, Kirwan
Haddow; Melia, Tait, Morris, McNaught, Stormont, Smith, Raby, Pratt, Copeland, Kirwan.
Feb 21 v Gravesend U (a) 1-3
Smith
Haddow; Erentz, Hughes, Jones, McNaught, Stormont, Smith, Levy, Kirwan, Copeland, Hyde.
Mar 5 v Stoke (h) 6-0
Cameron, Pratt 4, Kirwan
Haddow; Melia, Tait, Jones, McNaught, Hughes, Raby, Cameron, Pratt, Copeland, Kirwan.
Mar 17 v Corinthians (a) 3-1
Cameron 2, Kirwan
Haddow; Melia, Tait, Morris, McNaught, Jones, Smith, Cameron, Pratt, Stormont, Kirwan.
Apr 21 v Aston Villa (a) 3-4
Cameron, Copeland 2
Clawley; Erentz, Tait, Jones, McNaught, Stormont, Smith, Cameron, Pratt, Copeland, Kirwan.

1900-01
Sep 3 v Bristol R (a) 0-1
Haddow; Melia, Tait, Morris, McNaught, Stormont, Smith, Cameron, Brown, Pangbourne, Kirwan.
Sep 8 v Southampton (a) 3-1
Brown 3
Clawley; Melia, Tait, Morris, McNaught, J.L.Jones, Smith, Cameron, Brown, Stormont, Kirwan.
Sep 10 v Reading (h) 3-3
McNaught, Smith, Cameron
Clawley; Melia, Tait, Morris(Hughes), McNaught, J.L.Jones, Smith, Cameron, Brown, Stormont, Kirwan.

Sep 17 v Millwall A (a) 2-1
Cameron 2
Clawley; Melia, Hughes, Erentz, A.E.Jones, J.L.Jones, Smith, Cameron, Brown, Stormont, Kirwan.
Sep 24 v Richmond Association (h) 8-0
Smith, Pangbourne, Brown 4, Stormont, Kirwan
Clawley; Melia, Hughes, Erentz, McNaught, J.L.Jones, Smith, Pangbourne, Brown, Stormont, Kirwan.
Sep 27 v Notts C (a) 1-4
Brown
Clawley; Melia, Tait, Erentz, McNaught, J.L.Jones, Smith, Cameron, Brown, Stormont Kirwan.
Oct 3 v Reading (h) 1-1
Smith
Clawley; Melia, Tait, Erentz, McNaught, J.L.Jones, Smith, Cameron, Brown, Stormont, Kirwan.
Oct 8 v Notts C (h) 1-1
Brown
Clawley; Tait, Melia, Morris(Erentz), McNaught, Hughes, Smith, Moffatt, Brown, Stormont, Kirwan.
Oct 13 v Corinthians (h) 2-2
Smith, Brown
Clawley; Melia, Tait, J.L.Jones, McNaught, Stormont, Smith, Pangbourne, Brown, Cameron, Kirwan.
Oct 22 v Luton T (h) 1-3
Brown
Clawley; Erentz, Tait, J.L.Jones, McNaught, Stormont, Berry, Pangbourne, Brown, Cameron, Hyde.
Oct 31 v Queen's Park Rangers (h) 7-0
A.E.Jones, Cameron 2, Brown 2, J.L.Jones, Kirwan
Clawley; Erentz, Tait, Hughes, McNaught, Stormont, A.E.Jones, Cameron, Brown, J.L.Jones, Kirwan.
Nov 3 v Portsmouth (a) 3-1
Cameron, Brown, Kirwan
Clawley; Erentz, Tait, Hughes, McNaught, Stormont, A.E.Jones, Cameron, Brown, J.L.Jones, Kirwan.
Nov 5 v Cambridge University (h) 3-1
Hughes, Brown 2
Clawley; Erentz, Tait, Hughes, McNaught, Stormont, A.E.Jones, Cameron, Brown, J.L.Jones, Kirwan.
Nov 12 v Luton T (a) 0-1
Clawley; Erentz, Hughes, Moles, McNaught, Stormont, Smith, A.E.Jones, Brown, Pangbourne, Hyde.
Dec 17 v Preston NE (h) 1-1
Morris
Clawley; Erentz, Tait, Hughes, McNaught, Stormont, A.E.Jones, Morris, Brown, J.L.Jones, Kirwan.
Dec 29 v Newark (h) 3-0
Morris 2, Kirwan
Haddow; Erentz, Hughes, A.E.Jones, McNaught, Stormont, Moffatt, Morris, Brown, Kirwan, Hyde.
Jan 5 v Clapton (h) 3-0
Brown 3
Clawley; Erentz, Tait, Anson, Hughes, Stormont, Hyde, Morris, Brown, J.L.Jones, Kirwan.
Jan 8 v German Association (h) 9-6
Tait 3, Hyde, Morris 2 (1 pen), Brown 2, Kirwan
Haddow; Melia, Tait, J.L.Jones, McNaught, Stormont, Hyde, Morris, Brown, Moffatt, Kirwan.

386

Spurs played a German Association team from Berlin in January 1901. They beat the Germans in a high-scoring game at snow-covered White Hart Lane.

Feb 4 v Oxford University (h) 5-2
Erentz, Smith, Brown 2, Copeland
Clawley; Erentz, Tait, Morris, McNaught, Stormont, Smith, Cameron, Brown, Copeland, Kirwan.

1901-02
Sep 1 v Heart of Midlothian (h) 0-0
Clawley; Erentz, Tait, Morris, Hughes, J.L.Jones, Smith, Cameron, Brown, Copeland, Kirwan.
Sep 23 v Sheffield U (a) 1-3
Cameron
Clawley; Tait, Erentz, J.L.Jones, Hughes, Morris, Hyde, Copeland, Cameron, Gilhooley, Smith.
Oct 16 v Rest of Southern League (h) 2-0
Cameron 2
Clawley; Stevenson, Tait, Montgomery, Hughes, J.Burton, Gilhooley, Barlow, Woodward, Cameron, Kirwan.
Nov 13 v West Norwood (a) 3-1
Brown 3
Clawley; Erentz, Tait, Montgomery, McNaught, J.L.Jones, Smith, Cameron, Brown, Copeland, Kirwan.
Nov 25 v Cambridge University (h) 3-1
Brown, Kirwan 2
Clawley; Stevens, Tait, Montgomery, McNaught, J.L.Jones, Soulsby, Cameron, Brown, Barlow (Kirwan), Hyde.
Dec 2 v Army Association (h) 2-1
Cameron, Brown
Clawley; Stevenson, Tait, Hughes, McNaught, J.L.Jones, Haig-Brown, Cameron, Brown, Copeland, Kirwan.
Dec 14 v Corinthians (a) 0-3
Clawley; Erentz, Tait, Morris, Hughes, J.L.Jones, Smith, Barlow, Cameron, Copeland, Kirwan.
Jan 1 v Everton (a) 1-3
Smith
Griffiths; Erentz, Tait, Morris, Hughes, J.L.Jones, Smith, Copeland, Cameron, Kirwan, Woodward.
Jan 2 v Heart of Midlothian (a) 1-3
Scorer unknown
Griffiths; Erentz, Tait, Morris, Hughes, J.L.Jones, Smith, Copeland, Cameron, Kirwan, Woodward.
Apr 1 v Sheffield U (h) 3-2
Fitchie, Kirwan 2
Moles; Erentz, Tait, J.Burton, McNaught, J.L.Jones, Smith, Cameron, Copeland, Fitchie, Kirwan.
Apr 30 v Portsmouth (a) 2-0
Barlow, Copeland
Clawley; Erentz, Tait, Hughes, McNaught, J.L.Jones, Barlow, Cameron, Brown, Copeland, Kirwan.

1902-03
Nov 10 v Cambridge University (h) 2-1
Barlow, Houston
Clawley; Stevenson, Watson, Brown, Hughes, O.Burton, Warner, Gilhooley, Barlow, Houston, Chalmers.
Nov 15 v Corinthians (a) 3-1
Copeland 2, Kirwan
Clawley; Erentz, Tait, Brown, Morris, J.L.Jones, Gilhooley, Cameron, Woodward, Copeland, Kirwan.
Dec 8 v London FA (h) 2-2
Quinn, Houston
Williams; Stevenson, Watson, Brown, Morris, J.Burton, Gilhooly, Barlow, Houston, Quinn, Chalmers.
Dec 10 v West Norwood (a) 9-0
Barlow, Rainbird 3, Warner 4, Opp own-goal
Williams; Stevens, Tait, Brown, Bugg, O.Burton, Rainbird, Warner, Barlow, Quinn, Kirwan.
Dec 13 v Corinthians (h) 2-2
Houston, Chalmers
Williams; Watson, Tait, Morris, Hughes, J.L.Jones, Haig-Brown, Warner, Houston, Copeland, Chalmers.
Jan 22 v Cambridge University (a) 1-0
Gilhooly
Williams; Erentz, Watson, Brown, Hughes, Steven, Dryburgh, Gilhooly, Houston, Quinn, Chalmers.
Apr 6 v Queen's Park (h) 1-0
J.Burton
Williams; Stevenson, Tait, J.Burton, Morris, O.Burton, Haig-Brown, Gilhooley, Cameron, Hubble, Kirwan.
Apr 30 v Nottingham F (h) 2-1
Woodward 2
Clawley; Erentz, Tait, Hughes, Morris, O.Burton, Dryburgh, Gilhooley, Woodward, Copeland, Kirwan.

1903-04
Sep 23 v New Brompton (a) 0-3
Mearns; Stevenson, Archer, Brown, Bugg, O.Burton, Cameron, J.Jones, Gilhooly, Quinn, Chalmers.

387

Dec 7 v Burnley (h) 4-0
Warner, Badger 2, Cameron
Mearns; Watson, Erentz, Brown, McNaught,
O.Burton, Warner, Quinn, Badger, Cameron,
Chalmers.
Dec 12 v Corinthians (h) 5-1
Warner, J.Jones, Woodward 2, Copeland
Williams; Tait, Hughes, Morris, McNaught, J.L.Jones,
Warner, J.Jones, Woodward, Copeland, Kirwan.

1904-05
Sep 12 v Brighton & HA (h) 3-1
Stansfield, O'Hagan 2
Wainwright; Watson, Archer, George, McNaught,
Brearley, Walton, Swann, Stansfield, O'Hagan,
Kirwan.
Oct 31 v London FA (h) 4-1
Bull, O'Hagan 2 (1 pen), Swann
Eggett; Watson, Archer, George, Bull, J.Burton, Berry,
Swann, Glen, O'Hagan, Murray.
Nov 2 v Littlehampton (a) 7-0
Cameron 2, Copeland 2, McNaught, Warner 2
Williams; McCurdy, Tait, Morris, Hughes, McNaught,
Stansfield, Warner, Cameron, Copeland, Kirwan.
Nov 28 v Cambridge University (h) 2-2
O'Hagan, Opp own-goal
Eggett; Mccurdy, J.Burton, Hughes, Leach-Lewis,
McNaught, Gallacher, Warner, Glen, O'Hagan,
Kirwan.
Jan 19 v Corinthians (h) 0-2
Eggett; McCurdy, Gallacher, George, Bull, Hughes,
Walton, Stansfield, Glen, O'Hagan, Kirwan.
Jan 24 v Cambridge University (a) 4-4
Warner 2, Cameron 2
Williams; Mapley, Gallacher, Freeborough,
McNaught, Morgan, Warner, George, Cameron,
O'Hagan, Earle.
Apr 13 v Wanstead (a) 4-3
O'Hagan 2, Woodward 2
Williams; McCurdy, Gallacher, Morgan, Freeborough,
Hughes, Swann, Cameron, Woodward, O'Hagan,
Kirwan.
Apr 25 v Sheffield U (h) 0-0
Yates; Watson, J.Burton, Morgan, Bull, Freeborough,
Walton, Cameron, Stansfield, O'Donnell, Murray.

1905-06
Nov 27 v Cambridge University (h) 2-1
O'Hagan, Berry
Eggett; Chaplin, O.Burton, Brearley, Freeborough,
Darnell, Gaudson, Gibson, Berry, O'Hagan, Murray.
Dec 9 v Corinthians (h) 3-1
Walton, Kyle, Carrick
Eggett; Watson, O.Burton, Morris, Bull, Brearley,
Walton, Berry, Woodward, Kyle, Carrick.
Jan 24 v Cambridge University (a) 1-4
O'Hagan
Whitbourne; Chaplin, O.Burton, George, Freeborough,
Brearley, Berry, Stansfield, Leach, O'Hagan, Murray.
1906-07
Sep 13 v London Caledonians (h) 6-4
Steel, Chapman, Leach, Reid 3
Groves; Wilkinson, Rickham, Steel, McNaught,
Darnell, Stansfield, Chapman, Leach, Reid,
McDiarmid.
Sep 17 v Ilford (h) 4-4
Bird, Tait 2, Walker
Eggett; C.Watson, Wilkinson, Bird, McNaught, Jones,
Dow, Pickett, Tait, Walker, Walton.

Nov 12 v Cambridge University (h) 4-2
Bird, Eames 2, Spence
Kimball; J.Watson, C.Watson, Jones, McNaught,
Bird, Berry, Walker, Eames, Spence, Dow.
Nov 14 v Corinthians (a) 1-6
Brearley
Reilly; Chaplin, Tait, Morris, Bull, Hughes, Badenoch,
Hewitt, Stansfield, Reid, Brearley.
Nov 19 v Oxford University (h) 2-1
Payne, Whyman
Reilly; C.Watson, Harding, Jones, Darnell, Bird,
Walton, Hewitt, Leach, Payne, Whyman.
Dec 8 v Corinthians (h) 5-0
Woodward, Reid, Brearley 2, Timmis (og)
Reilly; Chaplin, J.Watson, Morris, Bull, Hughes,
Walton, Hewitt, Woodward, Reid, Brearley.
Apr 15 v C.W.Brown's XI (h) 2-1
Simonds, Hewitt
Eggett; Wilkinson, Burton, Darnell, Steel, McDiarmid,
Eames, Hewitt, Chapman, Simonds, Brearley.

1907-08
Feb 1 v Woolwich Arsenal (h) 0-1
Manning; Chaplin, Burton, Morris, Bull, Gray,
McNair, Pass, Woodward, Reid, Middlemiss.
Feb 22 v Chelsea (a) 1-1
Seeburg
Whitbourne; Chaplin, Burton, Steel, Bull, Darnell,
Walker, Pass, Seeburg, Pickett, Middlemiss.
Apr 30 v Clapton O (a) 0-2
Manning; Coquet, Dixon, Morris, Bull, Darnell,
Pickett, Minter, Seeburg, Payne, Jenkins.

1908-09
Apr 29 v Clapton O (a) 3-2
Tull 2, Curtis
Boreham; Leslie, Wilkes, Bentley, D.Steel, Darnell,
Curtis, Minter, Tull, R.Steel, Middlemiss.

1909-10
Sep 29 v Reading (a) 3-2
Tull 2, Minter
Boreham; Coquet, Wilkes, McFarlane, D.Steel,
Darnell, Curtis, Tull, Minter, R.Steel, Middlemiss.

1911-12
Feb 3 v Clapton O (h) 3-2
Minter, Elliott 2
Joyce; Webster, Brittan, Bentley, Lightfoot, Bowering,
Curtis, Minter, Elliott, Mason, Middlemiss.
Apr 18 v Northampton T (a) 0-2
Lunn; Webster, Brittan, Darnell, Kennedy, Bowering,
Curtis, McTavish J, Elliott, Bliss, Middlemiss.

1912-13
Apr 9 v Watford (a) 0-0
Joyce; Collins, Webster, Weir, Rance, Grimsdell,
Curtis, Minter, Cantrell, Bliss, Middlemiss.

1913-14
Feb 21 v Chelsea (h) 3-7
Sparrow, Banks, Bliss
McCleneghan; Collins, Pearson, Weir, Rance, Lightfoot,
Tattersall, Sparrow, Banks, Bliss, Middlemiss.
Mar 5 v Music Hall Artists (h) 3-2 (30-minute match)
Banks, Cantrell, Bliss
Joyce; Clay, Webster, Bowler, Steel, Grimsdell,
Walden, Banks, Cantrell, Bliss, Middlemiss.

1914-15
Oct 15 v Chelsea (a) 1-1
Sparrow
Watkins; Collins, Cartwright, Steel, Rance, Lightfoot, Tattersall, Banks, Sparrow, Lowe, Middlemiss.
Feb 6 v Fulham (h) 2-2
Steel, Cantrell
Eadon; Clay, Pearson, Weir, Steel, Lightfoot, Fleming, Lowe, Cantrell, Woodger, Middlemiss.

1915-16
Jan 29 v Clapton O (h) 0-1
Joyce; Clay, Ralston, Darnell, Rance, Barton, Morris, Lloyd, Bassett, Bliss, Steel.
Apr 24 v Norwich C (a) 1-1
McGregor
Watkins; Clay, Butcher, Elliott, Rance, Darnell, Morris, Lloyd, McGregor, Steel, Ramsay.
May 6 v Clapton O (a) 2-3
Bassett, Bliss
Jacques; Clay, Steel, Elliott, Rance, Barton, Morris, Bassett, Lloyd, Bliss, Hopkins.

1916-17
May 5 v West Ham U (a) 3-3
Potter, Banks, Barnard
Jacques; Clay, Feeburg, Elliott, Barton, Darnell, Potter, Bassett, Banks, Barnard, Casey.

1918-19
Aug 31 v Cpl H.Prices XI (St Albans) 1-1
A.Lindsay
Brandham; Thomas, Elliott, Beaton, Darnell, McCracken, Brooks, A.Lindsay, Barnard, Robson, Dockray.
Apr 26 v Clapton O (a) 1-6
Roper
Jacques; Draper, Ferris, Darnell, Rance, Robson, Rees, Minter, Roper, Simons, Middlemiss.
Apr 26 v Crystal P (a) 0-3
French; Clay, Craig, Thomas, Elliott, Tomkins, 'Slender'(Chester), Upex, Wilson, Banks, Dockray.
May 24 v Arsenal (a) 0-0
Jacques; Pearson, Clay, Tomkins, Rutherford, Barton, Dimmock, Innes, Minter, Powell, Furr.

1919-20
Dec 15 v Corinthians (h) 4-1
Cantrell 2, Wilson 2
Jacques; Pearson, McDonald, Smith, Rance, Skinner, Lorimer, Minter, Cantrell, Wilson, Dimmock.
May 8 v Norwich C (a) 4-0
Banks 2, Bliss 2
Jacques; Clay, Brown, Archibald, Smith, Grimsdell, Banks, Seed, Cantrell, Bliss, Dimmock.

1920-21
May 14 v Fulham (Camberley) 4-0
Grimsdell, Banks, Wilson, Bliss
Hunter; Clay, McDonald, Smith, Walters, Grimsdell, Banks, Seed, Wilson, Bliss, Dimmock.

1921-22
Sep 19 v Partick Thistle (a) 1-3
Wilson
Hunter; Clay, McDonald, Archibald, Walters, Grimsdell, Banks, Seed, Wilson, Thompson, Dimmock.
Sep 22 v Inverness Cal (a) 3-6

Grimsdell, Lindsay, Thompson
Hunter; Clay, McDonald, Archibald, Lowe, Grimsdell, Walden, Lindsay, Seed, Thompson, Dimmock.
Oct 6 v Corinthians (h) 2-1
Smith, Banks
French; Clay, McDonald, Smith, Lowe, Grimsdell, Lorimer, Seed, Banks, Bliss, Handley.
May 13 v Chelsea (Camberley) 1-1
Seed
Hampton; Clay, McDonald, Smith Walters, Skinner, Lindsay, Seed, Wilson, Thompson, Dimmock.

1922-23
Sep 11 v Corinthians (a) 2-1
Brooks, Hunter (og)
Jacques; Clay, McDonald, Skinner, Walters, Grimsdell, Walden, Handley, Lindsay, Dimmock, Brooks.
Oct 16 v Llanelly (a) 1-2
Whitton
Blake; Forster, McDonald, Poynton, Grimsdell, Lowe, Sage, Seed, Whitton, Dimmock, Handley.
May 7 v West Ham U (h) 5-2
Lindsay, Handley 3, Dimmock
Maddison; Clay, Forster, Smith, Walters, Grimsdell, Barnett, Thompson, Lindsay, Handley, Dimmock.

1923-24
Oct 25 v Norwich C (a) 3-2
Knott, Sharp 2
Blake; Ross, McDonald, Poynton, Sage, White, Handley Knott, Duffus, Sharp, Thompson.
Feb 2 v Chelsea (a) 0-0
Maddison; Bann, Forster, Smith, Walters, Duffus, Handley, Thompson, Osborne, Elkes, Brooks.
Feb 23 v West Ham U (a) 1-1
Thompson
Blake; Clay, Forster, Smith, Walters, Poynton, McCudden, Thompson, Minter, Elkes, Handley.
Mar 17 v West Ham United (a) 1-1
Lindsay
Maddison; Clay, Forster, Smith, Sage, Poynton, Thompson, Lindsay, Osborne, Elkes, Handley.
Apr 16 v Inter-Varsities (h) 7-1
Osborne, Lindsay, Elkes 2, Dimmock 3
Blake; Clay, Poynton, Smith, Lowe, Skinner, Thompson, Osborne, Lindsay, Elkes, Dimmock.

1925-26
Oct 22 v Norwich C (Bury St Edmonds) 2-3
Hargreaves 2
J.Smith; Bann, McDonald, Walters, Lowe, White, Walden, Lane, Hargreaves, Knott, Handley.
Mar 27 v Hull C (a) 0-5
Brittan; Bann, McDonald, Seed, Skitt, Grimsdell, Vanner, Minter, Lane, Elkes, Dimmock.
May 3 v West Ham U (a) 1-1
Blair
J.Smith; Bann, Richardson, B.Smith, Elkes, Lindsay, Thompson, Blair, Lane, Seed, Handley.

1927-28
Apr 25 v Ebbw Vale (a) 7-3
O'Callaghan 2, Lindsay, Armstrong, Dimmock 3
Spiers; Forster, Poynton, Lowdell, Skitt, Grimsdell, Thompson, O'Callaghan, Lindsay, Armstrong, Dimmock.
1929-30
May 1 v Yeovil & Petters (a) 6-4

Osborne 2, Harper 2, O'Callaghan, Dimmock
Spiers; Herod, Reddish, Skitt, Cable, Meads, Davies,
Osborne, Harper, O'Callaghan, Dimmock.

1930-31
Dec 8 v West Ham U (a) 2-1
Davies, Bellamy
Spiers; Lyons, Hodgkinson, Skitt, Messer, Meads,
Davies, O'Callaghan, Harper, Cook, Bellamy.
Feb 28 v Huddersfield T (h) 2-4
Harper, Goodall (og)
Spiers; Lyons, Hodgkinson, Skitt, Messer, Alsford,
Davies, O'Callaghan, Harper, Cook, Bellamy.

1933-34
Apr 30 v Luton T (a) 2-2
O'Callaghan, Hedley
Nicholls; Channell, Whatley, Day, Rowe, Meads,
McCormick, O'Callaghan, Hunt, G.W.Hall, Hedley.

1934-35
Apr 24 v Burton T (a) 2-2
Bell, G.S.Hunt
Hooper; Illingworth, Fullwood, Howe, Alsford,
Phypers, Bolan, Bell, G.S.Hunt, Duncan, W.Evans.

1938-39
Apr 17 v Arsenal (Colchester) 1-2
Duncan
Hooper; Ward, Whatley, Burgess, Hitchins,
Buckingham, Cox, G.W.Hall, Ludford, Duncan,
Medley.

1939-40
Sep 23 v Chelmsford C (a) 2-4
G.W.Hall, Ludford
Hooper; Howe, Whatley, Burgess, Hitchins,
Buckingham, Cox, G.W.Hall, Ludford, Sargent,
Tomkin.
Sep 30 v Chelsea (a) 2-4
Ludford, Medley
Hooper; Dorling, Whatley, Burgess, Hitchins, Howe,
Sargent, G.W.Hall, Ludford, Duncan, Medley.
Oct 7 v West Ham U (h) 0-2
Hooper; Dorling, Whatley, Burgess, Hitchins,
Spelman, Sargent, G.W.Hall, Ludford, Duncan,
Medley.

1941-42
May 25 v Crystal P (a) 5-3
Chisholm, Sainsbury, Gibbons, Edwards, Gregory (og)
Hooper; Ward, Tickridge, Chisholm, Hitchins, Hall,
Sainsbury, Broadis, Gibbons, Edwards, Ludford.

1942-43
Apr 17 v Queen's Park Rangers (a) 1-1
Ludford
Hooper; Ward, Whatley, Palmer, Howe, Buckingham,
Beasley, Milton, Ludford, O'Callaghan, Trigg.
Apr 24 v Charlton A (h) 2-1
Martin, Jones
Hooper; Ward, Whatley, Willis, Chisholm,
Buckingham, Beasley, Martin, Rowley, Hall, Jones.
Apr 26 v Fulham (h) 3-0
Rowley 2, Ludford
Hooper; Ward, Whatley, Howe, Chisholm,
Buckingham, Beasley, Martin, Rowley, Hall, Ludford.
May 1 v Clapton O (h) 4-3
Ludford, Holley 2, M.E.Sturgess
L.Sturgess; Ward, Whatley, Howe, Chisholm, Hall,

Ludford, Bennett, Holley, M.E.Sturgess, O'Callaghan.
May 8 v Arsenal (h) 1-2
Ludford
Hooper; Ward, Howe, Jones, Chisholm, Buckingham,
Beasley, Hall, Ludford, Clayton, Burley.

1943-44
Apr 10 v Millwall (a) 0-0
Ditchburn; Ward, Whatley, Durston, Gibbins, Evans,
Downer, Whent, Ludford, Beasley, Adams.

1944-45
Aug 19 v Coventry C (a) 1-3
Howe
Hughes; Ward, Willis, White, Page, Burgess, Walters,
Martin, Ludford, Howe, Beasley.
Apr 7 v Crystal P (a) 1-3
Opp own-goal
Hughes; Ward, Willis, White, Burke, Burgess, Walters,
Walker, Woodward, Gurr, A.E.Hall.
May 19 v Arsenal (h) 4-0
Walters, Flavell, Dix, Howe
Roberts; Ward, Willis, Ludford, Burke, Burgess,
Walters, Flavell, Lyman, Dix, Howe.
May 26 v Fulham (h) 2-2
Ludford, Burgess
Roberts; Ward, Willis, Ludford, Burke, Burgess,
Walters, Broadis, Lyman, A.E.Hall, Beasley.

1945-46
Mar 2 v Chelsea (h) 4-2
Foreman 2, Dix, Whitchurch
Hughes; Willis, Buckingham, White, Nicholson,
Ludford, Griffiths, Rundle, Foreman, Dix,
Whitchurch.

1946-47
Jan 25 v Arsenal (h) 2-0
Woodward, A.E.Hall
Hughes; Tickridge, Whatley, Woodward, Chisholm,
Trailor, A.E.Hall, Bennett, Duquemin, Dix,
Whitchurch.

1948-49
Jan 29 v Middlesbrough (h) 4-1
Burgess, Baily, Bennett, Jones
Ditchburn; Tickridge, Buckingham, Nicholson,
Woodward, Burgess, Walters, Baily, Duquemin,
Bennett, Jones.
Apr 25 v Hibernian (h) 2-5
Bennett, Duquemin
Ditchburn; Tickridge, Withers, Garwood, Clarke,
Trailor, Walters, Bennett, Duquemin, Baily, Medley.
May 9 v Cornwall County XI (Penzance) 2-0
Rundle, Medley
Ditchburn; Tickridge, Withers, Nicholson, Clarke,
Burgess, Walters, Bennett, Westwood, Rundle, Medley.

1949-50
Apr 24 v Chelmsford C (a) 4-1
Bennett 3, Duquemin
Ditchburn; Ramsey, Willis, Gilberg, Farley, Marchi,
Walters, Bennett, Duquemin, Rees, Medley.
May 1 v Hibernian (h) 0-1
Ditchburn; Ramsey, Willis, Gilberg, Clarke, Marchi,
Walters, Bennett, Duquemin, Harmer, Medley.

1950-51
Sep 18 v Lovells A (h) 8-0

390

Burgess, Scarth 2, Duquemin 3, Harmer, Medley
Ditchburn; Henty, Willis, Nicholson, Clarke, Burgess,
Walters, Scarth, Duquemin, Harmer, Medley.
Jan 27 v Cardiff C (a) 3-2
McClellan, Baily, Adams
Ditchburn; Ramsey, Willis, Garwood, Clarke, Burgess,
Walters, Murphy, McClellan, Baily, Adams.
Feb 6 v Combined Liège XI (Liège) 4-1
Walters, Murphy 2, McClellan
Ditchburn; Ramsey, Willis, Nicholson, Clarke,
Burgess, Walters, Murphy, McClellan, Baily, Medley.
Apr 23 v Hibernian (a) 0-0
Ditchburn; Ramsey, Willis, Nicholson, Clarke,
Burgess, Walters, Murphy, Duquemin, Baily, Medley.
Apr 30 v Chelmsford C (a) 7-3
Bennett, McClellan 4, Murphy 2
Reynolds; Willis, Withers, Brittan, Farley, Burgess,
Walters, Bennett, McClellan, Murphy, Medley.
May 16 v Racing Club de Paris (a) 4-2
Baily, Duquemin, McClellan, Medley
Reynolds; Withers, Willis, Bennett, Clarke, Brittan,
Walters, Baily, Duquemin(McClellan), Murphy,
Medley.

1951-52
Oct 10 v Copenhagen Combined XI (h) 2-1
Walters, Medley
Ditchburn; Ramsey, Willis, Nicholson, Clarke,
Burgess, Walters, Bennett, McClellan, Baily, Medley.
Mar 26 v FC Austria (Brussels) 2-2
Bennett, Duequemin
Ditchburn; Ramsey, Willis, Nicholson, Clarke,
Burgess, Walters, Bennett, Duquemin, Baily, Adams.
Apr 23 v Hibernian (h) 1-2
Ramsey (pen)
Ditchburn; Ramsey, Withers, Nicholson, Clarke,
Burgess, Walters, Bennett, Duquemin, Baily,
McClellan.
May 3 v Racing Club de Paris (a) 2-1
Ramsey, Bennett
Ditchburn; Ramsey, Withers, Nicholson (Robshaw),
Clarke, Burgess, Walters, Bennett, Duquemin, Baily,
Medley.
May 11 v Crittalls Athletic (Braintree) 8-1
*Walters, Uphill, Baily, Duquemin 2, Harmer,
McClellan, Opp own-goal*
Ditchburn; Willis, Gibbins, Bennett, Clarke, Wetton,
Walters(Uphill), Baily(Dowsett), Duquemin, Harmer
(Adams), McClellan.

1952-53
Oct 27 v Gloucester C (a) 1-2
Baily
Ditchburn; Ramsey, Withers, Robshaw, Farley,
Wetton, Walters, Bennett, Duquemin, Baily, Harmer.
Apr 16 v West Ham U (a) 1-2
Walters
Ditchburn; Baker, Withers, Nicholson, Clarke, Brittan,
Walters, Bennett, Laybourne, Baily, Medley.
Apr 20 v Reading (a) 4-0
Duquemin 2, Baily, McClellan
Ditchburn; Ramsey, Willis, Marchi, Clarke, Farley,
Brooks, Bennett, Duquemin, Baily, McClellan.
May 4 v Arsenal (a) 2-0
Bennett, Duquemin
Ditchburn; Baker, Hopkins, Wetton, King, Burgess,
Walters, Bennett, Duquemin, Baily, McClellan.
May 15 v Heart of Midlothian 0-2
Reynolds; Nicholson, Withers, Marchi, King, Brittan,

Brooks, Baily, Bennett, Harmer, McClellan.
May 30 v Racing Club de Paris (a) 1-1
Duquemin
Reynolds; Withers, Hopkins, Wetton, King, Burgess,
Walters, Bennett, Duquemin, Baily, Brooks
(McClellan).

1953-54
Sep 21 v Hibernian (a) 1-0
Wetton
Ditchburn; Baker, Withers, Bennett, Clarke, Wetton,
McClellan, Brooks, Duquemin, Baily, Owen.
Sep 29 v Racing Club de Paris (h) 5-3
Burgess, Hutchinson, Bennett 2, Duquemin
Ditchburn; Ramsey, Withers, Wetton, Farley, Burgess,
Hutchinson, Bennett, Duquemin, Harmer, Robb.
Oct 19 v Millwall (a) 2-0
Walters, Bennett
Reynolds; Baker, Withers, Nicholson, Clarke, Wetton,
Walters, Brooks, Bennett, Baily, Robb.
Oct 28 v FC Austria (h) 3-2
Walters, Duquemin, Harmer
Ditchburn; Ramsey, Withers, Nicholson, Clarke,
Burgess, Walters, Brooks, Duquemin, Harmer, Robb.
Apr 5 v Hibernian (h) 3-2
Burgess, Duquemin, Robb
Ditchburn; Baker, Withers, Brittan, Clarke, Burgess,
Hutchinson, Bennett, Duquemin, Harmer, Robb.

1954-55
Aug 14 v Lille Olympique (a) 1-1
Duquemin
Ditchburn; Ramsey, Withers, Wetton, Clarke, Brittan
(Walley), Dulin, Bennett, Duquemin, Baily
(McClellan), Robb.
Oct 11 v Queen's Park Rangers (a) 1-2
Ramsey
Ditchburn; Ramsey, Withers, Hills, Adams, Nicholson,
Dulin, Baily, Duquemin, Brooks, Spivey.
Oct 18 v Sportklub Wacker (h) 1-2
McClellan
Ditchburn; Ramsey, Hopkins, Nicholson, King,
Marchi, McClellan, Harmer, Dunmore, Brooks,
Gavin.
Nov 2 v Rot-Weiss Essen (h) 4-2
Ramsey 2 (1 pen), Brooks 2
Ditchburn; Ramsey, Withers, Nicholson, Adams,
Marchi, McClellan, Brooks, Dunmore, Baily, Gavin.
Nov 15 v Finchley (h) 2-2
Walters, Baily
Reynolds; Ramsey, Withers, Wetton, Price, Bennett,
Walters, Baily, Duquemin, Harmer, Robb.
**Nov 29 v Accrington S (a) 0-0 (abandoned after 52
minutes because of rain)**
Reynolds; Baker, McNally, Wetton, Clarke, Marchi,
Walters, Baily, Dunmore, Brooks, Dyson.
Mar 2 v Arsenal (h) 1-4
Robb
Reynolds; Ramsey, Hopkins, Blanchflower, Clarke,
Marchi, Gavin, Baily, Duquemin, Brooks, Robb.
Mar 9 v Racing Club de Paris (h) 6-0
Blanchflower, Marchi, Dulin, Duquemin, Brooks 2
Reynolds; Baker, Hopkins, Blanchflower, Price,
Marchi, Dulin, Harmer, Duquemin, Brooks, Robb.
Mar 14 v Hibernian (a) 1-1
McClellan
Reynolds; Baker, Hopkins, Blanchflower, Clarke,
Marchi, Gavin, McClellan, Duquemin, Brooks, Robb.
Mar 30 v FC Servette (h) 5-1

Gavin 2, Brooks, Duquemin, McClellan
Reynolds; Baker, Henry, Blanchflower, King, Marchi
(Woods), Gavin, Brooks, Duquemin, McClellan, Robb.

1955-56
Sep 25 v Aarhus Gymnastikforening (a) 4-3
Brooks 2, Stokes, Robb
Ditchburn; Withers, Hopkins, Blanchflower, Clarke,
Marchi, Walters, Brooks, Stokes, Baily, Robb.
Oct 12 v FC Vasas (h) 1-2
McClellan
Ditchburn; Baker, Hopkins, Blanchflower, Clarke,
Marchi, Walters, Brooks, Duquemin, McClellan,
Robb(Dyson).
Oct 24 v Plymouth A (a) 0-0
Ditchburn; Baker, Hopkins, Barton, Clarke, Marchi,
Walters, Brooks, Duquemin, Baily, Robb.
Nov 14 v Partick T (h) 0-1
Reynolds; Norman, Hopkins, Blanchflower, Ryden,
Marchi, McClellan, Brooks, Stokes, Baily, Dyson.
Dec 6 v Swansea T (h) 4-1
Dulin, Brooks, Duquemin, Baily
Reynolds; Norman, Hopkins, Blanchflower, Clarke,
Marchi, Dulin, Brooks, Duquemin, Baily, Robb.

1956-57
Sep 11 v Racing Club de Paris (h) 2-0
Marchi, Medwin
Ditchburn; Baker, Hopkins, Blanchflower, Clarke,
Marchi, Medwin, Harmer, Smith, Stokes, Dyson.
Dec 3 v Red Banner (MTK) (h) 7-1
Blanchflower, Medwin, Duquemin, Stokes 3, Robb
Reynolds; Norman, Hopkins, Blanchflower, Clarke,
Walley, Medwin, Harmer, Duquemin, Stokes, Robb.
Mar 19 v Combined Antwerp XI (Antwerp) 2-1
Medwin, Smith
Reynolds; Baker, Norman, Blanchflower, Ryden,
Marchi, Medwin, Harmer, Smith, Stokes, Dyson.

1957-58
Aug 3 v VfB Stuttgart (a) 2-2
Smith 2
Reynolds; Norman, Hopkins, Blanchflower, Ryden,
Walley, Medwin, Harmer, Smith, Stokes, Dulin.
Oct 14 v Hibernian (a) 2-5
Smith 2
Hollowbread; Baker, Hopkins, Blanchflower, Ryden,
Iley, Bing, Harmer, Smith, Walley, Dyson.
Oct 23 v Swiss National XI (Basel) 5-4
Smith 4, Dunmore
Ditchburn; Baker, Hopkins, Blanchflower, Ryden,
Iley, Bing, Smith, Dunmore, Brooks, Medwin.
Nov 6 v Bristol C (a) 3-4
Brooks 2, Harmer
Ditchburn; Baker, Hopkins, Ryden, Norman, Iley,
Medwin, Brooks, Smith, Harmer, Dyson.
Nov 11 v VfB Stuttgart (h) 3-2
Ryden, Smith, Robb
Ditchburn; Baker, Henry, Blanchflower, Norman,
Ryden, Ireland, Brooks, Smith, Harmer, Robb.
Mar 1 v Partick T (h) 4-1
Medwin 2, Brooks, Smith
Ditchburn; Hills, Henry, Blanchflower, Norman, Ryden,
Medwin, Brooks, Smith, Harmer, Jones(Dyson).
Mar 27 v Rotterdam Select XI (a) 4-1
Medwin, Brooks, Smith, Harmer
Ditchburn; Hills, Henry, Blanchflower, Laurel, Ryden,
Medwin, Brooks, Smith, Harmer, Dyson.
Apr 14 v Hibernian (h) 4-0

Ireland, Dunmore 2, Robb
Reynolds; Hills, Henry, Walley, Norman, Iley, Ireland,
Harmer, Dunmore, Clayton, Robb.
Apr 24 v Canto Do Rio (h) 4-1
Blanchflower, Smith, Clayton 2
Reynolds; Hills, Henry, Blanchflower, Norman, Iley,
Medwin, Harmer, Smith, Clayton, Dyson.

1958-59
Oct 14 v Bela Vista (h) 3-1
Stokes 2, Robb
Hollowbread; Baker, Hopkins, Dodge, Ryden, Iley,
Medwin, Harmer, Smith, Stokes, Robb.
Nov 10 v Hibernian (h) 5-2
Dunmore 3, Medwin 2
Hollowbread; Baker, Hopkins, Blanchflower, Norman,
Iley, Brooks, Harmer, Dunmore, Smith, Medwin.
Dec 8 v Bucharest Select XI (h) 4-2
Medwin, Harmer (pen), Stokes, Jones
Hollowbread; Hills, Henry, Dodge, Norman, Iley,
Medwin, Harmer, Smith, Stokes, Jones.

1959-60
Oct 21 v Reading (a) 5-2
Brooks, R.Smith, Jones 3
Hollowbread; Baker, Hopkins, Marchi, A.Smith,
Mackay, Medwin, Brooks, R.Smith, Dunmore, Jones.
Nov 16 v Torpedo Moscow (h) 3-2
Mackay, White, R.Smith
Brown; Baker, Marchi, Blanchflower(Henry),
Norman, Mackay, Medwin, White, R.Smith,
Dunmore, Jones.
May 2 v Crystal P (a) 2-2
Saul, R.Smith
Hollowbread; Barton, Henry, Blanchflower, Norman,
Smith J, Jones, Harmer, Saul, R.Smith, Dyson.
May 25 v Juventus (a) 0-2
Brown; Baker, Henry, Blanchflower, Norman, Marchi,
Medwin, White(Harmer), R.Smith(Saul), Mackay, Jones.

1960-61
Oct 24 v Army XI (h) 3-5
Allen, Aitchinson, Opp own-goal
Brown; Baker, Henry, Dodge, Norman, Marchi,
Aitchinson, Collins, Saul, Allen, Dyson.
Nov 14 v Dinamo Tbilisi (h) 5-2
Mackay 2, Medwin 2, Dyson
Brown; Baker, Henry, Blanchflower, Norman,
Mackay, Medwin, White, R.Smith, Allen, Dyson.

1962-63
Nov 14 v Zamalek Sporting Club (Cairo) 7-3
Medwin, White, Greaves 2, Jones, Dyson 2
Brown; Baker, Henry, Blanchflower, Norman, Mackay,
Medwin, White, Allen, Greaves, Jones(Dyson).
Jan 26 v Arsenal (h) 3-1
Greaves 2, Jones
Brown; Baker(Dennis), Henry, Marchi, Norman,
Mackay, Medwin, Clayton, R.Smith, Greaves, Jones.
Feb 2 v Portsmouth (a) 3-2
Mackay, Medwin, Greaves
Brown; Baker, Henry, Marchi, Norman, Mackay,
Medwin, Clayton, R.Smith, Greaves, Jones.

1963-64
Apr 28 v Coventry C (a) 6-5
White, Saul 2, Allen 3
W.Brown; Baker, Henry, Mullery, L.Brown, Marchi,
Jones, White, Saul, Allen, Dyson.

1964-65
Aug 8 v Feyenoord (a) 3-4
Greaves, Mackay, Dyson
Jennings; Knowles, Henry, Mullery, Norman, Beal, Jones, Greaves, Saul, Mackay, Dyson.
Sep 23 v Copenhagen Select XI (a) 1-2
Saul
W.Brown; Knowles, Henry, Mullery, L.Brown, Marchi, Robertson, Greaves, Saul, Jones, Possee.
Dec 8 v Leytonstone (a) 5-0
Allen 2, Dyson 2, Saul
Jennings; Baker, Dennis, Beal, A.Smith, Low, Weller, Clayton, Saul, Allen, Dyson.
Apr 27 v Anderlecht (a) 2-4
Greaves, Gilzean
W.Brown; Norman, Henry, Mullery, L.Brown, Clayton, Weller, Greaves, Saul, Gilzean, Jones.
Apr 29 Coventry C (a) 3-0
Mullery, Saul, Low
Jennings; Norman, Henry, Mullery, L.Brown, Clayton, Robertson, Saul, Low, Gilzean, Dyson.

1965-66
Sep 22 v Walton & Hersham U (a) 8-1
Mullery, Gilzean 4, Greaves 3
Jennings; Norman, Knowles, Mullery, L.Brown, Low, Robertson, Clayton, Gilzean, Greaves, Jones(Johnson).
Nov 18 v Hungarian Select XI (h) 4-0
Mackay (pen), Gilzean 3
Jennings; Norman, Knowles, Mullery, L.Brown, Mackay, Possee, Clayton, Saul, Gilzean, Robertson.
May 3 v WKS Legia (Warsaw) 0-2
W.Brown; Kinnear, Knowles, Mullery, L.Brown, Beal, Robertson(Johnson), Clayton(Mackay), Saul, Gilzean, Possee.
May 15 v Sarpsborg (a) 3-0
Gilzean 2, Weller
Jennings; Embery, Henry, Beal, Hoy, Mackay, Possee, Gillingwater(Johnson), Gilzean, Smith, Weller.

1966-67
Oct 10 v Dundee (a) 3-2
Mackay, Greaves 2
W.Brown; Clayton, Henry, Mullery, England, Mackay, Robertson, Greaves, Saul, Venables, Jones(Weller).
Nov 23 v Polish Select XI (h) 2-1
Greaves, Jones
Jennings; Beal, Knowles, Mullery, England, Mackay, Weller, Greaves, Gilzean, Venables, Jones.

1967-68
Aug 5 v Celtic (Hampden Park) 3-3
Greaves 2, Gilzean
Jennings; Kinnear, Knowles, Mullery, England, Mackay, Robertson, Greaves, Gilzean, Venables, Saul.

1968-69
Jul 31 v Glasgow Rangers (h) 3-1
Mullery, Collins 2
Jennings; Beal, Knowles, Mullery, England, Collins, Robertson, Greaves, Chivers, Venables, Gilzean.
Aug 3 v FK Austria (a) 2-2
Pearce, Greaves
Jennings; Kinnear, Knowles, Mullery, England, Beal, Robertson(Pearce), Greaves, Chivers, Venables, Jones.
1969-70
Aug 2 v Heart of Midlothian (a) 1-1
Morgan
Jennings; Beal(Want), Knowles, Mullery, England,

Collins, Johnson (Gilzean), Greaves, Chivers, Pearce, Morgan.
Aug 4 v Glasgow Rangers (a) 1-0
Pearce
Jennings; Want, Knowles, Mullery, England, Beal, Gilzean, Greaves, Chivers, Pearce(Pratt), Morgan.

1970-71
Aug 3 v Glasgow Rangers (h) 2-0
Gilzean, Morgan
Jennings; Evans, Knowles, Mullery, England, Beal, Gilzean, Perryman, Chivers, Peters, Morgan.

1971-72
Aug 7 v Heart of Midlothian (a) 1-2
Chivers
Jennings; Kinnear, Knowles, Mullery, England, Beal, Coates, Perryman, Chivers, Peters, Gilzean.
Aug 9 v Glasgow Rangers (a) 0-1
Jennings; Kinnear(Evans [Collins]), Knowles, Mullery, England, Beal, Coates, Perryman, Chivers, Peters, Gilzean.

1972-73
Jul 29 v Bournemouth & B A (a) 4-2
Kinnear, Perryman, Peters (pen), Pearce
Jennings; Kinnear, Knowles, Naylor, England, Beal, Gilzean, Perryman, Coates, Peters, Pearce.
Aug 2 v Aston Villa (a) 0-0
Jennings; Kinnear, Evans, Naylor(Coates), England, Beal, Gilzean, Perryman, Chivers, Peters, Pearce (Morgan).
Aug 7 v Celtic (a) 0-1
Jennings; Kinnear, Knowles, Coates, England, Beal, Gilzean, Perryman, Chivers, Peters, Pratt.

1973-74
Aug 8 v Ajax (Amsterdam) (a) 1-4
Peters
Jennings; Evans, Knowles, Pratt, Collins, Beal, Gilzean, Perryman, Chivers(Holder), Peters, Coates.
Aug 11 v Cardiff C (a) 3-1
Perryman, Gilzean, Peters
Jennings; Evans(Kinnear), Knowles, Pratt, Dillon, Beal, Neighbour(Holder), Perryman, Gilzean, Peters, Coates.
Aug 18 v Sunderland (a) 1-0
Neighbour
Jennings; Evans, Knowles, Pratt, Dillon, Beal(Holder), Neighbour, Perryman, Chivers, Peters, Coates.

1974-75
Aug 3 v Heart of Midlothian (a) 1-1
Pratt
Jennings; Evans, Naylor(Pratt), Beal, England, Conn (McNab), Pearce(McGrath), Perryman(Holder), Jones, Peters, Coates.
Aug 7 v Portsmouth (a) 2-0
Jones, Neighbour
Jennings; Evans, Naylor, Beal, Osgood, Holder (McNab), McGrath, Perryman, Jones, Peters, Coates(Neighbour).
Aug 10 v Fulham (a) 1-0
Peters
Jennings; Evans, Naylor, Beal, England(Osgood), Holder, McGrath, Perryman, Jones, Peters(Chivers), Coates.
Jan 24 v Watford (a) 3-2
McNab, Conn, Duncan

393

Jennings; Kinnear, Pratt, Beal, England(Osgood), Naylor, Coates(McNab), Perryman, Chivers, Conn, Duncan(Neighbour).
Jan 27 v Enfield (a) 2-1
Chivers 2 (1 pen)
Daines(Lee); Kinnear, Pratt, Beal, Osgood, Naylor, Neighbour(McGrath), Conn, Chivers, Peters, McNab (Coates).
Feb 26 v Red Star Belgrade (a) 1-0
Jones
Jennings; Kinnear, Knowles, McAllister, England, Naylor, Coates(Neighbour), Perryman, Duncan, Jones, Conn.

1975-76
Aug 8 v Bristol R (a) 4-1
Coates, Chivers 2, Jones
Jennings; Kinnear(Smith), Naylor, Pratt, Osgood, McAllister, Coates, McNab, Chivers, Jones, Neighbour (McGrath).
Sep 29 v Le Stade Rennais (a) 1-1
Young
Daines; Smith, McAllister, Pratt, Young(Walford), Osgood, McNab, Coates, Duncan(Robinson), Jones, McGrath(Naylor).
Oct 27 v Millwall (a) 1-3
McNab
Daines; McAllister, Duncan, Pratt, Young, Osgood, McNab, Perryman(Walford), Coates, Chivers, Neighbour(Brotherston).
Apr 21 v North Herts XI (Stevenage) 1-2
Armstrong
Daines(Kendall); Stead, McAllister(Smith), McNab, Young, Walford, Coates, Hoddle, Chivers(McGrath), Armstrong, Jones.

1976-77
Aug 10 v Swindon T (a) 1-3
Perryman
Jennings; Naylor, McAllister, Pratt, Young(Hoddle), Osgood, Coates, Perryman, McGrath(K.Stead), Conn, Neighbour.
Aug 16 v Royal Antwerp (h) 1-1
Armstrong
Daines; Naylor, McAllister, Pratt(Conn), Young, Osgood, Coates, Perryman, Armstrong, Jones, Neighbour.
Oct 9 v Arsenal (a) 2-1
Conn, Duncan
Daines; Naylor, Young, Hoddle, Pratt, Osgood(Keeley), Conn, Perryman, Moores, Duncan(Jones), Coates.
Oct 12 v Napredac Krusevac (a) 0-4
Daines; Naylor(Keeley), Osgood, Hoddle, Young, Pratt, Conn(McNab), Perryman, Duncan(Moores), Jones, Coates.

1977-78
Nov 22 v Arsenal (a) 3-1
Heffernan, Coates, Duncan
Daines; Naylor, Holmes(Heffernan), Coates, Osgood, Perryman, Pratt, McNab, Lee(Armstrong), Duncan (Moores), Taylor.
May 3 v Truro C (a) 8-2
Stead 2, Pratt, Duncan, Falco, Armstrong 2, Taylor
Daines; Naylor, Holmes, Stead, McAllister, Perryman, Pratt, McNab, Duncan(Falco), Armstrong, Taylor.
May 5 v Orient (a) 3-1
Jones, Duncan, Taylor

Daines(Kendall); Naylor(Stead), Holmes, Hoddle, McAllister, Armstrong, Moores, McNab(Pratt), Jones, Duncan, Taylor.

1978-79
Aug 5 v Aberdeen (a) 1-3
Taylor
Daines; Naylor, Holmes, Hoddle, Lacy, Perryman, Pratt, McNab, Duncan(Armstrong), Lee(Jones), Taylor.
Aug 8 v Royal Antwerp (a) 3-1
Hoddle (pen), Moores 2
Daines; McAllister, Gorman, Hoddle, Lacy, Perryman (Holmes), Villa, Ardiles(McNab), Armstrong, Moores, Taylor(Duncan).
Aug 10 v VVV Venlo (a) 0-1
Daines; Naylor, Holmes, Pratt, Lacy, Perryman, Villa (McNab), Ardiles, Duncan(Lee), Jones(Armstrong), Taylor.
Aug 12 v Bohemians (a) 4-0
Hoddle, Armstrong, Moores, Taylor
Daines; McAllister, Gorman, Hoddle, Lacy, Perryman (Holmes), Villa, Ardiles, Armstrong(Jones), Moores, Taylor.
Sep 19 v Aldershot (a) 1-1
Villa
Daines(Kendall); McAllister(Jones), Gorman, Naylor, Lacy, Perryman(Beavon), Villa, McNab, Lee, Pratt, Taylor (Moores).
Sep 26 v IFK Gothenburg (a) 0-1
Kendall; Hughton, Pratt, Hoddle, Lacy, Holmes, Villa (Armstrong), Ardiles(Beavon), Lee, Taylor, Jones.
Oct 9 v Saudi Arabian XI (Jeddah) 4-2
Lacy, Armstrong, Lee, Taylor
Daines(Kendall); Naylor, McAllister, Holmes, Lacy, McNab, Armstrong, Ardiles(Beavon), Lee, Pratt, Taylor (Galvin).
Oct 16 v Wolverhampton W (a) 1-2
Jones
Daines(Kendall); Naylor, Holmes, Lacy(Bowgett), McAllister, Armstrong(Hoddle), Villa, Ardiles, Jones, McNab, Pratt(Lee).
Dec 4 v West Ham U (a) 2-4
Holmes, Pratt
Kendall(Daines[Kendall]); Gorman, McAllister, Holmes, Lacy, Perryman, Pratt, Villa, Lee(Armstrong), Hoddle(Ardiles), Taylor.
Dec 18 v El Nasar (a) 7-0
Hoddle 2, Galvin, Ardiles, Beavon, Lee 2
Aleksic(Kendall); Naylor, Gorman, Hoddle, Lacy, Perryman, Pratt(Galvin), Ardiles(Beavon), Lee, Villa, Taylor.
Apr 24 v Queen's Park Rangers (a) 3-1
Villa 3
Aleksic; Lee, McAllister, Miller(Holmes), Lacy, Perryman, Hoddle, Ardiles, Jones(Armstrong), Villa, Pratt(Beavon).
May 11 v Gillingham (a) 3-2
Falco, Hoddle, Villa
Daines(Aleksic); Lee, McAllister, Holmes, Miller, Perryman(Gibson), Pratt, Ardiles, Falco(Jones), Hoddle, Villa.

1979-80
Aug 2 v Gillingham (a) 1-1
Hoddle
Aleksic; Lee, Lacy, McAllister(Miller), Smith, Hoddle, Perryman(Beavon), Pratt, Galvin, Villa, Jones(Falco).
Aug 4 v Oxford U (a) 1-2

Beavon
Aleksic; Southey, Smith, Mazzon, Miller, Perryman, Pratt(Hoddle), Galvin, Jones(Falco), Beavon, Villa.
Aug 7 v Dundee U (a) 2-3
Falco, Villa
Aleksic; Lee, Smith, McAllister, Lacy, Perryman, Pratt, Ardiles, Falco, Hoddle, Villa.
Aug 8 v Aberdeen (a) 0-2
Aleksic; Southey(Jones), Lacy, McAllister, Miller, Perryman, Pratt, Ardiles(Galvin), Falco, Hoddle, Villa (Beavon).
Aug 11 v Orient (a) 1-1
Hoddle
Aleksic; Lee, Smith, Miller, Lacy, Perryman, Pratt (Beavon), Ardiles(Jones), Falco, Hoddle(Galvin), Villa.
Nov 6 v Widad (Morocco) 4-2
Jones 2, Beavon, Hoddle
Aleksic; Hughton(Yorath), Smith, Pratt, McAllister (Lacy), Perryman, Ardiles(Galvin), Jones, Armstrong (Beavon), Hoddle, Villa.
Apr 15 v Crystal P (a) 3-2
McAllister, Armstrong, Taylor
Daines(Kendall); Hughton, McAllister, Naylor (Armstrong), Miller, Perryman, Ardiles, Jones, Hazard, Galvin(Taylor), Pratt.
May 5 v Bournemouth (a) 2-1
Gibson 2
Daines(Parks); O'Reilly, Hughton, Naylor, McAllister, Perryman(Mazzon), Hazard(Gibson), Jones(Falco), Taylor, Hoddle(Roberts), Galvin.
May 7 v Hertford T (a) 4-0
Roberts, Falco 3
Kendall(Daines); Hughton, Miller, Yorath, McAllister (O'Reilly), Perryman(Mazzon), Roberts, Taylor, Falco, Hoddle, Galvin.

1980-81
Jul 28 v Southend U (a) 1-1
Archibald
Kendall(Daines); Smith, Hughton(Holmes), Roberts, Miller, Perryman, Ardiles, Archibald, Crooks, Hazard, Taylor.
Jul 30 v Portsmouth (a) 2-1
Hughton, Falco
Daines; Perryman, Hughton, Yorath, Miller, Holmes, Ardiles(Roberts), Crooks(Gibson), Falco, Hoddle, Hazard.
Aug 2 v PSV Eindhoven (Beilen) 2-4
Ardiles, Taylor
Daines; Perryman, Hughton, Yorath, Miller, Holmes, Ardiles, Crooks, Armstrong, Hoddle, Taylor(Hazard).
Aug 4 v Glasgow Rangers (a) 1-2
Lacy
Daines; Smith, Hughton, Yorath, Lacy, Perryman, Ardiles, Archibald, Crooks, Hoddle, Villa.
Aug 5 v Dundee U (a) 1-4
Crooks
Daines; Smith, Hughton, Yorath, Miller, Perryman, Ardiles(Taylor), Archibald, Villa, Hoddle, Crooks.
Aug 8 v Swansea C (a) 0-1
Kendall; Smith, Hughton, Yorath, Miller(Hoddle), Perryman, Ardiles(Roberts), Crooks, Armstrong, Hoddle (Hazard), Villa.
Nov 17 v Weymouth (a) 6-1
Ardiles 2, Villa 2, Gibson, Dyer (og)
Daines; McAllister(Southey), Holmes, Smith, O'Reilly, Perryman(Crook), Ardiles(McAllister), Crooks(Gibson), Falco, Villa, Brooke.

Feb 2 v Jersey Select XI (a) 5-0
Ardiles, Archibald 3, Brooke
Aleksic(Daines); Perryman, Hughton, McAllister, Miller(Lacy), Roberts(Hazard), Ardiles, Archibald, Galvin, Hoddle, Brooke.

1981-82
Aug 8 v Glentoran (a) 3-3
Ardiles, Hoddle (pen), Falco
Aleksic; Hughton(Miller), Price, Roberts(Cooper), Villa, Perryman, Ardiles, Archibald, Galvin, Hoddle, Falco(Brooke).
Aug 10 v Limerick (a) 6-2
Archibald, Hoddle 4, Falco
Aleksic(Parks); Miller, Price, Roberts(Cooper), Villa, Perryman, Ardiles(Hughton), Archibald, Galvin, Hoddle, Brooke(Falco).
Aug 12 v Norwich C (a) 2-2
Brooke, Falco
Aleksic; Perryman, Price, Roberts, Miller, Villa (Cooper), Ardiles(Crook), Brooke(Dick), Galvin, Hoddle, Falco.
Aug 16 v Aberdeen (a) 1-0
Brooke (pen)
Aleksic; Hughton, Miller(Lacy), Roberts, Price, Perryman, Brooke, Archibald(Hazard), Falco(Dick), Hoddle, Galvin.
Nov 14 v Israel Select XI (a) 3-2
Hazard 3 (1 pen)
Parks; Perryman(Southey), Miller, Roberts(Smith), Hughton, Lacy, Ardiles(Dick), Galvin, Hazard, Gibson, Crooks.
Dec 22 v Plymouth A (a) 1-1
Hoddle
Clemence(Parks); Hughton, Perryman, Roberts(Lacy), Miller(Price), Hoddle, Ardiles(Hazard), Galvin, Villa, Falco, Crooks(Brooke).
Dec 29 v Sporting Lisbon (a) 2-3
Roberts, Villa
Clemence; Hughton, Price, Roberts, Villa, Perryman, Ardiles(Hazard), Falco, Galvin, Hoddle, Crooks.
Feb 22 v Jersey Select XI (a) 8-3
Hughton (pen), Hazard, Perryman, Falco 2, Gibson 2, Crooks
Parks; Hughton, Miller(O'Reilly), Price, Hazard, Perryman(Smith), Ardiles, Falco, Galvin(Gibson), Roberts, Crooks.

1982-83
Aug 3 v Scunthorpe United (a) 5-0
Falco 2, Gibson 2, Roberts
Clemence(Parks); Miller, Mabbutt, Roberts, Lacy, O'Reilly, Gibson, Brooke(Dick), Falco, Hoddle (Crook), Crooks(Cooke).
Aug 6 v FC Lausanne (a) 0-3
Clemence; Hughton, Miller, Roberts, Lacy, Mabbutt, Brooke(Crook), Archibald(Falco), Falco(Gibson) Hoddle, Crooks.
Aug 8 v Glasgow Rangers (a) 1-0
Mabbutt
Clemence; Hughton, Miller, Roberts, Lacy, Mabbutt, Brooke(Falco), Archibald(Gibson), O'Reilly, Hoddle (Crook), Crooks.
Sep 20 v Barnet (a) 1-2
Hazard
Parks(Webster); Mazzon, Dixon(Southey), Miller, Brooke, Perryman, Hazard, Crook, Falco, Villa, Crooks (Gibson).
Dec 20 v Borussia Mönchengladbach (Tel Aviv) 0-2

Clemence; Hughton, Lacy(Price), Roberts, Villa, Perryman, Mabbutt, Brooke(Cooke), Galvin, Falco, Crooks.
Dec 22 v Israel Select XI (Tel Aviv) 2-2
Brooke, Mazzon
Clemence(Thomas); Hughton, Price, Lacey(Culverhouse), Villa(Mazzon), Perryman, Mabbutt, Hazard, Galvin(Cooke), Brooke, Crook.
Mar 26 v Northerners (Jersey) 6-1
Hazard, Archibald 3, Brazil 2
Clemence; Perryman(O'Reilly), Hughton, Lacy (Ardiles), Roberts, Hoddle, Hazard, Gibson(Falco), Archibald, Brazil, Galvin.
Apr 19 v Bristol R (a) 3-2
O'Reilly, Perryman, Crooks
Clemence(Hughton); Hughton(Ardiles) O'Reilly, Roberts, Miller(Webster), Perryman, Mabbutt, Brazil (Villa), Galvin, Hoddle, Crooks.
May 17 v Trinidad & Tobago XI (a) 2-2
Archibald, Crooks
Clemence(Parks); Hughton, Price, Roberts, Hazard (Brazil), Perryman, Mabbutt, Archibald, Galvin, Hoddle, Crooks.
May 20 v ASL Trinidad (a) 2-1
Gibson, Brazil
Clemence; Hughton, Lacy, Mabbutt(Crook), Miller, Perryman, Gibson(Crooks), Falco, Galvin, Hoddle (Parks), Brazil.
May 23 v Charlton A (a) 4-4
Falco 4
Clemence(Parks); Price, Hughton, Perryman, Miller (O'Reilly), Roberts, Mabbutt(Crook), Brooke, Galvin (Hazard), Falco, Crooks.
May 30 v Aalesund (Norway) 3-2
Crooks 3
Parks; Hughton(Southey), O'Reilly, Hazard, Miller, Perryman, Gibson(Crook), Brooke(Culverhouse), Galvin, Falco, Crooks.

1983-84
Aug 2 v Hertford Town (a) 2-1
Archibald, Crooks
Clemence; Hughton(Crook), O'Reilly, Stevens, Miller, Brooke, Ardiles, Archibald, Galvin, Hoddle, Crooks.
Aug 4 v Enfield (a) 4-1
Roberts, Hoddle, Crooks 2
Clemence; Bowen, O'Reilly, Roberts, Stevens, Perryman, Ardiles, Archibald, Galvin, Hoddle, Crooks.
Aug 6 v Brentford (a) 4-2
Roberts, Brazil, Crooks, Whitehead (og)
Parks; Thomas, Bowen, Roberts, Stevens, Perryman, Ardiles, Brazil(Crooks), Falco, Hazard(Archibald), Galvin.
Aug 9 v Portsmouth (a) 3-1
Roberts, Galvin, Mabbutt
Clemence; Hughton, Thomas(Bowen), Roberts, Stevens, Perryman, Ardiles(Mabbutt), Brazil, Falco(Gibson), Hoddle, Galvin.
Aug 12 v Brighton & HA (a) 0-0
Clemence; Hughton, Thomas(Ardiles), Roberts (Thomas), Stevens, Perryman, Mabbutt, Brazil(Falco), Galvin, Hoddle, Crooks.
Aug 16 v Celtic (a) 1-1
Falco
Clemence; Hughton, Thomas, Roberts, Stevens, Perryman, Ardiles, Brazil, Galvin, Hoddle, Crooks (Falco).
Aug 17 v Dundee U (a) 1-1
Galvin

Clemence; O'Reilly, Galvin, Price, Miller, Hazard, Ardiles, Archibald, Falco(Brazil), Hoddle (Thomas[Roberts]), Mabbutt.
Oct 5 v Vale Recreation (Guernsey) 7-2
Hazard, Archibald 4, Brazil, Falco
Parks; Hughton(Bowen), Galvin(Crook), O'Reilly, Price, Perryman, Hazard, Archibald, Brazil, Falco, Brooke.
Mar 26 v Wimbledon (a) 5-0
Hazard, Falco 2, Crooks 2
Parks(Andrews); Thomas(Culverhouse), Hughton, Roberts, Miller, Perryman(Crook), Brooke, Hazard, Falco, Crooks, Dick.
May 1 v West Ham U (a) 1-4
Archibald
Parks(Corder); Culverhouse(Perryman), Hughton (Bowen), Roberts, Miller, Hazard, Ardiles, Archibald, Falco(Crooks), Mabbutt, Brazil.

1984-85
Aug 4 v Enfield (a) 7-0
Stevens, Brooke, Hazard, Crooks 4
Clemence(Parks); Stevens(Brooke), Hughton, Roberts, Miller, Perryman(Thomas), Ardiles(Bowen), Kempes, Galvin, Hazard, Crooks.
Aug 6 v Nice (a) 2-2
Miller 2
Clemence(Parks); Thomas, Hughton, Roberts, Miller, Mabbutt, Hazard(Bowen), Kempes, Galvin, Hoddle (Perryman), Crooks.
Aug 11 v Brentford (a) 3-0
Allen 2, Galvin
Clemence; Stevens(Mabbutt), Hughton(Bowen), Roberts, Miller, Perryman(Thomas), Ardiles, Falco (Allen), Galvin, Hazard, Crooks(Falco).
Aug 16 v Manchester C (a) 2-0
Roberts (pen), Galvin
Clemence; Stevens(Chiedozie), Hughton, Roberts, Miller, Perryman(Thomas), Ardiles(Mabbutt), Falco (Crooks), Allen, Hazard, Galvin.
Aug 18 v Sheffield U (a) 3-0
Allen 2, Falco
Clemence; Thomas, Hughton(Bowen), Roberts, Miller, Stevens, Chiedozie, Falco(Crooks), Allen, Mabbutt, Galvin.
Sep 12 v Real Madrid (a) 0-1
Clemence; Mabbutt, Thomas, Crook(Bowen), Stevens (Miller), Perryman, Brooke, Falco, Allen(Crooks), Hazard (Cooke), Chiedozie.
Oct 14 v Malta National XI (a) 1-0
Dick
Parks; Thomas, Perryman, Crook, Miller, Roberts, Brooke, Mabbutt, Falco(Culverhouse), Crooks (Cooke), Dick.
Nov 13 v Sutton U (a) 5-3
Crooks 3, Crook, Falco
Parks; Culverhouse, Miller(Brooke), Crook, Bowen, Perryman, Ardiles, Hoddle, Chiedozie, Falco(Baker), Crooks.
Mar 8 v Kuwait National XI (Amman, Jordan) 1-0
Crooks
Clemence; Stevens, Hughton, Roberts, Miller, Perryman, Chiedozie, Falco(Thomas), Galvin, Hoddle, Crooks (Hazard).
Apr 8 v Guernsey FA XI (a) 5-0
Clemence (pen), Falco 2, Crooks, Ardiles
Clemence; Thomas, Bowen, Culverhouse, Miller (Crooks), Crook, Ardiles, Falco, Leworthy, Hoddle, Chiedozie.

Apr 29 v Bristol R (a) 6-2
Cooke, Leworthy 3, Dick 2
Parks; Thomas(Samways), Culverhouse, Roberts, Miller, Perryman(Mabbutt), Ardiles(Cooke), Falco, Leworthy, Chiedozie, Dick.

1985-86
Jul 18 v Wycombe W (Bisham Abbey) 4-1
Thomas, Leworthy, Waddle, Galvin
Clemence; Thomas, Roberts, Hoddle(Cooke), Miller, Mabbutt, Ardiles, P.Allen, C.Allen(Leworthy), Waddle, Galvin.
Jul 24 v Chesterfield (a) 4-2
Roberts, Waddle 2, Chiedozie
Clemence; Thomas, Hughton, Roberts(Perryman), Miller, P.Allen, Ardiles, Falco, Waddle, Chiedozie, Galvin (Leworthy).
Jul 27 v AFC Bournemouth (a) 3-0
Miller, Falco, Galvin
Clemence; Thomas(Chiedozie), Hughton, Roberts, Miller, P.Allen, Ardiles, Falco, Waddle(Leworthy), Hoddle, Galvin.
Jul 31 v Plymouth A (a) 0-1
Clemence; Thomas, Hughton, Roberts, Miller, P.Allen, Ardiles, Falco, Waddle, Chiedozie, Galvin(Leworthy).
Aug 3 v Exeter C (a) 2-2
Falco, Hazard
Clemence; Thomas, Hughton, Roberts, Miller, P.Allen(Hazard), Ardiles, Falco(Samways), Waddle (Leworthy), Chiedozie, Galvin(Dick).
Aug 10 v Norwich C (a) 1-1
Leworthy
Clemence; Thomas, Hughton, P.Allen(Chiedozie), Miller, Perryman, Ardiles, Falco, Leworthy(Roberts), Hazard(Leworthy), Galvin(Dick).
Sep 10 v Fareham T (a) 6-3
Chiedozie, Leworthy 3, Cooke, Samways
Parks; Mabbutt, Thomas, Roberts, Miller(Galvin), Ardiles, Chiedozie, Leworthy, Falco(Cooke), Hazard, Samways.
Oct 14 v Maidstone U (a) 2-1
Falco, Galvin
Clemence; Stevens, Mabbutt, Roberts, Miller, Perryman (Grenfell), Ardiles(Moncur), Falco, Chiedozie, Cooke, Galvin.
Feb 10 v Jersey Select XI (a) 7-0
C.Allen 2 (1 pen), Thomas, Hoddle, Waddle, P.Allen, Mabbutt
Clemence(Jennings); Thomas, Hughton, Mabbutt, Miller, Ardiles(Crook), P.Allen, Chiedozie, C.Allen, Hoddle (Ardiles), Waddle.
Apr 6 v Glasgow Rangers (a) 2-0
Chiedozie, P.Allen
Clemence(Parks); Thomas, Hughton, Mabbutt, Miller (Ruddock), Bowen, Chiedozie(Samways), P.Allen, Falco, Waddle, Galvin(Dick).
Apr 22 v Chelmsford C (a) 8-2
Falco 5, C.Allen 2, Chiedozie
Clemence(Parks); Thomas, Ruddock, Roberts, Miller, Mabbutt, Pratt(Bowen), Crook, Falco, C.Allen(Close), Chiedozie.
May 9 v Brentford (a) 3-4
Chiedozie, C.Allen 2
Clemence; P.Allen, Hughton, Roberts, Mabbutt, Perryman, Chiedozie(Dick), Crook(Moncur), Galvin, C.Allen, Thomas.
May 12 v West Ham U (a) 1-5
C.Allen

Parks(Banks); P.Allen, Thomas, Roberts(Moncur), Hughton, Mabbutt(Polston), Chiedozie(Dick), Cooke, C.Allen, Crook, Galvin.

1986-87
Aug 4 v Aldershot (a) 3-2
C.Allen 2, Galvin
Parks; Stevens, Hughton(M.Thomas), Roberts (Hughton), Miller, Ruddock, Mabbutt, Galvin (Cooke), C.Allen(Falco), Hoddle(Bowen), Waddle.
Aug 8 v Brighton & H A (a) 4-0
Falco 2, Waddle 2 (1 pen)
Clemence; D.Thomas(Ardiles), Hughton, Roberts, Miller, Mabbutt, Waddle, Falco(Howells), C.Allen, Stevens, Galvin.
Aug 12 v Gillingham (a) 1-1
Falco
Clemence; D.Thomas, Hughton, Roberts, Miller, Mabbutt, Waddle, Falco, C.Allen(Howells) Stevens, Galvin.
Aug 19 v PSV Eindhoven (Barcelona) 1-1 (3-4 on penalties)
Falco (penalties scored by Gough, Stevens, Waddle)
Clemence; Stevens, M.Thomas, Roberts(Ardiles), Miller(Gough), Mabbutt, Waddle, Falco, C.Allen (P.Allen), Hoddle, Galvin.
Aug 20 v AC Milan (Barcelona) 2-1
Falco, Mabbutt
Clemence; D.Thomas, Hughton, P.Allen, Gough, Miller, Ardiles(Stevens), Waddle(Falco), Chiedozie, Hoddle(Mabbutt), Cooke.
Nov 4 v SV Hamburg (h) 5-1
Mabbutt, C.Allen 3, Claesen
Clemence; D.Thomas, Hughton, Ardiles(Polston), Gough, Mabbutt, C.Allen, Claesen, Waddle, Hoddle (Moran), P.Allen.
Dec 16 v Bermuda National XI (a) 3-1
C.Allen, Hoddle, Waddle (pen)
Clemence; D.Thomas(Polston), M.Thomas, Roberts (Howells), Gough, Mabbutt, C.Allen(Close), P.Allen Bowen), Waddle, Hoddle, Galvin(Ardiles).
Jan 20 v Linfield (a) 3-2
C.Allen (pen), D.Thomas, opp (og)
Clemence; D.Thomas, Stevens(Ruddock), Hodge (Galvin), Gough, Mabbutt, C.Allen, P.Allen, Waddle, Hoddle(Ardiles), Claesen.
May 28 v Millonaros, Colombia, (Orange Bowl, Miami) 0-1
Team unknown but included Dearden, O'Shea, M.Thomas, C.Allen, Howells, P.Allen and Hodge.

1987-88
Jul 23 v Exeter C (a) 1-0
Metgod
Clemence; Polston, Thomas(Metgod), Gough, Fairclough, Mabbutt, C.Allen, P.Allen(Waddle), Claesen(Galvin), Samways(Ardiles), Galvin(Hodge).
Jul 25 v AFC Bournemouth (a) 4-4
Waddle, Hodge, C.Allen 2
Clemence; Ardiles(Galvin), Thomas, Gough, Fairclough(Ruddock), Mabbutt(Polston), Metgod (Samways), P.Allen, Waddle, Hodge, Claesen (C.Allen).
Nov 10 v St Alban's C (a) 6-0
Samways, Close 2, Howells, Stevens, Stimson
Parks; Stevens, Thomas(Stimson), Ruddock, Statham, P.Allen(O'Shea), Samways(Moran), Ardiles, Howells (Samways), Close, Hodge(Moncur).
Dec 5 v Brentford (a) 0-0

397

Parks; Stevens, Hughton, Samways(Cook), Fairclough, Mabbutt, C.Allen(Johnston), P.Allen, Waddle, Moncur, Claesen.

Feb 15 v AS Monaco (h) 0-4
Parks; Statham, Ruddock, Moncur, Fairclough, Mabbutt, Moran(Stimson), P.Allen, Walsh(Howells), Samways(Metgod), Claesen.

Feb 19 v West Brom A (a) 1-4
Walsh
Parks; Statham, Hughton(Thomas), Fairclough, Fenwick, Mabbutt, C.Allen(Claesen), P.Allen(Hodge [P.Allen]), Waddle(Moran), Ardiles(Metgod[C.Allen]), Walsh.

Apr 15 v Hull C (a) 1-2
Walsh
Mimms; Statham, Thomas, Metgod, Fairclough, Mabbutt(Ruddock), Walsh, P.Allen(Hodge), Waddle, Samways(Howells), Claesen(C.Allen).

Apr 26 v Crystal Palace (a) 3-3
Hodge, Walsh, Claesen
Mimms; Statham, Thomas(Manuel), Fenwick, Ruddock, Hodge, Walsh, P.Allen, Howells(Moran), Samways, Claesen(Gray).

May 6 v Barnet (a) 2-1
Waddle (pen), Walsh
Mimms; Statham, Thomas(Manuel), Metgod(Howells), Fairclough(Ruddock), Mabbutt, Walsh(Gray), P.Allen, Waddle, Moran, Hodge.

May 10 v Euskadi (Bilbao) 0-4
Mimms(Parks); Statham, Thomas(Stimson), Fenwick, Metgod(Ruddock), Mabbutt, Walsh, Allen(Claesen), Waddle, Samways, Hodge(Howells[Moran]).

1988-89

Aug 7 v Dundee United (a) 1-1
Walsh
Mimms; Allen, Stimson(Hughton), Fenwick, Fairclough, Mabbutt, Walsh, Gascoigne(Statham), Waddle(Howells), Stewart(Gray), Samways.

Aug 10 v Reading (a) 1-2
Gascoigne
Mimms(Guthrie); Allen, Stimson, Fenwick(Butters), Fairclough, Mabbutt(Statham), Walsh(Howells), Gasgoigne(Moncur), Waddle(Robson), Stewart(Gray), Samways(Howells).

Aug 13 v Arsenal (Wembley) 0-4
Mimms; Allen, Stimson, Fenwick, Fairclough, Mabbutt, Walsh, Gascoigne, Waddle, Stewart(Gray), Samways(Howells).

Aug 14 v Milan AC (Wembley) 1-2
Fenwick
Mimms; Thomas, Hughton, Fenwick, Fairclough, Mabbutt, Walsh(Moran), Gascoigne, Waddle, Stewart, Allen.

Aug 16 v Chelsea (a) 0-0
Mimms; Thomas(Moncur), Hughton(Stimson), Fenwick, Fairclough, Mabbutt, Walsh(Gray), Gascoigne, Waddle(Stewart), Moran(Howells), Allen(Statham).

Aug 21 v West Ham United (a) 0-2
Mimms; Statham, Hughton, Fenwick, Fairclough, Mabbutt, Walsh, Gascoigne(Gray), Waddle(Moran), Samways, Allen(Howells).

Sep 6 v Swansea City (a) 3-0
Gascoigne, Howells, Gray
Mimms(Guthrie); Statham, Hughton, Fenwick, Fairclough, Mabbutt, Walsh, Gascoigne(Gray), Moran, Thomas(Howells), Allen(Moncur).

Oct 18 v Home Farm (a) 4-0

Brazil (og), Fenwick (pen), Howells, Stewart
Mimms; Stevens, Thomas, Fenwick, Fairclough (A.Polston), Mabbutt(Butters), Moran(Robson), Moncur, Stewart, Howells, Allen.

Jan 17 v AC Monaco (h) 1-3
Moncur (pen)
Thorstvedt; Butters, Hughton, Bergsson(Moncur), Fairclough(Thomas), Mabbutt, Howells, Gascoigne (Samways), Waddle(Walsh), Stewart(Robson), Allen(Nayim).

Mar 4 v Bordeaux (h) 1-2
Mabbutt
Thorstvedt; Butters, Bergsson(A.Polston), Fenwick, Moncur(Fairclough), Mabbutt, Walsh(Gray), Nayim, Samways(Moran), Stewart, Allen(Gilzean).

Apr 4 v Charlton Athletic (a) 3-4
Walsh, Stewart 2
Thorstvedt; Butters, Hughton, Bergsson, Nayim, Mabbutt, Walsh(Johnstone), Howells(Stevens), Statham(Theodosiou), Stewart, Allen(Cook).

1989-90

Oct 31 v Caen (Cherbourg) 2-1
Stewart, Howells
Mimms; Thomas(Gormley), Van den Hauwe(Hendon), Bergsson(Tuttle), Allen(Garland), Butters, Walsh (Statham), J.Polston, Samways(Howells), Stewart, Sedgley.

Nov 6 v Leicester City (a) 5-2
Gascoigne 2, Stewart 2, Sedgley
Thorstvedt(Mimms); J.Polston, Van den Hauwe (Hendon), Bergsson(Stevens), Allen(Garland), Howells(Butters), Walsh, Gascoigne, Stewart, Lineker(Robson), Sedgley(Gray).

Jan 26 v Plymouth Argyle (a) 3-0
Mabbutt, Gascoigne, Morrison (og)
Thorstvedt; Thomas, Hughton, Allen, J.Polston, Mabbutt, Walsh, Gascoigne(Moran), Stewart, Lineker(Nayim), Moncur.

Apr 3 v Brighton 1983 (a) 3-0
Gascoigne, Stewart
Thorstvedt; Bergsson(A.Polston), Van den Hauwe (Hughton), Sedgley(J.Polston), Howells(Thomas), Mabbutt, Walsh(Gray), Gascoigne, Stewart, Lineker(Samways), Allen(Moncur).

Apr 23 v Vålerengens IF (Bislet Stadium, Oslo) 1-1
Howells
Thorstvedt; Bergsson, J.Polston(Butters), Sedgley (A.Polston), Howells, Mabbut(Gray), Stewart (Moran), Samways, Nayim, Walsh, Allen(Garland).

1990-91

Aug 20 v Southend United (a) 4-1
Walsh, Stewart, Samways, Benjamin (og)
Mimms; Bergsson(Hendon), Van den Hauwe (Edinburgh), Sedgley(Tuttle), Samways(Thomas), Mabbutt, Stewart, Gascoigne, Nayim(Garland), Walsh(Lineker), Allen.

Oct 13 v Arsenal (a) 5-2
Stewart 3, Samways, Walsh
Mimms; Bergsson(Edinburgh), Van den Hauwe (Statham), Sedgley, Thomas, Tuttle, Stewart, Moncur, Nayim, Samways, Walsh(Van den Hauwe).

Nov 12 v West Ham United (a) 3-4
Stewart 2, Houghton
Mimms; Bergsson(Polston), Edinburgh, Sedgley, Edwards, Thomas(Tuttle), Stewart(Hendon), Moran(Houghton), Walsh(Smith), Samways, Allen.

1991-92
May 5 v Cardiff City (a) 2-0
A.Gray, Hendry
Walker; Allen, Sedgley, A.Gray(Houghton), Cundy
(Tuttle), Mabbutt, Stewart, Precki(McDonald),
Hendry(Gilzean), Howells, Nayim.
May 8 v Hull City XI (a) 6-2
Samways, Hendry 2, Barmby 2, Turner
Walker; Allen, McDonald(Caskey), A.Gray, Cundy
(Nethercott), Sedgley, Samways, Minton(Campbell),
Hendry(Hodges), Barmby, Turner.

1992-93
Jul 24 v Heart of Midlothian (a) 2-1
Durie 2
Walker(Thorstvedt); Fenwick(Austin), Van den
Hauwe(Edinburgh), Gray(Anderton), Cundy(Tuttle),
Ruddock(Sedgley), Nayim, Howells, Samways
(Cundy), Hendry(Durie[Ruddock]), Allen(Gray).
Jul 29 v Brighton & Hove Albion (a) 1-1
Samways
Walker; Edinburgh, Van den Hauwe(Tuttle),
Howells(Gray), Cundy, Ruddock, Nayim(Hodges),
Durie(Barmby), Samways(Beadle), Anderton, Allen.
Aug 1 v Glenavon (a) 1-0
Samways
Walker; Tuttle, Edinburgh(Austin), Gray, Cundy
(Howells), Ruddock(Cundy), Nayim, Durie, Samways
(Allen), McMahon(Anderton), Fenwick.
Aug 3 v West Bromwich Albion (a) 2-0
Hendry, Nayim
Thorstvedt; Austin, Edinburgh, Gray(Watson),
Fenwick, Ruddock(Cundy), Turner(Nayim), Durie
(Anderton), Hendry(Barmby), Howells, Allen(Samways).
Aug 5 v Sunderland (a) 3-0
Anderton 3 (1 pen)
Walker; Fenwick(Austin), Edinburgh, Howells,
Cundy, Ruddock, Anderton, Durie(Turner),
Samways(Watson), Hendry(Barmby), Allen.
Aug 8 v Watford (a) 1-0
Ruddock
Thorstvedt; Austin, Edinburgh(Landon), Howells
(Watson), Cundy, Ruddock, Nayim(Turner),
Hendry(Barmby), Samways(Gray), Anderton, Allen.
Aug 10 v Portsmouth (a) 2-4
Samways 2

Thorstvedt(Walker); Landon, Sedgley(Nethercott),
Howells, Cundy, Ruddock, Gray, Turner(Hendry),
Samways(Watson), Anderton(Houghton), Allen
(Barmby).
Sep 23 v Lazio (a) 0-3
Walker; Tuttle(Mabbutt), Edinburgh, Hendon,
Cundy(Nethercott), Ruddock(Fenwick), Sedgley
(Watson), Barmby(Hendry), Anderton, Sheringham
(Mahorn), Turner(Minton).
Oct 20 v Lazio (h) 0-2
Walker; Edinburgh, Van den Hauwe(Austin),
Samways(Howells), Mabbutt, Ruddock, Sedgley
(Watson), Durie(Turner), Barmby, Nayim, Allen
(Anderton).
Nov 10 v Swansea City (a) 3-3
Cundy, Sheringham, Legg (og)
Thorstvedt(Dearden); Austin(Nethercott), Edinburgh,
Samways(Barmby), Mabbutt, Ruddock, Cundy,
Durie(Hodges), Nayim(Watson), Sheringham(Mahorn),
Allen(McMahon).
Mar 28 v Crystal Palace (a) 3-3
Nayim, Ruddock, Barmby
Dearden; Austin(Bergsson), Edinburgh, Samways,
Mabbutt, Ruddock, Sedgley, Nayim, Moran(Gray),
Barmby, Allen.
Apr 23 v Real Zaragoza (a) 0-2
Walker; Bergsson, Edinburgh, Samways(Gray),
Nethercott(Allen), Ruddock, Sedgley(Turner),
Barmby(Hodges), Anderton(Watson), Nayim,
Allen(Fenwick).

Fiorucci Cup
On 27 April 1993 Spurs met Real Madrid and
Internazionale for the Fiorucci Cup. These matches
were only of 45 minutes duration and are therefore
not included in players' careers records but are detailed
below.
Real Madrid (h) 0-1
Walker; Bergsson(Fenwick), Edinburgh, Samways,
Mabbutt, Ruddock, Sedgley, Nayim, Watson
(Hodges), Moran, Allen.
Internazionale (h) 0-0 (Spurs lost 5-6 on penalties)
*Penalties scored by Gray, Ruddock, Sedgley, Nayim
& Hill.*
Dearden; Fenwick, Van den Hauwe, Gray, Nethercott,
Ruddock, Sedgley, Nayim, Hodges, Hill, Allen
(McMahon).

Testimonials, Benefits & Memorials

MOST of the matches detailed below were played as a reward for long and distinguished service to Tottenham Hotspur, although in some instances they were tributes to players whose careers had been brought to a tragic early end, such as John White and Peter Southey. Whilst most of the beneficiaries have been players, matches have also been staged for people like Bill Nicholson and Keith Burkinshaw who brought success as managers.

For many years Spurs would not grant testimonial matches although they often provided opposition in games for beneficiaries of other clubs. This policy was changed in the early 1970s, the first player so honoured being Jimmy Greaves.

Many Spurs players have been supported by testimonial matches organised by other clubs or private individuals, but as Tottenham did not participate in these games they are not recorded here.

In pre-Football League days some players did not have special matches arranged and beneficiaries were allowed to take the proceeds of ordinary Southern or Western League matches. These games are noted in the main League section.

JONES & STORMONT BENEFIT
Dec 11 1899 v Players of the South (h) 4-1
Stormont, Cameron, Pratt, Copeland
Haddow; Erentz, Tait, Jones, McNaught, Stormont, Smith, Cameron, Pratt, Copeland, Hyde.

T.H.BRADSHAW BENEFIT
Apr 2 1900 v Thames Ironworks (a) 3-0
Raby, Cameron 2
Clawley; Melia, Tait, Morris, McNaught, Jones, Raby, Cameron, Copeland, Roberts, Hyde.

SMITH & McNAUGHT BENEFIT
Oct 15 1900 v Millwall Athletic (h) 2-1
Hawley, Kirwan
Clawley; Erentz, Tait, J.L.Jones, McNaught, Hughes, Smith, Pangbourne, Moffatt, Hawley, Kirwan.

JACK OLIVER BENEFIT
Jan 14 1901 v C.W.Brown's XI (h) 4-2
Cameron 2, Kirwan 2
Clawley; Erentz, Tait, McNaught, Morris, Hughes, Smith, Cameron, Brown, Copeland, Kirwan.

J.JONES DEPENDANTS BENEFIT
Dec 15 1904 v George Robey's XI (h) 2-1
Cameron, Glen
Eggett; McCurdy, Tait, Morris, Bull, Brearley, Walton, Cameron, Glen, O'Hagan, Kirwan.

S.MOUNTFORD BENEFIT
Apr 2 1907 Spurs 1901 XI v Team of South (h) 1-4
Stormont
Clawley; Hughes, Tait, Morris, McNaught, Jones, Smith, Cameron, Brown, Stormont, Kirwan.

G.W.(WILLIE) HALL BENEFIT
May 7 1946 v FA XI (h) 4-1
Cox, Foreman 2, Medley
Ditchburn; Willis, Buckingham, Ludford, Nicholson, Burgess, Cox, Bennett, Foreman, Gibbons, Medley.

FRED SARGENT MEMORIAL
Sep 20 1948 v Chelmsford C (a) 5-1
Walters, Bennett, Duquemin 2, Jones
Markham; Tickridge, Withers, Ludford, Nicholson, Trailor, Walters, Baily, Duquemin, Bennett, Jones.

JOHN WHITE MEMORIAL
Nov 11 1964 v Scotland XI (h) 2-6
Marchi, T.White
W.Brown; Baker, Henry, Mullery, L.Brown, Marchi, Robertson, Greaves, T.White, Jones, Dyson.

JIMMY GREAVES TESTIMONIAL
Oct 17 1972 v Feyenoord (h) 2-1
Evans, Greaves
Daines; Evans, Knowles, Coates(Holder), England (Naylor), Beal, Gilzean(Pearce), Perryman, Chivers, Greaves, Peters.

PHIL BEAL TESTIMONIAL
Dec 3 1973 v Bayern Munich (h) 2-2
Pratt, Gilzean
Jennings; Evans, Knowles, Pratt, England, Beal, Gilzean (Neighbour), Perryman, Chivers, Peters(McGrath), Coates.

ALAN GILZEAN TESTIMONIAL
Nov 27 1974 v Red Star Belgrade (h) 2-0
Knowles, Gilzean
Jennings(Daines); Evans(Kinnear), Knowles(Pratt), McNabb, England(Dillon), Naylor, Gilzean, Perryman (McGrath), Jones, Peters(Neighbour), Conn(Coates).

CYRIL KNOWLES TESTIMONIAL
Oct 22 1975 v Arsenal (h) 2-2
McAllister, C.Knowles
Jennings(Daines); McAllister(Smith), C.Knowles, Conn, Young, Osgood, McNab, Coates, Chivers, Jones (P.Knowles[Naylor]), Neighbour.

JOE KINNEAR TESTIMONIAL
Mar 23 1976 v Brighton & H A (a) 6-1
Pratt, Stead, Osgood, Armstrong, Chivers, Jones
Daines; Naylor, McAllister, Pratt(Stead), Young (Keeley), Osgood, Coates(Armstrong), Brotherston, Chivers, Jones, Robinson.

PAT JENNINGS TESTIMONIAL
Nov 23 1976 v Arsenal (h) 3-2
Taylor, Greaves 2
Jennings(Daines); Osgood, Knowles(Gorman), McNab, Young(McAllister), Naylor, Taylor, Perryman(Pratt), Moores, Greaves, Coates.

400

JOHN PRATT TESTIMONIAL
May 12 1978 v Arsenal (h) 3-5
Perryman, Moores 2
Daines(Kendall); Naylor(Stead), Holmes, Hoddle, McAllister, Perryman, Pratt, McNab(Coates), Moores, Greaves, Cliff Jones(Taylor).

STEVE PERRYMAN TESTIMONIAL
Apr 30 1979 v West Ham United (h) 2-2
Villa, Ardiles
Aleksic(Kendall); Naylor, Smith, Miller(McAllister), Lacy, Perryman(Villa), Pratt(Lee), Ardiles, Jones, Hoddle, Greaves.

TERRY NAYLOR TESTIMONIAL
Apr 29 1980 v Crystal Palace (h) 0-2
Daines(Kendall); Naylor, Holmes(Lacy), Yorath, Miller, Beal(Hazard), Ardiles, Jones(Taylor), Chivers, Hoddle, Kinnear(Galvin).

BARRY DAINES TESTIMONIAL
May 11 1981 v West Ham United (h) 2-3
Hazard, Gibson
Daines(Aleksic); Perryman(Corbett), Mazzon, McAllister, Miller(Coates), Taylor(Gibson), Ardiles (Currie), Archibald, Villa, Hazard, Crooks(Falco).

PAUL PRICE TESTIMONIAL
Oct 12 1981 v Luton Town (a) 2-2
Hoddle, Crooks
Clemence(Aleksic); Perryman, Price(Mazzon), Roberts, Lacy(Corbett), Galvin, Hazard, Ardiles, Gibson, Hoddle, Crooks(McCabe).

BILL NICHOLSON TESTIMONIAL
Aug 21 1983 v West Ham United (h) 1-1
Brazil
Clemence; Hughton(Mabbutt), Thomas, Roberts, Stevens, Perryman, Ardiles(Hazard), Brazil, Galvin (Archibald), Hoddle(Price), Falco.

KEITH BURKINSHAW TESTIMONIAL
May 29 1984 v England XI (h) 2-2
Hughton, Brady
Jennings(Parks); Thomas, Hughton, Roberts(Stevens), Miller, Perryman(Hazard), Ardiles(Taylor), Crooks, Falco, Brady, Galvin.

PETER SOUTHEY MEMORIAL
Aug 20 1984 v Fulham (h) 3-1
Crooks, Allen 2
Clemence(Parks); Thomas, Hughton, Roberts (Bowen), Miller, Stevens(Crook), Chiedozie(Brooke), Falco(Crooks), Allen, Mabbutt, Galvin.

PAT JENNINGS TESTIMONIAL
May 8 1985 v Arsenal (a) 3-2
Crook, Falco 2
Clemence(Parks); Thomas, Mabbutt, Roberts, Miller (Galvin), Perryman, Crook, Falco, Leworthy, Hoddle, Dick.

GLENN HODDLE TESTIMONIAL
Aug 4 1985 v Arsenal (h) 1-1
Leworthy
Clemence; Thomas, Hughton, Roberts, Culverhouse, P.Allen, Ardiles(Crook), Hazard(Chiedozie), Leworthy, Hoddle(Samways), Waddle.

OSSIE ARDILES BENEFIT
May 1 1986 v Inter-Milan (h) 2-1
Falco, C.Allen
Clemence(Jennings); Roberts(Thomas), Hughton, Mabbutt, Miller, Galvin(Samways), Ardiles(Waddle), Falco, C.Allen, Maradona, Hoddle.

PAUL MILLER TESTIMONIAL
Aug 2 1986 v Glasgow Rangers (h) 1-1
C.Allen
Clemence; D.Thomas(Stevens), M.Thomas(Hughton), Roberts, Miller(Ruddock), Mabbutt, Cooke(Waddle), Falco, C.Allen, Ardiles(Hoddle), Galvin.

CHRIS HUGHTON TESTIMONIAL
Aug 10 1987 v Arsenal (h) 3-1
Thomas, C.Allen, Claesen
Clemence(Parks); Stevens(Polston), Thomas, Gough, Fairclough, Mabbutt, C.Allen, P.Allen, Waddle (Galvin), Hodge, Claesen.

TONY GALVIN TESTIMONIAL
Oct 20 1987 v West Ham United (h) 2-2
P.Allen, Archibald
Parks; Stevens(Polston[Hodge[Close]]), Hughton, P.Allen(Ardiles), Ruddock, Mabbutt, C.Allen, Archibald(Gray), Villa, Samways(Moncur), Galvin.

DANNY THOMAS BENEFIT
Mar 28 1988 v Manchester United (h) 2-3
Archibald, Hodge
Parks; Hughton(Moncur), M.Thomas, Roberts (Ruddock), P.Allen, Mabbutt, C.Allen(Moran), Archibald, Dalglish(Howells), Hodge, Barnes (Chiedozie).

DANNY BLANCHFLOWER BENEFIT
May 1 1990 v Northern Ireland XI (h) 2-1
Howells, Gascoigne (pen)
Thorstvedt(Mimms); A.Polston(Perryman), Thomas, Sedgley, Howells(Garland), J.Polston(Butters), Stewart(Gormley), Gascoigne(A.Polston), Nayim (Ardiles), Lineker(Walsh), Allen(Taylor).

RAY CLEMENCE BENEFIT
Aug 17 1990 v West Ham United (h) 4-1
Lineker 2 (1 pen), Gascoigne, Nayim
Clemence(Thorstvedt); Ardiles(Nayim), Edinburgh, Sedgley(Butters), Howells(Samways), Mabbutt, Stewart, Gascoigne(Moncur), Dalglish(Hendon), Lineker(Walsh), Allen.

EDDIE BAILY TESTIMONIAL
May 14 1993 v Enfield (a) 5-1
Sheringham 2, Anderton, Gray, Heald (og)
Walker(Dearden); McDonald(Campbell), Tuttle, Samways(Watson), Nethercott, Ruddock(Hodges), Sedgley(Gray), Hill(Turner [Caskey]), Anderton (McMahon), Sheringham(Mahorn), Hendry.

REPRESENTATIVE SPURS

The following list covers representative honours won by players whilst with Tottenham Hotspur. Many players gained such recognition before or after their time at White Hart Lane but they are not included here. Before 1924 there was only one 'Ireland' team, then the Republic began separate matches and that position is reflected here. The date given is the year in which the match was played and the figures in brackets the number of goals scored in that match. All matches are up to and including 1 May 1993.

Full Internationals

England

Allen C.D. (2 apps) 1987 v Turkey; 1988 v Israel.

Alsford W.J. (1 app) 1935 v Scotland.

Baily E.F. (9 apps, 5 goals) 1950 v Spain, Northern Ireland (2), Wales (2), Yugoslavia; 1951 v Wales (1), Austria; 1952 v Austria, Switzerland, Northern Ireland.

Bliss H. (1 app) 1921 v Scotland.

Brooks J. (3 apps, 2 goals) 1956 v Wales (1), Yugoslavia (1), Denmark.

Chivers M.H. (24 apps, 13 goals) 1971 v Malta, Greece (1), Malta (2), Northern Ireland, Scotland (2), Switzerland (1), Switzerland (sub), Greece (1), 1972 v West Germany, West Germany, Northern Ireland (sub), Scotland, Wales; 1973 v Wales, Scotland (1), Northern Ireland (2), Wales (1), Scotland, Czechoslovakia, Poland, USSR (1), Italy, Austria (1), Poland.

Clarke H.A. (1 app) 1954 v Scotland.

Clay T. (4 apps) 1920 v Wales; 1921 v Ireland; 1922 v Wales, Scotland.

Clemence R.N. (5 apps) 1981 v Norway; 1982 v Northern Ireland, Finland, Luxembourg; 1983 v Luxembourg.

Coates R. (2 apps) 1971 v Malta, Wales.

Dimmock J.H. (3 apps) 1921 v Scotland; 1926 v Wales, Belgium.

Ditchburn E.G. (6 apps) 1948 v Switzerland; 1949 v Sweden; 1953 v USA; 1956 v Wales, Yugoslavia, Denmark.

Fenwick T. (1 app) 1988 v Israel (sub).

Gascoigne P.J. (20 apps, 2 goals) 1988 v Denmark (sub), Saudi Arabia (sub); 1989 v Albania (sub) (1), Chile, Scotland (sub), Sweden (sub); 1990 v Brazil (sub), Czechoslovakia (1), Denmark, Uruguay, Tunisia, Republic of Ireland, Holland, Egypt, Belgium, Cameroon, West Germany, Hungary, Poland, Cameroon.

Greaves J.P. (42 apps, 28 goals) 1962 v Scotland, Switzerland, Peru (3), Hungary, Argentina (1), Bulgaria, Brazil, France, Northern Ireland (1), Wales (1); 1963 v France, Scotland, Brazil, Czechoslovakia (2), Switzerland, Wales (1), Rest of the World (1), Northern Ireland (4); 1964 v Uruguay, Portugal, Republic of Ireland (1), Brazil (1), Portugal, Argentina, Northern Ireland (3), Belgium, Holland (1); 1965 v Scotland (1), Hungary (1), Yugoslavia, Wales, Austria; 1966 v Yugoslavia (1), Norway (4), Denmark, Poland, Uruguay, Mexico, France; 1967 v Scotland, Spain (1), Austria.

Grimsdell A. (6 apps) 1920 v Wales, Scotland, Ireland; 1921 v Scotland; 1922 v Ireland; 1923 v Wales.

Hall G.W. (10 apps, 9 goals) 1933 v France; 1937 v Northern Ireland (1), Wales (1), Czechoslovakia; 1938 v Scotland, Rest of Europe (1), Northern Ireland (5); 1939 v Scotland, Italy (1), Yugoslavia.

Henry R.P. (1 app) 1963 v France.

Hoddle G. (44 apps, 8 goals) 1979 v Bulgaria (1); 1980 v Wales, Australia (1), Spain; 1981 v Spain (1), Wales, Scotland, Norway; 1982 v Northern Ireland (1), Wales, Iceland, Czechoslovakia (sub), Kuwait, Luxembourg (sub) (1); 1983 v Northern Ireland, Scotland, Hungary (1), Luxembourg; 1984 v France; 1985 v Republic of Ireland (sub), Scotland, Italy (sub), Mexico, West Germany, USA, Romania (1), Turkey, Northern Ireland; 1986 v Israel, USSR, Scotland (1), Mexico, Canada, Portugal, Morocco, Poland, Paraguay, Argentina, Sweden, Northern Ireland, Yugoslavia; 1987 v Spain, Turkey, Scotland.

Hodge S.B. (4 apps) 1987 v Spain, Northern Ireland, Turkey, Scotland.

Hunt G.S. (3 apps, 1 goal) 1933 v Italy, Scotland (1), Switzerland.

Knowles C.B. (4 apps) 1967 v USSR; 1968 v Spain, Sweden, West Germany.

Lineker G.W. (38 apps, 18 goals) 1989 v Sweden, Poland, Italy, Yugoslavia; 1990 v Brazil (1), Czechoslovakia, Denmark (1), Uruguay, Tunisia, Republic of Ireland (1), Holland, Egypt, Belgium, Cameroon (2), West Germany (1), Italy, Hungary, Poland (1), Republic of Ireland, Cameroon; 1991 v Republic of Ireland, Turkey, Argentina (1), Australia, New Zealand (1), Malaysia (4), Germany, Turkey, Poland (1); 1992 v France (sub) (1), Czechoslovakia (sub), CIS (1), Hungary, Brazil, Finland, Denmark, France, Sweden.

Mabbutt G.V. (16 apps, 1 goal) 1982 v West Germany, Greece, Luxembourg; 1983 v Wales, Greece, Hungary, Northern Ireland, Scotland (sub), Hungary; 1986 v Yugoslavia (1), Northern Ireland, Turkey, West Germany; 1991 v Turkey, Poland; 1992 v Czechoslovakia.

Medley J.D. (6 apps, 1 goal) 1950 v Wales, Yugoslavia; 1951 v France (1), Wales, Northern Ireland, Austria.

Mullery A.P. (35 apps, 1 goal) 1964 v Holland; 1967 v Spain, Austria, Wales, Northern Ireland, USSR; 1968 v Scotland, Spain, Spain, Sweden, Yugoslavia, Romania, Bulgaria; 1969 v France, Northern Ireland, Scotland, Mexico, Uruguay, Brazil, Holland, Portugal; 1970 v Holland (sub), Wales, Northern Ireland, Scotland (sub), Colombia, Ecuador, Romania, Brazil, Czechoslovakia, West Germany (1), East Germany; 1971 v Malta, Greece, Switzerland.

Nicholson W.E. (1 app, 1 goal) 1951 v Portugal (1).

Norman M. (23 apps) 1962 v Peru, Hungary, Argentina, Bulgaria, Brazil, France; 1963 v Scotland, Brazil, Czechoslovakia, East Germany, Wales, Rest of the World, Northern Ireland; 1964 v Scotland, Uruguay, Portugal, USA, Brazil, Portugal, Argentina, Northern Ireland, Belgium, Holland.

Osborne F.R. (2 apps, 3 goals) 1924 v Belgium; 1926 v Belgium (3).

Perryman S.J. (1 app) 1982 v Iceland (sub).

Peters M.S. (34 apps, 9 goals) 1970 v Wales, Northern Ireland (1), Scotland, Colombia (2), Ecuador, Romania, Brazil, Czechoslovakia, West Germany (1), East Germany (1); 1971 v Malta (1), Greece, Malta, Northern Ireland, Wales, Scotland (1), Switzerland, Greece; 1972 v West Germany, West Germany (sub), Northern Ireland (sub); 1973 v Scotland, Northern Ireland, Wales (1), Scotland (1), Czechoslovakia, Poland, USSR, Italy, Austria, Poland, Italy; 1974 v Portugal, Scotland.

Ramsey A.E. (31 apps, 3 goals) 1949 v Italy; 1950 v Scotland, Portugal, Belgium, Chile, USA, Spain, Northern Ireland, Wales, Yugoslavia; 1951 v Scotland, Argentina, Portugal, France, Wales, Northern Ireland, Austria (1); 1952 v Scotland, Italy, Austria, Switzerland, Northern Ireland, Wales, Belgium; 1953 v Scotland, Argentina, Chile, Uruguay, USA, Rest of Europe (1), Hungary (1).

Robb G.W. (1 app) 1953 v Hungary.

Roberts G.P. (6 apps) 1983 v Northern Ireland, Scotland; 1984 v France, Northern Ireland, Scotland, USSR.

Rowe A.S. (1 app) 1933 v France.

Seed J.M. (5 apps, 1 goal) 1921 v Belgium; 1922 v Ireland; 1923 v Wales, Belgium (1); 1925 v Scotland.

Smith B. (2 apps) 1921 v Scotland; 1922 v Wales.

Smith R.A. (15 apps, 13 goals) 1960 v Northern Ireland (1), Luxembourg (2), Spain (2), Wales (1); 1961 v Scotland (2), Portugal; 1962 v Scotland; 1963 v France (1), Scotland, Brazil, Czechoslovakia (1), East Germany, Wales (2), Rest of the World, Northern Ireland (1).

Sproston B. (2 apps) 1938 v Wales, Rest of Europe.

Stevens G.A. (7 apps) 1984 v Finland (sub), Turkey (sub); 1985 v Northern Ireland; 1986 v Scotland (sub), Mexico (sub), Morocco (sub), Paraguay (sub).

Stewart P.A. (3 apps) 1991 v Germany (sub); 1992 v Czechoslovakia (sub), CIS (sub).

Waddle C.R. (36 apps, 6 goals) 1985 v Romania, Turkey (1), Northern Ireland; 1986 v Israel, USSR (1), Scotland, Mexico, Canada, Portugal, Morocco, Poland (sub), Argentina (sub), Sweden (sub), Northern Ireland (1), Yugoslavia; 1987 v Spain, Northern Ireland (1), Turkey, Brazil, Scotland, West Germany; 1988 v Israel, Hungary, Scotland (sub), Colombia, Switzerland, Republic of Ireland, Holland, Sweden, Saudi Arabia; 1989 v Albania, Albania (1), Chile, Scotland (1), Poland, Denmark.

Walden F.I. (2 apps) 1914 v Scotland; 1922 v Wales.

Willis A. (1 app) 1951 v France.

Woodward V.J. (21 apps, 27 goals) 1903 v Ireland (2), Wales (1), Scotland (1); 1904 v Ireland, Scotland; 1905 v Ireland, Wales (2), Scotland; 1907 v Scotland; 1908 v Ireland, Wales (3), Scotland, Austria (1), Austria (4), Hungary (1), Bohemia; 1909 v Ireland (2), Wales, Hungary (2), Hungary (4), Austria (3).

Scotland

Archibald S. (22 apps, 3 goals) 1980 v Northern Ireland, Poland, Hungary (1), Sweden (sub); 1981 v Israel, Northern Ireland, Israel, Northern Ireland (1), England, Northern Ireland, Portugal; 1982 v Spain (sub), Holland, New Zealand (sub) (1), Brazil, USSR, East Germany, Switzerland (sub), Belgium; 1983 v East Germany; 1984 v England, France.

Brazil A.B. (2 apps, 1 goal) 1983 v Wales (1), England (sub).

Brown A. (1 app) 1902 v England. (Match later declared unofficial following crowd disaster).

Brown W.D.F. (24 apps) 1959 v Northern Ireland, Wales; 1960 v Poland, Austria, Hungary, Turkey; 1961 v Czechoslovakia, Northern Ireland, Wales; 1962 v England, Wales, Northern Ireland; 1963 v England, Austria, Northern Ireland, Norway, Wales; 1965 v England, Spain, Poland, Finland, Northern Ireland, Poland, Italy.

Conn A.J. (2 apps) 1975 v Northern Ireland (sub), England.

Durie G.S. (11 apps, 2 goals) 1991 v Switzerland (1), Romania, San Marino (1); 1992 v Northern Ireland (sub), Finland, Canada, Norway (sub), Holland, Germany, Switzerland, Italy.

Gilzean A.J. (17 apps, 8 goals) 1965 v Spain, Northern Ireland (2), Poland, Italy, Wales; 1967 v Wales (2); 1968 v Austria (sub), Cyprus (2); 1969 v West Germany, Wales (1), England, Cyprus, West Germany (1), Austria; 1970 v Northern Ireland, England (sub); 1971 v Portugal.

Gough R. (8 apps) 1986 v Bulgaria, Republic of Ireland, Luxembourg; 1987 v Republic of Ireland, Belgium, England, Brazil, Hungary.

Mackay D.C. (18 apps, 4 goals) 1959 v England, West Germany, Northern Ireland, Wales; 1960 v Poland, Austria (1), Hungary, Turkey, Wales, Northern Ireland; 1961 v England (1); 1963 v England, Australia, Norway, Northern Ireland, Norway (2), Wales; 1965 v Northern Ireland.

Roberston J.G. (1 app) 1964 v Wales.

White J.A. (18 apps, 1 goal) 1959 v Wales; 1960 v Poland, Austria, Turkey, Wales; 1961 v Czechoslovakia, Northern Ireland, Wales, Czechoslovakia; 1962 v England, Wales, Northern Ireland; 1963 v England, Northern Ireland, Norway, Wales (1); 1964 v England, West Germany.

Wales

Bowen R.M. (2 apps) 1986 v Canada (sub), Canada (sub).

Burgess W.A.R. (32 apps, 1 goal) 1946 v Scotland, England; 1947 v Northern Ireland, England, Scotland; 1948 v Scotland, England; 1949 v Northern Ireland, Portugal, Belgium, Switzerland, England, Scotland, Belgium; 1950 v Northern Ireland, Scotland; 1951 v Northern Ireland, Portugal, Switzerland (1), England, Scotland, Rest of United Kingdom; 1952 v Northern Ireland, Scotland, England; 1953 v Northern Ireland, France, Yugoslavia, England, Scotland; 1954 v Northern Ireland, Austria.

Day A. (1 app) 1933 v Northern Ireland.

England H.M. (24 apps, 2 goals) 1966 v Scotland, England; 1967 v England; 1968 v Northern Ireland, West Germany; 1969 v East Germany, Rest of United Kingdom, East Germany, Italy (1); 1970 v England,

Scotland, Northern Ireland, Romania; 1971 v Finland; 1972 v England, Scotland, Northern Ireland, England; 1973 v England, Scotland, England, Poland; 1974 v Hungary, Luxembourg (1).

Evans W. (6 apps, 1 goal) 1932 v Northern Ireland; 1933 v Scotland (1), England; 1934 v England; 1936 v England, Northern Ireland.

Hopkins M. (34 apps) 1956 v Northern Ireland, Scotland, England; 1957 v Northern Ireland, Czechoslovakia, East Germany, Czechoslovakia, East Germany, England, Scotland; 1958 v Israel, Israel, Northern Ireland, Hungary, Mexico, Sweden, Hungary, Brazil, Scotland, England; 1959 v Northern Ireland, England, Scotland; 1961 v Northern Ireland, Spain, Spain, Hungary; 1962 v Northern Ireland, Brazil, Brazil, Mexico, Scotland, Hungary; 1963 v Northern Ireland.

Hughes E. (12 apps) 1901 v Scotland, England; 1902 v Ireland; 1904 v England, Scotland, Ireland; 1905 v Scotland, England, Ireland; 1906 v England, Ireland; 1907 v England.

Jones C.W. (41 apps, 12 goals) 1958 v Northern Ireland, Hungary, Mexico, Sweden, Hungary, Brazil; 1959 v Northern Ireland, England, Scotland; 1960 v Northern Ireland, Republic of Ireland (2), Scotland (1), England; 1961 v Northern Ireland (2), Spain, Hungary (1), England, Scotland: 1962 v Northern Ireland, Brazil, Brazil, Mexico, Scotland; 1963 v Hungary (1), Northern Ireland (3), England, Scotland; 1964 v Northern Ireland, Scotland, Denmark, England (1), Greece; 1965 v Greece, Northern Ireland (1), Italy, USSR; 1966 v Scotland, England; 1967 v England, Scotland; 1968 v West Germany.

Jones E.N. (2 apps) 1948 v England, Scotland.

Jones J.L. (12 apps) 1898 v Ireland, Scotland, England; 1899 v Ireland, Scotland; 1900 v Scotland; 1902 v Ireland, England, Scotland; 1904 v England, Scotland, Ireland.

Medwin T.C. (27 apps, 6 goals) 1956 v Scotland (1), England; 1957 v Northern Ireland, Czechoslovakia, East Germany, Czechoslovakia, England, Scotland (1); 1958 v Israel, Israel, Northern Ireland, Hungary, Mexico, Hungary (1), Brazil, Scotland, England; 1959 v Northern Ireland, England, Scotland; 1960 v Northern Ireland (2), Republic of Ireland, Scotland, England; 1961 v Spain, Hungary (1), England.

O'Callaghan E. (11 apps, 3 goals) 1929 v Northern Ireland, Scotland (1); 1931 v Scotland, England; 1932 v Scotland (2), England, Northern Ireland; 1933 v Scotland, Northern Ireland, England; 1934 v England.

Price P.T. (14 apps) 1981 v USSR; 1982 v Spain, France, Norway, Yugoslavia; 1983 v England, Bulgaria, Scotland, Northern Ireland, Norway, Romania, Bulgaria, Yugoslavia; 1984 v Scotland (sub).

Rees W. (1 apps) 1950 v Northern Ireland.

Whatley W.J. (2 apps) 1938 v England, Scotland.

Yorath T.C. (8 apps) 1979 v Republic of Ireland, Turkey; 1980 v England, Scotland, Northern Ireland, Ireland, Turkey, Czechoslovakia.

Ireland

Kirwan J.H. (12 apps, 2 goals) 1900 v Wales; 1902 v Wales, England; 1903 v England, Scotland (1), Wales; 1904 v England (1), Wales, Scotland; 1905 v England, Scotland, Wales.

O'Hagan C. (5 apps, 1 goal) 1905 v Scotland, Wales (1); 1906 v England, Scotland, Wales.

Northern Ireland

Armstrong G.J. (27 apps, 5 goals) 1977 v West Germany, England, Wales (sub), Iceland (sub), Belgium (2); 1978 v Scotland, England, Wales, Republic of Ireland, Denmark, Bulgaria (1); 1979 v England, Bulgaria (1), England, Scotland, Wales, Denmark, England, Republic of Ireland (1); 1980 v Israel, Scotland, England, Wales, Australia, Australia, Australia, Sweden.

Blanchflower R.D. (43 apps) 1954 v England, Scotland; 1955 v Wales, Scotland, England; 1956 v Wales, England, Scotland; 1957 v Portugal, Wales, Italy, Portugal, Scotland, England, Italy; 1958 v Italy, Wales, Czechoslavakia, Argentina, West Germany, Czechoslavakia, France, England, Spain, Scotland; 1959 v Wales, Scotland, England; 1960 v Wales, England, West Germany, Scotland; 1961 v Wales, West Germany, Scotland, Greece, England; 1962 v Wales, Holland, Poland, England, Scotland, Poland.

Jennings P.A. (75 apps) 1964 v England, Switzerland, Switzerland, Scotland; 1965 v Holland, Albania, Scotland, England, Albania; 1966 v Wales, West Germany, England, Scotland; 1967 v Scotland, England; 1968 v Wales, Israel, Turkey, Turkey; 1969 v England, Scotland, Wales, USSR, USSR; 1970 v Scotland, England; 1971 v Cyprus, Cyprus, England, Scotland, Wales, USSR; 1972 v Spain, Scotland, England, Wales, Bulgaria; 1973 v Cyprus, Portugal, England, Scotland, Wales, Portugal; 1974 v Scotland, England, Wales, Norway, Sweden; 1975 v Yugoslavia, England, Scotland, Wales, Sweden, Norway, Yugoslavia; 1976 v Israel, Scotland, England, Wales, Holland, Belgium; 1977 v West Germany, England, Scotland, Wales, Iceland; 1985 v Turkey, Romania, England; 1986 v France, Denmark, Morocco, Algeria, Spain, Brazil.

McGrath R.C. (6 apps, 1 goal) 1974 v Scotland, England, Wales, Norway; 1976 v Israel (sub), Holland (1).

Rowley R.W.M (2 apps, 1 goal) 1931 v Wales (1), Scotland.

Republic of Ireland

Galvin A. (19 apps, 1 goal) 1982 v Holland; 1983 v Malta, Holland (sub); 1984 v Israel (sub), Mexico, USSR, Norway, Denmark; 1985 v Italy, Norway, Spain; 1986 v Uruguay, Iceland, Czechoslovakia, Belgium; 1987 v Belgium, Scotland, Bulgaria, Luxembourg (1).

Gavin J.T. (2 apps) 1955 v Holland, West Germany.

Holmes J.A. (12 apps) 1977 v France, Poland, Bulgaria, Bulgaria; 1978 v Turkey, Poland, Norway, Denmark, Northern Ireland, England; 1979 v Denmark, Bulgaria.

Hughton C.W.G. (50 apps, 1 goal) 1979 v USA; 1980 v England, Switzerland, Argentina, Holland, Belgium, France, Cyprus (1); 1981 v Wales, Belgium, Poland, France; 1982 v Holland, Spain; 1983 v Malta, Spain, Iceland, Holland, Malta; 1984 v Mexico (sub), USSR, Norway; 1985 v Italy, Israel, England, Spain, Switzerland; 1986 v Uruguay, Iceland, Belgium, USSR; 1987 v Bulgaria, Israel; 1988 v Yugoslavia, Poland, Norway, England, USSR, Holland, Northern Ireland; 1989 v France, Hungary, Spain, Malta, Hungary; 1990 v Wales (sub), Finland, Turkey (sub), Malta, Turkey.

Kinnear J.P. (24 apps) 1967 v Turkey, Czechoslovakia; 1968 v Poland, Austria; 1969 v Czechoslovakia,

Denmark, Hungary; 1970 v Poland, Sweden (sub); 1971 v Italy; 1972 v Iran, Ecuador, Chile, Portugal, USSR, France; 1973 v Poland; 1974 v Brazil, Uruguay, Chile, USSR, Turkey; 1975 v Switzerland, USSR.

Argentina

Ardiles O.C. (7 apps, 1 goal) 1981 v West Germany, Brazil; 1982 v Belgium, Hungary (1), El Salvador, Italy, Brazil.

Belgium

Claesen N.P.J. (9 apps, 6 goals) 1986 v Luxembourg (3), Bulgaria; 1987 v Portugal, Scotland (3), Republic of Ireland, Holland, Bulgaria, Scotland, Luxembourg.

Iceland

Bergsson G. (24 apps) 1989 v England 'B', USSR, Austria (twice), East Germany, Turkey; 1990 v Luxembourg, Albania, France, Czechoslovakia, Spain; 1991 v England 'B', Wales, Albania, Czechoslovakia, Turkey, Spain, France; 1992 v Greece, Hungary, Iceland, Greece, Russia; 1993 v United States.

Nigeria

Chiedozie J.O. (3 apps) 1984 v Liberia; 1985 v Tunisia, Tunisia.

Norway

Thorstevdt E. (23 apps) 1989 v Poland, Cyprus, Greece, France, Yugoslavia, Scotland; 1990 v Malta, Northern Ireland, Sweden, USSR, Hungary, Cameroon, Cyprus; 1991 v Cyprus, Romania, Italy, USSR, Czechoslovakia, Italy; 1992 v San Marino, Holland, San Marino, England.

Victory Internationals

Grimsdell A. (2 apps, 2 goals) 1919 v Scotland, Scotland (2).

Wartime Internationals

England

Buckingham V.F. (2 apps) 1941 v Wales, Wales.
Ditchburn E.G. (2 apps) 1944 v Scotland, Wales.
Gibbons A.H. (1 app) 1942 v Wales.
Hall G.W. (3 apps) 1939 v Wales; 1940 v Wales; 1942 v Wales.

Wales

Burgess W.A.R. (10 apps) 1939 v England, England; 1941 v England; 1943 v England; 1944 v England, England; 1945 v England, England, Scotland; 1946 v Northern Ireland.
Whatley W.J. (1 app) 1939 v England.

'B' Internationals

England

Bailey E.F. (3 apps) 1950 v Switzerland, Italy, Holland.
Clarke H.A. (1 app) 1954 v West Germany.
Ditchburn E.G. (2 apps) 1949 v Holland; 1950 v Switzerland.
Fairclough C.H. (1 app) 1987 v Malta.

Gascoigne P.J. (2 apps, 1 goal) 1989 v Switzerland (1), Iceland.
Harmer T.C. (1 app) 1952 v Holland.
Hoddle G. (2 apps, 1 goal) 1979 v Austria (abandoned), New Zealand (1).
Mabbutt G.V. (8 apps) 1989 v Switzerland, Iceland, Norway; 1990 v Algeria; 1991 v Wales, Iceland; 1992 v France, CIS.
Marchi A.V. (1 app) 1957 v Scotland.
Nicholson W.E. (3 apps) 1950 v Switzerland, Italy, Holland.
Robb G.W. (3 apps) 1954 v West Germany, Yugoslavia, Switzerland.
Roberts G.P. (1 app) 1984 v New Zealand.
Stewart P.A. (5 apps, 1 goal) 1989 v Switzerland (sub), Iceland, Norway; 1991 v Iceland (sub); 1992 v France (1).
Stokes A.F. (1 app) 1957 v Scotland.
Thomas M.A. (1 app) 1987 v Malta.
Walters W.E. (1 app) 1950 v Holland.
Withers C.F. (1 app) 1952 v Holland.

Republic of Ireland

McDonald D. (1 app) 1992 v Denmark.

Under-23 Internationals

England

Allen L.W. (1 app) 1961 v Wales.
Chivers M.H. (5 apps, 2 goals) 1968 v Scotland (1), Hungary (1), Italy, Hungary, West Germany.
Greaves J.P. (1 app, 2 goals) 1962 v Scotland (2).
Iley J. (1 app) 1958 v Wales.
Knowles C.B. (6 apps, 1 goal) 1964 v Wales; 1966 v Wales (1); 1967 v Scotland, Greece, Bulgaria, Turkey.
Morgan R.E. (1 app, 2 goals) 1970 v Bulgaria (2).
Norman M. (3 apps) 1956 v Scotland; 1957 v Romania, Czechoslovakia.
Perryman S.J. (17 apps) 1972 v East Germany, Poland, USSR; 1973 v Scotland, Denmark, Holland, Czechoslovakia, Poland, Denmark; 1974 v Wales, Scotland, Turkey, Yugoslavia, Czechoslovakia, Portugal, Scotland; 1975 v Wales.
Stokes A.F. (1 app, 2 goals) 1955 v Denmark (2).

Scotland

Conn A.J. (3 apps) 1975 v Romania, Denmark, Romania.
Robertson J.G. (3 apps, 1 goal) 1964 v France (1), Wales; 1968 v England.
White J.A. (1 app) 1959 v Wales.

Wales

Collins J.L. (5 apps) 1966 v England; 1967 v Northern Ireland (abandoned), England; 1968 v Northern Ireland, England.
Hopkins M. (1 app) 1958 v England.
Jones C.W. (1 app) 1958 v England.

Northern Ireland

Johnston R. Details unknown.

Under-21 Internationals

England

Allen P.K. (1 app) 1985 v Romania.
Anderton D. (3 apps, 3 goals) 1992 v Spain (1); 1993 v San Marino (1), Holland (1).
Butters G. (3 apps) 1989 v Bulgaria, Senegal (sub), Republic of Ireland (sub).
Cooke R.E. (1 app) 1986 v Denmark (sub).
Fairclough C.H. (2 apps) 1987 v Yugoslavia; 1988 v France.
Hendon I. (7 apps) 1992 v Hungary, Mexico, Czechoslovakia, France, Spain, Norway, Turkey.
Hoddle G. (12 apps, 2 goals) 1976 v Wales (sub); 1977 v Finland (sub); 1978 v Italy, Italy, Yugoslavia, Denmark (1); 1979 v Wales (1), Bulgaria; 1980 v Scotland, Scotland, East Germany, East Germany.
Jones C.H. (1 app) 1978 v Yugoslavia (sub).
Mabbutt G.V. (4 apps, 2 goals) 1982 v Denmark (2); 1984 v France; 1986 v Denmark, Italy.
Samways V. (5 apps, 1 goal) 1988 v Switzerland (sub), USSR (1), France, Denmark, Sweden.
Sedgley S.P. (1 app) 1989 v Sweden.
Statham B. (3 apps) 1988 v Switzerland, Denmark (sub), Sweden.
Stevens G.A. (6 apps) 1983 v Hungary; 1984 v France, France (sub), Spain, Spain (sub); 1986 v Italy.
Thomas D.J. (2 apps) 1984 v Italy, Spain.
Walker I. (8 apps) 1990 v Wales; 1992 v Hungary, Czechoslovakia, France, Spain, Norway, Turkey; 1993 v San Marino.

Scotland

Archibald S. (1 app) 1980 v Denmark.
McNab N. (1 app) 1978 v Wales.

Wales

Bowen R.M. (3 apps) 1983 v Norway; 1984 v Bulgaria, Yugoslavia.
Kendall M. (1 app) 1978 v Scotland.

Northern Ireland

Fitzgerald T. (2 apps) 1989 v Senegal, France.
Johnston R. Details unknown.

Republic of Ireland

Gormley E. (3 apps) 1989 v Senegal (sub), Bulgaria, France (sub).
McDonald D. (3 apps) 1991 v Poland, Poland, Turkey.
Turner A. (1 app) 1993 v Denmark.

Football League

Allen C.D. (1 app) 1987 v Rest of World.
Allen L.W. (1 app, 1 goal) 1962 v Italian League (1).
Ardiles O.C. (2 apps) 1987 v Rest of World (sub), Irish League.
Bailey E.F. (6 apps, 1 goal) 1950 v League of Ireland (1), Scottish League, Irish League; 1951 v League of Ireland; 1952 v Irish League; 1954 v Irish League.
Blanchflower R.D. (1 app, 1 goal) 1960 v Irish League (1).
Burgess W.A.R. (1 app) 1947 v Scottish League.
Clay T. (1 app) 1922 v Irish League.
Ditchburn E.G. (6 apps) 1947 v Scottish League, League of Ireland; 1948 v Scottish League, League of Ireland, Irish League; 1950 v Scottish League.

Elkes A.J. (3 apps, 1 goal) 1924 v Irish League; 1925 v Scottish League; 1927 v Scottish League.
Gough R.C. (1 app) 1987 v Rest of World.
Greaves J.P. (6 apps, 4 goals) 1962 v Italian League (1); 1964 v Scottish League (1); 1965 v Scottish League; 1966 v Scottish League (1); 1967 v Scottish League, League of Ireland (1).
Grimsdell A. (1 app) 1920 v Scottish League.
Hall G.W. (3 apps, 1 goal) 1934 v Scottish League; 1937 v Irish League (1); 1938 v Scottish League.
Howells D.G. (1 app) 1990 v Irish League.
Iley J. (1 app) 1958 v Scottish League.
Jones C.W. (3 apps) 1960 v Scottish League, Irish League, Italian League.
Knowles C.B. (1 app) 1968 v Scottish League.
Lunn T.H. (1 app) 1910 v Southern League.
Mabbutt G.V. (1 app) 1990 v Irish League.
Mackay D.C. (2 apps) 1960 v Scottish League, Irish League.
Medley L.D. (1 app) 1951 v Scottish League.
Metgod J.A.B. (1 app) 1987 v Irish League.
Middlemiss H. (1 app) 1910 v Southern League.
Mullery A.P. (2 apps) 1964 v Italian League, Irish League.
Nicholson W.E. (1 app) 1950 v League of Ireland.
Norman M. (1 app) 1964 v Italian League.
Peters M.S. (2 apps, 1 goal) 1970 v Scottish League (sub), Irish League (1).
Ramsey A.E. (5 apps, 1 goal) 1950 v Scottish League; 1951 v League of Ireland, Scottish League; 1952 v Irish League (1); 1953 v Danish Combination.
Robb G.W. (1 app) 1953 v Irish League.
Smith B. (1 app) 1922 Scottish League.
Spiers C.H. (1 app) 1930 v Scottish League.
Sproston B. (2 apps) 1938 v Irish League, Scottish League.
Stokes A.E. (1 app) 1957 v Scottish League.
Waddle C.R. (1 app) 1987 v Rest of World.
Walden F.I. (1 app) 1914 v Southern League.
White J.A. (1 app) 1960 v Irish League.
Woodward V.J. (2 apps, 3 goals) 1908 v Irish League (2); 1909 v Scottish League (1).

England v Young England

Bailey E.F. (1 app) 1955.
Ditchburn E.G. (1 app) 1957.
Greaves J.P. (3 apps, 1 goal) 1964 (1), 1965, 1966.
Knowles C.B. (2 apps) 1968, 1969.
Marchi A.V. (1 app) 1963 (sub).
Mullery A.P. (3 apps) 1965, 1968, 1969.
Norman M. (1 app) 1964.
Ramsey A.E. (1 app) 1955.

Young England v England

Chivers M.H. (1 app, 2 goals) 1968 (2).
Knowles C.B. (2 apps) 1965, 1966.
Norman M. (1 app) 1958.
Saul F.L. (1 app) 1966.
Venables T.F. (1 app) 1966.

England v Football League

Greaves J.P. (1 app, 1 goal) 1963 (1).
Norman M. (1 app) 1963.

Great Britain

Blanchflower R.D. (1 app) 1955 v Rest of Europe.
Burgess W.A.R. (1 app) 1947 v Rest of Europe.

Rest of United Kingdom

Bailey E.F. (1 app) 1951 v Wales.
Jennings P.A. (1 app) 1969 v Wales.
Medley L.D. (1 app, 1 goal) 1951 v Wales (1).

FA Charity Shield

Bailey E.F. (1 app, 1 goal) 1950 World Cup Team v Canadian Touring Team (1).
Elkes A.J. (1 app) 1925 Professionals v Amateurs.
Poynton C. (1 app) 1925 Professionals v Amateurs.
Ramsey A.E. (1 app) 1950 World Cup Team v Canadian Touring Team.
Walden F.I. (1 app) 1913 Professionals v Amateurs.

Miscellaneous

Bennett L.D. (Whilst guesting for Distillery) 1943 Northern Ireland Regional League v League of Ireland.
Bradshaw T.H. 1898 United League v Thames & Medway League; 1899 England XI v Scotland XI (Players' Union Funds).
Brown W.D.F. 1962 Scotland v Scottish League.
Channell F.C. 1935 England XI v Anglo-Scots.
Cullen J. 1898 United League v Thames & Medway League.
Greaves J.P. 1964 UEFA v Scandinavia (2).
Hall G.W. 1935 England XI v Anglo-Scots.
Holmes J.A. 1977 Republic of Ireland v League of Ireland.
Jennings P.A. 1973 All Ireland XI v Brazil, The Three v The Six; 1986 Rest of the World v Americas.
Joyce W. 1898 United League v Thames & Medway League (2).
Mackay D.C. 1961 Scotland XI v Scottish League; 1962 Scotland XI v Scottish League.
McKay K. 1898 United League v Thames & Medway League (2).
McNaught J.R. 1899 England XI v Scotland XI (Players' Union Funds).
Smith T. 1899 England XI v Scotland XI (Players' Union Funds) (1).
Walden F.I. 1916 England v Scotland (Military International).
White J.A. 1962 Scotland v Scottish League; 1964 Scotland v Scottish League.

Bill Brown

Top Twenty

Appearances
(Including substitute appearances)

Southern League
1. Tom Morris 239
2. Sandy Tait 207
3. John Kirwan 156
4. Edward Hughes 152
5. David Copeland 146
6. Harry Erentz 132
6. John L. Jones 132
8. John Cameron 118
9. Walter Bull 105
9. Vivian Woodward 105
11. James McNaught 104
11. John Watson 104
13. Joseph Walton 102
14. Tom Smith 94
15. Bob Stormont 93
16. George Clawley 83
17. John Brearley 70
18. John Chaplin 66
18. John Eggett 66
20. Ollie Burton 58

Football & Premier League
1. Steve Perryman 656
2. Pat Jennings 473
3. Ted Ditchburn 419
4. Cyril Knowles 402
5. Jimmy Dimmock 400
6. Glenn Hoddle 378
7. Gary Mabbutt 368
8. Maurice Norman 357
9. Alan Gilzean 343
10. Danny Blanchflower . . 337
11. Phil Beal 333
12. John Pratt 331
13. Arthur Grimsdell 324
14. Jimmy Greaves 322
15. Tommy Clay 318
15. Cliff Jones 318
15. Bill Nicholson 318
18. Alan Mullery 313
19. Ron Burgess 301
20. Mike England 300

FA Cup
1. Steve Perryman 69
2. Glenn Hoddle 48
3. Pat Jennings 43
4. Cyril Knowles 42
5. Alan Gilzean 40
6. Cliff Jones 39
6. Tom Morris 39
8. Jimmy Dimmock 38
9. Maurice Norman 37
10. Jimmy Greaves 36
10. Arthur Grimsdell 36
10. Chris Hughton 36
10. Sandy Tait 36
14. Gary Mabbutt 35
15. Ted Ditchburn 33
16. Danny Blanchflower . . . 33
16. Tommy Clay 33
16. Len Duquemin 33
16. Dave Mackay 33
20. Osvaldo Ardiles 32
20. Mike England 32
20. Bobby Smith 32

League Cup
1. Steve Perryman 66
2. Gary Mabbutt 53
3. Paul Allen 44
3. Glenn Hoddle 44
5. Pat Jennings 39
6. Ray Clemence 38
7. Chris Hughton 35
8. Martin Chivers 33
8. Cyril Knowles 33
10. Osvaldo Ardiles 32
11. John Pratt 31
12. Mike England 30
13. Mitchell Thomas 29
14. Alan Gilzean 28
15. Phil Beal 27
15. Jimmy Pearce 27
17. Vinny Samways 26
18. Graham Roberts 25
19. Terry Naylor 24
20. Tony Galvin 23
20. Paul Miller 23
20. Martin Peters 23

Europe
1. Steve Perryman 64
2. Pat Jennings 36
3. Mike England 35
4. Martin Chivers 32
4. Martin Peters 32
6. Phil Beal 30
6. Chris Hughton 30
6. Cyril Knowles 30
9. Alan Gilzean 28
10. Ray Clemence 27
11. Ralph Coates 26
11. Graham Roberts 26
13. Ray Evans 25
13. Mark Falco 25
13. Tony Galvin 25
13. Gary Mabbutt 25
13. John Pratt 25
18. Mike Hazard 23
18. Paul Miller 23
20. Steve Archibald 22

All Matches
(Includes 'Others')
1. Steve Perryman 1020
2. Pat Jennings 676
3. Gary Mabbutt 493
4. Glenn Hoddle 590
5. Ted Ditchburn 575
6. Cyril Knowles 571
7. Tom Morris 565
8. Ron Burgess 510
9. John Pratt 508
10. Tommy Clay 507
10. Alan Gilzean 507
12. Chris Hughton 499
13. Jimmy Dimmock 491
14. Phil Beal 483
15. Paul Allen 463
16. Maurice Norman 453
17. Danny Blanchflower . . . 437
18. Alan Mullery 429
19. Jimmy Greaves 420
20. Cliff Jones 418

Goalscorers

Southern League
1. David Copeland 51
2. Vivian Woodward 45
3. John Cameron 43
4. John Kirwan 40
5. William Joyce 33
6. Sandy Brown 30
7. Tom Pratt 25
7. Tom Smith 25
9. John Walton 23
10. Tom Morris 21
11. James Reid 20
12. John James 19
13. Herbert Chapman 16
14. Robert Clements 14
15. Alfred Warner 13
16. Alex Glen 12
17. Charles Hewitt 11
18. James Hartley 9
18. Edward Hughes 9
18. Harold Stansfield 9

Football & Premier League
1. Jimmy Greaves 220
2. Bobby Smith 176
3. Cliff Jones 135
4. George Hunt 125
5. Martin Chivers 118
6. Len Duquemin 114
7. Les Bennett 104
7. Jimmy Dimmock 100
9. Billy Minter 95
10. Alan Gilzean 93
11. Taffy O'Callaghan 92
12. Bert Bliss 91
13. John Morrison 90
14. Glenn Hoddle 88
15. Willie Evans 78
15. Frank Osborne 78
17. Jimmy Cantrell 74
18. Mark Falco 68
19. Gary Lineker 67
20. Sonny Walters 66

FA Cup
1. Jimmy Greaves 32
2. Bobby Smith 22
3. Alan Gilzean 21
4. Len Duquemin 17
5. Cliff Jones 16
6. Sandy Brown 15
7. Les Bennett 14
7. John Morrison 14
9. Les Allen 13
9. Bert Bliss 13
9. George Hunt 13
12. Jimmy Dimmock 12
12. Jimmy Seed 12
14. Martin Chivers 11
14. Glenn Hoddle 11
16. Jimmy Cantrell 10
17. Clive Allen 9
17. Garth Crooks 9
17. Charlie Handley 9
17. Own-goals 9

League Cup
1. Martin Chivers 23
2. Clive Allen 13
3. Martin Peters 12
4. Glenn Hoddle 10
5. Garth Crooks 9
6. Paul Gascoigne 8
6. Gary Lineker 8
8. Steve Archibald 7
8. John Duncan 7
8. Jimmy Pearce 7
8. John Pratt 7
8. Paul Stewart 7
13. Alan Gilzean 6
14. Jimmy Greaves 5
14. Mike Hazard 5
14. Graham Roberts 5
17. Paul Allen 4
17. Vinny Samways 4
17. Chris Waddle 4
17. Own-goals 4

Europe
1. Martin Chivers 22
2. Mark Falco 14
3. Alan Gilzean 13
3. Martin Peters 13
5. Bobby Smith 10
6. Ralph Coates 9
6. Garth Crooks 9
6. Jimmy Greaves 9
9. Steve Archibald 8
9. Terry Dyson 8
11. Cliff Jones 7
12. Tony Galvin 6
12. Graham Roberts 6
12. John White 6
15. Dave Mackay 5
15. Chris McGrath 5
17. Alan Brazil 4
17. Chris Hughton 4
17. Gary Mabbutt 4
17. Alan Mullery 4
17. Jimmy Pearce 4
17. Own-goals 4

All Matches
(Includes 'Others')
1. Jimmy Greaves 306
2. Bobby Smith 251
3. Martin Chivers 202
4. Len Duquemin 184
5. Cliff Jones 176
6. Alan Gilzean 173
7. Les Bennett 170
8. Bert Bliss 168
9. Mark Falco 152
10. George Hunt 151
10. Billy Minter 151
12. John Cameron 139
13. Jimmy Dimmock 138
14. Glenn Hoddle 132
14. John Morrison 132
16. Taffy O'Callaghan 121
17. Clive Allen 110
17. David Copeland 110
19. Sonny Walters 109
19. Albert Gibbons 109

408

Steve Perryman

Tottenham Hotspur
Pre-Football League Career Records

Player	Played	STHN LGE App	Gls	WEST LGE App	Gls	UTD LGE App	Gls	FA CUP App	Gls	OTHERS App	Gls	TOTAL App	Gls
ADELLINGTON E	1885-1886	-	-	-	-	-	-	-	-	3	0	3	0
AITKEN W	1893-1894	-	-	-	-	-	-	-	-	1	0	1	0
ALLEN J	1896-1897	4	0	-	-	9	1	-	-	11	2	24	3
ALMOND W	1895-1897	16	2	-	-	5	0	7	1	33	8	61	11
AMBLER CJ	1894-1900	22	0	-	-	14	0	12	0	85	0	133	0
AMOS R	1884-1886	-	-	-	-	-	-	-	-	6	3	6	3
ANDERSON J	1885-1892	-	-	-	-	-	-	-	-	11	0	11	0
ANSON	1900-1901	3	0	1	0	-	-	-	-	1	0	5	0
ARCHER AM	1903-1905	-	-	-	-	-	-	-	-	8	0	8	0
ATHERTON TH	1898-1899	2	0	-	-	3	1	-	-	9	3	14	4
AYRES	1889-1890	-	-	-	-	-	-	-	-	1	0	1	0
BADENOCH GH	1906-1907	1	0	1	0	-	-	-	-	1	0	3	0
BADGER HO	1903-1904	-	-	5	1	-	-	-	-	5	4	10	5
BAILLIE	1883-1884	-	-	-	-	-	-	-	-	2	0	2	0
BAILY W	1894-1895	-	-	-	-	-	-	-	-	3	1	3	1
BAKER	1893-1894	-	-	-	-	-	-	-	-	2	0	2	0
BALDOCK GR	1887-1893	-	-	-	-	-	-	-	-	10	1	10	1
BANNERMAN AC	1893-1894	-	-	-	-	-	-	-	-	4	1	4	1
BARBER	1891-1892	-	-	-	-	-	-	-	-	1	1	1	1
BARKER G	1894-1895	-	-	-	-	-	-	-	-	1	0	1	0
BARLOW J	1901-1903	6	0	9	6	-	-	-	-	13	5	28	11
BARNES	1891-1892	-	-	-	-	-	-	-	-	1	1	1	1
BASSETT G	1889-1892	-	-	-	-	-	-	-	-	12	3	12	3
BAXTER JM	1890-1893	-	-	-	-	-	-	-	-	11	7	11	7
BELL	1892-1893	-	-	-	-	-	-	-	-	4	5	4	5
BERRY F	1900-1901	1	0	1	0	-	-	-	-	1	0	3	0
BERRY WA	1903-1907	19	1	16	10	-	-	1	0	9	3	45	14
BEVERIDGE	1895-1896	-	-	-	-	-	-	-	-	1	0	1	0
BIRD C	1906-1907	-	-	-	-	-	-	-	-	3	2	3	2
BIRD J	1887-1888	-	-	-	-	-	-	-	-	2	0	2	0
BLACK D	1897-1898	20	8	-	-	15	6	2	2	19	9	56	25
BLAKE JJ	1905-1906	-	-	3	1	-	-	-	-	-	-	3	1
BOWYER	1893-1894	-	-	-	-	-	-	-	-	1	0	1	0
BRADSHAW TH	1898-1899	24	5	-	-	19	3	9	5	17	5	69	18
BREARLEY J	1903-1907	70	7	34	7	-	-	8	0	21	10	133	24
BRENNAN A	1894-1895	-	-	-	-	-	-	-	-	1	0	1	0
BREWSTER	1907-1908	1	0	-	-	-	-	-	-	-	-	1	0
BRIGDEN J	1891-1894	-	-	-	-	-	-	-	-	21	3	21	3
BRIGGS S	1891-1898	7	0	-	-	6	1	10	0	88	7	111	8
BROWN A	1900-1907	46	30	22	15	-	-	11	15	34	36	113	96
BROWN C	1902-1904	16	0	11	0	-	-	-	-	17	1	44	1
BROWN S	1895-1896	-	-	-	-	-	-	-	-	2	0	2	0
BROWN W	1895-1896	-	-	-	-	-	-	-	-	18	7	18	7
BROWN	1896-1897	-	-	-	-	-	-	-	-	5	1	5	1
BUCHAN	1895-1896	-	-	-	-	-	-	-	-	1	0	1	0
BUCKINGHAM W	1900-1901	6	0	2	0	-	-	-	-	-	-	8	0
BUCKLE R	1883-1895	-	-	-	-	-	-	-	-	53	25	53	25
BUGG	1902-1904	-	-	1	0	-	-	-	-	2	0	3	0
BUIST R	1895-1896	-	-	-	-	-	-	-	-	3	0	3	0
BULL H	1884-1893	-	-	-	-	-	-	-	-	30	0	30	0
BULL W	1904-1908	105	8	23	1	-	-	15	1	21	4	164	14
BUMBERRY TW	1884-1890	-	-	-	-	-	-	-	-	4	1	4	1
'BUNKS'	1893-1894	-	-	-	-	-	-	-	-	1	0	1	0
BURNE	1895-1896	-	-	-	-	-	-	1	0	1	1	2	1
BURROWS LY	1894-1898	27	1	-	-	21	1	12	0	59	1	119	3
BURTON JH	1900-1905	32	3	25	0	-	-	-	-	15	2	72	5
BURTON O	1902-1908	58	0	25	1	-	-	1	0	33	1	117	2
BURTON	1893-1896	-	-	-	-	-	-	-	-	2	1	2	1
BUTLER E	1895-1896	-	-	-	-	-	-	-	-	1	0	1	0
CADMAN M	1889-1892	-	-	-	-	-	-	-	-	5	0	5	0
CAIN R	1898-1899	24	0	-	-	19	1	10	0	16	0	69	1

Player	Played	STHN LGE App	Gls	WEST LGE App	Gls	UTD LGE App	Gls	FA CUP App	Gls	OTHERS App	Gls	TOTAL App	Gls
CALDECOTT	1894-1895	-	-	-	-	-	-	-	-	1	0	1	0
CAMERON J	1898-1907	118	43	33	16	19	7	25	7	99	66	294	139
CARRICK C	1905-1906	15	4	4	0	-	-	4	0	1	1	24	5
CARVER	1894-1895	-	-	-	-	-	-	-	-	1	1	1	1
CASEY HD	1883-1895	-	-	-	-	-	-	-	-	44	0	44	0
CATTELL C	1892-1893	-	-	-	-	-	-	-	-	3	1	3	1
CAWKILL	1884-1885	-	-	-	-	-	-	-	-	2	0	2	0
CHALMERS J	1902-1904	10	1	9	1	-	-	-	-	15	4	34	6
CHAPLIN JF	1905-1908	66	0	21	0	-	-	1	0	14	0	102	0
CHAPMAN H	1904-1907	43	16	15	4	-	-	7	1	6	1	71	22
CHERRIE	1895-1896	-	-	-	-	-	-	-	-	2	0	2	0
CLAWLEY G	1899-1907	83	0	31	0	-	-	12	0	61	0	187	0
CLEMENTS Jnr	1896-1897	-	-	-	-	-	-	-	-	3	1	3	1
CLEMENTS RW	1894-1898	21	14	-	-	16	6	9	4	83	47	129	71
COE	1896-1897	-	-	-	-	-	-	-	-	1	0	1	0
COLEMAN A	1893-1895	-	-	-	-	-	-	1	0	2	0	3	0
COLLINS JS	1894-1897	2	0	-	-	2	0	6	0	58	1	68	1
CONU	1885-1886	-	-	-	-	-	-	-	-	1	0	1	0
COOK HJ	1896-1897	-	-	-	-	-	-	-	-	1	0	1	0
COPELAND DC	1899-1905	146	51	60	21	-	-	20	3	77	35	303	110
COQUET E	1907-1908	6	0	-	-	-	-	-	-	1	0	7	0
COTTRELL F	1883-1896	-	-	-	-	-	-	1	0	48	19	49	19
COULSON W	1891-1892	-	-	-	-	-	-	-	-	3	0	3	0
COUSINS AC	1907-1908	2	0	1	0	-	-	-	-	-	-	3	0
CRAIG	1896-1897	-	-	-	-	-	-	-	-	1	0	1	0
CROSSLEY AJ	1888-1893	-	-	-	-	-	-	-	-	3	0	3	0
CRUMP WH	1895-1900	31	2	-	-	24	3	4	3	47	5	106	13
CUBBERLEY AW	1892-1895	-	-	-	-	-	-	5	1	43	6	48	7
CULLEN J	1897-1899	43	-	-	-	32	0	12	0	39	0	126	0
DARNELL J	1905-1908	34	1	21	0	-	-	1	0	9	0	65	1
DAVIDSON J	1897-1898	17	5	-	-	13	1	-	-	16	9	46	15
DAVIES RO	1889-1890	-	-	-	-	-	-	-	-	1	0	1	0
DAWSON J	1895-1896	-	-	-	-	-	-	-	-	3	0	3	0
DEVLIN J	1896-1897	21	2	-	-	12	2	3	0	24	1	60	4
DEXTER F	1883-1884	-	-	-	-	-	-	-	-	1	0	1	0
DICKIE RS	1894-1895	-	-	-	-	-	-	-	-	3	0	3	0
DINGWELL W	1891-1892	-	-	-	-	-	-	-	-	2	0	2	0
DIXON A	1907-1908	5	0	6	0	-	-	-	-	1	0	12	0
DOW W	1906-1907	9	3	5	0	-	-	-	-	3	0	17	3
DOWNIE E	1897-1899	11	0	-	-	9	0	-	-	18	0	38	0
DRYBURGH W	1902-1903	16	2	5	0	-	-	4	1	7	0	32	3
DRYSDALE	1890-1891	-	-	-	-	-	-	-	-	1	0	1	0
EAMES W	1906-1907	7	2	4	0	-	-	-	-	2	2	13	4
EARLE	1904-1905	-	-	-	-	-	-	-	-	1	0	1	0
ECCLES JW	1894-1896	-	-	-	-	-	-	6	3	22	6	28	9
EDWARDS A	1896-1897	-	-	-	-	-	-	-	-	3	0	3	0
EDWARDS F	1894-1895	-	-	-	-	-	-	-	-	1	1	1	1
EDWARDS HC	1893-1894	-	-	-	-	-	-	-	-	1	0	1	0
EGGETT JH	1904-1907	66	0	31	0	-	-	8	0	14	0	119	0
ELLIOTT A	1894-1895	-	-	-	-	-	-	-	-	1	0	1	0
ELLIS H	1891-1894	-	-	-	-	-	-	-	-	24	0	24	0
ERENTZ H	1898-1904	132	0	45	0	19	1	21	0	85 / 1	1	302 / 1	2
EVERDELL MJ	1894-1895	-	-	-	-	-	-	-	-	1	0	1	0
FENN	1894-1895	-	-	-	-	-	-	-	-	1	0	1	0
FINCH P	1900-1901	-	-	1	0	-	-	-	-	-	-	1	0
FINCHAM EJ	1893-1894	-	-	-	-	-	-	-	-	5	1	5	1
FISHER JT	1883-1884	-	-	-	-	-	-	-	-	1	0	1	0
FITCHIE TT	1901-1902	1	0	-	-	-	-	-	-	1	1	2	1
FLEMING W	1896-1897	2	1	-	-	-	-	-	-	3	2	5	3
FLOWERS	1895-1896	-	-	-	-	-	-	-	-	1	0	1	0
FORTNAM	1892-1893	-	-	-	-	-	-	-	-	3	2	3	2
FORTNUM W	1900-1901	2	1	-	-	-	-	-	-	-	-	2	1
FOX C	1891-1892	-	-	-	-	-	-	-	-	3	0	3	0
FREDERICKS GH	1902-1903	1	0	1	1	-	-	-	-	-	-	2	1
FREEBOROUGH J	1904-1906	2	0	12	1	-	-	-	-	6	0	20	1
GAIR	1896-1897	-	-	-	-	-	-	-	-	1	0	1	0
GALLACHER P	1904-1905	-	-	1	0	-	-	-	-	4	0	5	0
GAMBLE S	1892-1893	-	-	-	-	-	-	-	-	2	0	2	0
GARDINER	1896-1897	-	-	-	-	-	-	-	-	5	1	5	1
GAUDSON CG	1905-1906	-	-	1	0	-	-	-	-	1	0	2	0

Player	Played	STHN LGE App	Gls	WEST LGE App	Gls	UTD LGE App	Gls	FA CUP App	Gls	OTHERS App	Gls	TOTAL App	Gls
GEORGE JS	1904-1906	5	1	5	0	-	-	-	-	6	0	16	1
GIBSON W	1905-1906	-	-	-	-	-	-	-	-	1	0	1	0
GILDERSON E	1892-1894	-	-	-	-	-	-	-	-	2	1	2	1
GILHOOLY P	1901-1904	18	2	16	3	-	-	3	0	24	3	61	8
GILMORE J	1895-1896	-	-	-	-	-	-	2	0	2	0	4	0
GIPPS T	1907-1908	-	-	1	0	-	-	-	-	-	-	1	0
GLEN A	1904-1906	32	12	16	3	-	-	8	1	10	8	66	24
GODDARD H	1888-1889	-	-	-	-	-	-	-	-	1	0	1	0
GODFREY H	1894-1895	-	-	-	-	-	-	-	-	1	0	1	0
GOODALL D	1894-1896	-	-	-	-	-	-	4	4	18	13	22	17
GOODMAN A	1896-1897	-	-	-	-	-	-	-	-	1	0	1	0
GORMAN W	1893-1894	-	-	-	-	-	-	-	-	3	0	3	0
GRAY JA	1907-1908	15	0	5	0	-	-	1	0	3	0	24	0
GRIFFITH	1889-1890	-	-	-	-	-	-	-	-	1	0	1	0
GRIFFITHS FJ	1901-1902	9	0	7	0	-	-	3	0	4	0	23	0
GRIFFITHS	1893-1894	-	-	-	-	-	-	-	-	1	0	1	0
GROVES	1906-1907	-	-	-	-	-	-	-	-	1	0	1	0
HADDOW D	1899-1901	26	0	7	0	-	-	1	0	23	0	57	0
HAIG-BROWN AR	1901-1903	4	0	-	-	-	-	-	-	3	0	7	0
HALL AR	1897-1899	24	0	-	-	19	0	2	1	29	0	74	1
HARDING A	1906-1907	-	-	-	-	-	-	-	-	1	0	1	0
HARGREAVES	1897-1899	-	-	-	-	1	0	-	-	1	0	2	0
HARKINS H	1891-1892	-	-	-	-	-	-	-	-	1	0	1	0
HARSTON W	1883-1893	-	-	-	-	-	-	-	-	37	12	37	12
HART W	1892-1893	-	-	-	-	-	-	-	-	5	0	5	0
HARTLEY J	1897-1899	18	9	-	-	17	9	3	1	27	16	65	35
HATFIELD T	1896-1897	1	0	-	-	1	0	-	-	8	0	10	0
HAWLEY J	1900-1901	3	2	2	0	-	-	-	-	1	1	6	3
HAY W	1894-1897	-	-	-	-	-	-	1	0	4	0	5	0
HEPBURN AE	1891-1894	-	-	-	-	-	-	-	-	9	5	9	5
HEWITT C	1906-1907	30	11	8	1	-	-	5	0	6	3	49	15
HICKLING W	1905-1906	-	-	1	0	-	-	-	-	-	-	1	0
HICKSON	1898-1899	-	-	-	-	-	-	-	-	5	0	5	0
HOBSON	1896-1897	-	-	-	-	1	1	-	-	2	0	3	1
HOUSTON R	1902-1903	9	2	8	3	-	-	-	-	12	7	29	12
HUBBLE JC	1902-1903	-	-	-	-	-	-	-	-	1	0	1	0
HUDSON EG	1898-1901	1	0	-	-	-	-	-	-	-	-	1	0
HUDSON W	1887-1888	-	-	-	-	-	-	-	-	1	0	1	0
HUDSON	1898-1899	-	-	-	-	-	-	-	-	1	0	1	0
HUGHES E	1899-1908	152	9	62	4	-	-	31	2	73/1	5	318/1	20
HUGHES M	1895-1896	-	-	-	-	-	-	-	-	1	0	1	0
HUMBER C	1889-1890	-	-	-	-	-	-	-	-	3	2	3	2
HUNTER P	1894-1897	-	-	-	-	1	0	11	6	65	47	77	53
HURRY J	1891-1895	-	-	-	-	-	-	-	-	3	0	3	0
HYDE LJ	1899-1902	17	5	8	0	-	-	-	-	20	4	45	9
JACKSON	1893-1894	-	-	-	-	-	-	-	-	1	0	1	0
JANES	1896-1897	-	-	-	-	-	-	-	-	1	0	1	0
JENKINS	1907-1908	-	-	-	-	-	-	-	-	1	0	1	0
JOEL	1891-1892	-	-	-	-	-	-	-	-	1	0	1	0
JOHNSON A	1894-1895	-	-	-	-	-	-	-	-	1	0	1	0
JONES AE	1900-1901	8	1	10	5	-	-	-	-	7	1	25	7
JONES J	1900-1904	32	19	16	9	-	-	5	2	14	10	67	40
JONES JL	1897-1907	132	7	38	3	26	2	31	1	110	3	337	16
JONES R	1893-1894	-	-	-	-	-	-	-	-	1	0	1	0
JONES W	1906-1907	8	0	2	1	-	-	-	-	4	1	14	2
JONES	1894-1895	-	-	-	-	-	-	-	-	2	2	2	2
JONES	1896-1897	-	-	-	-	-	-	-	-	1	0	1	0
JOYCE W	1897-1899	40	33	-	-	33	21	12	8	34	31	119	93
JULIAN JW	1894-1896	-	-	-	-	-	-	5	0	27	3	32	3
JULL H	1891-1892	-	-	-	-	-	-	-	-	1	0	1	0
JULL JC	1883-1897	-	-	-	-	2	0	8	0	148	24	158	24
JULL TE	1894-1897	-	-	-	-	1	0	-	-	3	0	4	0
KEITH	1896-1897	-	-	-	-	-	-	-	-	1	0	1	0
KERRY AHG	1898-1899	-	-	-	-	-	-	-	-	2	0	2	0
KIMBALL SB	1906-1907	-	-	-	-	-	-	-	-	1	0	1	0
KING AH	1893-1894	-	-	-	-	-	-	-	-	1	0	1	0
KINGAN	1893-1894	-	-	-	-	-	-	-	-	1	0	1	0
KIRWAN J	1899-1907	156	40	63	16	-	-	24	2	102/1	39	345/1	97
KNOWLES J	1897-1898	19	0	-	-	14	0	1	0	16/1	0	50/1	0

Player	Played	STHN LGE App	Gls	WEST LGE App	Gls	UTD LGE App	Gls	FA CUP App	Gls	OTHERS App	Gls	TOTAL App	Gls
KYLE P	1905-1906	25	8	10	6	-	-	4	3	2	2	41	19
LANHAM CH	1895-1897	2	0	-	-	3	1	1	0	31	16	37	17
LATHAM	1896-1897	-	-	-	-	1	0	-	-	1	0	2	0
LATYMER	1888-1889	-	-	-	-	-	-	-	-	1	0	1	0
LAYCOCK	1894-1895	-	-	-	-	-	-	-	-	1	1	1	1
LEACH G	1905-1907	2	2	5	1	-	-	-	-	3	1	10	4
LEACH-LEWIS AF	1903-1905	2	0	-	-	-	-	-	-	1	0	3	0
LEAMAN S	1883-1890	-	-	-	-	-	-	-	-	2	0	2	0
LEE J	1907-1908	-	-	1	0	-	-	-	-	-	-	1	0
LEECH W	1898-1899	4	2	-	-	2	1	-	-	8	6	14	9
LEESE FJ	1891-1892	-	-	-	-	-	-	-	-	2	0	2	0
LEESE H	1891-1892	-	-	-	-	-	-	-	-	12	4	12	4
LEIGH AK	1900-1901	-	-	1	0	-	-	-	-	-	-	1	0
LEVY	1899-1900	-	-	-	-	-	-	-	-	1	0	1	0
LINDSAY J	1895-1896	-	-	-	-	-	-	-	-	4	1	4	1
LITTLEFORD A	1889-1890	-	-	-	-	-	-	-	-	5	0	5	0
LOGAN A	1895-1896	-	-	-	-	-	-	-	-	19	14	19	14
LOMAS J	1892-1893	-	-	-	-	-	-	-	-	2	0	2	0
LOMAS W	1883-1887	-	-	-	-	-	-	-	-	3	0	3	0
LOVIS F	1883-1894	-	-	-	-	-	-	-	-	23	3	23	3
LOVIS H	1892-1893	-	-	-	-	-	-	-	-	1	1	1	1
LOVIS J	1892-1893	-	-	-	-	-	-	-	-	1	0	1	0
LOVIS P	1892-1893	-	-	-	-	-	-	-	-	2	0	2	0
LOVIS S	1889-1893	-	-	-	-	-	-	-	-	5	1	5	1
McCONACHIE J	1903-1904	6	0	3	0	-	-	-	-	1	1	10	1
McCURDY W	1904-1905	12	0	10	0	-	-	-	-	7	0	29	0
McDERMOTT W	1896-1897	-	-	-	-	-	-	-	-	2	0	2	0
McDIARMID F	1906-1907	7	0	4	0	-	-	-	-	3	0	14	0
MacDONALD A	1893-1894	-	-	-	-	-	-	-	-	1	0	1	0
McELHANEY J	1894-1895	-	-	-	-	-	-	-	-	4	3	4	3
McELHANEY R	1896-1897	19	6	-	-	11	1	3	1	20	10	53	18
McGAHEY C	1893-1896	-	-	-	-	-	-	-	-	18/1	0	18/1	0
McINROY	1895-1896	-	-	-	-	-	-	-	-	1	0	1	0
McKAY K	1898-1899	18	5	-	-	14	5	9	1	12	14	53	25
McKENZIE LH	1894-1896	-	-	-	-	-	-	1	0	9	0	10	0
MacLACHLAN CF	1893-1894	-	-	-	-	-	-	-	-	15	2	15	2
McMILLAN	1905-1906	-	-	1	0	-	-	-	-	-	-	1	0
McNAIR WD	1907-1908	15	5	8	2	-	-	1	0	3	0	27	7
McNAUGHT JR	1898-1907	104	0	35	3	14	1	13	1	87	4	253	9
MADDEN J	1897-1898	2	0	-	-	4	0	-	-	2	0	8	0
MAIR J	1896-1897	2	0	-	-	7	0	-	-	10	0	19	0
MANNING GS	1907-1908	33	0	10	0	-	-	1	0	5	0	49	0
MAPLEY PJ	1903-1905	5	0	2	0	-	-	-	-	3	0	10	0
MARJORAM A	1895-1897	-	-	-	-	-	-	-	-	4	0	4	0
MARKHAM E	1892-1899	3	0	4	0	-	-	-	-	11	0	18	0
MARKHAM F	1892-1897	-	-	-	-	-	-	-	-	15	0	15	0
MARKHAM W	1892-1897	-	-	-	-	-	-	-	-	2	0	2	0
MARPOLE	1889-1890	-	-	-	-	-	-	-	-	2	0	2	0
MASON W	1884-1890	-	-	-	-	-	-	-	-	20	8	20	8
MASSEY FJ	1907-1908	-	-	3	0	-	-	-	-	-	-	3	0
MAYOR	1894-1895	-	-	-	-	-	-	-	-	1	0	1	0
MEADE TG	1897-1899	15	5	-	-	2	1	2	2	13	7	32	15
MEARNS FC	1903-1904	5	0	4	0	-	-	-	-	6	0	15	0
MEATES WP	1899-1900	-	-	-	-	-	-	-	-	1	0	1	0
MEGGS J	1892-1894	-	-	-	-	-	-	-	-	4	1	4	1
MELIA J	1898-1901	38	1	4	0	9	0	3	0	38	2	92	3
MIDDLEMISS H	1907-1908	25	8	2	1	-	-	-	-	2	0	29	9
MILARVIE	1896-1897	-	-	-	-	-	-	-	-	1	0	1	0
MILLARD	1891-1892	-	-	-	-	-	-	-	-	3	2	3	2
MILLER W	1891-1892	-	-	-	-	-	-	-	-	5	1	5	1
MILLIGAN	1896-1897	-	-	-	-	-	-	-	-	1	0	1	0
MILLIKEN J	1896-1897	19	6	-	-	11	3	3	0	20	5	53	14
MILLS J	1893-1894	-	-	-	-	-	-	-	-	9	1	9	1
MILNE S	1893-1894	-	-	-	-	-	-	-	-	11	2	11	2
MILNES FH	1905-1906	-	-	2	0	-	-	-	-	-	-	2	0
MILTON HA	1903-1905	1	0	3	0	-	-	-	-	-	-	4	0
MINTER WJ	1907-1908	9	4	-	-	-	-	-	-	1	0	10	4
MOFFATT J	1900-1901	6	3	2	0	-	-	-	-	4	0	12	3
MOLES WJ	1900-1903	4	0	3	0	-	-	-	-	3	0	10	0

Player	Played	STHN LGE		WEST LGE		UTD LGE		FA CUP		OTHERS		TOTAL	
		App	Gls	App	Gls	App	Gls	App	Gls	App	Gls	App	Gls
MONK CV	1891-1896	-	-	-	-	-	-	2	0	67	1	69	1
MONK S	1897-1898	-	-	-	-	-	-	-	-	2	0	2	0
MONTGOMERY	1901-1902	-	-	-	-	-	-	-	-	4	0	4	0
MONTGOMERY J	1895-1898	36	0	-	-	19	0	5	0	72	1	132	1
MOODY R	1892-1894	-	-	-	-	-	-	-	-	26	0	26	0
MORDIN WB	1893-1894	-	-	-	-	-	-	-	-	1	0	1	0
MORGAN C	1904-1905	-	-	1	0	-	-	-	-	3	0	4	0
MORRIS T	1899-1908	239	21	80	11	-	-	32	0	89	12	440	44
MURRAY WB	1904-1906	21	0	15	0	-	-	1	0	8	1	45	1
NESBIT	1893-1894	-	-	-	-	-	-	-	-	1	1	1	1
NEWBIGGING WM	1896-1897	10	2	-	-	11	4	3	3	23	14	47	23
NEWBURY	1893-1894	-	-	-	-	-	-	-	-	1	0	1	0
NEWBY W	1893-1895	-	-	-	-	-	-	-	-	19	1	19	1
NEWMAN	1894-1895	-	-	-	-	-	-	-	-	1	0	1	0
NIXON AC	1894-1895	-	-	-	-	-	-	-	-	1	0	1	0
OATES	1896-1897	-	-	-	-	-	-	-	-	1	0	1	0
O'DONNELL	1904-1905	-	-	-	-	-	-	-	-	1	0	1	0
O'HAGAN C	1904-1906	19	5	15	2	-	-	3	1	14	17	51	25
OLIVER J	1894-1895	-	-	-	-	-	-	-	-	1	0	1	0
OTHER AN	1887-1888	-	-	-	-	-	-	-	-	1	0	1	0
OWEN ML	1895-1896	-	-	-	-	-	-	1	1	3	0	4	1
PAGE G	1905-1907	1	0	1	0	-	-	-	-	-	-	2	0
PALMER	1892-1893	-	-	-	-	-	-	-	-	1	1	1	1
PANGBOURNE T	1900-1901	2	0	-	-	-	-	-	-	6	1	8	1
PARKER G	1888-1890	-	-	-	-	-	-	-	-	2	1	2	1
PASS JE	1907-1908	18	5	9	6	-	-	1	0	3	0	31	11
PAYNE	1888-1889	-	-	-	-	-	-	-	-	1	1	1	1
PAYNE E	1893-1899	20	6	-	-	11	1	14	6	95	49	140	62
PAYNE GC	1906-1908	7	3	4	2	-	-	-	-	3	3	14	8
PAYNE Jnr	1894-1895	-	-	-	-	-	-	-	-	1	1	1	1
PERRIN PA	1893-1894	-	-	-	-	-	-	-	-	1	0	1	0
PERRY	1889-1891	-	-	-	-	-	-	-	-	2	1	2	1
PICKETT AE	1906-1908	28	6	4	1	-	-	-	-	3	0	35	7
PILBROW W	1890-1891	-	-	-	-	-	-	-	-	1	1	1	1
PILCH RG	1903-1905	-	-	1	0	-	-	-	-	2	0	3	0
PRACEY A	1899-1890	-	-	-	-	-	-	-	-	1	0	1	0
PRATT T	1899-1900	30	25	-	-	-	-	1	0	29	29	60	54
PRYOR H	1894-1896	-	-	-	-	-	-	6	4	26	6	32	10
PURDIE T	1886-1889	-	-	-	-	-	-	-	-	2	3	2	3
QUINN D	1902-1904	1	0	3	0	-	-	-	-	9	2	13	2
RABY J	1899-1900	2	0	-	-	-	-	-	-	10	7	12	7
RAINBIRD HA	1902-1903	-	-	2	1	-	-	-	-	3	3	5	4
RANDALL W	1883-1887	-	-	-	-	-	-	-	-	11	6	11	6
REGAN CD	1895-1897	-	-	-	-	1	0	-	-	4	0	5	0
REID J	1906-1908	36	20	8	6	-	-	7	2	8	7	59	35
REILLY MM	1906-1907	19	0	6	0	-	-	7	0	4	0	36	0
RENALS JH	1893-1894	-	-	-	-	-	-	-	-	10	1	10	1
REYNOLDS	1894-1895	-	-	-	-	-	-	-	-	2	1	2	1
RICKHAM	1906-1907	-	-	-	-	-	-	-	-	1	0	1	0
RISLEY J	1894-1895	-	-	-	-	-	-	-	-	1	0	1	0
ROBERTS W	1899-1900	-	-	-	-	-	-	-	-	3	1	3	1
ROBERTSON	1896-1897	1	1	-	-	-	-	-	-	4	2	5	3
ROSE L	1892-1895	-	-	-	-	-	-	-	-	11	1	11	1
ROSS G	1895-1896	-	-	-	-	-	-	-	-	1	0	1	0
RULE AG	1898-1900	7	2	-	-	1	0	-	-	4	3	12	5
RUSSELL WH	1895-1896	-	-	-	-	-	-	-	-	1	1	1	1
SANDS	1900-1901	-	-	1	0	-	-	-	-	-	-	1	0
SCOTT WJ	1896-1897	-	-	-	-	-	-	-	-	3	0	3	0
SEEBURG MP	1907-1908	15	5	8	2	-	-	-	-	4	4	27	11
SHACKLETON J	1905-1906	3	1	6	0	-	-	-	-	-	-	9	1
SHAW WB	1893-1895	-	-	-	-	-	-	-	-	6	2	6	2
SHEARING W	1893-1894	-	-	--	-	-	-	-	-	1	0	1	0
SHEPHERD WJ	1891-1897	-	-	-	-	1	0	8	0	63	2	72	2
SHILLINGWORTH	1891-1892	-	-	-	-	-	-	-	-	1	0	1	0
SIMMONDS H	1893-1895	-	-	-	-	-	-	-	-	5	3	5	3
SIMONDS SR	1906-1907	-	-	-	-	-	-	-	-	1	1	1	1
SIMPSON H	1889-1895	-	-	-	-	-	-	-	-	17	1	17	1
SMITH AE	1903-1904	-	-	-	-	-	-	-	-	1	0	1	0
SMITH F	1894-1896	-	-	-	-	-	-	-	-	6	0	6	0

Player	Played	STHN LGE		WEST LGE		UTD LGE		FA CUP		OTHERS		TOTAL	
		App	Gls	App	Gls	App	Gls	App	Gls	App	Gls	App	Gls
SMITH T	1898-1907	94	25	18	4	18	2	20	2	75	22	225	55
SOULSBY T	1901-1902	-	-	-	-	-	-	-	-	2	0	2	0
SPENCE C	1906-1907	-	-	-	-	-	-	-	-	1	1	1	1
STANSFIELD H	1904-1908	48	9	27	3	-	-	6	0	17	4	98	16
STARK SG	1895-1896	-	-	-	-	-	-	-	-	1	0	1	0
STEEL D	1906-1908	32	1	9	1	-	-	1	0	5	1	47	3
STEVEN	1902-1903	-	-	-	-	-	-	-	-	2	0	2	0
STEVENS RC	1899-1903	-	-	2	0	-	-	-	-	3	0	5	0
STEVENSON J	1900-1904	4	0	10	0	-	-	-	-	11	0	25	0
STIRLING	1894-1895	-	-	-	-	-	-	-	-	5	1	5	1
STOKELEY	1896-1897	-	-	-	-	1	0	-	-	-	-	1	0
STORMONT R	1897-1907	93	8	13	2	33	8	14	1	83	5	236	24
SULLIVAN	1894-1895	-	-	-	-	-	-	-	-	1	0	1	0
SUNDERLAND	1896-1897	-	-	-	-	-	-	-	-	2	0	2	0
SWANN A	1904-1905	2	0	4	1	-	-	-	-	3	1	9	2
SYKES JL	1891-1896	-	-	-	-	-	-	-	-	56	14	56	14
TAIT AG	1899-1908	207	3	79	2	-	-	36	0	100	7	422	12
TANNAHILL R	1897-1898	11	3	-	-	5	3	2	0	10	3	28	9
TARBOLTON	1893-1894	-	-	-	-	-	-	-	-	1	0	1	0
TAYLOR S	1893-1894	-	-	-	-	-	-	-	-	6	2	6	2
THORBURN	1896-1897	-	-	-	-	-	-	-	-	2	0	2	0
THORNLEY JW	1892-1893	-	-	-	-	-	-	-	-	1	0	1	0
TURNER AD	1903-1904	6	5	3	0	-	-	-	-	4	1	13	6
TYLER W	1891-1892	-	-	-	-	-	-	-	-	11	5	11	5
TYRELL W	1883-1893	-	-	-	-	-	-	-	-	21	1	21	1
VAUGHAN	1903-1904	-	-	-	-	-	-	-	-	1	0	1	0
WAINWRIGHT W	1904-1905	-	-	-	-	-	-	-	-	1	0	1	0
WALFORD FS	1889-1891	-	-	-	-	-	-	-	-	8	0	8	0
WALKER RH	1906-1908	24	3	3	0	-	-	1	0	5	1	33	4
WALLER WH	1898-1900	4	0	-	-	1	0	-	-	-	-	5	0
WALTON J	1903-1908	102	23	49	12	-	-	14	4	23	9	188	48
WARD-LEAVER J	1894-1895	-	-	-	-	-	-	-	-	1	0	1	0
WARNER AC	1902-1905	47	13	22	3	-	-	5	0	20	14	94	30
WATSON A	1883-1884	-	-	-	-	-	-	-	-	4	2	4	2
WATSON C	1906-1907	-	-	1	0	-	-	-	-	3	0	4	0
WATSON J	1902-1908	104	0	47	0	-	-	23	0	26	0	200	0
WELCH A	1895-1896	-	-	-	-	-	-	-	-	1	0	1	0
WELHAM JW	1892-1895	-	-	-	-	-	-	3	0	50	2	53	2
WESTON S	1891-1893	-	-	-	-	-	-	-	-	8	4	8	4
WHITBOURNE JG	1905-1908	19	0	10	0	-	-	-	-	4	0	33	0
WHYMAN A	1905-1908	18	1	11	5	-	-	-	-	6	4	35	10
WILKINSON	1894-1895	-	-	-	-	-	-	-	-	1	1	1	1
WILKINSON J	1906-1907	2	0	-	-	-	-	-	-	3	0	5	0
WILLIAMS CA	1902-1905	37	0	20	0	-	-	5	0	24	0	86	0
WILLIAMS FG	1891-1892	-	-	-	-	-	-	-	-	1	0	1	0
WILLIAMS T	1895-1896	-	-	-	-	-	-	1	0	2	0	3	0
WILSON F	1896-1897	5	3	-	-	3	1	-	-	2	1	10	5
WOOD	1893-1894	-	-	-	-	-	-	-	-	1	0	1	0
WOODRUFF CL	1907-1908	5	3	-	-	-	-	-	-	-	-	5	3
WOODWARD VJ	1900-1908	105	45	15	7	-	-	20	5	24	25	164	82
YATES	1904-1905	-	-	-	-	-	-	-	-	1	0	1	0
OWN GOALS	1882-1908	-	8	-	2	-	3	-	1	-	8	-	22

Paul Allen

TOTTENHAM HOTSPUR
Career Records 1908-09 to 1992-93

Player	Played	LEAGUE App	Gls	FA CUP App	Gls	LG CUP App	Gls	EUROPE App	Gls	OTHERS App	Gls	TOTAL App	Gls
ACQUROFF J	1945-1946	0	0	0	0	0	0	0	0	2	2	2	2
ADAMS CJ	1950-1953	6	1	0	0	0	0	0	0	5/1	5	11/1	6
ADAMS D	1954-1955	0	0	0	0	0	0	0	0	2	0	2	0
ADAMS WH	1943-1946	0	0	1	0	0	0	0	0	11	0	12	0
AITCHISON BG	1960-1961	0	0	0	0	0	0	0	0	1	1	1	1
ALEKSIC MA	1978-1982	25	0	7	0	0	0	0	0	23/3	0	55/3	0
ALEXANDER S	1936-1937	9	1	0	0	0	0	0	0	0	0	9	1
ALLEN CD	1984-1988	97/8	60	11/1	9	13/1	13	3/1	2	32/6	28	156/17	112
ALLEN J	1932-1933	1	1	0	0	0	0	0	0	0	0	1	1
ALLEN LW	1959-1965	119	47	15	13	0	0	3	1	10	14	147	75
ALLEN PK	1985-	276/15	25	26/1	1	42/2	4	6/1	0	90/5	3	440/24	33
ALSFORD WJ	1930-1937	81	0	9	0	0	0	0	0	10	2	100	2
ANDERSON A	1944-1945	0	0	0	0	0	0	0	0	1	0	1	0
ANDERTON D	1992-	32/2	5	4/1	1	2	1	0	0	7/4	4	45/7	11
ANDREWS D	1983-1984	0	0	0	0	0	0	0	0	0/1	0	0/1	0
ARCHIBALD J	1919-1922	24	1	1	0	0	0	0	0	8	0	33	1
ARCHIBALD S	1980-1988	128/3	58	17/1	5	18	7	22	8	25/2	19	210/6	97
ARDILES OC	1978-1991	221/16	16	32	4	31/1	3	8/1	2	92/14	12	384/32	37
ARMSTRONG GJ	1975-1981	65/19	10	6/4	3	3/1	3	0	0	22/13	16	96/37	32
ARMSTRONG JW	1927-1930	28	5	5	0	0	0	0	0	12	9	45	14
ARNOLD W	1940-1941	0	0	0	0	0	0	0	0	1	0	1	0
ASTWOOD	1979	0	0	0	0	0	0	0	0	0/1	0	0/1	0
AUSTIN D	1992-	33/1	0	5	0	2/1	0	0	0	4/4	0	44/6	0
AUSTIN PC	1927-1928	1	0	0	0	0	0	0	0	1	0	2	0
AYRES	1917-1918	0	0	0	0	0	0	0	0	3	0	3	0
BAILY EF	1945-1956	297	64	29	5	0	0	0	0	56	21	382	90
BAKER PRB	1952-1965	299	3	27	0	0	0	16	0	58/2	0	400/2	3
BAKER S	1984-1985	0	0	0	0	0	0	0	0	0/1	0	0/1	0
BALDWIN A	1917-1918	0	0	0	0	0	0	0	0	1	0	1	0
BANKS JA	1913-1923	69	6	9	4	0	0	0	0	131	80	209	90
BANKS K	1985-1986	0	0	0	0	0	0	0	0	0/1	0	0/1	0
BANN WE	1923-1929	12	0	0	0	0	0	0	0	6	0	18	0
BARMBY N	1991-	17/5	5	3/1	3	2/1	0	0	0	5/6	3	27/13	11
BARNARD J	1916-1919	0	0	0	0	0	0	0	0	9	5	9	5
BARNES JCB	1987-1988	0	0	0	0	0	0	0	0	1	0	1	0
BARNETT FW	1922-1929	16	1	0	0	0	0	0	0	1	0	17	1
BARRON G	1942-1943	0	0	0	0	0	0	0	0	1	0	1	0
BARTON KR	1955-1964	4	0	0	0	0	0	0	0	2	0	6	0
BARTON P	1915-1919	0	0	0	0	0	0	0	0	91	6	91	6
BASSETT EJ	1915-1918	0	0	0	0	0	0	0	0	74	37	74	37
BAUCHOP JR	1913-1914	10	6	0	0	0	0	0	0	3	4	13	10
BAY	1918-1919	0	0	0	0	0	0	0	0	1	0	1	0
BEADLE P	1992-	0	0	0	0	0	0	0	0	0/1	0	0/1	0
BEAL P	1963-1980	330/3	1	30	0	27	0	30	0	62/1	0	479/4	1
BEAN R	1979	0	0	0	0	0	0	0	0	0/1	1	0/1	1
BEARMAN A	1916-1917	0	0	0	0	0	0	0	0	1	0	1	0
BEASLEY A	1942-1946	0	0	0	0	0	0	0	0	98	31	98	31
BEATON S	1917-1919	0	0	0	0	0	0	0	0	9	0	9	0
BEAVON MS	1978-1980	3/1	0	0	0	0/1	0	0	0	3/12	3	6/14	3
BEE	1918-1919	0	0	0	0	0	0	0	0	1	0	1	0
BELL S	1934-1937	15	6	1	0	0	0	0	0	1	1	17	7
BELLAMY WR	1926-1935	70	9	3	0	0	0	0	0	11	2	84	11
BENNETT F	1941-1942	0	0	0	0	0	0	0	0	3	0	3	0
BENNETT JK	1918-1919	0	0	0	0	0	0	0	0	4	1	4	1
BENNETT KE	1940-1941	0	0	0	0	0	0	0	0	6	1	6	1
BENNETT LD	1939-1955	273	104	22	14	0	0	0	0	83	52	378	170
BENTLEY FW	1908-1912	38	0	5	0	0	0	0	0	9	0	52	0
BERGSSON G	1988-	51/20	2	2/2	0	4/2	0	5/1	0	26/7	1	88/32	3
BING TE	1957-1958	1	0	0	0	0	0	0	0	2/2	0	3/2	0
BIRD	1917-1918	0	0	0	0	0	0	0	0	1	0	1	0
BIRNIE EL	1910-1911	4	1	0	0	0	0	0	0	1	0	5	1

Steve Archibald

Player	Played	LEAGUE App	Gls	FA CUP App	Gls	LG CUP App	Gls	EUROPE App	Gls	OTHERS App	Gls	TOTAL App	Gls
BLAIR J	1945-1946	0	0	0	0	0	0	0	0	2	1	2	1
BLAIR JG	1925-1928	29	15	1	0	0	0	0	0	2	1	32	16
BLAKE FJC	1918-1919	0	0	0	0	0	0	0	0	1	0	1	0
BLAKE HE	1921-1924	51	0	5	0	0	0	0	0	6	0	62	0
BLANCHFLOWER RD	1954-1964	337	15	33	4	0	0	12	2	54/1	6	436/1	27
BLISS H	1911-1923	195	91	21	13	0	0	0	0	99/1	64	315/1	168
BLYTH J	1936-1937	11	0	0	0	0	0	0	0	0	0	11	0
BOLAN LA	1933-1935	10	3	0	0	0	0	0	0	3	0	13	3
BOND DJT	1966-1971	20/3	1	0	0	2/1	0	1	0	8/1	2	31/5	3
BOREHAM F	1908-1910	20	0	0	0	0	0	0	0	15	0	35	0
BOULTON FP	1944-1945	0	0	0	0	0	0	0	0	1	0	1	0
BOWEN RM	1983-1987	14/3	2	3	0	0	0	0	0	7/14	0	24/17	2
BOWERING EG	1911-1912	7	0	0	0	0	0	0	0	2	0	9	0
BOWGETT P	1978-1979	0	0	0	0	0	0	0	0	0/1	0	0/1	0
BOWLER GH	1913-1919	3	0	0	0	0	0	0	0	3	0	6	0
BRACE RL	1983-1984	0/1	0	0	0	0	0	0	0	0	0	0/1	0
BRADY WL	1983-1984	0	0	0	0	0	0	0	0	1	1	1	1
BRAIN J	1931-1935	45	10	2	0	0	0	0	0	2	0	49	10
BRANDHAM J	1918-1919	0	0	0	0	0	0	0	0	1	0	1	0
BRAWN WF	1918-1919	0	0	0	0	0	0	0	0	1	0	1	0
BRAZIL AB	1982-1984	29/2	9	1	0	0/1	0	3/2	4	14/2	8	47/7	21
BRIGGS C	1942-1944	0	0	0	0	0	0	0	0	3	0	3	0
BRITTAN C	1950-1958	41	1	4	0	0	0	0	0	10	0	55	1
BRITTAN RC	1911-1914	42	0	2	0	0	0	0	0	9	0	53	0
BRITTON J	1925-1928	40	0	0	0	0	0	0	0	3	0	43	0
BROADIS IA	1940-1946	0	0	0	0	0	0	0	0	85	38	85	38
BROOKE GJ	1980-1985	49/24	15	4/8	1	4/1	1	6/5	1	21/7	7	84/45	25
BROOKS	1918-1919	0	0	0	0	0	0	0	0	1	0	1	0
BROOKS J	1952-1960	166	46	13	5	0	0	0	0	43	21	222	72
BROOKS S	1922-1924	10	1	0	0	0	0	0	0	6	2	16	3
BROTHERSTON N	1975-1976	1	0	0	0	0	0	0	0	1/1	0	2/1	0
BROUGH J	1908-1909	1	0	1	0	0	0	0	0	1	0	3	0
BROWN	1917-1918	0	0	0	0	0	0	0	0	2	0	2	0
BROWN DC	1909-1910	1	0	0	0	0	0	0	0	0	0	1	0
BROWN HT	1944-1945	0	0	0	0	0	0	0	0	3	0	3	0
BROWN IRJ	1909-1911	13	0	0	0	0	0	0	0	6	6	19	6
BROWN J	1936-1937	4	0	0	0	0	0	0	0	0	0	4	0
BROWN L	1963-1966	62	3	3	0	0	0	0	0	21/1	0	86/1	3
BROWN RE	1966-1967	1	0	0	0	0	0	0	0	0	0	1	0
BROWN RS	1919-1924	37	0	8	0	0	0	0	0	4	0	49	0
BROWN WDF	1959-1967	222	0	23	0	0	0	17	0	30	0	292	0
BROWNE J	1940-1944	0	0	0	0	0	0	0	0	4	0	4	0
BROWNE R	1942-1943	0	0	0	0	0	0	0	0	3	0	3	0
BRYANT B	1943-1944	0	0	0	0	0	0	0	0	7	2	7	2
BUCKINGHAM VF	1935-1949	208	1	26	0	0	0	0	0	77	1	311	2
BULL W	1908-1909	12	0	0	0	0	0	0	0	7	1	19	1
BULLING E	1910-1911	2	0	0	0	0	0	0	0	2	0	4	0
BULLY	1918-1919	0	0	0	0	0	0	0	0	1	0	1	0
BURCHELL GC	1939-1940	0	0	0	0	0	0	0	0	1	0	1	0
BURDITT FCK	1940-1941	0	0	0	0	0	0	0	0	1	0	1	0
BURGESS WAR	1938-1954	301	15	27	1	0	0	0	0	182	46	510	62
BURGON FA	1934-1935	4	0	0	0	0	0	0	0	0	0	4	0
BURKE C	1944-1945	0	0	0	0	0	0	0	0	15	0	15	0
BURLEY B	1942-1943	0	0	0	0	0	0	0	0	1	0	1	0
BURNETT J	1944-1945	0	0	0	0	0	0	0	0	1	2	1	2
BURTON O	1908-1910	38	0	4	0	0	0	0	0	5	0	47	0
BUTCHER G	1915-1916	0	0	0	0	0	0	0	0	1	0	1	0
BUTTERS G	1988-1991	34/1	1	1	0	2/1	0	0	0	12/9	0	49/11	1
CABLE TH	1928-1932	42	0	2	0	0	0	0	0	5	0	49	0
CAIN A	1918-1919	0	0	0	0	0	0	0	0	1	1	1	1
CALDWELL T	1916-1917	0	0	0	0	0	0	0	0	1	0	1	0
CAMPBELL S	1991-	0/1	1	0	0	00	0	0	0	0/2	0	0/3	1
CANTRELL J	1912-1923	159	74	15	10	0	0	0	0	20	11	194	95
CARTWRIGHT W	1913-1915	13	0	2	0	0	0	0	0	6	0	21	0
CASEY J	1916-1917	0	0	0	0	0	0	0	0	1	0	1	0
CASKEY D	1991-	0	0	0	0	0	0	0	0	0/2	0	0/2	0
CASTLE SE	1919-1921	5	0	0	0	0	0	0	0	1	1	6	1
CHANNELL FC	1933-1936	95	1	14	0	0	0	0	0	4	0	113	1
CHAPLIN A	1915-1916	0	0	0	0	0	0	0	0	4	0	4	0
CHAPMAN E	1942-1943	0	0	0	0	0	0	0	0	1	0	1	0

419

Player	Played	LEAGUE App	LEAGUE Gls	FA CUP App	FA CUP Gls	LG CUP App	LG CUP Gls	EUROPE App	EUROPE Gls	OTHERS App	OTHERS Gls	TOTAL App	TOTAL Gls
CHESTER A	1918-1919	0	0	0	0	0	0	0	0	2/1	0	2/1	0
CHIEDOZIE JO	1984-1988	45/8	12	5/3	2	7	0	7	0	22/6	5	86/17	19
CHIPPERFIELD J	1919-1921	15	6	0	0	0	0	0	0	2	0	17	6
CHISHOLM JR	1941-1948	2	0	0	0	0	0	0	0	79	1	81	1
CHIVERS MH	1967-1980	268/10	118	22/2	11	33	23	32	22	47/1	28	402/13	202
CLAESEN NPJ	1986-1988	37/13	18	1/5	2	7	3	0	0	11/3	5	56/21	28
CLARKE DH	1909	0	0	0	0	0	0	0	0	5	4	5	4
CLARKE HA	1948-1957	295	4	27	0	0	0	0	0	58	0	380	4
CLARKE RC	1972-1973	0/1	0	0	0	0	0	0	0	0	0	0/1	0
CLAY T	1913-1929	318	23	33	1	0	0	0	0	156	14	507	38
CLAYTON A	1916-1917	0	0	0	0	0	0	0	0	1	0	1	0
CLAYTON E	1957-1968	88/4	20	9	0	1	0	1	0	26/4	6	125/8	26
CLAYTON S	1942-1944	0	0	0	0	0	0	0	0	3	1	3	1
CLEMENCE RN	1981-1991	240	0	25	0	38	0	27	0	77	1	407	1
CLOSE SC	1985-1988	3/6	0	0	0	3	2	0	0	3/5	6	9/11	8
COATES R	1971-1981	173/15	14	11/1	0	19/3	1	26	9	48/9	6	277/28	30
COCKRAM AC	1983-1984	2	0	0	0	0	0	0	0	0	0	2	0
COLLINS J	1960-1962	2	0	0	0	0	0	0	0	1	0	3	0
COLLINS JL	1965-1966	2	0	0	0	0	0	0	0	0	0	2	0
COLLINS PJ	1968-1974	78/6	4	8/1	0	5/2	1	1/1	0	14/2	3	106/12	8
COLLINS T	1910-1915	115	1	9	0	0	0	0	0	11	0	135	1
COLQUHOUN DW	1931-1935	81	2	6	0	0	0	0	0	4	3	91	5
CONN AJ	1974-1977	35/3	6	2	0	1/2	1	0	0	11/5	3	49/10	10
COOK GW	1929-1931	63	22	4	2	0	0	0	0	6	6	73	30
COOK J	1987-1988	0	0	0	0	0	0	0	0	0/2	0	0/2	0
COOK RK	1949-1950	3	0	0	0	0	0	0	0	0	0	3	0
COOKE RE	1982-1987	9/2	2	1	0	1/1	0	1/2	0	4/11	2	16/16	4
COOMBER G	1917-1918	0	0	0	0	0	0	0	0	14	2	14	2
COOPER J	1981-1982	0	0	0	0	0	0	0	0	0/6	0	0/6	0
COQUET E	1908-1911	78	0	8	1	0	0	0	0	16	0	102	1
CORBETT PA	1980-1983	3/2	1	0	0	0	0	0	0	0/2	0	3/4	1
CORDER P	1983-1984	0	0	0	0	0	0	0	0	0/1	0	0/1	0
COUCHMAN HF	1918-1919	0	0	0	0	0	0	0	0	1	0	1	0
COX FJA	1938-1949	99	15	6	2	0	0	0	0	39	9	144	26
CRAIG	1918-1919	0	0	0	0	0	0	0	0	1	0	1	0
CRESSWELL W	1917-1918	0	0	0	0	0	0	0	0	11	0	11	0
CROFT T	1916-1917	0	0	0	0	0	0	0	0	2	0	2	0
CROFT W	1916-1917	0	0	0	0	0	0	0	0	3	0	3	0
CROMPTON A	1928-1930	15	3	0	0	0	0	0	0	9	5	24	8
CROMPTON GE	1910-1912	9	1	2	0	0	0	0	0	0	0	11	1
CROOK IS	1980-1986	10/10	1	0/1	0	1	0	0/2	0	13/22	2	24/35	3
CROOKS GA	1980-1985	121/4	48	21	9	19/1	9	15/1	9	42/14	30	218/20	105
CROSSLEY C	1916-1917	0	0	0	0	0	0	0	0	1	0	1	0
CROWL SR	1913-1918	1	0	0	0	0	0	0	0	15	1	16	1
CULVERHOUSE IB	1982-1985	1/1	0	0	0	0	0	0	0	5/8	0	6/9	0
CUNDY J	1991-	23/2	1	0	0	2	0	0	0	10/1	1	35/3	2
CURRIE AW	1980-1981	0	0	0	0	0	0	0	0	0/1	0	0/1	0
CURTIS JJ	1908-1913	84	5	7	0	0	0	0	0	25	7	116	12
DAINES BR	1971-1981	146	0	11	0	14	0	2	0	52/11	0	225/11	0
DALGLISH KM	1987-1991	0	0	0	0	0	0	0	0	2	0	2	0
DARNELL J	1908-1919	153	3	10	0	0	0	0	0	99	1	262	4
DAVIE J	1943-1944	0	0	0	0	0	0	0	0	1	0	1	0
DAVIES W	1929-1933	109	19	6	0	0	0	0	0	8	5	123	24
DAY A	1932-1936	13	0	1	0	0	0	0	0	4	0	18	0
DAY P	1979	0	0	0	0	0	0	0	0	1	0	1	0
DEARDEN K	1990-	0/1	0	0	0	1	0	0	0	2/2	0	3/3	0
DENNIS A	1964-1965	0	0	0	0	0	0	0	0	1	0	1	0
DICK AJ	1981-1986	16/1	2	2	0	0	0	3/3	0	7/11	4	28/15	6
DICKER LR	1952-1953	10	2	0	0	0	0	0	0	0	0	10	2
DILLON ML	1972-1975	21/3	1	1	0	1	0	2/1	0	3/1	0	28/5	1
DIMMOCK JH	1918-1931	400	100	38	12	0	0	0	0	53	26	491	138
DITCHBURN EG	1939-1959	419	0	34	0	0	0	0	0	122	0	575	0
DIX RW	1939-1948	39	5	4	0	0	0	0	0	54	14	97	19
DIXON K	1982-1983	0	0	0	0	0	0	0	0	1	0	1	0
DOCKRAY J	1918-1919	0	0	0	0	0	0	0	0	13	0	13	0
DODGE WC	1958-1961	6	0	4	0	0	0	0	0	3	0	13	0
DORLING GC	1939-1940	0	0	0	0	0	0	0	0	14	0	14	0
DOWERS J	1939-1940	0	0	0	0	0	0	0	0	2	0	2	0
DOWNER F	1943-1944	0	0	0	0	0	0	0	0	1	0	1	0
DOWSETT GJ	1951-1955	1	1	0	0	0	0	0	0	0/1	0	1/1	1

Martin Chivers

Player	Played	LEAGUE		FA CUP		LG CUP		EUROPE		OTHERS		TOTAL	
		App	Gls	App	Gls	App	Gls	App	Gls	App	Gls	App	Gls
DOYLE JJ	1915-1916	0	0	0	0	0	0	0	0	1	0	1	0
DRABBLE F	1909-1910	2	0	0	0	0	0	0	0	1	0	3	0
DRAPER	1918-1919	0	0	0	0	0	0	0	0	1	0	1	0
DUFFUS J	1923-1924	0	0	0	0	0	0	0	0	3	0	3	0
DUKE HP	1944-1945	0	0	0	0	0	0	0	0	3	0	3	0
DULIN MC	1954-1958	10	2	1	0	0	0	0	0	14	6	25	8
DUNCAN	1918-1919	0	0	0	0	0	0	0	0	1	0	1	0
DUNCAN A	1934-1943	93	22	10	4	0	0	0	0	81	22	184	48
DUNCAN JP	1974-1979	101/2	53	7	2	10	7	0	0	21/4	13	139/6	75
DUNMORE DGI	1953-1960	75	23	6	3	0	0	0	0	13/3	8	94/3	34
DUNN R	1944-1945	0	0	0	0	0	0	0	0	1	0	1	0
DUQUEMIN LS	1945-1957	275	114	33	17	0	0	0	0	66	53	374	184
DURIE GS	1991-	48	10	2	0	8	3	8	3	6/1	2	72/1	18
DURSTON	1943-1944	0	0	0	0	0	0	0	0	1	0	1	0
DYSON TK	1954-1965	184	41	16	6	0	0	9	8	30/5	13	239/5	68
EADON JP	1914-1915	5	0	0	0	0	0	0	0	1	0	6	0
EASTHAM S	1942-1943	0	0	0	0	0	0	0	0	1	0	1	0
EDINBURGH J	1990-	67/4	1	10	0	9/3	0	3	0	26/5	0	115/12	1
EDRICH WJ	1935-1937	20	4	0	0	0	0	0	0	0	0	20	4
EDWARDS M	1990-1992	0	0	0	0	0	0	0	0	2/6	1	2/6	1
EDWARDS RG	1941-1944	0	0	0	0	0	0	0	0	8	2	8	2
ELKES AJ	1923-1929	191	50	10	1	0	0	0	0	13	6	214	57
ELKIN BHW	1909-1911	26	0	2	0	0	0	0	0	6	0	34	0
ELLIOTT JE	1911-1920	13	4	0	0	0	0	0	0	135	11	148	15
EMBERY B	1965-1966	0	0	0	0	0	0	0	0	1	0	1	0
ENGLAND HM	1966-1975	300	14	32	2	30	0	35	3	37	1	434	20
EVANS A	1927-1929	5	0	0	0	0	0	0	0	2	0	7	0
EVANS J	1943-1944	0	0	0	0	0	0	0	0	1	0	1	0
EVANS N	1939-1940	0	0	0	0	0	0	0	0	1	0	1	0
EVANS R	1943-1944	0	0	0	0	0	0	0	0	1	0	1	0
EVANS RL	1968-1975	133/4	2	7	0	13	0	22/3	2	20/2	1	195/9	5
EVANS T	1929-1937	94	4	7	0	0	0	0	0	7	1	108	5
EVANS W	1930-1937	178	78	17	8	0	0	0	0	8	10	203	96
FAIRCLOUGH CH	1987-1989	60	5	3	0	7	0	0	0	24/3	1	94/3	6
FALCO MP	1977-1987	162/12	68	15	5	19/3	3	21/4	14	76/23	63	293/42	153
FARLEY BH	1949-1954	1	0	0	0	0	0	0	0	6	0	7	0
FEEBURY JH	1916-1917	0	0	0	0	0	0	0	0	1	0	1	0
FELTON W	1931-1934	73	1	2	0	0	0	0	0	3	0	78	1
FENWICK TW	1987-	90/3	8	7	0	14	2	4	0	30/3	5	145/6	15
FERRIER H	1945-1946	0	0	0	0	0	0	0	0	1	0	1	0
FERRIS	1918-1919	0	0	0	0	0	0	0	0	1	0	1	0
FINCH J	1941-1942	0	0	0	0	0	0	0	0	1	0	1	0
FINDLAY A	1920-1921	0	0	0	0	0	0	0	0	1	0	1	0
FINLAY DO	1942-1943	0	0	0	0	0	0	0	0	3	0	3	0
FITZGERALD A	1941-1942	0	0	0	0	0	0	0	0	1	0	1	0
FLACK DW	1940-1941	0	0	0	0	0	0	0	0	5	0	5	0
FLACK WL	1943-1944	0	0	0	0	0	0	0	0	2	0	2	0
FLAVELL R	1944-1945	0	0	0	0	0	0	0	0	15	2	15	2
FLEMING JB	1913-1915	19	3	0	0	0	0	0	0	10	5	39	8
FLEMING W	1917-1918	0	0	0	0	0	0	0	0	1	0	1	0
FLETCHER HD	1945-1946	0	0	0	0	0	0	0	0	1	0	1	0
FLINT K	1947-1948	5	1	0	0	0	0	0	0	0	0	5	1
FORD FGL	1945-1946	0	0	0	0	0	0	0	0	3	0	3	0
FOREMAN AG	1944-1947	36	14	2	0	0	0	0	0	18	25	56	39
FORMAN T	1910-1912	8	1	0	0	0	0	0	0	1	0	9	1
FORSHAW	1918-1919	0	0	0	0	0	0	0	0	1	0	1	0
FORSTER M	1920-1930	236	0	8	0	0	0	0	0	28	0	272	0
FRASER	1918-1919	0	0	0	0	0	0	0	0	1	0	1	0
FREEMAN E	1918-1919	0	0	0	0	0	0	0	0	2	0	2	0
FRENCH W	1918-1922	0	0	0	0	0	0	0	0	4	0	4	0
FRICKER F	1915-1916	0	0	0	0	0	0	0	0	1	0	1	0
FULLWOOD J	1934-1938	34	1	1	0	0	0	0	0	4	0	39	1
FURR WS	1918-1919	0	0	0	0	0	0	0	0	2	0	2	0
GALLOWAY SR	1928-1929	3	2	0	0	0	0	0	0	0	0	3	2
GALVIN A	1978-1988	194/7	20	23/1	2	20/3	3	25	6	88/14	16	350/25	47
GARBUTT H	1929-1930	0	0	0	0	0	0	0	0	4	7	4	7
GARLAND P	1989-1992	0/1	0	0	0	0	0	0	0	1/6	0	1/7	0
GARWOOD LF	1945-1951	2	0	0	0	0	0	0	0	3	0	5	0
GASCOIGNE PJ	1988-	91/1	19	6	6	13/1	8	0	0	28/3	13	138/5	46
GAVIN JT	1954-1956	32	15	2	1	0	0	0	0	9	3	43	19

Player	Played	LEAGUE		FA CUP		LG CUP		EUROPE		OTHERS		TOTAL	
		App	Gls	App	Gls	App	Gls	App	Gls	App	Gls	App	Gls
GEE	1918-1919	0	0	0	0	0	0	0	0	1	0	1	0
GEMMELL G	1913-1914	0	0	1	0	0	0	0	0	0	0	1	0
GIBBINS E	1943-1953	1	0	3	0	0	0	0	0	5	0	9	0
GIBBONS AH	1937-1946	27	13	6	5	0	0	0	0	115	91	148	109
GIBSON TB	1978-1982	16/2	4	5	1	1	1	0/2	1	7/10	9	29/14	16
GILBERG H	1941-1950	2	0	1	0	0	0	0	0	22	9	25	9
GILLINGWATER D	1965-1966	0	0	0	0	0	0	0	0	1	0	1	0
GILZEAN AJ	1964-1975	335/8	93	40	21	27/1	6	27/1	13	62/5	40	491/15	173
GILZEAN I	1988-1992	0	0	0	0	0	0	0	0	0/2	0	0/2	0
GIPPS T	1909-1910	0	0	0	0	0	0	0	0	2	0	2	0
GLEN P	1915-1916	0	0	0	0	0	0	0	0	1	1	1	1
GLIDDON G	1912	0	0	0	0	0	0	0	0	1	0	1	0
GOLDSMITH G	1934-1935	1	0	0	0	0	0	0	0	0	0	1	0
GOLDTHORPE E	1917-1919	0	0	0	0	0	0	0	0	17	9	17	9
GOODMAN A	1940-1945	0	0	0	0	0	0	0	0	2	0	2	0
GOODMAN AA	1919-1920	16	1	1	0	0	0	0	0	3	0	20	1
GORMAN J	1976-1979	30	0	2	0	0	0	0	0	5/5	0	37/5	0
GORMLEY E	1989-1990	0	0	0	0	0	0	0	0	0/2	0	0/2	0
GOSNELL AA	1910-1911	5	0	2	0	0	0	0	0	2	0	9	0
GOUGH RC	1986-1988	49	2	6	0	10	0	0	0	10/1	1	75/1	3
GRAY A	1991-	23/8	2	0	0	0	0	0	0	6/5	2	29/13	4
GRAY P	1986-1992	4/5	0	0/1	0	0	0	0	0	1/20	2	5/26	2
GREAVES JP	1961-1969	322	220	36	32	8	5	14	9	40	40	420	306
GREENFIELD GW	1931-1935	31	11	0	0	0	0	0	0	3	2	34	13
GRENFELL S	1985-1986	0	0	0	0	0	0	0	0	0/1	0	0/1	0
GRICE F	1935-1939	47	1	8	0	0	0	0	0	0	0	55	1
GRIFFITHS J	1945-1946	0	0	0	0	0	0	0	0	1	0	1	0
GRIMES W	1916-1917	0	0	0	0	0	0	0	0	3	1	3	1
GRIMSDELL A	1911-1929	324	26	36	1	0	0	0	0	57	11	417	38
GROVES VG	1952-1954	4	3	0	0	0	0	0	0	0	0	4	3
GRUBB AJ	1952-1953	2	0	0	0	0	0	0	0	0	0	2	0
GURR H	1942-1945	0	0	0	0	0	0	0	0	2	0	2	0
GUTHRIE PJ	1988-1989	0	0	0	0	0	0	0	0	1/4	0	1/4	0
HALL AE	1935-1947	41	10	4	1	0	0	0	0	37	11	82	22
HALL AG	1934-1936	16	3	5	0	0	0	0	0	3	5	24	8
HALL BAC	1933-1934	2	0	0	0	0	0	0	0	0	0	2	0
HALL FW	1944-1946	0	0	0	0	0	0	0	0	23	0	23	0
HALL GW	1932-1944	204	27	20	2	0	0	0	0	151	16	375	45
HALL J	1936-1946	53	0	5	0	0	0	0	0	9	0	67	0
HALLE W	1917-1918	0	0	0	0	0	0	0	0	1	0	1	0
HAMPTON CM	1921-1922	0	0	0	0	0	0	0	0	1	0	1	0
HANCOCK KP	1969-1971	3	0	0	0	1	0	0	0	4	0	8	0
HANDLEY CHJ	1921-1929	120	26	11	9	0	0	0	0	25	14	156	49
HANNAFORD C	1916-1917	0	0	0	0	0	0	0	0	1	1	1	1
HARBRIDGE CW	1918-1919	0	0	0	0	0	0	0	0	2	0	2	0
HARGREAVES H	1923-1926	34	7	0	0	0	0	0	0	5	6	39	13
HARES W	1942-1943	0	0	0	0	0	0	0	0	1	0	1	0
HARMER TC	1949-1960	205	47	17	4	0	0	0	0	51/2	18	273/2	69
HARPER EC	1928-1932	63	62	4	1	0	0	0	0	11	20	78	83
HARRIS H	1943-1944	0	0	0	0	0	0	0	0	3	0	3	0
HARRIS W	1909-1910	7	0	0	0	0	0	0	0	5	0	12	0
HARTLEY AF	1922-1931	7	1	0	0	0	0	0	0	6	4	13	5
HATFIELD	1918-1919	0	0	0	0	0	0	0	0	1	0	1	0
HAWKINS W	1916-1919	0	0	0	0	0	0	0	0	66	9	66	9
HAYES	1952	0	0	0	0	0	0	0	0	0/1	0	0/1	0
HAZARD M	1979-1986	73/18	13	7/3	2	11/3	5	22/1	3	41/17	11	154/42	34
HEDLEY F	1933-1935	4	1	1	0	0	0	0	0	4	2	9	3
HEFFERNAN T	1977-1978	0	0	0	0	0	0	0	0	0/1	1	0/1	1
HEGGARTY AE	1913-1914	0	0	0	0	0	0	0	0	1	0	1	0
HELLIWELL S	1927-1929	8	0	1	0	0	0	0	0	4	1	13	1
HENDON I	1989-	0/4	0	0	0	1	0	0/2	0	4/12	0	5/18	0
HENDRY J	1990-	5/9	3	0	0	1/1	0	0	0	10/4	5	16/14	8
HENLEY L	1940-1945	0	0	0	0	0	0	0	0	2	1	2	1
HENRY RP	1954-1967	247	1	23	0	0	0	17	0	51/4	1	338/4	2
HENTY R	1950-1951	0	0	0	0	0	0	0	0	1	0	1	0
HEROD ERB	1928-1931	57	0	2	0	0	0	0	0	10	0	69	0
HEWITSON R	1908-1909	30	0	4	0	0	0	0	0	3	0	37	0
HILL D	1992-	2/2	0	0	0	0	0	0	0	1	0	3/2	0
HILL W	1917-1918	0	0	0	0	0	0	0	0	2	0	2	0
HILLS JR	1954-1960	29	0	3	0	0	0	0	0	9	0	41	0

Jimmy Greaves

Player	Played	LEAGUE		FA CUP		LG CUP		EUROPE		OTHERS		TOTAL	
		App	Gls	App	Gls	App	Gls	App	Gls	App	Gls	App	Gls
HINTON WFW	1924-1926	57	0	7	0	0	0	0	0	6	0	70	0
HITCHINS AW	1937-1942	37	1	7	0	0	0	0	0	112	0	156	1
HOAD SJ	1916-1917	0	0	0	0	0	0	0	0	4	0	4	0
HOBDAY A	1913-1914	0	0	0	0	0	0	0	0	1	0	1	0
HODDLE G	1975-1987	371/7	88	47/1	11	44	10	17/4	1	88/11	22	567/23	132
HODGE SB	1986-1988	44/1	7	7	2	2	0	0	0	12/5	3	65/6	12
HODGES L	1991-	0/4	0	0	0	0	0	0	0	0/5	0	0/9	0
HODGKINSON H	1930-1932	56	0	2	0	0	0	0	0	5	0	63	0
HOFFMAN	1917-1918	0	0	0	0	0	0	0	0	1	0	1	0
HOFFMAN	1918-1919	0	0	0	0	0	0	0	0	1	0	1	0
HOLDER PD	1971-1976	9/4	1	0	0	0	0	0/6	1	3/6	0	12/16	2
HOLLEY T	1942-1943	0	0	0	0	0	0	0	0	1	2	1	2
HOLLIS RW	1952-1953	3	1	1	2	0	0	0	0	0	0	4	3
HOLLOWBREAD JF	1956-1964	67	0	6	0	0	0	0	0	9	0	82	0
HOLMES JA	1976-1981	81	2	9	0	2	0	0	0	25/4	2	117/4	4
HOOPER PGW	1934-1945	100	0	11	0	0	0	0	0	133	0	244	0
HOPKIN F	1915-1916	0	0	0	0	0	0	0	0	4	1	4	1
HOPKINS M	1952-1964	219	0	20	0	0	0	1	0	31	1	271	1
HOUGHTON S	1991-	0/10	2	0	0	0/2	0	0/2	0	1/2	0	1/16	2
HOWE LF	1930-1946	165	26	17	2	0	0	0	0	103	16	285	44
HOWELLS DG	1985-	122/30	15	8/3	1	17/3	2	6	0	31/25	8	184/61	26
HOWSHALL T	1945-1946	0	0	0	0	0	0	0	0	1	0	1	0
HOY RE	1965-1968	10	0	0	0	0	0	2	0	3	0	15	0
HUGHES WA	1944-1948	2	0	2	0	0	0	0	0	55	0	59	0
HUGHTON CWG	1979-1990	293/4	12	34/2	1	33/2	2	29/1	4	96/5	3	485/14	22
HUMPHREYS P	1909-1912	45	24	5	5	0	0	0	0	4	0	54	29
HUNT DA	1934-1944	17	6	2	0	0	0	0	0	5	7	24	13
HUNT GS	1930-1937	185	125	13	13	0	0	0	0	7	13	205	151
HUNT K	1916-1917	0	0	0	0	0	0	0	0	1	0	1	0
HUNTER AC	1920-1922	23	0	3	0	0	0	0	0	7	0	33	0
HUTCHINSON GH	1953-1954	5	1	0	0	0	0	0	0	2	1	7	2
ILEY J	1957-1959	53	1	4	0	0	0	0	0	9	0	66	1
ILLINGWORTH JW	1929-1935	10	0	2	0	0	0	0	0	8/1	0	20/1	0
INNES A	1918-1919	0	0	0	0	0	0	0	0	1	0	1	0
IRELAND JJC	1957-1959	3	0	0	0	0	0	0	0	2	1	5	1
JACK A	1917-1919	0	0	0	0	0	0	0	0	19	7	19	7
JACKSON H	1942-1943	0	0	0	0	0	0	0	0	2	0	2	0
JACKSON J	1944-1945	0	0	0	0	0	0	0	0	2	0	2	0
JACQUES W	1914-1923	123	0	15	0	0	0	0	0	125	0	263	0
JEFFREY G	1937-1939	1	1	0	0	0	0	0	0	0	0	1	1
JENKINS DJ	1968-1970	12/3	2	2/1	0	0	0	0	0	1	0	15/4	2
JENNINGS	1918-1919	0	0	0	0	0	0	0	0	1	0	1	0
JENNINGS A	1923-1924	0	0	0	0	0	0	0	0	1	0	1	0
JENNINGS PA	1964-1986	473	0	43	0	39	0	36	0	82/3	1	673/3	1
JINKS JJ	1945-1946	0	0	0	0	0	0	0	0	1	2	1	2
JOHNSON NJ	1965-1971	28/7	5	4	1	0	0	0	0	4/10	0	36/17	6
JOHNSTON R	1987-1990	0	0	0	0	0	0	0	0	0/2	0	0/2	0
JOLIFFE	1941-1942	0	0	0	0	0	0	0	0	1	0	1	0
JONES C	1934-1936	18	0	0	0	0	0	0	0	1	0	19	0
JONES CH	1974-1982	149/15	37	10/2	4	7/1	1	0/1	0	52/10	26	218/29	68
JONES CW	1957-1978	314/4	135	35/4	16	2	1	19	7	38/2	17	408/10	176
JONES EN	1942-1944	0	0	0	0	0	0	0	0	17	8	17	8
JONES G	1912-1913	8	0	0	0	0	0	0	0	3	0	11	0
JONES L	1942-1943	0	0	0	0	0	0	0	0	1	0	1	0
JONES WEA	1946-1949	56	14	2	0	0	0	0	0	7	2	65	16
JORDAN JW	1947-1948	24	10	3	3	0	0	0	0	1	0	28	13
JOSEPH L	1946-1947	1	0	0	0	0	0	0	0	0	0	1	0
JOSLIN PJ	1945-1946	0	0	0	0	0	0	0	0	4	0	4	0
JOYCE JW	1909-1916	73	1	8	0	0	0	0	0	32	1	113	2
KAINE WEJC	1925-1926	11	0	1	0	0	0	0	0	0	0	12	0
KEELEY AJ	1975-1977	5/1	0	0	0	0	0	0	0	0/3	0	5/4	0
KEMPES M	1984-1985	0	0	0	0	0	0	0	0	5	3	5	3
KENDALL M	1975-1981	29	0	6	0	1	0	0	0	9/18	0	45/18	0
KENNEDY JJ	1909-1912	13	1	0	0	0	0	0	0	4	0	17	1
KERRY AHG	1909-1910	1	0	0	0	0	0	0	0	0	0	1	0
KIERNAN T	1941-1942	0	0	0	0	0	0	0	0	2	0	2	0
KING A	1913-1914	19	0	1	0	0	0	0	0	5	0	25	0
KING DA	1951-1955	19	0	0	0	0	0	0	0	7	0	26	0
KING EF	1934-1935	1	0	0	0	0	0	0	0	0	0	1	0
KINNEAR JP	1965-1980	190/7	2	24	0	20	0	18	0	40/3	4	292/10	6

425

Player	Played	LEAGUE		FA CUP		LG CUP		EUROPE		OTHERS		TOTAL	
		App	Gls	App	Gls	App	Gls	App	Gls	App	Gls	App	Gls
KNIGHT JG	1928-1929	1	0	0	0	0	0	0	0	0	0	1	0
KNIGHTON T	1915-1916	0	0	0	0	0	0	0	0	4	2	4	2
KNOTT UJ	1923-1926	0	0	0	0	0	0	0	0	4	1	4	1
KNOWLES CB	1964-1977	401/1	15	42	1	32/1	0	30	1	62	3	567/2	20
KNOWLES PR	1975-1976	0	0	0	0	0	0	0	0	0/1	0	0/1	0
LACY J	1978-1983	99/5	2	12	0	11	1	4/1	0	37/5	2	163/11	5
LANDON C	1992-	0	0	0	0	0	0	0	0	1/1	0	1/1	0
LANE WHC	1924-1927	25	7	4	2	0	0	0	0	8	3	37	12
LAUREL J	1957-1958	0	0	0	0	0	0	0	0	1	0	1	0
LAWRENCE WH	1917-1918	0	0	0	0	0	0	0	0	5	1	5	1
LAYBOURNE	1952-1953	0	0	0	0	0	0	0	0	1	0	1	0
LEE C	1977-1980	57/5	18	6/1	3	2	0	0	0	20/3	10	85/9	31
LEE TWG	1973-1975	1	0	0	0	0	0	0	0	0/1	0	1/1	0
LESLIE TS	1908-1911	10	0	2	0	0	0	0	0	3	0	15	0
LEVENE DJ	1932-1935	8	0	2	0	0	0	0	0	1	0	11	0
LEWORTHY DJ	1984-1986	8/3	3	0	0	0/1	1	0	0	8/9	11	16/13	15
LIGHTFOOT EJ	1911-1918	62	2	5	0	0	0	0	0	17	0	84	2
LINDSAY AF	1917-1930	211	42	15	8	0	0	0	0	52	17	278	68
LINDSAY D	1917-1919	0	0	0	0	0	0	0	0	24	0	24	0
LINEKER GW	1989-1992	105	67	9	3	16	8	8	2	24/3	10	162/3	90
LLOYD H	1915-1919	0	0	0	0	0	0	0	0	41	7	41	7
LORIMER HH	1919-1922	5	0	0	0	0	0	0	0	8	0	13	0
LOW AR	1964-1967	6/2	1	0	0	0	0	0	0	3/1	1	9/3	2
LOWDELL AE	1927-1930	86	0	4	0	0	0	0	0	9	0	99	0
LOWE H	1914-1927	65	0	7	0	0	0	0	0	14	0	86	0
LUDFORD GA	1936-1950	77	7	6	1	0	0	0	0	192	83	275	91
LUNN TH	1909-1913	89	0	5	0	0	0	0	0	12	0	106	0
LYLE A	1909-1910	1	0	0	0	0	0	0	0	0	0	1	0
LYMAN CC	1937-1946	47	10	8	1	0	0	0	0	32	9	87	20
LYONS A	1930-1932	54	3	3	0	0	0	0	0	6	1	63	4
MABBUTT GV	1982-	355/13	27	33/2	4	51/2	2	22/3	4	105/11	15	566/31	52
McALLISTER D	1974-1981	168/4	9	16/1	0	13	1	0	0	55/3	3	252/8	13
McCABE M	1981-1982	0	0	0	0	0	0	0	0	0/1	0	0/1	0
McCALMONT	1918-1919	0	0	0	0	0	0	0	0	1	1	1	1
McCARTHY A	1940-1941	0	0	0	0	0	0	0	0	1	0	1	0
McCLELLAN SB	1950-1956	68	29	2	3	0	0	0	0	23/4	29	93/4	61
McCLENEGHAN H	1913-1914	0	0	0	0	0	0	0	0	1	0	1	0
McCONNON P	1909	0	0	0	0	0	0	0	0	2	2	2	2
McCORMICK J	1932-1946	137	26	13	2	0	0	0	0	20	2	170	30
McCRACKEN	1918-1919	0	0	0	0	0	0	0	0	1	0	1	0
McCUDDEN F	1923-1924	0	0	0	0	0	0	0	0	1	0	1	0
McDONALD D	1991-	2	0	0	0	0	0	0	0	2/1	0	4/1	0
MacDONALD RJ	1919-1926	109	0	16	0	0	0	0	0	25	0	150	0
McEWAN F	1939-1940	0	0	0	0	0	0	0	0	3	0	3	0
McFARLANE D	1908-1910	21	2	0	0	0	0	0	0	8	2	29	4
McFARLANE	1941-1942	0	0	0	0	0	0	0	0	1	0	1	0
McGLANACHLAN	1916-1917	0	0	0	0	0	0	0	0	1	0	1	0
McGRATH RC	1973-1977	30/8	5	0	0	1	0	7/1	5	8/7	0	46/16	10
McGREGOR T	1915-1916	0	0	0	0	0	0	0	0	1	1	1	1
McIVOR W	1918-1919	0	0	0	0	0	0	0	0	3	3	3	0
MACKAY DC	1958-1968	268	42	33	4	0	0	17	5	44/2	12	362/2	63
McMAHON G	1992-	0	0	0	0	0	0	0	0	1/2	0	1/2	0
McNAB N	1973-1979	63/9	3	2	0	5/1	0	0	0	26/8	3	96/18	6
McNALLY BJ	1954-1955	0	0	0	0	0	0	0	0	1	0	1	0
McTAVISH JK	1910-1912	40	3	2	0	0	0	0	0	3	0	45	3
McTAVISH R	1910-1912	10	3	1	0	0	0	0	0	4	1	15	4
McVEY J	1916-1917	0	0	0	0	0	0	0	0	2	0	2	0
MADDISON G	1922-1924	40	0	1	0	0	0	0	0	7	0	48	0
MAHORN P	1992-	0	0	0	0	0	0	0	0	0/3	0	0/3	0
MANLEY T	1943-1944	0	0	0	0	0	0	0	0	1	0	1	0
MANNION WJ	1941-1942	0	0	0	0	0	0	0	0	4	0	4	0
MANUEL B	1987-1988	0	0	0	0	0	0	0	0	0/2	0	0/2	0
MARADONA DA	1985-1986	0	0	0	0	0	0	0	0	1	0	1	0
MARCHI AV	1949-1965	232	7	16	0	0	0	12	0	57	3	317	10
MARKHAM S	1948-1949	0	0	0	0	0	0	0	0	1	0	1	0
MARSHALL A	1979	0	0	0	0	0	0	0	0	0/1	0	0/1	0
MARSHALL E	1942-1943	0	0	0	0	0	0	0	0	1	0	1	0
MARSHALL WH	1931-1932	1	0	0	0	0	0	0	0	0	0	1	0
MARTIN JR	1942-1945	0	0	0	0	0	0	0	0	45	15	45	15
MASON TL	1911-1912	7	1	0	0	0	0	0	0	1	0	8	1

Player	Played	LEAGUE		FA CUP		LG CUP		EUROPE		OTHERS		TOTAL	
		App	Gls	App	Gls	App	Gls	App	Gls	App	Gls	App	Gls
MASSEY FJ	1908-1909	1	0	0	0	0	0	0	0	1	0	2	0
MAZZON G	1979-1983	3/1	0	1	0	0/2	0	0	0	3/9	1	7/12	1
MEADOWS H	1951-1952	0	0	0	0	0	0	0	0	1	1	1	1
MEADS T	1929-1935	184	6	5	0	0	0	0	0	7	0	196	6
MEDLEY LD	1938-1953	150	45	14	1	0	0	0	0	90	28	254	74
MEDWIN TC	1956-1963	197	65	13	7	0	0	5	0	32	18	247	90
MEEK J	1935-1939	45	15	6	1	0	0	0	0	0	0	51	16
MESSER AT	1930-1932	50	2	2	0	0	0	0	0	4	0	56	2
METGOD JAB	1987-1988	5/7	0	0	0	2	0	0	0	7/6	2	14/13	2
MIDDLEMISS H	1908-1920	248	51	17	3	0	0	0	0	65	27	330	81
MILLER LR	1936-1939	56	22	9	4	0	0	0	0	0	0	65	26
MILLER PR	1978-1987	206/2	7	30/1	1	22/1	0	23	2	92/6	6	373/10	16
MILTON GW	1942-1943	0	0	0	0	0	0	0	0	1	0	1	0
MIMMS RA	1987-1991	37	0	2	0	5	0	0	0	20/5	0	64/5	0
MINTER WJ	1908-1926	248	95	19	6	0	0	0	0	66	50	333	151
MINTON J	1991-	2	1	0	0	0/1	0	0	0	1/1	0	3/2	1
MOGFORD RWG	1943-1945	0	0	0	0	0	0	0	0	8	0	8	0
MONCUR JF	1985-1992	10/11	1	0	0	1/2	0	0	0	9/21	1	20/34	2
MOODIE J	1944-1945	0	0	0	0	0	0	0	0	1	0	1	0
MOORES IR	1976-1979	25/4	6	0	0	3	2	0	0	11/7	9	39/11	17
MORAN J	1931-1932	12	0	0	0	0	0	0	0	0	0	12	0
MORAN P	1986-	14/17	2	3/1	0	1/4	0	0/1	0	8/22	2	26/45	4
MORGAN RE	1968-1973	66/2	8	6	2	3	1	2/1	1	12/3	5	89/6	17
MORRIS J	1915-1917	0	0	0	0	0	0	0	0	47	4	47	4
MORRIS T	1908-1913	63	2	7	1	0	0	0	0	13	1	83	4
MORRISON JA	1932-1946	134	90	21	14	0	0	0	0	35	28	190	132
MORTON JC	1908-1909	2	0	0	0	0	0	0	0	2	0	4	0
MOSELEY W	1943-1944	0	0	0	0	0	0	0	0	3	1	3	1
MUIR A	1942-1943	0	0	0	0	0	0	0	0	1	0	1	0
MUIR WR	1944-1945	0	0	0	0	0	0	0	0	1	0	1	0
MULLERY AP	1963-1972	313	25	33	1	18	0	10	4	55	10	429	40
MURPHY P	1950-1952	38	14	0	0	0	0	0	0	11	6	49	20
NAYIM	1988-1993	95/17	11	6/3	4	11/6	3	6	0	20/6	3	138/32	21
NAYLOR TP	1969-1980	237/6	0	17/1	0	23/1	1	13/6	0	66/8	0	356/22	1
NEIGHBOUR JE	1970-1977	104/15	8	10/1	1	14/3	1	6/3	1	24/10	4	158/32	15
NEILL T	1976	0	0	0	0	0	0	0	0	0/1	0	0/1	0
NELSON D	1942-1944	0	0	0	0	0	0	0	0	2	1	2	1
NETHERCOTT S	1991-	3/2	0	0	0	0	0	0	0	2/4	0	5/6	0
NEWMAN EH	1909-1914	31	6	2	0	0	0	0	0	1	0	34	6
NICHOLLS JH	1926-1936	124	0	5	0	0	0	0	0	10	0	139	0
NICHOLSON WE	1938-1955	318	6	27	0	0	0	0	0	50	1	395	7
NOBLE D	1941-1942	0	0	0	0	0	0	0	0	6	3	6	3
NORMAN M	1955-1956	357	16	37	2	0	0	17	1	42	0	453	19
NORRIS	1912	0	0	0	0	0	0	0	0	1	0	1	0
NUTTALL J	1917-1918	0	0	0	0	0	0	0	0	18	10	18	10
OAKES J	1944-1945	0	0	0	0	0	0	0	0	1	0	1	0
O'CALLAGHAN E	1926-1944	252	92	11	6	0	0	0	0	50	23	313	121
O'DONNELL F	1943-1945	0	0	0	0	0	0	0	0	13	8	13	8
OLIVER W	1913-1914	2	0	0	0	0	0	0	0	0	0	2	0
O'REILLY GM	1979-1984	39/6	0	2	0	4	0	2/2	0	14/4	1	61/12	1
OSBORNE FR	1923-1931	210	78	9	4	0	0	0	0	10	5	229	87
OSGOOD K	1973-1978	112/1	13	3	0	11	1	0	0	32/3	6	158/4	20
O'SHEA TJ	1986-1988	1/2	0	0	0	0	0	0	0	1/1	0	2/3	0
OTTEWELL S	1939-1940	0	0	0	0	0	0	0	0	1	0	1	0
OWEN AW	1953-1954	1	0	0	0	0	0	0	0	1	0	2	0
PAGE AE	1936-1946	56	0	1	0	0	0	0	0	31	0	88	0
PAGE R	1915-1916	0	0	0	0	0	0	0	0	3	0	3	0
PALMER	1942-1943	0	0	0	0	0	0	0	0	1	0	1	0
PARKER C	1943-1944	0	0	0	0	0	0	0	0	1	0	1	0
PARKS A	1981-	37	0	5	0	1	0	5/1	0	24/16	0	72/17	0
PARSONS J	1918-1919	0	0	0	0	0	0	0	0	1	0	1	0
PATON TG	1940-1941	0	0	0	0	0	0	0	0	4	0	4	0
PATTINSON	1918-1919	0	0	0	0	0	0	0	0	1	0	1	0
PATTISON JM	1942-1943	0	0	0	0	0	0	0	0	13	3	13	3
PEAKE WE	1917-1919	0	0	0	0	0	0	0	0	19	8	19	8
PEARCE JW	1968-1975	109/33	21	4/6	3	21/6	7	8/7	4	18/7	8	160/59	43
PEARSON J	1913-1923	47	0	3	0	0	0	0	0	7	0	57	0
PEARSON TU	1941-1942	0	0	0	0	0	0	0	0	2	0	2	0
PERRYMAN SJ	1969-1990	654/2	31	69	2	66	3	63/1	3	162/6	13	1014/9	52
PETERS MS	1969-1975	189	46	16	5	23	12	32	13	27	11	287	87

Alf Ramsey greets Danny Blanchflower on the day that the Irish star joined Spurs in December 1954.

Player	Played	LEAGUE App	Gls	FA CUP App	Gls	LG CUP App	Gls	EUROPE App	Gls	OTHERS App	Gls	TOTAL App	Gls
PHYPERS E	1934-1939	30	0	3	0	0	0	0	0	3	0	36	0
PIPER GH	1939-1941	0	0	0	0	0	0	0	0	4	0	4	0
PIPER RD	1962-1963	1	0	0	0	0	0	0	0	0	0	1	0
PITT SW	1965-1966	1	0	0	0	0	0	0	0	1	0	2	0
POLSTON A	1988-	0/1	0	0	0	0	0	0	0	3/9	0	3/10	0
POLSTON JD	1985-1990	17/7	1	0	0	3/1	0	0	0	9/7	0	29/15	1
POSSEE DJ	1963-1966	19	4	0	0	0	0	0	0	13/3	0	32/3	4
POTTER CB	1916-1919	0	0	0	0	0	0	0	0	22	9	22	9
POWELL A	1916-1917	0	0	0	0	0	0	0	0	1	0	1	0
POWELL J	1918-1919	0	0	0	0	0	0	0	0	1	0	1	0
POYNTON C	1922-1933	152	3	6	0	0	0	0	0	22	0	180	3
PRATT JA	1968-1986	307/24	39	23/5	2	27/4	7	24/1	1	81/12	16	462/46	65
PRECKI	1991-1992	0	0	0	0	0	0	0	0	1	0	1	0
PRICE H	1918-1919	0	0	0	0	0	0	0	0	9	3	9	3
PRICE J	1954-1955	0	0	0	0	0	0	0	0	2	0	2	0
PRICE PT	1981-1984	35/4	0	6	0	7	0	10	0	13/3	1	71/7	1
PRYDE RI	1944-1945	0	0	0	0	0	0	0	0	1	0	1	0
RALSTON A	1915-1919	0	0	0	0	0	0	0	0	102	0	102	0
RAMSAY A	1915-1916	0	0	0	0	0	0	0	0	1	0	1	0
RAMSEY AE	1949-1955	226	24	24	0	0	0	0	0	33	6	283	30
RANCE CS	1910-1921	105	1	7	1	0	0	0	0	150	12	262	14
REDDISH J	1928-1932	6	0	1	0	0	0	0	0	3	0	10	0
REES	1918-1919	0	0	0	0	0	0	0	0	1	0	1	0
REES W	1949-1950	11	3	2	0	0	0	0	0	1	0	14	3
REVELL CH	1941-1942	0	0	0	0	0	0	0	0	1	1	1	1
REYNOLDS RSM	1950-1959	86	0	9	0	0	0	0	0	43	0	138	0
RICHARDSON J	1925-1929	38	0	3	0	0	0	0	0	6	1	47	1
RINGROSE AA	1936-1939	10	0	0	0	0	0	0	0	0	0	10	0
ROBB GW	1951-1959	182	53	18	5	0	0	0	0	24	7	224	65
ROBERTS GP	1979-1987	200/9	23	27	2	24/1	5	25/1	6	81/6	10	357/17	46
ROBERTS RD	1944-1945	0	0	0	0	0	0	0	0	2	0	2	0
ROBERTS WT	1928-1929	4	2	0	0	0	0	0	0	0	0	4	2
ROBERTSON JG	1963-1969	153/4	25	18	3	2	0	4	3	31/3	12	208/7	43
ROBINSON	1917-1918	0	0	0	0	0	0	0	0	1	0	1	0
ROBINSON MJ	1975-1978	5/1	2	0	0	0	0	0	0	2/3	0	7/4	2
ROBSHAW HW	1951-1953	1	0	0	0	0	0	0	0	2/1	0	3/1	0
ROBSON J	1918-1919	0	0	0	0	0	0	0	0	2	0	2	0
ROBSON M	1987-1992	3/5	0	0	0	1	0	0	0	5/12	0	9/16	0
ROE TW	1925-1927	6	4	0	0	0	0	0	0	2	1	8	5
ROPER	1918-1919	0	0	0	0	0	0	0	0	1	1	1	1
ROSS JD	1920-1924	7	0	0	0	0	0	0	0	3	0	10	0
ROWE AS	1930-1938	182	0	19	0	0	0	0	0	9	0	210	0
ROWLEY JF	1942-1945	0	0	0	0	0	0	0	0	27	26	27	26
ROWLEY RWM	1929-1932	24	10	0	0	0	0	0	0	2	1	26	11
RUDDOCK N	1985-1988	7/2	0	1/1	1	0	0	0	0	9/9	0	17/12	1
	1992-	38	3	5	0	4	0	0	0	13	2	60	5
RUNDLE CR	1945-1949	28	12	1	0	0	0	0	0	9	2	38	14
RUTHERFORD J	1914-1919	0	0	0	0	0	0	0	0	2	0	2	0
RYDEN JJ	1955-1959	63	2	5	0	0	0	0	0	21	1	89	3
SAGE W	1919-1926	13	0	0	0	0	0	0	0	4	0	17	0
SAINSBURY R	1940-1942	0	0	0	0	0	0	0	0	2	0	2	0
SAINSBURY W	1941-1944	0	0	0	0	0	0	0	0	5	1	5	1
SAMWAYS V	1984-	126/28	8	12/1	2	22/4	4	6/1	0	52/12	10	219/46	24
SANDERS AW	1926-1928	13	7	0	0	0	0	0	0	0	0	13	7
SARGENT FA	1934-1946	96	25	16	8	0	0	0	0	32	6	144	39
SAUL FL	1959-1968	112/4	37	7	6	1	0	5	2	33/4	15	158/8	60
SAUNDERS	1917-1918	0	0	0	0	0	0	0	0	1	0	1	0
SAUNDERS W	1940-1941	0	0	0	0	0	0	0	0	3	0	3	0
SCARTH JW	1949-1952	7	3	0	0	0	0	0	0	5	4	12	7
SCOTT J	1928-1931	18	4	0	0	0	0	0	0	3	2	21	6
SEDGLEY SP	1989-	105/17	3	9/1	1	19/3	1	4/3	0	38/5	1	175/29	6
SEEBURG MP	1908-1909	1	0	0	0	0	0	0	0	1	0	2	0
SEED JM	1919-1927	229	65	25	12	0	0	0	0	30	7	284	84
SHARP B	1922-1925	3	0	0	0	0	0	0	0	3	3	6	3
SHARPE FC	1958-1959	2	1	0	0	0	0	0	0	0	0	2	1
SHERINGHAM T	1992-	38	21	5	4	4	3	0	0	3	3	50	31
SIBLEY A	1941-1942	0	0	0	0	0	0	0	0	3	1	3	1
SIMMONDS	1979	0	0	0	0	0	0	0	0	0/1	0	0/1	0
SIMONS HT	1918-1919	0	0	0	0	0	0	0	0	4	2	4	2
SKINNER GEH	1938-1946	1	0	0	0	0	0	0	0	15	3	16	3

Vinny Samways

Player	Played	LEAGUE		FA CUP		LG CUP		EUROPE		OTHERS		TOTAL	
		App	Gls	App	Gls	App	Gls	App	Gls	App	Gls	App	Gls
SKINNER JF	1919-1926	87	3	6	0	0	0	0	0	17	0	110	3
SKITT H	1924-1931	213	0	17	0	0	0	0	0	29	4	259	4
SLADE H	1916-1917	0	0	0	0	0	0	0	0	1	0	1	0
'SLENDER'	1918-1919	0	0	0	0	0	0	0	0	1	0	1	0
SLOAN T	1978	0	0	0	0	0	0	0	0	2	0	2	0
SMAILES J	1930-1932	16	3	0	0	0	0	0	0	0	0	16	3
SMITH A	1959-1964	0	0	0	0	0	0	0	0	2	0	2	0
SMITH B	1919-1929	291	9	28	1	0	0	0	0	50	3	369	13
SMITH GC	1945-1946	0	0	0	0	0	0	0	0	4	0	4	0
SMITH GM	1978-1982	34/4	1	0	0	6	0	0/1	0	19/3	2	59/8	3
SMITH IR	1975-1976	2	0	0	0	0	0	0	0	1/3	0	3/3	0
SMITH J	1959-1964	21	1	2	0	0	0	1	0	3/1	0	27/1	1
SMITH JMA	1925-1927	30	0	1	0	0	0	0	0	5	0	36	0
SMITH JR	1944-1945	0	0	0	0	0	0	0	0	1	0	1	0
SMITH K	1944-1945	0	0	0	0	0	0	0	0	1	0	1	0
SMITH P	1918-1919	0	0	0	0	0	0	0	0	4	0	4	0
SMITH N	1990-	0	0	0	0	0	0	0	0	0/1	0	0/1	0
SMITH R	1964-1965	0	0	0	0	0	0	0	0	1	0	1	0
SMITH RA	1955-1965	271	176	32	22	0	0	14	10	41/1	43	358/1	251
SMITH T	1943-1944	0	0	0	0	0	0	0	0	2	1	2	1
SMY J	1928-1931	17	6	0	0	0	0	0	0	2	0	19	6
SOUNESS GJ	1971-1972	0	0	0	0	0	0	0/1	0	0	0	0/1	0
SOUTHEY PC	1979-1983	1	0	0	0	0	0	0	0	2/4	0	3/4	0
SPARROW H	1913-1915	18	7	1	0	0	0	0	0	8	7	27	14
SPELMAN I	1937-1940	28	2	4	0	0	0	0	0	12	0	44	2
SPENCER A	1917-1918	0	0	0	0	0	0	0	0	1	1	1	1
SPERRIN J	1940-1942	0	0	0	0	0	0	0	0	16	4	16	4
SPERRIN W	1940-1944	0	0	0	0	0	0	0	0	28	6	28	6
SPIERS CH	1927-1932	158	0	11	0	0	0	0	0	17	0	186	0
SPIVEY D	1954-1955	0	0	0	0	0	0	0	0	1	0	1	0
SPROSTON B	1938-1939	9	0	0	0	0	0	0	0	1	0	10	0
STALEY R	1942-1943	0	0	0	0	0	0	0	0	1	0	1	0
STATHAM B	1987-92	20/4	0	0/1	0	2	0	0	0	13/5	0	35/10	0
STEAD K	1976-1977	0	0	0	0	0	0	0	0	0/1	0	0/1	0
STEAD MJ	1975-1978	14/1	0	0	0	0	0	0	0	17/9	3	31/10	3
STEEL A	1909-1910	1	0	0	0	0	0	0	0	0	0	1	0
STEEL D	1908-1912	131	3	12	0	0	0	0	0	23	1	166	4
STEEL RL	1908-1916	230	41	19	5	0	0	0	0	67	16	316	62
STEPHENS	1939-1940	0	0	0	0	0	0	0	0	1	1	1	1
STEVENS GA	1983-1990	140/7	6	13/4	0	19/2	0	15	3	35/8	4	222/21	13
STEVENS LWG	1941-1949	54	5	5	0	0	0	0	0	33	8	92	13
STEWART PA	1988-1992	116/5	28	9	2	23	7	8	0	43/2	20	199/7	57
STIMSON M	1986-1989	1/1	0	0	0	0	0	0	0	6/5	0	7/6	0
STOKES AE	1952-1959	65	40	4	2	0	0	0	0	20	20	89	62
STURGESS L	1942-1943	0	0	0	0	0	0	0	0	1	0	1	0
STURGESS ME	1942-1943	0	0	0	0	0	0	0	0	1	1	1	1
SWIFT WN	1944-1945	0	0	0	0	0	0	0	0	1	0	1	0
TATE JA	1912-1914	4	0	0	0	0	0	0	0	1	0	5	0
TATTERSALL WS	1911-1915	45	3	3	2	0	0	0	0	14	3	62	8
TAYLOR A	1929-1936	60	0	10	0	0	0	0	0	7	0	77	0
TAYLOR PJ	1976-1990	116/7	31	8/3	2	4/2	0	0	0	27/6	13	155/18	46
THEODOSIOU A	1988-1989	0	0	0	0	0	0	0	0	0/1	0	0/1	0
THOMAS DJ	1983-1987	80/7	1	4	0	11/2	0	8/4	0	48/7	4	151/20	5
THOMAS M	1982-1983	0	0	0	0	0	0	0	0	0/1	0	0/1	0
THOMAS MA	1986-1992	136/21	6	12	1	28/1	1	0	0	31/11	2	207/33	10
THOMAS WSL	1915-1918	0	0	0	0	0	0	0	0	25	6	25	6
THOMPSON A	1920-1931	153	19	13	2	0	0	0	0	39	12	205	33
THORSTVEDT E	1988-	138/2	0	13	0	20	0	6	0	33/3	0	220/4	0
THWAITES AW	1916-1918	0	0	0	0	0	0	0	0	11	3	11	3
TICKRIDGE S	1941-1951	96	0	6	0	0	0	0	0	49	0	151	0
TOMKIN A	1938-1940	4	0	0	0	0	0	0	0	2	0	6	0
TOMKINS EF	1917-1919	0	0	0	0	0	0	0	0	40	0	40	0
TOULOUSE CH	1948-1949	2	0	0	0	0	0	0	0	0	0	2	0
TOWNLEY JC	1927-1928	3	2	0	0	0	0	0	0	2	2	5	4
TRAILOR CH	1941-1949	11	0	1	0	0	0	0	0	6	0	18	0
TRAVERS G	1915-1917	0	0	0	0	0	0	0	0	6	2	6	2
TRIGG SA	1942-1943	0	0	0	0	0	0	0	0	1	0	1	0
TULL WDJ	1908-1911	10	2	0	0	0	0	0	0	8	5	18	7
TUNNEY E	1944-1945	0	0	0	0	0	0	0	0	1	0	1	0
TURNER A	1991-	7/11	3	0/1	0	0/2	1	0	0	4/5	1	11/19	5

431

Player	Played	LEAGUE		FA CUP		LG CUP		EUROPE		OTHERS		TOTAL	
		App	Gls	App	Gls	App	Gls	App	Gls	App	Gls	App	Gls
TUTTLE D	1989-	10/3	0	0	0	3/1	0	1	1	8/9	0	22/14	0
UPEX D	1918-1919	0	0	0	0	0	0	0	0	1	0	1	0
UPHILL DE	1950-1953	6	2	0	0	0	0	0	0	2/1	4	8/1	6
UPTON S	1912-1913	2	0	0	0	0	0	0	0	2	0	4	0
VAN den HAUWE	1989-	110/6	0	7	0	16	0	6	0	13	0	162/6	0
VANNER R	1925-1926	0	0	0	0	0	0	0	0	1	0	1	0
VARNEY M	1979	0	0	0	0	0	0	0	0	1	0	1	0
VENABLES TF	1965-1969	114/1	5	15/1	2	6	1	4	1	28/1	4	167/3	13
VILLA RJ	1978-1988	123/9	18	21	3	15/1	3	8/1	1	43/2	16	210/13	41
WADDLE CR	1985-1989	137/1	33	14	5	21	4	0	0	40/3	12	212/4	54
WALDEN FI	1912-1926	214	21	22	4	0	0	0	0	88	21	324	46
WALFORD SJ	1975-1976	1/1	0	0	0	0	0	0	0	7/4	0	8/5	0
WALKER D	1944-1945	0	0	0	0	0	0	0	0	1	0	1	0
WALKER I	1990-	36	0	0	0	3	0	2	0	13/3	0	54/3	0
WALLACE J	1940-1941	0	0	0	0	0	0	0	0	2	1	2	1
WALLEY E	1954-1958	5	0	0	0	0	0	0	0	7/2	1	12/2	1
WALLIS J	1940-1945	0	0	0	0	0	0	0	0	7	0	7	0
WALSH PA	1987-1992	84/44	19	4/4	0	9/7	2	1/3	0	38/13	15	136/71	36
WALTERS C	1918-1926	106	0	11	0	0	0	0	0	18	0	135	0
WALTERS J	1918-1919	0	0	0	0	0	0	0	0	1	0	1	0
WALTERS WE	1943-1956	211	66	23	5	0	0	0	0	113	38	347	109
WALTON J	1908-1909	24	2	4	0	0	0	0	0	2	1	30	3
WANT AG	1967-1972	46/4	0	3	0	3	0	0	0	18/2	0	70/6	0
WARD RA	1935-1946	118	10	17	1	0	0	0	0	243	17	378	28
WATKINS G	1914-1915	0	0	0	0	0	0	0	0	1	0	1	0
WATKINS W	1915-1917	0	0	0	0	0	0	0	0	3	0	3	0
WATSON K	1992-	4/1	1	0/1	0	1/1	1	0	0	0/9	0	5/12	2
WEBSTER FJ	1911-1915	83	0	4	0	0	0	0	0	16	0	103	0
WEBSTER SP	1982-1984	2/1	0	0	0	0	0	0	0	0/2	0	2/3	0
WEIR F	1912-1917	97	2	5	0	0	0	0	0	17	0	119	2
WELLER K	1964-1967	19/2	1	0	0	0	0	0	0	13/5	5	32/7	6
WESTWOOD JA	1948-1949	0	0	0	0	0	0	0	0	1	0	1	0
WETTON R	1951-1955	45	0	1	0	0	0	0	0	19	3	65	3
WHATLEY WJ	1932-1947	226	2	28	0	0	0	0	0	140	0	394	2
WHENT JR	1943-1944	0	0	0	0	0	0	0	0	3	1	3	1
WHITCHURCH CH	1945-1947	8	2	0	0	0	0	0	0	19	5	27	7
WHITE JA	1959-1964	183	40	19	1	0	0	17	6	14	6	233	53
WHITE RBW	1940-1946	0	0	2	0	0	0	0	0	167	4	169	4
WHITE SE	1923-1926	20	0	2	0	0	0	0	0	5	1	27	1
WHITE T	1964-1965	0	0	0	0	0	0	0	0	1	1	1	1
WHITTINGHAM A	1944-1945	0	0	0	0	0	0	0	0	1	1	1	1
WHITTON WA	1921-1923	0	0	0	0	0	0	0	0	2	2	2	2
WILBERT G	1939-1940	0	0	0	0	0	0	0	0	1	0	1	0
WILDING HTO	1928-1929	12	1	0	0	0	0	0	0	0	0	12	1
WILKES F	1908-1909	57	0	3	0	0	0	0	0	12	0	72	0
WILKIE RM	1956-1957	1	0	0	0	0	0	0	0	1/1	1	2/1	1
WILLIAMS CE	1941-1942	0	0	0	0	0	0	0	0	3	0	3	0
WILLIAMS JLJ	1912-1913	0	0	0	0	0	0	0	0	1	0	1	0
WILLIAMSON E	1916-1917	0	0	0	0	0	0	0	0	1	0	1	0
WILLIS A	1942-1954	145	1	16	0	0	0	0	0	112	1	273	2
WILSON A	1915-1916	0	0	0	0	0	0	0	0	10	0	10	0
WILSON C	1918-1923	55	27	7	6	0	0	0	0	18	15	80	48
WILSON JA	1943-1944	0	0	0	0	0	0	0	0	1	0	1	0
WITHERS CF	1947-1956	153	0	11	2	0	0	0	0	37/3	0	201/3	2
WOODGER G	1914-1915	0	0	0	0	0	0	0	0	2	0	2	0
WOODLEY VR	1939-1940	0	0	0	0	0	0	0	0	1	0	1	0
WOODRUFF CL	1908-1910	10	1	0	0	0	0	0	0	4	0	14	1
WOODS AE	1954-1955	6	0	0	0	0	0	0	0	0/1	0	6/1	0
WOODWARD HJ	1944-1949	63	1	4	0	0	0	0	0	9	1	76	2
WOODWARD VJ	1908-1909	27	18	4	0	0	0	0	0	2	0	33	18
WOOLCOTT RA	1969-1970	1	0	0	0	0	0	0	0	0	0	1	0
WORLEY LF	1959-1960	1	0	0	0	0	0	0	0	0	0	1	0
WORRALL E	1918-1919	0	0	0	0	0	0	0	0	11	0	11	0
WREN GC	1917-1918	0	0	0	0	0	0	0	0	1	0	1	0
WRIGHT AM	1950-1951	2	1	0	0	0	0	0	0	0	0	2	1
YORATH TC	1979-1981	44/4	1	7	0	7	0	0	0	7/1	0	65/5	1
YOUNG AE	1943-1944	0	0	0	0	0	0	0	0	3	0	3	0
YOUNG AS	1911-1912	5	3	0	0	0	0	0	0	0	0	5	3
YOUNG C	1912-1913	4	0	0	0	0	0	0	0	2	0	6	0
YOUNG WD	1975-1977	54	3	2	0	8	1	0	0	24	3	88	7
OWN GOALS	1908-1993	-	64	-	9	-	4	-	4	-	25	-	106

432